D1319913

BRITISH
CO-OPERATION

BRITISH
CO-OPERATION

BY

ARNOLD BONNER

THE HISTORY, PRINCIPLES, AND
ORGANISATION OF THE
BRITISH CO-OPERATIVE MOVEMENT

Published by the
CO-OPERATIVE UNION LTD.
HOLYOAKE HOUSE, HANOVER STREET, MANCHESTER

First published in September, 1961
Revised edition, 1970

©

Printed in Great Britain by the C.W.S. Ltd., South Reddish, Stockport

PREFACE

THIS book replaces *Co-operation*, by Hall and Watkins, familiar to and relied upon as a text book by students of the British Co-operative Movement since 1934. Much has happened since then but the qualities of the old book were such that there was a natural reluctance to replace it. Such extensive revision and additions, however, were eventually necessary that it became evident that a completely new book was required. W. P. Watkins, one of the joint authors, was of this opinion; the other, Fred Hall, died in 1938.

One of the valuable features of " Hall and Watkins," as it was known to students, was that it was written by men who were sincere co-operators of long experience in the Movement. The opinions expressed were consequently recognised as the opinions of co-operators from within and not opinions about Co-operation from without. It is hoped that this new book will secure the same recognition for it also gives a description of the Co-operative Movement as seen from within and tries truly to express the sentiments, hopes, and fears and the general social philosophy of the Movement.

The plan of the book is intended to simplify study and reference. Most chapters are divided into sections to facilitate the tracing of any one subject, e.g. membership, trade, the Co-operative Union, education, etc., through the book and yet can be studied for any period within the general context of that time. History has been severely pruned for reasons of space and because there are several easily accessible works on social, economic, political and working class history. Appendices are given to provide some original sources and to tempt students to further study and research in co-operative history, a subject whose interest and fascination increases the more deeply one delves.

It is impossible to thank all who have helped in the making of this book. Many are dead. All who knew Fred Hall will realise his influence upon the author of the book. Much of it is the fruit of discussions with all manner of co-operators during the last 30 years, especially with the members of the Co-operative College staff and officials of the Co-operative Union. Not the least important source was the Union dining-table at Balloon Street during the 'thirties. Here co-operative topics were daily discussed on the level to be expected from regular participants such as Fred Hall, George Walworth, J. S. Simm, Frank Jones, Edward Topham, Robert Southern, J. A. Hough, H. J. Twigg, and J. Jacques from the Union; George Darling and F. Lambert from C.W.S. Market Research; C. E. Tomlinson and W. H. Brown from C.W.S. Publicity; W. R. Richardson, Tom Crimes, T. W. Mercer, and F. Abbotts from the Co-operative Press; and W. R. Rae, the co-operative veteran of many fields and J. J. Worley, of the C.P.F., who were frequent visitors. All these contributed to the thought and literature of the Movement. The discussion was uninhibited and could be fierce. It was, however, always knowledgeable and provided an unequalled source of expert inside knowledge on co-operative topics past and present, of reminiscences of past co-operative workers and events, of the general sense and temper of the Movement.

More specific thanks are due to R. L. Marshall and W. P. Watkins for advice in planning the book and for criticism and suggestions in the writing of it. W. P. Watkins' assistance was invaluable in the chapter on International Co-operation. Miss Margaret Digby read and gave very helpful criticism on Agricultural Co-operation.

The Co-operative Union Editor, K. Hulse, besides editing and supervising the printing and publication also contributed useful suggestions. Special thanks are due to Desmond Flanagan, the Co-operative Union's librarian, who also conscientiously waded through the whole manuscript and from his encyclopaedic knowledge of the Movement corrected many slips, made valuable criticisms and suggestions and generally tried to keep it on the right lines. There was always the comforting thought that few errors would pass through their critical riddle.

Yet though I have tried to interpret and express the opinion of the Movement, I am of course personally responsible for what is written in this book. I hope readers of the book will find its reading as enjoyable as I did the writing of it.

A. BONNER

August, 1961.

CONTENTS

CHAPTER

CHAPTER		Pages
	Preface	v
1	Owenism	1
2	The Pre-Rochdale Co-operative Movement	22
3	The Rochdale Society of Equitable Pioneers	41
4	The Creation of a National Movement	59
5	The Co-operative Movement, 1870-1914 : Economic Development	87
6	Development of Organisation, Education and Ideas : 1870-1914	116
7	The Co-operative Movement, 1914-1939 : Economic Development	137
8	The Co-operative Movement, 1914-1939 : Other changes in Organisation and Development	174
9	Co-operation in the 1939-1945 War	209
10	The Co-operative Movement, 1945-1968. Economic Development	230
11	The Co-operative Movement, 1945-1970. Other changes in Organisation and Development... ...	268
12	Principles of Co-operation	304
13	The Organisation and Activities of the Retail Societies	331
14	The Business Federations	356
15	The Co-operative Union	379
16	Agricultural Co-operation	402
17	International Co-operation	429
18	Towards the Co-operative Commonwealth	472

APPENDICES

I	Biographical Dictionary	492
II	Conditions in the manufacturing towns contrasted with those in Owen's proposed villages	516
III	Model Rules for Co-operative Societies in 1832	518
IV	Early years of the Rochdale Pioneers Society	519
V	Laws and Objects of the Rochdale Pioneers Society	522
VI	Some early minutes of the Rochdale Pioneers Society	526
VII	Paper on the establishment of a Wholesale Society	529
VIII	Co-operative publications	534
IX	Provisions of the Industrial and Provident Societies Acts	537

INDEX

CONTENTS

CHAPTER

Page

Prelude

1   Owenism

2   The Pre-Rochdale Co-operative Movement   22

3   The Rochdale Society of Equitable Pioneers   41

4   The Creation of a National Movement   59

5   The Co-operative Movement, 1870-1914: Economic Development   87

6   Development of Organisation, Education and Ideas: 1870-1914   116

7   The Co-operative Movement, 1914-1945: Economic Development   147

8   The Co-operative Movement, 1914-1945: Other changes in Organisation and Development   174

9   Co-operation in the 1939-1945 War   206

10   The Co-operative Movement, 1945-1970: Economic Development   230

11   The Co-operative Movement, 1945-1970: Other changes in Organisation and Development   267

12   Principles of Co-operation   304

13   The Organisation and Activities of the Retail Societies   311

14   The Branches: Federations   358

15   The Co-operative Union   393

16   Agricultural Co-operation   402

17   International Co-operation   420

18   Towards the Co-operative Commonwealth?   442

APPENDICES

I   Biographical Dictionary   487

II   Chapters in the manufacturing town, contrasted with those in Owen's proposed villages   512

III   Model Rules for Co-operative Societies in 1832   514

IV   Early Acts of the Rochdale Pioneers Society   517

V   Laws and Objects of the Rochdale Pioneers Society   522

VI   Some early minutes of the Rochdale Pioneers Society   526

VII   Jargon the establishment of a Wholesale Society   529

VIII   Co-operative publications   534

IX   Provisions of the Industrial and Provident Societies Acts   537

INDEX

1 OWENISM

"It was from Owen that the working classes learned Socialism."

(*Max Beer*)

THIS book is concerned with the British Co-operative Movement, not with co-operation in general. Co-operation is much older than the Co-operative Movement; older indeed than man, for its practice is not confined to him. Bees, ants, beavers, lions, etc., co-operate. Co-operation simply means working together and one's opinion of whether some co-operative activity is good or not will depend upon the purpose of the activity and the means by which such co-operation is brought about or maintained. We should object to the co-operation of a gang of thieves for instance because of its purpose. We should object to the co-operation of a slave gang because of the means by which such co-operation is obtained. The act of co-operation is thus, in itself, neither good nor bad.

As the Co-operative Movement is only one instance of co-operation among innumerable others—joint stock companies, capitalist cartels, marketing board schemes, are all instances—we need to ascertain not so much the characteristics of co-operation in general, but the attributes, the characteristic features of the Co-operative Movement in particular. Although how and why people do or do not co-operate for any purpose is of obvious interest to a co-operator, we are concerned here with a particular movement.

A movement has been defined as " the series of actions and endeavours of a body of persons for a specific object," i.e., the pursuit of an ideal. Without objective, ideal or purpose there cannot be a movement. The ideals of the Co-operative Movement are the reason for its existence and from the pursuit of these are derived its principles and characteristic features; the body of persons consists of co-operators past as well as present; the series of actions and endeavours are its history. It would thus be impossible to describe or understand any movement without a study of its history.

The Co-operative Movement began with the Owenism of the early nineteenth century. Out of Owenism came the ideals, doctrines, myths, and much of the inspiration, which are associated with the Co-operative Movement. Instances of joint purchase and production and of community schemes and experiments can of course be found much earlier, hundreds of years earlier, but these are of little, if any, concern to the historian of the Co-operative Movement, for they neither originated nor constituted any part of that Movement.

THE BACKGROUND

The early nineteenth century was a period of considerable stress and strain. Great changes were taking place in the economic system, with consequent social effects. Population was not only increasing rapidly, but was also increasingly shifting its habitation. Many people left their native villages and moved to the growing towns and cities, industrial and mining districts in order to better their lot. Large numbers of these came from Ireland. All had to strike new roots, to discard old associations, old loyalties, former habits and ways of life. The construction of roads, canals and railways improved transport and communications and broke down the former isolation of many places. As this isolation was broken down, specialisation of districts upon particular products increased and dependence upon the outside world for employment and the supply of goods increased, and became subject to causes and persons unknown, and consequently feared. Many old and what had been supposedly secure and stable occupations declined, although new occupations and opportunities were increasing and developing. The way was opened to riches or to improved circumstances for some, to insecurity and poverty for others. To many, everything must have seemed in a muddle and the instability of the social order caused a feeling of insecurity.

There was also a political ferment. The new and heady wine of democracy could not be contained in the old bottles of the British constitution. There were strong demands for universal suffrage, freedom of speech and the Press and association, and the abolition of privilege. These demands gave rise to great popular movements and occasionally serious public disturbances. They were strongly resisted by those who had political power and used it to advance and safeguard their interests. Hence movements for political or social reforms had to impress by big, noisy and sometimes violent demonstrations, e.g., for parliamentary reform, the repeal of the corn laws, factory legislation. Such methods, inevitable in the circumstances, promoted revolutionary sentiments and at times what appeared to be revolutionary situations. The general sense of insecurity was thereby increased.

Much of the stress was due to the effects of the struggle against Napoleon and its aftermath. The country suffered from serious inflation, heavy and unjust taxation, the interruption of foreign trade during the war and from the deflation, speculative booms and catastrophic slumps which followed it. But the change of industrial system consequent upon the mechanisation of processes and the introduction of the steam engine, which is generally referred to as the Industrial Revolution, added to the strains and stresses in some ways, although it relieved them in others. It relieved them by increasing the output of wealth per head, enabling an increasing population to enjoy a rising standard of living. It added to them by the disturbances in the economic and social structure which it caused and the new problems it posed, the solutions to which were not easily or quickly found. Owenism originated in response to the factory system, drawing attention to the social and economic problems presented and offering solutions. We are concerned therefore mainly with the circumstances of the factory system in the early nineteenth century rather than with other economic, social and political phenomena of the day.

The change of system known as the Industrial Revolution was a change from a domestic system to a factory system. It was not as rapid as is often supposed. When Robert Owen died in 1858 it is probable that most people in the country had never seen a factory, certainly had never worked in one. Industries experienced their several industrial revolutions at different periods in the nineteenth and twentieth centuries, but the cotton industry had largely passed through its revolution by the end of the eighteenth century. Robert Owen's *Observations on the Manufacturing System* 1815, was written by one who had not only been an eye witness of that revolution but also actively engaged in it.

THE OLD DOMESTIC SYSTEM

The characteristic feature of the domestic system, or system of cottage industry as it is sometimes termed, was that the worker worked in his own home. Yet apart from the woollen industry of the West Riding, the worker was not an independent master craftsman, but a wage earner employed by a capitalist. The raw materials were provided by the capitalist, the product was his and the worker was paid wages by the piece for the work he performed. He was employed by the capitalist for the purpose of profit-making.

Pros. and Cons.

Many of the evils later associated with the factory system were common, e.g., low wages, payment in truck, unemployment, labour disputes, the exploitation of child labour. Weavers in the eighteenth century appear to have earned about one shilling per day of fourteen hours, women earned about two shillings and sixpence per week spinning yarn and a boy of six could earn a penny a day. Apprenticeship at its best was good, but it could be very bad indeed. Miss George's *London Life in the Eighteenth Century* gives instances as shocking as any to be found in the later factory system. But although the worker was poor, oppressed, insecure and obliged to labour long and hard for a pittance he had a measure of freedom. He decided the hours and pace at which he worked and he exercised his own judgement as to the manner in which he performed his tasks. The value of this freedom is shown by the workers' resentment at the factory system which denied it.

THE NEW FACTORY SYSTEM

The factory system is of course based upon the factory, a building housing the activities of several workers. These are employed by the owner of the factory and are subject to his orders and discipline. Usually the work is divided into many processes, each process being performed by a group of workers specialising thereon. The product of the factory is a collective product of all in the factory. It is necessary that each worker should perform his task, not at the time, pace or manner which pleases him best, but in accordance with the plan of production of the factory. This necessitates a factory discipline with somebody to plan and possessing the authority and power to compel those employed to conform to the plan. Such authority and discipline are essential to a factory no matter whether it be capitalist, communist, nationalised or co-operative. At this time the owner of the factory had this authority, and it was unchecked either by law or by trade unions. The power of the factory master was based on the dependence of the employed upon him for a livelihood.

THE FACTORY WORKERS

The factory worker spent the greater part of his waking hours in the factory, which could be a soul-destroying prison house. Edward Carpenter well described it in *Towards Democracy* as, " The great oblong, ugly factory, of five or six tiers, all windows, alive with lights on a dark winter's morning, and again with the same lights in the evening, and all day within, the thump and scream of the machinery, the thick smell of hot oil and cotton fluff, the crowds of drab-faced, drab dressed men, women and children—the mill-hands—going to and fro or serving the machines. And outside, the sad, smoke-laden sky, rows of dingy streets, waste tracts where no grass grows, tall chimneys belching dirt, and the same, sad outlook for miles." Discipline was maintained by keen supervision and threat of the sack and the imposition of fines for what were regarded as offences by the factory master, such as, in one recorded instance, for having a window open or for whistling at work.

And there could have been little good home life where the mother was in the factory for twelve hours a day:—" Too often the dwelling of the factory family is no home; it sometimes is a cellar, which includes no cooking, no washing, no making, no mending, no decencies of life, no invitation to the fireside." (*The Town Labourer*, J. L. and B. Hammond.) W. Cooke-Taylor, writing in 1842, drew attention to the need of the operative for rest and relaxation, and his difficulties of getting it:—" Nearly all legislation on amusements of the poor has been penal and restrictive; while a sour, jealous and selfish spirit has led to a series of encroachments on their comforts and enjoyments—the commons on which the labourers indulged in healthful sports are enclosed; policemen guard the streets and keep the highways clear; high walls enclose demesnes, and even the iron palisades that surround ornamental grounds are jealously planked over to prevent the humble operative from enjoying the verdure of the foliage or the fragrance of the flowers. . . . In these days to procure a book or a newspaper is easy enough; but it is not so easy for the operative to find a place in which he can sit down to read either. It is hopeless to try the experiment in the crowded lodging room or cellar, and in towns it is not possible to study in the open air. . . . The plain fact is, that in too many instances the only resource which the mechanic has for the excitement and emotions necessary to his existence is the public house. Excluded partly by law, but chiefly by the spirit of class, from nobler pleasures, he is driven to seek the joys of gin and brandy." (*Notes of a Tour in the Manufacturing Districts of Lancashire*, W. Cooke-Taylor.) Bad as were the conditions of the factory operative, he regarded them as preferable to those of the agricultural labourer. Families were known to endure incredible poverty and yet not apply for relief lest they might be sent back to the agricultural districts from which they had originated.

Factory Masters

The factory masters themselves were slaves to the new system. Competition between them was keen and ruthless. Many had little capital and were generally on the brink of failure. Competition for custom was truly a struggle for existence, in which failure meant a plunge back into the mass of wage earners from which many had painfully climbed. To sell cheaper than his rivals was thus a vital necessity to each, and to do so the factory master was impelled to drive his employees harder, increase the hours of labour, force down wages, and employ the cheaper and more docile labour of women and children. Any expenditure which did not yield a sure and quick return was avoided. Safety precautions and devices were neglected, children cleaned running machinery and suffered shocking accidents. Factories were ill-lit, ill-venti-lated, overcrowded, insanitary. Even factory owners who desired to improve matters felt powerless to do so, for they had to meet the competition of the worst employers. Robert Owen at New Lanark showed that good wages, fewer working hours, education and the improvement of morals and health did in fact increase efficiency and competitive power, but he had few imitators.

THE FACTORY TOWN

Without the advantage of steam power it is doubtful if the factory system would have extensively superseded the domestic system. Steam power also enabled industry to be concentrated in towns and the resulting concentrations of industry involved con-centrations of population. These concentrations sometimes resulted in new towns being built or caused old towns to grow very rapidly.

The factory town was a new phenomenon and there was neither knowledge nor administrative machinery to deal with the prob-lems presented. Sanitary engineering was not developed for instance to deal with the technical problems of sanitation, even if the realisation that such problems existed and the will to solve them had been present. Local government was generally inefficient, often corrupt, and a rapidly growing and large town had the same type of local authority as it had when only a mere village. Con-sequently towns grew unplanned, devoid of amenities, ugly, depressing, overcrowded, unhealthy, characterised by " steam, smoke and slums."

ATTITUDE OF ECONOMISTS AND UTILITARIANS

The changes in economic and social conditions stimulated thought upon them. This was often based upon concepts of natural rights and individual freedom, upon the belief in the superiority of natural law over government legislation. Although the excesses of the French Revolution had discredited its doctrines in the minds of many, the democratic ideals of liberty, equality and fraternity inspired many reformers with the desire for democratic, economic, social and political institutions.

Economic thought was based upon the concept of natural law. Adam Smith in his *Wealth of Nations* had expressed a contempt of governments' attempts to control and regulate commerce and industry. Such attempts in his opinion were based upon the folly and ignorance of governments and of merchants with axes to grind. He pleaded for the prevention of " the mean rapacity, the monopolising spirit of merchants and manufacturers who neither are nor ought to be the rulers of mankind," which had, " erected the sneaking arts of underling tradesmen into political maxims for the conduct of a great empire." Natural laws, left to themselves, would regulate economic affairs far better than could governments: " Without any intervention of law therefore the private interests and passions of men naturally lead them to divide and distribute the stock of every society among all the different employments carried on in it as nearly as possible in the proportion which is most agreeable to the interest of the whole society." Again he wrote: " The statesman who should attempt to direct private people in what manner they ought to employ their private capitals, would not only load himself with a most unnecessary attention, but assume an authority which could safely be trusted, not only to no single person, but to no council or senate whatever, and which could nowhere be so dangerous as in the hands of a man who had folly and presumption enough to fancy himself fit to exercise it."

Adam Smith and succeeding economists concerned themselves with discovering what these natural laws were. They referred to natural rates of wages, natural prices, natural rates of profit with the assumption that what was natural was best. A gloomy view, however, was taken by Malthus who held that as population naturally tended to increase faster than the means of subsistence, poverty was inevitable and irremediable unless the poor exercised a moral restraint as an effective check upon increase of population. Others of the classical economists also regarded the increase of population as being the cause of poverty and the obstacle to improving conditions, but held that it was practicable to limit the increase and " to raise the condition of the labourer to any state of comfort and enjoyment which may be desired." (*Elements*, James Mill.)

The classical economists of the 19th century held a philosophy known as Utilitarianism, its great exponent being Jeremy Bentham. It was based upon the principle of utility, i.e. all institutions (social, political, economic), laws and behaviour were to be

judged by the degree to which they promoted the happiness of
the greatest number. This philosophy permeated British political
thought in the 19th century and still exercises considerable
influence over all the major political parties. Although some of
its concepts favoured *laissez faire*, for instance, that every man
was the best judge of his own happiness and should be left as
free as possible to pursue it, yet others favoured the intervention
of the state, for the state should promote the happiness of the
greatest number, and legislation could and should be used for
the purpose. Thus while supporting *laissez faire* in many fields,
it provided the justification and the inspiration for reforms by
state intervention in others. The foundations of the modern
welfare state were laid by utilitarian reformers, Edwin Chadwick,
a fervent Benthamite, being the most industrious artificer. Thus
while the great political battles were being fought over free trade
and the corn laws, the modern historian can detect more subtle
changes, of more significance to the present. G. M. Young writes
that the most significant fact was " the emergence of a new state
philosophy of which the most overt tokens were the Factory Act,
the Public Health Act and the Education Minute of 1846. . . .
While an aristocratic fabric was quietly permeated with radical
ideas, an individualist society was unobtrusively schooled in the
ways of state control." (*Portrait of an Age*, G. M. Young.) A. V.
Dicey in *Law and Opinion in England* describes the debt of
collectivism to Benthamism and how the Benthamites " forged
the arms most needed by socialists." M. Beer in his *History
of British Socialism* also shows the debt of the modern British
socialist to the utilitarians, how " Webb stands on the shoulders
of J. S. Mill. He is the direct mental descendant of the last great
utilitarian."

Yet the socialistic elements in utilitarianism were unobtrusive
in the early 19th century, and although some working class
reformers, Francis Place, for instance, were ardent Benthamites,
others objected to the Benthamite doctrines of free competition
and the pursuit of individual self interest. Moreover some prominent economists and utilitarians, though by no means all of them,
adopted attitudes and expressed opinions which associated political
economy and utilitarianism with the inhuman poor law reform of
1834 and with opposition to factory legislation and to trade
unionism. They seemed to support and attempt to justify the
new order which was coming into being and which the working
classes did not find good. The new order and philosophy which
supported it were criticised on many grounds by formidable
critics, among them Robert Owen and his followers who became

known as Owenites or Socialists or Co-operators, and are today often referred to as " the Early English Socialists."

ROBERT OWEN, 1771–1858

The circumstances of the early 19th century created much popular discontent which expressed itself in riots, machine wrecking, secret drilling and popular demonstrations. Robert Owen expounded schemes of social reform which attracted some of the working classes and turned them from destructive to constructive purposes. According to Beer it was from Owen that the working classes learned socialism, " but it was essentially co-operative socialism and not militant socialism—his struggle was not primarily against usurpation and wickedness, but against error and ignorance " and " Owenite socialism though supplemented by deductions from the Ricardian theory of value was pacific, constructive, educational and non-political. Class warfare, passionate appeals to labour, demands for legal enactments and government reforms were regarded as not only futile but directly detrimental to the cause of the people." (*History of British Socialism.*)

Robert Owen first achieved fame as a successful captain of industry. But he was too big a soul and too fine a character to be content with the narrow conception of life and the ignoble, even if not sordid, ends of the typical business man of his day. In his later years writing of his experience at the New Lanark Mills, he stated, " I was completely tired of partners who were merely trained to buy cheap and sell dear. This occupation deteriorates and often destroys the finest and best faculties of our nature. From an experience of a long life, in which I have passed through all gradations of trade, manufactures and commerce, I am thoroughly convinced that there can be no superior character formed under this thoroughly selfish system." Owen was interested in higher aims of life than the accumulation of wealth. He was concerned with human happiness which he believed was determined by human character, and that human character was mainly determined by the conditions to which human beings were subject. He experimented at New Lanark to satisfy himself of the truth of his theories. When he began his career at New Lanark he found the workpeople there, " idle, intemperate, dishonest, devoid of truth and pretenders to religion, which they supposed would cover and excuse all their shortcomings and immoral proceedings." These characteristics of the workpeople, however, he believed to be due to the conditions under which they worked and lived. By changing these conditions he claimed to change their character and believed that what had been done successfully at New Lanark could be done with the whole of human society.

Owen was in his forties when he entered upon his public career of social reform. It was to be a long career, for he was writing and speaking, propagating his views even in the last year of his life and he lived to be 87. Yet the views he propagated throughout this long period were essentially the same as those he expounded in the first eight years of it.

Four essays entitled *A New View of Society, Essays on the Formation of Character* published between 1813 and 1816, contained his social theory. The first showed how poverty, misery and crime were due to ignorance of how human character was formed. The individual's character was made for him and not by him. " Any general character from the best to the worst, from the most ignorant to the most enlightened, may be given to any community, even to the world at large, by the application of proper means; which means are to a great extent at the command and under the control of those who have influence in the affairs of men." The second and third essays described how he had transformed New Lanark, and the fourth gave his scheme of national reforms, including the reform of the church and of the laws governing the sale of intoxicants, the discontinuance of the State lottery and the revision of the Poor Law.

Owen and his views attained some notoriety, particularly those which projected schemes for dealing with the unemployed and the poor. These were expounded in his " Reports," to the Committee of the Association for the Relief of the Manufacturing and Labouring Poor 1817, and to the County of Lanark 1821. Summarily, Owen held that the poor could not only be made self-supporting in Villages of Co-operation set up by the Government, but these, being modelled on New Lanark, would produce good characters and good citizens instead of the degraded paupers of the existing poor laws. Although at first he put them forward as a cure for unemployment and poverty he later advocated his Villages of Co-operation for universal adoption to replace capitalism and competition and provide the conditions for universal happiness, i.e. to replace the " Old Immoral World " by a " New Moral World."

Many notable people were attracted by Owen and were interested in his views, including the Duke of Kent (father of Queen Victoria), the Archbishop of Canterbury, Lord Sidmouth and the Benthamite circle of economists and utilitarians, viz. Bentham (who became one of his partners at New Lanark), James Mill, Ricardo, Malthus, Austin, Place, Brougham. Owen's attack upon all organised religions in 1817, however, aroused great enmity and opposition and provided the opportunity for some opponents to attack his views and schemes in general as being atheistical in origin and design. His views are summarised in the rest of this chapter.

OWEN'S OBSERVATIONS ON THE EFFECTS OF THE MANUFACTURING SYSTEM

In 1815 Owen published an essay with the above title as part of his campaign for a Factory Act to protect child labour in cotton factories. He therein expressed the view that the new manufacturing system generated a new character in the country's inhabitants, and this being founded upon a principle quite unfavourable to individual and general happiness would produce the most lamentable and permanent evils. The acquisition of wealth and the desire for continued increase introduced a fondness for essentially injurious luxuries and generated a disposition to sacrifice the best feelings of human nature to the love of accumulation. To succeed in this the lower orders had been subjected to a real oppression, to a situation more degraded and miserable than before the introduction of the new manufactures.

The inhabitants of every country were trained and formed in the main by circumstances and the character of the lower orders in Britain was formed chiefly by circumstances arising from trade, manufactures and commerce, the governing principle of which was immediate pecuniary gain. " All are sedulously trained to buy cheap and to sell dear; and to succeed in this art the parties must be taught to acquire strong powers of deception; and thus a spirit is generated through every class of traders, destructive of that open, honest sincerity, without which a man cannot make others happy, or enjoy happiness himself. . . . The employer regards the employed as mere instruments of gain, while these acquired a ferocity of character which unless judicious steps were taken to prevent its increase would sooner or later plunge the country into a formidable and perhaps inextricable state of danger." Owen objected to capitalism and competition on the grounds that they were not conducive to happiness because they promoted human character not conducive to such happiness. He had, however, other objections and one was that it created unemployment.

OWEN'S THEORY OF UNEMPLOYMENT

Before industry was mechanised, supply and demand were equal to each other, but the introduction of machinery, Owen argued, had destroyed this balance. Whilst machinery increased output it contracted the market by displacing labour and reducing wages so making the people's purchasing power insufficient to buy the goods produced. Exports would only relieve the surplus temporarily, for the mechanised methods of production would be adopted by other countries and so these export markets would disappear. If production continued to be for private gain conditions would continue to worsen and eventually become so intolerable that the workers would revolt and in a blind fury destroy everything. A system must be adopted in which consumption would keep pace with production. Co-operative labour and expenditure would be such a system.

These related theories of capitalist overproduction, unemployment, increasing misery and a final catastrophe, have survived to the present day. Although elaborated, modified and qualified, by various schools of thought and thus presented in various guises, the bald, crude statements of Owen remain the views of probably the greater part of the labour movement. The subject, however, requires a study which cannot be given here. Suffice it to say that the industrialisation of countries has not been accompanied by the phenomena which Owen prophesied. Wages have not fallen and, on the contrary, standards of living have risen except in countries which have not been industrialised, so that there has not been the continuous rise of unemployment or increasing misery which he prophesied. Even the revolutions which destroyed existing economic and social systems did not take place in advanced industrial countries, but in backward, undeveloped countries which had not passed through an industrial revolution.

OWENITE OBJECTIONS TO PROFIT AND IDEAS OF A JUST PRICE

In the Report to the County of Lanark, Owen expressed the view that the use of money created artificial and false standards of value. The natural standard of value was a unit of labour power. If commodities exchanged at their natural value, that is, according to the amount of labour required to produce them, there would be no profit upon price. "The adoption of this simple and natural device would remove all the evils from which civilised society now suffers."

Profit-making was the exploitation of some people by others and the aim of profit-making injured character. Owen declared: "profit upon price for individual gain and the accumulation of useless and unnecessary individual wealth brought into action the lower passions of human nature; and a false estimate of all things ensued and everything became valued by its cost instead of its intrinsic worth. Cunning and deception usurped the place of wisdom and sincerity." A propagandist Owenite body, the London Co-operative Society, gave the doctrine more clearly in the statement of its objectives in 1824. It sought to found a community on the principles of mutual co-operation and to restore the whole produce of labour to the labourer, to " Renounce all the evils of trafficking or mere commerce, likewise profit, which implies living on the labours of others, all our exchanges to be for fair equivalents, representing equal labour, and destined for immediate or gradual consumption and not for accumulation to command the labours of others."

These views were by no means original. The conception of a just price was an important part of Christian economic doctrine in the Middle Ages. Adam Smith in his *Wealth of Nations* had held that labour was the source, the determinant and the standard of value, that in the early and rude state of society which preceded the accumulation of capital and the appropriation of land the whole produce of labour belonged to the labourer, but that with the advent of the capitalist and the landowner, the produce of the labourer was divided into wages, rent and profits. Ricardo refined Smith's theories, but his theory of value was also a labour theory and he showed how the capital goods whose costs went into the cost of production, the buildings, machinery, materials, were themselves embodiments of past labour. This Ricardian theory of value was used by Owenites and by later socialists as a basis for theories of capitalistic exploitation of labour. It was developed into a somewhat ponderous but impressive theory by Karl Marx, but before Marx had shown any interest in socialism the essentials of his theories had been published by the individuals referred to as the " Early English Socialists."[1]

In general these held that labour had the right to its whole product but that private property in land and capital and the system of exchange resulted in labour being exploited by landowners and capitalists, rent and profits being extracted from the product and leaving only a pittance as wages for the labourer. Owen's remedy for this injustice was the Village of Co-operation, i.e. the Co-operative Community, and most of these early socialists agreed.

OWEN'S COMMUNITIES

Owen's plan of a community was of course first presented as a scheme for dealing with the poor. The community would have

---

[1] viz. John Gray (1799–1850) *Lecture on Human Happiness;* T. R. Edmunds (1803–1889) *Practical, Moral and Political Economy Most Conducive to Happiness and National Power;* John Minter Morgan (1782–1854) *Revolt of the Bees;* Thomas Hodgskin (1783–1869) *Labour Defended Against the Claims of Capital, Popular Political Economy;* William Thompson (d. 1833) *Inquiry into the Principles of the Distribution of Wealth Most Conducive to Human Happiness, Labour Rewarded or How to Secure the Whole Product of His Exertions, Practical Directions for the Speedy and Economical Establishment of Communities.*

consisted of about a thousand persons occupying from a thousand to fifteen hundred acres of land. They would practise co-operative house-keeping and the common training of children. Buildings would be erected in the form of a parallelogram enclosing a court-yard, and would provide a common kitchen, dining rooms, lecture room, schools, library, workshops, slaughter house, brew house, grain mill and individual quarters for separate families. The community would be largely self-supporting although some of its manufactures might be sold outside. It would cost about £100,000 to establish such a community. Later he elaborated the scheme and advocated it for general adoption, both as a means of right character formation and for remedying the injustices and evils of the existing social system. In the Report to the County of Lanark he expressed the opinion that there would be little need for money or private property, " It will be quite evident to all, that wealth of that kind which alone will be held in any estimation among them, may be so easily created to exceed all their wants, that every desire for individual accumulation will be extinguished."

The economists severely criticised these ideas. An article in *The Edinburgh Review* (1819), probably by Col. Torrens, held that the existing distress was due to the low expection of profits from trade, and the multiplication of Owen's parallelograms would not improve this. He argued that important factors had been over-looked by Owen in the working of the communities; for instance, they involved a big increase of population working on the land, but agriculture was subject to diminishing returns. If they were self-sufficing they could not enjoy the advantages of the division of labour and if they traded with each other and the outside world, then they would still be subject to the risks of occasional glutting of markets and stagnation of trade. Ricardo cross-examined Owen before a parliamentary committee in 1823, particularly on Owen's opinion that complete equality of reward would considerably increase production. The committee dismissed Owen's plan as impracticable " Except so far as its mechanism tends to the im-provement of public establishments, parish workhouses and great schools for the education of the lower classes."

Previous objections had been raised:— in a parliamentary debate in 1821, " The state of discipline recommended by Mr. Owen might be applicable enough to poor houses, but it was by no means agreeable to the feelings of a free nation " (Lord London-derry), and, " If Mr. Owen's system produced so much happiness with so little care, the adoption of it would make us a race of beings little removed from the brutes, only ranging the four corners of a parallelogram." (Jos. Hume.)

Attempts to found communities were made, the most important being at Orbiston (1825–1827), Ralahine (1831–1833), Queenwood (1839–1845), and " New Harmony " in the United States of America (1825–1827). All failed. That at Ralahine came to an end through the proprietor gambling away the estate. Reasons for the failure of the others were bad management, unsuitable colonists, insufficient capital and poor sites.

Apart from these, however, the community idea was doomed to failure as a means of attaining Owen's ideals. Technical and economic changes increasingly required larger productive units and markets than could possibly be provided by such village communities. These changes have resulted in great improvements in the ways of living and working which would have been denied to the village communities—and yet a good deal of the attractiveness of the community idea was the belief that work would be easier and living superior within them than without. Moreover, the culture and social life of the village community would have been inferior in many ways owing to the inevitable narrowness of experience, paucity of contacts with others and inability to support many cultural activities or develop them. Compare, for instance, the opportunities for cultural or social activities of the village with those of the city. Again the limitations on individual freedom in such small and compact communities would be inevitable and might well be intolerable.

It is significant also that the establishment of such communities would have been against the course of social evolution, which had been emancipating the individual from family and comprehensive communal obligations and dependency. On the other hand this emancipation has been accompanied by the growth of other more extensive, but specialised forms of community, often resulting in organisations which are national and even international in scope. Improved transport and communications together with economic development have caused a big increase in the communities of interest of individuals from some which were small and local, to others which are world-wide. This diversified growth of community is a social development which would have been hindered, perhaps prevented, by a universal adoption of Owen's village communities.

Nevertheless, with all their faults, many of which are more apparent now than then, the village community idea made a strong appeal to many working class people at the time, for it promised a considerable improvement in their lot. It promised clean and spacious dwellings, with good surroundings, good food, a shorter working day, pleasant occupations, security against sickness, unemployment and the poverty of old age, widow and orphanhood, and provision for the education and good upbringing of children. Whereas the manufacturing towns were " the abode of poverty, vice and crime and misery " the proposed villages " will ever be the abode of abundance, active intelligence, correct conduct and happiness." (Owen's letter to the London press in 1817.) *See Appendix II.*

OWEN AND THE FORMATION OF CHARACTER

Owen held that " That character of each of our race is formed by God or by nature and by society; that it is impossible that any human being could or can form his own qualities or his own character." This, as his critics pointed out, and Owen affirmed, relieved the individual of responsibility for his conduct and placed that responsibility upon society. Society being the great moulder of character it could produce the desired character by adopting the proper means.

The proper means commenced with the education of children, from the earliest infancy. " Children can be trained to acquire any language, sentiments or beliefs or any bodily habits and manners not contrary to human nature." He strongly condemned existing methods of education. Children learned to read, write, account and sew and yet acquired the worst habits, and had their minds rendered irrational for life. Reading and writing were merely instruments by which knowledge was imparted and were of little use unless children were taught how to make a proper use of them. Children were made to memorise instead of learning how to understand and the child who went to the top of the class was the one whose rational powers had been the soonest destroyed. " Three-fourths of the time which ought to be devoted to the acquirement of useful instruction, will be really occupied in destroying the mental powers of the children."

To Owen the real purpose of education was the formation of good character. He advocated beginning with groups of infants, " The precept or principle of action taught to them from their first day's entrance to the school (that they should always endeavour to make each other happy) the youngest infant easily conceived and was as easily induced, by the example of those previously instructed, to apply the precept to undeviating practice. And this principle and practice might be so deeply impressed at this early period on all infants that it would be a habit never to be forgotten or unused in the everyday transactions of life." (*The Life of Robert Owen*, by himself.) In the schools there would be no rewards nor punishments, for these incentives promoted false ideals and erroneous notions, leaving the character weak when the incentives were absent. The true incentive to study was the pleasure of learning. Every subject should be made attractive, and teaching as far as possible should be by conversation and the use of maps, pictures, natural objects, and games. Singing, dancing and " military evolutions " were to be a prominent feature. His methods were, of course, employed at New Lanark and aroused widespread interest, and of the many visitors most seem to have been impressed by the gentle, kindly, regular and diligent character of the children.

The education of children, however, was only the beginning of the process of forming character; the whole environment moulded it. Thus the existing system based on competition and the ruthless pursuit of self interest produced bad character. It was a selfish system and truth, honesty and virtue became mere names. (The ethics of modern advertising and salesmanship suggest Owen was not exaggerating.) Under it there could be no true civilisation for by it all were trained to oppose and often destroy one another by their created opposition of interests. " It was a low, vulgar, ignorant and inferior mode of conducting the affairs of society and no permanent, general or substantial improvement could arise until it was superseded by a superior mode of forming character and producing wealth." In the Villages of Co-operation, however, the right environment would exist. Equality and co-operation in every aspect of human life would result in the communities being free of the conflicting interests arising from the competition for place, privilege, wealth and employment, and not only would they be free of these malforming factors, but the common interest being obviously paramount, interest and duty would coincide and the social virtues be encouraged and promoted. " The arrangements to well-form the character of each will of necessity include the entire arrangements to well-form and conduct society; for there can be no part of society which does not enter into the formation of the character of everyone." (Owen's autobiography.) In his *New Moral World* he outlined a system which would cover the whole life and career of an individual, the nature of the education, amusement, exercise, work and duties being stated for each class of persons, classified according to age. To Owen, education was the formation of character. It comprehended all that affected a person's life, and it lasted from the cradle to the grave.

OWEN'S CLAIM TO SUPERIOR EFFICIENCY

Owen held that invention and discovery had already considerably increased productive capacity. He calculated that in 1816 cotton spinning machinery alone had " superseded the manual labour " of 80 million people. Inventions and discovery would continue, so that with his proposed arrangements the hours of labour could be continuously reduced whilst the quantities of goods were being increased. " The co-operative mode of living would secure great economies in production and consumption, so that greater ease and leisure would be available also." (Autobiography.) He dismissed the Malthusian theory of the tendency to over population on the grounds that the increase in output possible under his co-operative system removed all such danger, " It would defeat Malthus."

OWEN AND THE ECONOMISTS

The economists appear to have had a respect for Owen's sincerity and desire for social improvement, but little for his theories. Owen had a similar attitude to the economists. In his autobiography he observed, " From these political economists I always differed—they were liberal men for their time, friends to the national education of the people but opposed to national employment for the poor and unemployed or to the greatest creation of real wealth." " There was not a practical man among the party of modern economists. Their views and false principles have governed the administration of this country and have influenced public opinion for the whole of this century; and a more artificial and miserable existence or more hypocrisy is not to be found." " A few naturally strong-minded, active men, including Malthus, Mill, Ricardo, Col. Torrens, Hume and Place—the last possessing more energy and practical knowledge having risen from the working class, was the soul of the party—were well intentioned, clever, acute men, close reasoners and great talkers upon a false principle." (Autobiography.)

The disagreement between them was, of course, fundamental, for their objectives differed. First priority was given by the economists to the increase in the production of wealth and they believed this would be obtained by a freely competitive system in which each individual pursued his own individual self interest, and was responsible for his own decisions as to how he invested his capital, used his land, employed his labour, bought or sold his goods. Owen's first priority was the formation of character, he believed that the economist's system inevitably produced bad character with consequent evils. Whereas the economists believed that the distribution of wealth under their system would be roughly according to individual economic merit, Owen held that no individual could be responsible for his own character. It was determined for him in the main by society. Consequently the system of distribution of wealth favoured by the economists was unjust because it was society that made some lazy, careless, in-

competent. William Thompson, a disciple of Bentham, who became
an Owenite, came to the conclusion that the existing system of
distribution violated the principle of utility. The labourer only
got half the product of his labour, the rest being taken by the
landowner and the capitalist. Having no property in the product
of his labour the labourer was not moved to labour by the hope
of increasing happiness but by the fear of want. The insecurity
of the producer, i.e. the labourer, checked production, and so the
system was not only unjust but uneconomic.

OWEN AND RELIGION

Owen denounced all organised religions in 1817. He held that
" religions materially injured the finest qualities, and that, while
any of them prevailed, they would be a permanent obstacle to the
peace, progress in knowledge, charity and love, and happiness of
the human race. . . . Religions are today the great repulsive powers
of society; dividing husbands and wives, parents and children,
brothers and sisters; and are ever-burning firebrands wherever
they exist." (Autobiography.)

Owen was often denounced as an atheist, and there are even
some modern writers who describe him as such. Yet Owen himself denied that he was so. In his famous debate with Brindley at
Bristol in 1841 he stated, " I deny distinctly that I am either an
atheist or an infidel," and proceeded to explain his objections to
all organised religions, that in common with all laws they were
founded on " the error that man has within himself the power to
believe or to feel as he likes." He held that it was impossible to
know or to understand God, but he believed in God. Explaining
his views in his autobiography, he declared that there was an
element of truth in all religions, " This essence is the spirit of pure,
undefiled, universal love and charity for man, applied to daily
practice in voice, manner and act, and of love for that energy and
power which composes, decomposes, and recomposes perpetually
the elements of the universe and which is called God." " Un-
knowing in what form or manner the Intelligence and Power exists
which creates, uncreates and recreates all forms eternally throughout the universe—an Intelligence and Power far beyond the faculties of humanity hitherto to comprehend—yet I am compelled to
believe that this Intelligence directs all things within the universe
to produce the best possible ultimate results that the eternal
elements of the universe will admit." (Autobiography.)

His son, Robert Dale Owen, in *Threading My Way*, describes
and examines his religious views. He did not deny a world to come,
but man had no proof of it, could have no knowledge of it and

ought not to trouble himself about it. Therefore he omitted from his system as a motive to human conduct all reference to another life, believing men could be made to see how it was in their own interest to be temperate and industrious, just and kind and that in virtue of such insight and without other prompting they would act uprightly throughout life. " He regarded self love, or man's longing for happiness, rationally educated, as the most trust-worthy foundation for morals."

It is not surprising that Owen's religious opinions were mis-understood, distorted, and offensive to many who were sympathetic to his opinions on social reform, and also that they attracted some who were irreligious and more interested in attacking religion than social evils. Hence Owenism became associated with atheism and this was probably one of the main causes for its failure.

Owen's belief that the individual could not be held responsible for his character, his feelings and his actions, led him to conclu-sions on the institution of marriage which did further damage. He attacked it on the grounds that it forced people to " adopt a system of exclusion and mystery in all their domestic arrange-ments," which resulted in habits not conducive to good character. The training in family life was the worst training a child could have, for children were taught to consider their own individual family as their whole world, and to regard it as the duty and interest of all in the family to promote the advantages of all its legitimate members against those outside it. Parents were not the best persons to train their children and specially qualified experts were needed for this. Since men and women had no power to create their own feelings, or to love or hate at their own pleasure it was blasphemy against the laws of nature for man or woman to make any promises or engagements relative to their future feelings of affection." Therefore he denounced indissoluble unions and unions entered into from other motives than that of mutual affec-tion. Nevertheless, he believed that under his system permanent happy unions would be general, buttressed by regulations for marriage and divorce. These views were extravagantly and intem-perately expressed by Owen, and some of his followers were even more extreme in their expressions. Moreover, the conduct of some was scandalous to " The Old Immoral World." F. Podmore in his *Robert Owen* admits that " It was not difficult for an in-tolerant and unimaginative Christian to suppose that Socialism aimed at subverting alike social order, morality and religion; that its creed was mere blasphemy; and its motive forces greed and lust."

In these as in other matters Owen suffered from strong convic-tions based upon inadequate knowledge and lack of self-criticism.

Robert Dale Owen describes the disadvantages under which his father laboured. At 10 years of age he commenced work in London; at 45 he was worth a quarter of a million. This rapid rise to wealth and fame by his own unaided exertion was likely to encourage conceit in his own ability and judgment, and " He had been misled by prosperity, by benevolent enthusiasm, and there had been lacking, as a steadying influence, thorough culture in youth." He had none of the advantages of regulated study. " He read a good deal; but it was chiefly one or two London dailies with other periodicals as they came out. He was not, in any true sense of the word, a student . . . I never found, in his extensive library, a book with a marginal note, or even a pencil mark of his, on a single page. He usually glanced over books, without mastering them; often dismissing them with some such curt remark as, ' the radical errors shared by all men, made books of comparatively little value ' . . . . In this way he worked out his problems for human improvement to great disadvantage, missing a thousand things that great minds had thought and said before his time. . . . Thus while bringing forward principles of vast prac-tical importance that had been too much neglected by governments and individuals he forfeited, in a measure, the confidence of culti-vated men by evident lack of familiarity with precedent authorities on the same subjects."

Owen at first appealed to the upper classes and secured some attention and sympathy. His views on religion and marriage, however, alienated many, while economists and Benthamites, some of whom had also unorthodox views on religion and marriage, could not stomach his economics. A working class movement, however, developed which took from Owen what appealed to it, and rejected or ignored the rest of his doctrines. The *Co-operative Magazine* issued by the London Co-operative Society between 1826 and 1830, concentrated upon mutual aid and distribution. It carried co-operative ideas into all manner of working class organisations and they were discussed in the branches of trade unions, friendly societies, and mechanics institutes.

Although efforts at establishing communities failed, the idea gripped many working people and gave an objective for their am-bitions and efforts for a generation. When the idea of a community was discarded, and this was done only gradually, and when other means of attaining the ideals were adopted, the ideals still remained, viz., equality, social ownership, mutual aid, just prices, and the abolition of the profit-motive, and education in co-operation as a means of improving character. These Owenite ideals descended to the modern Co-operative Movement.

2 THE PRE-ROCHDALE CO-OPERATIVE MOVEMENT

"A slip of Owenism grafted upon a sound sense stock."

Quarterly Review, 1829.

ROBERT OWEN was out of this country in the period 1824–1829 attending to his New Harmony community in the United States of America and visiting Mexico and the West Indies. In his absence something approaching a recognisable Co-operative Movement was begun. Owen had maintained that to be successful a community must be established in the beginning in complete conformity with his scheme. To do so required the raising of the necessary capital before the scheme was commenced, and the amount required in Owen's opinion increased as time went on, until £240,000 was the figure stated. A group of working people could not possibly raise such a sum, and it was not likely that government or wealthy sympathisers would provide it.

However, there were others who believed that the communities could be established or developed much more cheaply and more easily than Owen believed. William Thompson estimated that five or six thousand pounds would be sufficient. In his *Labour Rewarded or How to Secure the Whole Product of His Exertions* (1827) he outlined a scheme by which trade unions could engage on constructive programmes which would develop from co-operative production into Owenite communities. In the *Co-operative Magazine* (1826) he exhorted the working classes to undertake co-operative production and exchange with each other at just prices thus eliminating profit, or workers of different trades to combine, form communities and " thus supply each others' wants, being producers and consumers, masters and employers, to each other." It was evident that if communities were to be established it could only be by the working classes' own efforts, but how could working people in those days raise the necessary capital? Dr. William King of Brighton showed them the way in his publication *The Co-operator*.

DR. WILLIAM KING AND *THE CO-OPERATOR*

Dr. William King, a medical practitioner of Brighton, promoted a Mechanics Institute in the town in 1825. This was one among many instances of his efforts to assist working people. Becoming interested in Owenite literature he communicated his interest to some of those who attended his classes. As a result two co-operative organisations were formed in Brighton in 1827, the Brighton Co-operative Benevolent Association and the Co-operative Trading Association. The first was to raise by small weekly subscriptions a fund for the purpose of assisting persons to join co-operative communities and to spread a knowledge of Co-operation. The second engaged in retail trade with the object of accumulating capital from its profits to eventually establish a community.

Much more important than the associations, however, were the interest and the ideas which King developed and expounded in his publication of *The Co-operator*, 1828–1830. This paper was published monthly and came to have a wide circulation, especially in the North and Midlands. It was written in plain, homely English, gave sound, practical advice based on common sense and Christianity, and exercised a profound and lasting influence on the Co-operative Movement. At the Fourth Co-operative Congress, October, 1832, the chairman, Thomas Hirst of Huddersfield, spoke of " That admirable and almost inimitable work *The Co-operator* . . . It would be a lasting disgrace to the co-operatives to suffer that work to sink into oblivion. It had converted hundreds, if not thousands to the cause, but he was sorry it was now out of print and scarcely a copy to be obtained." Others spoke of its importance and value, including William Pare, and a resolution was passed thanking Dr. King " for the useful instruction which he has conveyed, in the simple, yet truly eloquent language of the papers alluded to, on the important subjects of which they treat " and requesting a new edition. King could not provide this for the first edition had cost him £50, and he was not a wealthy man. Some of his readers, however, had the wisdom to bind copies and these continued to serve as " something of a text-book for the Movement." James Smithies had such a volume and he and the pioneers of Rochdale studied and discussed it. When they formed their Society in 1844 they were obviously very largely influenced by the ideas of Dr. King.[1]

DR. KING'S THEORIES OF CO-OPERATION

King accepted the Owenite myth of increasing misery and also argued that poverty, disease and crime were largely the consequences of the existing economic and social system. He believed,

---

[1] *Co-operation's Prophet* published by the Co-operative Union contains all the twenty-eight numbers of *The Co-operator*, together with some of King's correspondence bearing on Co-operation.

however, that working people were capable of remedying their conditions. The remedy for the workers' plight, King told them, was in their own hands. It was Co-operation. Union was strength, what one could not do, many might. " But before many can work they must join hand in hand; they must know their object and feel a common interest and a common tie." Under the existing system the workers competed with each other and regarded themselves as enemies of each other. They suffered from the introduction of machinery, unemployment and repeated reductions in wages. This was because they worked for others and not for themselves. Therefore they must work for themselves and enjoy the whole product of their labour. This, however, they could not do unless they had capital, and without capital they were obliged to seek employment of those who had.

His Remedy

As individuals they were powerless since each could not obtain the capital to employ himself. Co-operatively, however, they could provide capital to employ themselves and it could be raised by union and saving. Small weekly subscriptions to a common capital fund should be made. The large accumulations of workers' savings in friendly societies and savings banks showed what could be done. This co-operative capital, however, was not to lie idle or be lent to others to employ for their own profit. It must be so used as to multiply and accumulate capital for them to employ themselves. They must employ it in businesses of their own. He advised that they should start with a shop. They could commence this with a small capital and little experience. It could not fail if they bought and sold only for ready money and the members were loyal. Profits must not be distributed but must be added to the capital, so that the capital would continue to increase by the weekly subscriptions and the profits of the business. As the capital increased the society would increase the number of commodities traded in. As the wants of the members were limited, however, the time would arrive when the capital exceeded what was required by the shop. Optimistically, he held this would occur within a year. The surplus capital should then be used to employ a member to make shoes or clothes, etc., for the rest. He would receive the usual wages. The profits would be put to the common capital and so provide the means to employ other members. " In this way they will proceed, as the capital increases, to employ one member after another, either to manufacture articles consumed by the members or by the public." Thus eventually all the members would be self-employed through their society, and as they would have the whole product of their labour their capital would increase even faster. They would be able to purchase land and produce their own food-stuffs, build their own houses, provide their own schools, maintain sick and aged members and feed, clothe, and educate members' children. The society would thus evolve into a community.

The moral and religious principles of such a community must be Christian, because it was self-evident that the fundamental basis was to " love your neighbour as yourself . . . No man but a real Christian is fit for such a Community. In common life it is im-possible to act upon this principle. We must love ourselves first—our neighbours second. But in a Community our own interest is better secured in that of the Community than we could possibly secure to ourselves; therefore, interest and duty would go hand in hand." (*The Co-operator*. No. 1.)

The evolution of a community from a co-operative store was not the only method advocated. He drew attention to the wastage of working class savings in Friendly Societies and Trade Unions. These bodies invested working class savings in capitalist enter-prises at low rates of interest. This capital was used to employ workers, perhaps even the members of the societies and the unions, and return big profits to the owners of these enterprises. Trade unions also wasted working class savings in strikes. All these working class bodies should use their funds as capital in co-oper-ative enterprises of their own. These could develop into " co-op-erative colonies " of trade unions.

Essential Features

Education was a prime necessity, for the workers' plight was due to their ignorance. " The first step towards Co-operation and the first and the last step to make it successful is to remove this ignorance by every means in their power." The acquisition of knowledge was one of the first principles of Co-operation. The practice of Co-operation was itself educational but it also increased the need and the desire for knowledge. As soon as men assembled to discuss how their affairs were to be best managed their minds received new impulses, new ideas, new motives, and new objects. They had to exercise their judgments, to weigh and balance proba-bilities, to count profit and loss and to acquire knowledge of human character. All co-operators had to some extent to become men of business, and they could not do so without becoming men of knowledge. They would have to acquire knowledge of the com-modities in which they traded and of reasons for the variation of prices, and as they commenced manufacture and invested capital, " higher knowledge " would be forced upon them.

B

They must also learn and practise good business methods, seek for a quick turnover of stock, buy and sell for ready money only, keep accurate accounts and acquire habits of careful book-keeping, and these habits must be familiar to all or most of the members. He pointed out what might be considered rather obvious if it were appreciated in these days, that a membership ignorant of book-keeping cannot control a society and that the ability and knowledge to read and understand accounts is necessary for the control of any business.

As the benefits of Co-operation were derived from people attempting things for themselves in a co-operative manner it must be voluntary Co-operation. " Co-operation is a voluntary act and all the power in the world cannot make it compulsory, nor is it desirable that it should depend on any power but its own—the interference of governments would only cramp its energies and mis-direct them." He was opposed to revolution or the class war. Co-operation would be a stabilising element in society, it would remove the causes of revolution. Nor was Co-operation a com-bination of the poor against the rich, nor of workmen against masters. It was " but a rational application upon which every man acts and is directed to act, that of bettering his condition."

DIFFERENCES FROM OWEN

Dr. King differed from Owen in some important matters. Whereas Owen opposed and condemned all organised religions, King openly and firmly based his Co-operation on Christian doc-trine. He maintained that the spirit and ethics of the Gospels were the spirit and ethics of Co-operation. From the first number to the last, King expounded this opinion. Numbers 26 and 27 of *The Co-operator* were upon " The Bible " and " Christianity " res-pectively in which he enlarged upon this theme.

Owen condemned the family, but King regarded the family as the beginning and the basis of community: " the family was a community as far as it went, but the family affection ought to extend itself from private to public life, from the family to the world."

Owen was a Utopian socialist, that is, he planned an ideal com-munity in great detail and expected to build and start one complete and in full working order as one would build and start a machine or a factory. King, on the other hand, was an evolutionary as well as a Christian socialist. He showed how working people could start from their existing conditions and by the development of co-operative enterprise evolve a Co-operative Community. Moreover, King believed that working people had the capacity to do this by their own efforts. They could raise the capital and acquire the necessary knowledge and ability to manage their affairs by the practical experience of managing these co-operative undertakings. They would learn as they grew, starting with the smallest and simplest enterprise. The lessons learned in managing small under-takings would equip them to deal with larger ones. On the other hand, Owen had little confidence in working people, unless and until they had gone through his process of character formation. William Lovett in his *Life and Struggles* relates how Owen justified some undemocratic conduct of his to a congress committee by telling them that, " They were ignorant of his plans, of the objects he had in view and must consent to be governed by despots until we had acquired sufficient knowledge to govern ourselves." Owen sought the assistance of governments, no matter how despotic, and of wealthy men to provide the necessary capital for his schemes; King continually urged that the workers must rely on their own efforts, that the benefits of Co-operation were yielded by self-help through mutual aid.

Both, however, agreed upon the need for a change in the economic and social system so that human character conducive to happiness would be formed. King wrote " The greatest and most beneficial effects of Co-operation will be upon the moral character; and here those effects will be mighty. Practical Co-operation (as distinct from that absurd theoretic Co-operation which has been talked about so long to so little purpose) goes directly to improve the moral and religious character of men. This is the final end and consummation of the cause." (*The Co-operator*. No. 21.)

BIRTH OF THE EARLY CO-OPERATIVE MOVEMENT

King's *Co-operator* quickly had effects. It showed a practical way of escape from the new industrial and social order. Working people were accustomed to forming associations, to financing them by small weekly subscriptions, and to managing them democrati-cally, and his views on religion and the family would also be agree-able to them. Before the end of 1828, King knew of nine trading associations; by the end of 1829 he recorded one hundred and thirty; and when the publication of *The Co-operator* ceased in 1830, he claimed that three hundred societies were in existence.

Many co-operative productive undertakings had also been started; William Lovett mentioned societies handling " broad-cloth, silk, linen and worsted goods, shoes, hats, cutlery, furniture." These were formed in some instances by independent craftsmen working in their own homes, for co-operative purchase of raw material and sale of their products; in others there would be a workshop in which the members would be employed. The domestic system and handicraft methods were still common and facilitated the formation of such societies, but generally their existence was brief. Often they were started during a period of unemployment when the market was already glutted, or after or during a strike or lock-out. In either case the circumstances bringing the society into being were generally temporary and as they passed away, so did the societies. Others had more permanent objectives and were formed for the purpose of permanently escaping from the tyranny of the capitalist employer. These owed their origin to the influence of King's ideas, or of Owenite ones such as Thompson's. They were often started by Benefit Societies or Trade Unions.

A number of co-operative journals were in circulation propagating the ideals and methods of Co-operation. However, they were not official organs, often had only a local circulation, and were generally poorly written and produced. Yet a national Co-operative Movement was undoubtedly in being, but it still required national organisation.

PRE-ROCHDALE CO-OPERATIVE CONGRESSES

Steps towards forming such a national organisation were the holding of Co-operative Congresses, i.e., deliberate assemblies. (Holyoake stated that the term " Congress " was introduced by William Pare and its frequent usage by co-operators popularised what was an Americanism.) They were as follows:—

				Chairman
First	Manchester	May 26–28	1831	... E. Dixon
Second	Birmingham	October 4–6	1831	... R. Owen
Third	London	April 23–May 1	1832	... R. Owen
Fourth	Liverpool	October 1–6	1832	... T. Hirst
Fifth	Huddersfield	April 8–10	1833	... R. Owen
Sixth	London	October 7–12	1833	... R. Owen
Seventh	Barnsley	March 31–April 4	1834	... R. Owen
Eighth	Halifax	April 20–21	1835	... R. Owen

The first Congress was attended by delegates from 56 societies representing 3,000 members. Its principal achievement was the passing of a resolution to establish " The North-West of England United Co-operative Company " in order to furnish and stock a wholesale warehouse in Liverpool to serve co-operative societies to promote the sale and exchange of all articles of co-operative manufacture, and " to unite all the societies in this part of the kingdom into one body, for the mutual protection and advantage, and for the interchange of kind offices and benevolent actions." This was a practical resolution which shows the realisation of the need for an organisation of societies. Unfortunately the Movement was not strong enough at this stage to carry it out successfully.

The third Congress is regarded as the most notable. In it the attempts of Owen to dominate were defeated and the views of practical co-operators successfully asserted. The delegates had an obvious respect for Owen, for his benevolence, sincerity and good intentions, but they were by no means disposed to accept all his views. There is evident the desire and intention to prune and adapt Owenism and there was shown an impatience and dislike of what some delegates referred to as its " metaphysics."

Opposition to Owen

Throughout the Congress objections to Owen's religious views were made. John Finch (the " pioneer of co-operative wholesale trading " and who succeeded Owen as the governor of the Queenwood community) said he was sorry when persons declaimed against the religion of their country. " The principles of Co-operation are more in accord with the principles of the Gospel than are those of any other sect in existence." T. Hirst (who presided at the succeeding Congress) declared he was widely opposed to Owen on scriptural subjects; Carson of Wigan said people were deterred from joining the Movement by Owen's religious views, " in the part of the country from which he came, people co-operated from Christian principles." Nor did Congress agree with Owen's statement that " man's character was formed for him and not by himself." Skevington of Loughborough said he was not sent to discuss metaphysical questions and that his society would not sanction or receive any document which aimed at the subversion of Christian principles. Lovett agreed with Skevington. The Rev. Dr. Wade (Vicar of Warwick), who seems to have been adept at compromise, successfully moved an amendment so that the resolution which carried was: " That the character, under Divine Providence, is formed for each individual."

Owen's views on politics also aroused dissent. He submitted a proposed Address to the Governments of Europe and America, and on two points there was contention. One was the doubt whether it was much use appealing to governments and the view was expressed that governments could not produce the change which must be made by the peoples themselves. The other point of debate was Owen's opinion that the forms of government were of no matter. He was indifferent whether they were democratic, monarchical or despotic.

Congress showed it had a fervent belief in democracy, and was strongly opposed to any form of despotism. Owen's scheme of a

Labour Exchange Bank was opposed because it put all power in his hands and the committee would only assist him. It was pointed out that each of their societies was democratic—" How could such societies amalgamate with one that was a perfect despotism? " Articles of Agreement for the Formation of Community approved by Congress were emphatic that the government must be democratic and must abide by the votes of the majority although careful of the rights of minorities. Regular weekly meetings were to be held and good reasons were given for frequent meetings. They would " excite and maintain interest in the affairs of the community, keep alive the sympathy of all, inform, exercise and improve the intellectual faculties and afford an efficient preventive to all abuses of government."

Religious and Political Neutrality

It will be gathered that the Movement was not willing to be the instrument of Owen. The dissension arising from some of his views and the odium attached to them, with which the Movement did not desire to be associated, led to the famous resolution on religion and politics. It is significant that this resolution was moved by Owen and seconded by a clergyman, Dr. Wade, thus securing general approval.

It read, " Whereas the co-operative world contains persons of every religious sect and of every political party, it is resolved that co-operators as such, jointly and severally, are not pledged to any political, religious or irreligious tenets whatsoever; neither those of Mr. Owen, nor of any other individual." That the resolution was regarded as of considerable importance is shown by an addition to it—that it was to be the standing motto upon all publications the Congress might issue.

Model rules for co-operative societies drawn up by a committee appointed for the purpose were approved. These stated that the ultimate objective of all co-operative societies was community on land, and then proceeded along the lines advocated by Dr. King, viz. the weekly subscription until sufficient capital had been obtained to commence trade, purchasing at wholesale prices and selling at market prices and the provision then of mutual employment of members, schools, libraries and reading rooms. The capital should be indivisible, all profit being allowed to accumulate as capital, and credit should be neither taken nor given. A perusal of these rules shows a relation not only between them and King's *Co-operator* but also with the later rules of the Rochdale Pioneers.

The following Congress in October, 1832, felt the impact of the rapidly growing temperance movement, which was largely a working class movement in origin and composition. King had advised against holding meetings in public houses. If they could not do without beer and tobacco it was better to have a room of their own and he advocated societies getting licences and brewing their own beer in such instances. The type of man likely to be attracted by the Co-operative Movement was similar to that attracted by the temperance movement. Finch was a great temperance advocate and declared that co-operators should join temperance societies. Pare held that temperance societies were, like Sunday schools, Mechanics Institutes, Benefit Societies, etc., all pioneers for co-operatives. A resolution was carried unanimously calling on all co-operators to give every encouragement to temperance societies.

Subsequent Congresses show a steady deterioration in numbers and interest. It was doubted for a long time if the Halifax Congress was even held, for no reports of it could be discovered. A. Pahlman settled the question by finding reports of both the Barnsley and the Halifax Congresses (*Co-operative Review*, July, 1935). But the opinion expressed by George Simpson, a fairly reliable source, in 1879, that if it were held it was probably only local in character, is supported by the list of delegates given. There were only 21 delegates, all from the West Riding. Its principal business was the burial of the N.W. of England United Co-operative Company, which, it will be remembered, had been established by the resolution of the first Congress in 1831.

Failure of Wholesale Company

Great hopes had been held of this venture, but it appears to have started with too heavy overheads as a result of over-optimism regarding its prospects. In those days of poor transport a depot at Liverpool could not adequately serve societies throughout the country, and instead of an estimated trade of £500 per week, in the first twenty months trade only averaged £500 per month. In spite of reorganisation by the Huddersfield Congress, losses continued to be suffered and its trade decreased. At the Halifax Congress it appeared that only two societies, Halifax and Huddersfield, had done business with the Company since the previous Congress, and a loss of £20 had been suffered. It was decided to give up the wholesale establishment, dispose of the fixtures and stock, " pay off all the tradesmen's bills, and finish off all the Company's affairs in Liverpool in an honourable and tradesmanlike manner " and circularise all the co-operative societies remaining in existence, stating the position and asking their assistance to make up the losses. There appears to have been an adequate response and we can be proud with Pahlman that " The collapse of the experiment of the Co-operative Wholesale business did not leave any loss for persons outside the Movement."

Its collapse was due mainly to the collapse of the Co-operative Movement accompanying the failure of Owen's grandiose schemes of National Equitable Labour Exchanges and the Grand National Consolidated Trade Union. But the wholesale business was in difficulties from the start due to the timidity and lack of loyalty of the societies. Nevertheless, the experiment was remembered, it was referred to again and again in subsequent co-operative literature and remained present in co-operative thought. As a desirable objective it inspired some of the efforts at co-operative wholesale trading during the fifties, culminating in the establishment of the North of England Co-operative Wholesale Society in 1863.

EQUITABLE LABOUR EXCHANGES

At this time, many finished goods were the products of handicraftsmen. It was possible at times that some might well be unemployed yet willing and capable of producing goods required among themselves. What was needed was some organisation which would bring their products and demands together. Some trade unionists tried to do this by setting up what became known as Labour Exchanges. The *Co-operative Magazine* for September, 1827, contained a letter from William King (not Dr. W. King of Brighton), a well-known trade unionist, describing a " Union Exchange Society " which had been organised by some artisans. The out-of-work tailor who wanted shoes and the shoemaker who wanted a coat could be set to work by the Exchange to satisfy each other's wants.

Many co-operative societies at this period, moreover, were associations of workers of the same trade, and provided materials for unemployed members to work on, with the ultimate objective of employing all the members. The greatest difficulty, of course, was the disposal of the products. Labour Exchanges again appeared as a solution. Some Labour Exchanges or Exchange Bazaars were established to which co-operative societies sent their surplus produce for sale. One of the first of these was in Greville Street, Hatton Garden, started in 1830, which Lady Noel Byron helped with a donation of £100. At this time there were over 40 co-operative societies in London from which it could draw supplies. Other important ones were opened in London (in Portland Road and New Road, Marylebone, Oxford Street, Red Lion Square, the Rotunda and Blackfriars Road) in Birmingham, Glasgow, and Sheffield. These led to Robert Owen's inspiration to organise a system of National Equitable Labour Exchanges. He opened and acted as governor of the famous National Equitable Labour Exchange at Grays Inn Road in 1832.

They were termed " Equitable " because Owen intended them to effect exchanges at " true equivalents." He had given his opinion of what these were in his Report to New Lanark, 1820. He gave it again in a " Notice to the Public: Equitable Labour Exchange Institution of the Industrious Classes, Grays Inn Road " which was published in his paper *The Crisis* and in which he declared goods were to exchange " in the only equitable manner in which men can mutually dispose of their property with each other, viz. its value in labour for equal value in labour without the intervention of money."

Labour Exchange Valuation

The system designed to do this was complicated, but impractical and futile. Goods were brought to the Exchange and " deposited " and labour notes were given in exchange which the recipient could exchange for goods deposited by others. The labour notes received were equal in amount to the time it was estimated the commodity deposited should take to make. Thus it was held each depositor would be able to get back from the Exchange goods which had taken as much labour to make as those which he deposited; labour would be exchanged for labour and none would be able to make a profit out of others. There were, however, difficulties in such valuation for there had to be some valuation of the raw materials in the commodity, and some kinds of labour were more difficult, more skilled, or more scarce, and so commanded a higher price. The solution made was to convert the price of the raw materials into " hours of labour " by dividing that price by 6d., this being made the monetary value of a standard unit of labour. By similarly dividing by 6d. the current wages of the labour concerned it was ascertained how many hours of standard labour were equal to one hour of that labour. For example, if such labour commanded wages of one shilling per hour, every hour used on the product of such labour would be counted as two hours by the Labour Exchange. This, of course, was not equality, although it could be argued that it was equitable. It was not, however, practicable. Value in exchange is not determined by cost of production but by all that is involved in the interplay of supply and demand. This may be termed the market price though the freely competitive price would be more accurate. If a price higher than this is fixed, some of the supply of the commodity will remain unsold; and the market will become glutted. If the price fixed is lower than the

market price, the supplies in the market will all be sold before
everybody willing to pay that price is satisfied.

Defects

This in fact took place in the Exchanges whilst this system of
valuation was employed. Goods over-valued in comparison with
the current market price remained unsold and those under-valued
quickly disappeared. Moreover, there was consequently a tendency
for the supply of goods over-valued by the Exchange to increase,
since it was expected that a bigger value could be obtained by
supplying them to the Exchange than by selling them outside. It
was said that shopkeepers rid themselves of slow moving or un-
saleable goods by depositing them with the Exchange. Goods
undervalued by the Exchange, of course, would cease to be sent
there. It is significant that goods deposited at the Exchange in a
week generally exceeded those exchanged. This impracticable system could not continue and eventually the goods were valued, in
labour terms, at amounts similar to the current market prices.

The Exchanges on the whole seem to have operated much more
successfully than could have been expected. Men such as Lloyd
Jones and G. J. Holyoake writing many years afterwards held they
were very promising experiments which revealed a need they could
have met. There were large numbers of handicraftsmen who could
produce goods in their homes, and as Owen argued in *The Crisis:*
" Hundreds of thousands of persons of all the various trades in
existence rise every morning without knowing how or where to
procure employment. They can each produce more than they have
occasion for themselves, and they are each in want of each other's
surplus produce." The existence of the Exchanges may well have
induced many of these to produce goods which otherwise would
not have been produced, and yet which were needed and could
in fact be exchanged.

Limitations

The Exchanges, however, never satisfactorily solved the problem
of supplying foodstuffs, which most of the depositors wanted in
exchange for their products, and whilst meeting in some degree the
needs of handicraft small producers, did not meet the needs of the
factory worker. To handle foodstuffs and factory products required a much bigger and more elaborate organisation covering
the whole country, and a comprehensive national system of exchange embracing all kinds of labour and goods. Owen saw the
possibilities. The Exchanges were already dealing partly in the
products of co-operative societies and Owen devised a scheme for

a system of National Labour Exchanges, dealing with the products of co-operative labour, exchange to be for fair equivalents and devoid of profit-making. The co-operative societies producing for such exchange would be organised and financed by the trade unions. To effect this a national organisation of trade unions was necessary, and Owen, therefore, made a brief, and disastrous, incursion into trade unionism. He floated the Grand National Consolidated Trades Union.

TRADE UNIONISM

Wage earners had long realised the advantages of forming associations to protect and improve their wages and conditions. The Industrial Revolution increased the need for such association and, by concentrating wage earners into factories and factory districts created better opportunities for forming them. Their growth, however, was prevented by the Combination Acts of 1799 and 1800, but the repeal of these Acts in 1824 resulted in a rapid revival. These early associations were generally local in scope and outlook, but some of their leaders believed it was necessary to organise them on a national scale and there were ideas even of " one big union " to cover all wage earners. Some leaders were also ardent Owenites and had ambitions of making the trade unions into the instruments of workers' emancipation from capitalism. Moreover, the disappointment of many workers with the parliamentary Reform Act of 1832, which had denied the franchise to the working classes, caused hopes and interest to swing somewhat from political to industrial action. Hence Owen was able to find a ready hearing in the trade union world.

At the London Co-operative Congress in October, 1833, advertised as " The Co-operative and Trade Union Congress " in *The Crisis*, Owen made proposals for a Grand National Moral Union of the Productive Classes of the United Kingdom, and at a conference in London the following February, convened by Owen, the Grand National Consolidated Trades Union of Great Britain and Ireland was formally established. Although the big unions of the day did not join, the G.N.C.T.U. rapidly grew. " Within a few weeks the Union appears to have been joined by at least half-a-million members, including tens of thousands of farm labourers and women." (The *History of Trade Unionism*, S. and B. Webb.)

Owen's Plan

The objectives of the Union, however, were confused. Owen had a definite plan but it was not that of other of its leaders. Owen

declared that members of the Union had discovered that competition in the sale of their products was the cause of their poverty,
and this could not be overcome as long as they conducted their
affairs individually and in opposition to each other. They were
therefore to form national companies of production, each company
comprising all the individuals engaged in a particular trade or
manufacture. These companies would then exchange their products with each other " upon a principle of equitable exchange of
labour for a fair equal value of labour; and all articles, upon a principle of economy and general advantage, will be produced of the best
quality only." Later the master traders and manufacturers would
unite with these operatives and so even would the Government.

Others, however, notably James Morrison and J. E. Smith, who
were editors of *The Pioneer* (a trade union journal) and *The Crisis*
(the chief Owenite journal), exercised great influence. Whilst
believing in the desirability of the trade unions taking over production by a structure on Owen's lines, they also held that this
could not be done without a struggle, and the Grand National
must prepare itself to wage that struggle.

Meanwhile the rank and file had more immediate ends in mind.
They believed that as members of this huge organisation they had
it in their power to dictate to their local employers. Consequently
there were outbreaks of local strikes and lock-outs, which the
Union had not the means to support. Strong opposition from the
employers and the arrest and trial of the " Tolpuddle Martyrs "
resulted in the rapid collapse of the Grand National in the summer
of 1834. A strong contributory cause of this collapse was undoubtedly dissension in its leadership. Owen was opposed to the
class war which some desired the Grand National to wage, and
which *The Crisis* was advocating. He wound up *The Crisis* (1832–
1834) and replaced it by *The New Moral World* (1834–1845), dissolved the Grand National and replaced it by " The British and
Foreign Consolidated Association of Industry, Humanity and
Knowledge." In this collapse of 1834 disappeared not only the
Grand National, but Labour Exchanges and co-operative societies.
Owen had lost faith and interest in them.

Judgment of the Webbs

His scheme of co-operative production by trade unions organised as national companies was roundly condemned by Sydney and
Beatrice Webb in their *History of British Trade Unionism* as the
worst of all Owen's attempts to reduce his Socialism to practice.
They pointed out that a mere combination of workers as co-operative producers in a trade would no more abolish competition than

would a combination of all employers in a trade as a joint stock company. Such societies would in fact degenerate into capitalist enterprises and the scheme was not socialistic. If it had been carried out it " would have simply arbitrarily redistributed the capital of the country without altering or superseding the capitalist system in the least."

The idea lingered on, however, throughout the nineteenth century in trade union circles. It was revived in the syndicalist and industrial unionist movements in the early part of this century.

LAST PHASE OF OWENISM

Although the early Co-operative Movement disappeared in the catastrophe, it did not perish, for ideas, hopes and co-operators lived on. A few societies continued in being, and elsewhere there was the desire to try again. Owen, however, had never been enthusiastic about their forms of Co-operation. They were far removed from his ideal and he had no further interest in them. He devoted his energies to building up a purely Owenite organisation which, by education and propaganda, would prepare people for the Villages of Co-operation and The New Moral World. He and his followers became more concerned with and engaged in expounding the " metaphysics " which had annoyed some of those attending the early Congresses.

The Co-operative Congress at Halifax in April, 1835, was the last of the series of pre-Rochdale Congresses. Congresses, however, continued to be held by Owen. In May of the same year in which the Halifax Congress wound up the Co-operative Movement, Owen held a meeting in London which he termed a Congress, though anybody could attend and its deliberations were not of delegates. At this meeting he formed " The Association of All Classes of All Nations." Another Owenite movement had begun. A series of Congresses followed which Holyoake described as " Socialist " and the Congress of 1841 definitely adopted the term. The last of this series was held at Queenwood in June, 1846, another melancholy occasion, for the community was in process of liquidation and the delegates found themselves locked out by the trustees and had to meet in a tent.

At the Manchester Congress of this series held in 1837, another association, " The National Community Friendly Society," was formed to raise funds for the establishment of a community and a scheme for the spreading of Owenite ideas by " Social Missionaries " was set on foot. The country was divided into propaganda districts, each under a Social Missionary, appointed by the Central Board of the Society. These missionaries were very active, some

of them played a notable part in the later Co-operative Movement,
e.g. Lloyd Jones and Alexander Campbell, but G. J. Holyoake was
never a Social Missionary as is sometimes claimed for him.

Collapse

In 1838 the two bodies (the A.A.C.A.N. and the N.C.F.S.) were
joined into one body entitled The Universal Community Society
of Rational Religionists, a title shortened to The Rational Society
in 1843. Another body, the Home Colonisation Society, was
formed in 1840 to raise funds for the establishment of a community. The Queenwood community was already in being and the
efforts of the Rational Religionists were largely directed to raising
funds for it. Differences, however, arose as to how the community
should be run and for what purpose. Owen and the Home Colonisation Society desired a community of well-to-do Owenites,
hiring labour to do the hard manual work, whereas the many
working class supporters desired a community in which all would
work and share on a basis of equality. The consequent conflicts,
together with the failure of Queenwood, brought the Owenite
organisation to an end in 1845. Helping towards this was the split
on religious matters. The Rational Society had attracted militant
atheists and these sought to make the society into an instrument
for their purposes, against the opposition of Owen and his leading
followers, viz. Lloyd Jones, Fleming and Buchanan. The *New
Moral World* ceased publication and the Socialist Missionaries
found other occupations.

The organisation, however, had created quite a stir in its day.
The Bishop of Exeter attacked it in a speech in the House of Lords
in 1840. He sought to rouse alarm by drawing attention to this
" powerful and growing organisation," its sixty branches, the map-
ping out of the whole kingdom into fourteen districts each with
its complement of missionaries who regularly lectured in 350
towns, its weekly paper, the *New Moral World*, and a sale of
500,000 tracts within a year.

The Society itself made similar claims. Nearly all its branches
had lecture halls, called Social Institutes, with accommodation for
22,000 people. Lectures and discussions were held, generally on
Sundays. Most of the branches also held monthly or quarterly
" festivals," in which " music, dancing, recitations, songs, and
philosophical expositions are the means of entertainment." All
but four branches had schools or classes, some as Sunday schools,
some as day schools, and nearly all had libraries. These activities,
it must be remembered, were being carried out whilst other powerful and popular agitations were at their height, viz. the Chartist

movement and the Anti-Corn Law movement. Among the active branches was No. 24, the Rochdale branch. From this was to spring the modern Co-operative Movement.

CONCLUSIONS

We can now sum up the pre-Rochdale Co-operative Movement. It objected to the existing system, regarding it as the cause of bad character, poverty, crime and misery, and it objected to competition, to buying cheap and selling dear, to profit making. Although community was the ultimate objective, benefits could be obtained meanwhile by establishing and developing various kinds of societies operating in accord with co-operative principles. Character itself would be improved by practising Co-operation in these societies, by the knowledge and experience gained in managing them, by their educational efforts and by the encouragement and promotion of thrift, temperance and self-help. The temptation to make a class movement was resisted and these early co-operators appealed to men and women of all classes to co-operate for the good of all. They had a strong democratic sentiment, as shown by their schemes for governing societies, respect for individual freedom, tolerance, equality and their desire and efforts to develop feelings of fraternity. There was also a lack of confidence in the ability of any fundamental reforms being carried out by governments. Dr. King believed government assistance would do more harm than good and speakers at the Co-operative Congresses expressed similar beliefs. The Socialist Congress of 1841, in a rather patronising address to the Chartists, having noted their failures, declared that " The failures we anticipated, but we deeply deplore your sufferings consequent thereon " and went on to express the opinion that even if they attained the charter they " Would still be very far removed from the means to secure the relief they immediately required or permanent prosperity."

SOME REASONS FOR FAILURE

This early Movement failed from a variety of causes. Its second phase, the later Owenite movement, 1835–1846, termed the Socialist Movement, failed through internal dissensions, many arising from theological differences, and from the natural failings of Owen, who was now an old man. The Co-operative Movement, i.e. the Movement which sought its ends by establishing and developing co-operative societies and which held its last Congress in 1835, failed partly through internal weaknesses and partly from external events and circumstances.

Internal weaknesses of the individual societies were the lack of efficient business management and occasionally dishonest officials. The law was unsatisfactory and resulted in trustees having the effective control of societies with consequent frustration and dissatisfaction of the democrats in the societies. Dr. King's advice was not followed: profits were divided and not allowed to accumulate as capital and credit was given and societies consequently bankrupted. Accounts were not well kept. There was probably also much in John Finch's observations at the 1832 Congress that societies were failing owing to neglect of meetings, failure to make themselves acquainted with the principles and proceedings of the societies, leaving the management of their concerns to a few individuals and to a spirit of selfishness, engendered perhaps by the societies themselves: " Shopkeeping has no tendency to improve either their morals or their principles."

There were also external causes of failure. The struggle for the Reform Bill, the agitation for factory legislation, the revolt against the new poor law, and the Chartist movement, with their exciting mass demonstrations, great expectations, and the sense for those taking part of being involved in matters of great moment and of making history, must have made the little co-operative store or productive society appear humdrum and rather inconsequential affairs. These difficulties might have been overcome if Owen had not initiated his grandiose and impossible schemes. It may well be that if Owen had remained in America, the early Co-operative Movement would have grown and fulfilled its early promise.

3 THE ROCHDALE SOCIETY OF EQUITABLE PIONEERS

" They took their affairs into their own hands, and what is more to the purpose, they kept them in their own hands."

G. J. Holyoake.

ROCHDALE, situated on the boundary of Lancashire and Yorkshire, was an old town experiencing in the first half of the nineteenth century both the miseries and the benefits of the Industrial Revolution. Flannel manufacture had been its staple trade for centuries, but its numerous hand loom weavers found times increasingly hard as power loom competition increased, and as exports suffered from American tariff policy. Hat making, one of its most important industries, was in decline. On the other hand the cotton industry, introduced in the last decade of the eighteenth century, was growing, and so were coal mining and machine making. The new factories, however, and the coal mines attracted immigrant labour, much of it Irish, which probably further increased the discontent of the old inhabitants engaged in hand loom weaving.

That there was much discontent is shown by the frequency of strikes, which at times assumed a violent character, leading to the intervention of the military. Eleven hundred Halifax Volunteers, for instance, were brought into the town during a strike in 1808, followed by regular troops who remained stationed there until 1846. Another strike in 1829 culminated in disturbances which were suppressed by horse and foot soldiers, resulting in some fatal casualties, prison sentences, and the transportation for life of one of the leaders. Hand loom weavers were generally involved.

Rochdale's situation, and its woollen and cotton industries, brought it within the ambit of the West Riding of Yorkshire and of South East Lancashire, both troubled areas and the seed beds of various movements. It had consequently a lively, at times exciting, atmosphere. There was a strong radical element in the town and a reform meeting held a fortnight before Peterloo attracted an audience estimated at thirteen thousand. It was addressed by Tom Collier, son of " Tim Bobbin " and uncle of John Collier, one of the original Pioneers. G. D. H. Cole describes the strategic importance of the town in Doherty's attempt to form

a National Trade Union, and the part it played in the Chartist
movement, and in the Ten Hours movement. John Bright, the
great free trader, was a townsman, and Richard Cobden, another
great free trader, was its Member of Parliament for a period.
There was thus evidence of considerable political activity and of
exciting movements.

Early Co-operative Efforts

In the midst of this ferment there were attempts at Co-operation.
"The Rochdale Friendly Co-operative Society," a society of
flannel weavers with sixty members, was formed in 1830. It seems
to have had a small library, sent a delegate to the Birmingham
Congress of 1831, and addressed a letter to the Third Co-operative
Congress in 1832 asking for a flannel manufactory to be established
and for a permanent missionary system. This may have been a
fairly active group, for G. J. Holyoake states that the Rev. Jos.
Marriott, who served as chairman during the first Co-operative
Congress in 1831, "learned all his Co-operation in Rochdale."
Holyoake, however, is far from reliable. Probably proceeding from
this first venture was the establishing of a society which ran a
retail store in 1833. The shop was in Toad Lane, No. 15, a little
way below where the Pioneers were to open theirs. It managed to
survive until 1835, foundering upon the rock which wrecked most
societies—credit trade. Among those associated with this society
were certainly Charles Howarth, James Standring and John Aspden, later associated with the Pioneers.

In spite of this failure a small group of Owenites did not lose
their faith. They continued to meet, often in the home of James
Smithies, and kept contact with the wider Owenite movement. The
Rev. J. Marriott represented Rochdale at the Manchester Congress
of 1837. At the end of that year a meeting was addressed in the
Unitarian Chapel, Clover Street, by two prominent Owenites,
Fleming and Rigby, the outcome of which was declared to be
"The standard of socialism is thus planted in another town."
(*New Moral World.*) Similar meetings were held in neighbouring
towns, enabling a district meeting to be held on Christmas Eve.
Subsequent meetings continued to be held, the immediate objective
being to establish definite branches of the Universal Community
Society of Rational Religionists. Rochdale not only formed a
branch, No. 24, but in April, 1838, acquired the use of an annexe
to "The Weavers' Arms" in Yorkshire Street and named it The
New Social Institution. This was to be the centre of Owenite
activity in the town for some years to come, and the birthplace
and the first headquarters of the Rochdale Pioneers.

No. 24 Branch

Lectures were given there each week by Owenite missionaries or lecturers, usually from Manchester. Lloyd Jones, after a visit to the branch, reported that " The effects of the social principles are nowhere more agreeably manifested than in Rochdale. I have found them, strictly speaking, a social family, each endeavouring to promote the happiness of the rest. Almost every night in the week is devoted to the cultivation of the mental and moral faculties. A mutual instruction class is being formed in which the rudiments of general education will be taught by the members of the society. . . . A dancing class is also numerously attended. . . . In short this branch is so well organised that it cannot fail to have the most beneficial effect on all connected with it."

Yet although the branch made something of a local stir and could at times attract good audiences, its numbers remained small. They complained of persecution, that placards advertising their meetings were torn down and that brickbats were thrown against the doors of their institution. So strong was the prejudice against them that a temperance body thought it wise to inform the town that it " had no connection with the socialists."

At times debates were held with opponents and there was a notable one in 1839, when the local theatre was required to hold the audience. James Daly, secretary of the branch (later the first secretary of the Rochdale Pioneers), reported on the meeting that the socialist speaker had defeated his opponent, at least in argument. The meeting, however, voted that socialism was poor, mean, and low, defeated an amendment by T. Livesey (an Owenite socialist but also leader of the local radicals and a prominent Chartist throughout the life of that movement) " That socialism was the only system for effectually obtaining and securing the happiness of mankind " and passed a vote of censure on the Owenite. The voting was 3 or 400 to 12, Daly declaring the majority had " voted for the continuance of misery, crime and ignorance." Probably the twelve votes indicate about the full strength of the branch. Nor does it appear to have grown much. Another great debate was held in the theatre in 1841, on " The Relative Merits of Chartism and Socialism," the Owenites again suffering defeat. However, they were persistent, and opened a day and Sunday school, J. Daly acting as schoolmaster.

Support for Queenwood

In 1841 they were collecting money for the Queenwood community and some of them subscribed amounts that were substantial for working men in those days, e.g., John Collier, £5; J. Garside.

£21; W. Mallalieu, £5; A. Pilling, £10; James Smithies, £14; G. Healey, £20; J. Whitehead, £1. All of these men were later associated with the Rochdale Pioneers' Society.

The Queenwood experiment, however, did not proceed on the lines which many Owenites believed it should, and there followed the dissensions described in the previous chapter. It is possible that disappointment with the Queenwood venture caused the Rochdale branch, as it did other branches, to consider other ways of establishing a community. They were well acquainted with Dr. King's *Co-operator*, and some had been associated with the attempts to achieve communities by and through co-operative societies. It is not surprising, therefore, that they turned again to try this method, and circumstances towards the end of 1843 provided the opportunity.

The Hungry Forties

The eighteen-forties have gone down in history as " the hungry forties," and whatever the case elsewhere they were certainly hungry in Rochdale. In 1837 one hundred and eighty beasts were killed weekly in Rochdale, in 1841 the number was down to sixty-five or seventy. A number of local medical men stated that the labouring classes were suffering great and increasing privations, that great numbers were unable to obtain wholesome food in sufficient quantity to maintain them in health, that they were predisposed to disease and rendered unable to resist its attacks, and that many appalling cases of distress and suffering came almost daily under their notice. Sharman Crawford, the member for the borough, declared in the House of Commons in 1841 that in Rochdale there were 136 persons living on 6d. per week, 200 on 10d. per week, 508 on 1s. per week, 855 on 1s. 6d. per week, and 1,500 were living on 1s. 10d. per week. Five-sixths of those he spoke of had scarcely any blankets, 85 families had no blankets, 46 families had only chaff beds with no covering at all.

It will probably remain impossible to get certainty on all the circumstances responsible for the decision to form a society in 1844. It is certain, however, that there was a very active and zealous Owenite branch in existence which considered founding a society on lines similar to those advocated by Dr. King.

Start of the Rochdale Society

William Cooper gave an account to Professor Fawcett in 1866 of the founding and early history of the society. Reference to appendix[1] will show that he believed the failure of a weavers' strike

---

[1] *Appendix IV.*

and the subsequent effort to start a flannel weavers' productive society played its part. The Owenite branch was probably too small and the prejudice against socialism too strong for it to start safely a store-keeping enterprise, but its members appear to have successfully interested the weavers, some teetotallers and some Chartists in such an undertaking. The Owenites were undoubtedly the initiators and dominated the proceedings. They framed the rules, Charles Howarth and James Daly being deputed for the purpose, taking many from their own Owenite insurance society, " The Rational Sick and Burial Society " (established by the Manchester Congress of 1837), and as comparison will show, from the model rules of the 1832 Congress. Their plan, as shown in their statement of objects, was that of Dr. King, viz. to start with storekeeping and to develop it so as to provide self-employment of members and to grow gradually into a co-operative community.

A study of the interesting appendix in *A Century of Co-operation*, G. D. H. Cole, on " Who Were the Pioneers? " shows that the first list of subscribers contained a big proportion of weavers, which suggests that Cooper's opinion of the part played by the weavers in the origin of the society is probably correct. Many of these soon lost their interest, however, and dropped out before the meeting on August 15th, 1844, which formally established the society. Cole's final list contains thirty-four names, but this includes four arbitrators who were not members. Of these, certainly fifteen were Owenite socialists, including such active and leading personalities as George Ashworth, John Bent, John Collier, Wm. Cooper, James Daly, Wm. Mallalieu, James Smithies, Jos. Smith, Wm. Taylor, Charles Howarth, James Tweedale. Only ten were weavers. Nor must they all be pictured as half-starved operatives driven by the desperation of hunger to start a co-operative store. Most of them were comparatively well-paid skilled artisans, some in business on their own account. Idealism, the vision of a better social order, not hunger, inspired these men, but it would be wrong to assume that others who suffered from low wages and unemployment were consequently unmoved by anything but their own immediate suffering. There is sometimes a tendency, perhaps an inclination, to forget that the Pioneers commenced business with the purpose of pioneering the way to a new and better social order. Without that ideal the Society would never have been begun; without it the difficulties of the early years would not have been overcome, the efforts to promote and assist other societies never have been made, and the developments which created national organisations never thought of. In short, without an ideal there would have been no Co-operative Movement.

OBJECTS OF THE ROCHDALE PIONEERS

The objects of the Society were stated in "Law the First" of their rules as follows:—

The objects and plans of this society are to form arrangements for the pecuniary benefit, and improvement of the social and domestic condition of its members, by raising a sufficient amount of capital in shares of one pound each, to bring into operation the following plans and arrangements.

The establishment of a store for the sale of provisions, clothing, etc.

The building, purchasing or erecting of a number of houses, in which those members desiring to assist each other in improving their domestic and social condition may reside.

To commence the manufacture of such articles as the Society may determine upon, for the employment of such members as may be without employment or who may be suffering in consequence of repeated reductions in their wages.

As a further benefit and security to the members of this Society, the Society shall purchase or rent an estate or estates of land, which shall be cultivated by the members who may be out of employment, or whose labour may be badly remunerated.

That as soon as practicable the Society shall proceed to arrange the powers of production, distribution, education and government, or in other words, to establish a self-supporting home colony of united interests, or assist other societies in establishing such colonies.

That for the promotion of sobriety, a temperance hotel be opened in one of the society's houses as soon as convenient.

The close correspondence between this plan and that of King's and the early congresses may be observed. The ultimate object is the same—a co-operative community, so comprehensive in its scope that it would be a " self-supporting home colony." The plan of attaining it was also similar: first the raising of capital, then the opening of a store, later the provision of houses where co-operative living could be practised and developed (it will be seen that houses were to be provided for those desirous of living co-operatively). Manufacture and the cultivation of estates would provide self-employment and play their part in the development of the society into a community.

THE RULES OF THE ROCHDALE PIONEERS

A perusal of the original rules of the Society impresses one with the intention of the Society, although starting business in a very small way, to start in a businesslike manner. There is an absence of the rough and ready, makeshift, crude organisation which might have been expected. They had, of course, men amongst them with some experience, men who had studied and discussed King's *Co-operator* and who had attended conferences and congresses. Lloyd Jones stated that some went down to Queenwood for advice. Certainly they would be able to get advice and assistance from the Owenite missionaries and lecturers of Manchester.

After the statement of objectives, the rules proceeded to provide for the government of the Society. This was to be democratic. It was to be vested in a President, Treasurer and Secretary, three trustees and five directors, to be elected annually by general meetings of members. These officers were responsible to the membership. Quarterly general meetings were to be held at which the officers would give an account of their government and consider the audited financial reports. The officers and directors were to meet weekly " in the Committee Room, Weavers' Arms." The duties and responsibilities of each officer were specified and the rights and obligations of membership stated. Disputes were to be settled by arbitrators, " none of whom shall be directly or indirectly interested in the funds of the society " (a proviso overlooked by those who have included the arbitrators among the original " twenty-eight ").

Credit was to be neither taken nor given: " The officers of this society shall not in any case, nor on any pretence, purchase any articles except for ready money, neither shall they be allowed to sell any article or articles except for ready money. Any officer acting contrary to this law shall be fined in the sum of ten shillings and be disqualified from performing the duties of such office." (Rule 21.)

Profits were to be divided on what they believed to be an original device. At each quarterly general meeting the financial statement must state the amount of profit realised in the preceding quarter " which shall be divided thus: Interest at the rate of 3½ per cent per annum shall be paid upon all shares . . . the remaining profits shall be paid to each member in proportion to the amount of money expended at the store." (Rule 22.) This, of course, is the rule introducing the " dividend on purchase."

Nine rules were laid down to govern the management of the store, the times when it would be open, the appointment of a cashier and salesman: " The salesman to weigh, measure and sell, but not to receive payment, the cashier to receive payment, giving a receipt to the purchaser and keeping a check of such receipt, paying over the money drawn to the secretary at each weekly meeting." Purchasers were to be provided with printed forms containing the names of goods on sale; these would be filled up by the purchaser and handed to the salesman. He would hand them to the secretary " as a check on the cashier."

The rules were revised in 1845 and one of the revisions provided for monthly general meetings of members, the business of these meetings " To consist in the explanation of the principles, objects and laws of the Society to discuss the affairs and suggest any improvement for the consideration of the officers and board of directors." The need for greater flexibility in management was now realised, the rules governing management of the store were repealed and " The management of the store left in the hands of the officers and board of directors."

Not all the practices of the Pioneers were contained in their rules. There is no mention of sale at current market prices, of dealing only in pure, non-adulterated commodities, of giving true weight and measure or of political and religious neutrality. They adopted and evolved, however, what they found to be sound methods of conducting co-operative business which they communicated to the many societies seeking their advice, so that Rochdale practice became regarded as sound practice and generally adopted by most societies not only in this country but all over the world.

ROCHDALE PRINCIPLES

These rules and recommended practices have been summarised and from them abstracted what are termed Rochdale Principles. The original Pioneers themselves did not, however, draw up a statement of principles. As a consequence nearly every writer on the history of the Rochdale Pioneers who has attempted to state their principles has given a different list. Holyoake gave fourteen, which, however, he termed " features." In 1860, however, the Rochdale Society did make a statement in its annual almanac of the rules of conduct, the points of organisation touching the business transactions of the society. These were as follows:—

" The present Co-operative Movement does not intend to meddle with the various religious or political differences which now exist in society, but by a common bond, namely that of self interest, to join together the means, the energies, and the talents of all for the common benefit of each.

(1) That capital should be of their own providing and bear a fixed rate of interest.

(2) That only the purest provisions procurable should be supplied to members.

(3) That full weight and measure should be given.

(4) That market prices should be charged and no credit given nor asked.

(5) That profits should be divided *pro rata* upon the amount of purchases made by each member.

(6) That the principle of " one member one vote " should obtain in government and the equality of the sexes in membership.

(7) That the management should be in the hands of officers and committee elected periodically.

(8) That a definite percentage of profits should be allotted to education.

(9) That frequent statements and balance sheets should be presented to members.

Later, however, the International Co-operative Alliance found it necessary to have some definition in order to decide on the genuineness of societies applying for membership. Rochdale principles were generally accepted (except by the U.S.S.R.) as being essential, but there were differences of opinion as to what were the essential principles and on their interpretation. (See Chapter 12.)

COMMENCING BUSINESS

The first formal meeting of the Society was held on Sunday, August 11th, 1844. Miles Ashworth was elected president. He was a weaver, and it may have been to please the weavers that he was given this position. He was replaced by Charles Howarth at the next quarterly meeting. John Holt was elected *treasurer;* James Daly, *secretary;* James Tweedale, James Smithies, James Holt, James Bamford, William Taylor, *directors;* Charles Howarth, George Ashworth, William Mallalieu, *trustees;* John Bent and Joseph Smith, *auditors;* James Wilkinson, Charles Barnish, George Healey, John Garside, John Lord, *arbitrators.* A second meeting held in the Social Institute on Thursday, August 15th, resolved: " That the Society date its establishment August 15th, 1844."

Much, however, had to be done before the Society could commence business. Capital had to be obtained. This was raised by weekly subscriptions. With the addition of a loan of £6 from the Weavers' Association they had raised a capital of about £28 when they actually started business. The rules provided that each member might pay for their shares by instalments of 3d. per week; if three months in arrears they would be fined sixpence, if six months they were to be expelled. No member was to have more than fifty shares. A meeting on August 29th resolved that in order to raise capital more rapidly, no interest or profit arising from trade with the store should be drawn for the first twelve months after the Society commenced active operations, but " should be added to each man's stock to form additional shares."

Premises were obtained, the ground floor of a warehouse, No. 31

Toad Lane, at a rent of £10 per year for three years. After repairs had been made and simple fittings bought, there was little capital left for purchase of stock. Cooper, in later life, believed this was probably beneficial. It prevented speculative purchases which might have been ruinous. They started trade with 28 lb. of butter, 56 lb. of sugar, 6 cwt. of flour, a sack of oatmeal, and some tallow candles, the cost of the whole amounting to £16. 11s. 11d. This first stock of goods was speculative neither in nature nor quantity. This was well for men who had no experience in selling groceries or buying them wholesale.

The shop was opened on the evening of December 21st, 1844. During the next three months it opened on Saturday and Monday evenings only, but in March, 1845 it was opened on the evenings of every week-day except Tuesday, a proof of its progress.

Progress, however, was very slow. At the end of the first year the Society had increased membership to seventy-four, had sales amounting to £710, had increased the capital to £181, and had made a profit of £22.

DEVELOPMENT OF THE SOCIETY

A trade depression in 1847 might have wrecked the Society if it had given credit or allowed its share capital to be withdrawn. Several of the members were in difficulties and resorted to selling some of their shares to other members. However, although the capital of the society increased little during that year, it is significant that it did increase. Depression has not infrequently since then seemed favourable to co-operative expansion. The membership increased from 80 to 110 and the sales from £1,147 to £1,925, although the profits fell from £81 to £72. The successful weathering of this storm probably created confidence, for the next year saw its membership, trade, profits and capital show substantial increases, though industry was still depressed.

Some circumstances external to the society favoured its growth at this period. The disillusion of many Chartists by the fiasco of 1848, removed the enmity of some of them to what they regarded as a rival movement, diverting working class effort from the single aim of the " sacred cause." In 1850, The People's Institute, a literary society composed mainly of middle class people came to an end. Most of its library, consisting of 1,100 volumes, was bought by the Pioneers, and the Society became the foremost educational institution in the town. Much of its educational progress was due to Abraham Greenwood, who had been librarian to the institute. He joined the Pioneers' Society in 1846, and became a leading co-operator not only in Rochdale but also in the country, and the originator and designer of national developments.

Probably the failure of The Rochdale Savings Bank in 1849, however, gave the greatest impetus to the Pioneers' progress. This
bank had been the main depository for working class savings in
the town. The banker was also a manufacturer and had used the
savings deposits to meet the losses of his manufacturing business.
His death and the subsequent settling of his estate revealed the
calamity. The Pioneers' Society now appeared as the best
custodian of working class savings. It had built up confidence
in itself by its steady progress and its weathering of the trade
depression. Moreover, its democratic constitution was attractive
to the saver who desired to have some control over his savings
and to be able to keep an eye on how they were being used, for
each quarter a financial statement had to be presented to a general
meeting and the officers of the Society could be questioned upon it
by the members.

Membership increased from 140 in 1848 to 600 in 1850, and
capital from £397 to £2,300. These people had the good sense to
take their trade to where they had put their savings and trade
increased in the same period from £2,276 to £13,180 and profits and
interest from £561 to £991. Growth enabled an increasing range
of services to be provided. Drapery, tailoring, butchery and footwear were added, a newsroom and library provided, and the store
began to be opened daily in 1851.

THE CORN MILL SOCIETY

Retailing, however, was only to be the beginning of their venture.
The Pioneers were ready to take advantage of opportunities of
entering into production. One was provided by the attempt of
some Rochdale men in 1850 to start a co-operative corn mill on
similar lines to that of Leeds. Finding it difficult to raise the
necessary capital, they sought the support of leading members of
the Pioneers' Society, and removed their headquarters from "The
Weavers' Arms " to the Pioneers' premises in Toad Lane. The
capital then amounted to £6. A provisional board was appointed
which included a number of Pioneers; on September 18th, Charles
Howarth was elected secretary and he drew up the rules on similar
lines to those of the Pioneers' Society. The Society invested £100
in the Corn Mill Society and appointed representatives in whose
name the money was invested, for the law did not permit one
society to hold shares in another. The Brickfield Equitable
Pioneers' Society (a society about a mile from Rochdale) also
invested. A number of individuals were also persuaded, and
eventually a capital of £1,000 was raised. A mill was purchased
and the Pioneers increased their shares to £150 and made loans of

£284 in December. In January, 1851 the mill began to grind corn, and other societies began also to invest in it.

For some time, owing to mismanagement by the head miller who " had professed a practical knowledge of the business " the Society lost heavily. His discharge left the mill without a manager, and the committee had to manage the mill until the end of 1851. Although they had no experience or knowledge of corn milling, nevertheless a profit was made during the last quarter. Abraham Greenwood, President, did most of the work. His business genius, together with the loyalty of the Rochdale and the Brickfield Societies, who would sell no other flour than that of the Co-operative Corn Mill, kept it in business. The individual shareholders did much also, for they were afraid of losing their investments and they persuaded other societies to invest and to buy its flour. They had to overcome opposition in the societies which feared their investments would be lost and complained that trade suffered as members did not like the Society's flour. This dislike was due to its colour for, being pure, it was darker than the adulterated product of private millers. Eventually the Corn Mill Society won through. In 1852 it made a profit and by the end of 1853 its assets exceeded its liabilities.

A Joint Venture

The Co-operative Corn Mill Society is interesting as the first joint venture of consumers' societies. Its early members, between 1850–51, consisted of six retail societies and ninety individual members, including many of the original Pioneers and five women. By the end of 1852, twenty-two societies were dealing with the Society, and as confidence grew the number increased and they not only traded with but joined the Society. Most of these were within sixteen miles of Rochdale, but the Mill had a good trade with societies as far away as Crewe and Dudley.

It is also significant as indicating a departure from the policy of developing a " home colony of united interests." It was a policy rather of developing enterprises on a larger scale to meet the needs of several societies. The objects of the Society were simple and practical: " to manufacture flour and meal free from adulteration, and, after paying interest on capital invested, and expenses of management, to divide the remaining profits amongst members in proportion to their trade with the Society." There was no element in the purpose or organisation of the Society to suggest it was a " producer " society; it was consumer initiated and consumer owned and controlled, serving consumer interests.

THE MANUFACTURING SOCIETY

The Pioneers, however, were concerned with establishing what were definitely " producer " societies. Most notable of these was the Rochdale Co-operative Manufacturing Society. This was organised on what today would be regarded as " co-operative co-partnership " lines. The capital was subscribed by shareholders as in a joint stock company. The Pioneers' Society assisted them with funds, but each member was to take up two shares, but none more than twenty, of £5 each. They could be paid for by instalments of 1s. per week. Profits were divided equally between capital and labour after 5 per cent interest on capital and 7½ per cent for depreciation had been deducted. Profits were divided among the labour employed in proportion to their wages. Vansittart Neale, a Christian Socialist lawyer, who was to play a great part in the Co-operative Movement drew up the rules. Among the chief promoters were James Smithies, Abraham Greenwood, William Cooper and J. T. W. Mitchell. The last-named became Chairman of the Manufacturing Society—and was later to become President of the Co-operative Wholesale Society. In this position his strong support of consumer Co-operation and opposition to producer Co-operation made a definite and lasting impression on the organisation, policy and purpose of the British Co-operative Movement. His opposition to producer Co-operation may well have been a consequence of the history of the Rochdale Co-operative Manufacturing Society.

Success and Reversion

The Society was successful, profit sharing gave the workers a vested interest in its prosperity and consequently there was less need for supervision and expenses were less. John Bright was very favourably impressed by the scheme, believing that profit sharing would make the capital of the employer more remunerative, for the machinery would do more work and there would be greater economy in raw material. In 1859, however, the Society had so prospered that it was decided to construct a new mill. Additional capital was required and this was readily forthcoming. Unfortunately, many of the new shareholders were concerned solely with making a profitable investment and an agitation commenced to abolish the profit sharing with labour rule. This agitation achieved its object in 1862; profit sharing was abandoned, and the Society became nothing but a joint stock company with the sole purpose of making profits for its shareholders. The co-operative element was naturally shocked at this perversion of the enterprise. Abraham Greenwood declared that " The original promoters never lost confidence in the principle of profit sharing. It was the success of the society that attracted to it persons who only cared for the eternal ' divi.' These persons brought into the Society their money very rapidly for shares, thus raising the number of shareholders from 200 or 300 to 1,400. It was the new share-holding element that swamped the original promoters of what was then called ' Bounty to labour '." William Cooper also declared that " Nearly all the anti-bountyites are persons who joined the society after it had become a prosperous and paying establish-ment." He protested that people who simply wanted a return on their invested capital should have commenced a society after their own fashion for themselves. " It appears to me wrong for persons to enter a society with whose principles they disagree, and then destroy its constitution."

The outcome of this venture may well have been the undying opposition of J. T. W. Mitchell to schemes of producer Co-opera-tion and his preference for consumer ownership and control, which safeguarded co-operative productive enterprises from becoming the prey of what he termed " little capitalists."

OTHER ROCHDALE DEVELOPMENTS

Other co-operative enterprises started in Rochdale by men associated with the Rochdale Pioneers were the Rochdale Equit-able Provident Sick and Burial Society, the Rochdale Co-operative Card Manufacturing Society, a Co-operative Building Society, and the Co-operative Insurance Company (which later became the present Co-operative Insurance Society).

The Pioneers' Society also endeavoured to act as wholesaler for other co-operative societies during the 'fifties and then played the leading part in establishing the Co-operative Wholesale Society in 1863. Yet by 1863 it had only 4,013 members. Its achievements are indicative of what may be accomplished by even small societies if they are composed of members who elect leaders enterprising and resolute in co-operative purpose. This enterprise and resolu-tion were related in both cause and effect to its educational activities.

EDUCATION ACTIVITIES

The original pioneers who founded the society, the members of No. 24 Branch of the Rational Society, were, as keen Owenites, convinced of the necessity of education to achieve their purpose. Consequently the premises at Toad Lane were quickly put to educational uses. Lectures and discussions were held there on Sun-days and weeknights. When the whole of the building became available in 1848, the second floor was used as a reading room and steps were taken to form a library. From the organisation of these activities developed its education department.

Grants were made towards the library at quarterly meetings but these were apparently illegal. The alteration of the Society's rules consequent upon the passage of the Industrial and Provident Societies' Act in 1853 provided the opportunity to include a rule that 10 per cent of the Society's profits should be devoted to educational purposes. The Registrar, however, objected but eventually agreed to a rule that 2½ per cent should be so used. An education committee was formed, and it proved an enterprising and far-sighted body. Access to information is a requisite of study, and so a fine library was established. The construction of new central premises opened in 1867 provided adequate housing for the library, a splendid reading room, and other educational facilities on the second floor. Every branch shop was also provided with a news room, for the Society regarded its members not as customers but as co-operators whose minds, as well as their stomachs, required nourishment.

Lectures and Classes

A school for young persons was also conducted between 1850 and 1855, but more advanced education was provided after that year for people of more mature years, classes being held in political economy, mathematics and French. Courses of popular lectures were also provided, usually on historical subjects, which in those days at least, had generally the most popular appeal. Eminent scholars were brought to give these lectures, but their success revealed their defect, for they aroused an appetite for further knowledge which they could not satisfy. Serious continued class study was necessary for this and some of the members demanded it. A course of lectures on astronomy by Professor Stuart of Cambridge suggested the solution. In them was born the University Extension Class, according to Professor Sadler's *Manual on University Extension*. " It was at Rochdale that Professor Stuart invented ' The Class,' the period of conversational teaching, enlivened by brisk periods of ' heckling ' which has ever since been an important feature in the University Extension system." Its origin was simple. His lectures were illustrated by diagrams, which were left on the walls until the next meeting. Members attending a general meeting of the Society were so attracted that they stayed to discuss them and wrote to Professor Stuart to come to the lecture room before the next lecture in order that they might ask him some questions. " He did so, and thus began the first University Extension Class." In adult education, as in so many other matters, the Rochdale Pioneers justified their title of pioneers.

ROCHDALE'S PLACE IN HISTORY

The Rochdale Pioneers' Society is popularly supposed to owe its fame to being the first co-operative society. This, of course, is not so. Hundreds of societies were in existence before it, and some of these are even yet in being. Nor was it the first to employ the device of dividing profits in proportion to purchases. Yet Professor Clapham approved the general opinion that the modern Co-operative Movement began with the establishment of the Rochdale Society in 1844. No movement developed from these earlier societies and even if they maintained a continuous life, it was a stagnant one. " It is from the taking down of the shutters of the shop in Toad Lane, Rochdale, in December, 1844, that the effective Co-operative Movement of 19th century industrial Britain has always been dated and rightly." (*An Economic History of Modern Britain*).

The fame of the Pioneers rests on more than the invention of a successful system of running a co-operative store. They also founded a movement. They had a vision which was not restricted to their own locality and society or to their own day and generation and they sought to further the progress of the Co-operative Movement as a whole. A great deal was done in encouraging and assisting the promotion and growth of other societies. G. J. Holyoake wrote in the 'fifties: "Any readers of these pages who may contemplate forming stores in their own neighbourhood will, on application to the Secretary of the Equitable Pioneers' Society, Toad Lane, Rochdale, obtain the laws at present in force, and other printed documents from which executive details may be learned. . . . Many Members of Parliament, political economists and some distinguished publicists have made journeys of late to the Rochdale Store. The officers receive with courtesy and give information with enthusiasm to all enquirers. Indeed, they are often found travelling thirty miles from their homes to give evening explanations to some workmen's meeting desirous of information in practical Co-operation and of forming societies themselves." All in fact who desired knowledge of or advice upon co-operative societies sought it at Rochdale, just as in these days they seek it from the Co-operative Union.

These activities and the success of the Rochdale Society led to the establishing of many societies, usually in the same places which had tried co-operative experiments before 1844. Societies in these areas which still survived adopted the rules and methods of Rochdale and new societies did likewise. Thus co-operative societies came to conform to the Rochdale system.

Pioneers of National Ventures

Co-operative retailing was thus pioneered by them, but, of course, they did not stop there; they pioneered in co-operative production, wholesaling, insurance and education. Members of the Society played leading parts in founding and developing the co-operative national organisations. Abraham Greenwood drew up the scheme for the C.W.S., and was its first president, and the first committee of this Society also included James Smithies as treasurer, Charles Howarth (who had removed to Heywood) and T. Cheetham of Rochdale. William Cooper also played an active and prominent part in its foundation, Samuel Ashworth became its buyer and manager, and J. T. W. Mitchell became its chairman in 1874 and is generally recognised as its greatest chairman. He probably had a greater and more lasting effect on the Co-operative Movement than any other individual. Samuel Bamford, who, as editor of the *Co-operative News* (1875–1898) put this journal on its feet and was one of the great formative influences on the Movement, was also a product of the Pioneers, " distinguishing himself in the Equitable Pioneers' Science and Art Classes." The society played a leading part in promoting and organising the Lancashire and Yorkshire Conference Association, a precursor of the Co-operative Union, and amongst the sponsors of the first Co-operative Congress of the modern series in 1869 were Abraham Greenwood, J. T. W. Mitchell, and the Rev. Nassau Molesworth, Vicar of St. Clement's, Rochdale, the latter contributing a paper for Congress discussion. Professor Fred Hall, the first Principal of the Co-operative College and Adviser of Studies to the Co-operative Union, also came from Rochdale, and it was as a young man teaching classes in Co-operation for the Equitable Pioneers that he had the vision of a Co-operative Residential College, which he did much to bring about. Thus, the Rochdale Equitable Pioneers' Society not only began the modern Co-operative Movement, it also provided the men who largely made it.

C. Gide's Report

Professor C. Gide, the French economist and co-operator, paid a great tribute to the Rochdale Pioneers during a visit of delegates of the I.C.A. Congress to Rochdale in 1902. He then expressed the sentiments of co-operators the world over in appreciation and gratitude for the work of the Pioneers. Succeeding generations of co-operators would repeat them: "At the period when the Rochdale Pioneers formed your Society, there were not wanting in the world, either in France or in England, great economists and great socialists. Let me recall to your memory John Stuart Mill, Bastiat, Proudhon. Probably they had heard of what was actually going on in Toad Lane. But they never understood what kind of movement it was that was being prepared there, and they would have been astounded indeed, if anyone had told them that a day would come when no more disciples would be found for their learned systems, no more readers for their books, whereas the faithful followers of the Rochdale Pioneers would then number by millions.

"Oh, Pioneers! I thank you not only for having given us an admirable organisation, which has procured a little more comfort and material help in the battle of life to millions of beings, but above all things for having shown us by your example that all our sciences, all the science of learned men and of writers, all the science which is extracted from books and from laws, the sciences in the name of which we teach where we govern, is nothing worth in respect of clear foresight and creative power, by the side of the simple faith of some humble workers, who were absolutely without book learning, but who lived, worked, toiled and hoped resolutely even against hope." (I.C.A. Congress Report, 1902.)

4 THE CREATION OF A NATIONAL MOVEMENT

*" Nothing in progression can rest on its original plan.
We might as well think of rocking a grown man in
the cradle of an infant."*

Edmund Burke.

THE success of the Rochdale Society of Equitable Pioneers and the missionary zeal of some of its members revived the Co-operative Movement in districts where it had apparently died. This revival was also quickened by the formation and propaganda of Redemption societies. These were Owenite bodies adopting the methods advocated by Dr. King. Members of the societies subscribed one penny per week to a " Redemption of Labour Fund," which was to be an accumulation of capital to finance their self-employment on the land and in self-governing workshops. The largest and most active of these was a society at Leeds, founded in 1846. Lloyd Jones, the former Owenite missionary was among its leaders. It published a penny monthly journal, the *Herald of Redemption* later the *Herald of Co-operation*, edited by James Hole, and in 1848–1854 attempted a co-operative community at Garnlwyd, Carmarthenshire. Lack of capital caused failure, but attempts to raise capital for it led to the establishment of other Redemption societies. Some of these, including the Leeds Society, opened stores, the profits from which were to be used for developing the estate. The stores themselves, it was hoped, would provide outlets for the sale of the estate's produce. As interest in, and hope for, the community project waned many of these societies adopted the Rochdale system.

Growth

All societies at this time were small, often with only thirty or forty members. There are no reliable statistics relating to them, but there were at least 130 societies in 1851. Rochdale was then the giant with 700 members and a trade of £400 per week. Bacup had 400 members and £230 per week; Heywood, 340 members and £140 per week; and Halifax, 207 members and £50 per week.

Quite a number of societies were formed in 1850 and 1851,

mainly in Lancashire and the West Riding. This may have been
due to a quickening interest in social movements due to the
" Revolutionary Year " of 1848, as Thomas Hughes believed, but
there were probably other causes. Working men in those days
needed to make provision for themselves against the misfortunes
of unemployment, sickness, death and old age. Difficulties were
not confined to saving, but extended also to finding safe depositories for their savings. The failure of the Rochdale Savings Bank in
1849 was not exceptional and there were many such failures in the
following two or three years, due often to years of maladministra-
tion and neglect by the trustees and ingenious dishonesty by the
managers. Sick and burial societies were often unsound because
of defective actuarial calculations and expensive management. Co-
operative societies probably appealed to many thrifty working men
not only as a means of more economical domestic expenditure but
also as a good and safe investment for their savings.

The driving force of the Movement, as with any movement,
however, came from its idealists. These were strengthened by the
infusion of new thought by the body of men known as the Christian
Socialists.

THE CHRISTIAN SOCIALISTS

The 'thirties and 'forties were decades of considerable unrest
and occasional violent disturbances, e.g., the agricultural labourers'
revolt of 1830 and the struggles for the Reform Bill, for a Ten
Hours Bill, against the new Poor Law and against the Corn Laws.
The Chartist Movement brought together various elements which,
although having diverse objectives, were united in their opposition
to things as they were, and believed that their objectives could be
attained if the working classes obtained political power. These
manifestations of unrest shook some of the comfortable classes
from the complacency that all was well with the world. Disraeli,
in his *Sybil*, had drawn attention to the cleavage between the "two
nations," the rich and the poor, while novelists such as Mrs
Gaskell and Charles Dickens described the miseries and injustices
suffered by the labouring poor. Thomas Hood's *Song of the Shirt*
depicted the evils of the " sweating " system, and Mayhew's *Life
and Labour of the London Poor* gave graphic descriptions of the
lives lived by a considerable proportion of that city's population.
J. S. Mill, son of the classical economist James Mill and intellectual descendant of Bentham, was having doubts of the validity of
the assumptions of classical political economy.

There were also churchmen who found the system and its underlying philosophy objectionable on religious grounds. John Henry

Newman, leader of the Oxford Movement, denounced liberal political economy as " a categorical contradiction of our Lord, St. Leo and all saints " and, as already mentioned, there were clergymen and others such as Dr. King, Minter Morgan, John Finch, connected with the Owenite movement, whose objection to the existing system and ideas of reform were based upon their interpretation of Christian doctrine.

The term Christian Socialist, however, is generally applied to a group of clergymen and lawyers which existed from 1848–1854 and who so called themselves. A young barrister, J. M. Ludlow, first got the group together and the Rev. F. D. Maurice, Professor of Theology at King's College, London, was its leader. Its other notable figures were the Rev. Charles Kingsley, poet, novelist and its most stirring propagandist, and two who were to have a long and influential connection with the Co-operative Movement, Thomas Hughes and E. Vansittart Neale.

They believed that the evils of the day arose from the neglect of the Christian obligations of man to man, especially in their economic relations with each other. Selfishness and competition were condemned and they desired " God's order " which was an order of mutual love and fellowship, " an actually living community under Christ, in which no man has a right to call anything he has his own, but in which there is spiritual fellowship and practical co-operation."

Propaganda

The " Revolutionary Year " of 1848 and the Chartist fiasco on Kennington Common spurred them to action. They had a genuine sympathy for the disillusioned Chartists and sought to convert them to what they believed was a better way of social reform. A series of weekly tracts, *Politics for the People*, was published by them. Distinguished men contributed to these tracts, e.g., Maurice, Kingsley, Ludlow, the Archbishops Whateley and Trench, Bishop Thurlwall and Dean Stanley, but they were issued for only three months, and, although circulation reached two thousand, they did not reach the working classes for whom they were intended. *Tracts on Christian Socialism* followed in 1850, again failing the desired result, and these were succeeded by the *Christian Socialist*, a weekly journal, from November 2nd, 1850 to December 27th, 1851. The term " Christian Socialist " was deliberately chosen as a provocative challenge to " the unchristian socialist and the unsocial Christian." Kingsley also wrote two novels of social purpose, *Alton Locke* and *Yeast*, which attacked the sweaters of labour in town and country.

All this propaganda probably had some effect, but rather upon sympathetic middle-class people than upon the working-class unchristian socialists. More direct methods were employed and regular debates and discussions with working men were held at the Cranbourne Coffee Tavern. Here they met and gained the adherence of two men not without influence, Walter Cooper, brother of Thomas Cooper the Chartist poet, and Lloyd Jones, the former Owenite missionary. These two played prominent parts in the Christian Socialist ventures of The Working Men's Associations.

THE WORKING MEN'S ASSOCIATIONS

J. M. Ludlow was a young social reformer who was acquainted not only with English political economy but also with French socialism, then mainly influenced by Fourier (a Utopian Socialist) and Louis Blanc. The latter denounced competitive and capitalist industry and advocated self-governing workshops organised into self-governing industries. Ludlow persuaded the other Christian Socialists that similar associations could be started in this country and made to embody Christian association in industry. They proceeded to promote these associations by propaganda, initiative and loans.

Some societies, of which the Castle Street Tailors, London, was the first, had already been started before the establishment of The Society for Promoting Working Men's Associations in June, 1850. This Society consisted of a small number of " promoters," and the members of the associations who were termed associates. It was governed by a Council of Promoters and a Central Board which represented the associates. The Council raised funds and spread the idea of Co-operation and the Central Board assisted in forming new associations and in supervising and keeping them on the right lines.

The associations were democratic, the members electing from themselves a chairman, secretary, treasurer and council of administration. Executive power, however, was in the hands of a manager, and the Council of Promoters had the right to veto a choice of manager whilst their loans to the association remained unpaid. It was expected that by the time this was accomplished the association would have sufficient knowledge and experience to be entirely free, self-governing and successful. Profits would be divided amongst the associates every half-year after deductions had been made for repayment of loans and allocations to reserves. All work had to be done on the association's premises, there was to be no Sunday work, and the associations must be politically neutral.

Several associations were formed, not all directly by the Society for Promoting Working Men's Associations, but most had communication or some connection with it. The last number of the *Christian Socialist* gave a list of fourteen associations in London consisting of bakers, builders, needlewomen, tailors, silk weavers, printers, pianoforte makers and woodcutters. For the provinces the names of twenty-one associations are given, consisting of tailors, weavers, hatters, boot and shoe makers, ribbon weavers, engineers and saw makers, ten of them were in Lancashire, two in Yorkshire, two in Cheshire and three of them were Redemption societies.

Failure

Few of these societies had a long life. Some failed within a few months, others changed their character and became private profit-making businesses. The last to survive was the Salford Hatters, this being voluntarily disbanded in 1873.

Many valuable lessons can be learned from failures, and the reasons for failure in these societies were various. Those given by Walter Cooper, who was manager of the Castle Street Tailors, could be summarised as the lack of co-operative knowledge, purpose and will by the members. When times were good, " We called each other brothers, sang songs about ' labour's social chivalry ' and did wonders in the way of work and profit . . . . But the slack season came, for which we had not provided and brought with it those terrible evils, jealousy and disunion. . . . I believe all of us talked too much about rights, and thought too little about duties." The Report of the Society for Promoting Working Men's Associations in 1851 also blamed the co-operative deficiencies of the working-men associates:—

" The Society has for some time past determined to discourage advances of money to bodies of working-men about to start in association unless they have first shown some signs of preparedness for the change from their old life, and have subscribed some funds of their own . . . Working-men in general are not fit for association. They come into it with the idea that it is to fill their pockets and lighten their work at once, and that every man in an association is to be his own master. They find their mistake in the first month or two and then set to work quarrelling with everybody connected with the association, and after much bad blood has been roused, the association breaks up as insolvent and has to be reformed under stringent rules and after the expulsion of refractory members . . . we set up three sets of shoemakers in association, supplying in two instances the whole of the funds, in the other all but £5. None of the men were picked, we accepted them just as they came to us. We gave to them absolute self-government . . . Every one of these associations had quarrelled with and turned out its original manager within six months . . . Where the associations are successful the great danger which they and all who are interested in them have to guard against is exclusiveness. The associates find their own position greatly improved and fear to endanger it by taking in new members."

Reasons for Failure

There was neither the careful selection of members in the first place to undertake a form of co-operative enterprise which demands far more of its members than does consumer Co-operation, nor a period of education and training to prepare them for it. The disunion, bickerings and quarrels amongst themselves and with the managers and the lack of appreciation of the importance of the administrative, financial and commercial parts of the businesses were certain under these circumstances. One must not forget, however, that the factory system was still new and not as yet general and many were not accustomed to factory discipline and resented it and the managers who imposed it. Yet this does not account for the failures of such cases as the Padiham Commercial Mill Company, a society of weavers, and the Atlas Engineering Works, in which the members were well accustomed to factory work.

It was also a mistake, as the promoters realised, for them to advance the capital for these enterprises. There is a fairly general experience that co-operative societies fare best whose members have subscribed a substantial part, preferably the whole, of the capital themselves. The individual stake in the collective enterprise induces the necessary sense of responsibility and loyalty to obligations. There were also other difficulties, such as suppliers of raw materials and equipment refusing normal trade credits when aware that the enterprise was a co-operative one. There was, too, the great difficulty of finding a sale for the products. The customary channels in which business contacts were frequently made and knowledge of potential trade circulated, particularly the circles of businessmen in various spheres of social and business life, were not available to the working-class members of the association. Moreover, the associations had to compete with other producers and sometimes with each other, yet competition was regarded as an evil opposed to the ideal sought by the Christian Socialists.

E. V. Neale soon realised that the associations could not by themselves achieve that ideal. A more comprehensive scheme was required which would give greater unity and organised marketing. In a letter to the *Christian Socialist* he expressed the opinion that at that time the co-operative stores were more important than the associations and that they were more truly expressive of the principle of association, which was the union of conflicting interests. In the associations there was but a little attempt to reconcile the interest of the capitalist and the producer and none to reconcile those of producer and consumer.

NEALE'S PLAN FOR CO-OPERATIVE DEVELOPMENT

In April, 1851, Neale put forward to a conference of promoters and associates a scheme for the associations to be federated into a general union, the profits of all the associations to go into a common fund. " All the associates working in the same trade should form one association so that they might distribute the work more equally without entering into competition with one another." Nearly all the associates, however, objected to the proposal and it was dropped. Neale, however, was already putting a scheme for development into operation through the Central Co-operative Agency.

He had supplied the capital for the London Co-operative Stores which had started business in 1850 in Charlotte Street with Lloyd Jones as manager. This was transformed into a wholesale house, known as the Central Co-operative Agency although registered as Wooden, Jones and Co. (Joseph Wooden and Lloyd Jones were its directors). His scheme can be deduced from an appeal made to the trade unions for support for the institution which was " a legal and financial institution for aiding the formation of stores and associations, for buying and selling on their behalf and ultimately for organising credit and exchange between them." The Agency was intended to be the associations' market for their products and the source of supplies for the retail societies, serving also as banker, adviser, propagandist and promoter. It would reconcile the interests of producer and consumer and provide the means for the organic development of the Movement, which the associations and the retail societies lacked whilst they remained isolated from each other.

The agency prospered and progressed. Bigger premises became necessary and the agency moved to 356 Oxford Street. Unfortunately, these proved too big and expensive and Neale was obliged to wind the Agency up in 1857. A branch had been opened in Swan Street, Manchester, and a considerable trade done with the

northern societies. The Agency and Neale's scheme were pre-
cursors of much co-operative development later.

THE INDUSTRIAL AND PROVIDENT SOCIETIES' ACT, 1852

The formation and development of co-operative societies were
hindered by the lack of suitable legislation, and this the Christian
Socialists were quick to realise. Societies could obtain a legal
status by registering under the Friendly Societies' Act, 1846, but
this was unsatisfactory. The purposes of the society had to be
certified as legal by the Registrar of Friendly Societies, it could
only hold personal property through trustees, real property had to
be conveyed absolutely to the trustees and a society was thus
entirely dependent on their honesty in this respect.

There was also the awkward " Frugal Investment Clause." This
enabled retail societies to register under the Act, for by it, societies
for the frugal investment of their members' savings in purchasing
food, clothes, tools or other necessaries, were included as friendly
societies, but they were not permitted to trade with other than
their own members. Producer societies were thereby denied registration and they were in a very unsatisfactory legal position—
" each member could in most cases pledge its goods and credit and
steal its money without any legal remedy. If the number of members was less than twenty-five they were all partners, and as the
law then stood, every individual member had the power to pledge
the credit of the society and might have made away with the common stock, the only remedy being a suit in Chancery. If the
association numbered more than twenty-five, it placed itself out of
the pale of legal protection, unless it chose to register under the
Joint Stock Companies Act, the provisions of which being wholly
framed for bodies of persons subscribing capital merely, and not
labour, were totally inapplicable, and too expensive in any case
to be of any use." (Quoted in *Co-operative Production*, Ben Jones.)

The Christian Socialists managed to get the appointment of a
House of Commons Committee to consider and suggest means of
removing obstacles and giving facilities for safe investment of the
savings of the middle and working classes. A strong case was
presented; Ludlow, Hughes, Neale, Cooper and Lloyd Jones gave
evidence, their case being immeasurably strengthened by the
evidence of C. H. Bellenden Ker, a well-known authority on
company law, and John Stuart Mill, regarded as the greatest
economist of the day. The committee reported in favour of an
immediate measure.

Ludlow and Neale drafted a Bill and Robert Slaney, M.P., agreed to move it in the House. However, the Liberal Government fell in 1851 before it had been introduced and it was the succeeding Conservative Government which enacted it in its first session, the Royal Assent being given on June 30th, 1852.

Provisions

The Act permitted the establishment of societies for the purpose of raising, by voluntary subscriptions of the members, a fund for attaining any purpose or object for the time being authorised by the laws in force with respect to friendly societies or by the new Act, by carrying on or exercising in common any labour, trade or handicraft, or several labours, trades or handicrafts, except the working of mines, minerals or quarries beyond the limits of the United Kingdom, and also except the business of banking, whether in the United Kingdom or not. The rate of interest which societies might pay was limited to 5 per cent; dividends on purchases were specially authorised; and the balancing and auditing of accounts twice a year and the inspection of the accounts by members were to be provided for by the societies' rules. Shareholding was limited to £100 for each member, liability of members for debts was unlimited and continued for two years after ceasing membership; the transferability of shares was restricted; they could only be sold to the society itself or to another person with the consent of the board of management of the society; and only one acre of land could be held.

This first Act relating to co-operative societies as distinct from friendly societies or joint stock companies was a response to the demands of co-operators themselves for such legislation. Furthermore, it was drafted by co-operators themselves and, although not giving them all they desired, it gave most of what they believed they could get at the time. The most serious omissions were limited liability and facilities for federation, but the most important requisites for safeguarding the co-operative character of the societies were included, viz. members' control and the share capital provisions which would prevent the ownership of the society passing to a few individuals by their purchase of shares.

EFFORTS FOR CO-OPERATIVE UNITY

Many years afterwards, in 1878, Thomas Hughes declared that, " The passing of the Act formed a most important epoch in co-operative annals. The occasion was felt not only to justify but to necessitate an effort to consolidate the Movement, and the ground had been already prepared for such an effort. The northern stores had been visited by the promoters on several

occasions, and were all by this time in communication with the
London centre, had taken part in urging the passing of the Bill,
and were now eager to turn it to the best advantage."[1]

A conference was held in London in July, 1852, to discuss the
situation as it affected all co-operators. Twenty-eight societies
were represented, including delegates from Lancashire and Yorkshire, but the adhesion in writing of several other societies was
received. The provisions of the Act were explained and discussed,
and the promoters undertook to prepare an explanatory statement
and codes of rules and to circulate them amongst all co-operative
bodies in the kingdom. The conference also passed a resolution
which has often appeared as a Rochdale principle, " that this conference entreats all co-operative establishments, for the sake of the
general good, to sell all articles exactly for what they know them to
be, and to abstain as much as possible from the sale of all articles
known to be adulterated, even if demanded by the customers."

Committees were appointed to draw up plans for the establishment of wholesale depots for the supply of stores, to consider a
plan for a Co-operative Investment Society and to consider the
establishment of a newspaper. Conferences were held later at
Manchester and Leeds in 1853 and 1854. Christian Socialists then
ceased to act as an organised group. Maurice and Kingsley were
not happy with business activities and Ludlow was not attracted
by the incursions into trade, but Neale remained actively engaged
in connection with the Central Co-operative Agency.

The stimulus to closer union of societies had, however, been
given. John Bates of Bury appealed in the *Christian Socialist* for
the formation of a Co-operative Union and a Co-operative League
was formed at the beginning of 1852 to collect and diffuse information and ideas about Co-operation. The development of national
organisation, however, was in the first instance to be through
wholesaling.

EARLY CO-OPERATIVE WHOLESALING

There were many efforts at wholesale trading in the 'fifties.
Conferences convened by the Christian Socialists continued to be
concerned with it. That of 1852 (London) had passed a resolution
empowering a committee to draw up a plan for the establishment
of wholesale depots, and the conference at Manchester in 1853
drew up three interesting suggestions for dealing with the problem.

(1) Co-operative stores should contribute to a capital fund
according to their trade and membership for the purpose of

---

[1] " *Lecture on History and Objects of Co-operation.*" T. Hughes, 1878

starting and operating a wholesale society. This was regarded as too risky since the capital required would be large and they had not as yet the skill or knowledge for running such an enterprise successfully.

(2) The largest store in a locality should act as a wholesaler for the smaller ones around it. It would get the advantage of buying in greater bulk and some profit on the trade and the small ones would have less expenses in buying and a more reliable supplier than the ordinary wholesale merchant whose operations were "too frequently to the great detriment of struggling co-operative bodies." This was regarded as more practicable.

(3) A wholesale buyer should be appointed by a number of societies and provided with an office. Lists of goods required with the necessary money would be sent to him each month by the societies and he would then purchase in bulk and send to some appointed place for distribution to the societies.

This third scheme was strongly favoured. It required little capital and involved little risk; it would cut out middlemen; it would cover a larger district than would the second suggestion and so, having a bigger trade, be able to buy better; the smaller stores would be able to buy at the same prices as the larger, and the working men's associations could keep it well supplied with lists of articles they had available for sale. The scheme had been proposed in Bradford a couple of years earlier, but was never put into operation; nor did societies adopt this third scheme even although strongly recommended by the Congress.

WHOLESALE ACTIVITIES OF THE ROCHDALE PIONEERS

Meanwhile, the Rochdale Pioneers were also trying to establish and develop co-operative wholesaling, acting, in the opinion of Neale, upon the second scheme suggested at the Congress at which James Smithies was present. This Congress, however, was in 1853, whereas the Rochdale Pioneers had in fact decided on September 26th, 1850, to open a wholesale department and " to circularise all co-operative stores convening a meeting to consider the best means of purchasing our goods together." It commenced wholesale trading later in the year.

In 1851 a conference was held at Bury and Lloyd Jones was successful in persuading it to pass a resolution in favour of a Central Trading Department, and to appoint a committee to investigate the possibilities and draw up a report. The committee consisted of Lloyd Jones, James Smithies, William Bell of Heywood, and James Campbell of Manchester. Out of its deliberations

Lloyd Jones drew up a report, written by James Smithies, described as a prospectus for the Central Co-operative Agency. It
pointed to the growth of co-operative stores and the consequent
increasing need for the stores to co-operate for their purchases so
as to get into the wholesale markets. A wholesale co-operative
depot would give the individual stores, " the small ones as well as
the large, all the advantages to be derived from the extensive and
honest dealings " of such an undertaking. A capital of £6,000 to
commence was to be subscribed by the management committees
of stores; Manchester was to be the seat of the depot and, after
interest at 5 per cent had been paid on the capital, profits were to
be divided so that one-third would go to a reserve fund and two-
thirds returned to purchasers as dividend on their purchases.

Leeds Conference

The annual conference at Leeds of the Society for Promoting
Industrial and Provident Societies (into which the Society for
Promoting Working Men's Associations had transferred itself) was
held in the August of 1854. William Pare, an active leader of the
pre-Rochdale Movement was present and was elected to the
executive. Only twenty-three societies were represented, but they
included the Rochdale Pioneers. E. V. Neale presided, and its most
important business was a discussion on the need for a wholesale
centre for the purchase of general provisions in the north. The
committee urged the immediate adoption of such a centre and
suggested Rochdale: " by the length of time it has been established, and the amount of business it is doing, it naturally suggests
itself as the best one to be fixed on." It was also decided that the
next annual conference should be held at Rochdale in August, 1855.

The October issue of the *Co-operative Circular* contained a statement that the Rochdale Pioneers' Society, being desirous of
carrying out the resolution of the conference, was making arrangements for establishing the Central Depot and carrying out the
wholesale business which the conference had invited them to undertake. Their rules were being revised, they had taken stock and
made the necessary preparations, and now only awaited the sanction
of their members at the October quarterly meeting. Some of the
advantages of such a depot were pointed out—that the societies
would place themselves in a position of greater security from the
corrupt practices of trade of their own buyers and from the
exorbitant charges of middlemen.

The Society issued two almanacks for 1855, one for its own
members and one for distribution among other stores which contained the resolutions of the Leeds conference in respect of the

Central Depot and a statement that the Society had accepted the invitation and was prepared to accept any orders that might be sent. Some writers have taken this to be the beginning of whole-saling by the Rochdale Pioneers, but it was, of course, already engaged in such trade. The resolution of the conference, however, put the Rochdale wholesale department on to a better status, its wholesale department was no longer operating on a Rochdale decision alone and it was accepting a duty to which it had been invited by the wider Movement.

This, however, may have been responsible for the trouble which arose in the Society in connection with its wholesale department. There are generally some members in societies who object to their societies assuming any obligations excepting those to their own respective members, and there were some of these in the Rochdale Society. When the committee for the wholesale department was elected in April, 1855, the idealists appear to have been defeated, for only one of the original Pioneers was included. However, they regained control in 1856. Abraham Greenwood was made President in January of that year, and the quarterly meeting decided " the wholesale department be continued," but a committee of seven was to inquire into the system employed. This committee con-sisted of keen supporters of co-operative wholesaling, including J. T. W. Mitchell.

Unco-operative Enterprise

A conference was held in Rochdale in March, 1856, to consider the wholesale department. Greenwood was in the chair and it was proposed that the department should be converted into a federal agency representative of various societies. This presented legal difficulties, which could, however, be clumsily evaded as in the case of the Rochdale Co-operative Corn Mill. A definite plan was drawn up, and the Pioneers were willing to invest £1,500 in such a society, but the next conference which considered the plan was unable to agree upon it. Many difficulties appeared. How should the capital be raised? What price-policy should be adopted— market prices with the surplus distributed as dividend on purchases or cost prices plus a commission to cover wholesale expenses? Rochdale was accused by some delegates of charging unfairly and Rochdale made counter accusations of disloyalty and unpaid accounts. What was certain was the fact that the department was losing money and that the Rochdale Pioneers had to bear the losses. It was not surprising, therefore, that opposition within the Society to the department continued, and that finally, in 1858, its operations came to an end. William Cooper attempted to reopen it in 1859, but unsuccessfully, it being resolved " That the question of reopening the wholesale department be postponed for an indefinite period."

This attempt at wholesaling thus failed. Its failure was due to the nature of the enterprise being unco-operative even though the relations were between co-operative societies. There was no sharing of the risk, for the Pioneers' Society bore it all. The other societies, however, had no share in control and they perhaps naturally suspected that the department was run for the Pioneers' benefit and not for theirs. They could not feel the pride or the obligations of ownership in a venture in which they were customers but not genuine partners.

THE CO-OPERATIVE WHOLESALE SOCIETY

There were, however, some co-operators who realised that without some co-operative activity between societies the limits of co-operative progress would very soon be reached. A co-operative wholesale society of a truly federal nature was necessary if the Movement was to continue. E. V. Neale had preached this continuously from 1850, and there were many left who remembered the ambitions of pre-Rochdale Co-operation and its efforts at co-operative wholesaling and desired to revive them. There were also Rochdale Pioneers such as Greenwood, Smithies, Cooper, Mitchell, Howarth, Cheetham, with men of similar mould from other societies such as Hooson and J. C. Edwards of Manchester, Marcroft of Oldham, and Hilton of Middleton, who could see the need and were not to be prevented from pursuing their ideal.

In 1859, Greenwood, Hooson and Edwards decided to initiate a demand for amendments to the Industrial and Provident Societies' Act which would remove some of the legal obstacles to a federal wholesale society. They enlisted the support of Neale and Ludlow. The movement for such an advance was furthered by the publication of the *Co-operator*, under the editorship of E. Longfield for the first year. He was succeeded by Henry Pitman, who edited the paper until its end in 1871. Pitman's *Co-operator* was a powerful advocate for wholesale co-operation. Published monthly, it carried the arguments for a wholesale society more continuously, fully, widely and effectively than could ever have been done by the mere holding of conferences.

But conferences were necessary and were held. P. Redfern, the historian of the C.W.S., held that the C.W.S. sprang from a tea party held at Lowbands Farm, Jumbo, Middleton, in August, 1860. This theory was first advanced by W. Nuttall in 1869, but the Jumbo meeting has not been regarded as of importance by other historians of the Movement. From reports of the meeting in the *Oldham Chronicle*, the meeting was given a description of the Rochdale Co-operative Manufacturing Society, and the possibilities of further developments in co-operative cotton manufacturing were discussed. There is no mention of any discussion of amendments to the I. and P. Act nor of co-operative wholesaling, though it is probable these were discussed, for both subjects were very much in the air as they had been for some years past.

The *Co-operator* of October, 1860, appealed for a conference to be held to " collect the scattered fragments of these separate societies together and establish a strong and indissoluble union of co-operators." To begin with such a conference could discuss wholesale trading and assurance.

Preliminary Steps

A conference was held at Rochdale in November which appointed a committee to go further into the matter of amending legislation and co-operative wholesaling. It was a strong committee, consisting of idealists who knew how to get things done, viz. Abraham Greenwood and William Cooper (Rochdale), Marcroft and Hewkin (Oldham), Hooson and Dyson (Manchester), Hilton (Middleton), and C. Howarth (formerly Rochdale, now Heywood). To it were added Smithies, Stott, Cheetham (Rochdale) and J. C. Edwards (Manchester). This committee presented a report to a conference attended by delegates from most Lancashire and Yorkshire societies on Christmas Day in Manchester, 1860. It agreed on desirable amendments of the I. and P. Act, and Cooper, Greenwood and Stott were appointed to act with Neale in drafting a Bill. In 1861, further conferences were held to discuss the text of the Bill, which became law in August, 1862.

The Industrial and Provident Societies' Act of 1862 made possible the establishment of a federation of societies by enabling a society to hold shares in another. Thus there could be a society of societies. The legal maximum limit of £100 for a member's shareholding was raised to £200 but this, by an oversight, also applied to a society's shareholding. This difficulty, however, was removed by the amending Act of 1867 under which there was no limit to the number of shares a society could hold in another. As limited liability was given to shareholders, the legal difficulties of raising and investing co-operative capital were largely removed, although societies registered under the Act were prohibited from banking.

Anticipating the passage of the Bill the enthusiasts for co-operative wholesaling continued to hold conferences to discuss schemes and arouse support. After the enactment events moved quickly. A Christmas Day, 1862, conference was held in Oldham at which Abraham Greenwood read a paper describing his scheme for a co-operative wholesale agency operating on a commission basis. It was resolved " That we establish a wholesale depot or agency " and a committee was appointed to collect information and prepare a prospectus of a scheme to be submitted to a future meeting.

This was held in Manchester on Good Friday, 1863. It appears to have been a lively meeting. The proposal of J. C. Edwards that the Industrial and Provident Societies' Act should be extended to the Colonies and the store system spread to Canada and Australia was beyond the horizon of space and time of the assembled British co-operators and they regarded this as " off the point " and it was " remanded " for future discussion. Greenwood's scheme was then debated in detail: whether a wholesale was necessary; whether the scheme was practicable; whether the small societies would receive all the benefit; whether a wholesale buyer could satisfy all societies (Huddersfield and Halifax had different tastes in butter); whether he might not be bribed; and whether a depot was not to be preferred to an agency. This last question was dealt with by deciding it should be both, and the society be called "The North of England Co-operative Wholesale Agency and Depot Society Ltd."

C.W.S. Founded

The rules were submitted to the Registrar in August, 1863, and certified, the society being registered as the North of England Co-operative Wholesale Industrial Provident Society Ltd. W. Cooper, who had acted as secretary for the wholesale conferences, circularised the societies with the information and called a meeting at Manchester for October, at which societies were to join and take up shares. At this meeting officers and a committee were appointed. Societies joining the federation were to take up a share for every one of their members, the shares were 5s. each, and a deposit of 1s. per share had to be paid when the shares were taken up. The report of this meeting stated that fourteen thousand shares had been subscribed by forty-three societies. Thirty of these were in Lancashire and six in Yorkshire.

The initiative and enterprise which established the Society came from the group of societies in South East Lancashire, i.e. from Rochdale, Oldham, Manchester, and from smaller neighbouring towns and districts such as Middleton, Heywood, and Mossley. This had been true of the holding of conferences and the preceding agitation for amendment to the Industrial and Provident Societies'

Act. A statement of the cash received from societies to meet the expenses concerned with obtaining the amendment gave fifty-eight societies and of these forty-eight were Lancashire societies. These societies naturally supplied the first directorate—

President:	Abraham Greenwood, Rochdale.
Treasurer:	Councillor James Smithies, Rochdale.
Secretary:	J. C. Edwards, Manchester.
Auditors:	D. Baxter, Manchester; J. Hankinson, Preston.
Committee:	Charles Howarth, Heywood; T. Cheetham, Rochdale; J. Hilton, Middleton; W. Marcroft, Oldham.

These men had found it necessary to fight for the idea in their own societies, and not always successfully for Oldham refused to join so that Marcroft was replaced by J. Neild of Mossley. These men, with Cooper and Neale and other idealists, saw the Movement had no future unless some national unity and organisation were attained. The local limits of co-operative progress would soon be reached and a national field was necessary for the Movement to extend into production, banking, insurance, etc.

THE SCOTTISH CO-OPERATIVE WHOLESALE SOCIETY

Before the Owenite movements there were co-operative societies in Scotland, but as with similar societies in England they had no social philosophy and so were devoid of the idealism which tries to convert and so makes a movement. Hence they remained stagnant. Scotland, however, responded to the idealism of the early Co-operative Movement and played its part in it. Owen's great social experiment was at New Lanark; Orbiston near Glasgow was the scene of an attempt at an Owenite community; societies associated with the Co-operative Movement of 1828–1835 were formed; and branches of the succeeding Owenite movements were established in Glasgow, Paisley and Edinburgh.

There were Scotsmen active and prominent in these movements, notably Alexander Campbell, an Owenite missionary known throughout Great Britain. Campbell claimed to have invented the device of dividend on purchases, which he may well have done, although it seems to have been used in so many parts of the country before 1844 that probably many could also make a claim.

A letter of Campbell's to the *Co-operator* of November, 1862 to substantiate his claim, however, also throws light on his and Scottish activities during the genesis of the Co-operative Movement. He asserted that he had been advocating co-operative principles since 1818. In 1822 a co-operative baking society was established in Glasgow for which he drew up the rules and to which he advocated division of profits according to purchase. In 1829 he assisted in establishing the first co-operative society in

Glasgow, on the principle of dividing profits in proportion to purchases. He advocated the principle in lectures around Glasgow in 1830, and in 1831 the co-operators of Cambuslang adopted his plan. He lectured at Rochdale in 1840, and in 1843–1844.

The Movement in Scotland experienced similar fortune to that in England, the decline in the 'thirties and resurgence in the 'fifties and 'sixties. Some realised the need for a wholesale organisation, there were Scottish contributions to the correspondence in Pitman's *Co-operator*, and in 1863 the societies in the Edinburgh area established the Edinburgh Central Co-operative Association, which was a wholesale agency. It lasted for four years but was too limited in scope for successful development.

Failure of First Efforts

In 1863, however, the *Scottish Co-operator*, with John McInnes as its editor, appeared and played a similar part in Scotland to that of Pitman's *Co-operator*. It was soon advocating the establishing in Scotland of a wholesale organisation like that in England. A conference, among whose promoters was Alexander Campbell, was held in Glasgow in April, 1864 to " consider the necessity of establishing a wholesale depot or agency in Glasgow for the purpose of supplying co-operative societies in the West of Scotland and elsewhere with pure groceries and provisions from the best markets." Abraham Greenwood's paper which had outlined the scheme for the English wholesale was read and resolutions carried to establish a wholesale agency. Unfortunately, the Glasgow Society, which had taken the leading part, collapsed before the resolutions could be carried into effect and the attempt to establish a wholesale was not made.

McInnes, however, continued his campaign resulting in the calling of another conference at Glasgow in April, 1866. This was addressed by J. C. Edwards, cashier of the English wholesale. It decided that Scottish societies be advised to take up shares in the North of England Wholesale Co-operative Society and to give it the largest measure of support possible. Some Scottish societies did so, but Manchester was too far away to undertake wholesaling for Scotland successfully so that the desire grew for a branch or depot of the wholesale society in Glasgow. This view was expressed at a conference in June, 1867, at which J. C. Edwards was again present. He had to regret that the English wholesale was unable to meet their request but was willing to give all the help it could and would facilitate the transfer of shares of Scottish member societies in it to a Scottish wholesale society if one were established. This left the Scottish co-operators with no alternative but to found their own society and the conference proceeded to pass the following resolution:—

S.C.W.S. Founded

" That this conference, convinced of the advantage and necessity of a wholesale agency, and seeing that the North of England Co-operative Wholesale Society cannot extend a branch to Scotland, hereby appoint a committee to diffuse information, make the necessary arrangements for commencing a wholesale co-operative society in Glasgow, and in the meantime make use of the North of England Society for the supply of our wants as shall be deemed desirable."

The refusal of the English wholesale to open a Glasgow branch is often regarded as short-sighted. It must be taken into account, however, that, as the English society was by no means well established and not gifted with prophetic sight, it may have been well justified in its decision not to undertake an enterprise probably beyond its resources.

The Scots, however, proceeded now in a businesslike way, rapidly surveyed the situation and calculated the chances of success. Conferences were held in Glasgow and Edinburgh, January 1st and 2nd, 1868, and it was decided to establish a wholesale society, its first centre to be at Glasgow and its second at Edinburgh. By May, 1868, the Scottish Co-operative Wholesale Society was registered, and commenced business on September 8th, 1868.

THE CO-OPERATIVE INSURANCE COMPANY

The Christmas Day meeting of 1863 at Oldham which decided it was desirable to establish a wholesale depot or agency, also discussed the propriety of forming a life assurance and a guarantee society among members, and a sub-committee was appointed to inquire further into the matter. Nothing further was done, but the subject kept reappearing in the pages of the *Co-operator*. A conference called for Good Friday, 1867, was for the purpose of forming a Co-operative Insurance Company, among other matters. Many whose names should now be familiar were at this conference, Abraham Greenwood, William Cooper, J. C. Edwards, William Marcroft, James Smithies, Ed. Longfield, Henry Pitman, J. T. McInnes and E. T. Craig. The outcome of the conference was the setting up of the Co-operative Insurance Company in 1867 with headquarters in the premises of the Rochdale Pioneers. It was registered as a joint stock company as the Industrial and Provident Societies' Acts at the time did not provide for societies undertaking insurance business.

THE LONDON CONGRESS OF 1869

During the 'fifties and the 'sixties it was found necessary to hold many conferences of societies, to some of which reference has been made, in order to get the concerted action requisite for some co-operative advance, e.g., in securing satisfactory legislation and establishing wholesale societies and an insurance company. Other matters of common concern were also usually raised and the value of societies conferring together began to be appreciated. Loose forms of conference associations consequently developed, with elected conference committees to carry on activities until the holding of the next conference. The association in Lancashire and Yorkshire met annually and financed itself by a levy of a farthing per member on those societies who joined it.

The leading spirits of the Movement, however, realised that much more was needed. They desired a national movement with a permanent national organisation. Their inspiration was derived from the old ideals of the past, of the pre-Rochdale Co-operative Movement and Christian Socialism, quickened by the opportunities opened up by the success of Rochdale Co-operation.

William Pare, who had acted as secretary and played a very prominent role in the Co-operative Congresses of 1831–1835, commenced an agitation for a national organisation and annual congresses by a letter to the *Co-operator* in July, 1865. This stated, " It seems that one of the great wants at present is a thorough organisation of all the societies in Great Britain and Ireland for a common purpose. A ' Co-operative Congress,' as of old, should assemble annually to give and receive information on practical subjects. This should consist of the most experienced and intelligent from the several societies as delegates. The communication of facts as to the past and present, and the interchange of ideas and suggestions for improvements for the future would be the prominent feature of these assemblies. The Congress might have under its supervision the wholesale agency. It would inaugurate a missionary staff and other means of propaganda, and would, I trust, not neglect the great subject of education. . . . The Congress, too, should elect a central executive board or council, with a paid secretary, one of whose duties would be to superintend the missionaries and answer all inquiries as to the formation of new societies."

Arranging Congress

This was the opening of a correspondence on the subject maintained by Pare and others. Favourable opinion grew, but the first attempt to call a Congress in February, 1869, by a committee meeting in London under the presidency of E. V. Neale in August, 1868, met a disappointing response. Pare, however, convened a meeting in March of an "Arrangement Committee," again presided over by Neale, which proceeded to arrange a Congress to meet May 31st to June 3rd, 1869.

There were survivors from the Owenite movements on that committee besides William Pare, viz. Lloyd Jones, James Hole, Dr. H. Travis and G. J. Holyoake. Pare's explanation for the meeting being called had some of the old Owenite flavour. It was evident that some co-operative societies were becoming selfish and it was necessary to teach Co-operation to co-operators, and steps should be taken to prevent the great principles of Co-operation from degenerating into merely co-operative stores. He desired that the proposed congress should be a really important and effective affair from which should be dated the commencement of a new era. After a quarter of a century of shopkeeping it was surely time co-operators assumed a higher platform and a nobler task. He proceeded to suggest co-operative development into production, mining, agriculture and the establishment of self-supporting co-operative villages.

The "Arrangement Committee" secured the support of the " Conference Committee of the Lancashire and Yorkshire Co-operative Societies " and the Congress was duly held, the first of the modern series of congresses. Fifty-seven societies were represented, but of these only twenty-four were consumers' societies including the two wholesale societies and the Conference Committee of the Lancashire and Yorkshire societies. Three foreign societies were represented, two from Germany and one from Norway, this last by William Pare (who had worked as a commercial traveller in Scandinavia and appears to have had co-operative connections and probably did some propaganda there). Besides many productive societies there were nine trade unions including the powerful Amalgamated Society of Engineers. There was only a small representation from the North for the Northern societies had held their big conference at Leeds during March attended by representatives of nearly four hundred societies. The list of subscriptions shows, however, that many of these societies contributed to meet the expenses of the Congress.

The promoters were evidently desirous of bringing together all manner of working-class organisations into a co-operative fold, as the congresses of the early 'thirties had tried to do. They had been impressed by a resolution of the Trades Union Congress of 1868 " To utilise the organisation of the Trades Unions for co-operative purposes," and the trade unions had been invited to send delegates for more serious purposes than the making of fraternal speeches.

Congress Business

Congress proceeded by way of papers read upon subjects of concern to co-operators followed by discussions and the passing of resolutions. The titles of the papers read at this Congress are some indication of the various elements of Co-operation which it had brought together. There was a paper on " Trade Unions and Co-operation," the discussion upon which showed the trade unions to be indisposed to concerning themselves with co-operative production. William Allan said the Engineers' Society were not indisposed to co-operate, but they could not lend their funds to co-operative societies. There were many papers on co-operative stores and an important one dealing with the history of the C.W.S. An attempt at an Owenite revival was made, notably by the papers of Dr. Travis, who could reach the higher levels of Owenite metaphysics, and William Pare, who dug up the various projects of the 1831–1835 congresses, advocating self-supporting co-operative villages and the use of labour notes. These echoes from the past aroused interest and had a sympathetic hearing but no practical effect. J. T. W. Mitchell of Rochdale probably expressed the sense of the meeting: he " did not see any insuperable difficulty in the way of realising the better state of co-operative life which had been foreshadowed, provided we began low enough and proceeded by natural growth."

Development Proposals

Of more consequence were papers dealing with future developments, one on a general topic by Dr. J. Watts, and one advocating co-operative banking by W. Morrison, M.P., R. B. D. Morier and Canon Molesworth (the Rochdale " co-operative parson "). The suggestions for a national organisation were presented by Holyoake on "A London Co-operative Board " and part of Pare's paper in which he pleaded that the Congress should not end in desultory talk: it should give birth to a permanent and constantly acting body which would knit together in one compact whole the isolated societies and thus render them really helpful to each other in their immediate endeavours and lead them on to higher and nobler objects. Pare suggested such a body would frame a set of model rules for societies; acquire and disseminate by lecturers and tracts a knowledge of the best methods of commencing and conducting co-operative stores and productive establishments and of keeping and auditing accounts; advise in cases of difficulty and risk; arbitrate on differences and disputes between societies; seek to bring about amalgamations or federations for common purposes; and convene and arrange the business of an Annual Congress.

Holyoake's paper proposed the appointment of a London Co-operative Board to act as a sort of executive congress permanently meeting. In the discussion the need for some permanent organisation was evidently realised. J. M. Ludlow held that the country should be organised district by district or county by county into unions, meeting yearly by delegates, and at such meetings a central body should be elected which would command confidence and be able to enter into relations with co-operative bodies abroad. There should also be a committee in London for legal and legislative action and for general counsel.

Abraham Greenwood, who attended as delegate for the Co-operative Wholesale Society, in the main supported Ludlow, though he thought a Council in London co-operating with them in the North would best meet the case. He fully agreed with the need for county or district unions, as " even leading co-operators were often unknown to each other."

A resolution was carried to the effect that a provisional committee be appointed in London to act with the Conference Committees in the North and Scotland and convene a congress the next year, 1870. The composition of the committee which was appointed is interesting and significant of the weakness of the Co-operative Movement in the South at the time, for although it consisted of well-known, influential co-operators, they were not representative of Southern co-operative societies. Only one, E. O. Greening, out of the fifteen members, was a delegate of an English co-operative society. The rest consisted of friendly Members of Parliament, some prominent reformers, co-operative propagandists such as Holyoake and Lloyd Jones, and two trade union leaders, Allan and Applegarth (Allan had insisted the trade unions should be represented). Pare continued to act as secretary.

The danger was that this attempt would fail for the same reason as earlier efforts by the Christian Socialists had failed—because it was being done for co-operators instead of by co-operators themselves. To give weight to the venture it was essential that the Northern societies, the Rochdale movement, should be properly identified with the venture.

THE CREATION OF THE CO-OPERATIVE UNION

Realising the need for a national organisation and outlook, the Lancashire and Yorkshire Conference in 1870 agreed to merge itself in the Congress. The 1870 Congress was held in Manchester, had an attendance of 109 and was much more representative of the Movement than the first Congress had been even though 99 of those attending were from Lancashire and Yorkshire, and there was only J. McInnes from Scotland. This Congress elected a Central Board consisting of two divisions, the London Board, whose membership was the same as that appointed by the previous Congress with the addition of E. V. Neale, and the Provincial Board. Of this Board's fifteen members, eleven came from Lancashire, one from Cheshire, one from Yorkshire, and two from Scotland.

William Pare told Congress that a permanent secretary and a law clerk were necessary. The Central Board was given power to appoint whatsoever paid officers were necessary and societies were asked to subscribe not less than one penny per member to meet expenses. An appeal was sent out to 750 societies and 183, with 86,000 members, responded and provided £220. This was insufficient to maintain the suggested staff, but William Nuttall, head accountant of the N.E.C.W.S., and a member of the Provincial Board, undertook the secretarial duties on a part-time basis with William Pare.

The 1871 Congress was held at Birmingham and this attracted delegates from the Midlands, 73 out of a total of 113 attending. Yet the Lancashire and Yorkshire societies were still a large proportion of the subscribing societies, and the Provincial Board continued to be composed of Lancashire, Yorkshire and Scottish delegates with one from Cheshire. In the following year 198 societies subscribed £396, but the Central Board was authorised to co-opt two members from the Newcastle district, and during the year a Midland group of Provincial members was constituted.

Constitution

Membership of the organisation had now grown so that it covered the co-operative parts of the country and it became possible to organise on a more representative basis. In 1873, Congress was at Newcastle and it agreed to E. V. Neale's scheme by which the country was divided into five Sections, each Section being represented by a Sectional Board. They were the Scottish, Northern, North-Western, Midland and Southern. The first four replaced the former Provincial Board, and the London Board became the Southern Sectional Board. All the boards together constituted the Central Board. A committee consisting of two representatives from each Sectional Board, except the North-Western which provided three, was to meet quarterly. This committee was termed the United Board and was given power to control the salaried officers; supervise the Sectional Boards; organise inquiries and issue reports and publications. The United Board was thus the executive governing body, subject to Congress resolutions.

This system remained the basis of the constitution of the Co-operative Union until the reorganisation of 1932, although the number of Sections was increased later. In 1873, Nuttall resigned and E. V. Neale was appointed secretary. An office was rented at City Buildings, Corporation Street, Manchester. The organisation was becoming increasingly known as the Co-operative Union and it became registered as such in 1889 under the Industrial and Provident Societies Act.

THE " CO-OPERATIVE NEWS "

Little of the great work of creating a national Movement out of the hundreds of scattered societies could have been accomplished without the *Co-operator*. Yet as the Movement became organised and unified there was an increasing dissatisfaction with the paper. It was not under co-operative control and the editor, Henry Pitman, was a zealot in other causes besides Co-operation. Hence the paper contained fierce denunciations of tobacco, alcohol, and vaccination. There were several requests for a co-operative newspaper in the 'sixties and with the organisation of co-operative congresses the necessary steps were soon taken to give effect to them.

The Manchester Congress of 1870 discussed a paper given by Lloyd Jones on "A Co-operative Newspaper," in which he pointed out that every interest had some means of acquainting the world with its thoughts, intentions and progress. There were political, religious, professional and trade papers: even the gardeners could keep two or three journals going, and co-operators needed and were capable of sustaining a journal for similar reasons. Such a paper should give market and co-operative trade information; special news of the Co-operative Movement and general news; keep clear of theological and anti-theological discussions; but should be actively concerned with politics. Co-operators were necessarily concerned with the relations of capital and labour, in the future there would be political questions and the co-operative body could not remain silent upon them. The tone of the paper could be Liberal, since nearly all co-operators were Liberals.

The ensuing discussion naturally dwelt mainly on this political aspect. Probably Abraham Greenwood had the feeling of the meeting in pleading for tolerance. Co-operation must be conducted in a spirit of union, not of antagonism—"our object is the moral, social and industrial improvement of the labouring body, independent of politics." A resolution was carried that a newspaper devoted to co-operative interests should be established with as little delay as possible and referred the subject to the Central Board.

Decision to Publish

At the Congress of 1871 the subject was raised again as apparently nothing had been done to establish a paper. Discussion was concerned with the name, Lloyd Jones arguing for the *Citizen*, whereas McInnes favoured the *Co-operative News*. The disagreement over the title of the paper arose largely from disagreements over its purpose and content, and whether it should be published in London or Manchester. London might be the better centre for a paper such as Jones required, but Manchester was a better centre for a paper dealing mainly with co-operative news, as three-fourths of the membership was in Lancashire and Yorkshire, and the Co-operative Printing Society was situated in Manchester and would undertake its printing.

In 1871 the North of England Newspaper Company, with headquarters in Manchester, was formed to place " the co-operators of England in possession of a paper of their own." The first number of the paper appeared on September 2nd, 1871, and it was named the *Co-operative News*, and was printed by the Co-operative Printing Society. (This was the first of the co-operative printing societies now in existence. It was formed by a group of printers, mainly members of the staff of the *Manchester Guardian*, and before it had its own press it passed on its orders to the *Guardian*. Its first offices were on the premises of the C.W.S.)

William Nuttall, with other officers of the C.P.S., shared the editorial duties at first, Dr. John Watts writing the leading articles. J. C. Farn and Bailey Walker later served as editors but were succeeded in 1875 by Samuel Bamford, who continued in the office until his death in 1898. He, with the *Co-operative News*, was to play a great influential part in moulding the Co-operative Movement during the remainder of the nineteenth century. It still continues, the oldest working-class and democratically-owned newspaper in existence.

END OF THE BEGINNING

This survey has endeavoured to show how a Movement with high ideals and great ambitions became moribund in the 'thirties but so revived after 1844 that it was able to create national organisations in the 'sixties. The causes of failure in the 'thirties were many, but the underlying one was the failure to find a practical means of realising or even pursuing its ideals. Dr. King probably came nearest but even he was bemused by the conception of the small, self-supporting community as a desirable and practical objective. The dead ends of secularism and Queenwood into which the Owenite movement ran would have resulted in the complete disappearance of Co-operation as a movement if the small group of Rochdale Owenites had not turned to the discarded way advocated by Dr. King, although with modifications which by yielding more immediate benefits attracted a wider public.

A. D. Lindsay[1] saw in the Co-operative Movement an example of how progress is made, by " marrying the ideal with the possibilities of the concrete human situation." It is the fruit of idealistic revolt against the new industrial conditions, the revolt of Robert Owen, and after him of the Christian Socialists, such as Charles Kingsley and Thomas Hughes. "Without that idealism the Movement would never have come into existence. Without its continued success in enlisting in its service the loyalty and ideals of countless ordinary men and women, it would never have retained its economic efficiency. They thereby produced something very different from the concrete ideal pictured by the original inspirers of the Co-operative Movement. That marriage of the ideal with the concrete realities of the human situation has got to be performed again and again if we are to change our economic system as it is capable of being changed."

The societies founded on the Rochdale model would, however, have soon reached their limits of growth and lapsed into stagnation without the continuance of the powerful idealism which created the national organisations. This was formed of the currents of Owenism, Christian Socialism and the practical Co-operation of more ordinary folk which was evident in the early congresses. These currents merged in the Movement, often in the same individual. It is often imagined that the post-Rochdale co-operators were a different type of people from the pre-Rochdale ones and that different circumstances had produced different characters. Yet many of the leading figures who helped to shape and direct the later Movement were the same individuals who had played prominent parts in the old, notably William Pare, Lloyd Jones, Alexander Campbell, E. T. Craig, and there were, of course, many less well known. The leading figures of the original Pioneers were members of an Owenite branch.

---

[1] *Christianity and Economics;* the example is also used in his *The Modern Democratic State.*

Wider Horizons

With the success of Rochdale Co-operation, however, many became aware of greater possibilities, of wider horizons than the narrow confines of self-supporting communities. This was well expressed by Ben Jones, " It was quite possible to apply the principle of Co-operation, bit by bit, in sections, to all the circumstances of their lives, until a system of complete Co-operation should finally be evolved. They had begun to see that the effective force of machinery, with the necessary consequence of a more and more minute division of labour, and of a wider and still wider field of distribution from the centre of production was altogether irresistible; and that the idea of little, self-supporting colonies must give way to the infinitely grander idea that the whole world is one family, with members mutually dependent on their industrial exertions, and mutually benefiting by exchange of products." (*Co-operative Production.*)

The wider scope and more ambitious objectives were probably due to the influence of E. V. Neale who early saw the possibilities of developing Co-operation sectionally, but binding all by national organisations and common ethical principles. Yet it is significant that few of the schemes of Neale or his fellow Christian Socialists were successful. It was working men of Rochdale, Oldham, and hundreds of small towns and villages who actually and successfully established societies. It was idealists from this source who created the wholesales, the insurance company, and a co-operative newspaper. Without their assistance the Co-operative Union would never have been established. This was not due to any superiority of working-class ability or character, but to the vital element of self-help, of working-class organisations doing things for themselves instead of having things done for them.

With the foundations laid it becomes possible to observe the building of the structure upon them.

5 THE CO-OPERATIVE MOVEMENT, 1870-1914: ECONOMIC DEVELOPMENT

" If the old co-operators erred in sentiment, certainly the present ones err in the direction of materialism."
William Pare, 1870.

" Co-operation seems in some danger at the present time of losing itself through its own success."
E. V. Neale, 1870.

OPENING chapters described the first Co-operative Movement as a reaction to the Industrial Revolution. This failed, but was revived at Rochdale and developed into a national Movement with national organisations. Although the line of descent is clear, the new Movement, however, came to differ from the old. The early co-operators desired the creation of self-supporting, self-governing communities, insulated from the economic, social and moral evils of the "Old Immoral World," but the new Co-operative Movement gave up any intention of insulating itself from the outer world, though the Rochdale Pioneers and some other societies began with the ideal of establishing co-operative communities. Not the least service of E. V. Neale was his vision of transforming the existing system into a better one by the development of co-operative societies. The Rochdale system, discarding the community objective, adopted a similar approach to that of Neale, though there were inherent differences in ideals, not at first apparent, which became manifest as the national organisations began to develop. This programme of evolution, however, involved not a withdrawal or insulation from the world but an active and ever increasing participation in it. As Co-operation developed it consequently became increasingly affected by circumstances, economic, social, political and intellectual, external to itself. The danger that instead of reforming the world by its growth and influence it would be transformed by that same world into conformity with existing worldly ideas and practices was and is great, and has by no means been avoided in all instances. In this chapter an effort is made to show how the Movement fared in rapidly changing times.

THE BACKGROUND

Economically there was considerable progress during the period 1870–1914. The old industries such as cotton, wool, engineering, iron and steel, shipbuilding and coal continued to expand. Other industries such as clothing, footwear, paper and printing underwent their industrial revolutions. New industries arose, most notably motor vehicles and cycles, electricity, and many concerned with rubber and chemicals. Many domestic crafts were also increasingly transferred to the factory, for example, jam making, baking and laundry work. Exports increased from £233 million of home produce in 1871 to £454 million in 1911, and imports from £331 million to £680 million. Much of the increase in imports was in foodstuffs and this country became increasingly dependent on foreign supplies. There were big increases in imports of foods such as tea and sugar, which had always been imported, but there were also big increases in bacon and ham, beef, mutton, butter, cheese, eggs, potatoes and wheat. These imports raised the standard of living of most people, who fed better, and had more nourishing and varied diets than ever before. Some indication of growing prosperity is the increase of deposits in Post Office Savings Banks, from £17 million in 1871 to £176 million in 1911.

Growing Uneasiness

Yet there was also a considerable and growing uneasiness. Agriculture suffered a severe depression, which was of more concern to the country then than it would be now, for it employed a far greater proportion of the country's resources. Other industries were also meeting increasingly severe foreign competition at home and difficulties abroad due to the protectionist policies of other countries. Whereas in 1870, Great Britain had confidence in herself as the world's workshop, banker, carrier, the world's model of constitutional government and the world's leader in sound and enlightened commercial policy, in 1914 a good deal of that confidence had gone. Germany and the United States of America had each surpassed Britain in the production of iron and steel and were overtaking her in shipbuilding; and although she was still easily supreme in cotton and wool, the threat of an infant cotton industry in Japan was causing what proved to be justifiable alarm in Lancashire. Most disconcerting was that these rapidly developing industrial states were not based on free competition and free trade. Generally the current was running *against* international free trade and *with* economic nationalism and imperialism. There was consequently a natural uneasiness regarding the liberal foundations of British society and commercial policies as the rising states discarded them.

The "Great Depression" of the last quarter of the nineteenth century accentuated this uneasiness. There are no recorded general figures of unemployment,[1] but those recorded by trade unions of their membership are indications of general trends. These reveal several booms and slumps. Unemployment was a continuous worry in the minds of many although there were no depressions as severe as those of the 'seventies and 'eighties. It is significant that the terms "unemployed" and "unemployment" came into general usage during the 'eighties.

Yet in spite of boom and slump, there was considerable economic progress and some have indeed held that the pattern was a consequence of growth to meet a rapidly expanding world economy. Standards of living certainly improved towards the end of the century. Money wage rates according to Wood's index (1867–77 =100) rose from 93 in 1870 to 125 in 1900, but owing to the fall in prices real wages rose even more, from 95 to 147. The wage bill probably rose more than did wage rates, for there was a shift from the lowest paid occupations such as that of the agricultural labourer to higher paid work.

Between 1899 and 1914 export trade increased by 49 per cent, but according to Professor Bowley the national income only increased by 20 per cent and imports increased by 30 per cent. The considerable increase in the balance of payments was absorbed in foreign investments, these increasing from £2,000 to £4,000 million in the period, serving the country well in the Great War and its aftermath. This huge increase in foreign investment, however, was at the expense of the standard of living at home and real wage rates (1900=100) fell from 104 in 1899, to 91 in 1912.[2] This decline was largely responsible for the mounting labour discontent and the rise of militant and revolutionary labour movements such as syndicalism and industrial unionism, as well as the progress of Socialism and the Labour Party.

Changes in Structure

Competitive difficulties and fears resulted in attempts in some industries to lessen or eliminate competition by trusts or price fixing associations. These, however, were rarely successful in

---

[1] The heights and depths of unemployment were: 0·9 per cent in 1872; 11·4 per cent in 1879; 2·3 per cent in 1882; 10·2 per cent in 1886; 2·1 per cent in 1889–1890; 7·5 per cent in 1894; 2·0 per cent in 1899; 6·0 per cent in 1904; 3·6 per cent in 1906; 7·8 per cent in 1908; 2·1 per cent in 1913.

[2] *British Trade and Industry* by G. D. H. Cole.

D

meeting the expectations of their promoters. There was also a trend to larger scale production and to larger scale organisation. The former often results in an increase in the number of firms, each, however, more specialised; the latter is an increase in the size of firms, perhaps performing a larger range of operations and so less specialised. The growth in size was facilitated by the Companies Acts of 1855, 1862 and 1867, which eased and simplified the formation of joint stock companies and provided the boon of limited liability. Eventually the joint stock company became the typical form of business enterprise, but it did not do so rapidly. Many of the early companies failed and of the companies formed between 1856 and 1865, 54 per cent had ceased to exist 10 years later. Formation for many years proceeded by the conversion of family businesses or partnerships into companies as their owners desired to retire or to obtain additional capital for expansion.

The economic changes already mentioned caused changes in the commercial structure. As more food was imported more of it was handled in the first instance by big merchant importers and entered the country through a few big ports. This favoured, indeed necessitated, larger scale distributive organisations. The increasing concentration of industry also, of course, concentrated population and provided the mass markets for mass production. Producer retailers gradually disappeared in many trades, though not in all. Producers and consumers had increasingly to rely on distributive organisations to link supplies with final demands. Wholesalers increased in importance, often undertaking processes on a large scale previously performed by retailers, such as tea or tobacco blending and, of course, much weighing and packing.

Retail Changes

This trend of processes away from the retailer was increased by inventions which provided cheap paper, cardboard and printing. It became possible for manufacturers or merchants to pack their goods in attractive packets with their name or brand and also the price on them. By advertisements in the popular press and on hoardings a popular demand would be created for that brand, and the retailer had perforce to stock the brands his customers asked for and sell at a price not exceeding that advertised. Competition, however, was keen and price cutting resulted. Retailers being unable as in the past to manipulate prices, qualities and weights, sought to safeguard themselves by forming associations which made agreements with wholesalers and manufacturers to deny supplies to traders "guilty" of price cutting. In 1905, the Proprietary

Articles Trade Association objected to co-operative societies paying dividend on the purchase of goods covered by its agreements, on the grounds that these dividends were discounts. This helped to stimulate co-operative production.

It is impossible to give any accurate estimate of the number of shops or their increase during the period, but the structure of retailing was changing. Apart from the development of co-operative retailing, the big changes were the developments of multiple shops (i.e., a number of shops owned and controlled by one organisation) and departmental stores. Neither, of course, was new, but they developed in this period into important parts of the retailing structure. J. B. Jefferys has estimated that in 1875 there were 29 multiple shop firms with 978 branches and, in 1915, 433 firms with 22,755 branches. Some had grown very big; by 1914 there were 16, with over 200 branches each, seven with over 500 branches each, and two, both meat firms, with over 1,000 branches each. (*Retail Trading in Great Britain*.)

Some of these developments came from importers or manufacturers, for example, in tea, frozen meat, clothing, footwear, and medicinal goods, for the purpose of ensuring sales and controlling retail price policy. They had no faith in the independent retailer. Some of the commodities, tea or margarine, for instance, had insufficient trade to maintain a shop, so that other goods had to be added and the firms became engaged in the general grocery business. They had the advantage of buying on a larger scale than the unit shop, and sought other economies in standardisation of equipment, methods of selling and superior administration. They pushed their trade by concentrating on lines suitable for standardisation, low prices and advertising and in the grocery trades they took a leaf out of the co-operative book and stuck to cash transactions. The careers of these multiples were not always unchequered, Home and Colonial had four starts, Eastmans, an amalgamation of New York exporters and British distributors of meat, established in 1889, lost heavily during 1891-1894 and paid no dividend on ordinary shares for 13 years.

Department Stores

Departmental stores also had spectacular developments during the period, though from the nature of these businesses most developments are bound to be spectacular. A large shop carrying on several trades in departments under one roof, was not new. Flint and Palmers, in which Robert Owen worked as a youth, had some of the characteristics, and G. and W. Campbells of Glasgow had 64 attendants selling " every kind of soft goods " in the early nineteenth century. The modern type of department store, however, required a much larger market than existed then. Such markets developed in the early part of this century with the increase and concentration of population and the improvement of transport. Departmental stores began to be dominant features of London and the big provincial cities. Many had been family businesses with small beginnings, had grown big and had been converted into limited liability companies to raise the capital and bear the large risks of sinking an enormous amount of capital into a trading enterprise on one site.

Social Changes

Changes were also taking place in social life and character. Victorian life may have been narrow, but it was intense, real and earnest. It has been described as the most religious ever known. Self improvement was the aim of serious youth, and the improvement of others the aim of those of more mature years. Hence the vigour of all manner of voluntary associations for the improvement of character, mental as well as moral. This often involved a great deal of personal sacrifice of ease and comfort. J. T. W. Mitchell, whilst he was president of the C.W.S. (1874–1895), and engaged in the stress and worry of laying the foundations and building the structure of that organisation, never missed returning to Rochdale to conduct his Sunday School. He was not exceptional. Sabbatarianism was general and strict, all respectable people went to church or chapel on Sundays and others had to keep themselves out of sight and out of mind.

The foundations, however, of this hard working, thrifty and seriously dutiful Victorianism were already being sapped and mined. The Anglican church was riven by the Anglo-Catholic movement and Christianity was subjected to formidable attacks by free-thinkers now aided by their interpretation of the Darwinian theories of evolution. The pursuit of pleasure also became more acceptable. These changes became more marked after the turn of the century. They were assisted by the weakening of the churches themselves.

Education and the Press

Public elementary education was made general and free by the Acts of 1870, 1876 and 1891, but the system at its best only made people literate. There was little education in the real sense of the term, i.e., the development of the capacities to compare, analyse, criticise, understand and form rational judgements, but a profitable market was provided for those who could provide printed matter on a sufficiently low level. There were those, notably George Newnes, Alfred Harmsworth and Arthur Pearson, who saw the opportunity and took advantage of it. They provided a cheap and popular press which became the principal educational medium of the country. The policy, since this yielded most profits, was to give the public what it wanted—excitement, thrills and stunts. Headlines became the most important feature. Harmsworth (later Lord Northcliffe) has been described as " Boyish in his power of concentration upon the matter of the moment, boyish in his readiness to turn swiftly to a different matter and concentrate on that . . . boyish in the limited range of his intellect, which seldom concerns itself with anything but the immediate, the obvious, the popular." This description of its creator would also apply to his press and its public, which was widespread and included women and businessmen as well as the working classes, all suffering from intellectual immaturity as a result of lack of general education.

Fortunately, cheap printing and paper were also put to better uses. Editions of the classics were published at prices which put a good library within the reach of most. Many took advantage, developed studious habits and became well read. This was also furthered by the increase of free public libraries. Co-operative societies had often provided libraries as a means of educating their members and some of them were very fine indeed. Numerous libraries were founded, between 1886 and 1900, by Andrew Carnegie, the American steel millionaire who was born in Scotland, and a Public Libraries Act in 1892 facilitated the provision of public libraries by local authorities. A serious reading public provided a field for the growth of adult educational bodies. More significant even than the development of University Extension work was the formation of the Workers' Educational Association in 1904, and the establishment of Ruskin College in 1899, and the Plebs League in 1908. These bodies were mainly concerned with subjects—history, economics and political philosophy—which had a bearing on the big social problems of the day. From them came the leaders of working class opinion and working class organisations, the co-operative and trade union leaders and labour members of Parliament and members of local authorities. For them education took on the manner of a crusade, an essential, vital struggle necessary for success in the wider fields of social reform.

Social reform lagged until the return of a Liberal Government in 1906. The delay of this return was due to the disunity of the Liberal Party, arising from the issue of Home Rule for Ireland and its lack of passion for social reform. The Conservatives were in power from 1886, largely because there was no attractive alternative. Yet the conditions were favourable. The extension of the franchise in 1867 and 1884 had provided a preponderance of working class votes, the social conscience was pricked by the reports of inquiries exposing the shocking poverty of large sections of the population, the national income was increasing, reforms could be afforded, and T. H. Green had provided the philosophical basis for a Liberal collectivism. Yet it was the tariff reform campaign of Joseph Chamberlain which gave the Liberals their chance, for it split the Conservatives and united the Liberals. It also provided evidence that the country still firmly adhered to free trade. The Labour Party appeared in the House in 1906 as a political force with 29 members, and there were also 12 Liberal-Labour members and 14 miners. (The Miners' Federation was not affiliated to the Labour Party until 1909.) The Labour Party was an active and effective force, until it was hamstrung by the Osborne judgment of 1909, which threatened to deprive it of its lifeblood by declaring illegal the use of trade union funds for political purposes.

Revival of Socialism

The appearance of a Labour Party was largely due to the rise of a Socialist Movement. The modern British Socialist Movement began in the eighteen eighties with the foundation of the Social Democratic Federation, 1881, drawing its inspiration from Marx and following, apart from breakaways, the leadership of H. M. Hyndman. It was soon followed by the founding of the Fabian Society, 1884, which relied more on searching and scientific inquiries than upon philosophical speculations. Unfortunately the S.D.F. antagonised the trade unions by attacking their leaders and, financed by Tory money, by fighting two constituencies in 1886.

The Fabians were more successful in bringing Socialism into contact with the working classes. They did not regard Socialism as a thing apart to be introduced when " the day " arrived, but rather as a principle already at work. Their policy was to extend Socialism piecemeal, by gradual municipalisation and nationalisation bringing the economic system under social control through public authorities. Their method was to investigate a social problem, publish the results, make the public aware that a problem existed, and prepare and present a socialist solution. They hoped that their views would gradually penetrate and permeate all the political parties. These hopes have been realised to a surprisingly large extent, Fabianism playing the part in the twentieth century which Benthamism did in the nineteenth. Much of their influence was due to their Fabian tracts, which were a god-send to speakers at trade union branches and trades councils, and so spread socialist ideas in the trade unions. The tracts were effective because they were reliable in their facts and were brilliantly written, amongst the most notable contributors being George Bernard Shaw, Sydney Olivier, Graham Wallas, and Sydney and Beatrice Webb. It was soon realised that every social problem had historical roots and a good knowledge of social history, especially of the history of social institutions and organisations, was prerequisite to a rational appreciation of social problems. Little had been done, so the Webbs began their monumental labours in investigating the Co-operative Movement and in garnering facts to write their classic histories of local government and the trade unions. Although membership of the Fabian Society was small, only 150 in 1889, it exercised such influence that it largely brought about a socialist, trade union alliance.

The problem lay in a social democratic organisation (the S.D.F.) which did not attract the working class, and a Liberal-Labour organisation which did not pursue a Labour let alone a socialist policy. The solution was the creation of a party which would be both socialist and attractive to the working classes. This was sought by the establishment of the Independent Labour Party in 1893. It was free of the somewhat rigid dogma of the S.D.F. and has been described as radicalism adopting socialist policies. Socialism was to it an inspiration rather than a rigid body of doctrine and its appeal was largely emotional but effective. Robert Blatchford's *Clarion*, a journal begun in 1891, and his *Merrie England*, 1894, popularised socialist ideas. The result was a growth in the Trade Union Movement of a socialist body, whose increasing influence and power is shown by the carrying of socialist resolutions at the Trades Union Congress, often against the platform. It also was evident in and influenced the Co-operative Movement.

In 1899 the Trades Union Congress passed a resolution for a conference to be convened for the purpose of drafting a scheme for Labour representation in Parliament. The Co-operative Movement was invited to take part, but did not do so, and the conference meeting in February, 1900, consisted of representatives of the trade unions, the Fabians, the I.L.P. and the S.D.F. It set up what it termed a Labour Representation Committee, and this, although the term Labour Party was not adopted until 1906, was in fact a party for it was to have " a distinct Labour Group in Parliament, who shall have their own Whips and agree upon their policy," but were to co-operate with any party engaged in promoting legislation favourable to Labour and oppose any party having an opposite tendency. This gave it plenty of room for political manœuvre for it was not tied down to any socialist dogma, but the S.D.F., which desired an organisation openly committed to waging a class war, withdrew. Keir Hardie, however, believed that a Labour Party focusing attention upon labour interests and problems would inevitably move in a socialist direction. The future proved him right. At the time a more definitely socialist attitude would have lost the essential support of the trade unions, essential because only they could, and would, supply the necessary finance.

RETAIL SOCIETIES IN THE 'SEVENTIES

Steadily and continuously the membership, trade and capital of retail societies increased year by year from 1870 to 1914. The increase was not due to any great propaganda campaigns or advertising schemes, but to the gradually spreading realisation by working people of the benefits to be derived from forming and joining co-operative societies. Some features of the societies in the 'seventies are revealed in the evidence to the Select Committee on Co-operative Societies, 1878–1879,[1] from Dr. John Watts who had been connected with the Movement since 1840.

There were briefly, according to Watts, about 1,200 societies in the country, and 584 of these with 326,000 members were affiliated to the C.W.S. Two-thirds of the whole co-operative business was done in Lancashire, Yorkshire, Cheshire, and the more northern counties. They were run on the Rochdale system, which Watts regarded as the one, true form of Co-operation. By co-operative purchasing, wholesaling and extension into production, the members would get what he described as " honest " commodities virtually at cost, for although ordinary retail prices were charged, the difference was returned to the members as dividend on purchase. In a well conducted store this would amount to 2s. in the £1. The stores would not engage in undercutting, for this would destroy the difference, and so provident habits would cease to be encouraged by the accumulation of dividend savings. Instances were given of members accumulating useful nest-eggs by not withdrawing their dividends. The stores not only taught thrift, but also business habits to a large number of members by service on committees and they also engaged in a variety of valuable educational activities. Trade was estimated at £12,000,000 per

---

[1] *Report on Co-operative Stores* (1878–79).

annum and their Wholesale Society was already the biggest importer of Irish butter. Yet it was almost entirely a working class
movement and even the C.W.S., with its annual trade of
£2,705,000 was managed by a committee of working men who
met on Saturday afternoons and received a 5s. fee for their
attendance. " There may be a few of them who do not now
labour with their hands, but there is not one among them who
has not been brought up to some handicraft trade."

Holyoake, giving evidence before the same Commission, summarised co-operative practice which gave co-operative stores
advantages over their competitors and benefited their members.
They gave true weight and measure, and sold unadulterated commodities, " Our ambition is that Co-operation shall signify
genuineness in food and honest workmanship in articles of use.
We take no fees; we give no commission, we accept no credit;
and we permit no debt among our members . . . We make profits
by our methods of business. We buy largely in the wholesale
markets, we make no debts . . . we build our stores, and save in
rents; we need no advertisements, and we spend no money in
enticing custom. Then we care for our members; we set apart a
portion of the profits for their instruction, because you cannot
make co-operators out of the ignorant."

Some of these practices would appear of dubious wisdom to
modern co-operators. It must be taken into account, however,
that the societies were small, their membership was well informed
in Co-operation and consequently loyal, so that expensive sites,
advertising and other means of " enticing custom " were regarded,
and probably rightly, as unnecessary. There were no bad debts,
nor expenses of keeping customers' accounts and dunning them
for payment. Consequently the co-operative expenses of distribution were lower than those of the private traders. The dividends
of those years were literally the reward of co-operative loyalty.

GROWTH OF SOCIETIES

Statistics relating to co-operative societies before 1881 are unreliable, but the figures for that year give 971 societies with a total
membership of 547,000. In 1914 there were 1,385 societies and a
membership of 3,054,000. Societies were also growing in size:
in 1880, only three societies had more than 10,000 members
(Leeds, Manchester & Salford, Rochdale); by 1900 the top three
(Leeds, Bolton, Plymouth) had each more than 25,000; and in
1914 the top three (Leeds, Edinburgh St. Cuthbert's, Barnsley) had
each more than 40,000 members. The average size of a society
increased from 564 members in 1881, to 2,083 members in 1914.

Changes were becoming evident which were to have a marked effect in contemporary times. Co-operation in 1881 flourished mainly in the small towns and villages of the textile and mining areas, and co-operative activity was rare and of weakly growth in the big towns and cities with the exceptions of Leeds and Manchester. By 1914, Co-operation was established and showed promising growth in several towns and cities.

In the Midlands, Derby and Birmingham each had more than 29,000, and Leicester 21,765 members; in Scotland, Edinburgh had the largest society, and in Glasgow, the Kinning Park Society had 20,000 members, which with the membership of six other societies in the city gave a co-operative membership of close on 60,000. In the North, Newcastle-on-Tyne had over 27,000; in the South, there were three substantial societies in the metropolis, Royal Arsenal (Woolwich) 39,000, Stratford 34,000 and Edmonton 20,000; in Portsmouth, the Portsea Island Society had 12,000. Plymouth in the West was well established with over 42,000, but Bristol had only 17,000. Leeds, of course, was the biggest society in Yorkshire with 48,000, but Sheffield had a membership of 49,000 divided between two societies, Brightside & Carbrook, 29,000, and Sheffield & Eccleshall 20,000.

In Lancashire the largest societies were not as yet found in the cities and the Liverpool Society with 19,000 members was only half the size of that of Bolton. In the collection of townships commonly regarded as Manchester, the largest society was Pendleton with 29,000, and then came Eccles and Manchester & Salford with 18,000 each. The seven Manchester societies together had a total membership of 101,000. In every Section there were still many societies with only a few score members, though these were being reduced by amalgamation. The number of retail societies reached its peak of 1,455 in 1903, and in 1914 it had fallen to 1,385.

The trend towards amalgamation and the need for it were largely caused by the construction of electric tramways which extended the shopping areas of towns and of societies. There was a consequent increase in the overlapping of and competition between societies. To prevent or lessen this the Co-operative Union engaged in what was to prove a very long campaign of encouraging amalgamations and negotiating agreed boundaries between societies.

The main strength of the Movement remained concentrated in Lancashire, Yorkshire, Northumberland, Durham and the Scottish midlands, though after the turn of the century Co-operation was growing most rapidly in the Midlands. Even at the end of the period there were, however, still parts of the country in which Co-operation was non-existent or so very weak that they were aptly termed " co-operative deserts." Generally, these were in the agricultural counties of the English south and west, and the Scottish Highlands. For the greater part of this period the big cities were also co-operative deserts, but by 1914, Co-operation was rooted and growing in them, although measured by the proportion of membership to population it was still very small. For example, in 1911 co-operative membership in London was less than 1 per cent of the population, whereas in the county of Durham it was 13·3 per cent.

CAPITAL OF SOCIETIES

Share capital increased partly as a result of increased membership, partly as a result of greater working class prosperity and thrift, and partly as a result of greater confidence in co-operative societies as depositories of savings. Figures for the early years are unreliable, but in the 'sixties some well established societies were already embarrassed by an abundance of capital. The Rochdale Pioneers, for instance, took steps to compel some investors to withdraw their capital. The remedy for this was federal development by the expansion of the Wholesale Societies and the establishment of a banking department, which is dealt with later. There was a continuous yearly increase in the retail societies' share and loan capital, irrespective of boom and slump, from £6·05 million in 1881, to £44·94 million in 1914. The average per member also increased, though with slight fluctuations, from £10·96 in 1881, to £14·72 in 1914. Much of this increase was due to the accumulation of members' dividends so that the accession of new members reduced the average capital per member. Moreover, although many societies had a super-abundance of capital, others, especially new or young societies in the cities, suffered from a scarcity. The ease with which capital accumulated induced many societies to make rules restricting its growth, for example, by providing lower rates of interest on holdings over certain amounts.

It also discouraged societies from building up reserve funds, since to many the purpose of such funds was to maintain dividend rates during bad trading periods rather than to provide capital to finance development and growth. In 1883, the reserve funds amounted to £292,000, slightly more than 4 per cent of the share and loan capital; in 1901 to £1,066,000, slightly less than 4 per cent of the capital; and in 1914 to £2,912,853, which was 6·4 per cent of the capital.

Among the consequences of the reliance upon share and loan capital was the need to maintain a high liquidity of assets, for most of this share and loan capital was withdrawable at short notice. This discouraged societies from investing in the bricks, mortar and equipment involved in developing their own businesses and they preferred to have capital surplus to their own business enterprise and invest it elsewhere. A good proportion was invested with the Wholesale Societies, but much was also invested in what were regarded as safe investments such as government stocks, railways, and in Lancashire, cotton mills. Events were to show that even from a financial standpoint much of the capital invested outside the Movement would have been more profitably and safely employed in developing co-operative enterprises.

TRADE OF SOCIETIES

Trade also increased, from £15,411,185 in 1881, to £50,053,567 in 1900, and to £87,964,229 in 1914. A remarkable feature was the consistency in the sales per member, for this is affected by many circumstances. Among the most important are the increase in membership (new members generally purchase much less than the average, so that an increase in membership is apt to reduce the average trade per head) the prosperity of the members and changes in the value of money. Sales per member were £28·2 in 1881, at their lowest in 1887 at £25·8, and their highest in 1883 at £29·5. In five yearly averages the lowest figure was £27·1 in 1886–1890, and the highest in 1901–1905 was £28·9. When corrections are made, however, for changes in retail food prices, with few exceptions there was a yearly increase in the figure up to 1901, amounting to almost a 50 per cent increase on the 1881 figure. From 1901, however, the figure steadily fell and in 1914 the decrease was 14 per cent on 1901. This period, of course, was marked by a decrease in real wage rates whereas in the previous period they were rising, but the reason for the fall was more probably the increase in membership in districts which were not traditional co-operative strongholds and in which the average purchases were low enough to affect the national figures.

One reason for the comparative stability of trade per member was perhaps the preponderance of foodstuffs in co-operative trade, for this trade does not fluctuate with boom and slump as much as do many other commodities. According to figures given in *The Reasoner* in 1871, out of 291 societies every society was engaged in grocery, but only 54 had butchery, 88 drapery, 47 shoes and clogs, and 20 tailoring departments. The policy of aiming to make a specific rate of dividend perhaps dissuaded societies from undertaking lines of trade, such as butchery, whose rate of profit on sales was less than a predetermined rate of dividend. According to the General Co-operative Survey Report, in 1910, less than one-half of the societies had butchery departments and only 2·3 per cent had greengrocery. Many societies were too small to enter some other departments, there were only 46 per cent in tailoring, 30 per cent in millinery, 11 per cent in milk, 0·5 per cent in outfitting and only 0·5 per cent in funeral undertaking.[1]

DIVIDEND RATES AND POLICIES

The unsatisfactory development of the Movement was most probably due to the diversion of the aim of many societies to the making of high dividend rates. This may have resulted from management being increasingly in the hands of permanent officials. It would be difficult to assess the success of co-operative trading in terms of £ s. d., whereas private enterprise had a crude criterion in profits made. Practical businessmen, trained and experienced in private trade, attracted to the Movement by salary and security were perhaps apt to apply the standards of private business to co-operative business. As their committees were also often incapable of assessing the co-operative efficiency of the conduct of the business, this standard became accepted and managers aimed at high dividend rates.

High Dividends

Competition between societies also tended to force up the rates. This was possible because in many small towns and villages private trade was mainly in the hands of small shopkeepers who were too inefficient to compete effectively. They followed the lead of the societies in pricing, and so the societies were free to pay higher dividends by raising prices. Rates of dividend consequently often reached extravagant heights and round the turn of the century some societies were paying over 5s. in the pound. According to the figures of *The Reasoner* in 1871, the average dividend was 1s. 9d. in the £1, though one small society, Shawforth in Lancashire, paid 3s. 8d., and the average of the four northern counties was 2s. 1d. In 1879, 28 per cent of the societies recorded as paying dividend in the Co-operative Union statistics were paying between 1s. and 2s., 55 per cent between 2s. and 3s., and only 9·8 per cent between 3s. and 4s. In 1900 the percentage of societies paying between 1s. and 2s. had fallen to 20 per cent and the proportion

---

[1] *General Survey Committees Report*, 1919.

paying between 2s. and 3s. to 35 per cent; but 32 per cent were
paying between 3s. and 4s., and 6 per cent between 4s. and 5s.
Moreover, in certain sections of the Co-operative Union, the
Northern, North-Western (which included Yorkshire) and Scottish,
the pursuit of high dividends was even more pronounced. In the
Northern Section almost 50 per cent of societies paid between
3s. and 4s., and 12 per cent between 4s. and 5s.; in the North
Western rather less than 50 per cent paid between 3s. and 4s.,
and 7 per cent between 4s. and 5s.; and in the Scottish 41 per cent
paid between 3s. and 4s., and 10 per cent between 4s. and 5s.
In the Southern Section, on the other hand, 66 per cent of the
societies paying a dividend (not all were able to do so) paid between
1s. and 2s., and 17 per cent between 2s. and 3s.; only four
societies paid more than 3s., and 14 per cent paid less than 1s.

Looking back, the period appears as one of opportunities
wasted through such dividend policies. Often almost all surplus
was paid out in dividends and the inclusion of farthings and half-
pennies even in rates in excess of 3s. was quite common. Unsound
financial policies resulted, for reserves were not accumulated as
they could have been. Because of reliance on dividend to attract
trade and custom the improvement in service to the customer was
neglected. The obviously big profits possible from large scale
retailing, moreover, attracted capitalists into this trade and the
high dividend policies of co-operative societies also perhaps made
it much easier for the multiple firms to enter and develop in retail
trade.

These dividend policies, of course, were not unpopular amongst
the members. The domestic economy of many households relied
on the co-operative dividends for saving to meet expenditure on
items such as clothing, holidays, payment of rates, and provision
for bad times. Thrifty housewives preferred higher prices and
bigger shopping bills with the higher dividends later, to a lower
weekly expenditure which might only have meant more spent by
the husband on beer, sport and tobacco and less saved. Not all
wage earners, however, could afford such prices and saving, and
numbers of low paid and casual workers were consequently
deterred from co-operative membership and trade.

RETAIL SOCIETIES' PRODUCTIONS, 1870–1914

As societies grew bigger they were able to undertake productive
activities. The decline in home baking induced some to build and
equip bakeries; tailoring, dressmaking, furniture-making, boot-
making and repairs, farming and many other productive activities
were carried on. The General Survey Report of 1919 showed that

an amazing variety of productive activities from butter-making to window-cleaning were being undertaken before 1914. As the economical scale of production increased, some of these activities were being replaced by the factory production of the Wholesale Societies, e.g., dressmaking, tailoring, furniture, but by 1914 the retail societies were as yet little affected. Their productions increased from a value of £4,293,000 in 1900 to £15,705,000 in 1914.[1]

DEVELOPMENT OF THE C.W.S. IN WHOLESALING

The North of England Co-operative Wholesale Industrial and Provident Society Ltd., whose establishment was described in the last chapter, changed its name to the familiar Co-operative Wholesale Society by deleting Industrial and Provident in 1867, and North of England in 1872. It remained an Industrial and Provident society, but opened branches and developed trade all over the country so that " North of England " would have been a misnomer. Co-operative wholesaling had in fact been initiated in other parts of the country, in Northampton, London, Huddersfield and Newcastle. The advantages to be obtained from one wholesale, however, were obvious and because the C.W.S. was more widely and firmly based, it replaced these other ventures. Branches were opened at Newcastle in 1872, at London in 1874, and other depots or salesrooms followed: Liverpool (1875), Leeds (1882), Bristol (1884), Huddersfield and Longton (1885), Nottingham (1886), Blackburn (1890), Northampton (1890), Cardiff (1891), and Birmingham (1892).

Thus before the end of the century the country was covered by well-placed points at which the retail societies could be served by their wholesale organisation. One of the prime reasons why the Wholesale Society was established was the belief that the large-scale buying thereby made possible would result in various economies. Among these would be the cutting out of intermediaries or middlemen by buying in the first markets which produce entered or directly from the producer.

This soon necessitated the setting up of buying depots outside England. The first were in Ireland for the purchase of dairy produce—Tipperary (1866), Kilmallock (1868), Limerick (1869), Armagh (1873), Waterford (1873), and Tralee (1874). Then came New York (1876), Rouen (1879—the trade with which was conducted by the Society's own ship), Copenhagen (1881), Hamburg (1884), Aarhus (1891), Montreal (1894), Gothenburg

---

[1] *General Survey Committee Report*, 1919.

(1895), Denia (1896), Sydney (1897), Odense (1898), and Esbjerg (1905). Thus the C.W.S. had depots in Ireland, France, Denmark, Canada, the United States of America, Sweden, Spain and Australia, at which the foodstuffs of the English co-operator were bought through his co-operative organisations free of the speculators, merchants, agents, etc., with their various profits. The C.W.S., moreover, was not content merely to buy abroad. When the trade justified it, production itself was undertaken. It assisted the formation of the first co-operative dairy society at Drumcollogher in 1889, and took over another which was in difficulties at Castle-mahon in 1895. This was its first creamery and others followed, but trouble arose with the advocates of agricultural Co-operation in Ireland and this resulted eventually in their transfer—about one-third to societies and the rest to proprietors.[1] Bacon factories were also operated abroad, in Ireland at Tralee in 1901, and Denmark at Herning in 1900. Tea estates were purchased in Ceylon in 1913.

C.W.S. BANKING DEPARTMENT

Co-operators in the preceding generation had visions of the spread of co-operative trading and an extension of co-operative production which would gradually transform the economic system into a co-operative one.

E. V. Neale had seen the possibilities but also realised that the prerequisite was a central organisation or organisations, such as a wholesale society and a co-operative bank, to co-ordinate the activities of the various societies. He had a clear picture in his mind of what the pattern should be—retail societies covering the country, obtaining their supplies from a co-operative wholesale society and depositing their surplus capital with a co-operative bank. The co-operative wholesale society would purchase from productive societies owned and controlled by those employed in them and the co-operative bank would initiate and finance new productive societies to meet the consumers' needs. He outlined this scheme again to the Congress of 1870. It is doubtful if any other clear pattern of development was held.

The Rochdale Pioneers had as cheerfully established a federal consumers' productive enterprise in the Corn Mill as they had a producers' undertaking in the cotton manufacturing society. The Co-operative Wholesale Society, in the beginnings, had no firmly held, or even clearly seen, principles of consumer control and it, too, assisted the establishment of various productive societies. There were, however, some unfortunate experiences with these

[1] Ref. to Chap. XVI.

which resulted in co-operative production being developed mainly by the Wholesale Societies. This was a logical development of consumer Co-operation, but the issues and principles involved were not immediately clear. They began to emerge with the entry of the Wholesale Societies into production and the beginning of banking activities by the North of England Wholesale Society.

Establishing the C.W.S. Bank

The need for a co-operative bank had been long realised. At the first Co-operative Congress in 1869, papers on the subject were given by R. B. D. Morier (H.M. Charge d'Affaires at Darmstadt) and by the Rev. W. N. Molesworth of Rochdale. Thomas Hughes also dealt with it in his presidential address. It continued to be discussed at succeeding congresses, the Schulze Delitsch banks of Germany were thoroughly considered and papers by " a great authority on banking matters " (1870) and by " the head of a large joint stock bank " (1871) were given, the last advising that the Wholesale Society should begin to act as bankers. Conferences had also been held, the first at Bury in 1870, to discuss a paper by J. M. Ludlow. Congress resolutions had been carried in 1870, instructing the Provincial Section of the Central Board to consider the matter and prepare a scheme. Approaches were made to the friendly and building societies and the trade unions, but with no favourable responses. The Central Board came to the conclusion that the co-operative body " must depend on some action of its own in the way of banking," and that the nucleus of a bank might originate with the North of England Wholesale Society. Congress in 1871 decided that the Provincial Section should take action with a view to getting a banking system inaugurated through the North of England and Scottish Wholesale Societies. The Provincial Section deemed it better " that all possible pressure should be brought to bear on the Wholesale Society rather than seek to establish a separate institution." Their pressure was successful, for though the Whole-sale was naturally somewhat diffident at undertaking the apparently mysterious and hazardous business of banking, the impression given by Wholesale spokesmen at this period is of the coyness that is willing to be pressed.

This is not surprising, for they were fervent co-operative idealists with a great faith in the co-operative way and a growing conviction that this way was by the development of federal activities by the retail societies. The opinion has been expressed that this was a further departure from Owenism, but Owenism had been long left behind. It is of some significance that old

Owenites, such as Dr. Watts, Lloyd Jones and William Pare were strong advocates of the development of banking and productive activities by the Wholesale Societies, whereas those who came to oppose it in favour of production by producers' societies only and an independent bank did not derive their inspiration from Owen but from the Christian Socialists.

Four days after the 1872 Congress had dissolved, the Manchester sub-section appointed by Congress for the purpose approached the Directors of the Wholesale Society and in less than a month these had resolved to recommend to the quarterly meeting that the Society should commence and gradually develop a banking business. Some alteration of the law, however, was necessary, and although this was brought about through the efforts of W. Morrison, M.P., and Thomas Hughes, M.P., it was not until 1876. In the meantime the C.W.S. was carrying on, under the management of Abraham Greenwood, a loan and deposit business which was of doubtful legality, for the Industrial and Provident Societies' Act specifically excluded banking.

C.W.S. PRODUCTION

Opposition to the C.W.S. undertaking banking also developed. One of the principal reasons for the desire for a co-operative bank was to find a co-operative use for the rapidly growing surplus funds of the retail societies. Some expected that a co-operative bank would channel these supplies to finance the establishment and development of producers' societies, but there were others who believed that the funds would be better employed in the development of the Wholesale Societies' activities. The decision in 1872 that the C.W.S. should enter production, and in 1873 the beginning with the production of biscuits at Crumpsall and of boots and shoes at Leicester, aroused the opposition of those who favoured producer Co-operation. They realised also that a co-operative bank which was a department of the C.W.S. gave that body a commanding advantage as it would concentrate in its hands the capital of the retail societies available for investment.

In fact, the C.W.S., and many retail societies, burned their fingers in assisting producers' societies and taking part in some of their ventures during the 'seventies. About a couple of hundred were founded, most of which failed between 1862 and 1880. They were engaged in coal mining, textiles, printing and publishing, building, engineering and footwear. Many of the failures were associated with the onset of " The Great Depression," especially in coal mining and engineering, in which many capitalist enterprises also failed. The most spectacular was that of the Ouseburn Engineering Works on Tyneside, into which a good deal of co-operative capital had gone, for example Halifax Society lost £10,000 and the C.W.S. £8,000. Its failure in 1875, brought down in 1876 the Industrial Bank promoted by Dr. Rutherford, who also promoted the Ouseburn works and was at the head of both. This bank had been founded to finance Ouseburn when the C.W.S. was unwilling to invest more in the enterprise. It attracted deposits from both co-operative societies and trade unions, and some of these were shaken badly by the collapse. One society with a capital of £26,000 had £10,531 in the Industrial Bank. Other productive societies were also failing and more than two dozen had substantial overdrafts from the C.W.S., which now found itself in difficulties. Arrangements had to be made with its London bankers to carry over a debit balance of £50,000, and to meet one urgency financial assistance had to be obtained from the Rochdale Pioneers.

It is not surprising that these consequences of what were in essence speculative ventures induced caution in the retail societies and their Wholesale Society and an unwillingness to engage in productive enterprises which were outside their ownership and control and did not meet an already secured demand. The pattern of co-operative extension into production became one in which the market for a commodity was created by development in the retail societies, their demands for it were concentrated in the Wholesale Society and the demands eventually became large enough to sustain a productive enterprise on an economical scale. As the C.W.S. had both market and capital as a result of its wholesaling and banking activities, the extension of its productive enterprises had the appearance of a natural organic growth.

Reasons for C.W.S. Production

Many reasons could be found for the C.W.S. developing its productive activities, such as the co-operative employment of co-operative capital, the provision of co-operative employment (no light gain in those industries where " sweating " was common) and the advance to a comprehensive co-operative system which became known as a Co-operative Commonwealth. In some cases the factories of productive societies in difficulties were taken over, but probably the strongest and most frequent reason was to obtain greater reliability in the quality of the goods passing through the Wholesale to the retail societies. William Pare, for instance, in 1871 urged " that an important part of the co-operative prin- ciple was the production of a better class of goods; things made to wear and not to sell. Co-operators ought to take a pride in making their 'brand' an acknowledged sign of superiority." Complaints that the Wholesale Society sold adulterated goods, mustard being cited as an instance, were answered by Lloyd Jones that they were in the hands of the manufacturers of proprietary brands: "if the societies wished to sell pure mustard, it would be better that they should have a manufactory of their own." The advocates of producers' Co-operation also pleaded for trade with the distributive societies on the ground that there was little place for the producers of pure, unadulterated, honest goods in the competitive market.

The record of increasing productive enterprise by the C.W.S. during this period is an impressive one. Foodstuffs, footwear, clothing, bedding and furnishings, soap, printing and publishing, furniture, tobacco, general hardware, brushes, leather goods, boxmaking, umbrellas, glass, paints and varnishes were engaged upon. Some of the developments were in a vertical direction, taking in processes preceding the final stages of production, as with the weaving of cloth, fellmongering, currying and tanning of leather, fruit and vegetable growing and dairy farming.

Rarely did a year pass without some new productive enterprise being undertaken or an old one extended. Some years such as 1896, 1898, 1904, 1908, were exceptionally prolific. The value of C.W.S. productions increased from £133,106 in 1881, to £9,051,646 in 1914, and in the latter year the Society employed 20,000 people in productive enterprises. Such figures, of course, are but an index to the real gains—the provision of pure, unadulterated food, of good, honest hard-wearing footwear and clothing, and of well-made furniture and bedding. The products were what William Pare had asked for and C.W.S. products could be relied upon as being honest products. Moreover, 20,000 workpeople enjoyed the stability and conditions of co-operative employment which were distinctly superior to those which prevailed in private manufacture.

SCOTTISH CO-OPERATIVE WHOLESALE SOCIETY

The Scottish Wholesale Society had developed on similar, though not identical lines. There was the same pattern of development from groceries to dry goods, the increase in departments, the opening of branches and depots, Leith (1877), Kilmarnock (1878), Dundee (1881), and Edinburgh (1898). Overseas depots were established in Ireland and Canada. There was an unfortunate association with a co-operative productive society with some parallel to the C.W.S. and the Ouseburn venture, though the fingers of the S.C.W.S. were burned much more severely. In this case the S.C.W.S. became deeply involved in the affairs of the Scottish Co-operative Ironworks, an enterprise to find work for engineers victimised after an industrial dispute in 1872. Its collapse involved the S.C.W.S. in a loss of £10,427, more than its subscribed share capital. The loss was met by the retail societies levying themselves a penny in the pound of dividends, until the loss was wiped out and this was not accomplished until 1879.

As with the C.W.S., the lesson was learned—to engage in production to meet the retail society members' needs. This natural organic growth began with the manufacture of shirts in 1881, and was followed by clothing, furniture, footwear, building, printing, brushes, tobacco, engineering, tinware, soap, a variety of foodstuffs, paint, leather, umbrellas, jute and farming. A feature was the erection of several factories on one estate at Shieldhall, near Glasgow, this securing many economies in the provision of common services.

Another unique undertaking by the S.C.W.S. was the venture into direct retail trading. Local circumstances, not the least the opposition of landlords and shopkeepers, made it practically impossible for Co-operation even to start in the Highlands and the islands of Scotland. The S.C.W.S., therefore, decided to open retail branches in those areas, the first being at Elgin in 1908. Results, however, were disappointing during this period.

JOINT ACTION BY THE WHOLESALES

Both Wholesale Societies worked frequently together. At times business visits abroad were shared and a joint meeting was held in London in 1882, in connection with tea. An arrangement was made for joint consultation in 1890, leading to the formal establishment of a joint committee in 1900 which became responsible for tea, including the plantations in India and Ceylon, and for the cocoa and chocolate trade of both societies. Joint action with insurance was also taken. The Co-operative Insurance Company had been reorganised and renamed the Co-operative Insurance Society in 1899. There was dissatisfaction with the service it provided and the progress it made, and the development of insurance business by the C.W.S. aroused contention. This was eventually ended by the two Wholesale Societies taking over the C.I.S. in 1913.

ATTITUDE OF RETAIL SOCIETIES

As the trade of the Wholesales increased the opportunities for increased production also increased, not only by the extension of old enterprises but also by the creation of new. This led to an increase in the percentage of their own productions within their total trade which is shown by the following figures:—

Year	Sales £ mill.	C.W.S.			S.C.W.S.		
		Productions £ mill.	Percentage of Productions to sales	Sales £ mill.	Productions £ mill.	Percentage of Productions to sales
1881	3·574	·133	3·72	·986	—	—
1900	16·043	2·626	16·37	5·463	1·460	26·73
1914	34·910	9·051	25·93	9·425	3·139	33·30

(from General Survey Committee's Report, 1919)

The above figures showed substantial increases and they were not gained effortlessly. There was opposition to co-operative wholesale trading and production not only by private traders, but also within the Movement itself. Societies did not readily join in the early years, and their trade with the Wholesales appears to have been very grudgingly given. In 1871, it was estimated that the North of England Wholesale Society received only one-eighth part of the entire trade of retail societies. The reasons for this appear to have come from lack of co-operative knowledge and sentiment among societies' officials. Societies had been created rapidly. They appointed men as managers who, although experienced in retail trading, had been trained in private trade, had the outlook of private traders and were ignorant of, or out of sympathy with, the purpose of the co-operative societies. The Wholesale Societies had been founded, not without difficulty, by idealists, and appeared, or were made to appear, as the pipe dream of visionaries, to which the interests of the members of retail societies were sacrificed.

Disloyalty

" In many instances the hindrance lay in the power behind the throne," stated P. Redfern in *The Story of the C.W.S.* " ' In those old days,' says an old committeeman, ' the managers were the masters.' Many managers and societies' buyers had hastily concluded that if the Wholesale prospered their occupation would be gone . . . The buyers liked to bargain, to give orders and bestow patronage." For many years Congress discussions and the correspondence columns of the *Co-operative News* bore witness to the existence of this problem. Lloyd Jones, with the essential grasp of principle which every practical man must have, declared at the Congress of 1871: " Until the delegates infused a true co-operative spirit amongst their managers they would never get the

Co-operative Movement into a right condition. It was no use telling him that it was their members they had to contend against; it was their own servants they had to contend against. He found the managers and leading men more against doing their duty than he found the members."

The entry into production made the problem more serious, for it involved the investment of the Movement's capital in plant and buildings, and the achievement of some return upon this depended upon the loyalty of societies' buyers. This was by no means always forthcoming. Yet the changing conditions of the distributive trades with the advent of branded goods, large-scale advertising, joint stock enterprise with department and chain stores, the threat of monopoly and attacks by associations of private traders, made increasing reliance on the Wholesale Societies a matter of self defence, apart from the pursuit of co-operative ideals.

Manufacturers in general found the retailer a hindrance to large-scale production which required national markets with national uniform prices and national price policies. Some overcame the hindrance by opening their own retail outlets, some by national advertising of their branded products at prices fixed by themselves. They relied on their own ability to sell their products to the public and the retailer handed the branded packet over the counter to the customer in response to her requests, which had been stimulated by advertising and various devices of " salesmanship," e.g., door-to-door canvassing, distribution of samples and extravagant gift schemes.

Tea and Soap Struggles

Tea in prepacked blends was eminently suited to these practices, and crockery, jewellery, furniture and ornaments were given to purchasers of particular brands. This began in the 'eighties and developed with the years until the competition in gifts reached the stage when old age and widows' pensions were offered. At first these were paid, but later as claims increased they could not be met. Half-a-million women were purchasers and 19,000 widows were demanding their pensions. In 1905 it became a matter for the courts, and Justice Buckley described the scheme as " one for attracting married women to buy tea at 40 per cent above its market value by delusive and reckless promise of impossible pensions." Another dishonest practice of many private tea firms, was to weigh the packing and packet with the tea. Only concerted action by the whole of the Movement enabled co-operative trade in tea to survive and eventually attain a commanding position in it.

Soap was another commodity in which the Wholesales had to meet the competition of soap, plus gift coupon and bonus wrapper. This was intensified by the formation of a great soap trust in 1906, whose professed object was, of course, to " avoid the raising of prices to the public." The public, however, had its doubts and there was also a great outcry in the press. It was revealed that the size of the 1 lb. bars of soap had been reduced to 15 oz. One result was such a rapid increase in the demand for C.W.S. soap that there was difficulty in meeting it. Extensions to plant to meet this demand carried the risk of the plant becoming redundant when the hullaballoo died down. Conferences were called and hundreds of societies resolved to stock only C.W.S. soaps. The consequent reductions in orders on the private firms induced an attack on the Movement. Sir William Lever arranged a number of trap orders (a request for a Lever soap in the hope that a guileless assistant would supply C.W.S.) upon co-operative societies which sold only C.W.S. soaps, and then caused writs to be served upon 22 of them. The actions failed, and with the failure died the attempt to force co-operative societies to stock and sell Leverhulme's soaps.

These and similar efforts of private enterprise, however, made co-operators and their societies more conscious of the need for mutual reliance and loyalty to their federal undertakings and production of their own goods. These lessons were learned by hard experience whereas the attempts of co-operative theorists to teach them by voice and pen had been largely unheeded.

SIMILAR PROBLEMS IN SCOTLAND

The S.C.W.S. had also had to combat the concerted efforts of private traders to damage co-operative societies by organised boycotts. Children of members of co-operative societies were threatened with dismissal by some merchants and manufacturers, threats that in some instances were carried out. The master butchers at Glasgow decided that no co-operative society would be supplied from the Glasgow Dead Meat Market after June 25th, 1896; and they would have no dealings with anybody who sold to a co-operative society. An attempt was also made to prevent co-operative societies from bidding in the Cattle Market.

The response of the Co-operative Movement was interesting and significant. Both the Dead Meat Market and the Cattle Market were public property and subject to public control. To get this control exercised in the interest of the public instead of that of private traders, Glasgow co-operators, led and inspired by James Deans, Secretary of the Scottish Section of the Co-operative

Union, worked in conjunction with trade union and labour organisations to secure the election of members of the Corporation pledged to fair play for co-operators. Similar action was taken elsewhere. There was a struggle for public opinion. A defence fund of £20,000 was raised and a Co-operative Vigilance Committee exposed the designs and methods of the boycotters by propaganda and public meetings. In 1897, by-laws were passed which required auctioneers in the city markets to accept *bona fide* bids. The reply to this by private trade was to abandon public auctions and to deal in private rings. Some co-operative societies then began to buy direct from local farmers and the S.C.W.S. cattle buying department gave valuable help. The S.C.W.S. also arranged weekly supplies of cattle from Canada, and the co-operative butchery trade was built up as strong as ever.

As with other overt attacks on the Movement, this attempt proved beneficial. Not only was the loyalty of members strengthened, but a good deal of public resentment was aroused against the tactics of private trade, and interest quickened in the Co-operative Movement. During the three years of this struggle, 1894-1897, co-operative membership increased by 46,644, capital by £1,727,000, and trade by £3,554,000, an amount greater than the increase of the previous 16 years. This victory was due, it may be noted, to political action to get fair by-laws passed, to successful propaganda in winning over public opinion and to the ability to find alternative channels of supply because of the existence of the S.C.W.S.

CO-OPERATIVE CO-PARTNERSHIP

Many productive societies, as stated, foundered during the Great Depression and the experiences of this time led the Wholesale Societies to develop productive activities of their own. Those who regarded the Co-operative Movement's ideal to be the emancipation of the worker from wage-earning employment were not, however, content with this state of affairs. They struggled to get the Wholesale Societies' factories converted into the type of organisation they favoured, one element of which was profit-sharing. In this they were partially successful and the C.W.S. adopted the principle in 1874, but abandoned it, however, in 1886, though the S.C.W.S. retained it until 1914. The advocates of producer Co-operation, however, continued to press their case, to assist productive societies in being and to get new ones established.

In 1880, only 15 productive societies were still in existence, and they had no organisation for mutual help or for the propagation of their ideals. This was remedied by the formation of the Co-operative Productive Federation in 1882. Its objects were to promote unity of action amongst its members, secure capital for their use and find markets for their products. For several years, however, it was unable to do much. Out of it, in 1884, was formed the Labour Association, which devoted itself to education and propaganda, leaving the C.P.F. to concern itself with the business affairs of the societies. E. O. Greening was the leader, but had the support of old Christian Socialists in E. V. Neale, Thomas Hughes, J. M. Ludlow, and won that of trade unionists such as Henry Vivian and George Howell and of economists like J. Bonar and Alfred Marshall. The Co-operative Union agreed to the formation of a Co-operative Aid Association to encourage the formation of productive societies, and E. V. Neale drafted model rules for them.

Much had been learned from the experiences of the past, and the struggle and debates with the advocates of production by the Wholesale Societies led to a clearer definition of what the supporters of co-partnership had in mind. By it they meant a business organisation in which the wage earner had the right (and opportunity) to become a shareholder, the right to a share in the profits and the right to take part in the management. All three rights are essential. Co-partnership could be introduced by converting capitalist firms and by co-operative societies making their employees into co-partners. The Labour Association became increasingly concerned with the former task and so gradually drifted from the Co-operative Movement. During the early part of this century it devoted most of its activities to establishing housing societies known as Co-partnership Tenants' Societies.

Nature of Co-operative Co-partnership

Within the Co-operative Movement there developed Co-operative Co-partnership, i.e., the system practised by societies affiliated to the Co-operative Productive Federation. These accept the three co-partnership principles, but are also generally registered under the Industrial and Provident Societies' Acts; limit the rate of interest on shares; allow individual members one vote, and only one vote, each; pay a dividend out of their surplus to their customers; and in short are co-operative societies which also practise co-partnership.

The retail societies provided much of the capital by taking up shares in these societies and also formed the principal market for their products. Hall and Watkins found the co-operative co-partnership society to be " essentially a compromise between the

self-governing workshop and the consumers' co-operative undertaking of the ordinary type. It represents an endeavour to avoid the
defects and unite the advantages of both. It corrects the instability
of the self-governing workshop by introducing a body of shareholders who will support the authority of the management. It taps
sources of capital that the self-governing workshops could not
reach. It can develop, no less than the self-governing workshop,
the *esprit de corps*, the pride of ownership, the sense of responsibility, the spirit of give and take that contribute enormously to
business efficiency and smooth running." (*Co-operation.*)

In the 10 years following the establishment of the Co-operative
Productive Federation the number of co-operative co-partnership
societies trebled. Many of these were in the East Midlands footwear, hosiery and clothing industries, which were undergoing
their industrial revolution. Great progress was made in the years
1894 to 1899, through the zeal and ability of Thomas Blandford,
the general secretary of the C.P.F. He was successful in raising
capital, founded and organised the Federation's loan department,
organised exhibitions, developed propaganda, and began the
publication of the *Co-operators' Year Book*.

Yet, although the value of the output of these societies increased
from £885,000 in 1895 to £1,440,000 in 1914, the proportion of
this to co-operative retail trade fell from 2·61 per cent to 1·92
per cent in the same period. In 1914 there were fifteen textile
societies (including clothing and hosiery societies), fifteen footwear, eight metal trades (cutlery, watch-making, needle-making,
locks and cartgear), nine building and wood (mainly cabinet
makers), fourteen printing, three seeds and farms and nine others
(including " Temperance Male Nurses," Co-partnership Motor
Cabs, and a Fisherman's Ferry). Of the textile societies seven
were started between 1890 and 1901; of the footwear societies
eleven between 1890 and 1907; of the metal trades societies three
between 1892 and 1898; of the building and wood societies six
between 1891 and 1911; of the printing societies twelve between
1892 and 1909; of the seed and farm societies one after 1883;
and of the other societies six between 1896 and 1911.

It will be gathered that the eighteen-nineties and the first few
years of the nineteenth century were the period when most of
these societies were established. What is surprising is that the
movements for workers' control expressed in syndicalism and
guild socialism which appeared to be exercising considerable influence in the Trade Union Movement from about 1908 did not
result in efforts to establish workers' productive societies at a rate
equal to that of the previous decade.

6 OTHER CO-OPERATIVE DEVELOPMENTS: 1870-1914

> " *If you be guided by nothing better than mere commercial considerations, then Co-operation must prove a delusion and a snare, and the services and sacrifices of those who laboured in the past must have been given and rendered in vain.*"
> (*R. Fleming, Presidential Congress Address, 1914.*)

THE Co-operative Movement, of course, is much more than an organisation of business enterprises, indeed all its business is a means, not the end or purpose of its being. The previous chapter was concerned mainly with the development of co-operative business. This one deals with the wider aspects of the Movement, of the Co-operative Union, of co-operative education, the growth of auxiliary bodies, the conflict of ideals and the impact of new social thought.

CO-OPERATIVE UNION

The history of the Co-operative Union during this period is one of development of functions and constitutional change. It was active in promoting and assisting the growth of new societies. As these increased in hitherto co-operative deserts new Sections were created, the Western in 1878, the South-Western in 1895, and the Irish in 1889–1895. There was also an increase in the number of District Associations as societies came to realise the advantages of coming together for the discussion of matters of common concern and action.

Increasing activities necessitated increasing departmentalisation. It was impracticable for the Central Board to deal with every matter, especially those which required consideration between its periodical meetings. Special committees were therefore appointed. At first a Sectional Board was made responsible for some particular matter, the North-West Sectional Board, for instance, being entrusted with the management of the headquarters in Manchester and the Southern Sectional Board with keeping an eye on the activities of Parliament in London. This was not a satisfactory arrangement and was only tolerable on the grounds of economy.

Committees representative of each function came to be established as the financial resources of the Union increased. In some cases it was found desirable to have joint committees with the Wholesale Societies and one with the Trades Union Movement.

The Co-operative Union was also put on a sounder basis by its registration under the Industrial and Provident Societies Act in 1889. It was made thereby a federation of co-operative societies, each of which held a five shillings share with limited liability. The principal source of income remained the annual subscriptions and this became more satisfactory when it was decided in 1911 that all societies were to pay $1\frac{1}{2}$d. per member per annum—but with voting power proportionate to membership, i.e., one vote per thousand members. In the same year a new building, Holyoake House, Manchester, was opened as the permanent headquarters of the Co-operative Union. It was erected as a memorial to G. J. Holyoake, who had died in 1906.

Increase of Influence

The prestige and influence of the Union grew. Its highlights were the annual Congresses, and reports of these are indispensable to any serious study of the Movement. In them are found not only the records of the advance of Co-operation in all its various fields, but also insight into the dynamics of the Movement, the ideals and the currents of thought which started and shaped developments of function and form. Great issues were debated on high levels of principle, future lines of development were discussed and initiated, weaknesses of the Movement exposed, broad policy determined and the Movement's opinion on matters of national moment expressed.

Although less spectacular, the day to day activities of the Union were also important. Its general secretary, E. V. Neale, drafted the first set of model rules for societies. With Thomas Hughes he wrote *The Manual for Co-operators*, which gave a philosophy of Co-operation together with practical advice on the management of societies. He drafted a new Industrial and Provident Societies Act (enacted in 1893). Neale's successor, J. C. Gray prepared amendments which were enacted in 1913.

There were, however, many others, who would be described in these days as laymen and yet built on the foundations of the Movement. These were " the members of the seven Sectional Boards and the sixty-two District Conference Executives who spent untold hours of what might have been leisure time in nursing sickly societies, in bringing the wilful and refractory into safe co-operative paths, in stamping out the evils of credit, slipshod book-keeping and slack management, and in countless conferences, teaching, guiding and creating an enlightened co-operative opinion. The results of this work were to be seen in the work of the Congresses and the demeanour of delegates. Debates grew steadily less academic and more practical. As the Central Board's Report, the principal part of the agenda, grew larger, Congress became more businesslike in both temper and procedure. Moreover, it cared less and less to be patronised by the eminent and scholarly amateur in Co-operation, but preferred to be under the chairmanship of, and listen to the addresses of, men who had served a working apprenticeship in the Movement. If Congress by this lost something in imagination and width of view, it gained much in commonsense and its grasp of present realities." (*Co-operation*, Hall and Watkins.)

CO-OPERATIVE EDUCATION

Other co-operative societies followed the example of the Rochdale Pioneers' Society in its educational activities described in a previous chapter, organising classes in scientific, technological, art, commercial and general subjects. This was good work, but it often resulted in the neglect of co-operative education. Towards the end of the century, however, much of this educational activity began to be undertaken by local authorities, freeing for the first time all the educational funds and energy of the Movement for their primary purpose, the making of co-operators. This was not always realised or appreciated. Some societies confused education and recreation, and W. H. Watkins complained in 1897 that many were " spending with complacency, on tea parties, outings, social gatherings and other forms of diversion, funds intended to be applied to much more serious undertakings."

Fortunately, the Co-operative Union had from the beginning been intensely concerned with education in Co-operation. At the first Congress of 1869, Auberon Herbert stated that one of the great difficulties among co-operators was the want of education on the part of their managers and officers. He suggested as a remedy " a college, or training institution which should bring together under the same roof the students belonging to it." At the next Congress William Pare advocated co-operative colleges, stressing the danger to the Co-operative Movement " in its present phase of shop-keeping " of forgetting its purpose, of concerning itself only with saving and gains, these " being mistaken for the end instead of the means . . . than which nothing could be more disastrous." This Congress also passed a resolution urging all societies to use 2½ per cent of their surpluses on education.

As problem after problem was discussed at succeeding Congresses the need for effective co-operative education became increasingly clear. The difficulties of the Wholesale Societies and of co-operative production were largely due to the lack of loyalty arising from co-operative ignorance. William Nuttall of the C.W.S., for instance, declared in 1871, that "what was wanted were lecturers or something to enlighten co-operators ... buyers and sometimes committees were not imbued with the co-operative spirit; they had not studied co-operative literature and cared only for immediate profit."

Growing Need for Education

Arnold Toynbee of Oxford and Professor Stuart of Cambridge also declared that if the Co-operative Movement were to continue to pursue its mission it must educate its members with the object of making them good co-operative citizens. In a well known and memorable passage Professor Stuart stated in 1879: " If the mass of your members are not sufficiently instructed in economic science, in the facts of commerce, in the state of this and other countries, in the history of trade, in general knowledge, and in particular knowledge of what you aim at and how you seek it ... I say if the mass of your members are not sufficiently instructed in these things, there arises a real danger to the Co-operative Movement; your members become a hindrance and your possessions become a peril, and your productive endeavours will continue to be a failure, which they too often hitherto have been. Your Movement is a democratic movement if ever there was one. It therefore cannot repose on the good sense of a few; its success will depend on the good sense of the masses of your people ... First you must educate your members in your own principles and in those of economic science and in the history of endeavours like your own; and in the second place you must educate them generally. Education is desirable for all mankind: it is the life's necessity for co-operators."

The Central Board and Congress continuously discussed the question and in 1883 began to take practical steps by appointing an Education Committee to act as a central advisory body. Congress resolved that it wanted " the development of some system of education in Co-operation." Sectional Boards also set up committees. The objects of co-operative education were laid down as " primarily the formation of co-operative character and opinion, and secondarily, though not necessarily of less import, the training of men and women to take part in industrial and social reforms and municipal life generally."

The first attempt at class instruction in Co-operation seems to have been made in London in 1882 by Ben Jones, and a scheme for systematic instruction in the principles of Co-operation was drawn up by A. Acland. An inquiry conducted by the Education Committee into the educational activities of societies showed there was very little if any organised serious study. Funds were spent mainly on newsrooms and libraries, which were valuable, and on entertainments and excursions, which although serving useful purposes, were not educational. The central Education Committee proceeded to provide remedies. Outlines of lessons on Co-operation were prepared for teachers and pupils, a series of papers issued for reading and discussion at members' monthly conferences and efforts made to discover people willing and able to teach Co-operation.

Co-operative Union Efforts

A start was also made in the long neglected task of giving co-operative employees the opportunity to acquire the basic knowledge required for their work. Provision was made for the study of co-operative book-keeping and auditing, management and elementary and advanced Co-operation, the preparation of outlines and text-books. Correspondence courses began in 1890, E. V. Neale himself conducting a course in Advanced Co-operation on the basis of outlines published in the *Co-operative News*. Other subjects were gradually added. In 1900, 1,154 students enrolled and 582 sat for examination in Co-operation, Industrial History, Citizenship and Book-keeping.

Attention was also being given to the co-operative education of children. Junior co-operative clubs were formed in the nineties, junior classes in Co-operation started in 1898–1899 and a text-book for their use was published. In 1900, 942 children sat the junior examination.

Despite the work of a very active Education Committee there was such a great difference between what was being done and what was needed that a healthy dissatisfaction showed itself. Miss Margaret Llewelyn Davies, of the Women's Guild, one of the best minds and characters ever connected with the Movement, expressed this in a paper, first read to the annual meeting of the Women's Guild and considered by the Union's Education Committee in 1895–1896. She declared co-operative education to be two-fold:—

(1) Purely co-operative—being education in the principles and the work of Co-operation.
(2) General—by giving co-operators greater facilities for obtaining general knowledge and instruction, to better fit them for social duties.

The 1896 Congress decided that a Special Committee of Inquiry should inquire into and report on education for co-operators. As a result the Union's Education Committee was made more representative by the inclusion of Sectional Education Committees' Associations. It was also considered that the educational activities were too narrow in scope: " There is an absence of any systematic training in industrial and municipal subjects either by co-operative societies or by any outside body . . . . Here in the teaching of industrial economics and the duties of citizens, is the new pioneer work lying at the doors of co-operators."

There was undoubtedly a rising demand for such education consequent upon the growth of serious reading by working class people and increasing interest in social reform and the revival of socialism. Albert Mansbridge, a clerk employed by the C.W.S., started an important movement in adult education by a speech to the Co-operative Congress of 1898 which led to his giving a paper to a conference of co-operators at Oxford in 1899. His ideas of an alliance of co-operative, trade union and university extension effort, however, gained little support then, but he expounded them again in the *University Extension Journal* and this aroused a wider interest. His decision to initiate a new educational movement was " precipitated over a cup of coffee with Robert Halstead, secretary of the Co-operative Productive Federation."[1]

The Workers' Educational Association

In 1903 the Workers' Educational Association was founded. From the beginning it got a good deal of co-operative support. The first body to affiliate was Annfield Plain Co-operative Society. Robert Halstead was on the first executive committee and so were W. R. Rae, chairman, and C. E. Wood, secretary, of the Co-operative Union's Education Committee. At the end of the first year its membership consisted of 11 co-operative societies and 135 members. The first local branch was formed at Reading on the initiative of the Education Committee of Reading Co-operative Society in 1904. In March, 1905, a branch was formed at Rochdale as " The Rochdale Education Guild." Among the active personalities was Fred Hall, later to become the first Adviser of Studies to the Co-operative Union and Principal of the Co-operative College. He maintained an active interest in the W.E.A. for the rest of his life.

In Rochdale the idea of a class undertaking a long period of study under a university tutor still survived from the unsuccessful

---

[1] *History of the Workers' Educational Association* by T. W. Price.

E

approach of the Pioneers to Cambridge in 1871. In 1907, they approached Mansbridge, who was able to inform them that if an undertaking to study for a period of not less than two years was made by not less than thirty people the Association would try to provide a tutor. A meeting was held at which " Economic History " was chosen as the subject; and Saturday afternoons were decided on as the time. They were preferred to evenings as many were afraid that work and overtime would interfere with their continued studies. Forty-three students were enrolled, including one who sacrificed a promising career as a professional footballer. This was a generation with a proper sense of values! The first class was held on January 25th, 1908, with R. H. Tawney as the tutor. It was the first University Tutorial Class, and it would be difficult to over-estimate the consequences for the life of the nation of the development of this movement, for it affected politics, trade unions, education and cultural and social life generally, as well as the Co-operative Movement.

It was not, however, quite the movement Mansbridge had intended. The various bodies engaged, or which ought to have been engaged in adult education, continued along the lines of their own specific ideals although they were undoubtedly stimulated by the activities of the W.E.A. Co-operators, while actively collaborating both locally and nationally on provisions for general education, concentrated their separate efforts on subjects and activities directly connected with co-operative principles and organisation.

Lines of Co-operative Education

The general lines of development of co-operative education had been laid down by 1900, the curriculum was later widened and educational funds increased from £64,147 in 1900, to £113,226 in 1914. The number of students increased from 3,216 to 20,094 in the same period. This increase was largely due to the increase of enrolments in junior and intermediate co-operative classes (from 1,967 to 15,969), but also to the inclusion of new subjects for adults and employees. Syllabuses for adolescent co-operators were introduced (1908), Economics (1906), Secretaryship (1909), Apprenticeship and Management (1910), Elocution (1912), Literature (1912), Economics of Co-operation (1913) and for Special Classes for Women in Co-operation and Citizenship (1913).

The number of people interested in co-operative education and concerned with its growth naturally increased. For some years the Union's Education Committee had convened an annual conference of teachers to discuss their difficulties and problems. In

1908 the experiment was tried of adding to this a series of meetings dealing with other educational topics. Encouraged by its success, the following Easter a more widely representative gathering was held at Otley (1909). This is usually regarded as the first Easter Weekend. From 1934 it was described as the Easter Weekend Convention and has been held each year since, saving one or two breaks during the first world war. It brought together enthusiasts for co-operative education, extending their horizons from local to national problems and possibilities and naturally stimulating new developments. Among these was the foundation of the Co-operative Students' Fellowship, set up at the first Easter Weekend at Otley and later merged into the Co-operators' Educational Fellowship. This body, of course, helped to create and further the demand for the extension of co-operative education, particularly for a Co-operative College. Locally its members helped to form branches of Men's and Women's Guilds and to assist Guild branches by providing lecturers on co-operative topics. Some engaged on co-operative research.

THE CO-OPERATIVE COLLEGE

The idea of a Co-operative College had been present from the earliest days of the Movement. Suggestions for such a college or colleges were made in the Owenite publications and at their congresses and conferences. The idea soon reappeared in the modern series of congresses. William Pare spoke on it in the 1870 Congress and gave a paper at that of 1871. Auberon Herbert, as we have seen, desired a residential college for the co-operative education of managers. Hodgson Pratt and others made the same advocacy, and in 1890 the Union's Education Committee reported that it had given some consideration to the feasibility of commencing a co-operative school or college and that " there is lacking a suitably organised means for enabling our young people to study systematically the history, principles, objects and methods of Co-operation. There is no true co-operator . . . who denies the existence of an imperative need for this special study. These considerations have led us to suggest the formation of a co-operative school or college in which there should be a distinctive and systematic teaching of co-operative principles." Nothing came of this, but E. O. Greening and W. R. Rae (Chairman of the Education Committee 1901–1936) kept the subject before succeeding Congresses, while F. Hall was writing articles in favour of a college from 1905 onwards. The Easter Weekends and the Students' Fellowship spread the idea. A paper given by F. Hall to the Easter Weekend in 1912 gave the idea practical form as well as inspiration. A College Herald Circle was formed which carried on insistent propaganda until the Movement came to accept the idea.

Residential education needs to be experienced for its value to be assessed and it was in order to give some co-operators an appreciation of this value that the Education Committee was persuaded to organise the first Co-operative Summer School at Castleton in 1913. F. Hall was one of the principal promoters of this venture and indeed conducted the school. He later wrote: " the promoters knew that daily contact at a college not only stimulates discussions outside lecture hours of the subjects which the students are studying, but also leads to a general exchange of ideas which widens the students' outlook and also influences personal character and development." The success of this school was twofold, it increased the enthusiasm for a Co-operative College and also for subsequent Summer schools. Summer schools indeed came to play a considerable part in co-operative educational activity.

In May, 1914, a conference of the principal national co-operative organisations (the Co-operative Union, the Wholesale Societies, the C.P.F., the Secretaries' and Managers' Associations, the Co-operative Newspaper Society and the Guilds) heartily approved a proposal to establish a Co-operative College. The conference also pledged itself to continue as a provisional committee to undertake preliminary work, and asked the Co-operative Union to arrange for propaganda work on behalf of the College and to prepare for the realisation of the full scheme by developing educational work at Holyoake House and the Summer Schools. The outbreak of the Great War in the August of that year, however, put a halt to the scheme for some years.

THE CO-OPERATIVE GUILDS

A good deal of the life and vigour of the Movement in the thirty years preceding 1914 was due to the Women's Co-operative Guild. It was founded in 1883 as the Women's League for the Spread of Co-operation. Women, whether organised in guilds or not, are bound to play an important part in a consumers' Co-operative Movement, for women make most of the decisions which constitute consumers' choice. Housewives determine the pattern of family expenditure, which brands are bought, and whom they are bought from. The " sovereignty of the consumer " in practical terms is the sovereignty of the housewife holding the family purse. Yet women have been curiously ignorant or incapable of using a power which if organised would make that of the strongest trade union or capitalist monopoly appear trivial.

Before the advent of the Guild, few took an active part in the Co-operative Movement. Women did not attend the meetings of societies, sit on committees or attend conferences or Congresses. It required courage for the daughter of James Smithies to enter and use the reading room even of the Rochdale Pioneers' Society in the 'seventies.

Start of the Women's Co-operative Guild

In the closing decades of the nineteenth century, however, there were women determined that women should take an active part in public life. The movement for women's emancipation found a congenial field in the Co-operative Movement. Early in 1883 a feature entitled " The Women's Corner," edited by Mrs. Alice S. Acland was included in the *Co-operative News*. One of her articles suggesting meetings of mothers at which works on Co-operation could be read and discussed provoked a correspondence in which Mrs. M. Lawrenson of Woolwich put forward a plan for an organisation. By April, 1883, a League had begun with a membership of seven. By the end of the year three branches had been established—at Hebden Bridge (near Halifax), at Rochdale (with the daughter of Abraham Greenwood as secretary) and at Woolwich.

The League did not find that the greater interest and concern of women in the affairs of their local societies were always welcome. They had to overcome strong prejudice from men in general, and in particular from committees and officials who objected to the interference of customers with the way the shops were run. Fortunately, there were some prominent co-operators with broad and far-sighted vision to welcome the Guild movement. Abraham Greenwood, E. V. Neale, S. Bamford, and Ben Jones were sympathetic and helpful, and the wives and daughters of some leaders played an active part in Guild affairs. It was given financial assistance by the Union and until 1893, the annual meeting of the Guild was held at the Co-operative Union Congress and its annual report was included with the Congress Report.

It was intended that the Guild should prepare as well as induce women to take active parts in public life. For this reason each branch was run according to strict business procedure. The Guild's organisation on district and sectional lines, together with its annual congress, also educated women to take broader views and accustomed them to public speaking. They were encouraged to attend the general meetings of their societies, ask questions and take part in discussions.

Women consequently began to be elected to committees—to

education committees much more commonly than to management. In 1893, Mrs. Lawrenson and in 1894, Miss Catherine Webb
(author of what was for many years the standard textbook on
Co-operation) were elected to the Central Board of the Co-operative Union. Miss Spooner was Chairman of the United Board of
the Co-operative Union (1904).

At the Guild's coming of age in 1904, there was an impressive
list of co-operative offices held by women. Besides one in the
chair of the Co-operative Union, there were two on the Central
Board, two on the Education Committee, eleven on the Educational
Committees Association, thirty on management committees, two
hundred and thirty-eight on education committees, sixty to seventy
among the delegates to C.W.S. quarterly and divisional meetings
and sixteen among the delegates to the Co-operative Congress.

Work of the Women's Guild

A feature of the Guild's activities was its " campaigns." It
employed the Fabian tactics of making sure of its ground by study
and discussion, and then of shaping opinion and getting things
done by widespread and intensive propaganda. Early in its career
it was concerned with the use of co-operative capital and demanded
the employment of " surplus capital " in developing co-operative
enterprise. At first it was attracted to co-operative co-partnership
and profit sharing, but changed its views in favour of production
by the C.W.S., and then campaigned to further this. It kept an
eye on societies' loyalty to co-operative products, made matters
unpleasant in societies where that loyalty was lacking and strove
in various ways to " push the sales " of co-operative societies. It
worked to better the wages and conditions of co-operative employees, and agitated for and was eventually successful in carrying
a Congress resolution for a minimum wage. It examined the pre-
valence of credit trade in co-operative societies, condemned it and
campaigned against it. It examined dividend policies and condemned high dividends. The Guild was also actively concerned
with co-operative education. Its branches first undertook the co-
operative education of children and the part played by Miss M. L.
Davies in getting co-operative education organised systematically
has already been noted.

The Guild was also concerned with more general public issues.
It naturally played a prominent part in the campaign for women's
suffrage, but it was also active in supporting Free Trade, organising
a great demonstration in Manchester in 1903. On general social
welfare it actively concerned itself with the problems of housing,
the place of women, especially housewives, in the Health Insurance

Scheme, the health of school children, the employment of young persons, divorce law reform and old age pensions. It took part in the anti-sweating campaign and encouraged women to join trade unions.

Scottish women formed their own Guild in 1892, although groups of women connected with a few local societies, mainly in the Glasgow area were meeting before that. A good many of its efforts were devoted to raising funds for the establishment of convalescent homes. It began, however, after 1908, to take an increasing interest in political questions particularly those concerned with social welfare. Election to co-operative committees appears to have been more difficult than in England, and the first successful woman candidate, Mrs. Buchan in 1910, had been nominated thirteen times previously. In 1914, the Scottish Guild had 174 branches and 14,368 members.

TRADE UNIONISM AND THE CO-OPERATIVE MOVEMENT

From the beginnings in the early nineteenth century there were connections between the Trade Union and the Co-operative Movements and yet they remained distinctive in aims and methods. The Owenites, Dr. King, and later the Christian Socialists and their succeeding advocates of producer Co-operation had regarded the trade unions as possible means of furthering their aims, either by providing capital for producer co-operative undertakings or by undertaking production themselves. At the same time they decried the customary methods by which the trade unions struggled against the employers. Nor were their arguments unconvincing. George Howell, General Secretary to the Trades Union Congress could write in 1890: " If a portion of the £148,503 paid in out-of-work benefit in two years by the carpenters, engineers, iron founders and boiler makers had been employed in making doors and sashes, engines, boilers and mouldings, it would have been so much reproductive capital and have contributed something in the shape of experience towards the labour question. As at present constituted and managed, trade unions live from year to year on their capital, instead of imitating the commercial classes and growing rich out of profits."[1]

A more realistic attitude developed among co-operators. Beatrice Potter (later Mrs. Sydney Webb) in a paper given to a joint conference of trade unionists and co-operators in 1892, discussed the relations between the two Movements. She pointed out that both were necessary to working class progress, but that each had its own limitations. Even under consumers' Co-opera-

[1] *" Conflicts of Capital and Labour."*

tion or municipal enterprise, " without trade unionism there was
no security that the public benefit would not be made a source of
injury to a minority of producers," i.e. trade unionism was
necessary because of the employer-employed relationship, even if
the employer were a public body. On the other hand, " the ultimate decisions upon trade processes and industrial organisation
must inevitably rest, not with the producers of a commodity, but
with the consumers of it. The vague dream of investing trade
unions with control over their respective industries must be dismissed as a false ideal." She and Sydney Webb, of course, carried
out a life-long campaign against producers' control in any of its
forms, co-operative producers' societies, or syndicalism and
industrial unionism, and in the main they convinced co-operative
societies, trade unions and the Labour Movement. As co-operators changed their view of the role which labour could or should
play in their enterprises and as it was realised that consumer Co-
operation does not abolish the employer-employed relationship,
the way was clear for trade unionism among co-operative
employees.

Co-operative-Trade Union Relations

Since 1875 the Co-operative Union and the Trades Union Congresses have interchanged fraternal delegates. Closer relations
were sought and the Co-operative Congress of 1883 recommended
the appointment of a committee to meet periodically and confer
with a similar committee of the T.U.C.," to prevent disputes
between co-operative employers and employees, to bring about
that perfect understanding which ought to exist between these
influential working class organisations, and to effect a more rapid
development of co-operative production."

Arising from this, a joint committee was established but neither
co-operative societies nor trade unions used its services in the
settlement of disputes, although some guiding principles were
worked out—co-operative societies should observe trade union
hours and rates while disputes should be submitted to arbitration
before resort to strikes or lock-outs. Trade unionism amongst
shop assistants and clerical workers, however, was almost non-
existent so that retail societies were unaffected by collective bargaining with most of their employees. Shop assistants in general
suffered from long hours and low wages. Although conditions were
comparatively superior in co-operative employment, there were
bad spots which the Women's Guild helped to expose. It was stated
at the 1895 Congress that in some societies assistants worked 60–70
hours per week.

The A.U.C.E.

From 1891, however, co-operative shop assistants and office workers were organising in the Amalgamated Union of Co-operative Employees. Its methods were intended to be educational and pacific and to influence the Co-operative Movement to improve its labour conditions. But both the Co-operative Movement and the A.U.C.E. were affected by strong currents which moved throughout the whole Labour Movement. There were those who, regarding the Co-operative Movement as part of a wider working class movement, felt that it should be used to set the pace for improvements in labour conditions. Among labour objectives was that of a national minimum wage, and an agitation, therefore, developed, in which the Women's Guild was very active, for a minimum wage in co-operative employment.

In 1907 the Co-operative Congress passed a resolution, " that the time has arrived when the Co-operative Movement should establish a minimum wage for various classes of workers, below which societies should pledge themselves not to fall." Minimum scales were drawn up and adopted by the following Congress. Unfortunately, some societies did not recognise these scales, and the temper of the A.U.C.E., therefore, began to change. A strike fund was formed and pressure began to be exerted on individual societies to conform to the scale. This change in attitude caused co-operative officials to leave the A.U.C.E., and to establish the Co-operative Secretaries' Association in 1908, and the Managers' Association in 1912.

A.U.C.E. and T.U.C. Dispute

The A.U.C.E. ran into trouble, too, from other quarters—from the Trades Union Movement itself. British trade unionism is entirely unplanned, well described as " a sprawling, chaotic industrial movement." It is indeed, like the Co-operative Movement, more similar to an organic growth than to a planned machine. Unions were created to meet the needs of particular bodies of workers and each developed and adapted itself to meet changing needs and circumstances. Consequently considerable overlapping developed, several unions competing for the membership of the same workers. This led to much bitterness and conflict among the unions. The growth of the A.U.C.E. was bound to run into trouble of this kind. Every co-operative employee could have been a member of some other trade union, although owing to the unique nature of co-operative employment, few of them would have met his particular needs. Thus evolved the case for organising all co-operative employees in one union.

There was also, however, a case against. Co-operative employees were highly desirable members for trade unions. They suffered little unemployment, were comparatively well paid, and there was little danger of friction or disputes arising on the initiative of the societies. Thus the growth of the A.U.C.E. was not welcomed by the Trade Union Movement in general for it seemed to put co-operative employees into a privileged position. Matters were brought to a head in 1912 by a decision of the T.U.C. that where there was a union catering for an industry, the A.U.C.E. must hand over to that union those of its members who were employed in it. If put into effect this would have completely dismembered the A.U.C.E., so it left the Trades Union Congress.

THE MOVEMENT AND POLITICS

Although the Co-operative Movement expressed itself at times on current political questions and had prominent politicians address its Congresses, and although prominent co-operators engaged in politics, as a Movement it held aloof from party political alignment during the nineteenth century. This was partly due to fear by societies of becoming embroiled in party struggles and partly to the pre-Rochdale Movement's disbelief in political action as a means of effecting fundamental change. It was also due to the fact that political issues were not those on which co-operators as such were likely to feel strongly.

The circumstances which favoured political neutrality were, however, changing. As collectivism grew and movements for State Socialism came into being, political action presented itself as an alternative to voluntary co-operation. Moreover the Co-operative Movement appeared to some of the new socialists as another working class organisation which, together with the Trades Union Movement, could be formed into a Labour Movement with socialist leadership and objectives and the political means of attaining them. Hence there developed an agitation for the Co-operative Movement to enter politics.

Early Demand for Political Action

The suggestion was not entirely new. It had been raised after the Reform Act of 1867, and it occasioned a debate in the Congress of 1870, upon the policy which a co-operative newspaper should pursue. Lloyd Jones insisted that such a newspaper must adopt political views: "Co-operation could not be dissociated from politics." Every question, he argued, when treated fundamentally became a political one: "We must speak the truth boldly . . . and then Parliament, instead of tinkering at the condition of the people, would begin to set about the real work of procuring their political and social amelioration."

Others dogmatically asserted that since most co-operators were Liberal a co-operative newspaper should express Liberal politics. Abraham Greenwood said: " Let the Liberals set a noble example of Liberalism. Unless we know how to act broadly towards each other we shall remain divided. Co-operation is broad in its principles and must be conducted upon a broad policy—in a spirit of union, not antagonism. Our object is the moral, social and industrial improvement of the labouring body, independent of politics." This was the policy followed in general. Lloyd Jones, of course, was well ahead of his time and there was then no Social Democratic Federation, no Fabian Society, no Independent Labour Party, no political party with a programme of social reform.

During the 'eighties, political Socialism began to spread and affect working class organisations. It grew in the Trade Union Movement until it was successful in getting the T.U.C. to take steps to secure Labour representation in Parliament and eventually create the Labour Party. Efforts were made to induce the Co-operative Movement to take similar steps and two interesting and significant papers were given to the 1890 Congress. One by Miss M. L. Davies (Secretary of the Women's Guild), was on " The Relations between Co-operation and Socialistic Aspirations " and in this she showed the similarity of aim, pleaded for co-operators and socialists to draw closer together, and advocated the need for Parliamentary action. The other on " The True Relations between Labour, Capital and Consumption," by E. S. Bycroft, held that there was a strong and observable trend to State intervention and Socialism, that it would be folly for co-operators to ignore these signs of the times. Mr. Bycroft declared himself both socialist and co-operator and argued that Socialism included Co-operation. His views did not, however, commend themselves. Most speakers, and they included Greening, Mitchell, Holyoake and Neale, either condemned State Socialism outright or held that Co-operation was a much superior aim and method. It is significant, however, that the subjects should be presented and discussed; they were in the minds of co-operators.

Congress and Politics

They appear to have been thought over. At the Congress of 1891 several leaders expressed themselves in favour of some direct representation in Parliament. Ben Jones believed the slow progress of co-operators was because they were afraid to take Parliamentary action and they should get someone to represent them in the

House of Commons. G. J. Holyoake also thought the more direct representation they could get the better, whether the representatives were Liberals or Tories. J. T. W. Mitchell believed it absolutely necessary for co-operators as such to be represented in Parliament. In succeeding Congresses the subject continued to appear with reports that there were difficulties in getting M.P.'s to take " co-operative " Bills in hand, and co-operative representation was needed not only in the Commons but also in the municipal councils.

In 1897, a resolution in favour of direct representation in Parliament was passed by Congress. Maxwell, chairman of the S.C.W.S. had strongly advocated—" I am aware that many of my audience are ready to cry out ' no politics in Co-operation.' I do not seek to introduce politics into Co-operation, but to see more Co-operation introduced into politics." The discussion, however, showed that there was no intention of harnessing the Movement to any political party. The delegates wanted men in Parliament who understood and approved of Co-operation whether they were Conservative, Liberal or Radical. When the societies were circularised, however, for contributions, the difference between a Congress resolution and the opinion of the societies was shown. Only 160 societies out of 1,659 even replied. Of these 28 were favourable and were willing to subscribe in the aggregate £73; 24 were favourable, but required the consent of their members to subscribe sums amounting to £304 (including a S.C.W.S. subscription of £250); eight were favourable, but couldn't subscribe anything.

Subsequent Congresses discussed the matter but opposition grew, based mainly upon the fear that political activities would endanger the unity of the Movement and damage its trading interests. In 1900 a motion before Congress reflecting the trend towards the formation of a Labour Party asked Congress to pledge itself to " secure direct independent working class representation in the House of Commons." Congress defeated the motion by an overwhelming majority.

Proposed Alliance with Labour

In 1905, a further attempt to persuade the Movement to undertake political action was made when T. Tweddell, a director of the C.W.S., proposed a motion on behalf of the Parliamentary Committee. His speech, which was later published by the Co-operative Union, was a powerful plea for co-operative representation and for a political alliance with the T.U.C. This motion was carried, but a second which would have joined the Co-operative Movement to the Labour Representation Committee was hotly opposed, and an amendment was carried, by 801 to 135, that it was not advisable to be allied to any particular political party.

When circularised, the societies' response was again disappointing. Only 141 replied, and of these 129 were opposed to any system of co-operative Parliamentary representation and the annual contributions which were promised amounted to £25. In the light of these results the next Congress resolved the subject be dropped.

It was dropped until Mr. Tweddell picked it up again in 1908—but again unsuccessfully. The question, however, was kept alive at Congress after Congress. In 1913 it was brought to a head as a result of a joint conference of the Co-operative Union, the T.U.C. Parliamentary Committee and the National Executive of the Labour Party. A motion was consequently put before Congress favouring a closer union between the forces of organised labour and the Co-operative Movement, but an amendment was easily carried " strictly to maintain the neutrality of the Movement in regard to party politics."

Another joint conference of the Co-operative Union, the T.U.C. and the Labour Party was, however, held, and a scheme for a permanent joint committee drawn up which was to be submitted to the respective bodies. This scheme came before the 1914 Congress but was by no means welcomed. A motion of the C.W.S. was carried which showed this response in no uncertain terms. It instructed the Central Board to " maintain the neutrality of the Movement in respect of party politics, not to join in conferences with political parties, not to be officially represented at gatherings of political parties and not to employ co-operative men or money to the advancement of the Labour Party or political organisations or movements."

Thus twenty years continuous and persistent agitation for co-operative representation in Parliament and for alliance with the Labour Party had apparently ended in complete failure. The Great War which began in 1914, however, was to change this attitude to political endeavour.

THE CHANGE IN IDEAS

At the beginning of the period here reviewed, Congress reports show that although Owenite philosophy still echoed in co-operative circles, the ideas which motivated action were those associated with the Christian Socialists and those, half-formed or insufficiently defined, which were associated with Rochdale Co-operation and came to be termed " Consumer Co-operation." With the development of productive activities by the Wholesale Societies, two schools of thought emerged, one favouring ownership and control by producers, i.e., by the workpeople engaged in production, the other favouring ownership and control by the consumers of the product. The first is known as Producer Co-operation, the second as Consumer Co-operation. Until the last decade of the nineteenth century the contest between these two schools involved and shaped most co-operative thinking. Subsequently, although this contest was by no means finished, co-operators were increasingly concerned with the new socialist doctrines which presented problems of the relation between Co-operation and the various forms of Socialism and socialist movements and of the place of Co-operation in an increasingly collectivist state.

Neale's plan of co-operative development was upset by the entry of the C.W.S. into production. At the 1873 Congress, Dr. Watts gave a scheme of development in which the C.W.S. would extend co-operative production, " every extension being demanded by an already established trade." Ludlow also gave a paper in which he attacked the idea of consumer sovereignty. He declared that " consideration for the producer was the first stepping stone in the path of English Co-operation . . . we should raise the producer to his true dignity to subordinate mere consumption altogether to production . . . consumption was merely the animal element, production the divine . . . the main question was not whether consumers should get goods cheaper, but whether the men who spend themselves on the production of that article shall or shall not have the primary claim to the fruits of their labours. The question is not whether producers are to have better masters, but whether they are to be their own masters." E. O. Greening spoke at the 1874 Congress in a similar strain: " Our Movement was not started with the object of making money or supplying cheap goods, but of making men. The other things were subordinate."

Views of Hughes

The last great battle took place in the years 1887–1888. Judge Hughes was the champion of Producers' Co-operation. He outlined " the Wholesale System " as he saw it:—production of every article required by societies undertaken by the Wholesale, factories managed by its governing committee, the capital found by the Wholesale out of the surplus funds of our societies and the whole of the profits merged in the great " *pot au feu* " of the Wholesale and divided as dividend on purchases.

He objected to this system on various grounds. The extent and number of the enterprises required was utterly out of the capacity of any central body to manage efficiently; management by a distant committee would result in the old antagonism between employer and employed, and the workman had no share in either ownership or profits.

His alternative scheme was one in which the Wholesale would act as agent for every productive society, and not itself undertake production. He claimed that considerable advantages would result. The Wholesale would be free to devote itself to its true function, that of perfecting co-operative distribution; it would be able to enforce fair dealing, honest work and just prices, so that consumers would benefit; productive societies would benefit as injurious competition would be prevented; individual workers would benefit by the training in self-government and this with their accumulation of capital would avoid the subjection of one class by another.

Views of Mitchell

Against these views stood J. T. W. Mitchell, product of Rochdale Co-operation and chairman of the C.W.S. He also was an idealist —sincere and self-sacrificing, as were his opponents. The whole controversy was remarkable in that there was an absence of any form of, or possibility of, individual gain by any of the protagonists. Mitchell's case was that not only were there several instances where the C.W.S. had been " let down " by productive societies, but that all profits and incremental values should find their way into the pockets of the people and that dividend on purchases ensured this. He also wanted to raise men out of poverty and to make them co-operators and his form of Co-operation would do this better than any other method. The Wholesale Societies of England and Scotland had the highest right to make, as fast as they were able, everything that the retail societies sold. He supported his opinions by reference to co-operative history. The early co-operators had started with consumption, consumption ought to be the basis of the growth of all Co-operation.

Views of the Webbs

The most powerful, and probably the decisive case for consumer Co-operation was, however, given by Beatrice Potter, later Mrs. Sydney Webb, in her book *The Co-operative Movement*, 1889. She had made an examination of the Movement in fact as well as in theory. The Rochdale system won her favour because it contained the best parts of Owen and had made, by the introduction of the dividend on purchases and democratic control, a much more desirable and practicable system. She saw the Rochdale system as one which abolished the profit-making entrepreneur but retained the wage system, while producer Co-operation was one which aimed to abolish the wage system but retained profit-making. She found nothing ethical in producer Co-operation. If people worked harder and better in producer societies it was not in order to help others but to help themselves. Producers' societies were associations of profit makers and " an industrial organisation which substitutes for one profit-maker many profit-makers is not a step forward in the moralization of trade." She also regarded producer Co-operation as undemocratic. It would divide the community into self-governing circles of producers, which must either fight each other to the death or combine to impose price and quality on the public. The consumer interest on the other hand was the universal interest, and consumer Co-operation the most comprehensive system possible.

Sydney and Beatrice Webb had a great effect on co-operative thought. They gave what had been previously lacking, a theoretical basis and justification for consumer Co-operation. Their attacks on producer Co-operation effectively separated these two kinds of Co-operation from each other in the minds of many, but not all. On the other hand the Webbs were Fabian socialists and unwilling to accept voluntary Co-operation as the only means of solving every social and economic problem. They insisted on the need for Trade Unionism, political action and some obligatory Co-operation in the creation of a Co-operative Commonwealth. These views caused many co-operators to look upon the Co-operative Movement, not as a distinctive movement, but as part of a Labour Movement. Before 1914 there was a strong trend to a union of the Co-operative and Trade Union Movements and the Labour Party and to get the Co-operative Movement actively engaged in political action. There was a consequent tendency for co-operators to study political socialism and to try and discover ways of relating Co-operation to it. This led some to neglect the study of Co-operation and how political socialism could be made to conform to the ideals and principles of the Co-operative Movement. These tendencies became more manifest after 1920.

7 CO-OPERATIVE BUSINESS, 1914-1939

> " At no time was there a lack of specialists to diagnose the disease, the trouble was a general unwillingness to take the medicine."
> (" Co-operative Banking in India," G. M. Laud.)

> " A hundred years hence, school text-books and learned treatises will give more space to consumers' Co-operation, its constitution and ramifications, than to the rise and fall of political parties or the personalities of successive prime ministers."
> (S. and B. Webb " Consumers' Co-operation.")

THE history of our own times is the most difficult to study. We are in a jungle of detail which defies comprehension and there are conflicting ideas, ideals and movements, a variety of economic, social and political trends. Historical perspective is impossible. Yet of all history this is the most important to us, and despite the impossibility of seeing it as the future historian will, there are some outstanding features which cannot be ignored, such as the two great wars and the shift to collectivism.

THE GREAT WAR OF 1914–1918

One can, of course, only touch upon a very few of the items in that tremendous upheaval, the Great War of 1914–1918. Almost the whole world became involved. Mighty empires crashed and disintegrated, new nation states emerged, revolutions occurred or threatened and the very foundations of civilisation quivered. This book is concerned, however, not with these events, but with what by contrast is undoubtedly small beer, those matters which most directly affected the Co-operative Movement.

At first neither the country nor its leaders realised what war involved or the extent or nature of the efforts or sacrifices which would be demanded. It was looked upon as an affair almost entirely of military and naval operations during which the economic life of the country would continue as before with as little disturbance as possible. " Business as Usual," was a popular slogan to indicate the attitude it was hoped the general public would adopt. Attempts were made for some time to wage the war on the basis of a free economy, with appeals to people to put the public interest before that of their own individual economic self-interest. Men should volunteer for the armed services and appeals were made to labour and to employers to do the right thing, to consumers to ration themselves and to traders not to profiteer.

Gradually, however, the stern realities of the conflict compelled the Government to exercise increasing control. Freedom is one of the inevitable casualties of war. Conscription of men for the armed forces was introduced. Often private enterprise was unable to take the strain and proved itself untrustworthy. The Government had to assume management of the railways, shipping, transport, mining and the manufacture of munitions. Some manufactures were prohibited, others stimulated and subsidised, raw materials were rationed, prices fixed, imports and exports regulated and share issues controlled. By the end of the war the country was very close to what would now be termed a planned economy.

War Economy

As the Government became the largest employer of labour it encountered a host of problems. To solve these quickly and avoid stoppages and discontent it needed the co-operation of the trade unions. It became evident that collective bargaining and agreements were necessary to industrial peace. Trade unions became recognised as an essential part of the economy, whereas before the war many of them had been engaged in bitter struggles with employers to obtain even the right to bargain for their members. The trade board system was extended to cover occupations where trade unionism was weak or non-existent. To avoid continual wage disputes as the cost of living rose, the practice developed of automatically adjusting wages to changes in the Cost of Living Index Number. A Ministry of Labour was established in 1916 to deal with this and other labour problems.

Other general results were that the Government came to be regarded as responsible for the maintenance of industrial peace, the efficient conduct of industry and commerce and the welfare of the people. It became increasingly common for people to complain, if matters were not as they should be, " Why doesn't the Government do something? " Laissez faire was in short generally discredited and a collectivist attitude generally adopted.

This change was under a Government by no means disposed to collectivism. It was not due to any conversion to new ideas, but to the inescapable pressure of the facts of war. The alternative was defeat. Equally marked was the reluctant but gradually increasing protection of the consumer. As prices rose discontent increased. "Business as usual" for many meant taking advantage of whatever opportunities of profit were presented by the war.

Whereas in peace time a rise in the price of a commodity stimulated an increased supply of it, this was often impossible in time of war. Available supplies in peace time were shared out amongst the people according to their willingness and ability to pay the price. A diminution in supply would result in a rise in price until enough were compelled or induced to purchase less to equate demand with supply. The shortages of war time were such that this price mechanism became inadequate. Prices of necessities, if left unrestricted, would rise right out of the possible range of purchases for the poorer sections of the community. Controls were necessary but initially, at least, the President of the Board of Trade did not favour them. In a Parliamentary debate he stressed the dangers and difficulties of attempting to regulate prices and declared that the proper remedy for rising prices was rising wages! He was also convinced by his experience that governments could not buy half as well as individuals.

Food Control

Nevertheless, towards the end of 1916, he had to announce extensive powers of food control and the appointment of a Food Controller. This was Lord Devenport, a successful businessman, head of a firm of wholesale provision merchants and interested in some multiple concerns, a former chairman of the Port of London Authority and with the reputation of being a strong man. His efforts were pathetically futile. He sought to apply to the whole economy the lessons he had learned from his experience of running an individual business. Without any apparent knowledge of economic theory or principles he was incapable of taking a sufficiently comprehensive view. His efforts at dealing with one problem created graver ones.

Lord Devenport was succeeded in May, 1917, by Lord Rhondda who, with the assistance of J. R. Clynes, did gradually build up an efficient system of food control. A Costing Department examined the books of producers and traders to discover actual costs (which were found to vary a great deal) as a basis for price fixing. Local Food Committees were appointed by local authorities and although the Ministry hoped that private traders and co-operators would be kept off, in fact private traders, who had always been strongly represented on local authorities, were strongly in force on these committees. In November, 1917, 15 per cent of the members of these committees were farmers, 12 per cent private traders, and only $2\frac{1}{2}$ per cent were co-operative representatives. During the latter part of 1917, food queues began to appear. These had serious effects on morale and moreover workpeople had to absent themselves from work in order to join the queues to obtain food. This was remedied by rationing individual consumers. The Ministry itself came to undertake the business of buying, selling, transporting and distributing. Its Food Supply Manual, containing regulations and orders, in July, 1918, contained 700 pages.

It will be gathered that under the stress of war, grievous and urgent problems were settled by government action. The belief grew that many of the economic and social evils which had been tolerated before the war could be remedied by Government if the same zeal and resolution were shown in peace. There was also a feeling that after the great ordeal of the war had been passed there should be a substantial improvement in living conditions—" a land fit for heroes to live in," as Lloyd George expressed it. There was considerable promise. A Ministry of Reconstruction was created in 1917 to frame plans for the reorganisation of national life after the war, a Ministry of Health was established and two important Acts were passed, a great Education Act, and an Act enfranchising all men and women over thirty years of age.

CO-OPERATION DURING THE GREAT WAR

From the start of the war the Co-operative Movement showed a strong sense of public duty which it maintained throughout, despite a good deal of discouragement due to ignorance or hostility in official quarters. It attempted to keep down prices. For example, although the C.W.S. held great stocks of flour at the commencement of the war, it kept its price of flour down until these stocks were exhausted and it sold huge quantities to the army at pre-war prices, although big profits were there for the taking. For a period it sold Danish butter at 15/- lower than the market price and granulated sugar at 3/- per cwt. lower than the Government price, until private importation was stopped. It sold tea at $\frac{1}{2}$d. per lb. less than the legal price until made aware of a legal risk so incurred. Canned goods were sold at considerably below the current market price.

In order to obtain something like a fair distribution of scarce goods among their members, many societies adopted schemes of their own long before the Government introduced rationing. The difference in approach by trading concerns owned and controlled by their customers and those owned and controlled by proprietors engaged in business to make profit out of their customers was exemplified. Whereas it was in the interest of all members of a co-operative society that scarce goods should be distributed fairly among them, private traders had no such interest and they adopted all manner of devices to exploit the situation to their own profit. For example, those people whose custom was most desired got favoured treatment, or scarce goods were sold only to those who would also buy other goods.

Grievances

The societies, however, while organising fair distribution, could do so only among their own members and, moreover, they could not ensure their members getting fair shares of the whole national supplies. So they agitated for and sought to persuade the Government to introduce effective schemes of price control and rationing. The schemes at first adopted were very unjust to the third of the population in membership with the Co-operative Movement, but congenial to various types of private trader. Often the controls were manned by, or subject to the influence of representatives of private trade who were opponents of the Movement. Consequently co-operative societies did not get fair allocations of controlled goods and co-operators complained of the Wheat Commission, the Sugar Commission, and the milk, coal and butchers' meat control.

Not only was the Co-operative Movement's dignity affronted and its sense of justice outraged but it was also indignant at the losses caused by Government policy: " the Movement was deprived of the advantages of superior organisation which it had built up for the importation of wheat, bacon, butter, currants and other commodities; of its superiority in flour milling; and of its economy in wholesale distribution; finding itself constrained, to the relative gain of those who had been its rivals, to come down to the common level of quality, efficiency and distributive cost." (*The Consumers' Co-operative Movement*, S. and B. Webb.)

When conscription was introduced the Movement did indeed find itself in the hands of its enemies. Military Service Tribunals were appointed to decide on appeals against the conscription of men regarded by their employers as indispensable. These tribunals were generally composed of middle class men, some in trade themselves, many with friends and relations so engaged. As a consequence, appeals by co-operative societies met with scant consideration. One society had 102 men taken out of 104 and, in another instance, the military representative justified the taking of a branch manager on the ground that if the co-operative branch were closed a better living would be left for the village grocer. A private baker, as Chairman of a Tribunal exempted his own foreman baker from military service, and on the same day rejected the appeal of the local co-operative society for its foreman baker. One military representative actually stated that no harm would be done if by the withdrawal of all its male staff the co-operative store were shut down and its unfair competition with honest tradesmen brought to an end.

The incident which aroused most indignation and apprehension, however, was the subjecting of co-operative surpluses to an Excess Profits Duty. Co-operative surpluses had been long acknowledged by various Chancellors and declared by legal and fiscal authorities to be mutual savings and not profits. If co-operative societies were to concede that their surpluses were properly subject to E.P.D., they would acknowledge that these surpluses were profits. This would not only open the gate to further fiscal impositions but, more important, deny the validity of the co-operative system as an embodiment of the co-operative ideal of trade devoid of profit-making.

Attempts of the Movement to get some redress of grievances met with an indifference and a lack of sympathy which bordered on contempt. Co-operators began to believe that the reason was their own professed political neutrality. If, they argued, politicians have primarily their eyes on votes, a movement which professes political neutrality is a movement which can be safely ignored. This was of little concern before 1914, but it became increasingly important as the war proceeded and politics increasingly interfered with business—co-operative business included—dominating and controlling it. Moreover, the interference was not by noble-minded patriotic statesmen taking a true view of the nation's good, but by all manner of vested interests in exploitation, the natural enemies of the Movement. Political neutrality in these circumstances might bring the same fate as the pacifism of sheep among wolves and co-operators began to be convinced of the need for political representation.

Political Action

At the Swansea Congress, 1917, an amended resolution was moved and carried which declared that: " In view of the persistent attacks and misrepresentations made by the opponents of the Co-operative Movement in Parliament and on local administrative bodies, this Congress is of opinion that the time has arrived when co-operators should seek direct representation in Parliament and on all local administrative bodies. It therefore calls upon the Central Board of the Co-operative Union to take such steps as may be necessary to put into operation the terms of the above resolution."

A National Emergency Conference was called, and met in London in October to discuss a draft scheme for securing co-operative representation. It set up a Central Co-operative Parliamentary Representation Committee and also agreed to an Emergency Political Programme as " a definite expression of its general policy of industrial, social and economic reform." This consisted of eleven items. Nine were not distinctively co-operative and gave the Movement's views on profiteering, agriculture, taxation, banking, housing, education, foreign policy, demobilisation and the " democratising of State services." The remaining two stated the purpose of co-operative participation in politics: " (i) To safeguard effectually the interests of voluntary Co-operation and to resist any legislative or administrative inequality which would hamper progress. (ii) That eventually the processes of production, distribution and exchange (including the land) shall be organised on co-operative lines in the interests of the whole community."

A by-election at Prestwich in January, 1918, provided the opportunity for the first Co-operative candidate, H. J. May, to contest a parliamentary seat. Although defeated he polled well. At the 1918 Congress a constitution for a National Co-operative Representation Committee was approved, and in 1919 the Carlisle Congress converted it into " The Co-operative Party." By the end of 1920, 506 societies were affiliated to it and 180 local Co-operative Parties had been established.

The most important and significant effect of the Great War upon the British Co-operative Movement was this entry into politics. On the Continent the Movement remained politically neutral, but as the Report of the Emergency Congress stated; " every country in Europe has used Co-operation more freely, and valued it more highly as a national asset, than Great Britain." After an impressive recital of the part the Movement had been called upon to play in France, Switzerland, Russia and Germany, the report went on; " It is only in democratic enlightened Britain that Co-operation has been relegated to a back seat. Our government departments, ever tardy in co-operation with each other, have been united in their opposition to that Co-operation which is purely co-operative and of the people."

Business Progress

Despite the difficulties and handicaps the Movement continued to progress. Membership increased from 3,053,770 in 1914 to 4,131,477 in 1919; share and loan capital from £44,935,713 to

£74,411,306, and retail trade from £87,979,898 to £198,930,437.
A considerable rise in prices must, of course, be taken into account
as the cost of living index, standing at 100 in 1914, rose to 236 in
1919. The retail trade figure when adjusted to this change (which
yields a by no means accurate result) would be £84,292,556. It
must be remembered, however, that there were still many shortages
and rationing, particularly in the goods forming the backbone of
co-operative trade. Moreover the Movement's championship of
the interests of working-class consumers did something to raise
its prestige and to increase goodwill, and probably had something
to do with the phenomenal progress of the following twenty years,
when its membership and volume of trade (after adjustment for
price changes) more than doubled.

BETWEEN THE TWO WARS

The Great War made great changes in the country's economic
structure. To achieve victory it had been necessary to give to the
needs of war the first call upon manpower and resources. Civilian
needs came last and were only grudgingly conceded. Consequently there was a huge expansion of war industries and a severe
contraction of industries which met the normal requirements of
peace. A transition of this extent and nature could not have been
made except by the Government undertaking it. For a time there
was a planned economy, but planned for a generally accepted
supreme purpose, that of waging war successfully.

With peace another problem of transition was presented, that
of passing from a war to a peace economy. Demobilisation and
the contraction of war industries would result in millions of men
and women having to find new jobs, for instance. Their ability to
find employment would depend on the expansion of shrunken
industries to meet peacetime needs. Whereas war provides a
simple overriding objective for the direction of economic resources,
there is however, no such single, simple objective in peace.
Government economic planning in peacetime therefore appeared
to many to be impracticable as well as undesirable, the planned
economy of the war to be a temporary aberration, and a return
to pre-war *laissez faire* the speediest and the best way of recreating
a peacetime economic system.

There were, however, other opinions. Some saw the period of
transition from war to peace as a period of opportunity. Reconstruction, to them, did not mean a scrapping of all that had
been developed in wartime and a return to the pre-war competitive
struggles. It meant the diversion of wartime institutions to peacetime needs, the introduction of new systems, new industrial and

social relations and the prevention of the reintroduction of old evils—in short, reforms which would be difficult to effect in normal times because of the resistance of vested interests and the lethargy and indifference of the mass of the population. Ambitious schemes of reconstruction had in fact been prepared during the war and lavish promises had been made of a better economic and social order after victory had been obtained. Most of these schemes came to nothing. There was a strong desire for a return to " normal " conditions, and this was often regarded as a return to pre-war methods and circumstances. " Back to 1914 " was the ideal of many.

Aims of Labour

Labour, however, had no nostalgia for 1914. It presented a constructive programme, outlined by Sidney Webb in *Labour and the New Social Order*, in 1917. He regarded the war as the final breakdown of individualist capitalism. A new system must be erected upon the basis of the universal enforcement of a national minimum, the democratic control of industry, the revolution of national finance and the usage of surplus wealth for the common good. The private capitalist was to be progressively eliminated from the control of industry by a scientific reorganisation of the economic system upon a basis of common ownership and equitable distribution. Railways, mines and electrical power should be nationalised immediately—they were, of course, already under government management.

The period immediately following the armistice was unsettled and dangerous. The Coalition Government, 1918–1922, composed of Conservatives and Liberals trod warily. Discontent was checked by unemployment pay and promises of reconstruction and the motions of beginning to fulfil them. When it was judged the time was ripe, however, a different attitude was adopted. Although a Royal Commission (the Sankey Commission) appointed to inquire into the coal industry had a majority report favouring nationalisation of that industry, it became obvious that the Government had no intention of acting upon it. Moreover, according to the Webb's *History of Trade Unionism* the Government deliberately manœuvred a railway dispute and plunged the coal industry into premeditated strife. The onset of a severe slump also put labour on to the defensive. In spite of some hard fought strikes and lockouts, wages were reduced and trade union membership fell from its peak of 8,339,000 in 1920 to 5,421,000 in 1923. Government policy was now definitely that of recreating the pre-1914 system.

Economic Policy

A major and essential step towards this involved deflation. It was hoped by so doing to restore the international value of the £, especially in terms of dollars and secure a return to the International Gold Standard, with its accompanying stable currency exchange rates. Great Britain's dependence on international trade and her position as a creditor nation made this policy attractive, but adverse circumstances and events proved too strong for it to be successful. During the 'twenties, however, the effort was made, and was partly responsible for the unemployment of those years.

After the political and economic crisis of 1931 there was a change in approach and policy. The attempts to recreate the economic system of pre-1914 were abandoned. Free trade was replaced by protection, the International Gold Standard was departed from and the Government sought to control exchange rates by currency controls and manipulative dealings. Competition and free enterprise were also discouraged in some industries by schemes initiated and backed by the Government, e.g., in coal, agriculture, shipbuilding, transport. The 'thirties were a decade of national economic planning.

UNEMPLOYMENT BETWEEN THE WARS

Unemployment was the most marked feature of the period. It was of unprecedented gravity because of its extent and length. Every phase of life and thought were affected by it and some were dominated by it. The approach to economic, social and political problems is still under its influence, not only by governments and trade unions, but also by the millions of men and women who remember those dismal times. The following table shows its severity and fluctuations.

PERCENTAGE OF INSURED WORKERS UNEMPLOYED

	1914	=	4	
	1920	=	5	
Immediate Post-war	1921	=	17	Coalition Government
Effects	1922	=	15	
	1923	=	12	Conservative Government
	1924	=	10	Labour Government

	1925 =	11	
	1926 =	12	
	1927 =	9·7	Conservative Government
Gold Standard	1928 =	10·8	
	1929 =	10·4	
	1930 =	16·0	Labour Government
	1931 =	21·3	
	1932 =	22·1	
	1933 =	19·9	First National Government
	1934 =	16·8	
Protection and Rationalisation	1935 =	15·5	
	1936 =	13·2	
	1937 =	10·4	Second National Government
	1938 = 1939	13·3	

There are many explanations of this abnormal unemployment. The first crisis and depression were the direct effects of the war. Europe was impoverished and there were violent fluctuations of the exchanges, a deflationist policy and the difficulties of readjusting industry and trade to peace. These difficulties, however, had been overcome by 1924, world conditions generally improved and indeed there was something of a world boom between 1924 and 1929. Yet Great Britain did not share in this boom. It gradually became evident that its economic illness was not similar to pre-war cyclical depressions which were temporary and succeeded by booms, but was deep-seated and perhaps permanent. Even good times had 10 per cent unemployed, a proportion regarded as catastrophic before 1914.

Causes

Some of the blame is put upon the return to the gold standard in 1925, at the pre-war parity with the dollar. This over-valued the £, and so facilitated imports, but handicapped exports. It also made the conduct of financial policy very difficult, compelling the adoption of a tight monetary policy, with high interest rates and restriction of credit in order to prevent an external drain on gold reserves. On the other hand, the internal economy needed cheap and easy credit to finance expansion. If the level of costs could have been reduced the problem would have been considerably eased, but attempts to do so by forcing down wages proved too difficult and expensive.

An analysis of unemployment showed, however, that there were causes other than monetary ones. Four-fifths of the unemployed were found in five industries, cotton, coal, shipbuilding, wool and worsted, iron and steel. Each of these depended largely on exports. In 1914, cotton exported 80 per cent of its output, coal 20 per cent, shipbuilding 50 per cent, wool and worsted 50 per cent, and iron and steel $33\frac{1}{3}$ per cent. Cotton's difficulties arose from the rise of new and strong competitors in the East, and exports fell from 7,000 million yards in 1914, to 2,407 million yards in 1930. Coal's problem was one of an increased European productive capacity, a market with an inelastic demand, and a probability that the market would shrink. Shipbuilding had so increased its productive capacity to meet wartime demands that it was far in excess of peacetime needs. These industries were highly localised and a whole area might be dependent on one of them.

Thus, although the national average of unemployment was high, the figure for some localities was very much higher. There were towns with as high a figure as 80 per cent. People in these localities faced the prospect of never again earning a living. And these localities were not only the homes of the basic industries, they were also traditional strongholds of the Co-operative Movement.

A Labour Government held office from 1928 until the latter part of 1931, but found the economic difficulties too great to put its programme of social reforms into effect. The onset of a world-wide depression created a financial crisis which could not be met without departing from the gold standard. An attempt to do so caused the collapse of the Labour Government and its replacement by a National Government. This effected a revolution in British economic policy, bringing it back to a system somewhat akin to that of the seventeenth and eighteenth centuries. Its most important changes were the discarding of the gold standard and a definite departure from free trade on the one hand and State promotion of monopoly organisations as a means of economic planning on the other.

The relief from the restrictions of the gold standard eased matters, though subsequent currency restrictions and exchange regulations by the British and other governments were a handicap upon foreign trade. Protection could be of little, if any, help to either cotton or coal, or to the other exporting industries, and the monopoly organisations were designed to restrict trade, not to expand it, so that the revolution in economic policy was not one likely to lessen unemployment. Unemployment figures did fall, though it was not until 1937 that the figure was as low as that of 1928. The improvement was due partly to the upswing of the world cyclical movement and, from the mid-thirties, to the effects of rearmament.

RATIONALISATION AND ECONOMIC PLANNING

The difficulties of British industry in meeting post-war competition strengthened the opinion that it was inefficient. Much of this inefficiency was believed to be due to the faulty organisation, or lack of organisation, of industries as a whole. The remedy was held to be what was termed " rationalisation," defined by the Balfour Committee's Report as " the reduction in the number of types to be produced through a process of standardisation or simplification; mass production in the most efficient works and scrapping of inefficient works, elimination of redundant organisation whether in production or distribution, economy in transport through delivery from the nearest works and economy in the use of working capital."

Economists have often been sceptical of the economies claimed for monopolies, holding that the gains from the less-advertised powers to control output and fix prices are more certain and more potent attractions. Rationalisation, a new name for largely old-fashioned monopoly, required for success the acquiescence of an overwhelming proportion of the firms in an industry. This, however, could not be secured freely and an opinion grew that the State should step in and compel unwilling firms to submit to schemes approved by the majority of an industry and the Government.

State assistance was necessary not only to compel all within an industry into a scheme of reorganisation, but also to control imports competitive with its products. It would be obviously futile for an industry to reduce its output in order to raise prices if, because of increasing imports, the total supply on the market did not diminish.

All the major political parties were agreeable. Labour and Liberals believed unemployment and low wages were the results of inefficient organisation and Conservatives believed it was also a cause of bad trade and low profits. Ten years after the armistice there was almost a unanimous opinion that the days of free enterprise and competition were over and that " rationalisation " was to take its place. This later became known as " economic planning."

Labour and Co-operative Attitude

The support of organised labour for State-supported capitalist monopolies might be difficult to understand but it was based on the following reasons. Labour had come to make the inefficiencies of capitalism its main indictment and it was expected that a planned industry would remove many of these inefficiencies and be a step on the way to socialism. Planned industries, although capitalist at first, would be easier to take over by a future Socialist Government than would an unorganised, chaotic industrial system. Russia's first " Five Year Plan " made " planning " fashionable and it had a socialist tinge even if it was planning by capitalists for capitalist purposes. Moreover, planned industry would stabilise employment and perhaps yield higher wages.

Co-operative opinion was by no means so favourable. In this country the Co-operative Movement is mainly a consumers' movement and looks at matters from a consumer standpoint. Schemes to reduce supply and raise prices are unlikely to appeal to consumers, and the Co-operative Movement condemned all schemes of planning based upon the profit-making motive. It declared that any system of national economic planning should have as its objectives, the maximum use of national resources, the maximum output of goods and services, the equitable distribution of income, the fulfilment of the principles of economic democracy and reciprocal trading relations with other countries. (Co-operative Party Conference, 1935.)

Planning

Planning in the 'thirties, however, had very different objectives. There were several schemes but with one common feature—each scheme was designed to further the interests of those, or some of those, concerned with a particular industry, and those interests were to be furthered at the expense of the rest of the community. The Coal Mines Act of 1930, provided a system by which the coal owners were given powers to regulate the output of prices and coal. The Road and Rail Traffic Act, 1933, imposed regulations and a system of licences designed to prevent the development of road transport and so protect the railways and existing road interests. Joint action by the Import Duties Advisory Committee and the Iron and Steel Federation enabled the Federation to fix prices and control output of iron and steel. A tariff of 50 per cent protected the home market from foreign competition and levies on the industry were made to buy and scrap redundant plant, thus reducing productive capacity. In the cotton industry, a Spindles Board was set up in 1936 to buy and scrap surplus spinning plant in order to reduce its productive capacity. The flour-millers started in 1929 to buy and scrap surplus flour mills, and the woolcombers in 1933, to buy and scrap surplus woollen mills. The shipbuilders formed National Shipbuilders' Security in 1930 to buy and scrap surplus shipbuilding capacity, in four years destroying building capacity of one million tons.

Agriculture

Agricultural planning, being concerned with foodstuffs, affected the Co-operative Movement more directly. It was promoted under the Agricultural Marketing Acts of 1931, and 1933, the first passed by a Labour the second by a National Government. They were intended to restore the profitability of the industry by giving powers to the producers to control supplies and prices. Those producing some agricultural commodity could draw up a scheme and if, after it had been submitted to all the producers, a majority were in favour, a marketing board was set up with powers to fix the output of each producer and the price at which he could sell. The scheme would apply to all whether or not they agreed with it. Whilst foodstuffs could be imported freely, however, consumers still had some protection against the rapacity of food producers. This protection was removed by the Act of 1933, which gave the Boards powers to regulate imports.

Milk, bacon, pigs and potatoes came to have their respective boards. Established in 1933 the Milk Marketing Board had managed to raise the price of milk 10 per cent by 1937. A consequent increase in output was countered by selling the resultant surplus to school children at half the price and to manufacturers of such plastics as combs, ash trays, buttons, etc., at one-eighth the price. As surpluses increased, prices to manufacturers had to be reduced, thus upsetting the planned objectives. The Government, however, stepped in and agreed to pay a subsidy to milk producers so that a minimum price for manufacturers' milk could be guaranteed. " Irrational " consumers who might have preferred to pay a higher price for milk to drink than the manufacturers would pay to make it into buttons, were probably incapable of understanding the economics of the scheme, and need not be, and were not, considered.

Potato growers were able to restrict supplies more effectively. In 1934, all potato growers were registered, and any others deciding to grow potatoes had to meet a levy of £5 per acre for the privilege. The variations of nature were met by allowing only potatoes above a certain size to be sold for domestic use, and if there was a comparatively heavy crop the minimum size was raised, so that only the same quantity would be available for the domestic user.

Bacon

Bacon producers had to meet the difficulty that 85 per cent of supplies was imported and there was a strong preference for Danish bacon. Strong action was therefore needed to prevent British consumers buying the bacon they preferred. The method adopted was for the Bacon Marketing Board to decide how much bacon was to be consumed in the country. Imports were to be varied to maintain this predetermined quantity so that if home production increased, imports would be reduced by a corresponding amount. The effect of this was to cause the price of Danish bacon to rise as the imports of it were diminished. In the upshot the Danes got more for a smaller quantity of bacon, and the surplus was exported to Germany; so that in the main, British bacon planning benefited the Danish producer and the German consumer. The British consumer was the sufferer.

The Co-operative Movement did not regard this as desirable planning. To meet the preferences of its members it had its own bacon factories in Denmark, and co-operators enjoyed better bacon than most other people. Under the scheme, as the quotas of home bacon factories were increased and the imports of bacon cut down, the Movement was prevented from importing its own bacon from its own overseas factories and compelled to buy bacon from private British producers. Nor could it build factories of its own, for the Bacon Board regulated the output of each factory, and no new factories could be opened without its permission. Co-operative bacon curing was thus being planned out of existence.

In all these instances it may be observed that the intention was to restrict output to favour the interests of a section of producers. Now although a section may benefit by restricting its output and so increasing the value of its product, it is obviously impossible for all to do so. If all tried, the net result would be a smaller quantity of everything available for everyone. Yet every producer is part of a sectional interest which is opposed to the common interest. Sectional planning of the type of the 'thirties, favoured by some labour as well as some capitalist interests, was likely to result, as Barbara Wootton pointed out, " in a community more planned against than planning." (*Plan or no Plan.*)

POPULATION CHANGES

There were other important changes taking place in the economic and social background. Population increased, from 44 millions in

1921 to 48 millions in 1940—but the increase was of older people. The number of people below twenty years of age in 1946 was smaller than in 1901, and smaller than the number of people between 20 and 40. On the other hand, the number of people over 45 years of age increased by 65 per cent between 1911 and 1938. One aspect of this change in the age composition of the population was the smaller average size of families. The Mid-Victorian family had on the average 5½–6 live born children, that of 1925–1929 only 2.2.

These changes in social structure had, of course, various effects upon the ways of life and thought—and so also had the changes in the distribution of the population. There was a slight increase in the rural population in England and Wales, but a decrease in Scotland, and the urban population in all three countries increased. Of this urban population, in 1931, a substantial proportion, nearly 17 per cent, lived in towns with over one million inhabitants, but the biggest increase in the urban populations was in the urban districts of 20,000 to 100,000 inhabitants.

The decline of the old basic industries caused some reduction in the population of the areas where these had been located and an increase in the population of areas where new industries were developing. The Northern and Welsh regions lost population and the East and West Ridings and the North West were barely holding their own, but there were considerable increases in the Midland, London and South East, Southern and South Western areas. In particular, many of the northern industrial towns were losing population and even some of the cities, such as Liverpool, Manchester, Sheffield and Bradford.

From an economic viewpoint the distinction between a town and its surrounding districts, and even between towns, was becoming less marked. This was due to the rapid development of motor transport. People in what had been remote country districts were enabled to travel easily and cheaply to towns to do their shopping. Retail markets increased in area and, for some goods, covered many towns and vast masses of population. Some of the Manchester departmental stores, for example, drew customers from all over South East Lancashire and the North Midlands.

CHANGES IN THE PATTERN OF SPENDING

The development of regional market areas in place of many local ones had effects upon industry and the distributive trades. It encouraged the development of larger-scale production of consumer goods, with accompanying standardisation, branding and advertisement. In spite of increasing standardisation, the customer

F

had frequently a wider range of choice than ever before. This was due partly to competition and also to the larger market. The small townsman or the country villager, for instance, had less range in his choice of clothes or footwear when he was confined to the products of the local tailor or shoemaker than he found in the many competitive brands of standardised goods displayed for sale in the city or big town.

There was also a rising standard of life, in spite of unemployment. This was most marked among unskilled workers, for wartime increases had narrowed the gap between their wages and those of the skilled, and higher rates in general were maintained. Rent Restriction Acts kept one of the main items in family budgets low, and pensions, health insurance and unemployment benefits prevented the grinding poverty which afflicted many before 1914. Deflation also increased real wages since retail prices fell to a greater extent than did wage rates. Smaller families also allowed a greater proportion of a family income to be spent on various luxuries and a less proportion on prime necessities such as food.

In consequence of these changes, the pattern of spending also changed. Although there were increases, sometimes considerable, in consumption per head of such foodstuffs as butter, cheese, cocoa, fish, meat, eggs, tea, sugar, the proportion of income spent on food declined from 50.7 per cent in 1920 to 46.6 per cent in 1938. Sir John Boyd Orr nevertheless held in 1936 that the poorer sections of the population were undernourished, and that in fact the greater part of the population did not have sufficient milk, eggs, fruit, vegetables, meat and fish, though in most cases this was due to unwise spending rather than to inability to purchase.[1]

The amounts spent on confectionery, reading and writing materials and tobacco increased considerably, their proportion of total sales rising from 9·3 in 1920 to 14·4 per cent in 1938. The proportion of clothing fell from 24·6 to 19·4 per cent, though this was slightly higher than before 1914. There were other increases, all suggestive of more comfortable living, on all manner of household goods, entertainments, and travel—though, it is worth noting, the cost of travelling to daily employment was in many cases becoming a serious item.

CHANGES IN THE DISTRIBUTIVE TRADES

Because of the extent to which the Co-operative Movement in Great Britain has become involved in and dependent upon the distributive trades, changes in them are of particular importance. When the Movement had little competition to meet other than

---

[1] "Food, Health and Income" *Sir J. Boyd Orr, 1936*

that of independent private traders it had little difficulty in creating a much more efficient system than its competitors. It had the advantages—even if it did not fully exploit them—of larger scale and of vertical integration of retailing, wholesaling and production. During this century, however, large scale retailing has developed in the private sector and faced co-operatives with increasingly formidable competitors in the departmental stores and various forms of multiple traders.

The departmental stores increased in number, and increased their share of total trade a little. One feature was their establishment in the medium sized towns—in smaller versions, of course, than the great stores in the cities. The need to attract customers from wide areas led to heavy advertising expenses, various stunts, and the provision of amenities, which made such stores one of the most expensive types of trading. On the other hand the nature of the trade required very careful buying based on correct anticipations of demand, and these stores acquired knowledge and developed skills in buying and stock control which contributed considerably to retail efficiency.

Multiple Traders

The multiples, however, developed most rapidly. They were of various types. Some were chains of specialist shops, usually owned and developed by manufacturers or importers to give them control over retail policy and prices. There were also " local " multiples, i.e., chains of shops confined to a locality, and national multiples whose " chains " covered the whole country. There were, of course, great differences in scale of organisation. On the whole the most spectacular growth was that of the largest organisations; much of this was due to amalgamations. However, the smaller organisations, i.e., those with not more than two hundred branches each, grew almost as rapidly. Multiple firms in the grocery, footwear, pharmaceutical, newspaper trades continued to grow, and there were also developments in the milk and fish trades, furniture, electrical, jewellery and clothing. It has been estimated that in 1915 the multiple trade was composed of 72 per cent food, 15 per cent clothing (mainly footwear) and miscellaneous, but in 1939, food accounted for only 45 per cent, and clothing had risen to 26 per cent. (*Retail Trading in Britain, 1850-1950*, Jefferys.)

The most striking development and growth, however, was not of the specialist chain, but of the " variety " chain store, e.g., Woolworth, Marks and Spencer, Littlewood. These provided something of the attraction of the department store, having a large variety of commodities under one roof, but were free of its expensive amenities, advertising and services. They dealt in the cheaper commodities, openly displayed for customers to pick and choose, the assistants simply keeping an eye on the goods, wrapping them and taking the money. Such labour could be almost unskilled.

The multiples' methods were different from those of the old type of trader. They were not so much concerned with the full range of the needs of the consumer as with the more profitable lines which had a big and ready sale. The general trend to standardisation also had its effect and there was a diminution of technical skill required in retailing as most goods were in cans or packets. While clearly there was need for more commercial and business knowledge and skill, less was required of the assistant. As specialised knowledge and skill at the counter became unnecessary, overlapping of traders with each other increased. The grocer could sell patent medicines and the chemist dog foods, jewellery, etc. Shops, in fact, became less and less specialised, the variety chain store being the logical outcome.

Yet not all trade could be undertaken by the unskilled and ignorant. There was still a need for the trader who could advise the customer, and independent traders with the necessary skill and knowledge continued in business. All competed with co-operative societies, whose members required them to provide all the services of all the other forms of trading.

GENERAL CO-OPERATIVE SURVEY REPORT

Inflation and deflation, the general aftermath of war, unemployment, depressed areas, collectivism and economic planning, political enmity, monopoly and increasingly severe competition from various forms of capitalist trading all presented the Co-operative Movement with greater difficulties at the close of the Great War than it had previously met. These problems arising from circumstances outside itself were additional to those presented by its own internal growth, which were principally the increasing size and variety of its functions and the consequent pressures for integration and disintegration which demanded reorganisation. Awareness of the need for a realistic appreciation of the Movement and its relation to its environment, a dissatisfaction with co-operative progress, " especially so because of the rapid growth of capitalist combinations," the need for closer organisation and for " greater efforts to spread co-operative ideas and trade," led to the appointment by Congress in 1914 of a " General Survey Committee."

The resolution setting this up stated: " That this Congress, recognising the importance of efficiency and economy in its administrative work, and having a strong conviction that the progress of the Movement might be greatly accelerated, calls for a General Survey of the whole field of co-operative activities from its three main features, viz., education, production and distribution; and having due regard to their relative value, assign to each one its special sphere of action, and thereby give to the Movement generally that solidarity and flexibility so obviously lacking at present; and therefore instructs the Central Board to consider and report in terms of this resolution."

The constitution of the committee appointed did not meet with the approval of the Wholesale Societies, who declined to be represented on it or take part in its work, but answered its inquiries as to matters of fact. It was originally intended that the committee would be assisted by outside experts. Probably Sidney and Beatrice Webb were in mind for they had made a report on the Co-operative Movement for the Fabian Society in 1913 which aroused much discussion, but they were not called upon. The Committee relied upon its own resources (and there were some very capable and experienced men upon it) and the assistance of Co-operative Union staff. Fred Hall, appointed Adviser of Studies in 1915 was prevented by the war from undertaking the educational developments he intended and did a great deal of work for the committee instead. Interim reports were produced in 1916, 1917, 1918, and a final report in 1919, on which a Special Congress was held in 1920.

Although the war and the uncertainties which followed it made inquiries difficult and opinions of future developments hazardous, it is remarkable how the Survey Committee's Report shaped subsequent co-operative thought and action. Few new suggestions for the improvement of co-operative organisation and policy, have since appeared, except variations of ideas then put forward. The Report of the Independent Commission of Inquiry, 1958, shows similar opinions of the Movement's weaknesses and little new in remedies proposed. The gravest weakness, of course, is thereby exposed—the inability of the Movement to reform itself quickly.

Recommendations

The principal recommendations of the Committee included the reorganisation of the Co-operative Union, by giving representation to the Wholesale Societies on the Central Board, appointing a full-time executive, and giving the Co-operative Union power to expel societies which were deemed guilty of unco-operative conduct or refused to accept arbitration in regard to overlapping.

Education was not regarded sufficiently seriously by societies, many societies undertaking no educational work and many others spending their grants on activities of little educational value. Grants should be made, not as a percentage of surplus, but on a membership basis of not less than 1/– per member per year. Societies' education committees should include representatives of employees and auxiliaries and Educational Associations should be linked more closely with the Sectional Boards. The Co-operative Union's Educational Department should be strengthened to give stimulus, form and direction to the work of local societies.

Many fairly detailed recommendations were made regarding trade and finance. Retail societies should increase their range of services, and milk, laundry, fried fish, greengrocery, tobacco and sweets, newspapers, books and stationery, toys, furniture removing, funeral undertaking, hairdressing and window cleaning, etc., were instanced. A Mail Order business should be developed. There should be special societies for trade with the poorer classes on a basis of low prices and dividends. Federal enterprises for departmental stores and uniform designs for shops, packing and wrapping should be introduced. Membership should be increased by (a) the training and appointment of canvassers, well grounded in the principles, organisation and ideals of the Movement, (b) the appointment of organisers to propagate the idea of Co-operation where it was not well established, and (c) advertising with, every few years, a national co-operative advertising scheme. The loyalty of membership was to be increased by education, provision of rooms for social and recreative purposes, concerts and select libraries of co-operative and economic literature.

Overlapping

Overlapping of societies should be dealt with according to circumstances by (a) amalgamation and (b) arranging boundaries and securing loyalty to boundary agreements. Small societies in some cases should amalgamate; in others there should be co-operation with large neighbouring societies so that members of the small societies could obtain from the large societies goods which they could not obtain from their own. Large societies presented new problems of organisation and better methods of meeting these should be discovered by investigation. A sounder view of the respective functions of committees and officials should be taken and the official should have fairly wide powers, " so that he may exercise initiative as well as control." Officials were often seriously underpaid, a list of appropriate salaries should be prepared and there should be adequate facilities for training for these higher appointments.

Steps to increase the accumulation of capital and the use of a greater proportion of it in co-operative enterprise were advised. Reserves should be increased and the minimum to be held by a society should be 20 per cent of its share and loan capital. A special society for investing co-operative societies' surplus capital should be formed, and a separate national co-operative bank established in which the C.W.S. should merge its Bank and should have a large share of ownership and management.

It was recommended that goods be sold at current market prices or a little less, dividend rates be gradually reduced and differential dividends be paid where a high rate of general dividend prevented the opening of a department. All surpluses should not be paid out as dividends or allocated to reserves, but some part be put to collective uses such as collective life assurance, a pension scheme for members based on annual purchases, pension and superannuation schemes for employees and provision for members in cases of sickness, accident or distress.

Employees

A national minimum wage for co-operative employees should be fixed, women should receive the same wages as men for the same work and employees should be given full membership rights. Some societies should experiment with employee representation on management committees and societies should appoint " employment managers " (now termed " personnel officers ") to assist in choice of staff, keeping in touch with changes in the labour world, negotiating with staff and trade union officials and advising manager and committee on disputes, workshop conditions and welfare. Schemes of welfare work should be largely or entirely controlled by the employees and workshop committees and joint councils of employees and management committees be set up in all societies.

Production should be extended by the Wholesale Societies, separately and jointly; by the retail societies, for whom a long list of suggestions was given; by federations of retail societies; and by the co-operative co-partnership societies. Steps were also recommended towards extending co-operative control over raw materials and sources of supply, including the nationalisation of the land, mines and transport. An Agricultural Section of the Co-operative Union should be established; agricultural operations by retail societies encouraged; and federations, both local and national, of retail societies and farmers' societies formed for

buying agricultural requisites and selling agricultural produce.
International co-operative trade should be encouraged. Co-operative co-partnership societies were the appropriate organisations for developing production of goods for sale in the open markets of foreign countries. An International Co-operative Wholesale Society and an International Co-operative Bank were advisable, but pending their formation joint committees of Wholesale Societies with a common interest in purchase or production should be formed.

The recommendations of the Survey Committee were debated at Congresses and discussed at numerous conferences and gradually the ideas in them permeated the Movement. Such a radical reorganisation of a Movement as organic as the Co-operative Movement was and is, however, impossible. The importance of the Survey Committee's work is not to be measured by the number of its recommendations carried out. It drew attention to the issues involved, made many co-operators aware of new problems facing the Movement and convinced them of the need for an approach to its business problems based on economic reasoning and statistical information. Much action has indeed been taken since on lines similar to those recommended.

MEMBERSHIP AND SIZE OF SOCIETIES

Amalgamations reduced the number of retail societies from 1,357 in 1919 to 1,065 in 1940, whilst membership increased from 4,131,000 to 8,716,000. The average size of societies consequently increased. In 1920 the largest society was London with 96,659 members, Leeds came next with 92,212, and no other society had 90,000 members. Only 3·26 per cent of societies had a membership exceeding 20,000, though they accounted for 35·66 per cent of the membership, 52 per cent of societies had less than 1,000 members and approximately 84 per cent had a membership of less than 5,000.

In 1940 there were eight societies with a membership exceeding 90,000. London had 817,053 members, Royal Arsenal 332,567, Birmingham 234,765, South Suburban 200,640, Liverpool 131,442, and Leeds 129,455. Ninety-four societies had over 20,000 members, accounting for 8·83 per cent of societies and 61·89 per cent of the membership. Yet 30 per cent of societies had less than 1,000 members and every Section of the Co-operative Union contained some abnormally small societies of about 100 members. Many small societies, however, were to be found in areas where each village was in some degree isolated, dependent on its own resources and with a strong parochial sense.

Changes

These changes in the size of societies had their effects upon their character. In 1920 the typical co-operator was a member of a small society, but in 1940 he was a member of a big one, and although all societies are run on the same fundamental principles, there followed inevitable differences in the relation and attitude of the member. As a society grows bigger the typical member inevitably counts for less. There is a danger of loss of interest and concern and a smaller proportion of members attend general meetings and take part in electing committees to manage these vast business enterprises.

This provides the opportunity for groups with axes of their own to grind to obtain control of a society and use it for purposes other than co-operative ones. It also becomes increasingly difficult for the typical member to comprehend how the society is being run and, as his understanding lessens, so does his interest. The dangers were realised in the 'twenties, but the problem of maintaining sound and effective democracy in the medium and large societies has not been satisfactorily solved. Education in Co-operation is the obvious, indeed the only answer, but the educational resources were very far from being adequate to deal with the huge increases in membership between 1920 and 1940. The position might have been healthier if the proposals for dealing with increasing membership put forward by the Survey Committee had been put into effect.

Membership Pattern

The increase in membership was most marked in the Southern and Midland Sections where membership almost trebled between 1920 and 1940, from 1,253,000 to 3,709,000. As a result the three Northern and the Scottish Sections lost their preponderance: in 1920 they contained 62 per cent of the total membership and in 1940 slightly less than 50 per cent. The North had developed strong traditions of trading policy, favouring high dividends and the accumulation of reserves even if this meant also a high price policy. They had also developed habits of thrift and loyalty among their members. The Southern parts of the country had never found these policies practicable, adopted low prices and low dividends and with the rapid increase of membership could not rely on loyalty, which is of slow growth.

Co-operation was also growing more rapidly in the big towns and cities than elsewhere, again particularly in the Midlands and the South. This was gratifying in that it occurred where the competition of multiples and departmental stores was strongest. On the other hand, these big cities which had often been regarded previously as "co-operative deserts," clearly offered the best opportunities for rapid growth in those trades in which Co-operation was strongest. Moreover, the increase in membership of the big societies was partly to be accounted for by amalgamations and by expansion into rural areas and small towns.

This latter type of development has disadvantages. In previous times Co-operation was introduced into new areas by propaganda and education which induced people to join together in establishing a society of their own. Such new ventures represented increases in the number of genuine co-operators and the spread of co-operative ideas. When a large society opens a branch in such an area, it may rely solely on the attractiveness of its goods and service to obtain trade and membership. From a business standpoint the method may be successful, at least in the short run, but it increases the number of customers, not the number of co-operators. And the progress of the Movement depends in the long run upon the co-operators it makes, not the number of customers it attracts.

CO-OPERATIVE RETAIL TRADE

Trading figures showed an increase from £199 millions in 1919 to £272 millions in 1939. The real increase was more than this, as the general level of prices fell considerably. Adjusting these figures according to the Cost of Living Index, the trade in 1919

CO-OPERATIVE RETAIL TRADE, 1919 and 1939

| Section | 1919 | | 1939 | |
	Total in £ millions	Average per member	Total in £ millions	Average per member
Irish	1·8	49·11	2·1	34·3
Midland	22·9	41·90	42·2	32·5
Northern ...	29·1	61·12	21·8	33·3
*North Eastern ⎱ North Western ⎰	67·4	44·45	31·8 / 48·8	30·4 / 30·9
Scottish	41·5	67·33	43·8	46·4
Southern... ...	20·2	34·38	60·6	25·1
South Western ...	5·7	32·65	11·6	29·4
Western	10·0	58·72	9·4	37·3
Total	198·9	48·15	272·3	31·5

*In 1923 the North West Section was divided into a North West and a North East Section.

on 1914 values was £84 millions and in 1939, £173 millions. Average trade per member was £48·15 in 1919 and £31·5 in 1939, but when the adjustment is made for the difference in prices the figure on 1914 values is £20·40 for 1919 and £20·07 in 1939. Maintenance of the figure is commendable, for usually it falls with increases in membership since new members at first seldom purchase much from societies. It is significant, and gratifying, that their purchases generally increase with length of membership. Thus trade per member figures are highest in the areas where Co-operation has been established longest.

Comparison of Sectional rates of growth may be made from the table opposite:

Although the Southern Section had the most spectacular increases in membership, its average trade per member was the lowest of any Section. Both it and the Midland Section benefited from influxes of population, trade and industry. The Northern Section, though retaining a high trade per member made little progress, its real volume of trade being less in 1928 than in 1914. This was a consequence of the severe depression in the Section's staple industries of coal and shipbuilding, and of heavy unemployment. Similar circumstances account for the comparative decline in the Western Section which included South Wales, one of the most depressed districts in the country, in the North Western Section, affected by depression in cotton and coal, and in the North Eastern Section suffering from depression in the woollen industry. Scotland also lost ground comparatively, the reason here also being depression in coal and shipbuilding, although it continued to have the highest trade per member.

Trade Per Member

Conclusions must not be drawn too readily from comparisons of trade per member, for the statistics may be misleading. Societies' membership figures may exceed the true purchasing membership because their membership rolls are not kept up to date. A " cleaning up " results in a reduction in the membership figure and an increase in the figure of trade per member. Again, before 1914, many societies had rules restricting membership to one member per family. After 1920 these restrictive rules were being abolished and it was becoming increasingly common for more than one in a family to be members of a society. Thus, even if purchases per family remained the same the trade per member would fall. Families also were smaller and expenditure on foodstuffs, which accounted for over 80 per cent of co-operative trade in 1925 was reduced. There was also a considerable increase in the practice of having meals outside the home. This, with factory canteens and school meals, took some foodstuffs trade away from co-operative societies.

It would be interesting and valuable to trace and compare the development of the various trading departments in the Co-operative Movement but, unfortunately, the necessary information is lacking. The Co-operative Union did not make departmental analyses until 1928, and even then societies did not at first supply the information sufficiently broken down and correctly departmentalised. However, broad conclusions may be safely reached. There were considerable increases in some food trades which made grocery, bread and confectionery of less comparative importance. There were also more than proportionate increases in butchery, in greengrocery, fish and fruit, and in the " chemist " department.

Milk

Milk, in particular, was a trade which developed very quickly during the period. In 1919 the Movement was responsible for no more than 2½ per cent of the total liquid-milk distributive trade in England and Wales, but by 1930–1931 the proportion had increased to 14 per cent. In this year the quantity of milk distributed by 352 societies exceeded 100 million gallons, and they were the largest retail distributors of milk in England and Wales. " The Report of the Reorganisation Commission for Milk " 1933, paid tribute to the co-operative success in this sphere and also stated: " The fact that this great distributive organisation is, in essence, a consumers' movement has also assisted to keep down the margin between wholesale and retail prices and to modify the hardness of purely commercial principles in the middleman section of the industry." More briefly it had kept down profits.

In 1938 the trade had increased to 191 million gallons in England and Wales, and to 35 million gallons in Scotland. In money terms the trade increased from £7·71 millions in 1928 to £24·77 millions in 1939. The success was due to the speed with which the Movement realised the opportunities being presented for the large-scale distribution of milk by the development of motor transport and pasteurisation, and because it had the enterprise, capital and organisation to take advantage of them. A good deal of this was the result of the formation and activities of the Co-operative Milk Trade Association.

Dry Goods

In the dry goods trades there were increases in each department, but these were not satisfactory when the increase in membership

is considered—except for Furnishing and Hardware. Here, trade
in house furnishing increased largely as a result of the great housebuilding programme of these years, and the increase in the number
of families. As societies grow, larger departments can be opened
which would be uneconomical for small societies, and the failure
to make considerable increases more generally in the dry goods
trades suggested weaknesses which continue to concern co-operators.

Indeed the desire to increase these trades was responsible for
one great change in these years, i.e., in the attitude to credit
trading. Mutuality club trading (which in some societies took the
form more of savings than credit clubs) and hire purchase were
the principal means. The extent of the increase in credit trade is
indicated by the amount owing to societies by their members. In
1900 it was £655,943 or £0·38 per member; in 1920, £2,310,187
or £0·51 per member; in 1930, £5,306,041 or £0·83 per member;
and in 1939, £7,101,488 or £0·81 per member. Credit trading
probably helped some of the dry goods departments, notably
furnishing, but it was evidently far from a complete answer to
the problem of increasing co-operative dry goods trade.

According to J. A. Hough's estimates in *Co-operative Retailing*
the departmental trade increases of 1939 over 1931 were as
follows:

1939 Sales compared with 1931 Sales

1931 Sales = Index Base of 100

	Grocery, Bread, etc.	Butchery	Dairy	Greengrocery, Fish, etc.	Dry Goods	Chemist	Coal
Section with greatest increase	125 S.W. 147	126 S.W. 170	214 W. 447	144 W. 281	126 W. 155	248 S. 681	150 S.W. 152
Section with smallest increase	N.E. 110	Sc. & N.W. 110	Sc. 144	N.E. 103	N.W. 115	Sc. 153	N.W. 118

In constructing a Co-operative Index Number in 1935 it was
revealed that the eight most important commodities by sales value
were then Milk, Best Bread, Granulated Sugar, Danish Butter,
Danish Bacon, Empire Butter, Best Coal, Seconds Coal.

CAPITAL

The capital of the retail societies continued to increase, from a
total of share and loan capital of over £86 millions in 1920 to over

£201 millions in 1939. In spite of the huge increase in membership the average capital per member also increased, from £19·21 in 1920 to £24·32 in 1939. In only two years was there a decrease, the slump years of 1921 and 1922, though annual increases varied, being less in years of depression and greater in years of prosperity.

There were also changes in the comparative importance of the Sections as providers of capital. In 1920 the three Northern Sections and Scotland provided 66 per cent of the total retail capital, and in 1939, 52 per cent. The biggest increase was in the Southern Section, amounting to £35 millions, but capital per member still remained lower in this Section than in any other, viz., £18·5. The North Western, in spite of its depressed industries, continued to have the largest capital per member, £28·14. As a large proportion of co-operative share capital consisted of accumulated dividends, the lower rates of dividend in the South, together with the rapid increase in membership probably accounted for the lower figure.

Taken as a whole, however, the Movement had a superabundance of capital in relation to its current requirements, and many societies still had rules designed to restrict shareholding, since there was a dislike of societies being used for "investment purposes." Reserves, however, did not increase as the Survey Committee had advised. Although they increased from £5½ millions in 1920 to £15¼ millions in 1939, their proportion to share and loan capital increased only from 6·4 per cent to 7·57 per cent, far short of the 20 per cent recommended.

SURPLUS AND DIVIDENDS

Roughly speaking, the surplus is the difference between revenue and expenditure and in co-operative statistics the net surplus excludes the interest paid on share and loan capital since it is regarded as expenditure. This is in sound accordance with economic theory, but needs to be borne in mind when comparisons are made with organisations in which this practice is not followed. The greater part of this net surplus is returned to the members as dividend on their purchases, though some of it will be allocated to reserves and in some societies to bonus on wages, grants for education and charitable donations. Amounts paid out in dividends, however, are well indicated by the amount of net surplus for they are dependent upon and fluctuate with it.

The rate of net surplus to sales, which of course largely determines the rate of dividend on sales, was lower than in the period before 1914 and yet was maintained at a fairly high level. It amounted to 8·75 per cent in 1920, and to 9·85 per cent in 1939;

the lowest rate in the intervening period being 6·29 per cent in 1922, and the highest 10·27 per cent in 1931. The percentage of net surplus to share capital was 29 per cent in 1920, and 17 per cent in 1939. This decrease was due to the amount of share capital increasing in a greater proportion than the increase in trade, and than the amount of capital engaged in trade.

The Sectional figures give a very similar picture. Rates of net surplus to sales were, of course, much lower in the three Northern Sections and Scotland than in the pre-1914 period, but between the two great wars there was little change. On the other hand there was a tendency for the rate to increase in other Sections as the following table shows:

Percentage of Net Surplus to Retail Sales

Section	1920	1925	1930	1935	1939
Irish	5	4·35	5·45	5·04	6·3
Midland	7·04	7·65	9·09	9·16	9·85
Northern	9·14	9·86	10·03	10·36	11·00
North Eastern	...	9·45	10·64	10·23	10·11
North Western	8·82	9·81	11·04	10·84	10·89
Scottish	11·73	12·34	13·80	13·13	12·29
Southern	5·31	6·27	7·63	7·62	7·33
South Western	6·53	4·94	7·39	7·99	7·86
Western	7·36	6·24	7·78	9·01	9·06
Great Britain and Ireland	8·75	9·18	10·18	9·94	9·85

ECONOMIC SURVEY REPORT

The Movement, however was far from satisfied with the rate of progress and the adoption of the Ten Year Plan, which is dealt with later, showed the need for more information and for continuous research. In 1936 the Co-operative Congress passed a resolution instructing the Co-operative Union to undertake a comprehensive economic survey of the services provided by affiliated retail societies for the purpose of ascertaining progress compared with private trade, the preparation of a report indicating co-operative weaknesses, and drawing up a plan, which when endorsed by Congress, would require to be "implemented" by societies in membership with the Co-operative Union.

The survey was undertaken by the newly created Research Department under J. A. Hough, and a report was presented in 1938. This gave an excellent survey of the retail societies' trading services in the 'thirties and is a useful source of information for the period. Its conclusions were that although co-operative trade was increasing in both quantity and in proportion to national trade the progress was unsatisfactory, inasmuch as the trade of the multiples was increasing much more rapidly. The increase in co-operative membership should have provided a greater increase in co-operative trade and there was abundant evidence that a great amount of trade of the members was passing the Movement.

Much of this was due to the absence of, or to poor, facilities provided by many societies, " The Movement has not enough shops . . . or enough shops of the right kind in the dry goods departments." Many societies were too small to undertake an adequate range of trade and there was a lack of co-ordinated effort, " The Co-operative Movement, in some departments, cannot develop to the extent of competing successfully with other organisations on the basis of a large number of very small units."

Yet there was no unquestioning acceptance of the view that the large society was the answer to the problem of quickening co-operative progress. A table giving trade per member according to size of society showed a steady decline with increase in size. Some 947 societies with less than 10,000 members each, had a trade per member of £33·65, whereas the six societies with a membership of over 100,000 each had an average trade per member of £23·84. Moreover, the highest trade per member in dry goods was in Scotland, a Section of small societies, where it amounted to 4/5 per member per week, whereas that of the Midlands and the Southern Section amounted to only 1/9 per week.

Nevertheless, there were some big societies with a trade per member above the average, including one with £34·9, and some of the smaller societies had a trade per member below the average. One in the group 10,000—20,000 had only £16·82—although the record was made by a society of less than 10,000 members, with a figure of £94. This analysis led to the conclusion that " there is no connection whatever between the size of societies and average purchases per member."

The Report recommended that each society should proceed to examine its departmental trade and discover why members did not trade with each department to the extent of their capacity. The Co-operative Union should examine the position of societies in each Section with a view to making suggestions for their development and, where amalgamation was deemed necessary to secure economies or promote an extension of services, the area was to be surveyed and a special report prepared showing the advantages to be gained. If amalgamation were not found necessary, departmental weaknesses were to be pointed out with recommendations for the opening of new departments by individual societies, federal schemes, or inter-trading. This work was to be commenced immediately and carried out continuously.

WHOLESALE SOCIETIES

The development of the Wholesale Societies is inevitably largely determined by the retail societies who provide the capital, direction and trade. Trade and production grew as follows:

Trade and Production of the Wholesale Societies in £ millions

	1920		1930		1939	
	Amount	Percentage of Retail Trade	Amount	Percentage of Retail Trade	Amount	Percentage of Retail Trade
C.W.S.						
Trade ...	105·4	52·69	85·8	47·81	131·3	57·5
Production..	33·7	16·84	28·9	16·13	47·2	20·66
S.C.W.S.						
Trade ...	14·5	54·70	17·7	46·94	24·6	56·15
Production..	9·4	17·46	5·8	15·37	7·1	16·27
E. & S.J.C.W.S.						
Production..	...	...	0·89	0·41	0·86	0·32

The percentages given may be misleading if certain facts are not borne in mind. They are percentages of wholesale trade at wholesale prices to retail trade at retail prices, and thus in one respect underestimate the percentage of goods dealt with. In another respect the wholesale figures tend to over-estimate some for they also include items which do not enter into retail trade, e.g., sales of vehicles, office and shop fittings, sales to agricultural societies, and goods which are sent direct from manufacturer to retail societies but are invoiced through the Wholesales.

In spite of these difficulties, however, a comparison of the figures indicates that the trade and the productions of the Wholesale Societies were increasing rather faster than retail trade. Its pattern was naturally very similar, strong and weak in the same departments, preponderating in foodstuffs and making a relatively poor showing in dry goods. For example, in 1938 the butter sales of the C.W.S. amounted to £11,597,000, almost double its entire furnishing trade of £5,896,000 and more than double that of its drapery trade of £5,309,000. Its sales of soap at £2,099,000 were almost equal to its trade in footwear of £2,879,000.

Whether the weakness of the retail societies' dry goods trade was due to the weakness of the Wholesales' dry goods departments, or vice versa, was undecided. So too was the significance of the fact that the retail societies' weakest departments were those in which there was least loyalty to the Wholesales. Concern, however, at the Movement's relatively poor showing in these trades included the desire to increase co-operative production in them.

The C.W.S. was very enterprising during this period in increasing its productive activities. In every year, except 1927, some new productive undertaking was opened and, in some years, there were several. A good proportion of these were in foodstuffs, canning, dairies and aerated waters being of some significance, and in dry goods the Society carried forward the reorganisation and rationalisation of furniture manufacture and the manufacture of electrical appliances, including the appropriately named "Defiant" radio. By 1938, the C.W.S. had 182 factories, employing 46,292 people, the value of their production amounted to £43,869,805.

C.W.S. Bank

The C.W.S. Bank made a great advance from 55,171 accounts and a turnover of £496 millions in 1922 to 75,084 accounts and a turnover of £832 millions in 1939. Its customers did not consist only of co-operative societies but included churches, welfare institutions, miners' homes, trades and labour clubs, municipalities, trade unions and individuals. A few municipalities had accounts with the C.W.S. Bank in 1920, and the number had increased to 31 by 1938. In the same period trade unions accounts increased from 8,233 to 9,007—though this underestimates the growth of trade unions business with the bank as there was increasing internal centralisation in many trade unions and consequently fewer bank accounts for each trade union.

Individual depositors' accounts increased from 15,516 amounting to £2,070,673 in 1919 to 20,657 accounts amounting to £5,412,883 in 1938. The extent to which the bank was serving as a depository of individuals' savings is not measured by these figures alone, for there must be added in 1938 the 43,114 holders of the bank's deposit notes which amounted to £8,354,729. This increasing business was indicative of increasing confidence, earned by sound financial policies which put the security of the depositors' interests as the first consideration. Liquidity of assets and the avoidance of risky enterprises are among the principles of sound banking which the bank observed, whilst at the same time it served the proper financial needs of the Co-operative Movement.

C.W.S. Retail Society

A C.W.S. development which started in this period and which may prove in the future to be of considerable historical importance was the C.W.S. Retail Society. Difficulties of establishing and developing retail societies in North Wales, led to suggestions being made in 1927 that the C.W.S. should undertake retailing there, as the S.C.W.S. had undertaken retailing in the Highlands. A resolution was submitted to the Congress of 1928 declaring: " that the time is now opportune for the Co-operative Wholesale Society to undertake retail trade in areas where there are not sufficient facilities for the same, and requests the Co-operative Wholesale Society to take steps to this end in consultation with the Union." It was moved by A. Varley of the C.W.S. on behalf of the Joint Propaganda and Trade Committee (a joint committee of the C.W.S. and the Union). In his speech he suggested the need for C.W.S. retailing not only in areas where Co-operation was not established but also in rural areas where societies were small and weak, and in difficulties. N. S. Beaton of the S.C.W.S. gave the warning from Scottish experience that the opening of branches was not the same as starting societies: " Our methods must grow from the people; we cannot force a Movement upon them . . . People look upon these branches as something like a multiple shop."

Nevertheless, the resolution carried, but the C.W.S. did not submit a scheme to its members until 1933. The scheme, which was approved in 1934, was to establish a C.W.S. Retail Co-operative Society Limited. Its headquarters would be at Balloon Street, and its committee of management would be appointed by and from the C.W.S. Board. However, it would be made possible for local members to be gathered together and a local advisory committee appointed or elected with power to call local meetings. A three-quarters majority of the local members could convert the branch into an independent co-operative society owned and controlled by its membership. The C.W.S. guaranteed all individual share and loan capital and interest. In 1936 the first branch of the C.W.S. Retail Society came into being by the conversion of the Cardiff Co-operative Society.

The S.C.W.S.

The S.C.W.S. was also active in developing its productive activities and at the outbreak of war it had 58 factories and workshops employing over 10,000 people. Among the interesting developments were its entry into funeral furnishing in 1934, growing in two years into the largest funeral service in Great Britain; the production of electric lamps, in conjunction with the Swedish C.W.S., the Luma Lamp Factory being completed in 1938, the commencement of a chain of retail drug shops in 1937; and the reorganisation of its system of retail branches in 1934.

JOINT UNDERTAKINGS

The two Wholesales formed the English and Scottish Joint Co-operative Wholesale Society which was registered as a separate society in 1923. Its main activities were with tea, but it was also concerned with coffee, cocoa and chocolate.

Another joint undertaking of the two Wholesale Societies is the Co-operative Insurance Society, which was taken over by them in 1913. Its progress had been disappointing due to lack of capital and consequent lack of enterprise. In 1918, the Planet Friendly Society was taken over and an era of rapid progress began. It extended its branches of insurance, covering Fire, Life, Accident, Plate Glass, Fidelity, Burglary, Employers' Liability, Agricultural, Public Liability and Motor. The growth of the Society is indicated by the increase of its premium income, from £924,066 in 1919 to £9,058,751 in 1938, its assets increasing in the same period from £1,221,468 to £30,920,230.

CO-OPERATIVE CO-PARTNERSHIP SOCIETIES

The progress of co-operative co-partnership is indicated by the following table. It refers only to societies which were members of the Co-operative Productive Federation. All producers' societies were not members of this federation, but the most important and most of those which formed part of the Co-operative Movement were.

Progress of C.P.F. Societies, 1923–1940

Year	No. of Societies	Share and Loan Capital £	Reserve and Insurance £	Sales £ million	Surplus £	No. of Employees
1923	44	843,000	277,000	2·05	77,869	5,217
1930	43	1,053,000	387,000	2·74	138,770	6,970
1940	40	1,255,000	479,000	3·56	217,389	7,366

In 1930, of these societies eight were in the clothing trades, 17 in footwear and 12 in printing, and these three industries had

90 per cent of the trade of the societies. It will be observed that, apart from the number of societies, each column shows increases, but if reference were made to the whole of co-operative trade and employment, the comparative importance of these societies would be seen to be declining. The proportion of their production to co-operative trade or to co-operative production was less and the proportion of the number of their employees to all co-operative employees was less. Progress in co-operative production was in the main being made by the federations of retail societies, local and national.

The existing co-partnership societies were efficient, the severe slump of 1920–1922 was survived, the economic blizzard of the early 'thirties was weathered, but as a movement they ceased to grow. Few new societies were started and new industries were not entered. Yet the prospects appeared to be exceptionally favourable for the establishing of new societies. Capitalism, for instance, was productive of a large number of new enterprises, most of them small. Capital was abundant and there was a large, growing and sympathetic market. Superficially there was at the beginning of the period even an increasing popularity of ideas favourable to workers' control, e.g., syndicalism, guild socialism and industrial unionism. Yet it was fading idealism which was responsible for the failure to take advantage of the opportunities presented and the old urge to missionary endeavour appeared to have died.

No other branch of the Co-operative Movement depended so much for growth upon an altruistic idealism. For it is to the pecuniary interest of the consumer that the trade and production of the consumer societies should increase in volume and variety, and this interest in itself is an incentive to growth. There is no such pecuniary incentive for the member employee of the productive society to encourage the formation of societies in industries other than his own. The drive for the progress of this form of Co-operation depended upon an idealism transcending individual self-interest which the education and propaganda of these societies failed to maintain.

8 CO-OPERATIVE DEVELOPMENTS, 1914-39

> " *We can no more put our educational work out to be done by other people than we can put out our trade to be done by other people.*"   *F. Hall.*

> " *We are beginning to realise the fact of our entry into politics. The Movement is realising that it is an entity; that there is in this kingdom a body of people who consciously call themselves co-operators and who recognise that they form part of the great democratic movement which, in 1917, determined under the stress of external circumstances, to have a voice in what are called national affairs.*"   *W. H. Watkins.*

THE big economic, social and political changes of the period between the two world wars made great demands upon the adaptability and will to live of the Co-operative Movement. Governments of both right and left increasingly interfered with business and hindered and threatened co-operative expansion. The growth of large scale private enterprise in retailing reduced the most apparent material benefits of co-operative enterprise. There were rival movements for economic and social reform growing in influence and power. Within the Movement, labour became well organised and powerful, and determined to advance its own interests. The Movement itself was endangered by its age and success, which were likely to make it lethargic, tending to cling to obsolete methods and resist new, to take too much for granted in the way of support and understanding, be content with what had been achieved and indisposed to attempt new conquests and to be mainly desirous of a quiet and untroubled existence.

Although the response of the Movement to the challenge of the times did not satisfy the more enthusiastic co-operators, it did show a vitality and adaptability remarkable for so old, widespread and complex a Movement. The Co-operative Union was much expanded and its constitution changed, the Co-operative Party grew, so did the Guilds and the Youth Movement. The Co-operative Press sought to reach the general public of the whole nation. Co-operative education was increased to educate the rising generation of members, committees and staffs to the wider outlooks, a more scientific approach and better grasp of co-operative ideals and principles required by the changed circumstances.

THE CO-OPERATIVE UNION

The increase in size and activities of the Movement and increasing intervention of governments with business in general necessitated the growth and reorganisation of the Co-operative Union. As the activities of the Union had increased in the past, additional committees of the United Board had been set up to be responsible for their performance. A cumbersome and expensive structure was the consequence. In 1930, a Special Committee was appointed and on its report the Co-operative Union was reorganised in 1932. As there has been further reorganisation since then it is not necessary to go into detail. Summarily, the Central Board was to remain an entirely elected body on a Sectional basis; it was to meet before Congress to consider its Report to Congress and at Congress and at such other times as found necessary. Many of the old committees were abolished. In their place a National Executive Committee was set up, consisting of a direct representative from each Sectional Board and with the Chairman of the Central Board as its chairman. It was responsible for all the internal organisation of the Co-operative Union, its finance, appointments, administration and executive control.

Reorganisation

A new body, the National Co-operative Authority, was created to deal with the wider activities and policy of the Co-operative Movement and make decisions upon matters of national policy in the intervals between Congresses. It was believed that the influence of the Movement would be increased if it spoke " with one voice on questions of national policy and major public issues." To this end the National Authority was made representative of the national organisations—the National Executive of the Co-operative Union, four representatives of the C.W.S., two of the S.C.W.S., one of the C.P.F., one of the National Co-operative Publishing Society (the Co-operative Press), and two of the Co-operative Party. It was to meet at least quarterly.

Wide representation to include interested organisations was also provided in the constitution relating to the Education Department. A National Educational Council was constituted with representa-

tives from each of the Sectional Boards, each of the Sectional
Educational Committees' Associations, each of the Guilds and
from the National Co-operative Managers' Association, the Co-
operative Secretaries' Association and from the National Union
of Distributive and Allied Workers. The Council was to meet at
least three times a year. An Educational Executive of ten members
was appointed, five of whom, including the chairman of the
Council who would also be chairman of the Executive, must be
members of the Central Board. The Executive would meet
monthly for the purpose of transacting the executive and administrative work of the Education Department.

The constitution of the National Committee of the Co-operative
Party remained unchanged, it also was framed to represent all
co-operative organisations concerned with its political activities,
viz., the Sectional Boards, Sectional representatives of contributing societies, the Educational Council, the Wholesale Societies,
the C.P.F., the Joint Parliamentary Committee and the Guilds.

A more active and important part was visualised for the District
Associations. They were urged to interest themselves in the
development of co-operative trade and service, particularly in
connection with the establishment of new businesses.

New Departments

Besides the above changes in constitutional structure the Co-
operative Union experienced organic development in response to
the Movement's needs. The number of its departments increased,
a Labour Department and Adviser, 1918, an Agricultural Organiser, 1925, the Research and Statistical Department, 1936.

Increasingly numerous and complex labour problems at the end
of the first world war led to the appointment of a Labour Adviser
and the setting up of a Labour Department. Its functions became
those of assisting societies to meet the problems which confronted
them as employers, e.g., collective bargaining and negotiating,
drafting agreements, collecting and supplying information, and
advising.

The creation of an Agricultural Department and its subsequent
history shows the impact of various changes upon the development of the Co-operative Union. Agricultural Co-operation had
a difficult career which is described in another chapter. It was
faced with further disaster by the winding up of the Agricultural
Organisation Society in 1924, which left the agricultural societies
with no advisory union. It was suggested that the Co-operative
Union might undertake to guide and advise them. This suggestion
was taken up.

There were also other reasons. Retail societies' farming ventures were generally unsuccessful and the need for expert guidance and advice was realised. Co-operative idealists desired the development of all forms of Co-operation, and that all forms be united in the Co-operative Union. At first the department was administered by a joint committee of the Union and the C.W.S., but the C.W.S. withdrew in 1927. Although the expected benefits from expert advice on farming enterprises were realised the main functions of the department came to be determined by the Government economic planning of the 'thirties.

The agricultural societies had not the same social ideals and political sympathies as the Consumers' Movement and so did not join the Co-operative Union. But the great increase in the retail societies' milk trade brought thousands of farmers into business relations with these societies. The existence of an Agricultural Department enabled a national policy to be followed; it also enabled societies to have expert advice when setting up dairies or developing them.

In the 'thirties the introduction of marketing boards by the Government affected the supplies of some of the Movement's main commodities—dairy produce, meat, potatoes, pigs and bacon. In all these schemes co-operative interests were threatened. It was necessary to prepare co-operative cases for presentation to Reorganisation Commissions and Government Inquiries, to secure concessions, rights and immunities necessary to the practice and principles of co-operative trade. The Agricultural Department did this work, some of the most important the Union ever undertook, but certainly never visualised when the Department was first established.

Trade Associations

In 1930, following a pamphlet by A. Pickup and W. B. Neville, a Trades Advisory Committee was appointed by the United Board " to confer with the various Sections of the Movement with a view to the setting up of such Trades Advisory Bodies as may be found desirable to encourage, strengthen and develop the business organisation of the Movement." Its first report visualised the setting up of Trade Associations in Grocery and Provisions, Meat, Coal, Bakery, Laundry, Drapery, Boots, Outfitting, but progress in establishing these associations was much slower than had been expected.

The obvious need for a national policy led to the establishment of the National Co-operative Milk Trade Association in 1930. It was constructed on what was to become the customary Union pattern. Societies which were members of the Association elected a committee for their own Section, with a National Executive consisting of representatives from each Section, two from the Central Board and two from the C.W.S. The National Executive of the Association ranked as a committee of the Union and submitted its report to Congress. The Association's functions were mainly consultative and advisory, its decisions were recommendations to societies, not commands. It encouraged, by advice and help, societies desirous of entering or developing the dairy trade and promoted collaboration with the C.W.S. The Organising Secretary was the Agricultural Organiser to the Co-operative Union.[1]

A similar organisation, the National Co-operative Coal Trade Association, was formed also in 1930, at first due to the threat of monopoly by the Coal Merchants' Federation, based on the marketing provisions in the Coal Mines Act of 1930.

These two trade associations proved so useful that future developments were visualised by which a national policy and national efforts in other trades might be made. The Co-operative Meat Trade Association had an organisation similar to the Milk Trade Association, and it also found itself engaged with the consequences of new legislation and planning. Its Organising Secretary was the Agricultural Organiser. The Co-operative Drug Trade Association was another species, though of the same genus, consisting of a technical panel of chemists from the C.W.S. and the retail societies.

Legal, Finance Publications

The work and the importance of other departments considerably increased during the period. Legislation affecting co-operative societies continued to increase, multiplying the legal problems confronting societies and their need for legal advice and guidance. The Finance Department was also called upon more frequently as rating and taxation questions became more numerous and complex, a considerable addition being due to the Finance Act of 1933 which subjected co-operative societies to special income tax.

The Publications Department, besides the publication of books and journals, also handled publicity and Press matters for the Movement and advisory work thereon for retail societies. It also undertook a good deal of propaganda in defensive campaigns, such as that against the Finance Act of 1933, and big trade campaigns, such as Milk Publicity Week, the Window Display Competition, the National Propaganda Campaign, and the Coal Campaign all occasioned the publication of millions of special posters

---

[1] Congress Report 1930. Pp 85–87

and leaflets. By precept and example the Department also raised the standard and effectiveness of co-operative advertising. This was of no small consequence, for the quality of advertising affects public opinion of the advertisers.

TEN YEAR PLAN AND CO-ORDINATION OF PRODUCTION

Many in the Movement were concerned with securing a greater unity of co-operative effort and organisation in trade and production. The idea of all co-operative societies being merged into one national society continued to rise here and there, in spite of the criticism of the Webbs, which probably few of its advocates had ever read, or that contained in a Co-operative Union pamphlet on the subject by T. W. Mercer.

More promising was the adoption of a Ten Year Plan in 1935, to culminate in 1944. " Planning " had been popularised by the Five Year Plans of the U.S.S.R., and the idea of " planning " consequently appealed to some as being the essence of socialism; others believed in the greater efficiency of a concerted drive or that the plan with its annual targets for each society and organisation within the Movement would inspire new life and vigour for progress. The objective was " A Co-operative Movement serving the bulk of the homes of Great Britain, supplying most of the domestic requirements from co-operative factories and giving a range of services at least as wide as the best examples among present day societies." In more precise terms, trade and membership were to be doubled by 1944.

Targets were to be set each year in membership, trade and in the sale of co-operative products, for the whole Movement, each Section, District and society. National publicity and membership campaigns were planned and carried out in conformity with the general plan. In general the targets of increase allocated to the various Sections were hit until the outbreak of war in 1939 put an end to the scheme.

By and large the plan proved beneficial. Many societies were jolted out of a lethargic complacency and contentment with the position they had reached. At the Congress of 1937, it was said of the plan, " It has caught the imagination of our people, a very big thing in itself. A questioning spirit has been awakened in some quarters, co-operators are asking themselves whether they are doing all they ought to do in the way of securing new members and opening new enterprises, or whether they are simply jogging along waiting to be pushed into new developments by extraneous circumstances."

One of the consequences was the creation of a Research Department of the Co-operative Union and the making of an Economic Survey[1]. Another was a move for a co-ordination of all co-operative production. Efforts were being made from 1934 onwards by the Co-operative Union to get the Wholesale Societies and the C.P.F. to agree on measures of co-ordination. A Special Inquiry Committee was set up by resolution of the 1937 Congress to recommend methods to effect co-ordination. This, however, had to report failure to the Congress of 1939.

Co-ordination, to the Wholesale Societies seemed to mean absorption of the other productive societies; the wholesales professed they were not keen to do this, but that anything short of this was playing with the question. The Movement, expressing itself in Congress, believed that there could be co-ordination in such matters as purchase of raw materials, specialisation of factories, marketing of products, inter-trading[2]. Despite the efforts, lasting five years, and strong views expressed in Congress, it became increasingly evident that the parties concerned were unwilling to co-ordinate; only something in the nature of a shot-gun wedding could have effected it.

CO-OPERATIVE EDUCATION

Co-operative education developed considerably between the two wars, mainly as a result of the initiative of the Education Department of the Co-operative Union. Before the end of the war, a small number of whole time students were attending day-time classes at Holyoake House; this was intended to be the beginning of the Co-operative College.

It will be remembered that a meeting of all the co-operative organisations in 1914 passed a resolution approving the establishment of a Co-operative College and the taking of steps to that end. The war, of course, prevented further action, apart from the efforts of those who kept the ideal alive. In 1919 the time appeared ripe for definite action and at the Congress of that year Mr. W. Abbotts (Walsall) moved the following resolution:

"That this Congress is of the opinion that a Co-operative College is essential to the welfare and development of the Co-operative Movement and that no worthier memorial of the Peace and of those co-operators who have served and fallen in the war could be established than an institution for the dissemination of the principles of Co-operation and harmony in industrial and international relationships. It therefore instructs

[1] Report given in Congress, 1938, pp 54–89
[2] Congress Report 1938, pp 222–232

the Central Board to organise a fund forthwith for the establishment of such a College, to which co-operators and co-operative organisations may be invited to subscribe."

The resolution was passed and an appeal for £50,000 made. Contributions and promises were coming in when the slump of 1920 developed, prices fell, unemployment soared, share capital was withdrawn, dividends shrank and societies became naturally scared. A proposal that the C.W.S. should make a grant of £10,000 consequently met opposition. There were those who held that " advantage should be taken of existing institutions," oblivious of the fact that no existing institutions did, could, or would attempt to do what was intended of a Co-operative College. The issue was debated at C.W.S. quarterly meetings, four times adjourned, and was barely carried by 1,042 votes to 1,036 in July, 1921. A referendum of societies, however, was called for by Royal Arsenal Society, the depression had intensified meanwhile, and in January, 1922, the grant was annulled by 2,785 votes to 2,193. The £50,000 appealed for was consequently not forthcoming, only £17,621 was promised and £9,728 contributed. But on these slender resources the College was started.

The College Begins

Lectures were given in Holyoake House, which of course had never been designed for such a purpose. It was primarily an office building, yet classes were held and students studied in the midst of the office work of the headquarters of the Co-operative Union. Both students and staff found conditions certainly hard, and not until 1924 was a hostel provided for students' living accommodation. Holyoake House, however, had advantages; there was an excellent library (and there were also splendid reference library facilities in Manchester) and the College was right in the heart of the Movement.

Slowly the number of students grew, sustained by scholarships provided by local societies and the two Wholesales, and from the beginning there were students from abroad. Many of these students attained positions of responsibility and influence. By the time the second world war broke out five college students had been appointed to the tutorial staff of the Co-operative College, most of the principal administrative positions in the Education Department were filled by them, others were in important positions in other departments of the Union, one was a director of the C.W.S., another was a director of the S.C.W.S., and there were several filling responsible posts in both these bodies. There were also numerous secretaries, managers, education

secretaries and other officials of retail societies, and six had
become editors of co-operative newspapers at home and abroad.
The value, and the need for a Co-operative College had to be
shown by practical demonstration, and between the two wars the
College did that. Yet, as has been shown the ideal of a Co-operative College was as old as the Co-operative Movement itself.

Education Developments

The existence of the College enabled more systematic development of co-operative education to take place. Courses of study
could be prepared by its staff of specialist tutors and yet made to
blend into a harmonious whole. The writing of correspondence
courses involved a good deal of research in each subject and a
considerable body of organised knowledge was gradually developed.
This was disseminated through correspondence courses, and by
teachers of local classes. For the first time the Movement began to
have a supply of teachers with a reliable knowledge of its workings.

Studies were planned in a number of diploma courses, which
were developed in range and number as the resources of the
Department increased. The ideals of the Movement were kept to
the fore, the programme of the Education Department stating that
economic prosperity, social welfare and the moral progress of all
nations could only be achieved by the development of the desire
and of the ability to co-operate for the common good. It was the
need for such a development which must affect those concerned
with the direction and development of co-operative education.
" A right understanding of the past and the present is necessary
to those who would fit themselves for building a better future."
To this end " Industrial History, Economics, Sociology, Ethics,
Citizenship, Education and Co-operation " had their place in
the programme " whilst courses of study for those engaged in
co-operative business administration are also provided."

The Movement, in practice, however, was far more concerned
with those engaged in business administration than in the making
of co-operative social reformers. Yet, as had been recognised in
the early Congresses, the co-operative education of officials was
vital. In those days the pressing need was for officials, generally
and inevitably trained and experienced in private trade, to become
acquainted with the purpose and so understand the principles of
Co-operation. Societies were small, the range of their activities
narrow, their competitors generally ignorant and inefficient. An
intelligent man could pick up sufficient from his own practical
experience to manage a society reasonably well under those
conditions.

Employee Education

In the inter-war period those conditions, however, had passed. Societies were growing in size, many of them were big businesses with a wide range of activities presenting problems of organisation and finance for which individual practical experience alone was too narrow and limited to provide adequate experience. To attempt to learn by experience alone could be expensive in a small business, it would be ruinous in a large one. Moreover, the serious competitors of the co-operative societies were no longer the inefficient, small shopkeepers, but the big businesses of multiples, departmental stores and mail order firms managed by well-educated men.

Thus, as the Education Programme stated, " Co-operative business as a moral system of business must also remain an efficient system of business; and co-operative societies should provide adequate educational facilities for their employees so that the Co-operative Movement may be as efficient as its competitors."

Co-operative Congresses repeatedly passed resolutions expressing belief in the value of employee education, the need for adequately trained staffs and the desirability of making the holding of certificates a condition of new appointments or promotions. Technical or business efficiency, however, cannot be divorced in co-operative business from a knowledge of and a faith in co-operative principles, and this was realised and stressed in a resolution of Congress in 1933, which stated that " it is principally through the strengthening of faith in co-operative principles and through its own endeavours that the Co-operative Movement will attain its objects, and realising the importance to the Movement of the staffs of societies being imbued with co-operative ideals and keen in their desire for a Co-operative Commonwealth, expresses its approval of graded schemes of education in co-operative principles and technical training for co-operative employees."

Group Courses

Graded schemes had been developed to accord with the needs of the Movement as the resources of the Education Department increased and as the educational work it performed produced students capable of undertaking more advanced courses of study. Employee students proceeded through a series of group courses, each being complete in itself and yet a preparation for a succeeding stage. Each succeeding course was designed to give the student an increasingly intensive study of the work in which he was engaged, as well as new techniques, e.g., the compilation and use of statistics, and also an ever wider and deeper knowledge of the

Movement and of the legal framework and social and economic environment in which it operated. Thus he would gain an understanding of the purpose, the strengths and weaknesses of the Movement, of external forces and circumstances which favour or oppose its progress and of the nature of its competitors. He would come to appreciate that the conditions under which a society, or even a branch, operates, are constantly changing and that techniques and methods must be changed to meet them. To do so he must be capable of recognising and even foreseeing new problems, appreciating and analysing them and applying principles to discover solutions. His co-operative education was designed to develop such capacities. A similar scheme of graduated group studies was developed for office employees. As these courses required hard and sustained study over a long period, they were a test of character as well as of intellectual ability.

The study of Co-operation, at home and abroad with its social, economic and political environment was provided by a Diploma course in Co-operation.

Apart from the elementary stages of these courses of study there were seldom sufficient students in a locality to form a class, and even if a class had been formed it would often have been difficult and generally impossible to have provided a teacher. To meet this difficulty correspondence courses were provided. Even in the less advanced studies it was generally necessary to do this. Travelling teachers were, however, appointed who organised and conducted classes in salesmanship, and they selected suitable students who would be capable of teaching the subject later.

For the more advanced stages, correspondence courses were inevitable, save for the fortunate few who were able to attend the Co-operative College. Here the emphasis was upon the subjects of the Co-operative Diploma Course, which were less suitable for correspondence tuition, and yet which were regarded as necessary to produce co-operative leaders, even if in a business capacity. There was, as a result of the various efforts, a constant raising of the standards, not only of the examinations and consequently the studies, but also of what was expected of candidates for appointments and promotion. There was thus an induced tendency to the increased efficiency of staffs.

Member Education

The co-operative education of the general membership of the Movement was much less under the control and less subject to the driving force of the Co-operative Union. It could give leads by the preparation of syllabuses, exhortations, advice, provision of correspondence courses, text-books, summer schools and so forth, but apart from individual contact with students as in its correspondence courses, it had to rely on the active support of local societies, and this was often lacking. Its main concern was naturally education in Co-operation. Here it developed a series of graded studies in the History and Principles of Co-operation, viz., a Junior Grade, consisting of three stages, an Intermediate Grade for adolescent students and the Senior Grade consisting of three stages. The student thus had a good detailed knowledge of the Co-operative Movement before he attempted the final stage of the Senior Grade, which was intended to be concerned with wide and profound problems of various aspects of the Movement involved in a more advanced historical treatment and a critical survey. Correspondence Courses were only available for the Senior Grade, nor were examinations encouraged for the preceding ones. Besides many special co-operative subjects, syllabuses were provided to encourage the formation of classes for adults who wanted to study the Movement in a less exacting manner.

The Summer School movement continued to develop both in number and variety, and employees' schools and weekend schools were also started and developed. In 1938, summer schools for adults were held in Ireland, Brighton and Scarborough, attended by 268 students, an Adolescent School at Ambleside had 72 students and two Junior schools at Southport and Shornells were attended by 183 students. A school of a fortnight's duration was held for secretaries and cashiers attended by 40 students, and for salesmen and managers four schools were held attended by 167 students.

Joint Committee

The courses in Salesmanship and Management were subject to a Joint Committee on Technical Education, consisting of representatives of the Co-operative Union and the C.W.S. and formed in 1930. It was concerned with the training of apprentices, salesmen and employees on the managerial side in England and Wales, and the general dissemination of co-operative knowledge amongst employees, the expenses being shared equally by the two bodies. Classes taken by these students in book-keeping and secretarial subjects, however, remained under the control of the Education Department. As the Adviser of Studies and Principal of the Co-operative College was also the responsible official, the scheme fitted in well with the general scheme of the Education Department. The additional resources available made possible much of the extension of employee education during the 'thirties.

G

Convention

The Easter Weekends of the pre-war period grew from a small gathering of teachers and enthusiasts for co-operative education into an Easter gathering of substantial size whose name was changed to " Easter Weekend and Educational Convention " in 1935. It attracted the annual meetings of various educational bodies—the Co-operators' Educational Fellowship, the National Co-operative Men's Guild, the National Guild of Co-operators, the Co-operative Educational Secretaries' Association. The British Federation of Co-operative Youth and the Woodcraft Folk each organised a demonstration during the weekend. The main business, however, was the presentation of the Report to Congress of the Education Department, by courtesy of the National Executive. Opportunity to discuss this more fully than was possible at Congress was thereby provided, but, of course, no resolutions could be effective as the Department was responsible to Congress, not to the Convention. At the meetings of educational associations and societies' educational committees, resolutions on educational policy could be moved and discussed, but these also could not be binding on anybody. These meetings, nevertheless, were very valuable, they provided the opportunity for educationists to discuss educational policy and problems and to exert some influence on the Educational Council and Executive and societies.

Interest in and the desire for a common policy and joint efforts led to the formation of Educational Associations. In some areas there were District Associations, but a Sectional Educational Association was organised in each Section of the Union. Primarily they were federations of the education committees of retail societies, though generally Guild branches and other co-operative organisations were admitted to membership. They were credited with a high record of missionary work and education on behalf of co-operative education. In 1933, a National Association of Educational Committees was inaugurated and registered in 1937.

Youth

Apart from formal studies, valuable educational activities can be engaged in by associations for cultural, social, sporting and political purposes. Associations of co-operative youth termed Comrades' Circles, the first formed in 1907, had so progressed that in 1924 they were able to form a national body, " The British Federation of Co-operative Youth." It received financial aid from the Co-operative Union, and also advice and what guidance it would accept from the Education Department, a member of whose staff acted as joint secretary. A lively, vigorous but perhaps somewhat aggressively independent body, it undoubtedly assisted in producing co-operative leaders. In 1938 there were 231 circles with 8,000 members. Another body, the Woodcraft Folk, with uniforms and activities which were similar to some of the scouting organisations, was also formed, receiving official recognition and some assistance in 1932. Its membership in 1938 was 5,000.

There was a belief in the 'thirties that the junior classes and their studies and methods were out-dated, being too serious for the contemporary child. Some desired instead the formation of youth clubs with the accent on recreations, the co-operative message to be introduced by way of handicrafts, dancing, table tennis, etc. To further such on sound lines the Education Executive established a Youth Section and appointed a Youth Organiser in 1937.

Progress

All these efforts constituted and resulted in an unprecedented educational advance as is shown by the following table:

Year	Junior and Inter-mediate Classes		Adult Classes Social Subjects		Technical Classes		Total—all types of Classes	
	No. of Classes	No. of Students	No. of Classes	No. of Students	No. of Classes	No. of Students	No. of Classes	No. of Students
1918–1919	494	17,947	70	1,691	56	1,201	620	20,939
1930–1931	892	29,530	218	5,972	772	16,126	1,882	51,628
1938–1939	1,280	39,217	345	6,789	1,350	23,529	2,975	69,535

In 1938–1939 thirty-seven students were in residence at the Co-operative College, twelve of them came from abroad (S. Africa, Ceylon, Egypt, Denmark, Sweden, Iceland, U.S.A., India).

In 1936 co-operative education suffered a great loss in the death of W. R. Rae, who had been chairman of the committees responsible for the Education Department for 34 years, and a member of the Central Board since 1898. In 1938, a further severe loss was suffered by the death of F. Hall, the first Adviser of Studies and Principal of the Co-operative College. These two men had largely shaped the development of co-operative education and their deaths, together with the outbreak of war in 1939, marked the end of an era in its history.

THE GUILDS

All the Guilds grew in numbers and probably in influence. New guilds were formed, the Scottish Co-operative Men's Guild in

1922 and the National Guild of Co-operators in 1926, the latter deriving from earlier " mixed guilds " of men and women. All the Guilds had certain common features during the period. They performed a good deal of educational and propaganda work, were active supporters of the Co-operative Party, and engaged in various campaigns of a political nature, especially those concerned with foreign affairs and international peace.

Their most effective activities, however, were those concerned with the Co-operative Movement. The continued determination to increase the loyalty of the societies to co-operative productions and to increase the loyalty of the members to their societies, though less spectacular, had more effect than did demonstrations to change the policy of nations. Again, the experience of orderly debate and business procedure obtained in the Women's Guilds prepared many women for responsible positions in public life.

An experienced and eminent authority on social work stated in 1934 of the Co-operative Women's Guild: " The Guild set out to educate them first as consumers (a form of education singularly neglected by other sections of society) and gradually from this evolved its own method of adult education of women. The results of this method may be seen and admired at the impressive gatherings of the Guild, and in the undoubted influence of ' co-operative women ' on legislation bearing on problems affecting the home . . . Probably no organised body has done more to further the national protection of motherhood " and " adult education is not only wanted for the workers. Indeed, the aristocracy of the workers are in many ways better educated than the so-called educated classes. A meeting of the Women's Co-operative Guild provides a far more intelligent, better informed audience than many drawing room meetings." (*The New Philanthropy*, E. Macadam.)

The Guilds generally almost doubled their membership between the two wars. In 1938, the English Women's Co-operative Guild had a membership of over 87,000; the Scottish Women's Co-operative Guild of over 32,000; the National Co-operative Men's Guild, 10,000; and the National Guild of Co-operators, 5,000. The Irish Women's Guild, mainly centred around Belfast, and the Scottish Men's Guild, each had a few thousand members.

In 1920 the English Women's Guild had an impressive list of its members serving in public bodies, 28 were borough councillors, 200 were Poor Law Guardians, 22 were on Urban District Councils, 290 on Municipal Maternity Committees, 12 were appointed magistrates, one was on the Consumers' Council, three on Consultative Councils of the Ministry of Health, and large numbers were on local insurance committees, War Pensions Committees and Profiteering Committees. They were also gaining increased representation on co-operative bodies, 220 were on management committees and 662 on education committees, two were on the Central Board, one was on the Central Education Committee and one was a member of the Executive Committee of the Co-operative Party. Mrs. Cottrell just failed to be elected to the Board of the C.W.S. (she was successful in 1922).

In 1938 the numbers of the Guild's members on various public bodies must have been much larger: on co-operative bodies it had increased to 412 on management committees and to 930 on education committees (including 38 chairmen). Members of the Scottish Women's Guild also served on public and co-operative bodies, but the numbers are unavailable.

The Men's Guild was much smaller but its size belied its influence. One-tenth of its members were on co-operative committees, 592 on management and 412 on education committees. It had members on all the important national co-operative committees and boards, on the Central Board, the Educational Executive, the Co-operative Party, the C.W.S. Board, the directorate of the Co-operative Press, and the Co-operative Printing Society. On public bodies the list was also impressive, 297 were in elected public positions, 104 were J.P.'s and five were Members of Parliament.

The number of Guild members on public bodies is some indication of the part played by co-operators in civic life, although that part, of course, was much greater for there were many co-operators other than guild members also serving on them.

CO-OPERATIVE PARTY

The decision to seek co-operative representation in Parliament inevitably led to the creation of a Co-operative Party. Problems of constitution and organisation were presented—who would control the Party? how would it be controlled? how would it be financed? In 1918 a National Co-operative Representation Committee was set up representing various national co-operative organisations, and the Congress of 1918 resolved that the Co-operative Union " shall organise a special department which shall work under the National Representation Committee of the Central Board. There shall be appointed a person on the Union staff to act as secretary and head of the Department and the clerical staff and organisers necessary to secure the success of the department shall also be appointed. The appointments shall be made by the Executive of the Co-operative Union in consultation with the

National Co-operative Representation Committee." Thus the
Party staff were employees of the Co-operative Union and the
Party organisation was a department of the Union.

Of course, an effective party needed much more than that.
Active party workers, on whom any political party depends,
needed to be recruited and organised. Sectional and local councils
were created. In the Sections party work was promoted and
supervised by full-time organisers. Close contact with the Sectional Boards was maintained. Within the Sections there were local
parties and federations of parties. Difficulties presented by Parliamentary constituencies not being coincident with retail societies'
boundaries, of some societies within a constituency being affiliated
and some not, necessitated a flexible and complicated organisation.

1938 Constitution

In 1938 a new constitution was adopted. This retained the
National Committee and made it representative of the various
interests affected in such a way that it was likely to express the
political opinion of the Movement and yet give scope and opportunity to those which were particularly concerned with politics.
It consisted of eight members of the Central Board on a Sectional
basis, eight members elected on a Sectional basis by societies
subscribing to the Party fund, eight elected on a Sectional basis
representing local parties (not societies) and affiliated auxiliary
co-operative organisations, and representatives of the Union
Executive , the Wholesale Societies, the C.P.F., the Guilds and
the Joint Parliamentary Committee.

It was to be financed by contributions from affiliated societies,
grants from the national organisations, and special donations
from individuals or bodies.

A Party Conference was held at Preston in 1920, and from 1925
these Conferences have been held annually " to review the organisation and policy of the Party and to stimulate greater interest in
its work." Policy is discussed mainly on resolutions moved on
all manner of subjects of topical political interest. Delegates
attending any party's conference are generally far more zealous
and advanced than the average membership of such a party, and the
opinions expressed and resolutions passed are consequently hardly
representative of the party as a whole, so that few parties would have
their programmes determined for them by such conferences.

Party Conference

The Co-operative Party Conference, however, could not pass
" operative " resolutions any more than could the Education Con-

vention, but it could pass resolutions which " gave a lead " to the rest of the Movement. The National Committee was responsible not to the Party Conference but to the Co-operative Congress to which it presented its annual report, previously discussed at the Party Conference. Congress had thus the last word, and where differences or clashes of policy occurred, Party policy, as such, had to be abandoned. It might appear that since the Congress decision might be determined by societies not affiliated to the Party, or by delegates consisting of management committee people with little interest in political questions, it was unfair to the politically active that resolutions carried at the Party Conference could be overridden by Congress. Reflection would show the soundness, indeed the inevitability of this, if the Party were to continue to claim that it represented and expressed co-operative opinion.

The policies of the Co-operative Party were generally determined by that opinion, and that opinion was naturally affected by the ideals and interests of the Movement. It is sometimes regarded as reprehensible for a political party to be influenced by " interests," but any and every party is bound to be so affected. There is nothing reprehensible, however, if the interests are good interests and their influence is clear and above board. Co-operative interests in this country are those of the general consumer, they are not sectional or exclusive, for membership is open to all, and the policy of the Party is more subject to open debate than is that of any other.

Policy

In fiscal matters the Party favoured the abolition of tariffs, subsidies and restrictions upon the flow of trade and was opposed to commodity taxation in general. It continually pressed for the restraint of trusts and combines, and opposed the national economic planning of the 'thirties on the grounds that being based on the profit-making motive it would " perpetuate waste and existing inequalities of wealth and income, concentrate economic control in the hands of powerful self-seeking corporations and encourage nationalism and war." (*Co-operative Party Conference Report, 1935.*) Unemployment, it believed, could be cured and it projected schemes to that end; meanwhile, the unemployed should be treated fairly and not punished for the failings of an economic system which was neither their creation nor responsibility; it declared for the principle of " Work or Maintenance." Educational policy was based on the principle of equity. Reforms and developments were desired " to open up a

broad highway of education upon which can travel the so-called
' backward child ' as well as the talented one; and in which provision must be made to educate for communal living and communal
service as the highest ideal."

In international affairs it based its policy on the pursuit of
peace. This, it was held, involved the breaking down of barriers
to the intercourse of peoples, the development of International
Co-operation and the strengthening and support of the League
of Nations. It favoured disarmament conditional on effective
collective security. The weakening of the League of Nations and
the growing menace of Germany and Italy during the 'thirties was
recognised by others than Winston Churchill. In 1936, A. V.
Alexander warned the Co-operative Party Conference, " Copy-
book maxims will not save the world this time. . . . I prophesy
that unless you deal with him (Hitler) now, in two years' time
Germany will be in a position to say to you, ' This is where you
get off '."

Relations with Labour Party

There were such similarities of ideals, policy and supporters
between the Co-operative Party and the Labour Party that some
sort of alliance between them was probably inevitable. An
attempt to establish a formal alliance was made by negotiation
and preparation of a scheme and its submission to Congress in
1921. A great Press campaign had, however, been carried on, in
which concern for the Co-operative Movement was revealed in
unsuspected quarters and warnings against political alliances,
especially with the Labour Party, were given. The scheme was
rejected by Congress, but by the narrow majority of four votes.

In 1924, a Labour Government held office, and showed a respect
for the Co-operative Movement. A. V. Alexander was appointed
Parliamentary Secretary to the Board of Trade, and co-operators
were appointed to various advisory committees in the Board of
Trade, agriculture, housing, transport, and coal. Yet the programme of the Labour Party included the development of
nationalisation and municipalisation, possibly in fields where co-
operators were convinced that Co-operation was superior on
economic and social grounds.

The need for understanding and agreement was evident, and
the Congress of 1926 instructed the Executive of the Co-operative
Party to negotiate with the Labour Party. An agreement resulted
which was approved by the Cheltenham Congress in 1927, although the majority, 1,960 votes to 1,843 was a narrow one. This
agreement became known as the Cheltenham Agreement. There

was an immediate reaction. Efforts were made by other political parties to secure the defeat of candidates for management and education committees who were known to support the Co-operative Party, to cause societies to secede from the Co-operative Party, even to secede from the Co-operative Union. There was some measure of success, but generally it proved short-lived, for the Party continued to grow.

Increased concern with economic planning in the 'thirties created the danger of differences between the Labour and Co-operative Parties, for any national economic planning affects the Co-operative Movement in some way or other. Co-operators often favourable to such planning in general terms were very critical indeed of particular instances, e.g., the marketing boards. An invitation by the National Council of Labour to the National Co-operative Authority in 1935 to be represented was declined, but accepted in 1939, two representatives attending in a consultative capacity. In 1936 the Labour Party changed its methods of selecting and financing Parliamentary candidates which involved changes in relations with the Co-operative Party, hitherto governed by the Cheltenham agreement. These proposals, in the opinion of the Co-operative Party, involved such a loss of independence that they must be resisted. Negotiations for a new agreement were decided on in 1938, but the outbreak of war caused their suspension during hostilities.

Growth

It was a long and difficult struggle to found the Co-operative Party and, but for the circumstances of the Great War would probably have been unsuccessful. The task of building the Party, was not completed by the passing of resolutions at Congress. Each co-operative society is an autonomous body and decides for itself whether or not it should affiliate to the Party. Thus a struggle had to be waged in each society for affiliation. This was not easy, but in the long run the Party probably benefited, for in each affiliated society at least, a body of members came to exist who thoroughly understood the purpose of and need for a Co-operative Party; they had been forced to develop such an understanding in order to meet opposing arguments from every possible angle.

Moreover, in each affiliated society, a majority of the active, interested members, those who attended its general meetings, had to be converted to support of the Co-operative Party for affiliation to take place. Yet efforts at persuasion were often disappointing. Much more effective were the actions of the government, mainly the change of law in 1933 which made that part of the surplus which societies put to reserve subject to income tax, and the introduction of marketing boards. The rapid increase in membership in the 'thirties was probably largely a defensive reaction rather than a conversion to the belief that co-operative ideals could be attained by political means.

Growth of the Party is indicated by the following table:

Year	No. of Co-operative Societies	Societies affiliated to Party	Membership of Co-operative Societies	Affiliated Membership
1924	1,314	393	4,702,868	1,835,671
1931	1,188	434	6,590,020	3,522,566
1933	1,150	462	6,917,138	4,083,531
1934	1,135	477	7,202,721	4,410,368
1935	1,118	502	7,483,937	5,100,000
1940	1,065	516	8,716,894	7,511,072

The number of Co-operative Party members of Parliament varied with the fortunes of the Labour Party—one in the Coalition Parliament of 1918–1922; four in the short-lived Parliament of 1923 (Conservative Government); six in the Parliament of 1924 (Labour Government); five in the Parliament of 1925–1929 (Conservative Government); nine in the Parliament of 1929–1931 (Labour Government, in which A. V. Alexander was in the Cabinet as First Lord of the Admiralty); one in the Parliament of 1931–1935 (National Government); nine in the Parliament of 1935–1945 (National 1935–1940, Coalition 1940–1945).

Generally the Co-operative Members were active in Parliament on the big general questions of the day, but also defended consumer and co-operative interests which might well have otherwise been neglected. Their efforts were not always successful, which is not surprising when the proportion of Co-operative M.P.'s to 615 members of the House of Commons is considered, but they often exerted an influence out of proportion to their numbers, and there were many instances when it was of great value to the Co-operative Movement that its views were expressed directly and authoritatively on the floor of the House of Commons.

CO-OPERATIVE PRESS

As recommended by the Survey Committee, the English and Scottish Co-operative Newspaper Societies amalgamated (1921) under the name of the National Co-operative Publishing Society, changing this in 1935 to the Co-operative Press Ltd. The old desire for a co-operative daily newspaper remained alive and was increased by attacks upon the Movement by the Rothermere and Beaverbrook newspapers. The expenses, difficulties and risks involved in running a daily newspaper had, however, so increased that such a venture was shunned and an alternative taken, the acquisition of a co-operative Sunday newspaper. In 1929 *Reynolds* newspaper was purchased. It was a paper of Chartist origin and with a continuous radical tradition. S. R. Elliott, a former student of the Co-operative College, was its first co-operative editor.

Other co-operative publications, with the exception of the *Millgate* had been or were addressed to a co-operative public. *Reynolds* appealed to the nation at large. It had consequently to make a general appeal, to contain features not specifically co-operative, to express bold opinions on political issues as they arose, not after they had been debated at Conferences and Congresses, and it had to compete with powerful organs of the Press whose features and opinions were determined solely by whether they increased their circulations or not. To descend to the levels of such a Press would have been futile for any co-operative purpose, yet a circulation had to be gained if co-operative opinion were to be expressed to the general public. The problem was, and is, a difficult one. Co-operators at times complained that there was little of co-operative concern in the journal, but the value to co-operators of *Reynolds* proved to be not as a medium for the conversion of people to Co-operation, but as a means of defending the Movement from attacks and misrepresentation. There were times when its ability to do so was invaluable.

LABOUR RELATIONS

Before 1914, there was a growing desire in both trade union and co-operative circles for closer contacts with each other, a growing belief that they were parts of a wider labour movement with much in common. Co-operative objection to political alliances prevented the " fusion of forces " at this period, but the exigencies of war, as already shown, changed co-operative opinion. In 1917, a United Advisory Council of Trade Unionists and Co-operators was established consisting of six representatives of the Co-operative Union and six of the Parliamentary Committee of the Trades Union Congress (the T.U.C. had at this time no General Council and T.U.C. affairs between congresses were looked after by this committee).

A National Joint Conference of 700 delegates met in 1919 which adopted a programme of mutual assistance, declared the opposition of both Movements to trusts, State subsidies and protection, appealed to trade unionists to support co-operative trading, banking and insurance and for the Co-operative Movement to develop and gain greater control of raw materials. Both Movements benefited. Trade unions increasingly transferred their funds to the C.W.S. Bank and co-operative societies increasingly required their employees to be members of trade unions.

General Strike

Co-operative societies also gave considerable assistance to the trade unions involved in the great strikes of the railwaymen in 1919, and the miners in 1920 and 1921. They were naturally annoyed, therefore, when in the General Strike of 1926, their employees were called out in common with those of private employers, the C.W.S. being most affected. Co-operative employees were generally trade unionists and struck when called upon to do so, whilst private employers were often able to carry on with non-union labour, so that co-operative services were stopped, whilst some provided by private enterprise continued.

As the stoppage of co-operative services could injure none but the working classes, the strikers included, this action might be thought due to the confusion and lack of general organisation associated with the strike. The C.W.S. Bank even met " physical difficulties " in transporting the money for strike pay. In three weeks the Bank paid out £2,500,000 on trades union accounts, often only possible by the assistance of C.W.S. cars and drivers at the cost of friction with strikers themselves. But attempts to remedy matters by interviews with the General Council of the T.U.C. were fruitless; its strategy appeared to be to apply pressure on the Government by producing economic chaos. The assistance of the Board of Trade had then to be sought, on the advice of the General Council, so that the Co-operative Movement could continue to supply its members with food. This assistance was readily forthcoming, and to complete the ironies of the situation, the C.W.S. Bank's need to provide cash, not cheques, for strike pay, was made easier by the assistance of other banks. Naturally co-operators were incensed at the way in which they had been treated by the T.U.C.

Agreement with T.U.C.

However, co-operators know that co-operation must not be prevented by old sores and Congress in 1928 welcomed the establishment of a joint committee representing the T.U.C. and the Co-operative Union " to promote closer harmony and to prevent the repetition of events which occurred during the national strike of 1926." An agreement between the two Movements resulted,

which stated " that the relations between the Trade Union Movement and the Co-operative Movement with regard to questions
arising on terms and conditions of employment must be based
upon a different policy to that ordinarily applied to the ordinary
capitalist undertakings so far as strikes or lockouts are concerned.
Provided that the co-operative societies are recognising and applying recognised trade union rates of wages, hours and working
conditions, they shall be immune from strikes and lockouts in
respect of such matters."

N.U.D.A.W.

Inside the Co-operative Movement itself there had been a considerable development of trade unionism. It may be remembered
that the A.U.C.E. had to leave the T.U.C. in 1916, and other
unions were assisted in pressing their claims for membership upon
co-operative employees by the T.U.C. calling upon co-operative
societies not to recognise the A.U.C.E. Some co-operative
societies responded by requiring their employees to join unions
affiliated to the T.U.C., thus assisting that body in its struggle
with the A.U.C.E. However, in 1921, the A.U.C.E. amalgamated
with an affiliated union, the National Union of Warehouse and
General Workers' Union, and under the title of National Union
of Distributive and Allied Workers, became once more affiliated
to the T.U.C.

Meanwhile, labour troubles in the Co-operative Movement had
led to the creation of conciliation machinery, Conciliation Boards
being proposed and set up in 1916. When the A.U.C.E. ceased to
be affiliated to the T.U.C. the Joint Committee of Trade Unionists
and Co-operators was unable to act as an arbitrary body in
disputes in which the A.U.C.E. was engaged. Yet the A.U.C.E.
embraced most of the co-operative employees and the militant
policy it pursued resulted in its being engaged in most of
the disputes which mattered. Consequently, the societies had to
develop machinery other than that of the Joint Committee to
deal with them. The A.U.C.E. had pursued a policy of attacking
societies singly. To meet this, societies formed Hours and Wages
Boards, with the familiar structure of District organisations linked
together by Sectional Councils, for the purpose of collective
bargaining. The Labour Department of the Co-operative Union
was set up in 1918.

End of Joint Committee

With the post-war slump came a host of labour disputes. As
prices fell, unemployment increased, and wages were reduced. The

Co-operative Movement was not immune from these troubles, for the pressure of circumstances compelled it also to seek wage reductions. But the consequent disputes, after the formation of N.U.D.A.W., now came before the Joint Committee for settlement. Between September, 1921 and September, 1922, the Joint Committee considered 237 cases and made 81 awards which were carried into effect. The work, however, broke the back of the Committee. Its trade union members, whose unions were not directly concerned with co-operative labour, began to grudge the heavy inroads on their time which service on it demanded. Leading co-operators doubted its impartiality and competence.

Even co-operative employees, who actually came through the period much better than did other classes of labour, had no confidence in the Committee's trade union representatives, " The Trade Unionist members were themselves, or through their Unions, suffering heavy reductions in private industry. They saw no reason why the co-operative employees should fare any better," said Ellen Wilkinson, M.P., in *Trade Unionism Today*, 1939. In 1925, J. Hallsworth, general secretary of N.U.D.A.W. made such an attack upon the Joint Committee in the Trades Union Congress that it came to an end, the General Council of the T.U.C. refusing to appoint any more representatives.

A fresh start was possible and necessary with the ending of the Joint Committee. Negotiations continued over two years. The desire of co-operators that general principles should be laid down and that co-operative societies should not be subjected to strikes aimed primarily at capitalistic organisations was not met, but a new conciliation scheme was agreed upon. It was accepted by the Belfast Congress of 1926, and later by most of the trade unions concerned and approved by the Trades Union Congress.

National Conciliation Board

A National Conciliation Board was provided for, to be summoned when direct negotiations between a co-operative body and a trade union had broken down. The dispute had to be referred to the Board within seven days of the breakdown and the Board had to meet within fourteen days of reference. No lockout or strike was to be declared unless the dispute had been referred to the Board or the Board had not succeeded in finding a satisfactory settlement. It consisted of six co-operators, six trade unionists and an independent chairman.

All were chosen from panels. There was a special agreed panel of independent persons for independent chairman, e.g., lawyers, university professors. The co-operative panel consisted of four co-operators from each Section and four from each National Organisation in the scheme. The trade union panel consisted of four representatives of each union in the scheme.

In case of a dispute the trade union concerned selected from the panel the six trade union members, two of whom must represent unions not directly involved in the dispute. Co-operators likewise selected their six members from their panel, and two of these also must represent organisations not directly concerned. A decision could be arrived at by (a) a unanimous vote, (b) by a majority vote of both sides if the parties to the dispute agreed, (c) if neither of these was possible, by the arbitration of the chairman, if both parties consented and were agreeable.

The scheme proved successful and labour troubles were much less frequent and severe in the Co-operative Movement than else-where. It suffered, however, the disadvantage of not having the support of the C.W.S. or its subsidiaries, which believed that a Board so constituted, although suitable for retail societies, was not suitable for its labour questions.

C.W.S. and Trade Unions

The C.W.S., of course, employed a greater variety of labour than did the retail societies, and much of its labour, especially in its factories, was organised in trade unions which covered labour employed by private employers, with whom there were national agreements. In 1926 it was stated on behalf of the C.W.S. Board that it dealt with over seventy trade unions, but there were only half a dozen with which it had had any dispute, it observed the standard wages and conditions, " reductions or increases are con-ceded as they come forward," although it paid " better wages in the less protected trades than our competitors are paying—we want it understood that whatever variation takes place is to be recognised and applied by the Co-operative Wholesale Society."

It will be gathered that the C.W.S. did not desire to negotiate with co-operative labour as such, it was willing to recognise national agreements and where it felt necessary to improve upon them. As it could not join the various employers' federations which negotiated these national agreements with the trade unions whose membership included C.W.S. employees it could not take part in the collective bargaining involved. From a trade union as well as a co-operative viewpoint there were advantages in such a position. In the case of a strike the private employers would be subjected to more pressure if the C.W.S. employees remained at work, and trade consequently passed from them to the C.W.S., and the employees concerned were not drawing on the trade union strike funds. On the other hand, employees themselves might be unwilling to join trade unions in whose struggles they would not need to take direct part.

The belief that some employees did take that view resulted in the passing of a resolution in 1919 instructing the directors of the C.W.S. to " ensure that every employee who is eligible shall be a member of a trade union (recognised for affiliation to the Trades Union Congress)." This presented such difficulties that the Board resisted it, but opinion was adamant and insisted on its enforcement. A particularly dangerous situation, that of members of the A.U.C.E., was avoided by their return under the N.U.D.A.W. label to the T.U.C. fold. Not until 1925, however, were the numerous difficulties somewhat ironed out, and trade union membership made compulsory for C.W.S. employees. An attempt, in 1926, at a parallel compulsion for employees to become members of co-operative societies was fortunately defeated, a delegate rightly observing " How can you have Co-operation by compulsory methods? "

The C.W.S. was more seriously affected by the General Strike than were the retail societies, and it naturally desired to avoid repetitions of a similar character. This required the trade unions to recognise that employment by the C.W.S. was in a different category from capitalist employment. Not until 1938 was an agreement with the unions concerned made. This declared that the relationship of the Society with trade unionism differed fundamentally from that between trade unions and private enterprise, renewed the C.W.S. obligation to employ trade union labour only, the C.W.S. being promised exemption from any inter-union dispute, the C.W.S. pledged itself to demand trade union rates and conditions when making contracts with private employers and promised to try and secure the employment of trade union labour by such contractors. The unions undertook to assist the C.W.S. against low wage competition and that the C.W.S. should continue to follow variations in wages and conditions agreed upon in organised trades.

The unions concerned also came to an agreement with the C.W.S. on a system of conciliation for internal disputes similar to, but separate from, that which applied to the retail societies, and the Scottish Co-operative Wholesale Society operated a similar scheme.

Employee Representation

The Survey Committee's Report of 1919 considered the place of employees in co-operative societies and suggested that some societies should experiment with employees' representation on management committees. Many societies had rules preventing this and the common law, in practice, also did so. To make employees eligible for a management committee it was necessary for a specific rule to be made granting them this privilege. To obtain the inclusion of such a rule in the constitution of a society was not easy, but it was done in a number of societies, usually the bigger ones where an employees' vote could swamp that of the small proportion of interested members who attended meetings.

Regarded favourably by many leaders at the time of the General Survey, opinion was hardening towards the end of the period. This may have been due to experience or to the influence of Sydney and Beatrice Webb's long struggle against it. The Co-operative Union in 1939 declared: " While there may be exceptional cases, in the majority of instances it is not to the advantage of co-operative societies to permit employees to occupy seats on management committees," for the employees' interests " often conflict with those of the general membership " and " it is essential for the good government of societies that members of management committees should not have divided loyalties." If " co-operative societies still felt there should be an opportunity for employees to serve on management committees, the number should be restricted to not more than two, and the candidates should be chosen from and elected by the employees themselves and not by the general membership." Where this operated " no employee should have the right to vote for any other candidate." In 1939 about 80 societies had granted the privilege to employees to be eligible for election to management committees, and in sixty societies some employees had been elected, in most cases at elections open to the general membership in the usual way.

Wages and Conditions

The employees of co-operative retail societies enjoyed higher wages, a shorter working week and better prospects than the employees of private retailers. According to a Select Committee's report on shop assistants the average lengths of the working week for shop assistants were, bakers, 54 hours; butchers, 55; confectioners, 56; departmental stores, 48; drapery and clothing, 48; grocers, and provision dealers, 54. These are average figures, and many working weeks were, of course, much longer; some bakers worked a 75-hour week, some confectioners 80 hours, some departmental stores 60 hours, and some grocers 64 hours. In co-operative shops the maximum working week varied from 44 hours to 48 hours.

Ellen Wilkinson declared that " The combination of good wages and conditions, a high degree of remuneration and consequent security of tenure means that the Co-operative Movement gets the pick of workers in the distributive trade," but she refuted the opinion that the co-operative worker was selfishly concerned only with securing good conditions for himself: " Actually he is frequently found in the local Labour Parties and Trades Councils, a leading figure because he is used to dealing with the public and unlikely to be victimised by his employer." The Co-operative Movement in its position as an employer thus benefited the whole Labour movement.

CONTRIBUTIONS TO CO-OPERATIVE THOUGHT

There was a good deal published on the Movement during the period without there being any notable advance in co-operative thought. Sidney and Beatrice Webb's *The Consumers' Co-operative Movement* 1921, gave a descriptive and analytical survey with observations on organisation and structure which will be worth studying for a long time to come. But its fundamental ideas on purpose and principles and its insistence on consumer Co-operation and rejection of producer Co-operation, were the same as those of the earlier book by Beatrice Potter in 1891. The Webbs stressed consumer Co-operation as the practicable alternative to capitalism, i.e., " a means by which the operations of industry must be carried on under democratic control without the incentive of profit-making or the stimulus of pecuniary gain " and they theorised on the place of Co-operation in a socialist state.

S. and B. Webb

In their *Constitution for a Socialist Commonwealth* 1920, the Webbs discussed the place of voluntary consumer Co-operation in such a commonwealth and gave it a very big and important place indeed. There would be no limits on its expansion, although its primary field would be the production and distribution of goods for domestic consumption. Nationalisation, naturally a second best to the socialist, would be rare. Out of all the many hundreds of industries and services that went to make up the economic and social life of the nation, only half a dozen or so would need to be organised and directed nationally. As socialists the Webbs had a natural preference for social ownership and control, i.e., by societies, and regarded trade unions and co-operative societies as social tissue, " of actually greater importance than the State itself." They also held that it was in " the spontaneous undergrowth of social tissue, rather than in a further hypertrophy of the national government that will be found, for the most part, the institutions destined to increasingly supersede the capitalist system."

Unfortunately, few socialists or co-operators ever read works requiring the serious application which those of the Webbs demand, so that only slowly and gradually do their ideas permeate even the formative opinion of these Movements.

On contemporary questions affecting the Movement, the Webbs gave reasoned cases against the idea of a national society, against the merging of the Wholesales and the Co-operative Union, against employees sitting on management committees. They were strong defenders of dividend, but against high prices to provide it, and emphasised the need to improve the machinery of democracy in order to make democratic control more effective.

The translations of the works of some foreign co-operative thinkers affected the thought of co-operative students in this country. Most notable among these were the *Principles of Political Economy, Consumers' Co-operative Societies*, and *History of Economic Doctrines* (with M. Rist) by Professor Charles Gide; *The Co-operative Republic* by E. Poisson; and *Co-operative Ideals and Problems* by Anders Örne.

C. Gide

Gide was first attracted to the Co-operative Movement by an account of the Rochdale Pioneers, and his co-operative theories were firmly based on Rochdale principles. He saw consumer Co-operation as not only a means to a better economic system with a more just distribution of income but one which by abolishing the profit motive would facilitate moral progress, for it would abolish advertisement, lying, cheating, and inducements to extravagance. He saw the possibility of the growth of co-operative societies gradually transforming a capitalist order into a co-operative one, each co-operative society " already constitutes a little world organised in conformity with justice and social benefit, and it is sufficient to let it develop spontaneously, either by growth or imitation, to realise in the more or less distant future, the best of all possible worlds."

Gide was able to discern the fundamental ideals and principles, the nature of the Co-operative Movement, amongst all the welter of opinions, fashionable tendencies, attempted adoption of contemporary business practices, distortions of the co-operative idea which so often have befogged " outsiders " when attempting to make surveys of the Movement. He had a broader view of the Movement than had the Webbs, it was not confined to the consumer Movement, but included the producer Movement. He saw social values in this type of Co-operation similar to those which the great English economist, Alfred Marshall, had observed. He had confidence that both these forms of Co-operation together with agricultural Co-operation would eventually develop into and realise a complete harmony. Gide's thought was something of a synthesis of the consumer theories and those of the Christian Socialists.

E. Poisson

E. Poisson, active in the French socialist movement, a close associate of Jean Jaures, the great French socialist statesman, became friendly with Gide and took from him the ideal of a republic based on the principles of Co-operation. In his *Co-operative Republic* he expounded a theory of social evolution according to which the gradual development of Co-operation would transform capitalism into a co-operative system. Although it germinated in free competition and developed with capitalism, it developed a creative power of its own which operated in all social circumstances. The co-operative society was adapted to all natural states of society, not merely to those in which it first appeared. All races, all climates, all civilisations, were suitable for Co-operation. In essence, Poisson's ideal and theory of co-operative evolution were similar to those of Dr. William King and to that of the many co-operative idealists already mentioned. The *Co-operative Republic* was translated into English by W. P. Watkins in 1925.

A. Örne

In 1926, an English translation appeared of *Co-operative Ideals and Problems* by Anders Örne. He was prominent in the Swedish Labour as well as the Co-operative Movement. As financial secretary to the Government, Minister of Communications and Transport, Vice-President of the Swedish National Bank, and Director of the Post Office, he had considerable experience as politician, statesman and government official. As President of the Stockholm Society, for many years the editor of the newspaper *Kooperativa Forbundet*, and a member of the I.C.A. Executive he had also much co-operative experience. Although he had little time for the " Utopian " schemes of Robert Owen, holding that Co-operation arose out of the direct economic interests in goods and services of those participating, his conclusions regarding the nature of Co-operation, its ideals and principles were well within the traditional co-operative fold.

He found Co-operation to be the antithesis of capitalism in that capitalism was based on the motive of profit seeking whereas Co-operation was based on the direct interest of those co-operating. A great admirer and upholder of the Rochdale principles, he held that they contained all that was needed and nothing that was super-fluous for the foundations of a new form of every-day economy, " their application to business life would imply more startling changes than the bloodiest revolution ever wrought." He was a firm believer in democracy and in what democracy implies and depends upon—freedom and knowledge. Consequently he was opposed to monopolies, to economic planning which created them, and to the extension of the scope and power of the State.

The development of Co-operation was, to Anders Örne, the only means of creating a better economic and social order, free from the defects of capitalism and of state absolutism. A better order was not to be obtained by simply marking a cross in the proper place and leaving the rest to the government. Yet he also insisted on system and organisation within the Movement and the need for new ideas in the management of large societies which, in spite of the work of the Webbs and F. Hall, were not given adequate attention in the British Movement.

L. Woolf

Leonard Woolf in *Co-operation and The Future of Industry* 1918, and *Co-operation and Socialism* 1921, gave a socialist appre-ciation of the place of Co-operation in the progress to socialism and in a socialist state. He believed that Co-operation " contains within it the germs of a rational system of industry and that under that system the Movement would develop into the organ for carrying on industry democratically in the interests of the com-munity." He went further than the Webbs and argued that the whole of industry would be best controlled by organisations of consumers and he sketched the outlines of a Co-operative Com-monwealth. But he was not content that Co-operation should be left to expand by voluntary association alone. It should have the active assistance of the whole Labour and Socialist Movement to further such expansion. He held that " the co-operative system implied as its logical end an organisation of the whole community as consumers for the control of industry, and that such an organisation can be effected at any time by legisla-tion."

Thus Woolf advocated that Labour Governments should, instead of nationalisation or municipalisation, hand over services and industries to consumers organised in the existing co-operative system. Only thus could the profit-making motive be abolished and effective democratic control introduced, for he took a poor view of nationalised or municipal enterprises ever becoming truly socialist in nature or aim.

Woolf's solution, however, appealed to few socialists or co-operators. Socialists could still enjoy roseate dreams of nationalised industries managed with a hundred per cent efficiency, in which all labour would be keen to give its utmost for the good of the community, in which plant and machinery would always be the most modern and fluctuations in demands unknown, and in which economic, social and technical problems would be almost automatically solved. These dreams compared very favourably, of course, with the concrete realities of co-operative societies in existence, with their financial, labour and business problems, generally of a very mundane character and not to be solved by a brilliant speech, the coining of a catching slogan, or the passing of a resolution. Co-operators and the Webbs, on the other hand, objected to the discarding of the principle of voluntarism which Woolf's policy involved, and had no desire that their Movement or business should become the sport of politics.

F. Hall

These opinions of Woolf, however, had some influence, as many speeches at Co-operative Congresses and Conferences showed. But co-operators during the period were generally more concerned with the immediate problems of finance, trade, systems of management, the place of and relations with employees, the competition of the multiples, the obstacles imposed by marketing boards. A good deal of valuable and urgently necessary thought was given to these questions, and a more scientific approach was promoted, largely by F. Hall, whose *Handbook for Members of Co-operative Committees* was not only the reference book on many co-operative officials' desks, but also contained a good deal of co-operative philosophy in the advice given upon practical problems. Yet the big problems raised by the Webbs, Woolf, Gide, Poisson and Örne, were not considered or discussed adequately. The Movement became increasingly neglectful of ends, and concentrated upon means, which could not be understood without relating them to the ends which they should serve.

University Survey

A survey of the Movement was made by a group of University professors and lecturers under the auspices of the C.W.S., and published in 1938 as *Consumers Co-operation in Great Britain*.

Although it was not without factual errors and some of its opinions suggested a lack of understanding, possibly due to a neglect of the history of the Movement, it deserved far more attention than it ever received. This was partly due to the disturbed international situation in 1938 and 1939, with the outbreak of war in the latter year, to the size of the book, to its detailed nature, much of the detail being quickly out of date, and to the disinclination of the Movement to accept advice from outside.

On the whole the Movement came well out of the survey, but to many the most interesting and significant finding was in the concluding paragraph, " it is the only alternative scheme of economic organisation actually in existence in this country, and the only attempt at general economic planning on a large scale. It has achieved its present scope and dimensions without sacrificing anything of the principle of voluntarism. It may, therefore, be regarded as the possible middle way between *laissez faire* liberalism and rigid planning on a compulsory basis, and in this respect it has a strong claim to the allegiance of all those who believe that some form of economic planning is necessary, in the interests of order and justice, but who dislike the element of coercion in other systems which are offered for their approval."

The university survey thus agreed with the possibility and the desirability of a co-operative system replacing the existing one, thus supporting the claims of co-operative theorists from Dr. King onwards. A review of the book in the socialist journal *New Statesman and Nation* pointed out that the book had much to teach to those who were not co-operators. The vast majority of socialists were blind to the significance and possibilities of the consumers' Co-operative Movement because they were unconsciously themselves permeated by capitalist psychology, unable to dissociate profit from economics, unable to regard anything except the producer or production as the right basis in economic organisation. " Hence they are never able to see . . . that the consumer and consumption should be made the basis of Socialist organisation. Hence, too, their neglect of the Co-operative Movement as it stands before their eyes potentially the purest and most profit-proof form of Socialism and in fact the only Socialist alternative to the capitalist system which, in this country, exists and works successfully."

It was, however, unfortunate that only a small proportion of co-operators, too, realised the potentialities, significance and ideals of their Movement. " Outsiders " such as the Webbs, Woolf, or the University professors had far more confidence in the Movement than had many co-operators themselves. Some of these were in fact State socialists and regarded the Co-operative Movement as simply a fore-runner of state socialism. It was not surprising therefore that the vast majority of socialists continued in their blindness to the significance and possibilities of the Co-operative Movement.

9 CO-OPERATION IN THE 1939-45 WAR

" *The Co-operative Movement, like all other democratic movements, must be prepared to use to the full
its resources to assist in bringing the conflict to a
successful issue for the democratic cause.*"
(*Statement of the National Co-operative Authority,
September 8th, 1939.*)

THE outbreak of war in 1939 confronted the country with
similar problems to those of 1914, but it was better prepared
to meet them. Experience of the previous war provided knowledge
of the kind and nature of problems likely to be encountered.
Government and governed were also influenced by a different
social philosophy from that of 1914. *Laissez faire* had been
largely discarded, the economic planning of the 'thirties had
accustomed people to government planning, conscription for the
Forces was already in being, the country was well conditioned to
meet the economic and social consequences of modern war. Moreover, this war was more generally supported and regarded as just
than any other war in which the country had been engaged. There
was consequently a willingness to submit to war-time discipline
with its hardships, loss of freedoms and sacrifices because of the
belief that they were necessary to victory and that the consequences
of defeat would be even more grievous.

The crux of the problem was to devote as large a proportion
of the nation's resources to war purposes as possible without
inflation getting out of hand. A system of controls, many inter-
locking, developed, and there was even some degree of overall
control. Some of these were physical, e.g. of raw materials, some
financial and fiscal. Physical controls were usually directly imposed over the Movement and usages of men, plant, and materials.
Financial and fiscal controls were largely used to take away the
money income from the public which was surplus to that necessary
to purchase the goods permitted to be produced and sold at
regulated prices.

Rationing

Attempts to control food prices were made by fixing maximum
prices, both wholesale and retail, of all kinds of foodstuffs, by the

Ministry of Food. Legal maximum prices lead to all manner of abuses and evasions unless some means of sharing out available supplies is employed, i.e. rationing. It was anticipated that rationing of the basic foodstuffs would be introduced almost immediately, but owing to some administrative muddle this was not possible. Rationing did not come until January, 1940, then being applied to bacon, ham, butter, margarine and cooking fats, and sugar. In March of that year, meat, and in July, tea, were rationed. In 1941 cheese and preserves were included and an ingenious system of " points " rationing was introduced for goods, such as canned goods and dried fruits, which could only be legitimately bought if a requisite number of points coupons were handed over. Each consumer had a limited number of coupons, and a retailer's future supplies depended on the number of coupons he had acquired.

This eased the problem of allocating supplies on an equitable basis, gave the consumer some freedom of choice, and also made it possible to adjust demand to supply by changing the " points " value of a commodity without changing its price. In addition to these rations, children obtained midday meals in schools, many workers obtained meals in canteens, and a government enterprise, British Restaurants, also provided reasonably priced and, for wartime, nutritious and palatable meals.

Consumer goods other than foodstuffs were more difficult to control. Attempts at price-fixing were made at first by the Prices of Goods Act, 1939, which sought to restrict the prices of individual traders to increases justified by their individual increases of costs. This act was impossible to enforce. It was followed by the severer and much more effective Goods and Services (Price Control) Act, June, 1941, which gave the Board of Trade powers to fix maximum prices for any goods other than food, either new or second-hand and to fix maximum profit margins at all stages from manufacturer to retailer.

A rationing scheme on "points" was applied to clothes and footwear in 1941, but did not satisfactorily solve the problem of adequate supplies of cheap clothing to meet even the rationed demands.

Controls

The introduction of " Utility " schemes helped to solve this problem, and also those posed by the price control act of 1941. With clear specifications of goods whose prices and profit margins were to be fixed, the Utility schemes not only simplified the problems of price and profits control but also provided the public with good, cheap, and reliable goods.

Production of civilian goods was also cut down by prohibition, e.g. of housebuilding, and by a licensing system for scarce raw materials. The need for effective controls over the uses of raw materials increased as the war proceeded. A complicated system developed, under which licences to obtain raw materials were granted under schedules of priorities.

In a rough and ready fashion the controls worked, though there were many stories, probably exaggerated, of anomalies, bottle-necks, evasions and so forth. People also complained that the Government Departments concerned often lacked foresight, waiting until imminent danger of collapse in supply of a raw material forced them to take necessary steps. They also exhibited a good deal of tenderness for old vested interests. Boards which purchased and imported for the Government, valued the com-modity, arranged its distribution, and took the risk, nevertheless paid commissions to the former importing merchants, whose functions were now difficult to detect. "Instead of effecting all those real economies (in terms of plant and labour) in distribution which a monopoly position should give, the controls have, in many cases, simply superimposed a bureaucratic machine on top of the normal channels of trade which no longer perform any real function at all. The result is waste and inefficiency." (*The Raw Materials Controls*, G. D. N. Worswick.)

The task, however, was difficult, and the controls, although there were many defects, many due to circumstances impossible to remedy, did accomplish the main purpose of diverting raw materials from civilian to war industries. To produce a com-modity might require several licences from different authorities, so that whilst one control might be evaded, others would be effective. This system of control was generally effective in stopping production of less essential goods, but it also often resulted in frustration, holdups and waste of time and effort, and was a handicap to recovery after the war.

Labour

Among the effective controls was that of labour. As the demand for men and women by the forces, civil services, and war industries increased, the shortage of labour, especially skilled labour, became increasingly acute. Powers were given to the Ministry of Labour and National Service to direct any person to perform any service of which he or she was capable.

All adult persons had to register, all jobs had to be filled through the Employment Exchanges and people were directed to the work or to districts in which it was thought they would be best employed.

Millions of people were moved from their homes and transferred to war work in other parts of the country. Many had never worked in factories before. They had to be trained, organised, and the various social problems arising from their mobilisation and transference met. Without the active co-operation of the trade unions this organisation and transfer of labour could never have been made.

In such circumstances, labour, particularly skilled labour essential to war industries, could have forced up wages to extravagant heights. But the controls prevented employers competing for labour, prevented individual workmen changing jobs to " better themselves," and directed labour to the work required without having to offer higher wages to induce the change.

Thus, although there was no direct control over wages, there was control over the factors which influence or determine wages. Wages were increased as the cost of living rose, but a policy of stabilising the cost of living was followed, largely by price controls and subsidies.

Weekly wage rates, it is estimated, had risen at June, 1945 by 49 per cent on those of September, 1939. Earnings, due to overtime and bonuses, had risen by 80 per cent. During the same period the cost of living index, which underestimated the rise, had gone up by 32 per cent. From earnings, however, were deducted income tax and insurance, so the net money incomes of wage earners did not increase by as much as may at first sight appear.

Actually, with rationing and general shortages there was very little on which increased money income could be spent. Expenditure on food, clothing, household goods, was considerably reduced, clothing from £446 million in 1938 to £275 million in 1944 at 1938 prices, and household goods from £288 million to £100 million. As there was little which could be done with increased earnings, the recipients had money to save or burn, which some proceeded to do literally, the consumption of tobacco increased, and so did expenditure on entertainment. A huge quantity of surplus monetary purchasing power, together with unsatisfied desires produce black markets, which were by no means unknown, but fiscal and financial policies lessened this danger.

Taxation

Monetary purchasing power surplus to the requirements of the planned war economy was abstracted from the pockets of the public by taxation, forced bank loans to the Treasury, forced loans from the public (post war credits) and voluntary savings, encouraged by the National Savings Movement. Increased rates of old taxes and the introduction of some new ones were, however, the principal means of extraction.

Income tax was increased until the standard rate reached 10/- in the pound. Earned income and family allowances were reduced, resulting, together with the inflated rise of wages, in millions of wage earners coming within the scope of income tax for the first time. The old methods of tax collection would have been inadequate, it would have been impossible to have collected the tax annually from the millions of weekly wage earners. Moreover, if the inflationary pressure of the surplus wage income were to be lessened it was necessary that it should be taxed and collected weekly.

To overcome these difficulties the Pay As You Earn (P.A.Y.E.) system of tax collection on wage and salary earners was introduced. Although it operated efficiently, it had, and has, two serious objections. Firstly, there was the expense of calculating the tax weekly or monthly by the Inland Revenue authorities and by employers. Second, and of more importance, it induced less willingness to work. Additional earnings due to overtime or increased effort on piece work, were immediately subjected to tax, and were consequently discouraged whereas absenteeism, although resulting in less earnings, was partially compensated by a lower tax payment and so encouraged. The injurious effects of this, however, were not serious until the years after the war, when the incentives of belligerent patriotism had gone.

A new tax on profits, the National Defence Contribution, had been imposed in 1937, to this was added the Excess Profits Tax (E.P.T.) at first in 1939, 60 per cent, later in 1942, 100 per cent. They operated alternatively, according to whether current profits were reckoned as excessive or not. Profits were reckoned as excessive if they exceeded those of a certain pre-war year, 1935 or 1936, or the average of 1935 and 1937, or the average of 1936 and 1937. Only the excess was subjected to E.P.T. If, during the period when E.P.T. was levied, profits fell below the standard revenue, the deficiencies would be set off against tax already paid.

The popular justification for the tax was that none should make a profit out of the war, but although politically justified, it was inequitable and uneconomic, because firms making high profits before the war could continue to make them, while others, say in depressed industries or then under inefficient management, could not retain even normal profits. Thus some firms making low profits might be taxed 100 per cent, while others making high profits were free of E.P.T. The tax also removed a strong incentive to increased efficiency, discouraged investment and encouraged evasion. Bad practices and habits which developed in war time did not disappear when peace came. The tax had some peculiar and injurious effects upon the Co-operative Movement which will be dealt with later.

Another new tax was Purchase Tax, introduced in 1940 and imposed, at different rates, upon a wide range of goods. It was an attractive tax to the economic planners, for it enabled demands for particular goods to be increased or decreased by lowering or raising the tax upon them; it also enabled revenue to be raised from the wage earning classes without the ill-effects of raising equivalent amounts by increased income tax.

Little opposition was expressed to the tax except by the Co-operative Movement. The Glasgow Congress, 1940, passed a resolution of protest against the serious addition to indirect taxation upon clothing and other necessaries of life. The Co-operative Party fought the tax in the House of Commons, although in the main the Labour Party supported it. Co-operators feared that this tax would probably remain long after the emergency had passed. Their fears proved to be well founded.

Some indication of the increased burden of taxation is provided by a comparison of the yields of some of the principal taxes in 1938–1939 and 1944–1945. Income tax increased from £336 million to £1,317 million, death duties from £77 million to £111 million, N.D.C. from £22 million to £33 million, E.P.T. from nil to £477 million, Customs and Excise from £340 million to £1,076 million, the Ordinary Revenue as a whole increased from £927 million to £3,238 million.

Saving

Such heavy taxation, of course, curtailed spending, except by Government, and the increase of saving further contributed to that end. Much of this saving was loaned to the Government, the National Debt increasing from £7,247 million in 1939 to £21,473 million in 1945. " National " Savings, i.e. National Savings Certificates, Defence Bonds, Post Office Bank, Trustee Savings Banks, increased from nearly £30 million net receipts in 1938–1939 to £626 million net receipts in 1944–1945.

Other means of saving favoured by the small saver must also be considered. The cessation of house building and the property risks of war, naturally lessened the enterprise and activities of building societies, the numbers of share investors and depositors in them decreased, although the value of shares increased by £37 million, that of deposits decreased by £7 million. The income of life assurance companies increased from £137 million to £164 million;

the total funds of Friendly Societies from £155 million to £192 million; the share and loan capital of retail co-operative societies from £216 million to £325 million.

Foreign Trade

Another serious problem was that of Britain's foreign trade. The country needed to import not only foodstuffs but also vast quantities of raw materials and finished goods for war purposes. A big increase in agriculture, together with rationing reduced the need for imported food and feedingstuffs. But imports were vital, shipping difficulties due to submarine warfare and mines were not the only ones to be surmounted. The country had to persuade overseas suppliers to sell Britain their goods.

In many parts of the world, e.g., Africa, Egypt, India, supplies were obtained largely by running into debt for them, but the United States of America sought to prevent becoming involved by operating a " Cash and Carry " policy. Imports from the U.S.A. had to be paid for in cash, and carried in ships other than those of the U.S.A.

To obtain the necessary foreign exchange for this Britain had to export goods, and sell British investments overseas. All holders of foreign investments had to register their holdings and surrender them for British Government stock on demand. Britain's economic plans had, therefore, to include the maintenance of a strong export drive.

After March, 1941, the U.S.A. adopted the more helpful Lend Lease, under which Britain was able to borrow unlimited sums. But American exporters had objections to the competition of British exporters getting cheap raw materials through Lend Lease, so British exports were reduced to maintain goodwill, an action which was severely condemned later. It has been described as not merely audacity but downright recklessness for Britain, dependent for her living on abnormally large imports to surrender her visible export markets whilst her invisible exports also were withering away through the realisation of her overseas capital holdings and the destruction of her mercantile marine.

CO-OPERATIVE UNION DURING THE WAR

The Movement had to adapt itself quickly to the war economy barely outlined above. Although the Co-operative Union was in consultation with various Government Departments engaged in making War Defence plans before the outbreak, a continuous and ever-increasing spate of regulations, controls, rationing, new taxes, conscription and direction of labour, shifting of population, war damage, shortages, etc. faced every society and organisation with a host of new problems. The first requisite to their solution was the speedy provision of correct information.

To meet this need the Co-operative Union issued the *War Emergency Circular*[1], which notified societies within 24 hours of changes which would affect the running of their societies. Not only were information and advice given, but regulations were also explained, a time-saving device to over-worked officials who would otherwise have had to wrestle with the jargon and quasi-legal phraseology in which the regulations were expressed. The Publications Department was responsible for issuing the *Circular*, and the advisory departments of the Co-operative Union supplied it with much of the material. Indicative of the flood of regulations and of the service provided, it needed to be issued almost daily; in six years following September, 1939, 1,143 issues were made referring to 15,848 items.

The *Circular*, was of course, insufficient to meet all the needs for advice by societies. Each department of the Co-operative Union was subjected to requests for information as changes took place, each department had to be keyed up in anticipation of such requests immediately a change was made. And changes were of daily occurrence. Many of these were of serious consequence. Heavy rates of income tax and E.P.T., for instance, made the submission of correct returns and claims for allowances of increasing importance. The Co-operative Union gave advice, helped with returns, fought issues with the Inland Revenue, and recovered for societies hundreds of thousands of pounds in repayments of tax. Its advice, or assistance when societies were negotiating directly with the Inland Revenue, must have saved them many times more.

The Labour Department also found its advisory work multiplied as the male employees of societies were called up for military service or transferred to war work and then their female staffs subjected to similar call up and transfers. Societies' interests were fought for at the highest levels on lines of national policy when the call up of different classes was being considered or undertaken, at local levels and even in individual cases. With the replacement of regular staff by " substitute labour " and part-time workers, together with rises of wages, conditions of labour and wages problems also increased.

To deal with general problems a National Council of Hours and Wages Boards was established at the beginning of the war. It served many useful purposes and its work revealed the need for

---

[1] Later it became The *Co-operative Gazette*.

more national co-ordination in labour matters—over 300 wage agreements with trade unions covered the 250,000 people employed by the retail societies. It also represented the Movement in national bodies set up to deal with labour problems in their respective trades or industries. These Joint Industrial Councils agreed upon wage rates, which although not legal minima, as with Trade Boards, were in fact recognised as standard rates, and in the case of a dispute would have been so regarded by an Arbitration Court.

In the distributive trades, however, apart from the co-operative societies, trade union organisation was very weak; there was a large number of very small firms, so that probably a large proportion of distributive workers received less than the J.I.C. rates. The Co-operative Movement through the National Council was represented on eight Joint Industrial Councils. It had consequently a voice in determining J.I.C. rates, and tried to bring these up to co-operative levels, hoping for the time when there would be one uniform level of wage rates for all distributive workers, instead of a J.I.C. level and a co-operative level.

The Agricultural and Marketing Department was immediately concerned with interferences affecting the supplies of many important foodstuffs. Significantly the Government soon ceased to rely on the national marketing organisations of producers which had been set up in peace time for within a few months they had disappeared. There were many strong complaints from societies at first, due probably to the general muddle and lack of foresight of the Ministry.

Stocks of food were commandeered by the Government and distributed to retailers. Co-operators and their societies naturally objected when, as did happen in a case cited by A. V. Alexander in a Commons debate, a society had no supply of butter whilst multiples in the same town were selling C.W.S. branded butter.

A deputation from the Parliamentary Committee of the Co-operative Union met the Premier in 1939 to press for the introduction of sugar rationing although a section of the popular press was at the time opposed to rationing. However, as rationing was introduced and controls developed grievances lessened although they by no means disappeared. Close contacts by the Co-operative Union with Government Departments developed. The existence of the co-operative trading associations proved invaluable for they were able to consider general issues and make representations to a Ministry on behalf of the whole Movement. Considerable assistance was given to societies in negotiating general rulings regarding the flood of orders and instructions and in securing licences for the maintenance or increase of co-operative trade.

H

As agriculture became more profitable during the war there was a tendency for societies to engage in or increase their farming activities. The Agricultural Department did not encourage this, for the increased prosperity was due to abnormal conditions, subsidies, absence of foreign competition, and the long term prospects did not appear bright. It will be remembered that on the average the Co-operative Movement suffered a loss on its agricultural activities every year from 1919 to 1939. Profits were made during the war, but these reached their peak in 1943 and declined afterwards.

THE CO-OPERATIVE PARTY

The Co-operative Party supported war with Germany in 1939. It remained with the Labour Party as part of the official opposition until the formation of the Coalition Government under Winston Churchill in 1940, when A. V. Alexander resumed his old post as First Lord of the Admiralty. A political truce between the major parties was agreed upon in May, 1940, and consequently most public political activity was suspended. Yet the Party continued to grow and to build up and improve its organisation. The number of affiliated societies increased from 516 in 1940 to 668 in 1945 and affiliated membership from 6,161,000 to 8,833,000.

THE GUILDS

The Guilds went through a difficult period. Evacuation, war work, national service, commandeering of rooms, air raids, blackouts, made it difficult and in some areas, dangerous for groups such as Guild branches to meet. Membership consequently declined in catastrophic fashion.

In general the Guilds had been growing and developing very satisfactorily in the pre-war years, the English Women's Guild with 87,246 members in 1939 was within reach of its desired objective of 100,000 members. In 1941 its membership had declined to 49,122. From thenceforward it began to increase slowly, and in 1946 it was approaching 56,000. The Scottish Women's Guild did not suffer so severely. Its membership slumped from 33,000 to 22,000 in 1942 but then steadily increased so that in 1946 it had surpassed its pre-war figure with a membership of 39,046. The National Co-operative Men's Guild, with 15,000 members and on an average one new branch being opened each week on the eve of the outbreak, consoled itself after two years of war because it still retained three-fifths of that membership, one-third of which was serving in the forces.

Diminution of membership created financial difficulties and restricted Guild activities, but a survey of the history of each of the Guilds during the war shows considerable vitality, and to remain in being was itself an achievement for some. The Guilds were active in co-operative affairs, exercising their old influence, concerned with broader social and political issues, making men and women aware of the vast potentialities of the Co-operative Movement and engaging them in its voluntary service.

CO-OPERATIVE EDUCATION

Co-operative education received a severe setback. Most of its students were, of course, conscripted. Evacuation of children broke up junior classes and youth groups. Commandeering of halls and other premises by the military and civil defence services often made it impossible to provide suitable accommodation for classes. The educational schemes of some local education authorities collapsed and their facilities for co-operative classes with them. Air raids, blackout, difficulties of transport, overtime, and shift work, made it always difficult if not impossible for students to attend classes.

Not surprisingly some societies ceased educational activities. There was a rapid decline in the number of students, from a total of 69,535 in 1938–1939 to 13,466 in 1940; the most severe losses showing in the Junior and Intermediate classes which fell from 39,217 to 2,524 and in the Technical Classes which dropped from 23,529 to 7,101.

The Education Department of the Co-operative Union had to make rapid adjustments to wartime circumstances in order to keep in being the educational ideals and activities of the Movement. War did not remove the necessity for the continuance of the Movement making co-operators, but it did make it more difficult. Special war-time courses for individual home study by correspondence or by discussion study groups with correspondence, were provided in contemporary economic, social, international, and co-operative problems.

All these served useful purposes but it was significant that by far the most popular subjects were the co-operative ones. In spite of the world-wide nature of the war, the catastrophic effects of the collapse of international relations, and the economic and social problems confronting each individual and the country, co-operators attracted to study under Co-operative auspices were apparently more interested in their own Movement than in these wider issues. The courses appealed to many who had not previously attempted correspondence or group study although there was a decline in numbers taking them towards the end of the war, probably due to the attraction of a Rochdale Centenary course.

Special war-time correspondence courses were also provided for junior and " diluted " employees, but the numbers of these declined sharply after the first couple of years, and they were never as popular as the co-operative subjects. In spite of difficulties the standard correspondence courses after the first severe contraction maintained themselves and the numbers taking them were beginning to increase before the end of the war. Many students whilst serving with the forces continued their studies by correspondence tuition, and some who were prisoners of war also did so. There were cases of co-operative students in prisoner-of-war camps interesting other prisoners and small study groups being formed. In the 1944 Congress Report it was stated that, " In one camp a school has been constructed, classes organised and a small library of co-operative books built up."

The Co-operative College was the only adult residential college to remain open throughout the war, in spite of Holyoake House and the college hostels in Kersal being damaged in air raids. Tuition in the standard diploma courses continued, but in addition short-term courses were provided for Co-operative members and employees and for men of the Polish and Canadian forces. These short-term courses proved valuable, not only to the students but also to the College, for numbers of adult co-operators experienced and appreciated the value of residential study and became its good friends. Many of these later came to hold responsible and important positions in the Guilds, societies and national co-operative organisations.

In general, the Co-operative Union sought to keep the educational machinery of the Movement in being, to take advantage of whatever opportunities were presented for educational activity and to prepare for considerable educational advance when the war was over. The Educational Convention continued to be held each Easter week-end. Although adult summer schools were confined to and concentrated in Bangor, they were run successfully and became increasingly popular. Indeed after a sharp decline in 1940 attendance at summer schools increased until it attained a record in 1945.

Co-operative Youth

Co-operative Youth organisations were re-organised. All the youth organisations were brought into one National Co-operative Youth Organisation covering the age range 7–18 or 20. The British Federation of Co-operative Youth (B.F.C.Y.), however, remained outside; it changed its name to British Federation of Young Co-operators (B.F.Y.C.) and was to consist of young men and women between ages 18 to 20–25. It was hoped it would bridge the gap between the youth clubs and such organisations as the Guilds and the Co-operative Party.

In 1943 a new body was established, Co-operative Youth Centres, largely due to the initiative of the Co-operative Union Youth Organiser, J. L. Willson. This body intended to buy buildings which could be used as residential centres for co-operative youth. Tong Hall, an old mansion near Bradford was first purchased and opened, followed soon by Dalston Hall, near Carlisle.

Family life and discipline were seriously disturbed by absence of fathers in the services and mothers engaged on war work. The realisation of probable consequential dangers stimulated a considerable interest in youth organisations by the Government and the public. Although co-operative youth clubs were not founded for the purpose of remedying the deficiencies of parents, or finding tasks or recreations to occupy the time of idle hands, they benefited from the public interest stimulated in youth organisations. Local authorities, educational bodies, and others became aware of what was one of the major voluntary youth organisations in the country, and the Board of Education and the Scottish Board of Education made grants for the furtherance of its work.

The Educational Council also concerned itself with the problem of educational advance when the war was over. It united with the National Union of Teachers, the Workers' Educational Association and the Trades Union Congress in 1943 to form the joint Council for Educational Advance. Educational reform was in the air, an Education Bill was being drafted, there was need for influence, pressure and propaganda to bring about a truly progressive measure.

Even when the Education Act of 1944 had been passed, which in spite of various imperfections did make possible a real advance, the activities of such a body were still necessary. Immense powers to make or mar were put in the hands of the Minister of Education and, as a politician, what he would or would not do would be mainly determined by public opinion. Unfortunately public opinion in England has been lukewarm if not hostile to the education of the masses—hence the need for bodies to engage in the struggle for better education for all.

A New College

The Co-operative Movement, however, whilst taking part in this struggle was not unmindful of its own special responsibilities and example. The value of a Co-operative College had been shown before the war, there was still the need to provide a building and equipment adequate for residential education on a scale commensurate with the Movement's requirements. Schemes were being prepared and considered before the war, which the outbreak of war brought to nothing, but it was felt that 1944 was an occasion so suited to an appeal for funds for the purpose that even war must not prevent it being made.

It was hoped that the celebration of the Centenary of the Rochdale Pioneers would focus attention on their ideals and principles and it was " difficult to imagine a more fitting and lasting tribute to the Rochdale Pioneers than the establishment of a properly equipped college worthy of the British Co-operative Movement." Hence an appeal was made to the Movement in 1944 for a new college fund. The target was £250,000, which could be raised in seven years by subscriptions of 1d. per member per annum. More than half the amount was subscribed in a few months, but this came from the more progressive societies. By 1946 many societies had not contributed in any way and the fund was still far short of the target.

Meanwhile the Co-operative Union had, in 1945, purchased the mansion and estate of Stanford Hall, which had come into the market as a result of the death of its owner, Sir Julian Cahn. It consisted of extensive buildings, 300 acres of land, including tennis courts, cricket and football fields, swimming pool, and bowling green. There were excellent facilities for sport and recreation and buildings capable of adaptation for study and accommodation. The purchase price was £54,000 and the Education Executive was certainly justified in stating that " as the price of land is today and as building costs stand, it would be impossible for the Union either to build (in the event of permission being granted) or to acquire for £54,000 anything comparable with Stanford Hall." By the time building restrictions were removed and the building of a Co-operative College made possible, costs were very much higher. The Movement was indeed fortunate that the opportunity of purchasing a place such as Stanford Hall occurred when it did, and that the Union had the enterprise to take advantage of it. Nevertheless, Stanford Hall had still to be converted into a college—but the task and the expense of doing this belong to the post-war period.

RETAIL SOCIETIES DURING THE WAR

The retail societies though assisted by the services of their federal organisations had themselves to meet and solve the problems of wartime.   All faced depletions of staff, training of women, rationing and controls. Some, however, had mass evacuations with accompanying withdrawals of share capital and loss of trade. Folkestone, for instance, lost 70 per cent of its population and not surprisingly the Society's trade fell by 50 per cent. At one time, owing to mass evacuation, the registrations of the Royal Arsenal Society fell by 40 per cent and its trade by £2 million.

Many societies suffered damage to premises by air raids, some very heavily. Societies which suffered sudden destruction and loss were presented with serious problems of reorganisation which had to be solved quickly and effectively, for though bakeries and milk depots might be destroyed their members still required morning milk and bread. The metropolitan societies claim to have never missed a delivery, although houses were sometimes missing when the deliveries arrived.

A few instances illustrate the suddenness and severity of the problems sometimes confronting societies. Brightside and Carbrook Society had its great modern emporium with 45 departments, one of the finest buildings in Sheffield, and its administrative offices and equipment, destroyed in a single night. Clydebank in two evenings had 38 shops destroyed and 56 badly damaged. Greenock East End in two nights had all its shops damaged, its offices, bakery, hall and garage practically destroyed and its general manager, killed. Societies such as Plymouth, Exeter, Hull, Liverpool, Birkenhead, Brighton, and all the metropolitan societies, except Enfield Highway, experienced similar damage, offices, factories and workshops, shops, warehouses, bakeries, and laundries suddenly being damaged or destroyed.

The adaptability, loyalty and even courage of staffs were put to severe tests which revealed very high qualities indeed. Brighton had 27 shops damaged, yet no shop stopped serving customers for more than 24 hours. Grays Society had 86 shops damaged, but only one branch, and that by but an hour, failed to open at the usual time the following morning. One incident in the latter society illustrates the type of devotion which enabled co-operative services to be efficiently maintained. A milk roundsman buried in his shelter for three hours by a bomb explosion, was dug out at 3 a.m.—and was on his milk round at 7 a.m. Similar instances could be given by many other societies.

The case of Portsea Island, however, showed a capacity of the Co-operative Movement for quick and efficient reorganisation which is apt to be underrated. In one night this Society lost its central premises, grocery warehouse, despatch department, furnishing, dressmaking and tailoring workshops, offices, two grocery

branches, a hall, and its bakery, the largest in the South of
England. Emergency arrangements immediately came into operation. Supplies of bread were rushed from societies in London,
Brighton, Winchester, and Southampton, feeding not only Portsea
Island members, but the whole town, for every Portsmouth bakery
was out of action. Within three days the C.W.S. was sending
lorries with every sort of necessary goods. So quickly and efficiently did the Society adapt itself that its trade increased, doubling
its pre-war trade in butchery and drapery. Many of the other
blitzed societies also experienced increases of sales, probably due
to their superior organisation enabling them to recover more
quickly than did private traders.

Retail Trade

Co-operative retail trade increased in money terms during the
war but this increase was due to the rise in prices. Shortages and
rationing prevented any real increase. The change in the real
volume of trade cannot be accurately measured. Difficulties of
correcting volume of sales by price changes were increased, owing
to big changes in the pattern of spending making index figures
misleading. J. A. Hough, the Co-operative Union Research Officer,
however, by using some post-war statistics was able to make some
estimates of changes of trade on a departmental basis. These
showed a decrease in foodstuffs trade which reached its nadir in
1941, from whence it steadily increased, but even in 1945 did not
equal that of 1939, although its monetary value had increased from
£191·5 million to £237·7 million. Coal increased in real trade and
money values during the first year of the war and then decreased
year by year in real volume although increasing in money terms.
Dry goods sales decreased reaching their nadir in 1943; there was
a slight increase afterwards, but in 1945 the volume of real trade
was only 60 per cent of that in 1939, although its monetary value
had increased from £36 million to £41 million.

The percentage of co-operative trade to national trade increased
during these war years, in foodstuffs from 14 per cent to 15·46 per
cent, in coal from 13·05 per cent to 14·27 per cent, in dry goods
from 5·96 per cent to 6·9 per cent, and in footwear from 8·64 per
cent to 10·05 per cent.

War-time restrictions on supplies, qualities and prices hit some
private traders more severely than it did co-operatives, the expensive trade for high income groups being most seriously curtailed.
Advertising and expensive sales promotion schemes were also
practically stopped, and since co-operative trade had relied less on
these, and more on quality and service, it thereby benefited. More-

over, with uniform prices in both private and co-operative shops, the gain to the consumer of the co-operative dividend on purchase was clear, definite and indisputable.

Nevertheless, there were some significant features of co-operative trade which occasioned consideration by its students. J. A. Hough estimated the co-operative proportion of national food trade as not more than 17·5 per cent in 1945. In this group of commodities, however, milk amounted to 32 per cent, registrations for sugar, butter, margarine and cooking fats, preserves and cheese amounted to 25 per cent, bacon 23·5 per cent, meat, which was not sold by all co-operative societies, to 12–14 per cent, bread about 20 per cent, confectionery about 10 per cent. In the " points " trades, co-operative societies received about 16 per cent.

It will be noted that the co-operative share of trade was largest in those commodities such as sugar, milk, bread, for which advertising had not created a demand for particular " brands." With commodities controlled by the " points " system it was still often possible for the consumer to express a preference for particular brands, and this might account for the smaller share of co-operative trade, although the datum line system of distribution of points goods was probably more to blame. Under this system " points " goods were distributed among retailers according to sales in pre-war years. With growing membership, full employment and higher wages, societies were sometimes unable to meet the demands of their members for points goods. The difference between the registrations trade and the points trade of co-operative societies indicate the iniquities of the datum line system.

Capital

The following table indicates some of the main features of retail societies during the war.

War-time Statistics of Retail Societies £ million							
	1939	1940	1941	1942	1943	1944	1945
Share Capital ...	157	156	164	179	201	222	238
Loan Capital ...	44	44	47	51	58	65	72
Reserves ...	15	16	17	17	18	18	19
Small Savings ...	6	6	6	7	8	8	8
Owing for Goods	7	7	6	5	4	4	4
Net Surplus* ...	26	27	28	33	33	35	35
Percentage of Retail Trade ...	9·8	9·3	9·5	10·3	10·1	10·0	9·7

*Exclusive of share interest.

It will be observed that in the first year of the war there was a slight reduction of share capital (due to withdrawals of members evacuated from their societies' districts) but afterwards there was an annual increase, accompanied by a steady increase in loan capital. Reserves increased slightly by about a million pounds each year; the slightness of the increase was due to Excess Profits Tax falling on amounts put to reserve in excess of those so put before the war.

Societies had to be warned of the danger of increasing amounts put to reserve or depreciation, for the tax could have a snowball effect. J. S. Simm, of the Co-operative Union, showed how a society could within five years make the whole of its surplus subject to E.P.T. leaving nothing available for dividend (*Wartime Finance*). It was vital to societies that they must not become subject to E.P.T. so contrary to what would otherwise have been sound financial policy, societies making unusually large surpluses dare not increase the amounts put to reserve, they had to pay it out in dividends. Hence the small increase in societies' reserve funds during these years, in spite of the increases of surplus.

Probably a good proportion of the increase in share capital came from the increase in dividends, because leaving dividends to accumulate as share capital was an old, familiar way of saving for many co-operators.

The reduction in the amount owing for goods was largely due to a reduction in hire purchase trade, from £4,539,302 in 1939 to £1,693,457, indicative of the reduced trade in household goods.

THE WHOLESALE SOCIETIES DURING THE WAR

Besides maintaining essential services for the retail societies in the midst of war-time difficulties, the Wholesale Societies had much of their productive resources diverted to war purposes. Preparations were being made for this in consultation with Government departments before the outbreak of war. The record of achievement was a remarkable one, revealing a high degree of skill and adaptability of its workers and of organising ability by its administrative staffs.

C.W.S. clothing factories turned out 3,750,000 garments, including two million battledress suits, 500,000 R.A.F. garments, and over 250,000 greatcoats. Its cabinet works, upholstery, bedding, hardware, and tinplate factories produced millions of bomb and ammunition carriers, half a million mattresses, over 200,000 beds, 575,000 pillows and bolsters, 271,000 shelter bunks, 80,000 chains, 75,000 tables, 85,000 forms, 23,000 mosquito nets, 10,000 rifle parts, over 12,000 assault boats, aircraft components such as Mosquito and Hamilcar fuselages and wings, parts for aircraft rockets, for Bailey bridges, tanks, assault barges, electrical junction boxes and cable assemblies, and others too numerous to mention. The Birtley Tinplate works alone produced some 20 million components for the Army, Navy, and R.A.F.

The long and impressive recital of the huge and varied output of the C.W.S. factories during the war, is gratifying in its revelation of the immense productive resources at the disposal of the Movement. It is saddening, therefore, to reflect that the Movement itself had never utilised these resources to the full. The war-time demands of the Government were needed to do that, not peace-time demands from the Movement. Yet the war-time record showed the capacity for successful large scale mass production and the ability of the co-operative factories to more than hold their own if the volume of demand was sufficient to fully engage their productive capacity.

With premises all over the country the Wholesale Societies were certain to suffer damage from air raids, as indeed they did, mostly in Manchester, London, Cardiff, and Birmingham and in one air raid on Manchester the C.W.S. lost its Mitchell Memorial Hall.

Holyoake House, too, was badly damaged, its Assembly Hall being completely destroyed, and the Co-operative Union staff for a time had to be accommodated in the Co-operative College hostels at Kersal, themselves damaged on more than one occasion.

The trade of the Wholesale Societies increased in conformity with that of their retail society members, their trade increasing from £156 million in 1939 to £223 million in 1945. Although the percentage of wholesale to retail trade increased from 57·6 per cent in 1939 to 61·7 per cent in 1945 this was not an indication of increasing loyalty. It was partly due to the decrease in trade of various lines in which the percentage of wholesale trade had always been low, thus increasing the percentage of basic co-operative wholesale trade, and also to the " sellers' market " in which suppliers had the whiphand. As private trade suppliers had little natural sympathy with co-operative societies, in such circumstance the societies would have had raw deals or no deals at all, and societies had increasingly to rely upon their own Wholesale Societies for supplies of goods.

PRODUCTIVE SOCIETIES

The productive societies affiliated to the Co-operative Productive Federation encountered greater difficulties than did the consumer societies owing to their specialisation, and in some instances to wartime demands being much smaller than those of peacetime. Printing societies, for instance, were affected by limitations upon the sale of such printing lines as advertising, and by stringent restrictions on the use of paper. Clothing and footwear societies were also affected by the severe contraction of civilian trade, although this was made up to some extent by government contracts.

Hence the sales of these societies declined, from £3,562,000 in 1939 to £2,094,000 in 1945. Only the printing societies showed a slight increase of about £2,000, and this was due to an increase in prices, not an increase in volume of work. The number of employees decreased from 7,981 to 5,055 (by 1943 over 1,400 employees had joined the forces) and the membership from 14,497 to 13,911. Shortage of workers, especially skilled workers, was to be one of the greatest obstacles to recovery, another was the shortage of raw materials.

Yet the societies strengthened their financial position. Although share and loan capital fell from £1,170,000 to £1,117,000, reserve and insurance funds increased from £479,000 to £609,000, and in spite of the decreased sales, net surplus increased from £121,000 in 1939 to £231,000 in 1945 (in 1944 it was £274,000).

CO-OPERATIVE CENTENARY

Although the celebration of a centenary is often of more interest than historical significance, that of the foundation of the Rochdale Society of Equitable Pioneers is not to be ignored in a history of the Movement. It was celebrated not only in Great Britain but all over the world, evidence of the belief that the Co-operative Movement had its origin and inspiration in the ideals of these co-operators of a hundred years ago.

Owing to the highly critical stage the war had reached, celebrations fell far short of what had been intended in peacetime. Hopes of fulfilling the Ten Year Plan had disappeared with the outbreak of war. Nevertheless much was done, the Co-operative Union engaged L. du Garde Peach to write *Co-operative Century. A Pageant of the People*, which told the story of the Rochdale Pioneers in dramatic form. Societies all over the country gave it public performances, which were generally successful in attracting big audiences and informing and interesting the public.

G. D. H. Cole was also engaged to write a history of the Co-operative Movement, *A Century of Co-operation*, and the C.W.S. granted 20 annual scholarships, entitled C.W.S. (Centenary) Scholarships, tenable at the Co-operative College.

As the Centenary took place in the midst of preparations

for the landings in Normandy, when the future of democratic civilisation depended on victory or defeat, it was remarkable that the celebration aroused a nation-wide and unsurpassed interest. Even the B.B.C. mentioned it, if only for a quarter of an hour, in its Home and Forces programmes, although in the Foreign and Overseas programmes it dealt with the Centenary frequently and extensively and kept the people of the U.S.A., Canada, Australia, Europe, and the Middle East well informed of the nation-wide character of the celebrations.

10 THE CO-OPERATIVE MOVEMENT, 1945-1968. ECONOMIC DEVELOPMENT

" Peace should be built up on sound economic foundations. . . . We co-operators can help in the laying of such solid foundations and it is our duty to do so."
(Message of Swedish Co-operators to the British Co-operative Congress, 1946.)

THE AFTERMATH OF THE WAR

GREAT Britain emerged from the war on the victorious side but with resources seriously overstrained. The civilian population, if not exhausted were in a state of physical and mental tiredness which dulled both initiative and sense of responsibility. " I couldn't care less " was a phrase frequently heard which expressed the attitude to work and living to which many had sunk. But the country could not afford such an attitude, it was faced with a grim economic prospect. The costs of the war were not generally realised, but they had to be met, and there was no possibility of restoring the post-war standard of living for some years to come.

The real costs of war also include the hardships, suffering and losses experienced in its aftermath. The diversion of resources to war purposes resulted in failure to maintain and replace material equipment. Roads, railways, buildings, had been neglected, so had industrial plant and machinery not required for war purposes. Industrial efficiency was thus seriously impaired, although it was vitally important that it should be increased, for the country was so dependent upon foreign trade for foodstuffs and raw materials that it needed to increase exports to 75 per cent over those of 1938 in order to obtain the pre-war volume of imports.

This was due to the loss of income from overseas investments consequent upon their liquidation during the period of " Cash and Carry," and to the accumulation of foreign debts amounting to £3,000 millions. Moreover, during the period of " Lend Lease " the country had also sacrificed much of its export trade, which was now about 30 per cent of the pre-war level. Britain's war effort had in fact exceeded her economic strength: " the resources necessary for victory could not be mobilised without casting away resources necessary for the nation's livelihood when victory was achieved." (*British War Economy*, Hancock and Gowing.)

A Herculean task confronted the Government. An immense transition from war to peace economy had to be made, 45 per cent of the labour force was in the services and munitions industries, only 2 per cent in the exports industries, and less than 8 per cent in maintaining capital equipment. Industrial efficiency had to be restored and increased, exports had to be increased and some relaxation of strain on the population made.

At the General Election of 1945 the Labour Party was successful and a Labour Government took office. There were twenty-three Co-operative M.P.'s, of these A. V. Alexander was made First Lord of the Admiralty, A. Barnes made Minister of Transport, and R. C. Morrison was raised to the peerage to strengthen Labour in the House of Lords. R. A. Palmer, General Secretary of the Co-operative Union was also made a peer, assuming the title of Lord Rusholme.

LABOUR GOVERNMENT AND SOME POST-WAR PROBLEMS

International affairs during this period cannot be described here, but they had a considerable effect upon the activities of the Government in every other field and upon economic recovery. The outstanding feature was the menace of Russian expansion. This resulted in a very disturbed world, of serious concern to a country so dependent on foreign trade as Great Britain. The consequent maintenance and even increase of some armaments, caused great strains on countries at a time when economic reconstruction and social reforms were required.

Hence there was a continuance of conscription, shortages, controls, a strong tendency to inflation, increasing difficulty of securing a balance of foreign payments, increased taxation. It is against this background of cold war together with the aftermath of the previous hot one, that the economic and social achievements of this Government should be judged.

Before the war Britain continuously had an adverse balance of payments; Britain exported too little to pay for imports. But these deficits were negligible compared with the position facing the country in 1945. According to Lord Keynes, Britain faced a financial Dunkirk. It was estimated that this country faced a deficit in the balance of payments for 1946 of £750 millions. Without aid from the U.S.A., the country would be virtually bankrupt and the economic basis for the hopes of the public non-existent.

On August 14th, 1945, Japan accepted unconditional surrender and on August 17th, the U.S.A. announced the cessation of " Lend Lease " from September 2nd. This left Britain in a desperate condition indeed. Without American aid of some kind, the country would have to endure a severer austerity than during the war. However, a U.S. loan was offered and accepted. In the circumstances probably anything would have been accepted, and if the circumstances responsible for Britain's position were ignored the terms of the loan were not ungenerous. " Lend Lease " was written off, except for goods already in " the pipe-line," and credit given for £3,750 millions at 2 per cent to be paid off in 50 years beginning in 1951. The loan was exhausted by the end of 1948, 73 per cent of it went on food, ships and machinery, 11 per cent on food for Germany.

To add to Britain's difficulties the old pattern of international trade had been destroyed, and the new one involved greater imports from the New World and fewer from old sources of supply. This required Britain to obtain a balance in trade with these " dollar countries," necessitating a big increase in exports to them. As they had made great strides in increasing industrial efficiency during the war (their output of consumer goods increased) whilst Britain had been run down as one of the sacrifices for victory, this was not easy.

To do so required the continuance of controls. The sale of many British products in the home markets had to be prevented for they were required for export. It was also necessary to restrict imports from the dollar countries to bare essentials. This was attempted in some cases by taxation so heavy that it was expected to be almost prohibitive, as with tobacco, in others by the more effective restrictions of rationing, as with petrol. In spite of the efforts, the attempts to fulfil an obligation to restore the convertibility of the pound into dollars in 1947 failed after only five weeks convertibility. The Marshall Plan, 1947, however, came to Britain's aid, and in spite of serious defects, it did provide necessary assistance by the U.S.A. in rehabilitating the economies of Britain and Europe.

By controlled austerity, harder work and increased efficiency, the country was far more successful than had been expected or hoped. In 1946 British exports almost reached the 1938 level, in 1950 they were about 75 per cent above it, whereas British imports were about 10 per cent below those of 1938. This was in accordance with a Four Year Plan devised in 1948, which was to make Britain independent by 1952.

Unfortunately, the continuance of the controls and restrictions necessary for this tried the patience of a people who had endured much throughout the decade of the forties. Crises involving devaluation of the £, arising from external circumstances, such as a slight recession in the U.S.A., were due to the precarious nature of Britain's position; each one, however, increased the impatience of people desirous of freedom of choice, the abundance of goods, the pleasures and enjoyments associated with peace. A political opposition was by no means averse to stimulating an increase of this impatience, it was worth many votes at a general election.

Thus although the Labour Government successfully steered the nation through the greatest economic difficulties which it had ever encountered, it secured but a bare majority at the election of 1950, and was defeated in 1951. Moreover, it had associated itself in many minds with restrictions and austerity, an impression not quickly effaced. Yet in its short period of office it not only put the country back on its feet, it also carried through a vast programme of reforms.

LABOUR GOVERNMENT—PROGRAMME OF REFORMS

Several industries were nationalised, viz., coal, electricity, gas, transport, civil aviation, and also the Bank of England and Cable and Wireless, thus in the life of one Parliament nationalising most of what had been regarded as suitable for nationalisation by the Webbs in their book *The Constitution for a Socialist Commonwealth*.

Agriculture was encouraged, by what some regarded as extravagant and wasteful means. Prices of crops were guaranteed eighteen months ahead and of livestock four years ahead. Agricultural output increased: gross output (the amount of food coming off the farms) by 21 per cent in 1949–1950 over 1939, net output (amount of food less purchased feedingstuffs) by 46 per cent.

An important Agriculture Act was passed in 1947 which retained and consolidated many practices and provided for the re-establishment of marketing boards and introduction of marketing schemes. Tenant farmers were given practical security against dispossession except in cases of flagrantly bad farming, and price reviews were instituted under which prices were fixed so that, in the aggregate, farmers' net receipts would approximate to a determined figure. Prices of individual commodities could be raised or lowered to encourage or discourage their production. To provide money to invest in expansion, prices were fixed so as to yield an additional £40 millions per annum. Retail prices were not allowed to cover these fixed prices, however, differences between cost and retail prices being met by subsidies.

Food rationing continued, for scarcities were such that without it prices would have risen to heights inflicting hardship on people with low incomes. Prices were also kept down by big subsidies amounting to £462 millions in 1949. In spite of the scarcities the lower income groups were better fed than before the war. There were considerable increases in 1949 over 1938 in the weekly consumption of many nutritious foods, but big decreases in the more palatable foods such as bacon and ham, fresh and frozen meat, canned fish, butter and tea.

The health of the people was better than in the pre-war years, the death rate fell from $11 \cdot 8$ in 1938 to $10 \cdot 9$ in 1948, the lowest on record. The National Health Service Act was passed in 1946 and came into operation in 1948. This was a vast comprehensive measure which reorganised the various health services in the country. Its most striking feature was the free provision of treatment for disease, illness, etc., and of remedial appliances. The unexpectedly heavy demands (the service cost £366 millions instead of the estimated £200 millions) stressed the need for such a service and indicated some measure of the discomfort and loss of efficiency through people not having surgical and medical appliances, spectacles and dental treatment even when they required them. By July 1949, for instance, $4\frac{1}{2}$ million pairs of spectacles had been supplied.

A great improvement in social security was made by the Family Allowances Act (1945), the National Insurance (Industrial Injuries) Act, the National Insurance Act, and the National Assistance Act. These embodied in large measure the proposals advanced by Sir William (later Lord) Beveridge during the war. The National Insurance Scheme included everybody, all were to pay contributions, all were entitled to certain benefits, some to additional ones. Benefits were provided for unemployment, sickness, maternity, widowhood, orphanhood, old age, death.

British Labour movements have always been concerned with improving the education of the people. The Labour Government at once began to apply the Butler Act of 1944. In 1945 the school leaving age was raised to fifteen years, secondary school education was to be universal and free, state grants to universities were increased (£2 millions in 1938–1939, £17$\frac{1}{2}$ millions in 1948–1949). Although there were neither sufficient schools nor teachers to gain full benefits from the change, it yielded good results. In 1939, 80,673 sat for the School Certificate, in 1948, 113,192 sat; in 1939, 13,255 entered for the Higher School Certificate, in

1948, 29,731 entered; in 1938 there were 50,000 students at universities, in 1949 there were 80,000.

If steps had not been taken until the country " was ready for them " they would probably never have been made. They were taken because it was realised not only that a higher level of education was necessary for industrial and commercial efficiency, but also because it was necessary for the democratic control of an increasingly complex and high-powered state and essential to the growth of a more equalitarian society.

Throughout this century, and in some districts throughout the nineteenth century, there was a housing shortage. Private enterprise never provided houses of satisfactory quality in sufficient abundance to house the people. Between the two wars by heavy subsidising and municipal enterprise the problem was well on the way to being solved. But the great destruction of houses during the war (half a million destroyed or made uninhabitable, four millions damaged) and the cessation of housebuilding, made the shortage once more acute. There were also urgent needs for other buildings such as schools, hospitals, factories, and there were serious shortages of building materials and labour.

It was necessary, therefore, to exercise controls to secure priority for the more urgent social needs. Building by local authorities was given priority over private building in order that houses to let should be built. By February, 1951, 1,289,826 families had been rehoused, 848,652 permanent houses built, 157,146 temporary houses constructed, and 775,000 war damaged houses repaired.

The need for controlling the uses to which land is put was being realised before the war. During the war three important government reports were issued, the Barlow Report, the Scott Report and the Uthwatt Report. These showed the need for town and country planning on social, economic and strategic grounds. The Town and Country Planning Act, 1947, gave public authorities the powers for such planning. It gave them control of the use of land, of developments, and was intended to prevent profits being made from land speculation.

INCREASE IN GOVERNMENT EXPENDITURE AND TAXATION

This century has seen a huge increase in government expenditure, mostly due to war or preparations for war, and the growth of what Dr. Dalton described as our most impressive war memorial, the National Debt, from £8,163 millions in 1938 to £21,365 millions in 1945. Inflation, however, resulted in the increased real burden being much less than this increase in money burden. To meet this increase in expenditure there was a big increase in taxation which affected industry and commerce, investment, the pattern of expenditure and the distribution of income.

The total tax revenue increased from £3,141 millions in 1946 to £4,003 millions in 1951. This increase was obtained by increasing surtax, death duties, tax on undistributed profits, and profits tax (formerly N.D.C.). Inflation, also, by increasing incomes and expenditures increased the yield of many taxes. In the main the fiscal policy of the Labour Government was to lessen the burden on the smaller income receivers by increasing that of the richer. Thus the amount of tax payable by individuals with less than £1,000 per annum was reduced between 1946 and 1951 by reliefs, reductions and allowances. Yet such were wage and salary increases that the total amount of income tax paid by wage earners increased from £198 millions in 1946 to £265 millions in 1951, and of salary earners from £253 millions to £295 millions.

Employee insurance contributions increased from £17 millions to £27 millions (salary earners) and £64 millions to £152 millions (wage earners). These contributions were, of course, taxes in all but name. Employers' contributions increased from £84 millions to £205 millions. As the yield of direct taxes on income increased from £1,886 millions in 1946 to £2,359 millions in 1951, it will be seen that the bulk of this increase came from the employing and wealthier classes. The bulk of the increased yield from death duties, £143 millions to £194 millions, also fell on them; the exemption limit was, however, raised from £1,000 to £2,000.

The yield from indirect taxation also increased, but apart from some items of purchase tax, most of this fell upon luxury expenditure. Big increases in tax yields from 1946 to 1951 were, wines and spirits from £88 millions to £128 millions, tobacco from £438 millions to £622 millions, purchase tax from £161 millions to £338 millions. On the other hand, yields from beer fell from £276 millions to £261 millions, and from entertainments from £55 millions to £45 millions. Thus even indirect taxation, apart from tobacco tax, fell mainly on the better off, and the huge increase in tobacco tax was imposed for the purpose of cutting down consumption and so imports of tobacco from the dollar countries.

Purchase tax fell on a large variety of goods, many of a luxury nature, and even with the rest it is doubtful if their prices would have been less without the tax, for scarcities were so acute that the supplies available easily commanded the prevailing prices, and the cupidity of manufacturers and traders ensures a price as high as they can get.

MORE EQUITABLE DISTRIBUTION OF THE NATIONAL INCOME

The principal effect of the heavy and steeply graduated income tax and death duties was the more equal distribution of incomes, a change, however, mainly effected during the war. The following table is indicative of the change:—

DISTRIBUTION OF PERSONAL INCOMES, 1938 AND 1949

Income before tax	1938			1949		
	No. of Incomes	Gross Income	Income left after tax	No. of Incomes	Gross Income	Income left after tax
	(000)	£m.	£m.	(000)	£m.	£m.
Up to £250	N. A.	2,613	2,609	12,050	1,952	1,923
250–500	1,890	631	611	9,980	3,480	3,312
500–750	390	234	212	2,130	1,260	1,137
750–1,000	149	127	110	560	480	395
1,000–2,000	183	247	202	550	735	444
2,000–5,000	79	238	178	186	509	333
5,000–20,000	24	199	117	42	341	134
Over 20,000	2	87	30	2	70	9
TOTAL	N. A.	4,376	4,069	25,500	8,857	7,787

There were over 18 million people employed in 1939, most of them earning less than £250 per annum, the average weekly wage in certain industries selected by the Ministry of Labour was 53/3d. A glance at the above table will show a big shift into the £250–£500 and the £500–£750 ranges. It must be noted that the smaller incomes include those of juveniles, whilst husband's and wife's incomes count as one income. There are many pitfalls for those attempting to draw conclusions from income statistics, but a general drift is clear, viz., towards greater equality in incomes after deduction of tax.

Within the ranks of wage earners and salary earners there was also a levelling tendency. In 1938 the wages of the labourer in the building industry were about 75 per cent of those of the skilled man, in 1945 they were 81 per cent and in 1950 84 per cent, a similar change took place in engineering, from 75 per cent in 1938 to 85 per cent in 1950. Among salary earners there was a similar tendency, the lower paid getting bigger increases than the higher. The maximum salaries of Civil Service Principals increased only 14 per cent between 1938 and 1949, whilst those of clerical officers increased 29 per cent, those of graduate grammar school teachers increased by 28 per cent whereas those of certificated teachers in the elementary schools increased by 52 per cent. On the other hand, the lower salary earners improved their position less than did manual wage earners.

Wages as a percentage of total personal incomes increased as follows: 1938, 37·9 per cent; 1946, 37·2 per cent; 1950, 41·5 per cent. Salaries from 17·9 per cent in 1938 to 20·8 per cent in 1950; wages, salaries and pay of armed forces together rose from 59·6 per cent of total personal income in 1938 to 68·4 per cent in 1950. With full employment and increased and improved social services the working classes were in a better position in 1951 than in 1938 as compared with other classes.

INDUSTRIAL DISPUTES

During the war, systems of conciliation had so spread that 80 per cent of the employee population of Great Britain was covered by voluntary or statutory systems of wage regulation. Trade unions, affiliated to the T.U.C., had also grown from 4,669,000 members in 1938 to 6,671,000 in 1946, to 7,827,000 in 1951. The consequent better order in industrial relations resulted in less waste from industrial disputes. Whereas in the four years following the war of 1914–1918, 178 million days were lost in industrial disputes, in the years 1946–1950 only nine-and-a-half million days were lost.

A different economic policy was, of course, also responsible; controls were dismantled more slowly, and deflation, with consequent wage cutting disputes, not practised. Industrial production increased; in 1947 it was 15 per cent greater than in 1938, in 1948 it was 28 per cent greater, in 1949 37 per cent, and in 1950 50 per cent. As has been pointed out, however, Britain had to export more than before the war, but a remarkable recovery for the country as a whole was made during the period of the Labour Government.

THE ECONOMIC SITUATION
IN THE 'FIFTIES AND 'SIXTIES

The whole period was characterised by inflation, full employment, repeated balance of payments crises, and increasing Government intervention in the economy. Taking over from the Labour Government in 1951, the Conservatives proceeded to dismantle the remaining physical controls, such as the remnants of rationing, and to reintroduce monetary controls as a weapon of economic policy. Their attempts to control inflation were not notably more successful than those of their predecessors had been, however. A further feature of the whole period has been the general inability to reconcile faster economic growth, a repeated objective of all political parties, with balance of payments stability. Such objectives may be difficult to reconcile in favourable circumstances. British circumstances are not very favourable. Being such a large importer of raw materials, the initial stages of accelerated growth are inevitably accompanied by high imports, whereas exports take longer to manufacture and sell. Such a position can be borne for some time providing there are sufficient gold and foreign currency reserves to pay for these early deficits. Britain's foreign currency reserves have arguably not been large enough to bear that kind of burden for any length of time, particularly since sterling's international role made it liable to panic waves of selling in international currency markets and adequate reserves are necessary to support buying of sterling in such situations.

The methods used by successive Governments in dealing with these balance of payments crises—dearer money and higher taxes—have temporarily sacrificed growth and given rise to the now familiar stop-go cycle which has affected all businesses, not least retailing. A sudden enthusiasm for planning by the Conservative Government in the early 'sixties raised some hopes that this cycle could be planned out of existence. The aim of this type of planning, " indicative " rather than " imperative," was to speed up growth by co-ordinating public and private investment, and the strategy was based on friendly persuasion and the spreading of information rather than on physical controls. Such an approach was obvious from the early reports of the National Economic Development Council set up in 1962 and reached its high point with the publication of the National Plan in 1965 by the Labour Government's new Department of Economic Affairs. The Plan envisaged an overall growth of 25 per cent in the economy between 1964 and 1970 or an annual rate of growth of about 3·8 per cent. At the time of publication this was criticised as being far too ambitious and much of the document's forecasting was criticised as being too optimistic, particularly regarding the relative rates of growth of exports and imports. And certainly within two years if not less the document became a dead letter as the Government struggled anew with balance of payments difficulties using measures which completely upset the Plan's forecasts.

During the early 'fifties, it was possible, with some justification, to blame specific events for these recurring balance of payments crises—the Korean War, the Suez adventure, the position of the Deutschmark were each blamed in their turn. Such a position was becoming increasingly untenable by the early 'sixties and a growing number of voices were asking whether devaluation was not the answer. But in spite of increasing evidence that the exchange rate was becoming less and less maintainable (for example, the deficits were becoming larger in the " go " phases and the surpluses smaller in the " stop " phases), Governments did all they could to avoid devaluation. The Government's failure to deal effectively with the massive deficit they had inherited from the Conservatives (£406 millions on current account in 1964) led them to take severe disinflationary measures in 1966. The May budget was notable for the introduction of the Selective Employment Tax, said to broaden the basis of taxation and encourage more efficient use of labour, but probably far more effective as a means of reducing liquidity in all parts of the economy and of inducing a deflationary effect. This budget had been calculated to take something like £300 millions out of the economy in a full year—a substantial enough measure in itself. However, in July came the biggest " stop " of all time. Measures were introduced with the intention of reducing demand by another £500 millions which included a " freeze " of wages, dividends and prices and a cut-back in investment in the public sector.

Even these measures failed to cure the problem, however, and finally in November of 1967 the pound was devalued by 14 per cent. The subsequent recovery was slower than some economists had forecast partly because the demand for imports did not respond to price increases to quite the extent that had been anticipated, but by the end of the period the balance of payments position was much healthier. Whether the fundamental problem of more rapid growth with a healthy balance of payments position has been solved only time will ultimately tell.

Despite the crises and mismanagement of the last twenty years, however, living standards have risen continually and real wages have risen by about 70 per cent over the period. Prices have risen almost continually, by about a third in the 'fifties and a further third during the 'sixties, but incomes have generally outstripped prices so that during the 'sixties alone the average standard of living grew by one third. This progress has steadily modified the pattern of life for nearly everybody, particularly with regard to what they are able to buy.

CHANGES IN PATTERNS OF EXPENDITURE

Expenditure did not, of course, increase equally upon all goods. In the general increase in living standards of the past twenty years, for example, the rate of increase of expenditure on foods has not kept pace with the rate of increase of expenditure on many other goods, which is the pattern that is to be expected in a period of greater prosperity. In 1958 the average family spent 98/– a week on food, about a third of its total expenditure, in 1968 the amount spent had risen to 132/–, but this represented little more than a quarter of this family's expenditure. Another item in relative decline was clothing and footwear which represented slightly over ten per cent of the average family's budget in 1958 and a little under nine in 1968. On the other hand, expenditure on housing and related items such as fuel and lighting and household goods went up considerably from 67/– a week to 128/– which also represents an increase in the proportion of the budget —23 per cent to 26 per cent. Some of this increase is undoubtedly due to the fact, however, that the cost of housing went up considerably faster than the general cost of living. The most rapidly increasing item of expenditure is quite clearly that on motor vehicles. The average family spent 13/– a week in 1958 on buying and maintaining motor vehicles, four per cent of its budget. By 1968 they were spending 51/–, ten per cent of the budget.

Expenditure on convenience goods continued to increase. In the food trades, for example, this was reflected in the 'fifties by substantial increases in the sales of canned fruit, vegetables and soups. As far as vegetables are concerned, those of the frozen variety are now the most rapidly expanding. In the early 'sixties little over half a million tons of frozen vegetables were bought annually. Today the figure is nearer one and a half million. Forty per cent of all peas consumed are now of the frozen variety.

There were changes developing in transport, the extent and consequent effects of which it is too soon to predict. Railways suffered from a decline in traffic in the 'fifties which led to the closure of many uneconomic lines, generally branch lines. There was a slowing down of the rate of closure in the mid-'sixties and with the electrification of many longer-distance main lines some of the decline in traffic was reduced. Public motor transport also experienced difficulties, partly through the big increase in private cars which doubled in number to about ten million during the 'sixties alone. Thus, although there was a big increase in private cars, vans and lorries, there was a comparatively small increase in the licences of buses, coaches and taxi cabs. Non-motorists in these districts were faced with poorer travelling facilities than those of twenty years previously. This, together with traffic congestion in the big cities and towns, is having an effect, and is likely to have a greater effect in the future, on shopping habits.

POPULATION CHANGES

Population continued to increase, from 45 millions in Great Britain in the 'thirties to 49 millions in 1951, 51 millions in 1961, and 52 millions in 1966. The increase was partly due to people living longer, as in the pre-war period, but an unexpected feature of the post-war population viewed against the pre-war trend was that the number of births was increased.

There was little change in the territorial distribution of the population. Every region in England and Wales increased its population although with variations in extent. These net gains mask movements within regions too. The Tyneside, South East Lancashire, West Midlands and Greater London conurbations all lost population due to slum clearance, rehousing schemes and the general drift to the suburbs. Scotland suffered an overall slight loss of population between 1961 and 1966 after gaining in the 'fifties, but again the greatest loss was from the Central Clydeside conurbation.

DEVELOPMENT OF THE CITY REGION

The decline in the population of some of the cities may lead to wrong conclusions upon their importance. Few modern cities are attractive living places, so many desire to live outside the city where they work, and modern transport provides the opportunity. A city's offices, warehouses, shops, factories, workshops, schools and all manner of public institutions, however, constitute vast markets for goods and services many of which, including labour, are supplied by neighbouring towns and districts. Hence the concept of the city region, which extends beyond the fringe of the continuous built-up area to include towns bound together by their partial dependence on the conurbation's centre.

Such extensions may embrace very large areas, the Manchester region, for instance, would embrace most towns in Lancashire. The greatest of all, London, which Cobbett described a hundred and fifty years ago as the Great Wen, as a city region covers the greater part of South Eastern England. The effects of such development are many and various; on the one hand there is a huge mass market to absorb the products of mass production, on the other there is less spectacular but widespread, steadily increasing specialisation which furthers larger-scale production by disintegration and the multiplication of small, but highly specialised, firms. Professor Sargent Florence expressed the opinion that the bigger the size of the city the smaller was the average size of its industrial units.[1] The nature and extent of the developments in industry, commerce, retail trade, social and cultural life will depend upon how the accompanying transport problems of the regions are solved or attempted. Public transport, for instance, would probably provide a different pattern from that which would result if there were adequate roads and car parks.

UNEMPLOYMENT AND TRADE UNIONISM

Unemployment has never been a serious general problem during the period, the highest figures being in the 'fifties, 2·1 per cent in 1958, and in the 'sixties, 2·5 per cent in 1963. Since 1967, however, the figure has remained stubbornly at 2·4 per cent. The lowest figure was in 1955 with 1·1 per cent, probably an irreducible minimum. In some areas, however, the percentages were higher, notably in the North of England, Wales and Scotland and worst of all in Northern Ireland. Regional statistics of unemployment support the view that the rate of unemployment rose in direct correlation with distance from London.

The continued and general prosperity favoured the growth of trade unionism. Unions affiliated to the Trades Union Congress had a membership of nearly nine millions in 1968, an increase of about one million over the previous twenty years. Perhaps more interesting than the growth in membership, however, is the composition of the membership. The membership of manual workers rose very little, partly because of the decline of industries such as coal mining and the railways, but the membership of unions for white collar workers was increasing rapidly. And

[1] *At the Conference of the International Centre for Regional Planning and Development, 1959.*

not only were these unions growing in size, they were increasingly tending to affiliate to the T.U.C.

As a movement it sought to exercise pressure and influence on the Government, with what degree of success it is difficult to determine, although the strong opposition of trade unions to wage restraint and trade union law reform in the late 'sixties seem to have been of considerable influence. It is even difficult, however, to estimate its success in its primary functions of improving wages and conditions, for the circumstances were such that these would have improved in any case. Whether they would have improved as much or as quickly is debatable, for although earnings increased more than wage rates, and women, still largely unorganised, enjoyed increases in wage rates exceeding those of men's, and juvenile labour increased its rates and earnings in greater percentage than did men and women, it may still have been the pressure of organised labour which forced up not only its own earnings but that of unorganised labour also, for employers competing for scarce labour had to bid above the higher rates secured by trade unions.

There was increasing concern expressed during the period about the number of strikes although, when compared with other countries, Britain's strike record was not particularly bad. The heaviest loss was in 1957 when over eight million working days were lost and there were over four million in 1968. Normally, however, the figure seems to average between two and three million. Responsibility for, or even causes of, industrial stoppages are generally difficult, if not impossible, to discover. The rise of the shop steward movement seems to indicate shortcomings in trade union structure, particularly an element of overcentralisation and too much reliance on national collective bargaining. There were several moves during the 'sixties, however, towards more bargaining at company and even plant level. Besides the trade unions, it was increasingly suggested that management must bear its share of the blame and that the approach of British management towards industrial relations needed to be considerably improved.

THE DISTRIBUTIVE TRADES

The distributive trades are of exceptional interest to co-operators because co-operative enterprise in Great Britain is still primarily concerned with them. More reliable (though rather belated) information regarding them has become available from the Census of Distribution Reports. In 1961, there were 508,529 shops, but 58 per cent of them had a turnover of less than £10,000 a year and accounted for only 17 per cent of the total trade. These small businesses were usually family businesses, in which the family was seldom dependent on the income from the shop alone. The assistance of members of the family at week-ends and evenings when free of their own wage earning employment, the willingness to remain open when other shops are closed, especially on Sundays, the ability to provide a service in circumstances which make its provision by a shop with full time wage labour unprofitable, have enabled this type of business to survive against the competition of large scale retailing.

Yet the field of the independent shopkeepers continued to be encroached upon in the 'fifties by both the multiples and co-operative societies, but in the 'sixties almost entirely by the multiples, who continued to increase their share of total retail trade at the expense of both the independent shopkeeper and the co-operative society. The continued growth of the multiples has led co-operators to regard multiple competition as the only form worth much consideration.

PERCENTAGE SHARES OF RETAIL TRADE BY FORM OF ORGANISATION
1950–1966

	1950	1957	1961	1966
Co-operatives	11·4	11·9	10·8	9·2
Multiples	21·9	24·9	28·9	35·0
Independents	66·7	63·2	60·3	55·8

Multiples are indeed engaged in the type of trade, in both class of goods and customer, especially suited to co-operative enterprise. They have continually increased their trade faster than retail trade as a whole. From 1961 to 1966, for example, total retail trade increased by 23 per cent and that of multiple retailers by 49 per cent. In the 'fifties their most rapid advances were in the field of non-foods where it was said that the advantages of size were most marked but in the 'sixties their progress in the food trades has been remarkable. Again between 1961 and 1966, for example, the total sales of all food shops increased by 19 per cent, those of multiple food shops by 59 per cent.

There are, in fact, so many kinds of multiples that generalisations referring to them all may be misleading. The methods, advantages and disadvantages, and problems of a small multiple with a dozen shops, localised in character, are likely to be different from those of a national multiple with more than a thousand shops; those of a multiple of specialised shops are likely to be different from one engaged in many different trades; one which manufactures most of its own goods from one which manufactures none.

A not uncommon feature in retail history, the gradual drift away from specialisation by specialised shops into more general trading is to be observed in multiple development. They have increased the range of goods traded in through concentrating on the more profitable lines, which are not those which yield the highest profit on sales. They are run primarily to make profit for their shareholders, not to serve any and every need of the consuming public.

The war years forced the big variety chain stores off the rather stupid specialisation on trade in goods below a certain price, once believed to be the key to their success. Relieved of these limitations their increase and growth have been spectacular. Trading in mass produced standardised goods, their scale of trading enables economies of buying, handling, accounting, control of stocks, use of unskilled labour, and so on to be made.

Some of the larger multiples have, without undertaking production themselves, been able to control production because of the big orders they offer to producers. They are so big that the producers are willing to produce to the specifications and needs of the multiple and accept advice and even guidance to obtain more efficient production. An efficient co-ordination of supplies with demands is thus secured, with the retail element dominant.

Other Retailers

One form of action taken by independent retailers to counter-act their declining share of trade has been the formation of "voluntary chains" sponsored in the main by wholesalers. These attempt to achieve the same kind of relationship between independent firms that exist between the head office of a multiple and its branches, particularly so as to secure a guaranteed market for the wholesaler who is then offered some security for forward planning purposes and is able to undertake various marketing activities for the retailer members. Since each firm remains legally independent, the relationship can never be quite as close as within a single organisation but by a combination of contractual agreements and financial incentives a considerable degree of success has been achieved, particularly in the food trades. By the mid-'sixties, these chains had achieved about the same turn-over in grocery as co-operative societies.

Among the forms of trading suffering severely from the war, but which have made a spectacular recovery since, is mail order trading. There are different forms of this, from the direct Press advertisement to the elaborate catalogue trade. By far the largest part of this trade (85 per cent in 1961) is concentrated through part-time agents working for a small number of firms responsible for an overwhelming proportion of the trade. Its recovery is such that its growth has been constantly faster than that of any conventional retail outlets. Between 1961 and 1966, for example, when all retail sales increased by 25 per cent, those of mail order houses increased by 84 per cent. Mail order trade increased from £47 millions in 1950 to £128 millions in 1958, and an estimated £480 millions in 1968.

Departmental stores were long regarded as the most progressive and efficient form of retailing, and most co-operative societies had ambitions for departmental stores of their own. Many realised their ambition, and in many towns the most imposing retail premises were co-operative. But in general, departmental stores have not increased; their share of total retail trade in fact decreased from 6 per cent in 1950 to 5 per cent in 1957 and has not significantly changed since. While all retail sales increased by 25 per cent from 1961 to 1966, those of departmental stores increased by 20 per cent. There have been short periods when this situation has been reversed as in 1960–61 and indeed in the past two years, but these have generally been transitory, appearing to depend upon particular circumstances. More stringent hire purchase terms, for example, seem to favour department stores.

Credit Trade

Hire purchase, although preferable to some other forms of credit trading, was regarded with disfavour for many years by co-operators and others. The increasing Americanisation of the British distributive techniques, however, made it generally acceptable.

But however attractive a form of trade this was to the consumer, it presented opportunities of gain by extortionate terms and other abuses of which some private traders were not slow to take advantage. So many co-operators came to feel that if consumers were intent on credit trading it would be better if undertaken by their own organisations and so under their own control and free from profit-making and consequent exploitation. Co-operative societies thus undertook hire purchase and a club credit trade but apart from household textiles, and clothing and footwear, a larger, often a much larger, proportion of multiple trade was hire purchase or other instalment system, than was co-operative. Some multiples depended almost entirely on such trade.

The inflationary effects of credit trading necessitated the imposition of restrictions upon it by Government during the post-war years. The total amount of hire purchase debt and other credit instalments increased from £360 millions in 1956 to £740 millions in 1959 and to its highest point ever in 1965 when it stood at over £1,200 millions.

Since then, however, the Government has attempted to restrain hire purchase as part of its general disinflationary policy and in 1968 the hire purchase debt stood at about £1,100 millions. These restrictions particularly affected sales of consumer durables and of motor cars.

SOME CHANGES IN METHODS OF RETAILING

Perhaps the biggest changes in retailing since the war were the introduction of self-service and the supermarket. Self-service retailing had been developed in the U.S.A. and Canada, and the idea came from there. It was tried out tentatively by London Co-operative Society during the war, but it was Portsea Island Society which first went into it in a big way, and whose success interested the Movement and started a widespread and considerable conversion to this method of retailing. In 1950, 90 per cent of all self-service shops, were co-operative. In the rapid growth of self-service retailing in the next twenty years, however, that lead soon disappeared and by 1960 co-operative societies owned less than half of all self-service shops and by 1968 the figure was nearer one quarter.

Supermarkets are an extension of the self-service idea, being large stores (of at least 2,000 square feet sales area) operated mainly on self-service lines selling the whole range of foodstuffs plus basic household requirements. There are pressures both from the supply and the demand side for such changes. On the supply side there are certain managerial economies and reduced labour costs, for example, and on the demand side the convenience of one-stop shopping and the preference for price competition. Again, while co-operative societies were early into this field, the development of the multiples has been such that during the 'sixties the proportion of all supermarkets operated by co-operative societies has tended to decline.

Among the consequences of these trends are the reduction in the importance of personal salesmanship and an increase in the importance of advertising and the pack. Manufacturers try to sell their products by advertisements in the Press and on television, for the retail salesman in self-service is silent. This gives a big advantage to the big manufacturer who can afford to advertise on a large scale. It has also been suggested that this will tend to shift competition from quality and price to effectiveness in advertising and attractiveness of package.

In retailing, however, this would not appear to have happened. In fact, it is more plausible to argue that price competition has increased particularly since the abolition of resale price maintenance in 1964, but even before then retailers were ignoring manufacturers' prices. Indeed, it is arguable that the change in the law was merely a catalyst for a process that was happening anyway as large retailers undercut their competitors' prices and dared the manufacturers to cut off their supplies. The Co-operative Movement had always opposed resale price maintenance in principle and had effectively broken it by the device of dividend, but it was the larger multiples who created the immediate issue. The traditional supporters of the practice, the small retailer, no longer had the economic or political power to prevent its erosion and final abolition.

Nevertheless, despite the increasing price competition in some sectors of retailing, there was growing uncertainty amongst some consumers in the face of other modern marketing techniques. Deprived of the assistance of knowledgeable retailers, some consumers felt the need for impartial investigation and advice about the pretensions of manufacturers in regard to their products and during this period there has been action, both voluntary and governmental, to provide some consumer protection. On the voluntary level, following the example of consumers in the U.S.A., associations of consumers were formed to undertake investigations into manufacturers' claims. The original one was the Consumers' Advisory Council in 1954 which published " Shoppers' Guide " from 1957 to 1962 and was joined by the Consumers' Association in 1957, a far more successful body in appealing to consumers. It now claims well over half a million members and publishes the widely read magazine " Which? " Local consumer groups have appeared in a number of cities and towns.

Government action has included the appointment of the Molony Committee on Consumer Protection in 1959 which prompted the setting up of the Consumer Council in 1963, wholly supported by public funds and appointed by the President of the Board of Trade " to review the problems experienced by the consumer and to devise and advance means of resolving them." Various legislative measures taken to protect the consumer have included the Weights and Measures Acts, the Hire Purchase Acts, and most recently the Trade Descriptions Act. Then, at the local government level, a few authorities have set up consumer protection departments where consumers who have complaints about goods or services and have not been able to get satisfaction can take their problems.

J

RETAIL SOCIETIES—MEMBERSHIP AND SIZE

A remarkable feature of the Movement's history is the steady growth of membership ever since accurate figures became available in the 1870's and this growth is something everybody came to take for granted. This was a process which was bound to end, although whether the deceleration of growth in the 1960's was permanent or temporary only time will tell. After the increase in membership of 2,432,000 from 1948 to 1958, there was a net increase over the country as a whole of 200,000 from 1958 to 1968 with net decreases in some Sections and national decreases in three of the years, 1965, 1967, and 1968. It should be pointed out, however, that the figures are somewhat suspect. In the past, some societies have been somewhat tardy in bringing their membership registers up to date with the result that membership figures were often overstated. In addition, with the large number of societies it was inevitable that there would be people who were members of more than one society, so again the official figures would tend to overstate the number of people who belonged to co-operative societies. This was well brought out in 1965 when official national membership figures fell by 214,336. In the same year, London Society had been through its membership records and as a result its membership alone had been reduced by 308,490. Nevertheless, allowing for any exaggeration, which is probably much less than it was in 1958, the 1968 membership figure of 12,794,228 is something of which the Co-operative Movement can be proud.

SECTIONAL MEMBERSHIP, 1948–1968

Section	1948 thous.	1958 thous.	1968 thous.
Irish	113	162	209
Midland	1,552	2,032	2,465
Northern	818	998	1,013
North Eastern ...	1,181	1,355	1,183
North Western ...	1,807	1,973	1,838
Scottish	1,180	1,398	1,374
Southern	2,744	3,682	3,664
South Western ...	767	994	1,048
Total...	10,162	12,594	12,794

Since the Second World War, the Midland Section has become the second greatest in membership. Until as late as the 1940's the Northern, North Eastern, North Western and Scottish Sections had provided half of the total membership but this is clearly no longer the case. During the 1950's the Southern and

Midland Sections were growing at about the same pace, but during the 'sixties the Midland Section has gone way ahead in growth although this is partly explicable in terms of London's review of membership in 1965.

The number of societies continued to decrease as a result of amalgamation, from 1,030 in 1948 to 918 in 1958 to 539 in 1968, a fairly substantial decrease in twenty years, with an obvious acceleration in the 1960's. If the branches of Co-operative Retail Services and Scottish Co-operative Retail Services and the areas of the S.C.W.S. Retail Branches were not treated as separate societies in the statistics, the number of retail societies in 1968 would have been 495. With the impetus of the Co-operative Union's Regional Plan (referred to in more detail elsewhere) the number of societies has been decreasing even more substantially and rapidly, so that in mid-1970 the number was down to 435.

This reduction in size of societies with the increase in membership has naturally resulted in an increase in the average size of society. In 1948, 11 per cent of societies had more than 20,000 members each, embracing 65 per cent of the membership, in 1968, 26 per cent of societies were in this category with 82 per cent of the membership. In 1948 there were eight societies with membership over 100,000, in 1958 eighteen and, in 1968, 25 which together had about 43 per cent of the total membership. There were still 231 societies of less than 5,000 members each but they included less than four per cent of the total membership.

CO-OPERATIVE RETAIL SERVICES

After the war, the C.W.S. Retail Society adopted the less question-begging and cumbersome title of Co-operative Retail Services Ltd. Its organisation is described in a later chapter. When the Congress of 1928 passed a resolution which led to the C.W.S. undertaking retailing, its object was to get the C.W.S. to establish and develop Co-operation in " Co-operative deserts." But it may be remembered from a previous chapter that the C.W.S. did not regard this as the function which its entry into retailing would serve. It believed that such an entry would enable it to manage earlier and better those societies which found themselves incapable of managing their own affairs. Only when indebted to the C.W.S. was it able to exercise control over their management. At the time, 1928–1934, the C.W.S. had 14 societies under its direct management and 40 other societies under supervision by its officials. This was the problem to which the C.W.S. directed its attention.

Most of the growth of C.R.S. took place after the war. In 1943 it had seven branches (each branch a former retail society) with an aggregate membership of 38,000, in 1948 there were 24 branches with 111,000, and in 1958, 35 branches with 296,000 members. After that period C.R.S. branches no longer necessarily coincide with former retail societies since a process of rationalisation was begun, but in 1968 there were 29 branches with 1,022,000 members. During the 1960's some fairly large societies joined C.R.S., 1965 being a notable year when Bristol took its 130,000 members and Reading took its 60,000 members into the organisation. Some co-operators have not been happy at this form of development which is at variance with some of the prized features of the co-operative way, but neither could they have been happy to contemplate the alternatives. The hard fact is that without the C.R.S., the areas of these societies in many instances would have lapsed into co-operative deserts.

In fact, the economic progress of C.R.S. over the past ten years has been quite encouraging. In 1958 the average trade per member of the C.R.S. was £52 compared with a national average in England and Wales of £75. By 1968 the C.R.S. figure was £72 (an increase of 38 per cent) while the national figure was £82 (an 11 per cent increase). Similarly with share capital, while national average shareholding per member has been falling, the average shareholding of C.R.S. members has been increasing and is now higher than the national average.

SCOTTISH CO-OPERATIVE RETAIL SERVICES

As mentioned in an earlier chapter, the Scottish Wholesale Society had been involved in retailing for some years through the S.C.W.S. Retail Branches, the main intention of which was to provide co-operative services where local circumstances prevented residents providing these services for themselves. In 1967, however, it was decided to set up, in addition, Scottish Co-operative Retail Services on similar lines to the English model with the difference that it was suggested that S.C.R.S. could serve as an embryo of a national Scottish Co-operative Society. In its early days it is clearly acting as an ambulance service for ailing societies, however. At the end of 1967 it had four areas with a total membership of 6,554 and at the end of 1968 nine areas with 119,361 members. The fact that the average purchases per S.C.R.S. member in 1968 were about £61 in comparison with a Scottish average of £115 and that the average shareholding in the S.C.R.S. was about £8 in comparison with the national

average of £14 gives some indication of the kind of societies
S.C.R.S. is having to take over at this stage.

POST-WAR CO-OPERATIVE RETAIL TRADE

A bird's eye view of the retail societies is provided by the
following table:—

RETAIL SOCIETIES' TRADE, CAPITAL AND SURPLUS, 1948-1968
(£ millions)

	1948	1958	1968
Trade	502·6	997·7	1,095·0
Share Capital	245	251	204
Share, Loan and Sundry Funds	336	356	355
Reserves...	21·9	37·6	49·0
Credit to Members	11·5	29·5	42·4
Net Surplus including Share Interest... ...	46·7	66·7	42·0
Share Interest	6·6	7·3	6·6

Retail trade was almost doubled in monetary terms from 1948
to 1958, but of course the rise in prices and the increase in
membership must be taken into account. Nevertheless, the
increases recorded in the 1950's are in marked contrast to the far
slower rate of increase in the 1960's. In fact, some recent years
have seen a decline in trade but over the past five years or so
total trade has hovered around the £1,100,000,000 mark.

Even in the 1950's, however, concern was being expressed by
co-operators about the figures of total trade. Although the
national volume of trade was substantially bigger in 1958 than in
1948 or pre-war, when the increases in income and expenditure of
co-operative membership during the 'fifties were taken into account,
the increase in co-operative trade was disappointing, particularly
when compared with the increases in trade recorded by the
multiples. It was the feeling that the Movement was not
progressing as rapidly as it should which led to the setting up of
an Independent Commission of Inquiry in 1955 whose report was
published in 1958.

This Report paid a good deal of attention to this disparity of
growth. It found four main weaknesses, not very important if
the Movement were content with its existing share of the trade,
but if the Movement were to increase its share they needed to be
taken most seriously and corrected rapidly. The weaknesses were
an inadequate number of outlets, especially in dry goods, an
unsatisfactory distribution of these outlets, again especially in dry
goods, and certain faults in range and quality of goods sold.

Uneven development had resulted in some districts in the
North having too many grocery shops and others, in the South,

having too few. The earlier development of the Movement in the North than in the South and a social background which was evidently more conducive to Co-operation had led to an unbalanced geographical distribution of co-operative trade.

CO-OPERATIVE TRADE BY SECTIONS, 1948–1968

	1948		1958		1968	
	Trade £ mills.	Average per Member £	Trade £ mills.	Average per Member £	Trade £ mills.	Average per Member £
Irish	6	53·5	12	76·4	17	80·7
Midland	76	48·7	169	83·2	216	87·7
Northern	47	57·9	93	93·2	87	86·0
North Eastern ...	56	47·2	108	79·7	88	74·0
North Western ...	83	46·0	141	71·6	150	81·8
Scottish	88	74·5	157	111·9	159	115·6
Southern	107	39·1	236	64·1	285	77·9
South Western ...	39	50·8	81	80·5	93	88·5
	502	49·5	997	79·2	1,095	85·6

	Trade Increase				Increase per Member			
	1948–1958		1958–1968		1948–1958		1958–1968	
	£m.	%	£m.	%	£	%	£	%
Irish	6	100	5	42	22·9	43	4·3	6
Midland	93	122	47	28	34·5	71	4·5	5
Northern	46	98	—6	—6	35·3	61	—7·2	—8
North Eastern ...	52	91	—20	—18	32·5	70	—5·7	—7
North Western ...	58	70	9	6	25·6	56	10·2	14
Scottish	69	77	2	2	37·4	50	3·7	3
Southern	129	121	39	16	25·0	65	13·8	21
South Western ...	42	105	12	16	29·7	58	8·0	10
	495	99	91	9	29·7	60	6·4	8

By 1948, the Southern Section was the largest Section in terms of membership and as one would expect, the largest in terms of trade, but in terms of trade penetration (measured by average purchases per member) was the least successful. Since 1948 the figures indicate quite clearly that the Midlands and southern part of England are the most rapidly growing in terms of total trade and that differences in average purchases per member are not as marked as they used to be.

It has been argued that this is a natural levelling-up process, that the greater the initial trade penetration the less potential there is for further expanding either total trade or trade penetration. While not wholly discounting this factor, the Independent Commission showed that other variables correlated just as well with trade progress, such variables as having a low proportion of small societies in the Section or the proportion that reserve allocations bears to total sales.

But while regional variations in trade progress give clues to the shortcomings of co-operative organisation and business practices, a more disturbing feature of the period after the Commission's report has been the inability of the Movement generally even to hold its own, let alone make any progress. The Commission had been concerned with the Movement's failure markedly to increase its share of total retail trade, particularly its non-foods trades, for during the 'fifties the Movement's sales of foodstuffs had more or less expanded at the same pace as national food sales. During the 'sixties, however, the co-operative food trade has failed to maintain that record.

CO-OPERATIVE DEPARTMENTAL SALES, 1948–1968

(£ millions)

	1948	1958	1968
Grocery, Bread and Confectionery	261·2	531·7	545·4
Butchery	33·3	75·3	72·3
Greengrocery, Fruit and Fish	12·2	18·3	11·3
Dairy	56·8	117·4	155·1
Total Food	363·5	742·7	784·1
Drapery	43·1	66·5	73·5
Men's Wear	12·8	19·7	20·8
Footwear	15·0	17·8	18·1
Furnishing, Hardware and Electrical	24·9	65·9	92·0
Total Dry Goods	95·8	169·9	204·4
Coal and Fuel	21·2	40·0	34·3
Pharmacy and Optical	9·0	20·9	26·4
Other Departments	13·1	24·3	45·8
Total Sales	502·6	997·8	1,095·0

Thus, while the Co-operative Movement had managed to double its sales of food (at current prices) between 1948 and 1958, over the next ten years the expansion in food sales was negligible. According to the Censuses of Distribution, the sales of food shops increased by 19·1 per cent between 1961 and 1966. This represents a 2·8 per cent increase by co-operative societies, a 6·5 increase by independent retailers, and a 59·6 per cent increase by multiple retailers, which would suggest that the advantages deriving from large scale operations, most apparent in certain non-foods trades in the 'fifties, have now also become very apparent in the foods trades as well.

The figures for dry goods give little more ground for encouragement. Again between 1961 and 1966, the sales of non-food shops in general increased by 26 per cent, those of co-operative societies by 14·6 per cent, those of independent retailers by 18·3 per cent, and those of multiple retailers by 42·9 per cent. As is obvious from the table, however, there were considerable variations in the fortunes of different non-foods departments, the worst results coming in exactly those departments, Men's Wear and Footwear, that the Independent Commission had warned would have to be organised on a far larger scale if they were to meet the competition of the multiple chains. Indeed, these national chains have become even more concentrated than they were in the 'fifties.

The relative decline in co-operative food sales slightly influenced the pattern of co-operative trade:

DEPARTMENTAL PERCENTAGES OF CO-OPERATIVE TRADE
1935–1968

	1935	1948	1958	1968
Grocery, Bread and Confectionery ...	57·7	52·0	53·2	49·8
Butchery...	8·5	6·6	7·5	6·6
Greenfruit and Fish	1·6	2·4	1·8	1·0
Dairy	7·7	11·3	11·7	14·1
Total Food	75·5	72·3	74·4	71·6
Drapery	7·9	8·6	6·6	6·7
Men's Wear	2·7	2·5	1·9	1·9
Footwear	2·5	3·0	1·7	1·7
Furnishing, Hardware and Electrical...	3·2	5·0	6·6	8·4
Total Dry Goods	16·5	19·1	17·0	18·7
Coal and Fuel	4·5	4·2	4·0	3·1
Pharmacy and Optical...	0·6	1·8	2·0	2·4
Other Departments	2·7	2·6	2·4	4·2

A survey of this table suggests little change in the general pattern. Foodstuffs and dry goods had nearly the same proportion in 1958 as in 1935. Since 1958 the proportion of foodstuffs has declined somewhat but, as pointed out, this has taken place in a situation of a declining volume of trade. Between the Census of Distribution of 1957 and that of 1966 expenditure in retail outlets on foods increased by 39·1 per cent and expenditure on non-foods increased by 51·2 per cent. Continuation of this trend would mean that spending on non-foods would be greater than that on foodstuffs by the late 'seventies. There is no evidence of such a trend in the pattern of co-operative sales.

It is arguable that the pattern of co-operative trade is very different from the pattern of national consumer expenditure because the Movement established a strong foothold in the foods trades before faced with strong competition whereas in dry goods they never had such a start over the multiples. Thus the trend has been for many co-operative members to buy much of their food from their own shops, but their clothing and footwear from the shops of the multiples. It was estimated by the C.W.S. Market Research in 1955 that if co-operative members gave the same share of their spending to co-operative dry goods trade as they did to co-operative grocery the Movement's dry goods trade would be trebled. The continuing, largely changeless pattern of co-operative trade was consequently to be deplored; it is not surprising that it engaged much of the attention of the Independent Commission. It is to be regretted that the problem has not substantially changed.

There were signs, however, that towards the end of the period in question things were improving particularly as a result of some of the activities of the reorganised Wholesale Societies. In England and Wales, for example, the national marketing campaigns carried out by the C.W.S. with intensive television and newspaper–magazine advertising was having an impact and many societies were participating in " Operation Facelift," a C.W.S. sponsored scheme to give co-operative shops a bright, modern, uniform appearance. The full impact of these activities came too late to appear in a full year's trade figures (although there was an increase in co-operative trade in 1968 in contrast to 1967's fall) but preliminary figures for 1969 show encouraging signs. It should be noted that at least some of any improvement in the sales figures for the category " Grocery, Bread and Confectionery " for 1969 will be due to an increase in the sales of cigarettes and tobacco. The quick and ready response of the Movement to the ending of resale price maintenance on these commodities in September of 1968 was a credit to its forward planning and had a marked effect on sales figures, but it is unlikely that societies will be entirely satisfied with an increased reliance on commodities that have such low profitability.

At this stage, however, it is unrealistic to expect any rapid, immediate improvements. The concentration of the Movement's resources into larger, more economic units, whether they be regional retail societies or reorganised, streamlined federations, and the rebuilding of the Movement's reputation are essentially long-term operations, the full results of which cannot reasonably be expected for some years.

CAPITAL OF RETAIL SOCIETIES IN THE
POST-WAR PERIOD

Co-operative finances were not subject to the same degree of stress and strain after the second world war as they were after the first. After the first, members in dire straits as a result of the post-war slump withdrew their savings from their co-operative share accounts in order to make ends meet; after the second there were withdrawals, not to meet dire need, but to buy the goods which war had denied them. Withdrawals began as restrictions on goods were diminished or abolished. Amounts withdrawn were substantial in amount but a very small percentage of the whole so that there was no embarrassment. Nor was the period of withdrawal a long one; share capital fell between 1947 and 1951 and total capital funds (share, loan and sundry funds) fell between 1948 and 1952. Then, during the remainder of the 'fifties, capital funds continued to increase year by year although at a lesser rate than they had before the war.

Since 1961, however, there has been a reversal of this trend. Every year since then has seen a decline in share capital, loan capital, and small savings so that in total members are holding about £63,000,000 less capital in co-operative societies in 1968 than they were in 1961. In the same period, sundry funds have increased by about £38,000,000 to £116,000,000 in 1968 (compared with £204,000,000 share capital). The substantial proportion of these sundry funds consists of loans from employees' superannuation funds (£89,000,000 in 1968), which have assumed a marked significance in the finances of societies, particularly considering their growth rate in comparison with other sources of capital. This could be dangerous in view of the possibility, for example, that a new State scheme could be introduced better than that at present offered by societies or restricting any contracting-out; the possibility of some more stringent regulations about occupational pension schemes requiring a greater spread of risk by diversifying investments; the possibility that as trustees of their employees' superannuation funds, directors of societies could find themselves personally liable should any loss be incurred.

The consequences of E.P.T., as has been shown, deterred societies from adding to their reserves as much as they would have liked during the war. Indeed, the treatment of undistributed surplus as a profit liable to tax and distributed surplus as a collective saving not liable to tax has usually tended to deter societies from building up reserves, and taxes which are designed to encourage business to plough back profits, like the pre-1958 Profits Tax and Corporation Tax, have the opposite effect on co-operative societies that they are designed to have on private business. Under such schemes companies and/or their share-holders pay more tax on dividends than on undistributed profits; co-operative dividends are not liable to tax but undistributed surplus is.

Nevertheless, after the war the reserves of societies began to accumulate again, although not at a particularly satisfactory rate. The Co-operative Union Financial Policy Committee's Report in 1952 stressed the importance of a more rapid build-up of reserves and the Independent Commission were concerned about the low level of reserve allocation in co-operative societies, advising that a greater proportion of surplus should be put to reserve. The published reserves in 1968 stood at £49,000,000, equivalent to 24·05 per cent of share capital as against the 1948 figure of £21,900,000, 8·9 per cent of share capital.

Co-operative societies certainly obtained capital at very low cost, partly due to the effects of inflation, share interest amounting to just over £5 millions in 1938 and to just over £6·5 millions in 1968. In that period trade had increased from £263 millions to £997 millions, so that the burden of share interest on its trade was much less in 1968 than in 1938. Share interest in 1938 amounted to 3·35 per cent of its share capital, in 1968 to 3·23 per cent; in proportion to trade 1·9 per cent in 1938 and 0·6 per cent in 1968.

Co-operative societies, of course, were never intended to be used for capital investment purposes; they were non-profit making organisations so the intention has been to pay capital a fair reward for the service it yielded and use the surplus in ways to eliminate profiting from members' trade. The decline in share capital since 1961 and the fact that the return on share capital is about the same as it was in 1938 suggest that many members no longer consider their return a fair one, however. It has been argued in the past that the kind of people who invest in co-opera-tive societies and the amounts of money they invest are not much affected by interest rates. Security and liquidity, on the other hand, are of much more importance. This may well have been true at one time but with increasing prosperity it would appear that people are becoming rather more interest conscious. Another view is expressed that in the Welfare State and affluent society people are less interested in saving. This is quite untrue; the fact is that the better-off people become the more they are able and the more they do save. The expansion of institutions anxious to use people's savings—building societies, insurance companies, unit trusts—are the living proof. Equally, the expansion of the building societies would seem to disprove the view that in an inflationary situation, people are not interested in fixed value securities.

Yet in this time of expanding savings, members have been withdrawing their capital. Part of the explanation would certainly be the low interest rates paid by societies. Interest rates on share capital, for example, rarely compete with those paid by building societies. There is certainly a case for looking at these very closely but probably an even stronger case for looking at loan capital and raising longer term loans at higher rates of interest, a policy adopted by many societies already. There is the danger that capital will merely be switched out of share accounts into loan accounts, but, as the Co-operative Union has pointed out, that is better than losing the capital altogether. In any case, interest rates are not the whole story. Confidence in a society's security and future, a society's trade performance, the impression of competence or otherwise given to the public will also clearly be of some importance, and again, where any doubts have been cast on these, as they have in a number of cases, the task of rebuilding confidence is essentially a long term process.

SURPLUS AND RATES OF DIVIDEND

During the 'fifties, the general situation was one of larger amounts being returned to members while concern was being expressed about declining dividend rates. In 1948 the total surplus excluding share interest had been £40 millions and the average dividend rate 1/5½d., in 1958 total surplus was £59 millions and the average dividend 1/0¼d. Charging lower prices for goods is bound to reduce the profit on sales although the quicker turn-over that one hopes to achieve as a result of those lower prices should increase the total amount of profit and the rate of profit on capital.

However, the trend during the 'sixties has been rather different since both total surpluses and dividend rates have been declining. Between 1958 and 1968, the total surplus fell by £23 millions to £35·5 millions and the average dividend rate for 1967 (the last year for which it was calculated in s. d.) stood at 6¾d. The pressures of competition, particularly in the food trades, made it difficult for many societies to pay an attractive dividend or any at all in a few cases, and there have been many societies who have adopted new measures. Some societies have dropped the payment of dividend altogether in some or all of their food shops and have substituted a deep, cut-price policy. There is nothing essentially unco-operative about this. Whether people receive the economic benefits of co-operative trading immediately or at the end of the accounting period is largely a matter of taste and possibly business prudence. The criticism is that non-members get exactly the same benefits as members.

Another technique has been the adoption of dividend stamps by many societies where customers receive a number of stamps, proportionate to the value of purchases made, which they can save by sticking into a book. When a book is complete they have the choice of exchanging the book for cash, using it to buy goods from the society's stores, or depositing it in a share account. In most societies, the book acquires a greater value in each of the respective uses. From the society's point of view this method has the considerable advantage of being much cheaper to operate than the more conventional dividend systems, it encourages spending with the society and it has been argued that customers like the method. On the other hand, societies are, for the first time, contracting to pay a dividend before they have made it. In principle at least, co-operative dividend has always been regarded as a residual. If there is a surplus left at the end of the accounting period then it may be distributed amongst the members. In practice most societies attempted to make a certain rate of dividend but if they failed to make it, they had made no contracts about it. In fact, the rate of dividend that dividend stamps represent is so low that societies would have to be in very dire straits not to be able to meet it, but the practice does nevertheless mark a departure from previously recommended co-operative practice.

CREDIT TRADE

The table on page 253 showed a continual increase in credit trade between 1948 and 1968. The average amount owing per member in 1948 was £1·14, in 1958 £2·37, and in 1968 £3·31. Allowing for increases in prices and the increase in credit trade generally, the increase is insubstantial. The percentage of members' indebtedness to trade increased slightly from 2·3 per cent in 1948 to 3·9 per cent in 1968. In view of the small part of co-operative trade represented by goods characteristically bought on hire purchase and other types of credit, such figures are hardly surprising.

LOCAL FEDERATIONS

Retail societies have often discovered that some service or trade has an economical scale of operation bigger than is possible for the individual society. The solution to this problem is federation, a number of societies establishing a federal society to undertake that particular trade or service, run on Rochdale principles, the societies being the members. Some of these federations are national, such as the Wholesale Societies and the Co-operative Union, but there are also many local federations, principally for dairies, bakeries, laundries, solid fuel, footwear repairing, funeral furnishing and drugs.

Year	No. of Societies	Share Capital £m.	Loan Capital £m.	Reserve and Insurance Funds £m.	Trade £m.	Surplus £m.
1948	82	2·8	4·3	0·73	12·7	1·1
1958	87	7·1	5·8	1·35	32·7	2·0
1968	56	4·9	3·8	2·05	44·6	1·2

The heavy reduction in the number of these societies since 1958 is mainly, but not entirely, accounted for by the reduction in the number of bakery societies which, together with many individual retail societies who previously undertook their own baking, have given over their operations to the C.W.S. Bakery Division.

THE WHOLESALE SOCIETIES

The progress of the Wholesale Societies is indicated by the following table:—

		(In £ millions)				
Year	Trade (Wholesale)	Value of Productions	Share Capital	Reserves	Number Employed	
					Distrib.	Product'n.
C.W.S.						
1948	252	78	20·1	19·0	8,933	41,044
1958	463	143	30·1	22·9	10,708	40,873
1968	483	141	31·5	47·5	7,582	27,976
S.C.W.S.						
1948	55	20	2·3	3·5	2,479	13,673
1958	90	25	4·7	7·0	2,777	13,453
1968	85	16	5·0	13·7	2,217	6,720

As one would expect, the trading fortunes of the Wholesale Societies are closely tied to those of the retail societies. Thus, during the 'fifties, trade increased fairly steadily but during the 'sixties this progress has been very unsteady and in the case of the Scottish C.W.S. has been reversed. Even where wholesale trade has increased, it has been in less proportion than has retail trade. In 1946, the proportion of wholesale trade, at wholesale prices, to retail trade at retail prices was 61·5 per cent, in 1958 55·4 per cent, and in 1968 51·9 per cent. These figures are a very rough guide, for all the trade of the Wholesale Societies is not with retail societies and some of that which is, does not come directly into retail sales, e.g., sales of vehicles, shop and office fittings.

The composition of retail societies' trade is also reflected in the Wholesale Societies' trade. For example, the C.W.S. Food Division was responsible for 77 per cent of all C.W.S. sales in 1968 (and for 93 per cent of its grand trading profit before the deduction of unallocated expenses). Within the Food Division, groceries are by far the largest single item. All other departments outside of this Division are relatively unimportant although each is responsible for trade running into millions of pounds; the most substantial are housewares and optical, drapery, and coal.

Production by the Wholesales showed a steadily rising curve until 1958. In fact, from 1953, C.W.S. production was rising faster than its sales but its progress in many directions was disappointing and some factories were working below capacity. But again, since 1958 the problems have become more apparent. The value of Wholesale productions went up unsteadily until the mid-'sixties but the value of C.W.S. productions has declined steadily since 1965 when they had stood at £160 millions and those of the S.C.W.S. since 1960 when they had been £25 millions. In both cases the cutback in production has been the result of quite deliberate policies since the reorganisation of the Societies involved close and rigorous scrutiny of productive and distributive units with the purpose of eliminating those that are unprofitable. This examination resulted in the closure of some factories and the reorganisation of others. In the case of furniture production, the decision was taken to cease altogether and to concentrate on the marketing of furniture. There were those that argued that in this process the Wholesales were sacrificing long-term advantage for the sake of short-term expediency but, on the other hand, it was certainly true that several factories had not been profitable for some time and the example of many of the Movement's competitors, particularly in the dry goods trades, suggested that buying power was at least as important as productive facilities for getting goods made to specification at acceptable prices.

The failure was one that had long been recognised in principle, namely that the Movement's potential was far from being fully realised because retail societies were not fully utilising the concentration of buying and production available in their federal societies. Whether the blame for that situation lay with the retail or the Wholesale societies was debatable but the essential issue was to solve the problem. Following the failure of the Movement to set up a single national advisory, wholesaling, and productive federation on the lines proposed by the National Federation Negotiating Committee in 1964, both Wholesale Societies sponsored investigations into their effectiveness. Both the C.W.S. Joint Reorganisation Committee (consisting of equal numbers of C.W.S. directors and elected representatives of member societies) and the S.C.W.S. Review of Organisation (undertaken by the Board of Directors with the assistance of a management consultancy firm) concluded, as the N.F.N.C. had done, that closer relationships were going to have to be developed between retail and wholesale societies if the Movement were going to progress or even survive as a major retailing force.

Thus, in the acceptance of the reorganisation proposals, the retail societies have at least nominally recognised their identity of interest with the Wholesale Societies. Under the terms of the new relationship, the Wholesale Societies explicitly recognise that their primary function is to serve the retail societies and to obtain and organise the supply of goods to societies on a co-ordinated basis " with the principle of service rather than of profit as its guide." For their part, retail societies undertake to work together in the co-ordination of merchandise ranges " and to give effective undertakings of continued trading support." The intention of such a scheme is to achieve the integrated marketing approach that increasingly appears to be a precondition of success in contemporary retailing and since the reorganisation of the Wholesales, considerable progress seems to have been made in this direction. The C.W.S., for example, has introduced the new " Co-op " symbol now used by almost all retail societies as well; has eliminated the wide variety of brand names used for its productions replacing them by the generic brand name, " Co-op"; has redesigned all packaging for its products; has conducted a large number of national marketing campaigns in both foods and non-foods; and has introduced " Operation Facelift," to give as many co-operative shops as possible a modern and uniform appearance.

While other departments of the Wholesales experienced difficulties, however, the Banking Departments continued to grow. The number of current and deposit accounts held in the C.W.S. Banking Department rose from 73,382 in 1939 to 125,301 in 1948, 163,410 in 1958, and 237,395 in 1968. Its facilities were such that it appealed increasingly to others than co-operative societies. Most trade unions and many public authorities, friendly societies, various mutual organisations and thousands of individuals were holding accounts with it. In fact, this amount now far exceeds the amount held by co-operative societies. Its current account turnover increased from £2,138 millions in 1948, to £5,042 millions in 1958, to £13,362 millions in 1968.

The S.C.W.S. Banking Department had 3,949 accounts in 1948 with a current account turnover of £103 millions, 6,114 accounts with a current account turnover of £508 millions in 1958, and in 1968 7,348 accounts and £567 millions current account turnover.

There have been suggestions from time to time that the Wholesales' Banking Departments should be set up as separate organisations. A minority report coming from the Inquiry Committee set up in 1953 to inquire into the financial control and management of the C.W.S., for example, recommended the setting up of a separate Co-operative Bank although such a bank was to be owned and controlled by the C.W.S.; the majority report, however, held that "the attempt to make the Bank a separate entity at the present time would be wrong." This remains the case to the present although the C.W.S. Banking Department is now known as the Co-operative Bank.

C.I.S.

Part of the case for a separate bank was the success of the Co-operative Insurance Society, which was owned by both Wholesale Societies but run as a separate venture. Its premium income rose from £21,709,000 in 1948, to £47,702,000 in 1958, and to £88,271,000 in 1968. All classes of insurance were effected, though Industrial Life, Ordinary Life and Motor predominated. Its reserve funds increased from £86 millions in 1948 to £464 millions in 1968.

CO-OPERATIVE PERMANENT BUILDING SOCIETY

All building societies are in essence co-operative, but the C.P.B.S. was always regarded as being particularly so. Founded in 1884, it grew slowly until 1919 when the vast extension of home ownership in the inter-war years enabled it to grow rapidly. In 1939, its assets amounted to £39 millions and it had 150,000 borrowing and investing members. Little could be done during the war, but it has made exceptional progress since and is now the third largest building society in the country.

(£ millions)

Year	Members	Shares	Loans	Reserves	Advances on Mortgage
1948	181,012	35·5	14·5	2·6	14·1
1958	537,562	181·6	14·2	5·7	30·2
1968	908,236	533·8	9·0	19·2	114·6

It was also helpful in assisting co-operative efforts such as Self Help building projects and co-operative housing societies.

However, the C.P.B.S. withdrew from membership of the Co-operative Union in March, 1970. Apparently it was the desire of the C.P.B.S. by this means, and possibly also by a change of name at some future date, to separate its identity from the Consumers' Co-operative Movement. This brought to an end an historical affinity which the Co-operative Union regretted.

CO-PARTNERSHIP SOCIETIES

The co-operative co-partnership societies were mainly engaged in industries, clothing and footwear, which did not enjoy the general expansion of the 'fifties. Heavy weather indeed was experienced through a sudden boom in prices and acute scarcity of raw materials caused by the Korean Wear, and then a sudden slump, with heavy losses on stocks due to the war's ending. The following table gives some indication of their position:—

PRODUCTIVE SOCIETIES

Year	No. of Societies	Share and Loan Capital £m.	Reserves £m.	Sales £m.	Net Surplus £m.	No. of Employees
1948	46	1·191	1·124	2·692	0·477	6,640
1958	41	1·793	1·569	6·463	0·319	4,898
1968	30	1·409	1·846	6·185	0·159	3,375

The last years of the decade of the 'fifties were not happy ones for these societies, which experienced reductions in share and loan capital, sales, net surplus and number of employees, though there was a pleasing increase in their reserves. Most of their trade was with co-operative societies, although the printing group and some of the " miscellaneous " societies had a substantial trade outside the Movement. It was saddening to many co-operators to witness this shrinking of trade, for co-operative trade had been regarded as exceptionally stable.

A severe blow was also suffered in 1959 by the defection of two large societies from membership of the Co-operative Productive Federation. This resulted from events following the Report of an Independent Committee of Inquiry set up in 1958. The C.P.F. had experienced difficulties through rising costs due to inflation, a falling off in subscription income due to the falling surpluses of member societies, a severe decline in income from the Joint Invoice Scheme, and the honouring of a guarantee of a society which went into liquidation. The Committee expressed the opinion that the Joint Invoice scheme was likely to shrink still further and recommended an increase and change in method of subscription and various curtailment of activities to reduce expenses. Increased subscriptions and the prospect of less service appear to have been the reason for the withdrawal of the two societies.

The decline of the late 'fifties continued throughout the 'sixties with about a quarter of the societies disappearing altogether. Although the increase in reserves almost compensated for the loss of share and loan capital, it allowed societies to merely remain where they were before. Sales declined considerably particularly when allowance is made for increases in prices and net surplus fell dramatically. The largest decline in numbers occurred amongst footwear societies who were reduced from twelve to seven. By 1968 only a third of these productive societies were members of the Co-operative Productive Federation.

11 THE CO-OPERATIVE MOVEMENT, 1945-1970. OTHER CHANGES IN ORGANISATION AND DEVELOPMENT

> " In the teeth of the opposition of big business the Co-operative Movement has made immense progress. It sets high standards of service. It stands for fair dealing and good quality. It strives for the consumer against the monopolists; it has done away with exploitation by returning trading surplus to the customer. Above all, it shows that voluntary Co-operation is a marriage of high democratic principle and sound practical commonsense. Voluntary Co-operation should be free to expand in the interest of the consumer."
>
> (*Co-operative Union Statement on Agricultural Marketing Policy, 1952.*)

THE previous chapter described some of the economic and social background of the post-war period and the business reactions of the Co-operative Movement to it. There were, however, other features and other reactions perhaps more important in the long run. Among the features was an accentuation of collectivist economic planning, which, it should be observed, may be neither socialist in purpose nor method. This demanded an examination of co-operative ideals and principles, of the *raison d'etre* of the Movement, and a defence of its right to exist and to grow. The nature of the business, social, and political problems facing the Movement, as well as others presented by its own growth, required reorganisation of the Movement as a whole, as well as of its parts. This is the subject matter of this chapter.

CO-OPERATIVE UNION POST-WAR REORGANISATION

The nature and functions of the Co-operative Union make it susceptible to every economic, social, and political change. Embodying nearly all co-operative societies in the country, with the exception of most agricultural societies which prefer to remain outside the Movement, its reactions and responses are those of the Movement as a whole. Hence the history of the Co-operative

Union during this period epitomises much of the history of the Movement, too, at this time.

As has been shown, it was a period of considerable change and consequently the work and functions of the Co-operative Union increased. Controls continued for many years, new ones were introduced, old ones were amended and ended. Problems were created on which the guidance and advice of the Union were required; similarly there were fiscal and legal problems created by a spate of legislation. Problems were created by the revival of statutory marketing schemes. Inflation brought financial and labour problems. The re-emergence of the problems of reorganisation and co-ordination, problems created by the policies and projected schemes of political parties, the need to prepare and present cases to defend the interests and cause of Co-operation before government committees, political parties, and the public in general, all these increasing demands upon the services of the Union resulted in its expansion and growth and reorganisation.

Post-war reorganisation began in 1946 with the setting up of a special committee on " Congress Procedure." It submitted a full report dealing with preparations for Congress, choice of date, place, president, representation, submission of resolutions and amendments, the conduct of Congress, standing orders, length and programme of proceedings. In the main its proposals were accepted by the Congress of 1947 which also took steps to reorganise the constitution of the Co-operative Union.

These were induced by some constitutional uncertainty of the spheres of operation of the National Executive, the National Authority, the Joint Parliamentary Committee, with consequent danger of overlapping in policy matters and the belief that the Movement was not exercising the influence on the Labour Government which it should. Government economic planning and its probable extension increased the need for the Co-operative Union to be able to act quickly and as an authoritative body. A resolution was carried which declared that " the present machinery of the Co-operative Movement is not capable of bringing to bear our full weight upon the Government and its policy " and instructed the National Executive to produce proposals for " an effective quick-acting body, empowered to represent the whole of the Movement."

Proposals intended to put this resolution into effect, however, were not accepted by the Congress of 1948, but another resolution was carried which instructed the National Executive to amend the rules and constitution of the Co-operative Union along certain defined lines. Some hoped that the proposals would include the abolition or the reduction in size of the Central Board, but the upshot in 1949 was an enlargement of the Central Board by 18 representatives; of the C.W.S. (8), the S.C.W.S. (4), the Co-operative Press (2), the C.P.F. (2), and the Co-operative Party (2).

New Constitution

A new executive called the " Central Executive " was brought into being consisting of representatives of the Central Board (two from each Sectional Board and one from the Irish Executive) and the chairman of the Central Board, four from the C.W.S., two from the S.C.W.S., one from the Co-operative Press, two from the Co-operative Party, and one from the C.P.F. The National Co-operative Authority and the Joint Parliamentary Committee were abolished, but at its first meeting in 1949 the Central Executive decided to establish two principal sub-committees, the General Purposes Committee, replacing the National Executive, and the Parliamentary Committee replacing the former Joint Parliamentary Committee.

Constitutional changes were made, too, in the Trade Associations, in the Co-operative Party, and in the constitution of the Education Department which will be dealt with later.

The constitutional changes of 1949 had brought representation of the national federations into the Co-operative Union, thus making it a more widely representative and so authoritative body, but the expansion of the Central Board did not conform with the streamlined constitutional machinery which some desired. Thus, in 1952, the Central Board was abolished by Congress and the Central Executive was made the principal authority of the Co-operative Union, although an annual meeting of the Sectional Boards was to be held at each Congress. Some regretted this abolition on historical grounds: the Central Board was older than the Co-operative Union itself, and in name and conception went back to the Owenite movement which preceded Rochdale, being indeed revived by William Pare in the eighteen sixties.

The Movement, however, is too businesslike to have undue respect for ancient monuments, and the defence of the Central Board rested on a claim that it was vital to the democratic control of the Co-operative Union. Its use and importance had indeed been stressed by the National Executive in the 1949 debates, although the Wholesale Societies would have even then preferred its abolition. However, the case against it held that the expenditure of time and money it involved was not justified by the purpose it served, the Central Executive was in fact doing the work, and the

Central Board was a piece of redundant machinery. Nevertheless, it had strong support and the resolution to abolish it was carried only by the very narrow margin of 5,703 votes to 5,594.

There was a good deal of unhappiness at this decision, the Sectional Boards felt their status had been lowered and they had lost power to determine policy. This feeling showed itself at the first annual meeting of the Sectional Boards with the Central Executive, which passed a resolution asking the Central Executive to find some basis for collective action by the Sectional Boards. This would have meant the revival of the Central Board in some other form, so the Central Executive in effect declined.

Amendments

A Committee of Inquiry into the machinery of the Union set up in 1954 expressed general approval of it when it reported the following year. To bring the Sectional Boards more into the picture, however, it recommended that members of the Sectional Boards should receive the minutes of all the national committees including those of the Central Executive. Matters of major policy, when practicable, were to have prior consultation by the Sectional Boards on each of which there would be their two representatives on the Central Executive.

This situation was modified in 1962 when the membership of the Central Executive was changed slightly. It was felt that retail societies ought to be directly represented on the Executive as well as indirectly via the Sectional Boards, so the representation from each of these Boards was reduced from two to one and each Section, with the exception of Ireland, was given one representative who may or may not be a member of the appropriate Sectional Board and who was to be elected by the societies in the Section.

In 1960 the Development Committee had been set up (see section on the Independent Commission Report) as a special committee answerable to Congress and responsible for the Development Department among whose functions were to make a sustained study of consumer trends and make recommendations as to co-operative action for changes in methods and organisation and consideration of new enterprises, the scrutiny of specific development proposals of retail societies, and the consideration of financial problems. In practice, the Committee itself felt it was overlapping with the Central Executive and the Trade Associations so in 1962 the Development Committee was abolished and the Central Executive adopted the pattern of sub-committees which remained until 1970. In addition to the by-now familiar General Purposes Committee, responsible for the management and administration of the Union, and the Parliamentary Committee, responsible for the promotion and examination of legislation, a third sub-committee was introduced, the Trade Advisory Committee, with much the same functions as the old Development Committee but with a responsibility not only for the Development Department but also for the Food Trades Department and the Dry Goods Trades Department.

Inflation, and the increase in activities, necessitated increases in subscriptions to the Union in spite of many economies. Before the war each member society paid a subscription of 2d. per member, a rate increased to 3d. after the war and over the next twenty years reached 6d. in 1965. Since then it has been maintained at the same rate, a rare example of price stability.

CO-OPERATIVE UNION AND POST-WAR LABOUR GOVERNMENTS

Because of its close links with the Labour Party, the Co-operative Movement has generally welcomed the two periods of Labour Government in Britain since the last war. The support given by the Co-operative Movement was probably stronger for the 1945–51 administrations than the 1964–70 ones but this was probably part of a wider mood of greater expectations in 1945 than in 1964. Despite the different contexts of the two periods, however, some of the themes of the two periods are remarkably similar.

Many of the measures of nationalisation and improvements in social security undertaken in the first period were welcomed by the Movement which had indeed been advocating such measures for many years. The Movement was also keen to assist the Chancellor of the Exchequer in preventing further inflation, feared as a menace to national recovery. In February, 1948, the Government issued a " Statement on Personal Incomes, Costs, and Prices " which urged voluntary restraint on wages, profits and prices. It was recognised that success in the attempt to peg wages depended not merely on stabilising prices but in reducing them. Quick action was necessary, and in February and March the National Co-operative Authority devised a scheme and appealed to all retail societies to make it effective. Certain price reductions were recommended in sugar, bacon, margarine, cheese, butter, preserves, and bread. The Wholesale Societies agreed to payment of bonuses to societies who made the recommended price reductions.

Despite criticisms of the Authority's initiative, the policy was overwhelmingly accepted by Congress and put into effect by societies containing the vast bulk of the membership. Average national rates of dividend fell by 3d. between 1947 and 1949.

As a gesture the action was possibly to be commended and it is conceivable that only the Co-operative Movement was capable of such action. But it could be little more than a gesture without effective Government action to restrain costs such as rising wages. This was not forthcoming to the necessary extent. In any case, without corresponding savings or tax increases, the reduction of certain prices had no effect on the level of total demand which would simply be switched to other goods. Indeed, the reduction in dividends resulting from the price reductions could well have marginally reduced savings from retained dividend and released some cash for more immediate expenditure.

In fact, the Authority reported to Congress in 1949 that: " Almost immediately after the operation of the policy, substantial wage increases had to be conceded to the trade unions (including those in co-operative employment) and then followed additional costs involved in the new scheme of Social Insurance." Exhortations by Government and the setting of a good example by the Co-operative Movement were utterly inadequate to stem the inflation.

There were other matters which made the Co-operative Movement critical of Government policy and administration, such matters as licensing systems which prevented the Movement from building new shops and factories, and the introduction of new taxes like the 1946 Profits Tax which included co-operative societies' undistributed surplus as a profit. Many co-operators had expected a more understanding attitude from a Labour Government.

The return of a Labour Government in 1964 after thirteen years in opposition was again largely welcomed by the Co-operative Movement and the Government started with a considerable amount of Co-operative goodwill. The Government again felt the need to exercise a restraining influence on prices and incomes and again the Co-operative Movement was willing to assist although on this occasion it is notable that the Movement's efforts were of a rather less precise character than they had been in the forties. A letter sent to all societies by the Co-operative Union early in 1965 was in part a narration of the reasons given by the Union to the Minister of Agriculture for recent unavoidable price increases. However, the letter also expressed the Union's support for " the Government's desire for the maximum possible price stability and urges all societies to examine their costs and trading methods with a view to containing price rises to the maximum extent possible. It is for each society to determine what contribution it can make to the national effort at this time . . ."

Any feeling that the Movement's goodwill towards the Government was returned, was rudely shattered the next year when Selective Employment Tax was introduced which placed a severe and continuing strain on the Movement's support for the Government. This, together with the withdrawal of investment allowances for retailers earlier the same year, put considerable pressure on the finances of co-operative societies. Further increases in the tax in 1968 and 1969 increased this pressure and caused some people to doubt the wisdom of giving any kind of support to the Government. But officially the Co-operative Union maintained its support while doing all in its power to make its opposition to Selective Employment Tax as effective as possible, short of asking or advising Co-operative M.P.'s to vote against the tax in the House of Commons.

AGRICULTURAL MARKETING SCHEMES

Pre-war grievances of the Co-operative Movement against the Government's agricultural policies also continued. In spite of the privileges, subsidies, rate reliefs, protection, and marketing schemes between the wars and the abnormal war conditions, British agriculture was still in a precarious position. Its prosperity was due to artificial conditions—guaranteed minimum prices for producers and maximum prices for consumers, the gap between the two being filled by heavy Government subsidies. These conditions might well change.

Desiring a prosperous and stable agriculture the Labour Government was unfortunately attracted to the pre-war schemes of Producer Marketing Boards and was even contemplating Import Boards as a further protection. The Co-operative Movement was alarmed at the general vagueness of the proposals and at the obvious dangers to the consumer, the creation of monopoly powers and profits and the raising of prices. Yet in spite of co-operative protests an Agricultural Marketing Act was passed in 1949 for the purpose of re-establishing Producer Marketing Boards.

The Government was still, however, largely engaged in trading in foods, it was the sole purchaser of all wheat, milk, eggs and meat and whilst this continued the consumer had some safeguard, but in 1954 all food was derationed. The Government was divesting itself of all trading functions. A danger was that as the Government stepped out, producer monopoly schemes would step in, entry having been prepared by the Marketing Act of 1949. The National Farmers' Union was soon active in preparing and submitting schemes. It had seemed to exercise a far more effective influence over even a Labour Minister of Agriculture than did the Co-operative Union. Indeed the Congress Report of 1951 suggested that it would be better to negotiate with the N.F.U. in preparation of schemes than to appear at different public enquiries to object to them.

Co-operative Policy

In 1952 the Co-operative Union issued a statement on Agricultural Marketing Policy, in which it summarised and recapitulated its objections to such schemes from 1931 onwards. It was not opposed to organised marketing, it favoured schemes which improved quality, effected economies and related production to market requirements, but it did criticise the purpose, scope, and procedure of the Marketing Acts, by which only producers could submit schemes, and vote upon them and the majority on a Board must be producers.

Yet their functions were not confined to those which only concerned producer interests. They might buy and sell, regulate quantities and grades, determine the channels of distribution, fix prices and regulate wholesale and retail margins. Other interests could only object at public inquiries, their role could never be other than that of critics and opponents, " at no stage in the preparation of a marketing scheme is adequate provision made for bringing together all parties to arrive at an agreed solution." Thus the whole approach to and the introduction of a scheme was in a most unhealthy atmosphere of sectional interest.

It seemed sinister that in drafting the Monopolies Bill (1948) provision was made for excluding agricultural marketing schemes from its scope. Co-operative opinion was in favour of Reorganisation Commissions being set up by the Ministry of Food (likely to look at matters from a consumer angle) and the Ministry of Agriculture jointly, and that the promotion of a scheme should depend on Government assent and not on the decision of a Minister of Agriculture or the National Farmers' Union. Naturally the Movement preferred the growth of genuine agricultural Co-operation and pointed out how this was growing. Membership of agricultural co-operative societies in 1949 amounted to 70 per cent of farmers, and their sales to £56 million. Most of these societies were members of the C.W.S.

Actually the worst fears of the Co-operative Movement were not realised. The Government, after 1954, showed an unwillingness to establish Boards with the powers permitted by the Act of 1949, and several schemes submitted by the National Farmers' Union were rejected. In fact, Government policy was more in accord with that which had been advocated by the Co-operative Movement, and since 1958, the Co-operative Union has not found it necessary to make any major policy statements on agricultural marketing schemes, although of course the Grocery and Provisions Trade Association and the Parliamentary Committee of the Union have maintained their watching brief to safeguard the interests of Co-operative members and consumers generally. Thus, for example, in 1967 when there was pressure from the Milk Marketing Board and the National Farmers' Union on the Government to withdraw from its controlling position on milk, the Union made its position clear that it felt that the Ministry of Food should remain responsible for the milk industry on the grounds that the Minister was responsible to Parliament and was specifically charged with watching the interests of consumers. In the event of the Ministry withdrawing from this position, the Union would press " for the establishment of an Independent Milk Commission assisted by a Statutory Advisory Committee representing manufacturing, wholesaling, processing and distributive interests." This was simply a re-expression of the Co-operative policy stated in the policy statements of 1952 and 1958.

In the concluding paragraph of the statement on Co-operative Policy on the Agricultural Marketing Acts, 1958, the policy is succinctly expressed, " that there is ample justification for the view that the Agricultural Marketing Acts now provide an obsolete and inadequate framework for devising marketing arrangements appropriate to current conditions. In horticulture, livestock and bacon, action has been taken outside the Agricultural Marketing Acts and in both the Milk and Eggs Schemes the original pattern has been profoundly modified so as to provide a larger place for other trading interests than is envisaged in the basic Acts—every commodity should be looked at separately and the marketing framework adopted of a type specially designed to cover the distinctive features of each trade. This framework must take into account the interests of consumers and distributors as well as producers."

CO-OPERATIVE UNION AND TAXATION

The Co-operative Union continued to be concerned over fiscal matters; it continued its campaign against Purchase Tax in the interests of consumers in general, but was also involved in disputes over the liability of co-operative societies to Profits Tax, imposed after the cessation of E.P.T. in 1946. In framing this tax the unique features of co-operative financial structure had been overlooked and its imposition was not only unjust but opposed to the purposes of the tax as expressed by the Chancellor. Representations were made and the Finance Act of 1947 made some valuable concessions, although the Movement was not happy at the assumptions on which the tax was still imposed. Later in 1947 the tax was increased and all manner of anomalies were exposed. Some societies found their liability increased by 17 times, others only doubled.

Nevertheless, private trade carried on a Press campaign against what it regarded as preferential treatment for co-operative societies, to which the Co-operative Union replied. Perhaps because of the feelings expressed by private trade, however, co-operative grievances were not met by the Chancellor.

In 1958 these grievances were increased by the Finance Act which replaced the two rates of Profits tax, 3 per cent on undistributed and 30 per cent on distributed profits by a flat rate of 10 per cent. As co-operative societies had been taxed at the 3 per cent rate, they experienced an increased rate of tax whereas other businesses enjoyed a tax relief. Societies paid an additional £1,500,000 tax by this measure.

In 1964, in the first Budget of the new Labour Government, the Chancellor announced his intention of introducing a Corporation Tax to be levied on companies and other corporate bodies in place of the existing Income Tax and Profits Tax. There was some attempt to get co-operative societies treated differently from companies for the purposes of this tax but no success was achieved and indeed there seemed to be some relief that the principles on which the taxation of societies were based were not changed, namely that dividend was to be treated as a trade discount and share and loan interest was to be allowed as a deduction in arriving at the income for Corporation Tax purposes.

Grievances about the system of taxation have been concentrated almost entirely on Selective Employment Tax since its introduction in 1966. As a result of this tax, all employers paid a flat rate contribution on all their employees as part of their National Insurance contribution. For employers in service industries the payment was a net burden and was never seen again, but employers in manufacturing industry received their contributions back after six months together with an extra premium (equal to an extra 30 per cent), while employers in certain other industries such as agriculture and construction simply received their original contributions back. The premium to manufacturing employers has since been withdrawn (except for the regional employment premium in development districts) but this has done nothing to lessen the Co-operative Movement's opposition to the tax.

Consistent opposition has been maintained to the principles of the tax, particularly its discriminatory nature. When the tax was introduced one of the supporting arguments put forward was that it was desirable to correct the bias of indirect taxation towards manufactured goods. There may well have been some truth in that argument for certain services but it certainly did not apply to distribution since the incidence of any tax on goods fell on the consumer so Purchase Tax, for example, is as much a tax on distribution as it is on manufacturing. A more curious argument used by the Chancellor at the time was the allegation that it was desirable that the numbers engaged in manufacturing should be increased and those in services decreased, implying there was something preferable about producing goods to producing services, an argument not seriously entertained by economists for many years. Even if it were true that too many people were engaged in distribution, the only area in which it could be maintained was in the proliferation of small one-man shops who were not touched by the tax, since it was not applied to the self-employed.

The net cost of S.E.T. to retail societies in its first full year was £8,200,000, equivalent to 2·09d. per £ of sales. Since then the rate has been increased twice, from 25/- to 37/6 to 48/- for men and from 12/6 to 18/9 to 24/- for women. Professor Reddaway, undertaking a survey for the Chancellor on the effects of S.E.T. on prices, profit margins, and productivity, suggested that since the introduction of the tax productivity in distribution had increased more than would have been expected on the pre-1966 experience. Similarly prices and margins had risen more slowly. Opponents of the tax were not necessarily convinced, however. Reddaway himself admitted the difficulty of separating the effect of S.E.T. from other factors such as the ending of resale price maintenance which worked in the opposite way on prices to S.E.T. And with regard to productivity, opponents pointed to the increasing rate of investment in retailing in the mid-sixties both by retailers and property developers which could reasonably be expected to lead to improvements in productivity particularly since much of this investment was in bigger and more efficient shops.

The Co-operative Union, recognising that simply opposing the

tax was not enough, made its own proposals for alternatives to
S.E.T. mainly in terms of a general payroll tax and a wealth tax.
The most likely alternative, however, appeared increasingly to
be a tax on value added on the model of the indirect tax system
of the European Common Market, apparently favoured on
principle by the Conservative Party and a likely condition of
entry to the Common Market. The Co-operative Movement had
its misgivings about this too and declared its opposition to the
tax at the 1970 Congress.

The size and complexities of the taxation system so increased
the demands of societies upon the Co-operative Union for assistance and advice that a special department of Taxation was set up
in 1954. Previously this work had been performed by the Finance
Department. A good deal of its work continued to be negotiations
with the Inland Revenue on behalf of societies to get their assess-
ments reduced. As the assistance and advice of the Union became
more generally followed, these cases and the amounts recovered
naturally tended to decrease, although it amounted to £198,000
for 140 societies in 1953. The amount was down to £41,000 for
100 societies in 1956 but then began to rise, amounting to £71,000
for 106 societies in 1958, and throughout the 1960's has remained
at about £70,000. All the saving to societies by the work of this
Department, of course, can never be measured, for it is impossible
to estimate the savings made by taking its advice.

LABOUR PARTY POLICIES

In general it will be gathered that the Co-operative Movement
had reason to be concerned with Government activities. Not
infrequently injustice has been inflicted, not of intent, but through
ignorance or carelessness. Few Cabinet Ministers, and fewer
permanent heads of Government Departments, have been men
to whom the Co-operative Movement was any more than a name,
it had not the part in their every day experience as it had in that of
a substantial proportion of the community. It was perhaps a
consequence of this that there was the tendency to overlook the
interests of co-operators or even the existence of the vast co-operative enterprise.

Labour Party politicians have seemed as guilty of such oversight as those of any other party. It had been hoped that Co-
operative representation on the National Council of Labour
would keep both the Labour Party and a Labour Government
aware of its existence and acquainted with its point of view before
the drafting of programmes and legislation. In fact, the Council's
role as interpreted by both the Labour Party and the Trades

Union Congress has been one of meeting to deal only with specific questions as they arise which really means that it can only effectively discuss events which have already taken place. The Council scarcely has a continuing existence and has been characterised by flurries of activity, most recently, for example, concerned with the introduction of Selective Employment Tax, another example of the situation where the decisions had already been taken and where it did little more than provide the Co-operative Union with the opportunity to reiterate its opposition to the tax.

The agreement that had been made with the Labour Party in 1946 had also provided for machinery for the necessary consultation. Part I of that agreement had set up a Joint Policy National Committee consisting of equal numbers of the Central Executive of the Co-operative Union and the Executive Committee of the Labour Party. It was envisaged that this would make no binding decisions but would provide opportunities for the discussion of matters of common interest.

Had this machinery been used, then the Labour Party could not have embarked on programmes in ignorance of items which would meet co-operative opposition. In fact this machinery had never worked and under the new agreement of 1958, which is still operative, this machinery was scrapped and not replaced. Clause 3 of this new agreement, however, declared that for the purposes of consultation on political policy matters which may affect their mutual interests the National Executive of the Labour Party and the Central Executive of the Co-operative Union should establish such machinery as may be found mutually convenient, but clause 4 provides " It is understood that the authority of either body to reach policy decisions is in no way impaired."

The Co-operative Union report suggested that this was more flexible and convenient; in practice it had been found better to have joint discussions by personnel specially experienced in the questions arising, rather than by the six-a-side committee for policy discussions under the old agreement. Yet the prime difficulty was not met, that of the Labour Party formulating and publicly announcing policy before consultation with the Co-operative Movement on matters of considerable import to it. Thus there was some concern on the part of the Co-operative Movement about certain aspects of the Labour Party policy statement, " Signposts for the Sixties," which gave the impression that the Labour Party was more favourable to dealing with the production end of industry rather than the consumer end in considering questions of public ownership. Ten years later a perhaps rather more encouraging sign was the statement in " Labour's Economic Strategy " that " The Government should embark on a comprehensive study of the Co-operative Sector. It should establish a Co-operative Development Agency with research facilities and resources to promote fresh development in Co-operatives." Yet even on an issue such as this the Co-operative Union had not been consulted and the Union found it necessary to initiate discussions with the Labour Party to discover exactly what they had in mind.

The 1958 agreement also provided for the imposition of limits upon the number of sponsored Co-operative Parliamentary candidates, the number to be settled after each General Election after consultation. Co-operative Parliamentary candidates must also agree that, if elected, they would join the Parliamentary Labour Party and act in accordance with its standing orders. There was a corresponding provision in the 1946 agreement, but in the new agreement there was recognition of the special concern of Co-operative Members of Parliament in matters affecting the economic interests of the Co-operative Movement. When differences arise there is provision for consultation between the Co-operative Movement and the Labour Party " to ensure that, if possible, mutually acceptable decisions are reached."

Co-operative Grievances

Yet the Co-operative Movement had to make frequent complaints of non-consultation whilst the Labour Government was in power, the issue arising at Congress after Congress. One of the complaints was the failure to include co-operative representatives on important committees, or to consult the Movement, although employers' association, such as the Federation of British Industries, and the trade unions through the Trades Union Congress were so consulted. Co-operators held that neither the T.U.C. nor the F.B.I. could represent the point of view of the Co-operative Movement. Yet, engaged as producers, distributors, and consumers, contacting half the people in the country, it insisted it was as important a unit as the F.B.I. or the T.U.C., and demanded to be regarded as equal partners with the Labour Party and the trade unions in building a new order. It was unpleasantly aware that it was not always so regarded.

When an Economic Planning Board was set up in 1948, it consisted of representatives of the Federation of British Industries, the British Confederation of Employers, the Trades Union Congress, heads of Government Departments and members of the Central Economic Planning Staff, but included no representative of the Co-operative Movement. The Movement was dissatisfied; it had a wealth of experience in retailing, wholesaling, manufacturing, banking, insurance, international trade, and considered that on the grounds of economic achievement and consumer representation it should be represented on the Economic Planning Board. The reasons given for its non-inclusion were also galling—" that many other special interests were excluded from the Planning Board because their inclusion would have made the Board unwieldy."

To regard the Co-operative Movement merely as a " special interest," albeit it was the oldest, numerically the strongest, and with the greatest record of achievement of any part of the Labour Movement, was tactless, if not insulting. However, whilst the Co-operative Movement complained, it gave the Labour Government loyal support, and yet kept consistently before the Labour and Trade Union Movements its own co-operative solution— mutual ownership of trades and services in which individual preferences must be paramount.

An emergency resolution passed at the Congress of 1949 contained a paragraph stating the co-operative view: " Congress is of the emphatic opinion that the co-operative method of voluntary organisation should be recognised as an integral part of the national economy and should be capable of expansion in meeting the increasing requirements of consumers. The Movement must use its utmost power to preserve the right of co-operators to maintain and develop their own resources under their own democratic control in the satisfaction of their needs and in keeping with co-operative purpose and practice."

This, of course, was no intrusion into a socialist philosophy held by the Labour Party. The Labour Party was a comprehensive party embracing many different socialist schools of thought and the co-operative view was no newcomer among them. Much of the intellectual foundation of the Labour Party had been constructed by the Webbs, and in their " Constitution for a Socialist Commonwealth " they had a place for voluntary consumer Co-operation much greater than possibly the Co-operative Congress of 1949 contemplated. Moreover they laid down its right to expand and even enter industries already nationalised; and although State Socialist ideas were for the time predominant, hence the co-operative reaction, these had been denounced as State Capitalism by the extreme left before 1914.

Co-operative Statements

To state and explain its views more fully, a statement of policy, *The Place of a Co-operative Movement in a Collectivist Economy,* was prepared and published in 1950. This was, and is, an important document. It described the achievements, structure, principles, and purpose of the Movement, stressing its social character, and explaining the dangers to it of certain controls, planning, and nationalisation in some detail. It criticised the draft programme of the Labour Party *Labour Believes in Britain* as containing no indication of a planned socialist progression. Although discussions with the Labour Party had taken place, there had been nothing akin to negotiations. Although there was disagreement with some items in this programme, there was no fundamental conflict; the Co-operative Movement agreed with the stated objectives of the Labour Party Constitution, and pointed out that this stated " common ownership " not nationalisation.

Co-operation was claimed as a superior form of common ownership to nationalisation on the grounds of better democratic control and the more equitable distribution of surpluses. It asked for prior consultation before the Labour Party made public declarations on issues of vital importance to the Co-operative Movement. And it also gave a gentle reminder that the Labour Government might be followed by Governments of a different political complexion who could follow a policy of denationalisation. Thus there was a danger that co-operative enterprises might go through a process of nationalisation and then be converted into private enterprises on denationalisation.

The statement also said: " The Co-operative Movement does not object in principle to public authorities embarking on new enterprises on non-monopolistic lines, provided such enterprises are not privileged and provided also that due regard be paid to the potentialities of the Co-operative Movement. Without proper consideration such developments would result in wasteful duplication of services or payment of compensation to the detriment of the taxpayer and the consuming public. The Co-operative Movement is prepared at all times to assist public authorities by utilising its economic resources and knowledge in the national interest . . . Each Government proposal put forward for a specific commodity or service shall be fully examined and considered from a co-operative point of view."

The co-operative case continued to be pressed both in general and in relation to particular instances of public control. In 1953 a second statement of general co-operative policy entitled *Social Ownership and Consumer Problems* was issued. It claimed that co-operative societies were the most socially democratic trading institutions in operation, that the co-operative idea was not limited to these but capable of far wider recognition and application, that

" nationalisation " is not necessarily identical with " socialisation,"
and although a suitable form of socialism in some cases, is not
suitable for general application. " Nationalisation may only be a
convenient slogan to avoid the necessity of new thinking."

The statement then proceeded to suggest lines along which new
thinking might proceed, of the means by which co-operative
democracy might continue to expand, even in a collectivist system.
Then it directed attention to immediate problems, outlining a
consumer approach to monopolies, resale price maintenance,
indirect taxation, especially Purchase Tax, marketing of agricultural produce, meat supply and distribution, and milk policy.
Other spheres of co-operative endeavour were also outlined, as
co-operative co-partnership, agricultural societies, co-operative
housing societies. It discussed the spheres of nationalisation and
municipal enterprise, and made criticisms of their existing forms,
particularly the weakness of democratic control.

At the Labour Party Conference of 1955 a resolution was adopted
instructing its National Executive in conjunction with the Co-
operative Union to compile a policy statement on the role of the
Co-operative Movement in the formation of a socialist society.
A statement to help the Labour Party Executive was prepared by
the Co-operative Union and presented in 1958 as *Co-operation and
Socialism*. This pointed out that the Labour Party, Trade Union
Movement, and Co-operative Movement have much in common,
origins in the same social strata, intermingled membership, efforts
to defend the consumer, emancipate the worker and promote social
betterment. It sought to correct any mistaken ideas that the Co-operative Movement was a gigantic, fully integrated and unified commercial enterprise. It stressed its objectives, short and long term,
and its characteristic features. The various types of co-operative
organisation were described and some of their achievements given,
both in Great Britain and overseas.

Coming then to the main argument, what part could the Co-
operative Movement play in the formation of a socialist society,
the statement pointed out there could be no simple answer for it
involved the perception of definable objectives and possible limits
of co-operative expansion. Neither of these could be perceived.
It also involved pre-knowledge of the kind of society which might
develop under socialist governments. Nobody had such fore-
knowledge, it was impossible to envisage the ultimate form of a
socialist society. Co-operation evolved organically, it was not
opposed to nationalisation and municipalisation except in so far as

they prevented co-operative expansion. This was due to co-operators believing their own methods had proved to have tremendous social advantages over other proposals.[1]

NATIONAL MEMBERSHIP SCHEME

A National Membership Scheme was initiated as a result of a recommendation by the Co-operative Reorganisation Inquiry Committee in 1945; though the preparation and inauguration took some time and the Scheme was not launched until January, 1949.

Under it members of societies who joined the Scheme could purchase from other member societies and receive dividend on those purchases. It was hoped that the Scheme would not only encourage co-operators to purchase from other societies when within their areas, but would also help to promote the sense amongst individual members of being associated with a national Movement. The Scheme also provided for the easy transfer of members' capital when they changed societies.

Several amendments were made to the scheme during the 'sixties, however. In 1962 it was recommended by the Co-operative Union that only single checks of £1 or over should be recorded for National Membership purposes primarily because of the work and expense involved in processing a large number of small value checks. But in January of 1963 a sample survey of societies by the Union revealed that most societies wished to record all checks regardless of value so Congress of that year rescinded its previous decision and reverted to the original system.

A more radical change took place in 1966 when Congress accepted that the scheme should be changed so that members were required to claim dividend from the selling society rather than having it automatically credited through their own society as had been the practice up to that point. This possibility had been turned down by Congress in 1962 but a number of societies had been unilaterally varying the scheme claiming that with the introduction of computers to deal with their cash control and members' purchase records, the costs of dealing with National Membership purchases was out of proportion to their other costs for check processing.

---

[1] The Co-operative Party also expressed the co-operative viewpoint strongly in many issues of its *Monthly Letter* and its successor, *Platform*, and in such publications as *Building the New Britain* 1951, *Socialisation of Coal Mining* 1952, *The People's Industry* 1952, *Challenge of our Times* 1956, *Co-operation and Modern Socialism* 1958, *Housing* 1959, *Social Ownership and Control* 1961, *Social Ownership in the 'Sixties* 1965, *Public Monopoly and the Consumer* 1968, *Taxation and the Consumer* 1969.

This change, and the reasons for making it, radically curtailed the operation of the Scheme, and with the number of societies paying dividend by stamps increasing rapidly, the Scheme has become virtually extinct in practice if not in name. On the other hand, the Dividend Stamp Scheme does allow stamps acquired at any society to be redeemed at the purchaser's own society, if it is in the Stamp Scheme.

INDUSTRIAL AND PROVIDENT SOCIETIES' ACTS

A much needed reform in the Industrial and Provident Societies' Act was made in 1952, which raised the shareholding limit from £200 to £500, and the deposits in small savings accounts from 10/– to £2 as the maximum deposited at any one time and from £20 to £50 as the maximum held by a single depositor. A larger measure had been intended, but the Labour Government had not been able to find time for it (the Government was in fact very hard pressed) during its period of office, and the shortened version was enacted by the succeeding Conservative Government.

Further amendments were made by the Industrial and Provident Societies' Amendment Act in 1954. This was due to a Co-operative M.P. securing the right to introduce a Private Members' Bill. Its most valued provision was the protection given to the use of the term " Co-operative," although it only applied to new societies or companies, the term could continue to be used by organisations already using it before the passage of the Act. Other provisions dealt with amalgamations and transfer of engagements and many minor matters. Resulting from these amended acts the text of the Model Rules for Co-operative Societies by the Co-operative Union was revised in 1955.

In 1960 a Co-operative M.P. was successful in introducing another private member's Bill enabling societies, if they wish, to raise the maximum shareholding for an individual member from £500 to £1,000. The Act, which came into force in 1961, also gives power to agricultural and horticultural co-operatives to make advances of money to their members without security

The main Industrial and Provident Societies Act of 1893 and all subsequent amending Acts were brought together into the consolidating Act of 1965 under which all societies are now registered. An amending Act of 1967 facilitated the borrowing of money by co-operative societies and a further Act passed in 1968 was primarily concerned with accounting procedures and the position of auditors.

THE INDEPENDENT COMMISSION

The Movement had long felt that its economic progress was hindered by defects in its overall organisation. As might be expected in such a complex of organisations as the Co-operative Movement, there was a feeling within each organisation that the rest were not pulling their weight. Retail societies complained of the inefficiency of the Wholesales and the Wholesales complained of inefficiency and lack of loyalty of the retails. Much of this feeling became centred on co-operative production. On both idealistic and purely business grounds the extension and increase of co-operative production was desired. But such a development required a confidence and loyalty between co-operative producers and retailers that was lacking.

Before the war appeals had been made to co-ordinate production. Unfortunately, many took this to mean the co-ordination of co-operative productive organisations, whereas the real necessity was a more effective co-ordination of co-operative retailing and production.

Failure to obtain co-ordination of the productive organisations led to Congress passing a resolution in 1954 requesting the Central Executive to set up a Special Committee to investigate and report to Congress the following year on the subject of closer collaboration between the C.W.S., the S.C.W.S., and the C.P.F., and the development of the marketing of co-operative productions on a joint national basis. The Central Executive complained that the terms of the resolution were too vague, but acting in the spirit of the resolution got the three organisations together to see if collaboration and joint marketing could be secured. They could not, however, agree and in a lengthy joint letter to the Central Executive stating this, also emphasised the difficulties and waste caused by the lack of support of retail societies to co-operative productions, declaring, " the time is overdue when an independent commission should be set up to examine every facet of co-operative structure."

Sharing this view and acting upon it the Central Executive at the 1955 Congress moved the establishment of an Independent Commission of suitable persons, not engaged in co-operative management or administration, to survey the whole field of co-operative production and marketing and to prepare a report making recommendations to secure the greatest possible advantage to the Movement from its manufacturing, wholesale, and retail resources. The principal objections raised in Congress were to the proposed manning of the Commission by independent persons, that the ground had been covered many times before and was thoroughly well known and that the reasons for lack of co-ordination were not lack of knowledge but lack of willingness.

The three federations (C.W.S., S.C.W.S., C.P.F.) of course supported what was in effect their own proposal. R. G. Gosling, speaking for the C.W.S., declared they were unanimous in the view that the time had come for an impartial examination, " We say this, that regardless of the consequences to the C.W.S., the C.P.F., or the S.C.W.S., we want an impartial examination of what is happening and to be told where we are wrong and how we can work in alliance with you for the better fulfilment of the co-operative task." The resolution was carried by 8,926 votes to 2,743.

The Commission was duly appointed, its chairman being the Rt. Hon. H. T. N. Gaitskell, leader of the Labour Party, a former Chancellor of the Exchequer, and former head of the Department of Political Economy of London University. Other members of the Commission were chosen[1] as having (a) academic/economic knowledge and authority, (b) industrial experience with knowledge of organisation in large-scale undertakings and (c) specialist knowledge of the Co-operative Movement and familiarity with its production and marketing problems.

C. A. R. Crosland, a well-known Labour politician and socialist author, was appointed secretary. Within the terms set it was a well-chosen commission; what it lacked, however, and could not include, were members such as the Webbs, with a life-time study, contacts and understanding of the Movement as well as their nose for constitutional problems and the ability to solve them. For the problems involved were more constitutional than economic, as subsequent debates showed.

Special Congress

In 1958 the Independent Commission Report was presented to the Co-operative Congress, then explained and discussed at Co-operative Union Sectional Conferences before being debated at a Special Congress in November of the same year. It was a

---

[1] **Prof. D. T. Jack,** Professor of Economics, Durham University. **Dr. J. B. Jefferys,** Secretary of International Association of Department Stores, author of two standard works on retailing. **Col. S. J. L. Hardie,** former member of British Transport Commission, Chairman of Iron and Steel Corporation, 1950/1952. **J. T. Murray,** Industrial Consultant, Member of Scientific Advisory Council, formerly manager of a large textile firm. **Alderman F. Pette,** former General Manager of Middlesbrough Society and President of N.C.M.A., Chairman of Peterlee New Town Development Corporation. **Miss Margaret Digby,** Secretary of Horace Plunkett Foundation and of Federation of Agricultural Co-operative Producers in Great Britain and Ireland. Author of many books on Agricultural Co-operation. **Lady Margaret Hall,** Tutor in Economics, Somerville College, Oxford.

lengthy report requiring more study, consideration of consequences, debate on desirability and practicability of recommendations, examination of conformity with co-operative ideals and
principles than was possible within six months. Haste, however,
was explicit in the resolution, a time-table had been laid down to
which events had to conform.

The Special Congress debated the Report on a series of resolutions and amendments. Those dealing with price policies, dividends, reserves, interest rates, liquidity, capital accumulation,
place and functions of boards of directors and officials expressed
views long advocated and had an easy passage through Congress.
Perhaps their passage was too easy, keener debate might have
impressed retail societies with the importance and necessity of
carrying them into effect.

The great debate took place on the proposal to establish a new
federal society, a Co-operative Retail Development Society
(C.R.D.S.). Its functions were to be research, advice and the
initiation of developments. Research on selling methods and
techniques, management structure and organisation, trends and
developments in retail trading and consumer expenditure would
enable it to act as a central economic planning unit. It would also
serve as a recognised channel of approach and source of advice for
societies needing capital.

Believing that the dry goods trades required retailing organisations on a national scale, the Report recommended the creation of
national chains of specialist shops, and the C.R.D.S. would decide
on and plan their establishment.

Although opposed by the Central Executive, a resolution was
carried requesting the Central Executive to initiate negotiations
with the Wholesale Societies and to submit a report to the 1959
Congress on the measures taken to constitute, organise, and finance
the C.R.D.S. This was not a resolution committing the Central
Executive to establish C.R.D.S., but to prepare a scheme which
the 1959 Congress could accept, amend or reject.

Even this tentative step barely commanded sufficient support,
the resolution being carried by the narrow majority of 6,516
votes to 6,425. A more definite resolution, however, was then
carried by an overwhelming majority of 9,527 votes to 2,737.
This affirmed that the Co-operative Union was the organisation
primarily responsible for advisory services and called upon the
Central Executive to expand the services of the Labour, Finance,
and Research Departments, to develop new advisory services

necessary to promote co-operative trade and to institute the charging of reasonable fees for specific services requested by a society.

Implementation of Resolutions

Another important resolution endorsed the basic principles for the amalgamation of retail societies and requested the Central Executive to assume responsibility for conducting a detailed national survey of the whole problem. Such a survey was badly needed. The haphazard growth of societies occasioned much waste and inefficiency by no means confined to the obvious evils of overlapping. Amalgamations had been recommended by the Commission to create societies big enough to develop a full range of services on an economical scale. This would not mean, of course, a uniform size of society, for circumstances differ, but it would mean that only one society would operate within a shopping area. As the previous chapter showed, shopping areas are now often very big indeed.

Detailed surveys were necessary to determine the most desirable groupings for amalgamation and the Co-operative Union entered upon this task in 1959. It was completed and the *National Amalgamation Survey* report was published in September, 1960. Its conclusions were made on the assumption that they would form a long-term basic plan for the concentration of societies into autonomous units of sufficient size to allow the efficient and economic operation and development of co-operative retail outlets. If carried out the recommendations would have reduced the number of societies from 875 to 307. Societies with less than 10,000 members would have been reduced in number from 625 to 90. The most difficult task, however, remained, that of persuading vigorous, flourishing societies to amalgamate with others. Success was in fact very limited. Five years after the publication of the survey there were still 704 societies, 447 with less than 10,000 members, and in 1968, when the Amalgamation Survey was superseded by the Regional Plan, 539 with 316 in the smaller category.

Meanwhile the committee constituted in accordance with the resolution of the Special Congress of 1958 was engaged in negotiations with the Wholesale Societies in preparing a scheme for a C.R.D.S. It was not able to report before 1960 when Majority and Minority Reports were submitted to Congress. Both accepted the need for the services recommended. The main differences regarded the control of chain shops and whether retail development services should be undertaken by an autonomous division of the Co-operative Union or by the extension of the existing Co-operative Union structure by creating a new department.

These issues, however, had already been largely decided. In 1959, retail societies had agreed to a C.W.S. scheme of chain shops, the first in footwear, and the Special Congress resolution had stated that the Co-operative Union was the proper body to provide advisory services. The Majority Report accepted these decisions. There was, however, a fierce debate between the respective supporters of the two reports at the Congress of 1960, but the Majority Report was accepted by a majority of 8,432 votes against 4,742.

As a result the Co-operative Union set up a new Development Committee and Department in 1960. After two years operation the Development Committee was abolished since it was felt to be overlapping with the Central Executive and the Trade Associations.

THE REGIONAL PLAN

As will be obvious, it had been the official object of the Co-operative Union for some considerable time to reduce the number of retail societies and to reap the benefits of larger scale operations. The General Survey Report published in 1919–20 had seen the benefits of larger societies, for example. The most recent attempt to get societies to conform to a rational and national plan of amalgamation had been the Amalgamation Survey of 1960 following the recommendations of the Independent Commission. By the late 'sixties, however, there was little doubt in anybody's mind that it had been almost completely ineffective in a period when the Co-operative Movement's competitors in retailing were becoming larger and were taking a larger share of the market.

Against this background, the Co-operative Union published in 1967 the " Regional Plan for Co-operative Societies," a plan designed to reduce the 467 societies in England, Wales and Ireland to 50 regional retail societies. (Responsibility for a survey in Scotland was left to the Scottish Sectional Board and the S.C.W.S. who, while supporting the concept of regional societies, felt that at that particular point of time a set plan would be unnecessarily rigid, particularly in view of the status of most of Scotland as a Development Area with all that that involved in terms of industrial and population movement.) Based on the same principles as the Amalgamation Survey, the Regional Plan takes these principles several steps further to create societies considerably larger than those envisaged in the earlier scheme. Each of the projected regional societies is contained within an area in which the inhabitants do virtually all of their shopping thus cutting out the wasteful duplication of resources arising from a situation where a number of societies within the same area attempt to provide all the required services even when inhabitants of each society's area commonly move into another society's area to do part of their shopping, most notably for non-foods. Each of the projected regional societies has as its focal point a town or conurbation with a population of at least 100,000 and a substantial intake of dry goods trade, and is designed to be of optimum size (having due regard to geography, transport and the flow of trade) to secure substantial economies in the purchase and sale of food and dry goods. Such societies should also be in a position to make more economic use of increasingly scarce capital, be better able to employ specialist managerial personnel, and be better able to cope with local industrial and population changes in contrast to the typical small society which is sometimes dependent on the employment provided by one industry for its prosperity or is unable to cope with influxes of population because it is too small and has insufficient capital.

Put before the 1968 Congress, these proposals were overwhelmingly accepted and then began the spadework of effecting the proposals. Although progress has not been as fast as some people might have liked, looked at historically the progress of mergers has been fairly fast since 1968. Compared with the 467 societies covered by the Regional Plan, there were, in April 1970, 312 societies, a reduction of a third.

There has been some feeling, however, that even societies of this size will be inadequate and in the North East of England the Regional Plan has been superseded by the considerable progress made in the formation of the North-Eastern Co-operative Society which is intended to cover the whole of County Durham, most of Northumberland and part of north Yorkshire. This society involves what would have been seven societies in the Regional Plan but there are special problems in this area which makes it something of a special case, for example the decline of the old staple industries of the area, the introduction of new ones and the subsequent growth of new residential areas and indeed towns which make it necessary to plan development over the area as a whole. In addition, the C.W.S. has a special interest in that it has a great deal of capital invested in the regional warehouse at Birtley, Co. Durham and hence has a more pressing interest than usual in the success of retail societies at the local level. Thus, not surprisingly, the C.W.S. has played a considerable part in sponsoring this new society.

INTEGRATION OF THE NATIONAL FEDERATIONS

Accompanying the moves towards the rationalisation of the pattern of retail societies, there have been attempts to rationalise Co-operative structure at the level of the national federations. At the Congress of 1962 a resolution was overwhelmingly accepted instructing the Central Executive to set up a joint committee " to initiate negotiations to amalgamate the functions of the Co-operative Wholesale Society, the Scottish Co-operative Wholesale Society, the Co-operative Productive Federation and the Co-operative Union with the object of creating a single National Federal Organisation to be responsible for the productive, wholesaling, technical, financial and all other advisory services required by the Movement."

The National Federation Negotiating Committee, as the committee became known, consisting of representatives of the four federations mentioned in the resolution plus three representatives of retail societies, presented an interim report to the 1963 Congress and its final report in 1964. During the course of the Committee's work, the C.P.F. had withdrawn, feeling that the proposed National Federation would be a predominantly consumer organisation in which they did not want to lose their identity although they were prepared to become members of the new federation. Nevertheless, the rest of the Committee reported in favour of the merger of the remaining three bodies. This, it was argued, would give rise to a number of advantages. For example, a single co-operative supplier for a national market would be created; all co-operative productions would become available for the whole of the British Co-operative Movement; a means would emerge of rationalising national co-operative productive and distributive resources; overlapping and duplication of services and functions would be avoided; and the achievement of unity in the national structure of the Movement would engender a sense of common purpose. If these were to be fully realised, however, there would have to be greater co-ordination between wholesaling and manufacturing activities and retail society requirements than was generally the case at that time. The committee recommended that the commitment to education and to politics be continued by the new federation, more or less in their existing form.

The S.C.W.S. and many of the Scottish retail societies were not able to accept the recommendations mainly because they feared that in any process of rationalisation, particularly of

productive resources, it would be they who would suffer dispro-
portionately. The N.F.N.C. had anticipated these objections and
had tried to introduce safeguards into their report but they were
not sufficient to satisfy Scottish fears. In fact the proposals were
accepted by Congress but the general meeting of the S.C.W.S.
later rejected them so nothing came of the report directly although
the reorganisation of the two Wholesale Societies in 1965 was
largely the result of the failure of this attempt at integration.

As early as 1966, however, discussions had been taking place
between the Co-operative Union and the C.W.S. regarding the
possible overlapping of trade advisory functions being developed
by the C.W.S. and developing from these early discussions, the
possibilities of merging the Union and the Wholesale Society
came to be discussed. A resolution passed by the 1969 Congress
welcomed these discussions and asked for a report and recommendations to be made to the next Congress. The S.C.W.S.
maintained its opposition to a merger so the committee considering the problems consisted only of Union and C.W.S. representatives with observers from the S.C.W.S. and it was faced with
the difficulty of incorporating the Scottish part of the Movement
and of continuing services which did not readily fit into the
C.W.S. structure. The solution of the Joint Committee was for
the Co-operative Union to transfer its engagements to the C.W.S.
and for the latter body to fully incorporate certain services
previously provided by the Union into its own activities. These
would be the Food Trades Department of the Union, the Dry
Goods Trades Department, the Development Department, and
the Organisation and Methods Section of the Finance Department.
In addition, the Milk and Fuel Trade Associations would be more
closely connected with the C.W.S. and the remaining trade
associations would be discontinued and replaced by Technical
Panels to be appointed by the C.W.S. to enable the C.W.S. to
have consultative arrangements with its member societies. This,
it was argued, would eliminate the duplication of trade advisory
services that it was alleged was taking place and would enable the
C.W.S. to play a more central part in the national planning of
co-operative trading policies. Other services, however, were
either not duplicated or needed to be maintained as a service to
the whole of the British Movement. To maintain these, it was
recommended that the C.W.S. and the S.C.W.S. should set up a
Joint Policy Committee, to consist of eight representatives from
the C.W.S., two from the S.C.W.S., and nine from the retail
societies, to have general responsibility for all the remaining
departments from the now defunct Co-operative Union, although

there would still be the special committees for Wages, Conciliation, Educational, and Political matters and there would be a
separately appointed Parliamentary Committee instead of the
previous one which was a sub-committee of the Central Executive.
After considering the proposals, however, the Central Executive
felt that they could not accept them fully, arguing that the
complete disappearance of the Co-operative Union might not be
acceptable to the Movement at that stage. Instead the Central
Executive introduced proposals which achieved much the same
effect in a rather simpler manner, namely that the Union should
continue to exist but that the trade advisory services and trade
associations mentioned above should be transferred to the
C.W.S. In addition they recommended that the Union's Central
Executive should be reconstituted so as to be composed in the
same way that the Joint Policy Committee would have been,
with a separately appointed Parliamentary Committee. These
latter proposals were accepted by the 1970 Congress.

THE CO-OPERATIVE PARTY

Some of the big political issues confronting the Co-operative
Movement, state collectivism (which may be socialist or capitalist)
and relations with the Labour Party have already been described.
In these struggles the Co-operative Party, of course, was in the
forefront. Its work consisted of research, (to discover the facts
on which rational policy could be based); education (to equip
members with the knowledge and the attitude of mind which is
necessary for a rational approach to questions); propaganda (to
influence public opinion) and direct participation in the work of
Parliament by its members in the two Houses.

The Movement as a whole had become convinced of the value
of the Party; in 1945 there were 668 societies affiliated to the
Party with a membership of 7,511,072, amounting to 82·66 per
cent of the Movement's membership. This affiliated membership
steadily increased during the 'fifties as the Movement's membership increased, but with the decline in the growth of Co-operative
membership in the 'sixties, the Party's affiliated membership
remained fairly stable. As a result of the number of societies
being reduced by amalgamations the number of affiliated societies
fell quite substantially. In 1959 there were 604 societies affiliated
with a membership of 10,942,421 amounting to 87 per cent of
the Movement's membership. In 1969 there were 292 societies
with 11,144,497 members, 85 per cent of the total membership.

By the General Election of 1945 the number of Co-operative
Members of Parliament was increased from nine to 23. Subsequent

elections were not so fruitful, agreements with the Labour Party on Parliamentary candidatures making it difficult to increase co-operative representation. The results of post-war elections are shown below:—

GENERAL ELECTIONS
Co-operative Party

Year	Candidates	Successful
1945	34	23
1950	33	17
1951	38	16 + 3 by-elections.
1955	38	19 + 1 by-election.
1959	30	16
1964	27	19
1966	24	18
1970	28	17

The 1945 and 1950 and the 1964 and 1966 elections resulted in Labour Governments in which Co-operative Party members held Ministerial positions. In the first of these Administrations, A. V. Alexander was First Lord of the Admiralty and later Chancellor of the Duchy of Lancaster and A. Barnes was Minister of Transport and, in addition, the Party had four Parliamentary Secretaries and four Parliamentary Private Secretaries. In the 1966–1970 Government, three members of the Group were Ministers, George Darling as Minister of State at the Board of Trade until 1968, John Stonehouse as Minister of Aviation and later as Postmaster General, and J. Dickson Mabon as Minister of State at the Scottish Office. One other member was a Parliamentary Secretary and seven others were Private Parliamentary Secretaries. Another, Sydney Irving, was Deputy Chairman of Ways and Means and Deputy Speaker.

In the Parliamentary struggle the Parliamentary Group of the Co-operative Party, besides being engaged on general issues on the side of the Labour Party, also kept a watchful eye on matters directly affecting co-operative interests, and defended these on the floor of the House, which, of course, also frequently meant expressing opinions from the standpoint and defending the interests of the consumer.

Among the matters on which the Parliamentary Group were particularly active were a long campaign against the injustice and anomalies of Purchase Tax and S.E.T. and bills and acts relating to resale price maintenance, monopolies and restrictive practices, Profits Tax, Corporation Tax, hire purchase and rentals, transport, shop hours, food, agriculture, television, local government, Industrial and Provident Societies, night baking, tariffs on food and vegetables, food and drugs, rating and valuation, sugar, dentists, opticians, advertisements, slaughterhouses, weights and measures, National Insurance, consumer protection, and of course the annual Budgets.

This recital, by no means a complete record, gives some indication of Government intervention in business, including Co-operative business, and emphasises the need for Co-operative representation in Parliament to express the views and defend the interests of co-operators and consumers in the constitutional manner and place for the purpose.

CO-OPERATIVE EDUCATION SINCE THE WAR

In October, 1945, the Co-operative College and Education Department were moved from Manchester to Stanford Hall, near Loughborough. Such an uprooting and transplanting would have been difficult at any time, and circumstances increased the difficulties. The cessation of hostilities in 1945 was quickly followed by a big increase in the demands of the Movement upon the Department. Correspondence students increased from 1,156 in 1944-1945 to 2,216 in 1946-1947 and the number of college students from 25 in the first term at Stanford Hall to 82 in the first term of 1946-1947 and to over a hundred in subsequent years.

During the war the resources of the Department had shrunk, both it and the College had been without a Head since 1943 and both tutorial and administrative staffs had been seriously reduced. Text-books of all kinds and even paper were difficult to obtain.

Lieutenant-Colonel R. L. Marshall, O.B.E., M.A., was appointed Director of Studies and Principal of the Co-operative College in 1946 and commenced his duties with the Department in the summer of 1947.

Reorganisation of the Department began in 1948 with the approval by Congress of a new constitution submitted by a special committee. An acceptable new constitution had been difficult to prepare, for previous proposals had been rejected in 1945 and 1946, and the one approved in 1948 was the fruit of two years' inquiries and negotiations. It had to fit within the new constitution of the Co-operative Union and yet bring within it all the organisations actively concerned with education.

The existing National Education Council and Education Executive were abolished and in their place " The National Co-operative Education Association " set up. This brought within one organisation the whole of the educational work of the Co-operative Union at national and Sectional levels. At the latter level were Sectional Educational Councils. Each of these consisted of four representatives of the Sectional Boards, and four (later increased

to six) members elected by committees responsible for education
in societies within the Section, and one from each of the Sectional
organisations of the Guilds, provided it had not less than 500
members in the Section. A National Executive was elected by the
Sectional Education Councils, two from each Section, one of
whom must be a Sectional Board representative and one from the
rest. This constitution of the Executive was changed in 1968 and
is referred to in the later chapter on the organisation of the
Co-operative Union. Each Sectional Secretary of the Co-operative Union was also secretary to the Educational Council of his
Section. The new constitution was intended to effect a close
integration of Co-operative Union machinery and of societies and
organisations engaged in educational activity.

The Education Department was then reorganised. Its head,
R. L. Marshall, was named Chief Education Officer, responsible
for all the educational staff and services of the Co-operative
Union, supported by various specialised National officers as well
as by the full-time tutors of the College. In each Section a
Sectional Education Officer was appointed "responsible for
educational assistance to local societies and organisations in all
the educational provisions of the Union, including the Co-operative Youth Movement, day release and day continuation education
and all other forms of further education, including technical and
other education." These officers not only served as a source of
speedy and reliable advice, often by personal contact, to societies
and students, but also helped to inspire and initiate educational
developments and to further the carrying out of the policies of the
Education Executive. In particular they acted as advisers and
agents for the Sectional Educational Councils.

Development was hindered by financial stringency. Inflation
had put the Co-operative Union into financial difficulties to which
reference has already been made, and it was necessary to curtail
expenditure of each department. The Education Department was
restricted, in 1952, to an allocation from Co-operative Union
funds of £30,000. Fortunately the new constitution eased the
position, for the societies in membership with the National
Co-operative Education Association had realised the need for
national development and in 1950 agreed to contribute to a national
fund on the basis of 10/– per thousand members. The fund,
however, was not to be used to finance Union services already in
operation but "for the work of initiation, experiment, and
development, particularly in direct service to local societies which
cannot be supported from the Co-operative Union's income."
Nevertheless, some of the work that the Department would have

liked to have done has remained very much restricted by financial circumstances as it has shared the difficulties of the Union as a whole and indeed the Movement as a whole.

There was no scarcity of ideas and needs for which the fund could be used; the problem was the familiar economic one—of allocating scarce resources to a variety of ends. Educational projects of any worth are generally bound to be long-term ones, so that the economical expenditure of the fund required both an over-all and a future survey. In 1955 a Five Year Plan for education expenditure was drawn up and tentative decisions made. The allocation of funds fell roughly into five parts, Co-operative College National Scholarships, Technical Education, Adult Education, Youth Work, Grants to Auxiliaries.

In 1956 the Easter Conference of the N.C.E.A. unanimously agreed to this Five Year Plan for concerted action put before them by the Education Executive under the title of " A Plan and a Challenge." It brought before societies the educational work in which they should be engaged, classifying it under Technical (or employee) for the needs of the staff, Adult (or member) with particular emphasis on co-operative studies in consumer education, and Co-operative Youth. Each was challenged by a target in each activity based on the average attainment of activity by societies of similar size.

Guidance was given by the plan for it reminded societies of the priorities of educational activity, a class in Co-operation, for instance, is more important than choral or dramatic activities. Nevertheless, it sought to induce societies to have balanced programmes in which nothing was neglected. At the end of the first Five Year Plan in 1961, results were sufficiently encouraging to continue the scheme for a further five year period. The following tables give the situation at the beginning of the scheme, at the end of the first five years, at the end of the second, and the most recent figures.

EMPLOYEE EDUCATION

Category	1955/56	1960/61	1965/66	1968/69
Evening Classes with C.U. syllabus	4,117	7,153	3,516	1,412
Evening Classes with non-C.U. syllabus	1,548	2,465	2,652	1,328
Day Release...	3,567	6,399	4,737	3,910
Other (Short Practical) Training...	14,180	23,165	13,334	11,185
Postal Tuition	2,501	3,814	2,999	1,991
Totals	25,913	42,996	27·238	20 216

MEMBER EDUCATION

Category	1955/56	1960/61	1965/66	1968/69
Classes in Social Studies (including Co-operative) ...	2,108	4,982	2,395	1,578
Classes other than Social	7,205	6,098	4,317	5,278
Short Lecture courses	22,831	25,252	13,950	11,727
Cultural Activity Groups	9,329	9,467	10,479	11,094
Totals	41,473	45,799	31,141	29,677

As is obvious from the figures, the promise of the first five years of " Plan and a Challenge " was not maintained in the second. There was in fact a quite rapid decline in 1964–65 in staff education which was explained as a result of societies being forced to reduce their establishments in an attempt to contain wage costs, a high rate of staff turnover, and a trend to more part-time employees at the expense of full-time. These trends would appear to have intensified since the introduction of S.E.T. Nevertheless, the evidence of diminishing attention being paid to education and training at a time when some competitors were becoming more aware of the benefits of training is to be deplored. The decline in member education more or less accompanies the decline in staff training and is more evidence of societies concentrating on the apparently more pressing problems of trade and finance. Whether the relative neglect of education and training will eventually affect trade and finance, however, unfortunately only time will tell.

However, one measure that may force societies to take action on staff training is the Industrial Training Act of 1964 under which Industrial Training Boards can be set up for specific industries to encourage and promote the training of staffs. These Boards are financed by levies on employers in the industry concerned who may have the levies returned at a later date if they undertake or utilise systematic staff training facilities approved by the Board. Boards covering the Movement's activities (mainly the Distributive Industry Training Board and the Food, Drink and Tobacco Industry Training Board) were not set up until 1968 but there is little doubt that the impact, if only financial, of these Boards will soon be felt by societies who will have an added incentive to undertake staff training on a wider and more effective scale.

THE CO-OPERATIVE COLLEGE

Apart from provision for national scholarships the restrictions upon the expenditure of the N.C.E.A. National Fund prevented it from being used to equip Stanford Hall or on College development. The College was soon in financial difficulties for there was neither adequate capital nor income to maintain, equip, or develop it. Continuing inflation added to the difficulties and heavy and continuous deficits brought matters to a head in 1950.

Congress in that year agreed to the setting up of a Committee of Inquiry to investigate the educational and financial structure of the College. The strong and representative committee appointed recommended that it was best " to place the burden on the Move-ment as a whole by asking the Co-operative Union to call for an additional subscription of ¼d. per member per annum by retail societies and a corresponding increase in the subscriptions of the national federations and other members." Congress accepted the recommendations and for the first time the College finances were put on a satisfactory footing.

The College was further adapted and equipped, particularly with the completion in 1956 of a new wing of study bedrooms. Its numbers of sessional students settled at 100 and the students come into residence for at least one full session from October to July. They undertake studies in retail management and secretaryship for the awards of the Co-operative Union and in social studies for the Diploma in Political, Economic, and Social Studies awarded by the University of Nottingham to external students (introduced in 1953) or the Co-operative Union Diploma in Co-operation. Additionally the College took the initiative in 1964 in the Management Development Scheme which is designed to recruit potential managers from universities and colleges and give them a year's Co-operative training at the College and in societies with a guarantee of a post at the end of the course.

Among the other important developments was the provision of a special course for students from developing countries. This arose in the first instance from an approach by the Colonial Office at the end of the war regarding facilities for training men from Colonial Government Co-operative Departments. Twelve students from nine different countries arrived to take the course in 1947–48. As the course became more widely known so did its appeal. Students entered it from Co-operative organisations other than Government Departments and from countries outside the Commonwealth. In 1968–69 there were 40 overseas students, 30 from Commonwealth countries. In addition to the Co-opera-tive Union awards, a new provision from 1968 was the Diploma in Co-operative Development (Overseas) awarded by the Lough-borough University of Technology to meet the needs of some of the more advanced students. This was the first British provision on a university level of a course covering the problems of economic and social development with concentration on the role of Co-operation and the problems involved in its promotion.

Among the developments, however, perhaps the most important was the provision of a special course for students from under-developed territories. This arose in the first instance from an approach by the Colonial Office at the end of the war regarding facilities for training men from Colonial Government Co-opera-tive Departments. Twelve students from nine different territories arrived to take the course in 1947–1948. As the course became more widely known so did its appeal. Students entered it from co-operative organisations other than Government Departments and from countries outside the Commonwealth. In 1958–1959 there were 35 overseas students in the course, 25 from Govern-ments of the Commonwealth.

These overseas students were a valuable element in the College. They brought knowledge, experiences and outlooks strange to the British student and to each other, thus widening the horizons of all and generating some understanding of each.

Several of these students served their countries and the Move-ment well on their return. Some became Ministers, heads or deputy heads of Government Departments, general secretaries or managers of co-operative organisations, a few became Principals of or lecturers in Co-operative Colleges, many contributed to journals and most engaged in some kind of educational activity. Thus the Co-operative College became a source of ideas and in-spiration to Co-operative Movements in many parts of the world.

THE CO-OPERATIVE AUXILIARIES

The Guilds and the British Federation of Young Co-operators encountered great difficulties after the close of the war. While co-operative membership was still increasing, the membership of the auxiliaries in England and Wales fell from 103,000 in 1938 to 56,000 in 1958 and 34,000 in 1968. The B.F.Y.C. was particu-larly badly hit, its branches falling from 66 in 1948 to 39 in 1958 with a membership of 150 and it finally went out of existence in 1960. Similarly the National Co-operative Men's Guild declined from a membership of 11,530 in 1938 to 1,488 in 1959. In the early 'sixties it converted itself to a mixed auxiliary under the title of the League of Co-operators but finally in 1967 joined the original mixed guild, the National Guild of Co-operators.

This decline, which had become most obviously apparent during the 1950's, caused concern amongst earnest co-operators. A Working Party, consisting of representatives of the auxiliaries and of the Co-operative Union and the C.W.S., was formed in

1958 to investigate the position and issued a report in 1960. The Education Executive also, in 1959, sponsored an enquiry into their functions and activities, undertaken by B. Groombridge who was experienced in this type of investigation. His report[1] made out a strong case for their continuance, stating " if they did not exist, it would be necessary to create them, to check oligarchy, to improve co-operative democracy, to involve working class people in the whole texture of society, and to develop self-confidence."

Some of the recommendations of the Groombridge Report have since been carried out. For example, there is more emphasis on programme planning and more purposeful activities and the College and Education Department of the Union have mounted a regular series of leadership training courses for the auxiliaries. Following logically from the report's recommendations the auxiliaries have followed a national programme theme each year, such as the Regional Plan, and co-operators and local goverment.

Nevertheless, membership has continued to decline although the rate of decline per year shows some indication of slowing down. There are one or two encouraging signs too. A small number of societies, for example, are experimenting with Young Mothers Groups, affiliated to the Women's Guild but aimed specifically at the younger woman. Another small group of societies have Young Members' Organisations, experiencing considerable teething troubles so far, but with the possibility of undertaking the same kind of role as that undertaken by the B.F.Y.C. in the past.

END OF HISTORICAL SECTION

This book has shown how some fundamental social problems were emphasised by the Industrial Revolution. How the early co-operators sought to solve these problems and achieve their ideals but found no practicable way of doing so until the Rochdale Pioneers discovered how, " to marry the ideal with the concrete realities of the situation," which the Movement has had to do again and again.

In its history the Co-operative Movement has witnessed the rise and fall of many social and political movements, has been advised and exhorted by advanced contemporary thinkers, from outright *laissez faire* at one time to outright planned economy at another. It has experienced booms, slumps, and prolonged depressions, economic and social changes, great wars and their aftermaths,

---

[1] Published as a Co-operative College Paper, *Report on Co-operative Auxiliaries*, 1960.

changing forms of competition, occasionally the favour, more frequently the indifferences, sometimes the enmity of governments.

Yet it has continued to grow, never spectacularly but persistently and continuously, because it meets the needs of the common people and continues to pursue its high ideals in ways which do not ask of the ordinary man and woman efforts and sacrifices which they are not prepared to make continuously and permanently.

Speaking at the Rochdale Congress of 1892, G. J. Holyoake found the reason for the continuance of the Co-operative Movement to be that it was necessary and just. " The Rochdale system of Co-operation was the littlest, the obscurest, the most unfriended, the most disregarded, most condemned, the least hopeful, the least likely to succeed of any system ever to be devised by man. Yet it has not ceased to be. On the contrary it continues to grow and it is even now the most prosperous system yet devised for the amelioration of the workers of England. How did the Pioneers bring this to pass? What was their inspiration? They had no learning of the schools, but they had that genius which enters the hearts of honest men. They know that it makes all the difference in the world whether you put truth first or second. They put principle first, and profit second, believing that principle was the foundation of all honourable profit, and the only honest source of it. It was not dividend which mainly inspired them, for they had never seen it and they detested the competitive underhandedness by which they saw others acquiring profit. Let us keep to their methods and we shall see the day which they desired to see—when the penury of the many shall terminate and the scandalous fortunes of the few be impossible, under the co-operative law of the common interest, inspired by goodwill and governed by equity."

This passage of Holyoake is as apposite of the Movement today as it was when made.

12 PRINCIPLES OF CO-OPERATION

> " *Without honesty and devotion to principle there can
> be no progress in public affairs.*"
>
> G. J. Holyoake.
>
> " *Direction is more important than speed.*"
>
> Fred Hall.

THE history of the Co-operative Movement provides material which elucidates its principles. Not only are principles revealed by the study of the Movement's practices, but also the recognition and observance of principles in solving problems, in deciding what was or was not done, and thus shaping the form and determining the course of the Movement. The recognition of principles implies an objective or ideal from which they are derived, they are rules which must be observed if the ideal is to be attained. If changed, there is a change in the objective pursued, progress towards the former ideal stops. Hence the observations of Holyoake and Hall at the head of this chapter.

From this history it will be seen that the ultimate aims of the Co-operative Movement have not changed though the means of pursuing them have changed. Owen's community schemes have, for instance, been long discarded as impracticable ways to the Owenite ideal but the Owenite ideal remains. Owenites, Rochdale Pioneers, and Christian Socialists, had similar ideals, though advocating different ways of attaining them. All were opposed to the prevailing system because it promoted social evils, selfishness, the exploitation of man by man, bad character and consequent unhappiness.

They desired an economic system based upon common ownership and mutual aid, in which none would be in a position to exploit the rest, in which equity, individual freedom and a strong sense of fellowship would be the basis of social relations, in which sympathy with, care for and the desire for others' happiness would be promoted in each individual, i.e. a system conducive to good character and consequent happiness.

Throughout the history of the Movement these underlying ideals may be detected. A previous book on Co-operation stated,

" Co-operation has other aims than economic ones. The earnest co-operator seeks to apply co-operative methods to all purposes of social life, and does so because he believes that in working for the common good, man's highest qualities are enlisted and developed; and in the employment and development of these qualities the man himself becomes a better man and the quality of the human race is improved." (*Co-operation*, Hall and Watkins.)

Not all co-operative societies were started with ultimate social ideals in mind, not all co-operators have them. But as Dr. King pointed out the practice of Co-operation itself teaches lessons, affects character and has its economic and social effects. If, for instance, co-operative societies of all kinds so developed that all economic activities were undertaken by them, the economic system would be co-operative, and the approach to economic and social problems would be co-operative, even though the founders and adherents of each society had only limited aims and were devoid of the larger vision.

It is instructive to consider the theories of two great European co-operators, Anders Örne of Sweden and Professor Charles Gide of France. Each approached Co-operation from a different point than had British Co-operation. Neither was the product of British co-operative thought, which was considerably affected by Owenism, but their theories and conclusions were very similar.

ÖRNE'S CO-OPERATIVE IDEALS

Örne brusquely put aside the ideals of social Utopias, he found the driving power of co-operative undertakings to be simply economic interest. Individuals found a direct interest in co-operating to provide goods and services for themselves instead of relying on provision by others whose primary aim was profit. " The antithesis of Co-operation is profit-seeking economy, organised in the form of undertakings whose proprietors regard the production and distribution of goods merely as the means whereby to procure gain for themselves."

The two distinctive ends, one the welfare of the consumers, the other profit acquisitions by the owners of capitalist enterprises resulted in different economies, not only materially but also in intellectual approach. He held that the profit motive had become so exalted that it had come to appear as the true purpose of economic activity. This mentality affected economists, businessmen and statesmen, even in parties that considered themselves socialist, e.g. protection against competition, compulsory cartels, and prohibition of new enterprises.

Consumers' Co-operation because of its close and comprehensive relations had boundless possibilities of development. It was an alternative to profit-seeking enterprise on the one hand and to modern Utopias, State-planned economies, on the other. " Salvation in our opinion must be sought in a new organisation—first by a co-operation of individuals free from any element of compulsion, with self-responsible, improved relations for meeting human needs, and then by the new spiritual outlook which such a change must gradually evolve. In its present phase the consumers' co-operative type of undertaking is of universal interest and magnificent promise as the herald of a new order." Although basing Co-operation solely on the economic interest of the consumer, the ultimate social ideal was similar to that of the long line of British co-operators.

GIDE'S CO-OPERATIVE IDEALS

Professor Charles Gide, an economist as well as a French co-operator of international repute, arrived at similar conclusions. The immediate aim was to satisfy the needs of members better and more economically than was done by existing institutions, but there were further and higher aims, " the attainment of greater justice in economic relations." He pointed out that the Rochdale Pioneers (whose history first inspired him) were not content with seeking from Co-operation an increase in comfort for the poorer classes, but found in it an instrument of economic transformation, not only in the sphere of exchange but also in production and the division of wealth, for in their system capital would have no profits. " Co-operation therefore means nothing less than an economic system destined to supersede capitalism by mutual aid, by one more like the earlier domestic systems " (in earlier times the household had largely produced for its own needs, grown its own food, made its own bread and jam, butter and cheese, spun, wove, made its own clothes). A consumers' society was like an enlarged family, undertaking similar functions for itself. Örne, whose childhood was spent in just such a peasant household, had a similar idea.

Gide, with Örne, and British co-operators, also had hope of Co-operation furthering moral progress by abolishing the pursuit of profit as the motive of economic activity and replacing it by the aim of satisfying needs. " Whilst abolishing advertisement, lying, cheating, and inducements to extravagance, it will succeed in establishing in business a reign of truth and justice." Co-operation to him was also an end in itself, " It is a living organism and the results already achieved contain the germs of all the possibilities

to be wished for in a latent state—Each co-operative society
which obeys the laws which it has made for itself already constitutes a little world organised in conformity with justice and social
benefit, and it is sufficient to let it develop spontaneously, either
by growth or imitation, to realise in the more or less distant
future, the best of all possible worlds."

Ernest Poisson, a successor of Gide, in his *Co-operative Republic*
expounded a theory of social evolution, showing the interrelation
between economic and social change and how a new system is
brought about by the gradual transformation of an old one. He
claimed that " the institutions which form part of the essential
conditions of a transformation of society are definitely to be found
in the consumers' Co-operative Movement."

GENERAL ACCEPTANCE OF ROCHDALE PRINCIPLES

Although the approach was thus from different standpoints
there was also a general acceptance of the validity of Rochdale
Principles. Örne wrote: " Whenever we decide to establish an
undertaking of a real co-operative type—we must of necessity
apply Rochdale principles from stem to stern. This assertion is
proved to the hilt by practical experience, replete with warning
examples of disastrous attempts to apply other methods and forms
of administration." Not only did the Principles " contain all that
is necessary and nothing superfluous," but they were applicable
to all forms of co-operative enterprise, "with only a slight
alteration in terms, not in economic import."

Gide also declared that the experience of three-quarters of a
century had been unable to add much to the Principles and that
thousands of societies since formed had found themselves bound
to copy the Rochdale rules almost literally—" one of the most
remarkable phenomena in economic history." And Professor
Lambert (Liege University) has declared: " Far from becoming
outmoded the Rochdale Principles represent, in their essence,
everything that is new and hopeful in our modern civilisation."
(*A Fresh Analysis of Rochdale Principles*, 1958.)

Despite the almost universal nominal acceptance of the Rochdale Principles, however, there has been considerable dispute and
differences of opinion as to what were the essential principles and
on their interpretation. Faced with the need to have some
definition in order to decide on the genuineness of societies
applying for membership, in 1931 the International Co-operative
Alliance set up a Special Committee to enquire into the application
of the principles and to define them. This committee reported to

the I.C.A. Congress of 1934 finding the principles "founded in the constitution, rules, and practice of the original society founded in Rochdale in 1844 " to be:

1. Open Membership
2. Democratic Control
3. Dividend on Purchases
4. Limited Interest on Capital
5. Political and Religious Neutrality
6. Cash Trading
7. Promotion of Education

The findings of the committee were discussed at the Congresses of 1934 and 1937 by representatives of twenty-six countries and finally approved by them with only two dissentients. The first four of these principles were then used by the I.C.A. in framing its rule governing eligibility for membership which is limited to *bona fide* co-operative societies. Thus, in a sense, only the first four of the above principles were regarded as absolutely essential although for a number of years when reference was made to the Rochdale Principles, most co-operators thought of all seven.

But the passage of twenty-five years and the changes taking place during that period caused some people to doubt whether all of these principles were still valid and as the result of a resolution passed at the 1963 I.C.A. Congress a Commission was set up (the late Arnold Bonner was one of its members) with the task of ascertaining the extent to which the principles were observed today and of considering whether they met the needs of the Co-operative Movement in the modern world. The Commission reported to the 1966 Congress and recorded that their task had proved to be one " not so much of revision, as of clearing up confusion and removing unnecessary rigidity rooted in un-balanced or oversimplified interpretations . . . "

They recommended that " the following should continue to be considered as essential to genuine and effective co-operative practice both at the present time and in the future as far as can be foreseen:—

1. Membership of a co-operative society should be voluntary and available without artificial restriction or any social, political, religious or racial discrimination, to all persons who can make use of its services and are willing to undertake the responsibilities of membership.

2. Co-operative societies are democratic organisations. Their affairs should be administered by persons elected or appointed in a manner agreed by the members and accountable to them. Members of primary societies should enjoy equal rights of voting

(one member, one vote) and participation in decisions affecting their societies. In other than primary societies the administration should be conducted on a democratic basis in a suitable form.

3. Share capital should only receive a strictly limited rate of interest, if any.

4. Surplus or savings, if any, arising out of the operations of a society belong to the members of that society and should be distributed in such manner as would avoid one member gaining at the expense of others.

This may be done by decision of the members as follows:—

(a) By provision for development of the business of the Co-operative;

(b) By provision of common services; or,

(c) By distribution among members in proportion to their transactions with the society.

5. All co-operative societies should make provision for the education of their members, officers and employees and of the general public, in the principles and techniques of Co-operation, both economic and democratic.

6. All co-operative organisations, in order to best serve the interests of their members and their communities, should actively co-operate in every practical way with other co-operatives at local, national, and international levels."

This formulation was debated at the 1966 Congress and over-whelmingly accepted. One subsequent amendment concerns the fourth principle where some disagreement arose over the use of the words " surplus or savings." As a result of a change of rule at the 1969 Congress, this principle now begins " The economic results arising out of the operations of a society . . ." All six of these principles are incorporated into the I.C.A. rule governing eligibility for membership.

MEMBERSHIP

By voluntary membership is meant that members join a society of their own free will, in distinction to what the Webbs termed " Obligatory Co-operation," i.e. the co-operation which one is obliged to undertake by authority, as in many state and municipal undertakings. There was nothing relating to voluntary member-ship in the original Rochdale Rules, except that each member was " at liberty to withdraw " from the Society.

The I.C.A. Report of 1934 stated that " the idea of obligatory membership of a co-operative society never entered into the conception of the Rochdale Pioneers neither in planning their Society nor its subsequent development.

That of 1966 stated that " . . . (the individual's) decision to apply for membership should normally be the result of his unfettered appreciation of co-operative values and consideration of his economic advantage, including that of his dependants. He should be free also to withdraw from a co-operative when he finds that he no longer has any need of its services or when the co-operative is unable to supply his needs." This freedom cannot be absolute, however, since once a member, a person accepts certain obligations which should not be lightly overthrown and there may be occasions when the refusal of a small group of people to become members of (say) a marketing or supply society may threaten to sabotage a land reform or land reclamation programme, in which case a government may be justified in enforcing membership on a recalcitrant minority. Nevertheless, the need for recognising voluntary membership as essential to co-operatives was generally stressed.

Actually the Co-operative Movement throughout its history has recognised and valued voluntary membership and voluntarism in general as fundamental to the co-operative ideal. Dr. King, for instance, wrote: " Co-operation is a voluntary act, and all the power in the world cannot make it compulsory; nor is it desirable that it should be dependent on any power but its own. For if Co-operation (as seems likely) be the form which the greater part of the world is destined to assume, the interference of governments would only cramp its energies and misdirect them."

Hughes and Neale stated in their *Manual for Co-operators:* " Co-operation is essentially a voluntary system. Its root has been traced back to that deepest of all principles known to us—free, that is self-governing, reasonable, will; only by free self-help can Co-operation procure for man the good claimed as being capable of being produced by it."

Anders Örne was equally definite, " Co-operators are jointly convinced that only in an atmosphere of perfect freedom can trustful and confident co-operation and a real and universal solidarity spread and prosper."

Gide also recognised Co-operation as an expression of and dependent upon freedom: " It makes no appeal to revolution or coercive legislation, but relies on the moral forces of individual energy and the spirit of solidarity . . . Its motto is a two-fold one: self-help . . . and each for all . . . the desire to seek freedom not only for oneself but for others and by others. It is to moral inspiration that Co-operation owes its progress, as much as, and perhaps more than, to its practical advantages."

The Co-operative Union's statements on policy to which reference was made in Chapter XI also emphasised the voluntary nature of the Co-operative Movement, the first one declaring: " The Movement has developed to its present stage in an atmosphere of free association and it is not the desire of co-operators that opportunities of free association should be reduced. Rather do they look forward to increasing opportunities of extending the co-operative method to wider fields." (*The Place of the Co-operative Movement in a Collectivist Economy*.)

Individual freedom is regarded as necessary to the improvement of character which has always been regarded as the ultimate goal of Co-operation. But individual freedom cannot exist in a world of individual selfishness, co-operation is necessary to provide the opportunities for a full life. Only by voluntary co-operation is it possible to enjoy the advantages of associated effort and yet have the freedom necessary to exercise the mental and moral faculties so as to develop the character essential to a better social order. Voluntarism is a fundamental principle of the Co-operative Movement because it is essential to its ideal.

By open membership is meant that the society is not exclusive, " it must be open to all to whom it can be of service " (Örne). Without this principle societies would lose their co-operative character and degenerate into profit-making concerns. A retail society, for instance, could consist of a few members who traded to make profit out of other people, a productive society could consist of a few members employing many workpeople, to make profit out of them. Cases of such are not unknown in co-operative history. Open membership would have prevented them.

Other important consequences proceed from this principle, besides the maintenance of its non-profit-making character. A society's share capital cannot be a limited amount as is that of a joint stock company, for new members will be required to take up shares. The value of its shares will never rise above their par value since new shares can always be taken out at that value. Hence there are no "capital gains" nor speculation in co-operative shares.

A consumers' society has the most universal appeal for it can be of service to everybody. All benefit from an increase in membership, for each new member brings some additional capital and trade. Increased capital enables increased facilities to be provided, and enjoyed by all. Increased trade reduces expenses per pound of trade, thus also benefiting all.

Open membership is necessary for progress to the co-operative ideal. Poisson regarded " indefinite extensibility of membership "

as one of his laws of co-operative evolution. " Every consumer
has not merely the duty of being a co-operator but the right. In so
far as the co-operative society claims to supersede completely private trade, nothing else can be expected. It is no longer a special
association, but a public body which cannot refuse anyone the
right to live, that is, to consume."

Nevertheless, the rules of the Rochdale Pioneers provided for
the rejection of candidates for membership and for the expulsion
of members whose conduct was prejudicial to the interests of the
society. This is not unreasonable, for individuals may be seeking
to injure or impede the work of the society. But it does not
infringe the principles of open membership, if refusal of membership is solely on co-operative grounds, and not on others which are
irrelevant to the purpose of the society, e.g. nationality, race,
religious or political creed.

Consumer societies will find little cause to close the gate of
membership to any individual but other kinds of society may need
to be careful as to whom they admit, for example, a credit society,
on strictly co-operative grounds, would be right to exclude moneylenders, a marketing society to refuse membership to unreliable
producers, a productive society to restrict membership to those
employed in it. On reflection it will be seen that none of these
contravenes the principle of open membership.

Professor Lambert analysing Rochdale Principles found the
open membership principle to be important and also that it " bears
out the altruistic spirit of Co-operation, since the social wealth
built up by the exertions of past and present generations is made
available to any members who may enter the co-operative at some
later date. In other words, it is exactly the opposite of the wealth
that people accumulate for themselves or for a small group."

DEMOCRATIC CONTROL

A co-operative society is an association of persons with an
undertaking in common for specific purposes. Control of the
undertaking by the persons associating is necessary if the specific
purposes are to be served and served efficiently. Such control is
democratic control. Except in the case of very small societies the
control cannot be exercised directly, so the members elect a
committee or board to do it for them.

A board of directors, however, cannot possibly manage a society,
it has neither time nor ability to do that, nor is it necessary that it
should. For it can and does employ persons who as a result of
training and experience have acquired the special capacities to
perform the managerial functions. This does not, however, relieve

the board of the responsibilities of control; each director is indeed subject to legal responsibilities which should deter him from treating his office lightly. The board exercises control by its powers to appoint, promote, and dismiss those employed by the society, especially its chief officials. They are responsible to the board, the board is responsible to the members.

The duty of the board is to see that the society is managed by its officials honestly, efficiently, and in accordance with co-operative principles, i.e., in the interests of the members. Its main functions are those of supervision of management, judgment of performances and results, and policy making. In the case of consumer societies, the boards represent the consumer interest and it is their duty to see that the society is managed in the interests of consumers.

Place of the Member

As the board is elected by and from the members, who, of course, are the consumers of its services, it should be zealous and conscientious in the performance of these duties. The constitutions of societies are devised, however, to enable the membership to control the boards. Firstly, each member has one vote and none more than one. This prevents a few members, or a board, having enough votes to outvote the rest of the membership, and thus be able to ignore the interests or desires of the membership. It is necessary that every member should be able to exercise influence upon the management and " one member one vote " is essential to this.

" One member, one vote " is, however, very far short of being a complete formula for democratic control. It is necessary for democratic control that the voter should have alternatives to vote for, e.g., rival candidates for office, and sufficient knowledge of persons and policies to be able to form a rational judgment upon them. This requires an educated membership, adequate provision of information, and opportunities for discussion of the society's affairs with those responsible for its management.

Efficient societies attempt the co-operative education of their membership in a variety of ways dealt with in another chapter. Information of the society is provided by periodical statements of accounts, often referred to as " balance sheets," by stories in local newspapers or society journals. Information of the Movement as a whole, necessary to an appreciation of the place, policy, and progress of any individual society, is provided by national co-operative journals of which the *Co-operative News*[1], published

---

[1] *The Scottish Co-operator in Scotland*

weekly, is undoubtedly the Movement's newspaper, and is indispensable for a knowledge of current affairs.

General Meetings

The General Meetings, however, are the most important part of co-operative constitutional machinery. They are held periodically according to rule, a few quarterly (at one time this was general) but more often half-yearly, or annually. Any member who cares to attend can do so and express his opinion upon any matter on the agenda. The principal business is generally the consideration of the accounts, and the opportunities for questions upon these enables all the activities of the society to be questioned and commented upon.

The business, however, is not confined to this consideration, and the general meeting may discuss and authorise new departures, allocation of funds for education, political activities, charitable grants, alteration of rules. As a member may give notice of motion to instruct the board to do or refrain from doing something, or, if he can get support of a sufficient number of members required by rule, can get a special meeting called, it will be seen that the individual member can exercise a good deal of influence in his society if he cares to make the effort.

The fact that the committees must meet the members in the general meetings, face their probings, questions, and criticism, is probably the most effective control. For it is this which makes the membership's influence felt at every board meeting, presenting the potent question to every director and official on every issue—" What will the members think? " If the general meetings do have this effect, then there is effective democratic control.

For many years past attention has been drawn to the small proportion of members attending general meetings and voting in co-operative elections. Both of these circumstances are to be deplored, but it does not follow that democratic control is ineffective. As the Webbs pointed out, " the self government of the co-operators is manifested more in the continuous supervision and criticism maintained over the executive by small bodies of members than by frequent changes in the composition of the executive by spasmodic mass votes. Thus, the co-operative democracy really acts directly on the executive," and " the fact that the meeting consists only of a few hundred members gives even a greater opportunity to the pertinacious critic who . . . is conscious that he is voicing the complaint of an unnumbered host of articulate and absent members." (*The Consumers' Co-operative Movement*, S. & B. Webb.)

Although the effectiveness of the general meeting depends more upon the quality than upon the numbers of the members attending it, numbers do matter. For the general meeting is not only a means by which members can question the executive, it is also a means by which the members can be informed and inspired. The early co-operators realised the value of the general meeting in helping to create a knowledgeable and loyal membership.

In its early days, for instance, the Rochdale Society tried to ensure a good attendance by making general meetings the occasions of tea parties, for which each member was charged whether he attended or not, and using the meetings as an educational medium, the proceedings being opened by the chairman or some member of the board giving a short address on some co-operative ideal or principle.

Although appertaining to communities, the Co-operative Congress of 1832 gave reasons for the frequent holding of general meetings which are still generally applicable—to excite and maintain interest, to keep alive the sympathy of all, to inform, exercise and improve the intellectual faculties, to afford an efficient preventive to all abuses of government.

The large membership of some societies, and the great areas they cover make it impossible for any general meeting to contain any but a minute fraction of its members. To overcome this some of the new regional societies have adopted the device of district meetings. This has its drawbacks for each district meeting is a section of the whole general meeting, hence they must have the same agenda, so there can be little opportunity for initiative from the floor, and there is danger of a consequent sense of frustration and powerlessness which may result in indifference, apathy, and abstention. Professor Lambert advised a two-tier system of meetings, primary meetings held in districts, but with full powers to make proposals and hold discussions, and a higher level meeting of delegates from the districts which would settle issues, but major questions would first of all have been put to the primary meetings.

The general meeting is, or should be, the hub of the democracy of the society. If a satisfactory number of members is to attend, it must be interesting and have and exercise powers which make it worth while attending. The powers are there, it is usually the interest which is lacking. Lambert made suggestions for increasing this, amongst which were—managers should be chosen not only for their organising powers but also for their ability to explain co-operative problems to members in a clear, interesting way, statements to meetings should deal not only with the past but look to the future and discuss the society's prospects in the year ahead, " Co-operators must learn once more to strive for victory "; the meeting should not confine itself to the affairs of its own society, but should hear about and discuss the progress of the Movement in their own country and the world.

Elections

The election of the board of directors is, of course, of the utmost importance. There are many interests and problems involved; for instance, who should be eligible to vote. Various qualifications have been and are employed to restrict it to those who are genuinely concerned with the society's interests. Shareholding is an obvious qualification, but the size of the minimum shareholding for eligibility to vote is questionable. Too high a minimum may disenfranchise many who are good members except for shareholding, too low may enable issues vitally affecting the society to be decided by people who have little or no stake in it.

Co-operators have naturally strong feelings against capitalist control, and so the minimum shareholding is very low, in some cases one share not even paid up is sufficient. But this may overlook the duty of the members to provide the capital, without which the society could not function.

The Rochdale Pioneers in their desire for equity allotted one vote to each member, but their original rules also provided for equal shareholding, there was to be equity of duties as well as of rights. Equity of shareholding is at present impossible, but the responsibility of each member to provide some share of the capital needs to be stressed, and a minimum shareholding, not beyond the means of any of its members, would help to do so.

Another qualification sometimes favoured is that of minimum purchases. Such a qualification restricts the vote to those who use the society to some extent for the purpose for which it exists and denies it to those who join a society solely for the purpose of using it to pursue some other end. Moreover, such a qualification might make a vote more valued and relate it to the performance of the duty of the member of dealing with his society.

Methods of voting are also important to the effectiveness of democratic control. When societies were smaller, voting generally took place at the general meetings, and this had the advantage of restricting it to the informed and active members, though the packing of meetings by interested parties in some particular issue was not unknown. In the case of large and widespread societies, without district meetings, such a system, however, in effect disenfranchises a large proportion, perhaps the majority of the members.

To overcome this, various devices have been introduced, none of them entirely satisfactory. In some cases ballot boxes are in the branch shops, and members can vote as they do their shopping. Many of such votes may be lightly given and may be influenced by the assistants or branch manager, a danger if an employee candidate is concerned. Balloting at centres, under disinterested supervision, is preferable.

Postal ballots at first sight may appear to be a solution, as a high proportion of members vote. But many of these members may never attend a meeting, may be utterly uninformed of what they are voting upon, and consequently affected by the press or other influences, seeking to persuade people to vote in ways not in the interests of the society or the Movement. Again, postal ballots give an advantage to those candidates who have some publicity value or influence, and these may not be the best people for committee work. Where there are also rules prohibiting candidates canvassing for votes, the system may be very unfair.

The underlying evil, which makes all these schemes defective is, of course, the apathy and ignorance of the average member. A poor system could be made to work well by a good membership, a good system will not work well with an apathetic and ignorant membership.

Eligibility of Candidates

Eligibility of candidates for election has also been a subject of dispute. A member of the board of a co-operative society fills an important and responsible position. Large societies are very big businesses, working with millions of pounds of capital, with millions of pounds of turnover and employing thousands of work people. The decisions of their boards affect the lives and fortunes of their thousands of employees, members, employees in federal organisations, and the public at large. In a less degree, so do the decisions of the boards of smaller societies. Qualification of eligibility for such powerful positions is of obvious importance.

Many societies have rules requiring a minimum length of membership and some measure of concern with and loyalty to the society, such as minimum purchases over a period, a minimum shareholding (these qualifications often being substantially higher than members' qualifications for voting).

There are also many disqualifications, such as being, or the spouse being, engaged in some business competitive with the society; participating in the profits of any contract with the society except as a member of a corporate body; relatives employed by the society.

Employment by the society was a disqualification by the rules of many societies, but in practice employees were, and are, prevented by common law from sitting on boards of directors, since whilst they were on such a board they would not, without infringing the law, be able to continue drawing wages or salaries as employees. For they are in the same position as directors of joint stock companies and " A director is precluded from dealing on behalf of the company with himself and from entering into engagements in which he has a personal interest conflicting, or which may possibly conflict, with the interests of those whom he is bound by fiduciary interest to protect." (Dr. San Garde, Solicitor for the Co-operative Union in the *Co-operative Review*.)

This obstacle to employees being elected to boards of directors may be overcome either by the general meeting voting the employee director a remuneration as a *director* or by the inclusion of a rule in the rules of the society specifically providing that employees may be members of the board of directors. There must, that is, be a special provision in the rules to enable an individual to be a member of the board of directors and at the same time occupy a paid position in the society. Whether it is wise and proper for employees to be eligible for election is a matter of debate, many societies have included rules making it legally possible, the membership itself decides whether they are in fact elected.

Board of Directors

There is not space in a book of this type to deal in detail with the powers, duties and responsibilities of boards. These are defined by law and the rules of the society, powers conferred upon them cannot be withdrawn except by alteration of the rules, and the members cannot override a decision of the board if the rules empower the board to make such a decision. As regards their functions, much depends upon circumstances, e.g. the competence of officials and the board's confidence in them, it is impossible to draw up a satisfactory line of demarcation between directorial and managerial functions.

In general, however, the advice given in the *Handbook for Members of Co-operative Committees* (F. Hall) is sound, " Committees too frequently try to manage a society. This is not their function. Their function is to direct and guide policy. It is the manager's function to manage. The managers have, or should have the technical and expert knowledge. The committee will be advised by their experts and should be able to judge which of the alternative courses suggested by their advisers is the right one to follow. They should also be able to judge from the records and statistics placed before them whether the society is being well managed or not. Hence sound judgment of men and measures is a most important qualification. Given this, the more a committee man knows of the technical side of the society's business the better; but he should not let his knowledge tempt him to interfere with the management of departments, for he will, by so doing, weaken the sense of responsibility in the managers of those departments and probably create friction."

The Independent Commission, however, whilst agreeing that committees should not attempt to manage, considered the functions of supervision, judgment, and determination of policy could be performed much more easily and quickly, it recommended the abolition of sub-committees, and held that monthly meetings should be enough. In large societies it recommended the election of a Members' Council of 60–70 members, which would meet twice a year. It would be the highest authority in the society, approving the report and balance sheet, with sole power to alter rules, and electing the board of directors. (Somewhat similar to the " two-tier " system advocated by Lambert.)

In fact, most of the geographically large regional societies have a system of district or divisional general meetings which are all sections of the general meeting. In the newer regional societies, most have district committees which are little more than advisory and consultative bodies but which send some of their members forward to the central Board of Directors. The Members' Council or Congress, which is fairly common in other countries, is unknown in retail societies in this country.

It will be gathered that the ideal of effective democratic control has not been reached in the Co-operative Movement as yet. But it is held as an ideal and sincere efforts continue to be made to attain it. This is because of the realisation that it is essential to Co-operation, most of whose difficulties arise from defects in the working of its democracy. The democratic principle has indeed been regarded by many as the most important of all co-operative principles, and of Co-operation itself as the attempt to develop an economic democracy.

LIMITED INTEREST ON CAPITAL

The principle of limited interest on capital would be better stated as a rate of interest on capital fixed by rule. It is closely related in purpose to the principle of dividend in proportion to business done with the society, for the objective is the same— to prevent profit going to capital. At the same time there is recognition of the value of the service performed by the provision of capital and this is paid for by a fixed rate of interest, sufficiently high to attract an adequate amount. Being paid for this service, capital has no further claims on any surplus. If the amount of capital needs to be increased or decreased, the rule fixing the rate of interest may be altered. This change of rule, however, requires the consent of the members. Interest on share capital is generally regarded by co-operators as an expense of the undertaking.

DISPOSAL OF SURPLUS

There are those who have regarded payment of dividend on purchases as the most important principle and distinctive feature of Co-operation. Although the practice did not become widespread until after the establishment of the Rochdale society of 1844 it had been used before but amongst a number of other practices. Theoretically, the net surplus or savings made by many societies in the pre-Rochdale Movement were to be kept indivisible and added to the societies' capital in order to assist their development into self-supporting communities. Practically, division of at least some of that surplus was fairly widespread without any uniformity of method. Equal division, division according to capital contribution, division according to transactions were all practised. The Rochdale Pioneers chose the last method for the cogent reason that in order to attract members they had to offer some short-term advantage in the contemporary economic environment. This decision was largely a result of a previous decision concerning price policy when they had decided to sell goods at the current market price, administratively the most convenient policy.

There is little doubt that the payment of dividend gave rise to several advantages. It encouraged people to become members and to purchase from their society. It was often a source of saving and an incentive to thrift, encouraging self-reliance among sections of the working class. The accumulated dividend, besides being useful to the individual member, also proved to be a useful source of capital. Finally, Beatrice Webb argued that the payment of dividend on purchases established Co-operation on the foundation of pure democracy in the sense that payment according to shareholding or division amongst the workers would encourage limitation of membership thus leading to a limited number of individuals (capitalists or workers) assuming the government and obsorbing the profits. With the payment of dividend on purchases there was on the other hand the desire and the incentive to encourage as wide a membership as possible.

It should be noted, however, that there has been a tendency

to distort the purpose of dividend. Strictly speaking the surplus available for distribution is a residual remaining after various other claims have been met. In practice there are usually attempts to stabilise the rate of dividend. On the one hand, members come to reckon on a constant rate and on the other managers tend to budget for a constant rate including it in their calculation of prices thus effectively turning the system upside down. Perhaps arising from this, there has also been a tendency to regard the dividend rate as an indicator of the economic efficiency of a society with the result that managers are reluctant to reduce rates and have drawn on reserves to maintain the rate, a very unsound business practice.

In fact, in considering the question of use of surplus one problem to be solved is that of balancing the interests of the individual members and those of the society as a whole. In Britain there has perhaps been a tendency to stress the interests of the former at the expense of the latter with regard, for example, to paying out as high a dividend as possible and neglecting to build up the society's own capital by putting a proportion of the surplus to reserve. It is arguable that in the past when societies could rely on members keeping at least a part of their dividend payment in their share accounts this did not particularly matter since the society still had the use of the money for some time. Nevertheless the money was still withdrawable and if the society had neglected to build up its own capital it could be faced with considerable difficulties if there were a run on share capital for any reason. But because of the stress on dividend on purchases as a principle (and immediate economic self-interest which undoubtedly bolstered the principle) many British societies have tended to pay more attention to dividend payments than to reserve allocations.

The fact that dividend on purchases is not absolutely essential to co-operative societies (and is therefore not a principle) can be quite easily indicated by instancing a society that allows its members to purchase at prices so near to cost that no margin remains that is large enough to be worth distributing. This is generally the trend in advanced industrial economies like Britain already where competition is strong and dividend rates display a downward trend because profit margins are being squeezed. In addition there is evidence that the consumer prefers the more immediate benefit of lower prices than the delayed dividend payment. The fact that societies give their members more immediate economic benefits such as lower prices or dividend stamps does not make them unco-operative.

A further fact is that societies may devote all or part of their net surplus to the provision of services for the common enjoyment of all their members, as being more useful to them than the equivalent in cash, because the members could not provide them economically as individuals. Thus societies may provide educational services, recreational facilities, collective life insurance and so on and could devote all of their surplus to such provisions without endangering their status as a co-operative society. The crucial point is that whatever is to be done with a society's surplus is detemined by democratic decision by the members according to their judgment of what is just and expedient. The principle regarding dividend on purchases is not that it should be paid but that if there is a surplus to be distributed and if the members decide that the surplus should be distributed then it should be distributed on the basis of transactions.

Non-profit making

Co-operators have at all times and places regarded their enterprises as being non-profit undertakings, since co-operators make nothing at the expense of anybody else. Thus the Webbs argued that " profits in co-operative trading go to neither capital nor labour, they cease to exist. The Consumers' Co-operative Movement is in fact based on the elimination of ' profit on price'." (" *The Consumers' Co-operative Movement.*")

This is most clearly seen when the device of dividend is used. The Report of the Departmental Committee on Income Tax in 1905 declared: " The suggestions made to us that the dividend which is paid to members of these societies constitutes a profit which would properly be taxable rest we think on a misapprehension of the nature of dividend. The so-called dividend arises from the fact that the prices charged by the society to its members are in excess of cost price. If the goods were distributed at exact cost price there would be no dividend . . . But the societies, for what they consider good reasons, prefer to fix a scale of prices which leaves a margin above costs. Thus an adjustment has to be made periodically and the balance between cost price and distributing price is divided amongst the members in proportion to their purchases. This dividend is clearly not profit, but merely a return to members of sums which they have paid for their own goods in excess of cost price."

Even where there is no dividend, however, when the surplus is used in some other way, the fact that the benefits received by co-operative members are entirely of their own making and not gained at the expense of others means that the surplus is different

in kind from the profits of a capitalist organisation. In some
countries it is taken to the extreme that if a co-operative society
is wound up the reserves are regarded as being indivisible so
after creditors are repaid, members receive their nominal shareholding back and if anything surplus remains, it is given over to
a co-operative fund administered by the governmental Co-operative Department or to another co-operative society or to some
other approved body. In these circumstances, a member of a
co-operative society can never get more out of the society than
he puts in.

PROMOTING EDUCATION

The purpose of co-operative education needs to be kept in mind
if it is to be understood as a principle. The early co-operators
were in no difficulty, they were engaged in pursuit of an ideal, and
the making of co-operators was essential to it. Education in
Co-operation was thus an essential of the Movement, and it is
bound to remain the core of its educational work. A knowledge
of the world within which the Movement operates is, however,
also necessary, and the study of history, economics and politics
cannot therefore be neglected, nor can a study of the techniques
of business be neglected by its employees.

For the co-operative viewpoint, which is that of users, is different
from the common viewpoint which is that of profit making. Hence
with different purposes in view the techniques are likely to be
different. Commodities designed and produced to serve best the
needs of the consumer would be different from those designed and
produced in the interests of the profit maker. A beast cut up to
yield the most profit will be cut up differently from one cut up in
portions most satisfactory to the consumer.

The arts of salesmanship and advertising will perhaps differ
more than any other as between those of consumer Co-operation
and private trade. If co-operative employees and officials are to
engage in co-operative business efficiently, they must understand
it, and realise the essential differences between co-operative and
other business. What is good business practice for the one, for
instance, may be bad business practice for the other, for their
purposes are not only different, they are frequently opposed.
Hence the need for co-operators to undertake their education not
only in the ideals and principles of Co-operation, but also in the
techniques of their business.

The co-operative education of membership is also essential. For,
as a democratic movement, its leaders, policies, and progress will
depend on the quality of its membership. " In a democratically

organised form of trading there is specially necessary an intensive business and administrative educational activity so that the members may exert their full influence and that wisely and to their mutual benefit. The average man, illiterate in economics, sees no contradiction in refusing to capitalise his own undertaking adequately while at the same time demanding from it the most magnificent results. Economic superstition and darkness of this kind must be eliminated, and every co-operative society must undertake that task if it is to have any future." (Anders Örne.)

The membership must also be educated in co-operative ideals and principles so that they may judge policies and performances from the co-operative angle. Only by so doing will a co-operative approach be made and co-operative ideals pursued. Thus co-operative education is a fundamental principle of the Movement. The I.C.A.'s conclusion was that " in the last analysis the principles embody the spirit of Co-operation, which has to be awakened and renewed in every fresh generation that takes over the work of the Movement from its predecessors. That awakening and renewal depend, more than anything, upon the care and assiduity with which each generation keeps the torch of education aflame."

CO-OPERATION AMONG CO-OPERATIVES

An idea which has always been implicit in Co-operation—it is after all only an extension of the fundamental co-operative idea of association for mutual benefit—was found in the I.C.A. Report of 1966 to be worth stating as a principle of Co-operation. This kind of co-operation has been the customary way in which Co-operatives have advanced from one stage of the productive process into the next, for example, from retailing into wholesaling and production, or from selling on the home market into exporting.

While it has always been an important idea, however, it is becoming increasingly important with changing economic circumstances. The Movement's most effective competitiors are large-scale concerns, vertically and horizontally integrated, and it must be expected that the trend will continue towards oligopoly and monopoly, not only nationally but inter-nationally. Any vestiges of competition will be among these large concerns and the Co-operative Movement is potentially among the largest. To be effective, however, there must be more co-operation among Co-operatives themselves for the benefit of members and the community at large. Thus the Movement needs to concentrate its power in larger units by applying consistently without restriction, from the local to the international plane, the principle of co-operation among co-operatives, to prove its greatness and act successfully against monopoly. As the I.C.A. Commission wrote, co-operative societies " must act as members of a common united effort to realise the objectives and ideals of the movement as a whole."

POLITICS AND RELIGION

The historical chapters described how the idea of political and religious neutrality emerged in the British Co-operative Movement and why in some measure it was departed from. The I.C.A. report of 1934 considered that it should be retained as a principle but the 1966 report felt unable to give it the same absolute authority. Part of the principle as it was originally understood is now dealt with in the principle concerning membership, that is that there is no discrimination on grounds of politics or religion. Otherwise, the word " neutrality " is itself not entirely satisfactory, carrying as it does overtones of passivity and indifference, qualities that co-operatives cannot afford to nurture when their own interests are at stake. From that point of view, " independence " is a far better description of the desirable position.

The Commission suggested there were two factors to be taken into account when considering political action. On the one hand, Co-operatives needed to choose the methods which would be most effective, on the other, they needed to choose those which would secure the maximum of consent and support among the members, the overriding consideration being that any weakening of a co-operative's unity impairs its power to act effectively, not merely in the political field, but in all other fields as well.

Thus a co-operative's position on this question will depend on the circumstances. In certain cases, neutrality will be the right and proper policy, in other cases, political activity will be justified.

BUSINESS PRACTICES

Under this heading the 1966 Report considered two practices which had at some time or other been considered principles of co-operation, cash trading and honesty in trading, neither of which the Commission could give the universal validity of being a principle, but both of which it considered extremely important guides to business practice.

Cash Trading

Contrary to much popular co-operative belief, the Rochdale Pioneers did not introduce the prohibition of credit simply to protect themselves as a trading organisation, although that was undoubtedly a consideration. In addition they were concerned with the well-being of their members as individuals. They, and many co-operators after them, considered indebtedness as one of the great political and social evils. A man in debt was not a free man, and freeing and keeping the working classes from debt was necessary for their emancipation. Credit societies in agricultural areas have much the same purpose, that of freeing the peasant farmer from the servitude of private debt which may be lifelong.

With increasing prosperity, however, conditions change. Higher earnings, greater spending power, greater security of employment, all make credit rather less of a danger to the individual and possibly to the co-operative as a business organisation. Indeed, in these conditions, co-operative societies were forced to provide credit facilities if they were going to retain their members' custom. Nevertheless, honesty in trading is important here and co-operatives have the duty to provide credit on fair and economical terms, a practice which some private traders have not been noted for. Co-operatives also have the responsibility towards themselves and their members to decide carefully when, and in what manner, it would be permissible to rely on credit, especially in regard to articles of consumption.

The important thing is that societies should look at the question of cash and credit policy not only from the standpoint of their own business advantage, but also from the standpoint of the true economic and moral interests of their members. And societies would be failing in their educational duty if they did not take care to instruct their members in the issues involved, so that they make intelligent decisions which will later justify themselves by their consequences, in terms of both co-operation and good household management.

Honesty in Trading

To say that this is no longer a principle of Co-operation may give a rather unfortunate impression. What is meant, of course, is that it is no longer distinctively co-operative.

The reasons why the Rochdale Pioneers found it necessary to emphasise this practice are known well enough. Partly due to the efforts of the British Co-operative Movement, the practices of adulteration that were part of the competitive situation of the mid-nineteenth century have now disappeared. This is not to say, however, that the need for vigilance on the part of the Co-operative Movement has disappeared. The sand may have disappeared from sugar but few people would claim that as a result trading has become completely honest. The inflated claims of advertisements, the package or container that misleads, are indications of the continuing need for protecting the consumer amply manifested in the rise of consumer protection organisations in several countries. There would still seem to be the need, therefore, of an organisation like the Co-operative Movement which can not only agitate and protest but supply economically practicable alternative products which are genuine and reliable, for whether honest trading is regarded as being a distinctive co-operative principle or not, it is certainly a logical consequence of consumers co-operating to provide the means to satisfy their wants.

LOYALTY

Loyalty to the society does not appear as a principle in previous statements, probably because it is implicit in Co-operation itself; if there were no loyalty there would be no Co-operation. But possibly because it was so obvious as to be taken as generally understood there is sometimes a tendency to overlook its fundamental importance. For example the Independent Commission did not consider that the retail societies should be under any obligation to " buy out of loyalty " from the Wholesale Societies. A similar opinion was expressed by Auberon Herbert in 1877 and convincingly answered by Lloyd Jones who explained the nature of distributive Co-operation, viz. the capital was provided by the members, but the custom that made the capital fruitful was given *as a duty* by the members, and the surpluses and dividends came as a result of the faithful performance of this duty. The relation between the Wholesale and the individual society was the same as that between the individual member and his retail society, it was the same business carried a step further in the same hands, " to be sustained and made profitable by the same sense of duty." He pointed out that the Wholesale was an organisation of retail societies and their obligation was in fact an obligation to each other, just as the obligation of the individual member to purchase from his society is an obligation to his fellow members. This sense of duty and an understanding of duty were necessary to the vitality and progress of Co-operation even as a business. Without it there would be waste and losses, to be suffered by all the members, whether retail societies in the case of wholesales, or by the individual members in the case of societies.

Gide has described the many economies yielded by co-operative trading; it could provide for the needs of its members with certainty, it had not to run the risks of bad speculation and of consequent bad stock, it did not need luxurious premises or expensive sites, but these economies were dependent on its members being conscientious and loyal in purchasing from the store. The heavy expenses of selling goods, often exceeding their costs of production, largely consist of the expenses of attracting the public to buy them. It is not unknown for a pack to cost more than the goods it contains, and to have occasioned a good deal more scientific thought and research. Competition is often in the attractiveness of the packs rather than in the quality of the contents. If co-operators were loyal to their societies and their societies loyal to their co-operative suppliers, they would be spared such expensive follies.

As co-operators, both individuals and societies, lose their sense of duty, however, co-operative trade becomes more similar to that between private traders and their customers. Expenses consequently rise as similar methods come to be employed to persuade co-operators to buy from their own businesses. Thus, lack of loyalty causes the distinctive advantages of Co-operation to be lost. Loyalty is perhaps of even more importance to some other forms of Co-operation, marketing societies, for instance. Lack of loyalty is probably the principal cause of failure among these. A society with a loyal membership is impregnable. One in which there is no sense of obligation amongst its membership is weaker than a capitalist concern.

Lloyd Jones expressed this: " It is not the capital that makes success, though it is necessary to success. It is not management which brings profit, though the best management should be secured, but that living sense of duty which carries to the centre that custom without which the whole Movement could never be anything but a perishing and corrupting body without a soul."

Loyalty is indeed a fundamental principle of Co-operation, generally recognised but surprisingly seldom stated.

UNDERLYING PRINCIPLES

An examination of the above principles reveals an underlying social philosophy. Voluntary and Open Membership and the Promotion of Education are expressions of the more universal principle or ideal of Freedom.

Fixed Interest on Capital, Equitable Use of Surplus, Honest Trading, and Loyalty, are all expressions of Equity.

Freedom and Equity are two main principles of Democracy, but there is an equally important third, Fraternity. All are interdependent, none can exist without the others. Fraternity, however, cannot be embodied in rules, it is the attitude of each member to the rest, it can be promoted and encouraged, it cannot be imposed.

Dr. King devoted a whole issue of his *Co-operator* to fraternity under the heading of " The Spirit of Co-operation." He believed Co-operation would remove the obstacles to friendship namely— self interest, rivalry, jealousy, and envy. It promoted sympathy, tolerance, understanding, and affection. These would be of gradual growth but " The Spirit of Co-operation is the spirit of friendship and brotherly love, which, though small at first in the infancy of the society, will gather strength and stature as it grows."

Some cynics will smile at King's claims for Co-operation, but the difference between the ideal and the reality is some measure of the Movement's failure and is to be deplored. The need for fraternity is undeniable, without it Co-operation will not work satisfactorily, nor will it progress. Its lack reveals itself in the apathy and indifference of members to the democratic control of their societies, in the lack of loyalty, in failure to subject narrow sectional interests to the good of the whole; in short, a good many of the weaknesses of the Co-operative Movement are due to its losing what Dr. King rightly described as "The Spirit of Co-operation."

In the welter of statistics on capital, trade, expenses, etc., and the concern with financial, trading, production, and organisational problems, this vital matter is overlooked at the Movement's peril. For the most important products of the Co-operative Movement are co-operators and if it fails to produce these it may well end with producing nothing, for it cannot exist without them.

13 THE ORGANISATION AND ACTIVITIES OF THE RETAIL SOCIETIES

> *" In the subtle power of the Co-operative Faith we discover the secret of that administrative success of the British Co-operative Movement which perplexes the ordinary man of the world. Officers earning less than the market rent of their ability, chairmen and committeemen accepting nominal fees, watch nevertheless with integrity and zeal over the interests entrusted to their care."*
>
> *Beatrice Potter.*

AS will have been seen in the historical chapters the co-operative retail societies are the primary, basic societies of Consumer Co-operation, and the best known type of society in Great Britain. The progress of most other consumer co-operative organisations is dependent upon them, for they provide the trade, capital and directorates of these other bodies. They set the pace and determine the direction of the Co-operative Movement in general, for nothing can succeed without their co-operation.

With possibly a few exceptions these consumer societies and other types of co-operative societies are registered under the Industrial and Provident Societies Act and so subject to their provisions, to which reference will be made during this chapter. An appendix gives a summary of the Act. Seven members are required as the legal minimum membership of a society. The legal minimum age of membership is 16 years. Other societies and companies are legally eligible for membership.

Although they vary in size from small societies of a few score members to societies with over a hundred thousand, and one, the London Co-operative Society, with over a million, they all embody the principles described in the preceding chapter and are recognisably members of the same species, all having the same characteristic features which distinguish them from other forms of business enterprise. Amongst these is the ownership and control of the co-operative business by its customers, who are the members of the society.

MEMBERSHIP

In the main, though not entirely, the membership consists of wage earners and their wives. Much depends on the locality. Where Co-operation has been long established, it is usual for co-operative membership to be a fair cross section of the community with most people members of the society, as reference to and comparison of the Census figures and those of societies' membership in the Co-operative Union Statistics will show. In others, probably rare, where Co-operation is comparatively new, there may be few other than wage earners in membership. Although salary earners are often diffident in taking part in what they regard as working class organisations experience shows that in time they become attracted to and members of various kinds of friendly society, building societies, co-operative societies and even trade unions. At all times men and women from these classes have been active and prominent in the Co-operative Movement, both locally and nationally.

Holding that all are consumers and that everyone has a consumer interest, the consumer Co-operative Movement has resolutely refused to become a class or sectional movement and appeals to all. Membership is practically open to everyone over 16 years of age, although the rules of some societies fix a higher age limit. Entry is easy, it is usually possible at any branch shop or the offices of a society. A small sum, generally 1/-, as a membership fee is all that is necessary for enrolment, although a minimum shareholding is necessary for full membership rights. This, however, may be paid in instalments or by crediting the member's share account with what is due as dividend on purchases.

The composition of the membership is important for it will affect the nature of the trade a society undertakes, both as regards kinds and qualities of goods, the services expected and provided, the style and equipment of its shops, its financial structure, directorate and policy.

CAPITAL

Capital is raised by means of shares, loans of various kinds and allocations to reserves from surpluses. Wage earners require depositories for their savings which are secure and which can be drawn upon easily and quickly. Co-operative societies have met these needs by accumulating large amounts of liquid assets which can be readily converted into cash, and by making their share capital withdrawable. This withdrawability has attracted working class savings, but has hindered development by making societies timid of sinking capital in the fixed assets of bricks, mortar, fittings and machinery.

This difficulty of acquiring the necessary fixed assets for expansion can be overcome by accumulating reserve capital (better described by continental societies as " Own Capital "), and this is the policy long recommended by the Co-operative Union. Reference to the statistics in the historical chapters will show with what success. Retail societies' capital in excess of what is required for their own businesses is generally invested with their wholesale societies though a considerable amount is also invested in various kinds of government and municipal loans.

Inquiries suggest that there is a considerable difference between the typical shareholding and the average shareholding. A maximum shareholding is laid down by law (£1,000), the object being to prevent a few obtaining a dominant ownership in a society (which, in spite of one man one vote, could be dangerous owing to withdrawability of share capital), and the rules provide for a minimum shareholding, which is kept down to a low figure so as to present no obstacle to membership. A high proportion of membership has little more than the minimum holding. This is due to lack of education of societies' membership, many are unaware of their relationship to the society, and that the co-operative business is run on the members' money.

An increase in the typical shareholding would strengthen societies not merely by adding to their capital resources, but would lessen the risk of large proportions of share capital being withdrawn at once; strengthen the common bond of a common capital, and increase the sense of ownership and so concern in the societies' affairs of the typical member. It is highly desirable that each society should be self-financing and so have the self-reliance and responsibility associated with co-operative enterprise, and that each member should have a sufficient stake in the enterprise to promote a realisation of responsibilities and obligations to his society. " Where thy treasure is, there will thy heart be also."

Under the I. and P. Acts each member accepts the liability to subscribe share capital, although the value of the minimum share is fixed by the society's rules. There is a legal maximum shareholding of £1,000 for individual members, but no legal maximum for a society's shareholding in another. Members enjoy limited liability, that is, their liability to the society and its creditors is limited to the shares they have taken up. Each, of course, is liable for the minimum shareholding, and each is liable for the balance of any share not fully paid up. A member's liability extends for one year after he has withdrawn from a society so far as any debts of the society existing at the time of his withdrawal are concerned providing the contributions due from existing members are insufficient to meet them.

In these days it is extremely rare for a society to be unable to meet its debts, or for a member to have to pay the balance of shares he holds, or for an ex-member to repay share capital he has withdrawn. But the legal obligation is there and it is well for all concerned to realise the member is something more than a customer. It is the members who carry the risks of the enterprise.

MANAGEMENT

A retail society's affairs are administered by elected boards and appointed officials. As a retail society consists of its members, it is the duty of boards and officials to administer these affairs in the interests of the members. The machinery of democratic control exists to ensure this. These circumstances—the purpose of the society and its democratic constitution—make it more difficult to manage than a private business, for the purpose of a capitalist concern is clear and single, that of making profit for its owners. This simplifies the formulation of policy and the judgment of performances. Managers and directors, being responsible to the owners, whose interest is simple and direct, know what is expected of them, that is, actions and decisions which will increase profits.

A co-operative society has no such single purpose in view or single interest to serve. The interests of members are many and diverse. Members are both shareholders and customers and some are employees. Thus at one and the same time it is demanded that share capital be secure, easily withdrawable and yield a good rate of interest, that shops be conveniently sited (and what is convenient for some is inconvenient for others) be the most attractive, best equipped and stocked in the locality, provide the best service (often including delivery), offer the best qualities of goods with the widest range of choice, pay higher wages for shorter working weeks than do other traders, charge the lowest prices and yet with all this pay a good dividend on purchases.

These demands will all be voiced through the democratic machinery of a society and boards and officials are thus kept aware of the many interests they are expected to serve. Concentration on any one to the neglect of the others will result in trouble. Although all are not of equal importance, it is necessary for the good management of a society that each is considered and given its proper weight so that the right balance and harmony is secured. This requires a good knowledge of the members, their needs, desires, inclinations, general sentiments, which a management truly representative of the members is likely to have, and a board of experts and specialists is not.

Place of the Board

It has often been suggested, and in fact Congresses have approved of the suggestion (by acceptance of the General Survey Committee's Report in 1919 and resolutions of the Special Congress at Blackpool in 1958), that boards of directors should confine themselves to determining policy and leave the officials to perform the managerial functions, for which they were appointed and are paid. These functions require a knowledge and experience which the layman cannot have, hence the need to employ those who possess them. J. S. Mill expressed it as, " The ideal of democracy is that the people shall be masters, but employ servants more capable than themselves."

This ideal, however, is not easily attained, for the separation of policy (making and supervision) from managerial functions is not to be performed by lines of simple definition. That boards of directors may be prone to waste time by discussing petty details and neglecting or inadequately discussing big issues was drawn attention to by G. J. Holyoake in his *History of the Rochdale Pioneers*, and the fact that these complaints can continue to be made for a hundred years indicates that the problem is not a simple one. Nor is it confined to co-operative committees. Reference to " Parkinson's Law " suggests it is a common defect.

The Independent Commission of Inquiry suggested the proper functions for a board were: First, the selection of the chief officials, their salaries and conditions of work. " In the existence of this power lies the ultimate guarantee of democratic control," but not the appointment of officials below top level. Secondly, the laying down of general policy on prices, dividends and reserve allocations. Thirdly, it should decide the rate of interest to be paid on members' capital. Fourthly, the sanctioning of all capital expenditure above a certain level and generally the plan of capital development for the coming year or years. Fifthly, the approval of a capital Budget showing in detail how this plan is to be financed. Sixthly, it must receive from its chief official and carefully scrutinise, regular trade and statistical reports designed to give maximum information and the most scientific check on efficiency. Lastly, it must provide a continuous liaison with the membership.

From these suggestions it will be gathered that the Commission's opinion was that a board of directors should roughly confine itself to the determination of policy, the appointment of officials to carry out that policy, and the supervision and judgment of their performance. How far the board's activities will extend depends principally upon their confidence in the competence and integrity of their officials, and successful management will depend largely upon the confidence of the officials in the board. This confidence has to be won, it cannot be other than the fruit of experience of relations with each other.

Much " depends upon the good sense of both committees and managers in carrying out their respective duties. If the former interfere too much with the manager they may spoil him as a manager, discourage him, stifle his initiative and perhaps cause him to resign. If the manager assumes an authority which belongs to the committee, he is likely, sooner or later, to come into conflict with the committee and ultimately with members of the society. Tolerance, sympathy, confidence and goodwill on both sides are essential to harmonious working; and if these exist there will be few occasions when differences will arise." (*Handbook for Co-operative Committees*, F. Hall.)

Every society must have a board which is subject to obligations imposed by the Industrial and Provident Societies Act, and by the rules of the society. Its powers are indicated and limited by these rules. If a power is given to it by the rules its decisions within that power cannot be overridden by the members, e.g. appointment and dismissal of employees. Hence the importance to all concerned, including members, of having a knowledge of the society's rules.

Only one committee, i.e. the management committee, or board of directors, is recognised by law, but the members may and often do appoint other committees such as an education committee and a political committee. The powers of these committees are also conferred and limited by the rules of the society, by law, and decisions of members' meetings. As these committees are not the legal committee of the society, any property they acquire must be acquired in the name of the society and therefore through the board of directors, which is the legally recognised committee of the society.

The best size of board will depend partly upon the size of the society, a large society is likely, for instance, to have sub-committees, and to lighten this burden a larger board is required than in the case of a small society. But in all cases it is necessary to keep committees small enough to enable matters to be discussed. Not less than seven, not more than 12, is advised.

Sometimes it is suggested that the service required on the boards of large societies is beyond what can reasonably be expected of part-time members and that full-time salaried boards of directors have become necessary. This view, however, has not been widely accepted. F. Hall pointed out that the overwork of boards is largely their own fault. They try to follow the same lines of control as when the society was small, they try to manage the society instead of supervising it. With the right systems of control involving the consideration of reports and statistics, the board even of a very large society could perform its proper functions without any undue burden.

If whole-time committees were appointed there would be the danger of these becoming in fact if not in name whole-time officials, with an official viewpoint, unresponsive to and unrepresentative of the general membership. The size of salary paid would also be important if the right kind of person were to be attracted. It would need to be high enough to attract the best ability, but the higher the salary the greater the danger of attracting people who would canvass and pull strings for the sake of the job and its salary rather than for the sake of serving the society. Moreover, persons of business ability prepared to serve on part-time committees might be unwilling to throw up good positions in the outside world for a place on a full-time committee subject to the uncertainties of re-election in a short period. (*Handbook for Members of Co-operative Committees*.)

Place of Officials

The actual management of a society is bound to be in the hands of officials. In general, the practice of having two more or less equal officials at the top of the management structure— the General Secretary and the General Manager—which was common until fairly recently has been replaced by a system where there is one official clearly at the head of the structure, usually known as the Chief Executive Officer.

Primarily, this official is the link between the society's board and its appointed management. As such he becomes the centre of communication in the society passing on information and instructions from both the board and himself to the society's management and in turn passing back to the board reports and information from the management. In addition, he becomes the primary co-ordinator of management activities throughout the society, since he is the only official concerned with the management (rather than the direction) of the whole organisation.

Because of his position vis-a-vis the board and the rest of the management, the chief executive officer bears the main responsibility of interpreting the board's policy decisions to his managers, ensuring that those policies are fully understood by them and seeing that they are carried out. The task of actually translating the policy into management instructions and procedures will also essentially be his, either alone or working with the appropriate managers.

In making its policy decisions, the board cannot work in a vacuum. Thus another of this official's responsibilities is to prepare reports for the board based on the information, budgets and trading developments reported to him by lower management. The board's policy decisions are likely to be based in the main on these reports. In fact, although the ultimate responsibility for policy must lie with the board, there is no doubt that they will rely to a greater or lesser extent on the advice of their chief official in coming to their decisions. Thus another extremely important function is to act as adviser to the board and in some ways this may be the most crucial of his functions. Some people would argue that in the present business environment, lay boards of directors cannot hope to formulate policy; all they can do is decide it, that is on the basis of alternatives laid before it by its chief official and probably acting upon his advice they make a choice.

In some societies, a chief executive officer is also responsible for the main secretarial duties in the society, in others the duties are embodied in another official. The secretary, whether he be chief executive or another official, is the official mouthpiece of the society. He receives official communications to the society and signs official communications and notices on behalf of the board and society. He is also responsible for keeping the society's accounts, preparing its balance sheet, conducting general correspondence and organising the office, and is official custodian of the society's seal, cash and books.

Directly below the chief executive officer in the management structure come the departmental managers (sometimes known today as divisional managers). In some societies these managers still have some degree of direct responsibility to the board but increasingly they are responsible to the chief officer who is the primary source of contact between board and management.

As the name implies, the departmental manager is responsible for a particular trading department, grocery, butchery, footwear, electrical and so on. In this function the departmental manager will be more of a technical specialist than the chief officer and less of a " pure " manager but he is nevertheless responsible for the overall co-ordination and management of his department. He will have the responsibility of applying policy in his department, and of seeing that it is run efficiently within the limits set by those policy decisions. This will lead to a concern with the sales figures for the department, with its profitability and hence its expenses relative to its revenue, and he may also be involved in the buying function although he may have a specialised buyer for this purpose. Like every other employee in a supervisory capacity, he will equally be an important link in the chain of communication passing on information and instructions from above and information and advice from below. In this capacity the departmental manager may play a part in the formulation of policy since he will be passing advice up to the chief officer on technical and trading developments affecting his department and policy decisions are likely to be made bearing this information and advice in mind.

PRICES AND DIVIDEND

Although in general the prices of goods will be fixed by the managers, the board will expect to see a satisfactory surplus from each department at the end of the trading period. This surplus will depend in the first place upon the difference between the buying prices and the selling prices, this difference being described as the gross surplus. But this gross surplus must cover the expenses of selling, including a share of the over-head expenses of the society. When these expenses have been deducted the remainder is the net surplus which is available for disposal as dividend, grants, allocation to reserves, etc.

The higher the selling price in relation to cost price the higher will be the gross surplus on each sale, but managers have not this easy solution to their problem of getting a satisfactory surplus. If the prices fixed are too high the goods will not be sold, or will sell so slowly that expenses per £ of sales will be high. The prices of goods are determined by the interplay of supply and demand, and although owing to the imperfections of retail markets we may find some differences in the prices of the same goods in various shops, in general there can be little difference, taking differences of retail services also into account, if all the retailers are to remain in business. Thus the power to fix prices is very limited.

Unfortunately, societies have often been obsessed by rates of dividend, i.e., the ratio of what is paid out in dividend to the value of the sales. The whole financial and trading policies of some societies have consequently been subordinate to and determined by some dividend policy, i.e., the attainment of some predetermined rate of dividend. The rate of dividend is determined by the rate of profit on sales, but the rates of profit on sales of different commodities are by no means equal. There is a tendency to equality of returns on capital, but owing to differences in the rates of turnover of different commodities, this inevitably results in differences in rates of profit on sales.

Thus a commodity which has a quick turnover, such as meat, will yield a much lower rate of profit on sales than one with a slow turnover such as furniture, yet it may yield a higher rate of profit on the capital employed. This is the general reason why the net margin of surplus per £ of sales of some departments is always higher than that of others, even though in slow turnover departments other costs may be higher, e.g., floor space per £ of sales.

Other ill-effects of making a specific rate of dividend the main target of a society may be unsound financial policies, such as insufficient allocations to reserve, or even drawing upon reserve to pay the dividend, inadequate depreciation and expenditure upon maintenance of property. Also there is the inclination of officials, boards and members to believe all is well if " the dividend is made," whereas this may be a cloak covering many inefficiencies.

Dividend on purchases has been and is a strong attraction to co-operative trade, indeed the corresponding surplus in private trade is the sole attraction to all and every manner of private trader to engage in it, but some co-operative societies came to rely too much upon the dividend, and neglected to provide efficient retail service. Yet the facts stared them in the face, the most severe competition they had to meet came from the multiple firms, and as these paid no dividend on purchases, it was obvious that many people attached a greater importance to efficient service than they did to dividend on purchases. Assessment of the efficiency of a society is not an easy matter, it involves consideration of many matters, but increasing trade is a better criterion than the rate of dividend on purchases.

Fortunately, the general trend to " small profits and quick returns " has been contracting the rates of profits on sales and co-operative societies have been forced to adapt their policies to this general trend. Hence the long continued fall in average rates of dividend during this century. This has opened up for co-operative societies fields of enterprise in which the rate of profit on sales is now not less than the rate of dividend aimed at. For a long period the lower rates of dividend corresponded with larger amounts of dividend and for some societies still do and often represent higher rates of return on capital. The constant decline in dividend rates, however, has led some societies to adopt other methods of passing on the financial benefits of co-operative trading to members (referred to in Chapter 10) mainly those of paying no dividend in certain departments but charging very low prices or of using dividend stamps.

BALANCE SHEET AND STATISTICAL RECORD

The balance sheet at the end of each trading period (usually annually, with interim statements quarterly or half-yearly) reveals the results of the society's operations during that period. Boards and managers cannot wait until then to ascertain whether the society or any of its departments is working satisfactorily or not. It is customary for the board, or a sub-committee, to have a report from each departmental manager submitted to its weekly meeting. The better the organisation the more useful is the form of statement prepared and the more accurately are the trading results of the week given. In a well-organised society it is possible to tell within small limits what rate of dividend could be paid if the accounts were made up at that moment. Such weekly surveys are necessary to reveal defects so that they can be quickly remedied.

The balance sheet which the society publishes and which is discussed and submitted for approval at the general meeting brings into a focus the results of the society's operations and the position of the society at the date it was drawn up. Dr. King long ago held that an understanding of a society's book-keeping was necessary to effective democratic control, and that is as true today as when King wrote. It is the discussion of the balance sheet at the General Meeting which gives the membership the opportunity to query and discuss the society's operations.

The Industrial and Provident Societies Act requires each society registered under it to forward to the Registrar by March 31st in each year an Annual Return in a form prescribed by the Registrar showing the receipts and expenditure, funds and effects of the society. Along with the Return there must be a copy of the auditor's report and a copy of each balance sheet made during the period covered by the Return. The society is also required by the Acts to provide gratuitously a copy of the last Annual Return issued by the society to every member or person with an interest in its funds. A copy of the last balance sheet with the report of the auditor must always be hung in a conspicuous place in the society's registered office. A society must also forward every third year a Triennial Return showing the holdings of each person in the society and this also must be signed by the auditor. Every society is thus compelled to appoint an auditor and by the Acts he must be an approved auditor, i.e., on a list of auditors drawn up by the Treasury. In practice, the Treasury confines these appointments to certain bodies of professional auditors and accountants.

The legal compulsion to draw up an Annual Return, the right and opportunity of each member to inspect the Annual Return and balance sheet gives every member the opportunity to satisfy himself of the soundness of the society and its business results, members have also the legal rights to inspect their own accounts and the books containing the names of members of the society. Members also may demand a copy of the rules on payment of the usual charge for them. Upon the application of ten members of twelve months' standing the Registrar is empowered to appoint an accountant or actuary to inspect the books of the society and report thereon.

Upon the application of one-tenth of the whole number of members or of 100 members in the case of a society exceeding 1,000 members, the Registrar, with the consent of the Treasury may appoint inspectors to examine into and report on the affairs of the society; or call a special meeting of the society. To safe-guard societies and the Registrar from needless inspections, applications for such an inspection must be supported by evidence showing good reasons why an inspection should be made or a special meeting called, and that the applicants are not actuated by malicious motives. The applicants may also be required to give security for the costs of the proposed inspection or meeting. All the expenses might, indeed, have to be defrayed by the members applying, though the Registrar may order them to be paid out of the funds of the society, or by the members or officers, or former members or officers, or in such proportions as he may decide. (Ref. to *Handbook to the Industrial and Provident Societies Act*, Chappenden.) These safeguards against needless or malicious applications are necessary, but in this, as in other matters, it will be seen that the Industrial and Provident Societies Act was drawn up to safeguard the rights and interests of the members.

TRADING ACTIVITIES

Co-operators are and have generally been proud of their respective societies' achievements. This pride often showed itself in building the biggest and finest shop in their town or village. Many of these can still be seen. Often the most prominent building in a town, with the exception of some churches and the Town Hall, is the central premises of the co-operative society. Co-opera-tive policy in production has generally been to produce goods free from scamped, shoddy or jerry work, goods of a sound quality which could be relied on to last. Their buildings also were of this type. But needs and circumstances changed, shopping centres shifted, new techniques of retailing were introduced, and the well-built solid, freehold properties, the pride of the past, became relics of late, sometimes mid-Victorianism, often unsuited to the shopping or office requirements of modern times.

Even these buildings, however, are still superior to most of the premises in which private retailing is carried on, as a casual stroll round almost any town will show. The incursion of new traders into old co-operative districts, however, resulted in the erection of large shops with garish frontages, which although an offence to the eye also attracted it, and custom. Co-operators, spurred on by their traditional determination to have better shops than anyone else, and also lately by their introduction of supermarkets and self-service, responded by the building of new premises, the modernisation of old and the closing down of shops in demolition areas.

These impressive and prominent departmental stores, supermarkets, etc., however, are not all. There has been a considerable building of smaller branch shops, of neat and pleasing appearance, and the expansion of co-operative trading into districts and villages new to Co-operation has generally brought a higher standard of shop, service and hygiene into them. This is as it should be, for co-operators should be able to provide better for themselves than others will do for them for profit, and it is well that they make the general public aware of it. Good shopping facilities are an effective means of doing so.

The historical chapters showed how the range of trade of co-operative societies has continuously increased, remarkably so since 1920. The Co-operative Union census of co-operative shops and services in 1955, in addition to the customary foodstuffs trades, which have also increased in range, gave interesting and significant evidence of an increasing number of societies engaging in new trades such as radio, television and electrical and in expanding in trades previously little engaged in by co-operative societies, such as funeral furnishing and monumental masonry, paints and wallpaper, pharmacy, optical, dental, chiropody, hairdressing, painting and decorating, sports outfitting, photographic studios, bookselling, furniture removal, motor coach and car hire, travel bureaux, ballrooms, petrol stations and wine shops, even chimney sweeping and window cleaning. A large society can undertake a wider range of services than can a small: with the trend to larger societies the prospects of the co-operator being able to obtain any goods or service he desires from a co-operative society become very close.

The growth in the economical scale of operations in production, however, has reduced opportunities in some fields for retail societies. Much of the bespoke tailoring, dressmaking and millinery production has been ousted by the factory, a change in fashion has closed down or reduced the clogmaking and repairing departments of Lancashire societies, baking has also ceased by many as the scale of operations has become too big for them, so has cabinet-making and jam-making.

These changes are inevitable, but often new opportunities for production may arise. It is desirable that they should, partly because such production finds co-operative employment for co-operative members, partly because co-operative control is conducive to greater reliability of the product, and partly because the increased surplus arising from production increases the rate of dividend. For example, with bread, if the society merely sells bread the only surplus arising is that on selling. If it also bakes the bread, to the surplus on selling is added the surplus on production, so that to the same amount of retail bread sales there is a larger amount of surplus. This, of course, is still obtained if, when the retail society ceases to bake bread, it has its bread baked and provided for it by a federal enterprise of which it is a member.

EDUCATIONAL ACTIVITIES

A co-operative retail society needs to engage in activities other than retailing. Education is the most important of these, for ultimately the performance of any of its other activities will depend upon the education of its members and employees.

Skill and knowledge are necessary for successful management at all levels; they are also necessary for most of the tasks of all employees. There is a considerable body of knowledge, largely consisting of the systematised experience of management in various businesses and of the techniques of various forms of retailing, which is drawn upon in the study of various subjects which are abstracted from it. Instruction is provided by classes and where the number of students is insufficient to form a class, by postal tuition with the Education Department of the Co-operative Union. It is necessary and urgent that the knowledge and routine of specialised work should be learned by a society's employees.

But this is the easiest task of the educationist. More difficult is that of developing the judgment so that objective views be taken and rational decisions made, of encouraging imagination and initiative so that problems are anticipated and original solutions found, of cultivating co-operative character and inspiring zeal for the co-operative cause. Paraphrasing a well-known observation of Cromwell's Ironsides, they must know what they work for, and love what they know. These ends can be partially achieved by formal educational means, but more influential is the example of senior officials, older employees, committeemen and members. Successful co-operative trading requires a different approach to the business of retailing, and a different approach from both sides of the counter.

An educated membership is necessary for the success of the society as a democratic business organisation. For the membership is sovereign, exercising control not only through the general meetings and elections but also by its purchasing power and ownership of capital. Managements of societies must provide what the members demand in the shops, as regards both goods and service. A co-operatively educated membership would demand well-designed and well-made goods, and promote pride in co-operative service by appreciating good salesmanship, not the aggressive salesmanship beloved of private enterprise, but the salesmanship which benefits the customer. It would also ease management by a reliable loyalty, thus eliminating much of the risk and expense involved in anticipating demand.

Moreover, the boards of directors and other committees are elected by and from the membership and the quality of these committees will thus be largely determined by the quality of the membership. These committees affect management, so also do the general meetings, for the views expressed there, or likely to be expressed there, will influence the decisions of committees and the activities of officials. If this member influence is to be beneficial and not injurious, the membership must take wide views, considering all the interests of the society and be capable of forming rational judgments. It must consider the various interests and realise the need to balance and harmonise them including the long-term interests of the society, submitting questions to the rule of a prudent and reasoning intelligence, the hallmark of the educated man or woman.

" Actually democracy both in the State and in the free organisation is almost entirely a matter of training the individual. Such training must aim to develop both mental self-reliance and a sense of solidarity and responsibility without either of these attributes overshadowing the other." (*Co-operative Ideals and Problems*, Anders Örne.)

Seeking to evade democracy in the hope that it can be ignored, and so the burden of management be lightened, is fatuous. If the membership is loyal, it is so because it understands the purpose

M

and organisation of the society, but such a membership will exercise its democratic rights. If it has not this understanding it will be disloyal and management will be faced by the difficulties of wooing the custom of fickle members and hampered by the pressures and intrigues of a small number of members who care to use its democratic machinery for the purpose of furthering sectional interests or the ends of militant minorities. This brings disaster.

The task of education in a retail society is thus not only to provide the instruction and training to employees necessary for the performance of their tasks. That is its easiest work. It also has to educate staff and membership in the ideals, principles and arts of Co-operation.

The Education Committee

It has long been agreed that if this necessary work was to be done it was better that a special committee, i.e., an education committee, be elected to undertake it—not that such work is a matter of indifference to the board of directors, but because it has not the time to give it adequate attention. There is an evident need for both these committees to work in harmony with each other. To do so it is necessary for each to remember that they are servants of the same people and working for the same object.

Sometimes a necessary liaison is effected by one or more members of the board sitting also on the education committee. To obtain the active support of those specially concerned with the activities of the committee, representatives from the Guilds and employees may also be included, as recommended by the General Survey Committee. It is desirable, of course, that the directly elected members of the committee should be in a majority. Other means of affecting the necessary liaison are regular meetings with the board of directors, at least quarterly, and meetings with guilds and employees.

Much of the work and organisation undertaken by the education committee will fall upon its secretary. It is desirable that this official should be appointed by the committee, and that he should not be a member of it. In societies with a membership of over 20,000, it has long been urged that the work and activities require a full-time appointment for the position of education secretary if the duties are to be adequately performed.

According to F. Hall the work of an education committee should be without limit; inevitably it will become engaged in social and propaganda work as well as educational activities.

Its primary educational work is the provision of facilities for the study of Co-operation. This involves the organisation of classes. It is unwise to provide one class to meet the needs of adolescents, employees and adult members, the beginner at co-operative studies and those who have made previous studies. Yet this is what is often attempted. And failure is inevitable.

The various types of possible students and their respective needs require consideration and special provision made for them. Co-operation and its problems cannot be understood without some knowledge of the economic, social and political environment in which it operates so that facilities for what are termed " social studies,"—economics, politics, history, etc.—need also to be provided. It is increasingly necessary that the co-operative consumer should be an educated consumer, capable of sound choices, considering the essentials of commodities and ignoring the irrelevances frequently stressed by advertisement, so that steps to educate the consumer in choosing and in the economical use of income need also to be made. And lastly there must be provision for the training and education of the society's employees.

To meet these various needs the efficient society will have many means. It will have the organisations of the Co-operative Youth Movement—the Playways (7–10 years), the Pathfinders (11–14 years), the Youth Clubs (15–20 years), and perhaps junior classes in Co-operation and junior choirs.

Classes for adults will be held on various co-operative subjects, probably working to the syllabuses of the Co-operative Union, and on various social subjects, perhaps in collaboration with such bodies as the W.E.A. or the L.E.A. Discussion groups may also be held, popular lectures given, week-end schools provided and the sale and distribution of co-operative periodicals or other literature undertaken.

Employee training and education will be provided by initiation courses for new employees, by short practical courses dealing with some of the elementary manual skills and selling techniques of the salesman, and by classes for more sustained study, particularly in the subjects of the group certificate and diploma courses of the Co-operative Union for employees with any ambition. In many cases day release classes in the subjects taken by juniors may be provided by the L.E.A. or if no such provision is made, the society should be pressing for it. When there are insufficient students to form a class, as is likely in advanced subjects even in large societies, correspondence courses may be taken, and this should be encouraged. It is common for societies to pay fees for such courses on such conditions as the completion of a proportion of the lessons and sitting for or passing the examination.

Advice is needed by students regarding subjects to take and

courses to follow. The education secretary will be regarded as the person to approach and should be capable of giving such advice. Arrangements must be made for the holding of examinations, and the education committee is generally required to make them. If the education committee has done its work well there will be a number of capable, keen and ambitious students, desirous of the more advanced studies possible at the Co-operative College. Probably the society may offer scholarships tenable at the College, and the committee be wholly or partially responsible for awarding them. A similar duty will fall on them in selecting people for the various summer schools, or other special residential courses and many societies provide scholarships for these.

In addition to these formal provisions, societies may have choirs, dramatic and orchestral societies. Some of these reach very high standards and compete successfully at competitive festivals. A society with an active and efficient education committee will thus be playing a valuable part in the cultural life of the local community.

It will be gathered that a live and progressive society will be engaged in a large variety of educational activities, often by their nature making considerable calls upon the time of committeemen. Hence the need argued for an education committee, and for a full-time education secretary in societies of more than 20,000 members.

The Education Secretary

In such a society the education secretary in addition to the normal secretarial duties of convening committee meetings, conducting correspondence, recording minutes, keeping accounts and preparing financial statements, preparing memoranda and maintaining a filing system, will be engaged in organising a wide variety of educational activities. He will organise classes, i.e. find classrooms, arrange times of meeting, approach and persuade potential students to join them (the most difficult and important task), find suitable teachers, (owing to past neglect of education, also difficult), keep an eye on the conduct of classes and arrange for the holding and supervision of examinations.

In addition, he will be organising conferences, one-day and week-end schools, choirs, concerts, dramatic performances, film shows, youth clubs and children's groups, perhaps holiday camps and tours. He will also prepare and place advertisements, arrange for printing, act as liaison officer with the board of directors, chief officials, employees and auxiliaries, negotiate with the local Director of Education and such bodies as the W.E.A. and be the channel of communication of his committee with the

Sectional Education Council and the Education Department of the Co-operative Union.

A good deal of his work will be in the evenings and week-ends. His life will be a busy one, but also full and rewarding if he regards himself as dedicated to a cause. Unless he so regards his position he is unlikely to remain in it. The furtherance of co-operative education and so of the Co-operative Movement depends very largely on these men.

POLITICAL COMMITTEES OR " SOCIETY CO-OPERATIVE PARTIES "

With the rise of the Co-operative Party many retail societies have become engaged in political activities. Political activities, however, require political organisation and there are complexities which prevent this being as simple and straightforward as organising other activities of the society. These complexities are the boundaries of the society not coinciding with those of electoral constituencies and agreements and relations with the Labour Party.

As regards boundary difficulties, in some cases a society's area may cover more than one parliamentary constituency, indeed some may cover several, as does the London Co-operative Society, or parts of several, in others a parliamentary constituency may include several societies. To meet these difficulties the Co-operative Party has framed four constitutions of what are termed Society Co-operative Parties.

Section A provides for a Party governed by a committee responsible to and directly elected by the members of one society.

Section B provides for a Party which is governed by a committee representative of the various committees and organisations of one society.

Section C is a constitution to cover a number of societies acting together in a number of parliamentary constituencies.

Section D is a constitution to provide for county constituencies in which a number of Society Parties and societies are within a county constituency.

In C and D the activities are akin to federal activities, and no individual society can have sole control or all its own way. There can, therefore, be no direct control by the membership of any individual society. In Section B the members of the committee will be responsible to the organisations and committees whom they respectively represent, and again there is no direct control by the membership, although in practice there may be more effective control by the society. Only in Section A is there a direct responsibility to the membership, and even in these cases there is also an inescapable responsibility and obligation to the Party as a whole, each constitution makes the Society Parties responsible for carrying out national policy and observing the conditions of membership laid down by the National Committee. Each Society Party is governed by a Council, and all members of it must sign the following declaration:

" I declare myself a Co-operator, assert my belief in the Co-operative Commonwealth, and agree to accept the programme, policy and constitution of the Co-operative Party national and local. I will do all in my power to promote the political policy of the Co-operative Party as declared from time to time and approved by the Co-operative Congress. I am not a member of any political organisation which sponsors or supports Parliamentary or local government candidates in opposition to the candidates either of the Co-operative Party or of any other Party with which it has an electoral agreement."

A member of any political party other than the Labour Party could not honestly sign this document.

Agreements with the Labour Party provide for the selection of candidates for local government and for parliamentary elections. Co-operative Members of Parliament or of local government bodies must have been approved by the Labour Party, form part of the Labour Group, and are subject to Labour Party discipline. This may create complications.

The political activities of the society will consist of arousing and maintaining political consciousness so as to create an active and efficient political organisation. Co-operative knowledge and experience have a good deal of value to contribute to public affairs, but to do so co-operators in a locality must build " a robust organisation, proud of its identity and confident of its ability to help build up a powerful democratic political movement " in their own district. " The agreement is neither a perambulator for the politically immature nor a bath chair for the politically infirm. It is intended to help Parties grow into healthy and active maturity without endangering the unity of our three great democratic movements." (*Facing The Future Together*, J. Bailey.)

Co-operators on local bodies are in a position to discover and expose discriminations against co-operative societies. Contacts with the society's departmental heads enables informed support of or opposition to the local body's regulations relating to food storage, treatment and inspection, and contracts. Town planning, administration of trading departments, the management of finance, municipal housing, are also subjects on which the special experience of co-operators should be valuable.

Affiliation fees to the Co-operative Party are a fixed sum per member per annum, but neither this, nor any society grants to the Society Party, can be paid unless provided for in the rules or by resolution of a general meeting. Thus the membership of any society has the ultimate control over that society's political activities, although this cannot be a control of detail, and is subject to the limitations necessarily imposed by affiliation to the Co-operative Party.

THE AUXILIARIES

In addition to the work of the educational and political committees, a lively and progressive society will have lively and progressive auxiliaries, i.e. Guild branches, Youth Groups, and perhaps a branch of the Educational Fellowship. These undertake educational activities of a varying nature and quality, but their educational contribution is not confined to lectures and discussions.

Many members learn in the auxiliary bodies the correct procedure of meetings and the conduct of affairs in a business-like way. And they learn these arts by practising them. In many, perhaps most instances, there is no other opportunity of learning by experience. Thus many women who have played an active part in public life served their apprenticeship by " going through the offices " of a Guild branch, gaining the capacity and so the confidence which served them well elsewhere. The majority, however, can obviously never become members of co-operative or other public committees, but they raise the standard of the general meetings of the society and improve the quality of the general membership.

These members of the auxiliary bodies have their interest in the society stimulated, and interest of the members is the first and vital step to effective democratic control. Also they learn that the society is something more than a trading concern, that it is part of a social movement. Again interested co-operators often find in the Guilds the only means by which they can apply their intellects and energies in the Movement continuously from week to week. In these bodies contacts are made, friendships built up, the sense of a co-operative fellowship realised.

Although intangible this is probably their most valuable contribution, for the fraternal bond is the vital bond of societies. As Aristotle observed, " Where love is based on the useful, the love is not of each other for what they are, but only in so far as each gets some good from the other . . . and the useful is nothing permanent, it varies from time to time."

Thus a strong and enduring society cannot be built up on material interests alone, on the benefits yielded by trading activities. Writing of the ideal society which is the objective of the Co-operative Movement, Beatrice Potter stated: " But the social value of this form of society would not consist solely or even principally in a more equitable diffusion of the necessaries and comforts of life. If this were all, it would be a poor result for generations of human effort; a goal unworthy of the disciples of Robert Owen. For Co-operators have always been inspired by the ancient doctrine of human fellowship, by the new spirit of social service, by a firm faith that the day would come when each man and woman would work, not for personal subsistence or for personal gain, but for the whole community." (*The Co-operative Movement in Great Britain.*)

It is in the auxiliaries that this doctrine of human fellowship is fostered and expressed, wherein " fellow co-operators " comes to mean something other than fellow customers or fellow shareholders. Hence the importance which thinking co-operators attach to such bodies as the Guilds, even to small and struggling branches.

The auxiliary bodies are generally assisted by grants, use of rooms, assistance in provision of speakers, etc., usually by the education committee. But they are independent bodies, and generally jealous of their independence. Although assisted, sometimes generously, they could not exist without some of their members giving freely a good deal of time and effort to their organisation and administration.

SIZE OF SOCIETIES

Few inferences of much value relating to the comparative virtues of large and small societies can be drawn from the general statistics of averages and percentage increases. Of more practical value is a survey of each district to enable the making of what the soldier would describe as an appreciation of the position. Having all relevant circumstances presented it would then be possible to make a rational judgment of what amalgamations, and even transfers of territory from one society to another, could be made with advantage. This, of course, is what the Independent Commission recommended and was effected by the Amalgamation Survey of 1960 and the Regional Plan of 1968.

The idea that there is an optimum size of society can be dismissed at once, the optimum size of society in a sparsely populated territory such as Wales is obviously different from that of a densely populated territory such as London.

Small societies, indeed small businesses, are not without their advantages. They are easier and cheaper to manage and more subject to democratic control. The board of a small society can fully comprehend its business, whereas it is doubtful if any human intelligence could have an equal comprehension of the affairs of very large societies, and the difference in the comprehension of the average member would be even more marked.

As a society grows bigger the place of the individual member becomes correspondingly smaller. In a small society he can affect the policy of the society by expressing his opinions at a general meeting, his support of the society's activities is important, he feels it is valued and he is inclined to give the loyalty he knows is expected. Disloyalty lets his neighbours down.

In a big society the individual member may feel he counts for little. He is one amongst scores of thousands, his support of the society's activities will be neither noticed nor missed. If he attends a general meeting he may not know a single soul there; in a small society he would know everybody.

Consequently, in the large societies there is not the same personal knowledge or sympathy, either between the members themselves, or between the members and the board or between the officials and employees; the sense of common interests and obligations is weaker, the society seems to regard the individual more as a customer than a member, the bonds of co-operative fellowship are lacking.

On the other hand, small societies by their very nature have serious limitations. Operating in a small area, they are subject to all the risks which affect that particular area, e.g., strikes, unemployment, the decline of an industry or even a firm on which all the area is dependent. A large society covering an area in which many industries are carried on has these risks spread so that no single one is ruinous, as it may be to the small society.

In addition, there seem to be various economies of scale which are as applicable to retailing as to any other industry. Initially some services can only be provided if there is a large enough scale of operation, so there are some things that small societies cannot do but there may well be economic advantages in doing the things they do do on a larger scale. It would seem to be in co-operators' own interests to do this without any pressure but unfortunately it has taken the evidence of the multiple chains to persuade co-operators on this point.

There is also the argument that a few large societies will make more rational use of resources than a proliferation of small

societies. The tendency for dry goods trade to be concentrated
in the centre of trade catchment areas, for example, has not
fully been recognised by co-operative societies in the past and
the pattern has frequently been for a number of societies to
exist within a trade catchment area each providing dry goods
shops when much of this trade, and probably an increasing
proportion, was moving out of any one society's area into the
nearest city or large town. One of the intentions of regional
societies, of course, is that the Movement's dry goods shops can
be concentrated in the areas where most of the dry goods trade
is done.

It is this kind of duplication which has probably been a more
important problem for co-operative societies than actual overlapping of boundaries where societies have competed for all the
trade of the same people. There have been examples of this
happening in certain parts of the country but it has probably
never been much more than a marginal problem and is one that
scarcely exists today. A more serious and, until full regionalisa-
tion, continuing problem is the unnecessary duplication of dry
goods shops within trade catchment areas.

Quite apart from its trading advantages, the larger society may
well have other advantages. The range and quality of its educational services, for example, could be greater than those provided
by smaller societies and the evidence would seem to indicate that
the societies with the most impressive educational records tend
to be larger ones. Democratic control may give rise to difficulties
but experiments with more appropriate structures could provide
an adequate democracy and, because of its size, the pool of
directorial ability and talent will be larger in a regional society.

RELATIONS WITH THE CO-OPERATIVE MOVEMENT

A good retail society will not confine its whole attention to
affairs within its own boundaries. It has common interests with
other societies and these often require common action to safeguard or to further them. Hence the establishment of federal
trading bodies, as local federations and the Wholesale Societies,
and the Regional, Sectional and National organisations of the
Co-operative Union.

The retail society should take an active interest in these bodies,
sending good delegates to their meetings, voting with care for
candidates for office, giving adequate consideration to resolutions,
giving full and interesting reports to the membership of the society
on these federal activities. A new venture by the Wholesale
Society, or the closing down of a factory, or Congress resolutions,

for instance, are matters of concern to the membership of every retail society and they should be made acquainted with them.

The next chapter deals with these federations, which are, of course, largely extensions of retail societies' activities on to a national plane. But the study of a retail society cannot be divorced from them, for as they are dependent upon the retail societies, so each retail society is dependent upon them. Few, if any, retail societies could stand alone, and there would certainly be no Co-operative Movement without its national organisations.

14 THE BUSINESS FEDERATIONS

"*The free association of autonomous democracies in free and autonomous federations is one of the most valuable contributions of the British Co-operators to the art and science of democratic organisation.*"

("*The Consumers' Co-operative Movement.*" S. & B. Webb.)

"*Throughout the ascending scale of the federal structure each higher organisation is created and administered by and for those below it. In the final analysis, it is not the top organisation but the small basic units that are sovereign.*"

("*Co-operation and Post-War Relief*", I.L.O.)

THE organisation of the British Co-operative Movement has not been made to the blueprint of any genius of administration or constitution making. It is, like many other British institutions, more in the nature of an organic growth, responding to changing needs and circumstances by developing new shoots, by the withering away of what has become unnecessary but withal by the continuous thickening and toughening of the main limbs. As it is still growing, still developing, still adapting, any analysis of its organisation unrelated to its history would leave out of account what is literally its vital element—its power and process of growth and change. However, this book has described such growth and change of the retail societies and their federal developments, in their activities as well as their organisation. This chapter deals with the present organisation of the main co-operative business federations.

THE CO-OPERATIVE WHOLESALE SOCIETY

The Co-operative Wholesale Society with, in 1968, a share and loan capital of nearly £70 million, sales of £483 million and productions of £141 million, is one of the biggest businesses in the country. It is engaged in wholesaling every kind of commodity dealt in by the retail societies, and producing many of them, has depots and estates overseas, is engaged in banking and, in co-operation with the S.C.W.S., in insurance. Yet this enormous and complex business depends upon the purchases and savings of individual consumers, mostly of the working classes, and is an example of what can be achieved by the co-operation of people with small incomes.

Its organisation and methods embody the co-operative principles described in Chapter XII, it is democratically controlled and non-profit making. It is a federal society the members of which are other co-operative societies. With a long and wide-spread practical experience unequalled by any other co-operative organisation in the world, its opinions and advice may be disputed but they are far too weighty ever to be ignored.

MEMBERSHIP AND CONTROL

Its membership is important for reasons similar to those of the importance of the membership of retail societies—their demands and loyalty dictate its policy and methods. Membership consists of co-operative retail societies, agricultural societies, service and productive societies and federations, and overseas societies. These member societies own and control the C.W.S.

Control is exercised by the society members through their power of electing the Board of Directors, through general meetings, and through the need for the Board to submit any proposal not covered by the rules to a referendum of the societies.

Following the reorganisation of 1965, the Board of Directors will ultimately consist of thirty part-time, unpaid directors. (At the middle of 1970 there were still in addition twelve full-time directors remaining from before 1965 who did not opt to take an executive appointment at the time of reorganisation. In the process of time these full-time directors will all retire and not be replaced.) The part-time directors are elected for three years and their terms of office are so arranged that one third retire each year. A retiring director is eligible for re-election providing he is renominated by his society.

Candidates must be either a member of the Board of Directors or must be the chief official of the nominating society and, should they cease to be either of these, must leave the Board. No society is allowed to have more than one representative on the Board. Canvassing by or on behalf of candidates is prohibited, the only official information about the candidates being that which the Returning Officer sends out with the voting papers, and the information is based on replies to a questionnaire. Candidates, however, have other means of making themselves known, by attending and speaking at conferences, Congress, general meetings of the C.W.S., serving on various co-operative committees and so on.

Elections

The system of voting in the election of directors is somewhat complicated owing to the different sizes of member societies, to the desire to ensure that each part of the country is fairly represented and that the nominees of small societies have a reasonable chance of election.

It would be ridiculous to apply the principle of one member, one vote, in the elections of federal bodies whose members are of very unequal size, e.g., to allow the London Co-operative Society with over one million members only one vote and a society with a few score members also one vote, would not be equal representation. Each society must have a shareholding corresponding to its membership, so that votes proportionate to shareholding would approximate to size of membership, and this system of allocating votes was at one time employed.

But co-operators have always been prejudiced against any suggestion of capital control and the system was changed to the present one where volume of trade is the main determinant of the number of votes exercised by a society. Each member society has one vote by virtue of being a member, one additional vote for the first £12,500 worth of goods purchased from the C.W.S., and an additional vote for every complete £25,000 beyond that amount.

To obtain a fair representation of each part of the country, representation is on a Sectional basis, the Sectional boundaries corresponding with those of the Co-operative Union.

The Metropolitan area is treated separately as in most Co-operative Union committees. Thus the electoral areas are (with their current representation): Northern (4), North-Eastern (3), North Western (5), Midland (6), Southern (6), South Western (3), Metropolitan (3).

Nomination of candidates is confined to the nominee's own society in the Section in which the vacancy occurs. Each candidate then submits to national election and, according to the number of vacancies in the Section, those candidates with the highest number of votes proceed to the Board. Before 1965 the national elections were conducted on a transferable vote system, but since then an ordinary ballot has been used. The number of seats for each Section is based on that Section's trade with the C.W.S. and is subject to quinquennial review.

Members' Meetings

The C.W.S. members' meetings used to be held quarterly, but
following the recommendations of a special committee of inquiry
in 1953, the rules were altered so that they are now held half-yearly.
In order to keep the meetings down to a reasonable size, simul-
taneous meetings with the same agenda are held in London,
Manchester and Newcastle. Prior to the meetings a report on
the trading activities, etc., of the C.W.S. is circulated to member
societies and the principal business of the meetings is the discussion of the report.

A director will be in the chair, supported by other directors
and some senior officials of the C.W.S. The chairman will introduce the report in a brief speech drawing attention to items
considered worthy of special attention. Questions and comments
follow, criticising, praising, warning, advancing constructive
suggestions and so on. A good proportion of the delegates will
be societies' directors and chief officials, though many societies
also send " members' delegates " elected from the rank and file
at their general meetings.

At such C.W.S. meetings the delegates are generally well
informed, the discussions are to the point, the delegates receive
authoritative explanations, and the directors are left in no doubt
regarding societies' opinions for—" The delegates are for the
most part, not merely themselves consumers, but what is more
valuable, also expert representatives of the consumers, trained
in the very business of detecting their fellow members' complaints
and desires, and discovering the means by which they can be
met." (*The Consumers' Co-operative Movement*, S. & B. Webb.)

Formal motions from societies will have had previous notice,
and these, with the Report will be voted upon. The proposed
dividend on purchases, and at the annual meeting, the balance
sheet must also be approved by resolution. It will be gathered
that these meetings are vital parts of the system of democratic
control, exercising real influence on the conduct of the C.W.S.,
and on the attitude of the society-members to the C.W.S.

The C.W.S. Board

The old full-time board had the final power of policy making
but through a system of other committees and sub-committees
had some managerial functions as well. The Joint Reorganisation
Committee reporting in 1965 were of the opinion that the
directors had made the best of difficult circumstances and had
endeavoured to adjust their methods to the needs of changing
times and a constantly increasing business. Nevertheless, they

considered that a clearer distinction had to be made between the functions of policy making and those of management and that if the closer, interdependent relationship of retail and wholesale they advocated were to be effective then a new form of control would have to be introduced.

Hence their recommendation that the full-time Board of (at that time) 21 directors be replaced by a part-time Board of thirty directors who would all be practising directors or managers of retail societies. This is designed to lead to a closer understanding between the retail and wholesale sides of the Movement and end the division of interests which has embarrassed the C.W.S. ever since it was formed.

As a policy-making body the C.W.S. Board meets for one day each month. It is felt that no more than this is necessary since policy is a fairly long-term affair and certainly will not change from day to day. The background of the directors ensures that they are extremely knowledgeable about co-operative business affairs and in touch with the needs of retail societies.

Responsible to the Board for the management of the Society is a Chief Executive Officer with three Deputy Chief Executives and a number of Group Managers. The functions of the Board are similar to those of a Board of any co-operative society: to be the statutory authority responsible for the control of the business and for determination of policy; to appoint and, if necessary, remove the Chief Executive Officer and in consultation with him appoint some of his immediate subordinates; to approve the annual operating plans and capital expenditure programmes; to receive monthly progress reports; to present reports and balance sheets to Shareholders' Meetings; and to appoint representatives to other bodies.

CAPITAL

Each constituent society is required to subscribe capital according to the number of its members. The minimum is one transferable £5 share for each two members, but the current arrangements *permit* present member-societies to subscribe one £5 share per member and *require* new members to do so. It may be noted that this is in excess of the individual member minimum shareholding of many retail societies though, of course, much below the average shareholding. Yet there must be many individual members of retail societies who have less capital invested in their societies than those societies are obliged to invest in the C.W.S. in respect of them.

As the C.W.S. has not too much share capital the inference may be that some retail societies' minimum shareholdings are too low. In many cases these minima are the same as in 1939, since when inflation has reduced the value of the £ to about one-quarter of its then value. Share capital alone would be insufficient to finance the activities of the C.W.S., it also employs loan capital and has built up healthy reserves.

The Co-operative Bank[1] functions as banker not only to the Co-operative Movement but also for the majority of trade unions and many public authorities, friendly societies and individuals. It has, therefore, the primary duty of any banker of safeguarding its depositors. This necessitates the holding of assets possessing adequate security and liquidity. Thus its banking resources are no more suitable to be tied up in long-term productive or trading ventures than are those of other banks.

Nevertheless within the limits of prudence, the Bank does something to redistribute the surplus capital of some societies by receiving it as deposits and lending it as overdrafts to societies which are short of capital. Overdrafts are, however, essentially short-term loans and not a proper means of financing long-term ventures, hence the long-term capital shortages of some societies are not likely to be met by a Bank redistribution of capital. They can only be properly met by the members of such societies investing more in them. No society should rest content with anything short of self-financing.

By concentrating the surplus capital of the societies as deposits in the Co-operative Bank, the societies obtain the advantages of the principle of " massed reserves " and so a more economical employment of capital. Every society needs to hold some liquid assets to meet probable demands for withdrawal of share capital. If each society were completely independent, each would need to hold a proportion of liquid assets to meet possible withdrawals, which in the aggregate would far exceed what was necessary.

When the Independent Commission reported in 1958, withdrawals had never exceeded 3 per cent of members' capital per annum, a situation which remained true until 1967. Even before 1967, however, individual societies had had to meet much heavier withdrawals than that, so each tended to keep a proportion of liquid assets with such possibilities in mind.

Deposits with the Co-operative Bank can be such assets but the Bank does not need to keep as large a proportion as do the individual societies for in normal circumstances a run on share capital against which each society must make provision is not likely to affect the Movement as a whole, although there have

---

[1] In July, 1970 it was announced that the Co-operative Bank was to become a separate limited company in its own right, with capital wholly owned by the C.W.S.

been notable examples of national runs on capital. But normally, a heavy run on a few societies would only be a small proportion of the liquid reserves of the Bank.

Thus by concentrating capital the societies increase their financial strength at less expense and release capital for more remunerative purposes. These may be in the form of loans by the Bank to its trading and productive enterprises (and their use in these ways of course benefits the retail societies), loans to assist retail societies to meet temporary financial difficulties, or in investments.

DISTRIBUTION OF SURPLUS

The Rochdale principle of sharing the surplus in proportion to purchases is followed. As the dividends on wholesale trade go to swell the disposable surpluses of the retail societies and so to increase the dividends which they pay to their members, the individual members of retail societies share in the surpluses yielded by wholesale trading.

Their interest in co-operative enterprise does not end there. For many years the C.W.S. has paid a rate of dividend on purchases plus an additional dividend on purchases of C.W.S. productions. This additional dividend is justified in equity, as part of the C.W.S. surplus is yielded by its productive enterprises. Thus the individual member of retail societies shares in the surpluses yielded by retailing, wholesaling, and in the case of C.W.S. productions, by production. If C.W.S. production extended to the primary processes of production so that it produced the commodity from first process to last, the co-operative purchaser of such a commodity would, after the return of his dividend, be obtaining it free of profit tribute to anybody. The individual member of retail societies has thus an interest in the extension of C.W.S. production. It is the surest, perhaps the only, way of emancipation from the exactions of profit makers.

WHOLESALING

The historical chapters described the development and the nature of the Society's wholesaling activities. This chapter is concerned with general considerations. Wholesaling is necessary to the distributive trades owing to the localisation of industry, specialisation by producers and the numbers of retailers engaged in selling a large variety of commodities. These circumstances render it impossible in most cases, and expensive and wasteful except in a very few, for the retailer, even the largest, to make direct contact with producers, or vice versa.

Consider, for instance, the thousands of items dealt in by a large retail society, and the fact that there are often several firms producing any one of those items. Imagine the number of interviews with travellers and the amount of correspondence with each, if there were no middlemen, no wholesalers, to bring the supplies into contact with the demands. Suppose, for instance, ten firms produced a commodity and a thousand retailers sold it. Direct contacts would number at least ten thousand (10 x 1,000), involving ten thousand visits by travellers to retailers or retailers to producers, or ten thousand lots of correspondence, despatch, inspection and comparison of samples, etc.

A wholesaler can provide a much better service at less cost. His warehouse can contain and display the product of each manufacturer for inspection and comparison by the retailers, or his travellers can carry around samples of each. It is because of the economies of wholesaling that the wholesaler continues to exist. Neither producers nor retailers keep him in business because they love him, but because they cannot do without him.

The service being essential it was to the advantage of retail societies to co-operate to perform it for themselves. It still is. One of the reasons why co-operative societies established the C.W.S. was the unreliability of private wholesalers, both as regards prices and quality of goods and deliveries. The C.W.S., operating on a larger scale than is possible for any retail society, can employ specialist buyers, subject goods to tests in its research laboratories, assess qualities and secure a reliability in most instances beyond the reach of the individual retail society.

Moreover, buying in much larger bulk it can secure better terms, have goods made to specification, obtain the economies of bulking, by-pass chains of middlemen, and make direct contacts with producers, even if this involves establishing depots overseas. And, of course, the wholesalers' and other middlemen's profits which would otherwise go into other pockets are saved.

Nor are the advantages of co-operative wholesaling limited to those societies who purchase from it. For private wholesalers know they have the C.W.S. to beat, and societies disloyal to the C.W.S. obtain better terms than would be the case if there were no C.W.S., just as non-unionists obtain better terms than would be the case if there were no trade unions. It has not been unknown for societies' buyers to present private wholesalers with C.W.S. price lists in order to get those better terms, indifferent to what their position would be if their fellow retail societies did the same and eventually there were no C.W.S. price lists to bargain with. As with the retail societies, the full benefits of Co-operation cannot be obtained unless full loyalty is given to their joint enterprise by those co-operating.

The disloyalty of some injures the rest, it causes increasing expenditure on sales promotion, increases overhead expenses per £ of sales, makes demands unstable and so the speculative risks, and losses, of trade are greater than they need be. Lastly, by reducing trade, the economies of larger scale operation are lost.

The C.W.S. is literally the creature of the retail societies, and it would be a biting commentary on their own business abilities if it were true that acting together they could not perform these wholesaling functions for themselves as efficiently as the private wholesalers will do for them. Pride alone should discourage disloyalty.

PRODUCTION

One of the first and most enduring of co-operative ideals was self employment. The Owenites, King, the Rochdale Pioneers, the Christian Socialists, J. T. W. Mitchell, were all strong advocates of it. Although some differed as to the means of attaining it, the objective was common to all. Many retail societies in the early days engaged in productive activities, but as has been seen the increasing scale of economical production lessened the scope of productive enterprise for them. In an increasing number of cases a national scale of operations became necessary and consequently a national market was necessary to sustain them.

With the existing structure of the Movement the C.W.S. was the obvious organisation to undertake such production. It had the knowledge of designs, qualities, quantities, prices, from its wholesaling activities; it already had a trade in the commodity with the retail societies; it had the capital available to finance such ventures; it had such a variety of enterprises that a new one could be carried during the inevitable early period of teething troubles. Hence it is not surprising that most of the extension of co-operative production has been by the Wholesale Societies, and that co-operators would look to them for its further extension. Without national organisation, co-operative production would be impossible, and the Co-operative Movement would suffer from arrested growth as the limits of retailing expansion were reached. The pursuit of the co-operative ideal necessitates the extension and expansion of co-operative production.

Apart from the pursuit of its ideals the extension of co-operative production had business attractions. It tended to increase rates of dividend, found a co-operative use for co-operative capital, and enabled the Movement to control the quality and delivery of the products and conditions under which they were produced. It freed societies from having to submit to terms (such as not being allowed to pay dividend) imposed by producers. It safeguarded societies and allowed them to protect others from the malpractices of capitalist monopolies. Lastly, to be confident of adherence to the principle of honest trading, co-operators needed to produce their own goods, for only then could they be sure that the goods they sold were pure, unadulterated, and not finished in ways calculated to deceive the customer into thinking they were better than they were. Co-operative production is thus necessary to make the application of co-operative principles complete.

The Independent Commission considered that the Movement should concentrate its resources on expanding its retailing and wholesaling and the production of basic foodstuffs, other than the primary processes of agriculture. This advice was not based upon the view that co-operative production of dry goods was undesirable, but that the Movement could make better use of its limited resources by concentrating on the lines stated. Dry goods were so various, of changing patterns, designs, etc., that at the best only a fraction of what is demanded could be produced. It would be more advantageous for the Movement to exercise its power as a large scale central buying organisation, for "with one or two exceptions the most formidable retail competitors have no factories of their own." This has tended to be the approach of the C.W.S. during the 'sixties, typified by its decision to cease the production of furniture and to concentrate on its marketing.

CO-OPERATIVE RETAIL SERVICES

The origin and growth of Co-operative Retail Services Ltd., originally named the C.W.S. Retail Co-operative Society has already been described. Here its constitution is given.

The C.R.S. consists of the C.W.S. and of former retail societies which have ceased to be independent retail societies and are now branches of C.R.S. One branch may cover a large city and have many shops, another might only cover a village with one shop. Each branch has a committee elected by the members of the branch at a branch meeting.

Government of the C.R.S., however, is by the Board of Directors. This consists of twelve members, six appointed by and from the Board of Directors of the C.W.S., and six elected by the branch committees. For this election the branches are grouped in sections; the branches in each section nominate persons they desire to represent them, but the election is by national ballot by all the branches of the society.

According to Rule 60, this Board could have complete government in its hands, but it may of course depute (or withdraw) powers to the branch committees. It is responsible for the control of all business carried on by the Society and to " engage, remove or discharge all managers, salesmen or employees of any description " and " to fix their duties, salaries or other remuneration." Thus all the officials and employees of the branches are responsible to the Board of Directors.

A meeting of members is held in the area of each branch each half-year at which the balance sheet and accounts for the branch are submitted and discussed. Here the individual members may criticise, approve or make suggestions, but the actual power of the meeting is confined to the election of members of the branch committee and of delegates to the general meetings of C.R.S.

Branch Committee

A branch committee will meet regularly with an official or officials of the branch in attendance, receive and consider statistical data on current trading operations and make suggestions which may be considered favourably by the officials or if higher authority is required, by the Board of Directors of C.R.S. An interested and capable branch committee may thus exercise a good deal of influence, although the employees and officials are not responsible to it. It has, however, complete autonomy in Co-operative Union matters and in the election of delegates to C.W.S. meetings and voting in C.W.S. affairs.

There are shareholding and purchasing qualifications for membership of a branch committee, not more than one employee of the society at any time may be a member of a branch committee. The functions of a branch committee as defined by rule are to visit premises; bring before the Board of Directors of C.R.S. anything relating to quality or price of goods or the conduct of business which appears to it to be faulty; make recommendations to the Board of Directors with regard to trading results, admission of new members, appointment of staff, and development of the branch; and incur capital expenditure on behalf of the branch to such an extent and for such purposes as the Board of Directors shall from time to time determine.

General Council

To establish contact between the Board of Directors and the branches, which are scattered over the country (though mostly in Wales and the West country) and between the branches themselves, a General Council is held quarterly. It is attended by a member from each branch committee and members of the Board of Directors. Although it has no executive power, being restricted to receiving and discussing reports from the Board of Directors and submitting recommendations to it and to general meetings of the Society, the opportunity of discussion and explanation is held to be productive of understanding and of a degree of agreement which would otherwise be difficult to secure.

General Meetings

General meetings are held annually, usually in London. Each branch is entitled to be represented at the general meetings by three delegates, at least one of whom is the member of the branch committee who is its delegate to the General Council, one is appointed by the branch committee and one is elected by the members of the branch. On a ballot vote at general meetings, voting power is scaled according to the membership of the branch but the C.W.S. has a voting power equal to that of all the branches.

The functions of the ordinary general meeting are to receive reports from the Board of Directors, auditors or any other officers on the Society's business, and the state of affairs at the date thereof; to elect the auditors of the society and to transact other general business of which 14 days' notice has been given.

Finance

The C.W.S. guarantees the repayment of share and/or loan capital held by members, payment of interest on shares and loans held by members, and payment of a certain rate of dividend to members. Separate accounts are kept covering the operations of each branch, which after making adequate provisions, normally pay the dividend it distributes. However, to enable the guaranteed minimum rate to be paid by branches where surpluses are too small for this there is a central fund called " The Mutual Aid Fund," to which each branch subscribes *pro rata* to its sales.

Capital is subscribed by the individual members and also by the C.W.S., Rule 6, stating that " The Co-operative Wholesale Society Ltd. shall be entitled and may be required by the committee to hold as many shares as will make its holding equal to one half of the total number of shares issued from time to time." This does not mean that the C.W.S. does supply half the capital, but it is entitled to do so. As, however, it has a preponderance of voting power on the Committee, the Committee is hardly likely to request what the C.W.S. would prefer to refuse. In 1968, out of a total share and loan capital of £22,478,738 the individual members subscribed £14,498,738 and the C.W.S. £7,980,000.

It is thus not the provision of capital by the C.W.S. which has induced societies to merge themselves into the C.R.S., for the individual members continue to supply the bulk of the capital employed. It is generally due to difficulties which the individual members have no confidence in their society to surmount. With C.W.S. guarantees of their share and loan capital, interest and dividend, the members are quite willing for the worries and responsibilities of running their society to be taken over by C.R.S.

This may disappoint the co-operator who looks for more from Co-operation than trading and financial benefits. It hardly provides the character forming visualised by Dr. King, or reaches the " self help " admired by G. J. Holyoake for instance. But it is doubtful if the membership concerned is sufficiently advanced in Co-operation for anything more onerous.

Few people do not prefer to be free of worry and responsibility and C.R.S. provides the material fruits of Co-operation to the individual member without imposing any responsibilities. It is therefore not surprising that the Co-operative Retail Services Survey Committee (1959) reported that " no case has ever arisen in which a branch of C.R.S. has ever desired to have its identity restored . . . . It is curious that there is interest in it from outside C.R.S. and not from within."

The rules, however, make it most difficult if not impossible in practice for a branch to recover its independence as a society. A requisition to that end must be signed by one-fourth of the members who together own not less than two-thirds of the capital of the branch, the new society would have to pay to C.R.S. the purchase price of the property and assets plus the total losses, if any, incurred in running the branch, and any member's share capital in C.R.S. could not be transferred from C.R.S. to the new society without written consent.

The rules of C.R.S. allow for part of its surplus, not exceeding 1 per cent of net profits after providing for depreciation to be put to an Education Fund for promoting instruction, culture or recreation. The amount would be recommended by the Management Committee and approved by ordinary general meeting. It would be spent " in such manner and in such proportion between one branch and another as the Committee may from time to time direct, and in the absence of any such direction any branch education committee may apply any proportion allotted to it as it may determine."

A branch education committee may be provided for by the

management committee. Its members may be elected by the members of the branch and/or appointed by the Committee. With the sanction of the Committee the branch education committee may appoint a branch education secretary, his remuneration being determined by the Committee.

There is also provision in the rules for political activities, but branches are not obliged to engage in these, or educational activities. It is left to the option of the members of the branches.

Neither the C.W.S. nor C.R.S. have pursued an aggressive policy of enlarging C.R.S. There is a natural willingness to consider approaches by retail societies who through one cause or another are interested in a merger. Each case, however, comes before a Standing Joint Committee of the Co-operative Union and the C.W.S., and various alternatives are considered, such as amalgamation with neighbouring societies, before there is agreement to merging in the C.R.S.

OTHER RETAIL DEVELOPMENTS OF THE C.W.S.

In the main the C.W.S. performs services for and trades with organisations, but it has some direct contacts with individual co-operators. Many, for instance, deal directly with the Co-operative Bank, and many use the services of the Co-operative Travel Service, which is a tourist agency for travel at home and abroad. A subsidiary company, Travco Hotels Ltd., owns and operates a number of hotels and holiday homes at the leading resorts.

Federal developments have taken place in milk processing and in baking, in which the C.W.S. has taken part. The increasing scale of economic operation necessitated an increase in the size of bakery plant and a market of a size far outside the range of most societies. Unfortunately, some societies were indifferent to the need to push the sales of bread and confectionery of federal bakeries. An approach in 1958 was made to the C.W.S. to take over, in full, Lancashire Co-operative Bakeries, a federation in which it had an interest. It agreed to do so on condition that the C.W.S. should have the authority to pursue house-to-house delivery of bread, confectionery and biscuits in the area. This was agreed to, and the C.W.S. entered upon another sphere of direct retail contacts with individual consumers, the engagements of the Lancashire Co-operative Bakeries being transferred to the C.W.S. in January, 1959.

To facilitate the new arrangements the C.W.S. established a Bread and Confectionery Division. Other bakeries have also been taken over subject to similar conditions. Long-term agreements are made with the societies concerned which include provision for dividends.

It will be remembered from Chapter XI that the Independent Commission recommended the establishment of national chains of specialist shops and that the first chain should be in footwear. Further, the 1960 Congress decided that the C.W.S. and S.C.W.S. should proceed with the establishment of such chains in partnership with retail societies which wanted to participate. Accordingly, Society Footwear Ltd., was established in 1961 for the purpose of running a chain of footwear shops.

In 1962, it acquired a private chain of shops and part of another chain with the result that some of the shops were in the areas of societies that were not members of Society Footwear. A few of these societies agreed to join the chain but others did not. In 1963, the Society changed its name to Shoefayre Ltd., and, while in some areas it carries on footwear operations for local societies as the Independent Commission had envisaged it would, in many other areas it operates with no visible co-operative link and in competition with the local society. This certainly was not the intention of the Independent Commission's recommendations.

National Co-operative Chemists

This society is a federation of the C.W.S. and " such other societies as shall be admitted by the directors." Its aim is to develop the pharmacy trade on a national scale, and seeks to do so by the transfer from retail societies of existing chemists departments, setting up new branches or purchasing the goodwill of established businesses. As in the case of similar developments by the S.C.W.S., the establishment of a branch is conditional upon the consent of the local society.

A retail society consenting to the establishment of a N.C.C. branch in its area, enters into an agreement with the N.C.C. that it will not undertake similar business during the continuance of the agreement apart from the sale of prepacked drugs, etc., in its grocery branches. The N.C.C. pays to each retail society in whose areas it operates a discount calculated upon the trade of the N.C.C. shops. The rate of discount is based upon the earnings of the N.C.C., but is not less than $7\frac{1}{2}$ per cent of its retail trade; the retail societies, however, pay dividend upon their members' purchases from the N.C.C. shops.

Each society, other than the C.W.S., which is a member of N.C.C., holds a number of shares fixed by the Board of Directors, subject to a maximum of one share for every 10 members. The

C.W.S. is entitled to hold a number of shares equivalent to the total number of shares held by other societies. Upon admittance into membership a retail society is required to take up five fully paid up £1 shares, but there is provision of further shareholding when N.C.C. pharmacies are established in its area. When this takes place the society member contributes share capital equal to 50 per cent of the capital expenditure incurred.

General meetings are held annually. Each society member has one vote for every £1 share. N.C.C. has a Board of 10 members, five appointed and removable from time to time by the C.W.S. Board and five elected by the retail society members. No person other than those appointed by the C.W.S. Board, can be a director unless he is a member of the board or secretary, manager, or managing secretary of a member society.

Retail Advisory Services

Particularly since the reorganisation of the C.W.S., with the re-emphasised feeling that the Wholesale Society was there to serve the retail societies and indeed that the survival and success of the C.W.S. depended upon the survival and success of the retail societies, it has provided the retail societies with an increasing range of advisory services. It was the feeling that these trade advisory services were overlapping those provided by the Co-operative Union that led to the transfer of the Union's Food Trades Department, Dry Goods Trades Department, Development Department, and Organisation and Methods Section to the C.W.S. in 1970. With these changes, the C.W.S. became the primary agency for the provision of trade advisory services in England and Wales.

THE SCOTTISH CO-OPERATIVE WHOLESALE SOCIETY

Much of what has been written of the C.W.S. is true of the S.C.W.S. and there is no need to go over similar ground in describing the aims, place and activities of the S.C.W.S. There are, however, some differences to which attention must be drawn.

The objects of the Society as stated in its rules, are " to carry on all or any of the following businesses, industries or trades," a list being then given. The possibility of any future development being omitted is met by the clause " to carry on any kind of trade or industry; as may be determined from time to time."

Membership is open to all co-operative societies registered under the Industrial and Provident Societies' Act (even those outside of Scotland). At one time employees over the age of 21 also had the entitlement to become members of the Society through the Association of Shareholding Employees but this is a fast declining category. In 1948 there were 287 such employee members, in 1958 144, and in 1968 36.

Shareholding is, of course, a condition of membership and minimum shareholding is based upon the number of members of the member society. Each member society must take up not less than one share in respect of each member and increase the number of its shares annually as its members increase. Shares are now £5 each.

All shares are transferable, not withdrawable, although there is provision for repayment of shares at the discretion of the Board of Directors.

Control

General meetings are held on Saturdays in June and December, the December meetings in Edinburgh, the June meetings in Glasgow. At the meeting held in June the Board of Directors submit a report and annual balance sheet.

Voting is on a different basis from that of the C.W.S. Each society has one vote in virtue of membership and additional votes up to a maximum of 50. The maximum number of votes is held by the society with the largest net purchases from the S.C.W.S. for the preceding quarter; all other societies having votes in the same proportion to 50 votes that their purchases have to those of the society with the largest purchases. Societies may have as many delegates as the number of their votes.

The Board

The Board of Directors is elected by and from the member societies. It will eventually consist of nine members including the President, all of whom serve in a full-time salaried capacity. (At present it is in the process of being reduced from 12, by retirement and resignation. In 1969 there were still 11 directors.) Each is elected for a period of three years. There is a maximum age limit, each must retire at the quarterly meeting following his 65th birthday. The President is elected by the member societies.

A candidate for election to the Board of Directors must be nominated by a member society and can only be nominated by one society; a society cannot nominate a member of another society unless the proposed nominee is not being nominated by his own society. The nomination paper amongst other information states the duration of the candidate's membership in the Co-operative Movement, positions held in the Co-operative and

Trade Union Movements and on public boards and committees, this is circulated with the first voting paper. Any form of canvassing or soliciting votes " by any person whatsoever . . . whether with or without the candidate's knowledge " incurs the penalty of disqualification. Societies nominating a candidate, however, may circulate a statement on his qualifications not exceeding 500 words, and he may, if invited, appear before a board or a group of boards of management to discuss his candidature.

All candidates for office on the Board of Directors, other than retiring members seeking re-election, must be under 52 years of age and must have been *bona-fide* purchasing members of at least five years' standing of a member or member societies. Not more than one member of any society may hold office on the Board at one time. Employees of the S.C.W.S. are not allowed to hold any office on the Board, but may be nominated. If elected, their employment, of course, would terminate. Directors would be disqualified from holding office if they held any other office or place of profit on the S.C.W.S., or were concerned in or participated in the profits of any contract with the S.C.W.S.

Three or more auditors are elected, each for a period of three years, retiring in rotation each year.

Activities

The activities of the S.C.W.S. are similar to those of the C.W.S.; it has depots and salesrooms at home and overseas, produces many of the goods it sells, and has a Banking Department. It also operates directly, both laundry and funeral furnishing undertakings, and has agreements with local societies for the setting up of chemists' shops. It has also a retail branch service, whose origin and development were described in a previous chapter.

According to its rules, " In communities where no retail co-operative society in membership of this Federation is established, retail branches may be formed and carried on under the control of the Board of Directors. The Board of Directors shall have power to pay a dividend to all purchasers from such retail branches. Purchasers shall have no part in or control over the business of retail branches and the Board of Directors at any time, if and when they think proper, shall be entitled to discontinue any branch without consulting the purchasers." The Board has the power to promote any of these branches into a retail co-operative society registered under the Industrial and Provident Societies Acts.

In addition to these S.C.W.S. retail branches, there has been since 1967 Scottish Co-operative Retail Services on lines very similar to C.R.S. in England and Wales. It will be noted then that the two ventures are different in purpose and organisation. The purpose of the S.C.W.S. retail branches is to carry co-operative business into co-operative deserts and so to pioneer co-operative enterprise. There are no branch committees. So far S.C.R.S. has provided an ambulance service for ailing retail societies whose directors remain as area committees. It has been suggested, however, that S.C.R.S. could provide the nucleus of a national Scottish Co-operative Society.

THE CO-OPERATIVE TEA SOCIETY

Formerly the English and Scottish Joint C.W.S., the Co-operative Tea Society (still a partnership of the C.W.S. and the S.C.W.S.) carries on a number of productive enterprises at home and abroad and also deals in overseas produce. It has tea packing and blending factories in Great Britain and tea estates in India and Ceylon. About one fifth of the tea consumed in Great Britain is provided by this society. It also has coffee, cocoa and chocolate factories, and overseas depots in India, Ceylon, and Africa.

THE CO-OPERATIVE INSURANCE SOCIETY

The C.I.S. also is a joint venture of the two Wholesale Societies. It effects all classes of insurance and has grown to be one of the largest insurance enterprises in the country. As a co-operative enterprise it does not, of course, operate for private profit.

The whole of the profits of the Life Department are used to improve policyholders' benefits. Profits on the other branches are payable to co-operative societies as dividend on their fire, general and collective premiums paid during the year.

Individual co-operators placing their own fire and general insurances with the C.I.S. benefit by obtaining these at lower rates than are generally charged by other companies.

THE CO-OPERATIVE PRODUCTIVE FEDERATION

The history of the productive and co-operative co-partnership societies has been traced in earlier chapters. Although fewer than in previous years, several of these are members of the Co-operative Productive Federation. Its headquarters are in Leicester, and most of the member societies are in the East Midlands.

According to C.P.F. rules, " membership of the Federation shall consist of societies or companies who, unless exempted by resolution of a general meeting, shall hold not less than one share for each five of its own members;" " Societies or companies only shall be admitted whose rules admit the workers employed by them to membership and to the participation in the division of profits in respect of their wages."

Management of the C.P.F., is a part-time one, consisting of president and ten committee members, one half of whom retire annually, but are eligible for re-election. The offices of president, auditors and arbitrators are filled annually.

Two general meetings are held each year at each of which a financial statement is presented, and at one the officers of the Federation are elected. Society members are represented by one delegate for every £10 or part of £10 subscribed, but no society may be represented by more than three delegates.

The rules of the C.P.F. state its objects as follows:—

" The special objects of the federation are to carry on the industries, businesses and trades of commercial agents, supervision and advising agents, bankers and general dealers both wholesale and retail. Also to provide for the appointment of organiser or organisers or other means, for the purpose of propagating the principles of co-partnership in such a manner as may appear advisable to the Executive from time to time. The objects of the Federation shall include dealings of any description in land."

An amendment gave the Federation power to act as guarantors or trustees for its member societies. This was a dangerous provision and on one occasion caused a crippling loss. It will be noted that, as is customary with the objects rule of organisations, the declared objects are more numerous and comprehensive than are the objects in practice pursued. Its activities are educational and propagandist, advisory in financial and general matters, protective of societies' interests, and assistance to obtain capital and trade.

Constituent societies of the C.P.F. are usually also members of the Co-operative Union, of which the C.P.F. is also a member. It is represented at Congress, of which it has on some occasions provided the President. It used also to be represented on the Union's main committees but in recent years its representation on the Central Executive and the Party's National Committee has disappeared, leaving it represented only on the National Executive of the Dry Goods Trade Association which has now been put under the aegis of the C.W.S. These appointments were significant of the recognition by the Movement of the potential of the form of Co-operation represented by the C.P.F. Through this representation it often played an active and influential part in the Movement as a whole, although in capital, trade and membership the C.P.F. societies are together inferior to many individual retail societies. In this, as in many other matters, the Co-operative Movement demonstrated the value it attached to ideals.

THE CO-OPERATIVE PRESS

Publications within the British Co-operative Movement are issued by many organisations—the Co-operative Union, the Wholesale Societies, the International Co-operative Alliance, retail societies, the Guilds, etc. But each and all of these on some matters is bound to speak to a brief, for instance on issues directly affecting their own organisation. There is, therefore, a case for an independent Press in the Co-operative Movement, independent in the sense that it is not subservient to any one organisation, but is open to fair discussion and criticism of each and all of them. Such is the Co-operative Press Limited, originating and developing, as earlier chapters described, from " The North of England Newspaper Company Limited."

The Co-operative Press Limited is a registered Industrial and Provident Society. It is a federation of all types of co-operative societies, 537 in number in 1968, mainly retail societies, but also including the Co-operative Union, the two Wholesale Societies, the C.P.F., the Women's and the Men's Guilds and some trade unions.

It is governed by a board of nine directors elected by constituent societies. Voting is by postal ballot, votes being proportionate to membership, share capital and trade done with the Co-operative Press. Election is for a period of three years, and there is an age limit of 70 years.

Half-yearly shareholders' meetings are held. Divisional meetings are held in London, Newcastle-on-Tyne, Glasgow or Edinburgh, with the final meeting the following week at Manchester.

The number and diffusion of membership makes it unlikely that any single co-operative organisation could obtain control over it, nor could its publications be transferred to any outside body without a voting majority of its shareholders agreeing thereto, which is improbable. As the Co-operative Press does not receive any subsidy designed to influence or control the policy of its journals, it is able to fulfil its function of an independent press within the Co-operative Movement. General control over all publications is vested in the Board of Directors with executive control exercised by its chief officials.

The policies of its journals are subject to criticism at the half-yearly meetings. It is interesting and significant that criticism at these meetings has more often been of quality and standard, than of profitability. Not that the members are indifferent to finance, but the approach has often been that a high level of journalism is the essential condition, it is the work and duty of the Board and officials to make the enterprise pay within that condition.

This is not easy, for the British public is largely literate only in the sense of being able to read and write. There is not a large market for a press which seeks to describe events fully and objectively, which tries to induce its readers to think, and is concerned with moral issues. Profits are bigger and more easily obtained by papers providing highly coloured and low-level articles on sex, on sport, on small incidents likely to arouse high feelings and on all manner of stunts appealing to the emotions, prejudices and vices of their readers.

The principle of honest trading is, however, more important in food for the mind than it is in food for the body, and co-operators being concerned with the effects of consumption rather than with profits from supply, could not descend to the levels of the popular press without betraying their ideals and principles. Hence the attempt to make their old Sunday newspaper, *Reynolds News*, reach the level, gain a similar prestige and exercise the same kind of rational influence as do papers like the *Guardian*, the *Observer*, and the *Sunday Times*. Declining sales forced the Press to adopt a more tabloid format to attempt to recapture lost circulation, and in 1962 the *Reynolds News* became the *Sunday Citizen*. Neither of these two papers could have existed without the help they obtained from the rest of the Movement through the Collective Advertising Scheme. Even that, however, was insufficient to maintain the *Sunday Citizen* which ceased publication in 1967.

The other publications of the Co-operative Press are designed for specifically co-operative readers. The *Co-operative News* (weekly) is indispensable to any serious co-operator. It gives what its title indicates, news of the Co-operative Movement, of the affairs of all types of co-operative organisations and the discussion of topical problems. The *Scottish Co-operator* serves a similar purpose for Scotland.

Co-operative Management and Marketing (monthly) contains articles on a level demanding serious consideration by its readers. It is intended for officials, directors and students and deals with the topical business problems facing them and with the broader economic and social matters which are the context of these problems.

N

As with so many other co-operative matters, success cannot be commanded by the efforts of the central organisation alone. It demands the loyalty and efforts of the local societies. A Co-operative Movement with a membership of over 12 million should not be worried over circulation problems. Nor would it be if local societies seriously concerned themselves with the sale of co-operative periodicals. Private newsagents, for instance, were often more active and more successful in selling *Reynolds News* than local societies are in selling the *Co-operative News;* in former days *The Millgate*, a cultural review, had a good circulation, but its sales depended on private, not co-operative salesmen. Yet the formation of a co-operative climate of opinion is of vital concern to any and every co-operative society.

15 THE CO-OPERATIVE UNION

" Democracy cannot afford to dispense with complication in its administrative machinery because only by an extensive variety of parts, and a deliberately adjusted relation among those parts can there be any security, for the personal freedom and independence in initiative of the great mass of individuals "
(*"Constitution for a Socialist Commonwealth."*
S. *and* B. *Webb.*)

"IF the British Industrial Co-operative Movement possesses a sense of unity today it is largely due to the existence and work of the Co-operative Union. We have seen how individual societies groping their way to success through experience that was often sad and sometimes fatal, felt the need of a central organisation to which they could turn for advice and assistance. That need the Co-operative Union supplies. Although societies today in their greater strength no longer need the kind of help and advice which young and struggling societies require, even the strongest of them would suffer if it were isolated from the rest of the societies. . . . Experience has shown that instead of united action having become less necessary as societies have become larger it has become more necessary. There has consequently been a continuous expansion of the activities of the Co-operative Union." (*Co-operation*, Hall and Watkins.)

The history of the Co-operative Movement since the above passage was written in 1934 would serve to emphasise the opinions then expressed. The Movement has had to stand as a movement against governments, adverse legislation, war-time and post-war bureaucracies, political parties, and trade unions as well as against the various machinations of business opponents. Besides the performance of these defensive functions there has been an increasing need for the co-operative education of members, officials and staff as societies grew bigger, with more complex organisations and subject to the impact of political, economic and social events and movements.

There has also been need for increasing research so that the various currents affecting the Co-operative Movement could be ascertained and their strength measured. Moreover the Union has been the means by which new ideas and developments have been introduced, discussed, modified and amended, adopted or rejected. To a large extent, as the historical chapters showed, the history of the British Co-operative Movement as a movement, in modern times, is largely the history of the Co-operative Union.

OBJECTS OF THE UNION

As stated in its rules the objects of the Union " are to carry on the trades of accountants, booksellers, commercial and general advisers, publishers and arbiters in matters arising between societies which cannot be settled locally, and of propagating co-operative principles and ideas, and the organising of co-operative work in all its branches, whether such work be in connection with industries, trades, or business, or for the promotion of education and other objects and purposes of a similar character with a view to the ultimate establishment of a Co-operative Commonwealth."

It will be seen that its objects are wide, varied and far distant, all being related and directed to the distant ideal of a Co-operative Commonwealth. Most organisations state their objects as widely as possible so as to have all possible activities in the future as well as the present legally covered, although some of the objects may be unrelated to any current activity. In this case, however, every one of the objects stated does in fact cover some Union activity or other.

This history has already described these activities; a good deal of the work of all departments is of an advisory character—legal, financial, fiscal, commercial, labour, political, educational; it has pioneered a good deal of reorganisation; it is a bookseller and a publisher of books, pamphlets, periodicals, reports, through these media providing general advice and information to societies and engaging in publicity and propaganda and it engages in a wide variety of educational activities.

Also, as it represents, with the exception of agricultural Co-operation, all branches and organisations of co-operative activity, its pronouncements on co-operative and other subjects are regarded as expressions of the opinions of the Co-operative Movement as a whole. These pronouncements, however, are seldom made without there being considerable discussion and debate at various levels, so that the Union not only pronounces opinion, it is within the Union that the representative opinion is formed. With such a variety of functions, all democratically controlled, the organisation of the Union is bound to be complex.

MEMBERSHIP

The Union is open to "all Industrial and Provident Societies, Joint Stock Companies and other Bodies Corporate, which have for their object the promotion of co-operative principles and ideas," i.e., of genuine co-operative societies. It consists of nearly all the retail societies, local federations, the Wholesale Societies and their joint enterprises, co-operative co-partnership productive societies, the Co-operative Productive Federation, the Co-operative Press Ltd. (until 1970 the Co-operative Permanent Building Society) and many special and productive societies connected with consumer Co-operation. Agricultural societies, however, with a few exceptions, have kept aloof, and housing societies have their own federation.

Applications for membership are made to the General Secretary who submits them to the General Purposes Committee of the Union, whose approval is necessary for their acceptance. Each applicant for admission is deemed "to accept as the principles by which all its business transactions shall be guided—the desire to promote the practice of truthfulness, justice and economy, in production and exchange

(1) By the abolition of false dealings

    (a) Direct, by representing any article produced or sold to be other than what it is known to the producer or vendor to be

    (b) Indirect, by concealing from the purchaser any fact known to the vendor material to be known by the purchaser, to enable him to judge of the value of the article purchased

(2) By conciliating the conflicting interests of the capitalist, the worker, and the purchaser, through the equitable division among them of the surplus commonly known as Profit

(3) By preventing the waste of labour now caused by unregulated competition.

It should be observed that all members of the Co-operative Union are deemed to have accepted in (1) a principle intended to safeguard the individual customer, and which in the description of Rochdale principles was described as Honest Trading. Also in (2) are the Rochdale principles of division of surplus in proportion to transactions and limited interest on capital. Another important Rochdale principle, that of Democratic Control, is implicit in rule 10: "No society shall be admitted unless its management is of a representative character."

Under rule 8, provision is made for a society amalgamating with another to apply for retention of its Union membership, providing that "no branch shall be so recognised unless it is vested to a substantial degree with the function of managerial control." The rule also enables branches of C.R.S. to be members of the Co-operative Union.

The Union has power to expel members. Rule 10 states that "no society shall be allowed to remain in membership with the Union which does not abide by its rules, conform to its aims and accept the decisions of the Central Executive confirmed by Congress. Any disagreement that may arise through overlapping or any other matter which cannot be settled by consultation between the parties shall, in failure of conciliation, be submitted to persons appointed by the Co-operative Union Limited and their decision shall be deemed final by all parties."

Each member of the Union is required to hold one share, value 25p, and to make an annual contribution to the Union's funds. In the case of retail societies this contribution is based upon their membership, at present it is $2\frac{1}{2}$p per member, but this rate has been altered in the past and, of course, may be in the future. The Central Executive decides the rates of contributions payable by other kinds of societies, federal, productive, agricultural "or any other form whatsoever."

Membership of the Union is voluntary, like the membership of any co-operative society. Each society has joined of its own free will, each society may withdraw. This fact has important consequences upon the constitution, policies and activities of the Union. It cannot, for instance, be a governing body, it cannot be happy with simple majority decisions on matters vital to any of its members, it must always seek what the Webbs described as "the highest common measure of agreement."

CO-OPERATIVE CONGRESS

The final authority of the Co-operative Union is its general meeting—the Co-operative Congress. According to rule it must be held annually during the three days commencing with Monday in Spring Bank Holiday week, at a place determined by the Central Executive.

It consists of all members of the Central Executive and Sectional Boards, representatives of the Regional Councils, three representatives of the Co-operative Party (any of the foregoing may speak, but have no votes) and delegates from societies which are members of the Union. Every retail society member is entitled to send one delegate, but if it has more than 3,000 members it is allowed to send more than one, the number being according to a graduated scale of membership with a maximum of eleven. Other societies, whose subscriptions are fixed by the Central Executive, have their number of delegates also fixed by the same body.

Voting is one vote for each retail society by virtue of membership plus additional votes for each thousand members on which it contributes. The full voting power of any one society is exercised by one of its delegates, though all its delegates may address Congress. The voting power of other than retail societies is decided by the Central Executive.

The President of Congress is elected by the Central Executive. This is regarded as the greatest honour the Movement can bestow and expresses an appreciation of capacity and character proven by experience in service to the movement.

Congress proceedings are regulated by rule and include—

(a) The opening address. This is made by the President of Congress, and is usually known as the inaugural address. These addresses have played an important part in the Movement's history, not seldom initiating changes or movements for change, and frequently setting the tone not only for Congress but also for the Movement during the Congress Year.

(b) The discussion of the Report made by the Central Executive. This includes the reports of the Union Departments, the Parliamentary Committee, the National Wages Board, the Education Executive and the Co-operative Party. In addition there may be Special Reports on some subjects.

These reports cover the work of the Co-operative Union during the year. They are printed, together with the accounts of the Union and sent out to societies at least 21 days before the first day of Congress. Amendments to the report of the Central Executive must be sent to the General Secretary not later than ten days before Congress, and they must be sent out forthwith to societies.

Thus the activities of the Union can be thoroughly examined and discussed by societies before Congress meets; it would be impossible to get through the immense range of business otherwise.

In Congress, each report is introduced by a member, usually the chairman, of the committee concerned, then delegates discuss the report. The discussion is replied to, usually by the chief official of the appropriate Union department.

(c) The declaration of election results.

(d) The discussion of any papers, or proposals, directed or authorised by the Central Executive or the Standing Orders Committee.

(e) The discussion by the Congress of any matters arising out of (b) and (d).

(f) The discussion of any proposal submitted by any society-member or national committee of the Union sent in not later than ten weeks before the first day of Congress, providing the Central Executive decides it comes within the scope of Congress business. Amendments must be received not later than thirty-five days before Congress.

(g) The Election of Auditor.

Congress is formally a business meeting dealing with the affairs of a federal co-operative society, viz., the Co-operative Union. Much of the business done is of vital importance to societies and to the Movement as a whole. Its greatest value however is probably educational and inspirational.

Delegates, even long seasoned ones, cannot fail to be inspired by the singing of the opening hymn of Congress by a thousand voices, followed by the introduction of overseas delegates from various parts of the world. For a time at least the idealistic nature of the Movement is uppermost, and one is impressed by the sense that the Co-operative Movement is no mean movement, either in aim or scope. As the various reports are introduced and discussed delegates are made aware of the many problems confronting the Movement of which each of their societies is a part. They hear a variety of opinions expressed upon them, a concern and interest in matters exceeding those of any one society is demanded, they are brought to realise that they are members of a Movement whose bounds are world wide. Moreover, and of some consequence, fellow co-operators from all parts of the country meet. Friendships are made and renewed, for in the informal gatherings of Congress are made many of those fraternal bonds which do much to hold a Movement together.

Yet the power of Congress must not be overrated. It is not a parliament of the Movement in the sense of being a legislative body. As pointed out in an earlier chapter the only operative resolutions it can pass are those relating to the affairs of the Co-operative Union itself. It cannot command or instruct any of its members to do anything, a Congress resolution is not binding on any of the retail societies or the federal bodies, they are each responsible to their own members, not to Congress.

There have been many instances in the Movement's history where a resolution has been comfortably carried in Congress but which has for long failed to gain the adherence of societies' boardrooms. If those resolutions had been binding they would probably never have been carried. As it is, progressive minds may carry a resolution in Congress, and so give a valuable, often an indispensable, lead to societies. The fact that Congress has discussed and approved some matter is in itself a powerful argument in persuading a society to adopt it. Congress is thus often able to act as a pacemaker to the Movement. If its resolutions were binding it would seldom be able to do anything effective until the mind of the whole Movement, not merely of Congress delegates, was made up. This would generally mean that it would proceed at the pace of the slowest.

CENTRAL EXECUTIVE

The affairs of the Union are administered by the Central Executive and the Sectional Boards, to which there shall be assigned such areas as Congress may direct from time to time.

The Central Executive, it will have been gathered, is the prime national committee of the Union. Since Congress 1970 it consists of eight representatives of the C.W.S., two from the S.C.W.S., and nine members elected by societies in each Section (the Metropolitan area being regarded as a Section for these purposes) and from Ireland. Each of these retail society representatives must be a member of the appropriate Sectional Board or of the Irish Regional Council. The Central Executive appoints its own chairman annually from amongst its own members who is also regarded as Chairman of the Co-operative Union.

The Executive meets at such times and places as it fixes from time to time, but generally there are quarterly meetings. At these meetings it transacts business referred to it by Congress or which it decides to undertake itself. Questions of major policy will certainly be considered by it and all the ultimate decisions on policy and management questions are made by the Executive.

In 1969, the Central Executive formed an Economic and Taxation Committee to meet on an *ad hoc* basis, consisting of four Co-operative Union representatives, three from the C.W.S., two from the S.C.W.S., one from the Co-operative Party and one from the Co-operative Insurance Society. The newly constituted Central Executive in 1970 decided that this Committee should continue its work and also that a General Purposes sub-committee of the Executive would deal with the detailed management affairs of the Union as it had done before the 1970 Congress decisions.

PARLIAMENTARY COMMITTEE

From 1949 to 1970 the Union's Parliamentary Committee was a sub-committee of the Central Executive but in the changes of 1970 it was made into a separate committee of the Union. It now consists of one member appointed by and from each Sectional Board, one member from the two Metropolitan Regional Councils combined, one from the S.C.W.S., one from the C.W.S., one from the Co-operative Press, two from the Central Executive and two from the Co-operative Party.

The Committee keeps its eye on Parliamentary Bills and legislation to detect if they contain any thing affecting co-operative interests. An average of something like twenty Bills a year require detailed attention and consultation with other Union departments and federal organisations. In addition a close watch is maintained on the private bills of local authorities which sometimes contain clauses dangerous to the many interests of co-operative societies in their respective areas, for example, the licensing of mobile shops, street trading, weights and measures.

There are also matters arising from the operation of legislation, marketing boards, criticisms of various government and local government activities, and the securing of representation on many government bodies.

SECTIONAL BOARDS

The Co-operative Union divides Great Britain into seven Sections, viz., Northern, North Eastern, North Western (which includes Ireland), Midland, Southern, South Western (an amalgamation of the old South West and Western Sections) and the Scottish Section. Each of these elects a Sectional Board by and from the member societies, with the constitutional provision that in England and Wales each Regional Council in the Section will be represented on the Board, or, where there is only one society in a Region, that society will be represented. These bodies are directly concerned with matters affecting the welfare of societies within their own Section. Their primary work is to co-ordinate co-operative activities within the Sections, to implement the Regional Plan, to operate the Sectional wages machinery, hold meetings and conferences, advise societies, seek to reconcile differences between them, in short to do the Union's work and watch over the Union's interests in their respective areas.

If a society meets any difficulties it will often consult its Sectional Board. The Boards meet normally in alternate months and as each of them has representatives on the Central Executive and various national committees, the Boards, and through them the societies, are kept in close touch with national policy. In turn, the Central Executive and its national committees are also kept well informed of the sense and feeling of the Boards and, of course, through them of the societies.

There is a constant current of information and opinion flowing in each direction, from the centre to the Sections and from the Sections to the centre. The minutes of the Central Executive, and Parliamentary Committee are circulated to the Sectional Boards. By rule the Central Executive is obliged to hold an Annual Meeting during the period of Congress of all members of the Sectional Boards and representatives of the Irish Executive to " review the work of the Central Executive, to express opinions thereon, to submit suggestions for consideration by the Central Executive." Also: " Should extraordinary circumstances arise which in the view of the Central Executive justify a joint meeting between the Central Executive and the Sectional Boards for the purpose of consultation, such meeting may be held under arrangements made by the Central Executive."

Each Sectional Board has a full-time Secretary. Expenditure on Sectional work is limited to the amounts fixed by the Central Executive for any financial year. The Central Executive decides whether any activity or proposed activity of a Sectional Board is within the objects of the Co-operative Union.

It will be seen that Congress is the sovereign authority of the Union. The Central Executive, and so the whole administration of the Union, is responsible to Congress, not to the Sectional Boards or to any joint meeting of the Boards. This is direct democracy, for Congress is the assembly of all the member societies.

REGIONAL COUNCILS

With the advent of the Regional Plan, the old District Councils became defunct and were replaced by Regional Councils, one for each of the regional groupings proposed by the Plan. Each Council consists of one or two representatives of each society in the Region, preferably the President and/or the Chief Executive Officer. The primary function of these Councils is to seek ways and means of merging the societies in the Region in accordance with the Plan, so eventually it is hoped the need for them will disappear. In the meantime, they are charged with the task of seeking to rationalise the use of management and capital within the Region and of standardising accounting and administrative procedures. They also have certain functions concerning wages taken over from the old District Wages Boards and may arrange conferences to consider trading, financial and development problems. Through their representative on the appropriate Sectional Board, each of the Regional Councils is linked with the Co-operative Union.

TRADE ASSOCIATIONS

Until 1970 Trade Associations for Bakery, Dry Goods, Fuel, Laundry, Meat, Milk, Grocery and Provisions, and Technical Panels for Publicity, Pharmacy/Optical and Transport were part of the Union organisation.

The objectives of the Trade Associations were to unite in single representative bodies the organisation of their respective trades in the Co-operative Movement; to provide mutual help by consultation, exchange and interchange of ideas; to work for full co-operation with the Wholesale Societies, and in appropriate trades with the member societies of the Co-operative Productive Federation; to promote measures in the interest of the consumer; to examine Bills or Orders which affect the trade and tender opinions thereon to the Parliamentary Committee; to assist in the preparation and presentation of cases on behalf of the trade to Government departments or other responsible bodies; to act as negotiators on matters of price and policy.

At the 1970 Congress it was decided that their activities should become the responsibility of the Wholesale Societies.

WAGES MACHINERY AND THE LABOUR DEPARTMENT

The historical chapters described the development of the machinery for collective bargaining by retail societies.

Until 1969 there was a fairly elaborate structure of District and Sectional Wages Boards below the National Wages Board, but their functions are now undertaken by the Regional Councils and Sectional Boards. The reason for this change was the argument that most wage agreements were now made on a national basis and one of the chief functions of both the District and the Sectional Wages Boards had become that of collecting opinion on national proposals and passing them up the structure, a function of which the Regional Councils and Sectional Boards were just as capable, particularly in view of their composition with a predominance of presidents and chief officers. The Regional Councils have the power to set up Personnel Committees which are concerned with a wider range of staff matters including training.

In Scotland the District Wages Boards and the Sectional Wages Board continue and in England, the old Metropolitan District (now Regions 36 and 37), which has long been regarded as a Section for wages purposes, retains its Wages Board.

The National Wages Board is formed of two representatives from each Sectional Board in England and Wales, two representatives each from the Scottish Sectional Wages Board and the Metropolitan Wages Board, and two representatives from the Central Executive. Before entering into negotiations the National Wages Board consults with retail societies, Regional Councils and Sectional Boards and thereafter meets the Trade Union side. The results of the negotiations are also circulated generally by way of a recommendation for acceptance. The final decision on ratification rests with the constituent societies, so there is the machinery for providing an opportunity for societies, Regions and Sections to express their opinions and exercise their influence but no sectional interest can override the larger overall national interest.

When negotiations between the co-operative side and a trade union fail to bring about a settlement the parties usually have recourse to the National Conciliation Board. Twenty-one trade unions were signatories to the original agreement setting up the National Conciliation Board for the Retail Co-operative Service, but this number is now somewhat less by reason of amalgamation and fusion on the Trade Union side. The Board normally comprises six co-operative employer representatives and six worker representatives, together with Joint Secretaries and an Independent Chairman. There is also a national panel comprising ten members from each side, appointed on the co-operative side by the National Wages Board. This panel deals with all national differences.

The Independent Chairman for each meeting of the Board is selected from a special panel agreed between the Central Executive and the trade unions, and his primary function is to endeavour to assist the Board to reach a decision by conciliation.

The Board has functioned for over 40 years, and during this period it has met on over 600 occasions and dealt with more than 1,000 individual cases. In most cases the Board reached a decision, in others the decision was left to the arbitration of the Chairman and there were other cases (few in number) where no decision was reached because either one party or the other to the difference was unwilling to accept arbitration.

In passing, it should be mentioned that during the period of the second world war, compulsory arbitration was enforced by statutory legislation. Therefore, during this period finality was assured in all cases heard by the Co-operative Conciliation Board. With the repeal of the statutory legislation the position in the retail co-operative service reverted to the pre-1939 practice and the chairman can now only give an arbitration award if both parties to the difference agree that he should do so.

On the whole the machinery has worked well, strikes and lock-outs being almost unknown within the Co-operative Movement.

The Labour Department is concerned with the administration of the Wages Board machinery as a whole and acts as the secretariat to the National Wages Board. It is usual for an officer of the Labour Department to assist Sectional Boards when dealing with wages matters and generally accept responsibility for the conduct of negotiations with a trade union. Wage claims in particular involve the Department in collecting statistical and economic data for the consideration of the National Wages Board which, in conjunction with the views, opinions and suggestions from its constituents, enable policy to be determined. In addition, the Department must keep a careful watch on the deliberations and decisions of more than a score of Statutory Wages Councils and voluntary Joint Industrial Councils which lay down minimum wages and conditions in many trades covering both private and co-operative employees. The Co-operative Movement is represented on all these bodies by both experts and laymen. Generally co-operative wages and conditions are superior to these minima, but it is obviously necessary that societies should be kept informed of their legal obligations in matters of this kind, particularly as it is impossible in practice to ensure that changes in wages and conditions of service can all take place at one and the same time.

The Department has also important advisory services to perform relating to all manner of labour problems such as dismissals, appointments, promotions, demotions, the interpretation of agreements, the Shop and Factory Acts, National Insurance, superannuation schemes, incentive payment schemes, working hours, and the Joint Advisory Councils.

EDUCATION

The history and changes of organisation of the Education Department were shown in earlier chapters, here is summarised its organisation at present, i.e., under the constitution adopted by Congress in 1948.

Congress then agreed to the setting up of the National Co-operative Education Association, its membership to consist of all registered societies engaged in co-operative educational activities which are members of the Co-operative Union. Its objects are:

(*a*) To unite in a single organisation the work of educational promotion within the Co-operative Movement.

(*b*) To provide a medium of mutual help and consultation on all matters affecting the educational interests of the Co-operative Movement and their advancement.

(*c*) To secure effective co-operative representation on committees of other organisations and to establish joint committees in advancing the interests and organisation of educational work.

The N.C.E.A. is organised Sectionally. In each Section of the Co-operative Union there is a Sectional Education Council consisting of four members appointed by and from the Sectional Board, and six representatives (who must be education officials or members of committees engaged in educational work) elected by committees responsible for education in societies. (Generally these will be education committees, but in some societies the board of directors is responsible for education.) In addition there is one representative appointed by each of the Sectional organisations of the auxiliary bodies, i.e., the Guilds within the Section, providing the body has at least 500 members within the Section. The society representatives on the Sectional Councils are elected biennially and no society may have more than one elected representative on a council.

The Councils must meet at least once a quarter and are committees of the Co-operative Union. Their annual reports are included in the Sectional Boards' Reports to the Annual Sectional Conference.

The functions of the Councils include:

(1) To stimulate and assist the development of co-operative education in all its aspects.

(2) To carry out the policies of the Education Executive and to be responsible for submitting to the Education Executive representations for further national policies and developments.

(3) To undertake responsibility at Sectional level for all educational activities—conferences, schools and classes, etc.

(4) To work in close association with the Sectional Education Officer.

The education officers at Sectional level are appointed by and responsible to the Education Executive. Some of these have a general educational responsibility, others are staff training specialists, others member education specialists. They are all experts in co-operative education, serving as advisers to societies and to individuals, also acting as agents of the Councils and the Education Executive.

The Education Executive is a national committee of the
Co-operative Union and is the governing body of the N.C.E.A.
It consists of four representatives of Sectional Education Councils
in England and Wales (other than representatives of Sectional
Boards) elected by the member societies in the appropriate area,
three representatives of Sectional Boards from Sections which did
not secure representation by the first method, one representative
from the Scottish Co-operative Education Association and one
from the Scottish Sectional Board, two representatives from the
C.W.S., one from the S.C.W.S., one from the Central Executive,
and up to four co-opted members with special experience of or
interest in Co-operative education. The chairman and vice-
chairman are appointed by and from the Education Executive at
its first meeting after Congress each year.

Subject to the Central Executive and the rules of the Co-
operative Union, the Education Executive has full executive
powers in controlling the affairs of the National Co-operative
Education Association and the Education Department of the
Co-operative Union, including the Co-operative College.

Within the same limitations the Education Executive holds an
annual Education Convention, generally at Easter. Proposals for
consideration are received under regulations determined by the
Education Executive, and any proposals adopted may be implemented by the Education Executive subject to approval by
Congress. The Education Executive submits a report to Congress.
However those specifically interested in co-operative education
will already have had the opportunity of considering and discussing the Education Executive's Report to Congress at the Education Convention held at Easter.

The Education Convention continues to be the highlight of
co-operative educationists. It is generally attended by nearly
500 delegates and " visitors." Only delegates, of course, have
voting powers, but the presence of " visitors " is valuable and
significant, reminiscent of the time when the " Easter Week End "
was a gathering of enthusiasts for co-operative education seeking
information and inspiration. These are still prime purposes, the
discussion on the Report must enlighten many, and the revival
of the practice of the giving of papers, followed by discussion,
on special subjects must also help. As with Congress however
a good deal of the value of the Convention is in the informal
discussions, the friendships made and renewed, and the sense of
unity of purpose in the pursuit of high ideals which is kept alive.

It may be observed that the constitution was intended to bring
within one organisation all co-operative interests relating to co-

operative education. Of course, every co-operative interest and activity is related to co-operative education, and the constitution shows the appreciation of this in the representation of the Sectional Boards on the Sectional Education Councils and the Education Executive. The Education Executive moreover is subject to the Central Executive and responsible to Congress, and the finances and staff of the Education Department are subject to the control of the General Purposes Committee. Thus while enlisting and organising the services of those specially interested in co-operative education the general control of the whole Movement is maintained.

The income of the Executive consists partly of fees for College, schools, correspondence courses, examinations, etc., also of a share in the subscription income of the Co-operative Union. In addition there is a special subscription paid by committees in the N.C.E.A. at the rate of 10/- per 1,000 members. This goes to the N.C.E.A. Fund. This fund is for experiment and for the development of direct service to society committees. The Executive is accountable for this fund, not to Congress but to the annual N.C.E.A. Conference.

The work of the Education Department is recorded in the annual reports to Congress and is described in the historical chapters. It may be summarised and described as

(a) *Advisory:* Advice and help to local societies is given to local societies on all manner of educational matters, both from headquarters and by the Sectional Education Officers, e.g., formation of classes, relations with local education authorities and other bodies, holding of schools and conferences, speakers, etc. Much advice of a general kind is provided by publications such as the monthly *Member Education Bulletin* and *Staff Training and Education Bulletin*, circulars, leaflets, and perhaps most important, the annual Prospectus, which is a summary of the provisions of the Department for long term courses, correspondence courses, syllabuses (61 in 1969), regulations regarding certificate and diploma courses, arrangements for examinations.

(b) *Planning:* It prepares schemes, some long term, others short, for the education of adult members and youth and for the education and training of various classes of employees. Many of these plans require the direct and active participation of local societies for success. Class work, for instance, is the essential base of educational activities. The Department provides syllabuses, conducts examinations, grants certificates and scholarships, assists teachers, and prepares text-books for such classes, but the work of forming classes is inescapably that of the local societies. The plans often, however, involve the Department in more direct participation.

(c) *Preparing Material For Study.* The Department, often together with the Publications Department of the Union, prepares and supplies study material such as text books, study outlines, and discussion guides. These cover topics for both employee and member education and are supplemented by various visual and other aids as films and film strips, tape recordings, etc.

(d) *Teaching.* The Department is a teaching body, and not only for the College which we have described earlier. It also teaches through Summer Schools and correspondence courses. It provides postal tuition for students unable to attend a local class, generally because no local classes in the subjects are available. These correspondence courses are not only invaluable to students, they also provide valuable first-hand information to the Department on the capacities and difficulties of students. Since these students are in all parts of the British Isles, the information and experience relating to these students is broader than could be obtained from any single locality. Its Summer Schools are held for employees, officials, board members, advanced students, teachers, members and youth, and both short and long term residential courses are all run at the Co-operative College, Stanford Hall.

(e) *Examination.* The Department is an examining body and examination papers are set in practically all subjects in the Department's Prospectus. Nearly 4,000 papers were submitted for examination in 1969, a creditable achievement for the students concerned inasmuch as they worked through their postal tuition or class subjects, very often in their own time. Paper qualifications, which are statements of examination successes, have their limitations, but they are indicative of personal qualities not without value in the business world, viz., farsightedness in seeing the need to equip oneself to take advantage of future opportunities, enterprise in undertaking a course of studies, and resolution and tenacity in completing it. Examinations are a more effective control of subjects studied and standards set than are syllabuses or class inspections, and as an examining body the Union is able to exercise some control in these vitally important matters.

(f) *Research.* A good deal of research is always being undertaken by the Department's staff, in relation to the educational and youth problems of the Movement and also into the wide range of subjects covered by its activities. This is necessary to improve its courses and to keep them up to date with changing circumstances and needs, new techniques, new theories, new knowledge, and developments in the Co-operative Movement and outside it. In addition, it undertakes or sponsors research into specific problems or matters of general concern to the Movement which are unlikely to be undertaken by the departments of the Union or the Wholesale Societies. The results of such research projects are often published in "The Co-operative College Papers."

THE CO-OPERATIVE PARTY

Earlier chapters have described the growth and changes in the constitution of the Co-operative Party. It is led and governed by a National Executive Committee, whose objects are defined by the constitution of the Party as " to secure direct co-operative representation in Parliament and on local and other administrative bodies in accordance with the decisions of the Co-operative Congress; and to undertake, in furtherance of these objects, such propaganda or other work, either alone or in co-operation with other committees or organisations, as may be desirable with a view to the establishment of a Co-operative Commonwealth."

The National Executive Committee is a committee of the Co-operative Union and is responsible to the Central Executive and through it to Congress. It consists of one member elected from each Section (including the Metropolitan area), totalling eight, by contributing societies or Society Parties, one member from the C.W.S., one from the S.C.W.S., one from the Co-operative Press, two from the Central Executive, and not more than two co-opted members from the Guilds and the C.P.F. Two of the Parliamentary Group (Co-operative M.P.'s) usually attend as observers.

Thus the National Executive Committee is so constituted that almost every important section of the Co-operative Movement is represented on it. Each member of the National Executive Committee must sign a formal declaration asserting belief in the Co-operative Commonwealth and agreeing to accept the programme, policy and constitution of the Co-operative Party, and that he is not a member of any political organisation which sponsors or supports parliamentary or local government candidates in opposition to the candidates either of the Co-operative Party or any other party with which it has an electoral agreement.

The functions of the National Executive Committee are those which the national organisation of any political party undertakes, viz., preparation and statements of policy, advice and help to local organisations, propaganda and education, administration of

Party funds, selection of parliamentary candidates, the convening of an annual conference. In addition there is the undertaking of such other work as may be remitted to it by the Central Executive of the Union, the submission of a report on its work during the year to the Central Executive for inclusion in the Congress Report, and the framing and submission of resolutions for consideration by the Central Executive of the Union as to whether such resolutions shall be submitted to Congress. If agreement cannot be reached, there is provision to refer the matter to a Joint Committee which would have the power to decide whether and in what form a resolution should be submitted to Congress.

It will be gathered that the Movement as a whole through the organisation of the Co-operative Union has effective control over the Party. This is strengthened by other factors. The National Executive Committee must submit its minutes to the Central Executive, the National Executive Committee is responsible to the Central Executive and to Congress for the use of the Co-operative Party Fund, the staff of the Party is appointed by the Central Executive in consultation with the National Executive Committee of the Co-operative Party.

The Annual Conference is usually held at Easter. It consists of representatives of societies subscribing to the national funds of the Co-operative Party, society co-operative parties, voluntary parties and party federations. An Annual Report is prepared by the National Executive Committee and consideration of this, with statements of policy, special reports and motions submitted by organisations entitled to be represented composes the business of the Conference.

The Co-operative Party Conference has no authoritative powers. Resolutions passed by it do not bind or commit the Co-operative Movement or even the Co-operative Party. This is not undemocratic, for the Conference is not representative of the Movement. Moreover, it is unwise for any political party to be subject to and bound by the decisions of such conferences.

A famous authority on democratic government explained this as follows, in every party there are zealots " who care more for the principles or aims of the party than for immediate victory. These are the men who do the unpaid work in the constituencies and keep the local party machinery going. They summon the meetings of associations and generally carry their resolutions in the local meetings of the party which are attended by its more ardent members. Their enthusiasm, often coupled with inexperience, makes them eager to go full steam ahead, and their activity often enables them to commit the party, at its larger gatherings, to a policy more extreme than is pleasing to the bulk of the members. The more prudent chiefs sometimes try to slow down the pace, but are not always able to do so in time, so it may befall that the party is officially pledged to proposals in advance not only of public opinion generally, but even of the average opinion of its own members. The result is that the moderate members drop away and may possibly drift into the opposite camp . . . party spirit often appears to be hotter, and party antagonisms more pronounced, than is really the case, for in a large nation the mass of the electors take their politics more coolly than is realised by those who derive their impressions from newspaper reports of party meetings."[1]

The determination of policy by political enthusiasts would be particularly dangerous in the Co-operative Party, for although there may be a fair unity of opinion in the Movement on matters directly affecting the Movement, it is unlikely that there will be such unity on a variety of other political issues, international affairs for instance. There would thus be a real danger of the Party splitting from or splitting the Movement. Hence the value of Congress having the last word, for this assembly is more representative of the typical co-operator, and indeed more representative of the general electorate, than any political gathering is likely to be. Moreover, Co-operative Party policy, endorsed by Congress, can be fairly claimed to be the political expression of the Co-operative Movement, otherwise such a claim would be unfounded.

The Party Conference, however, is vitally important. Political issues are examined and debated there far more thoroughly than they could be in Congress, and resolutions passed will play a part in forming opinion and giving a lead to the Movement as a whole, and they may, of course, be approved by Congress. But as with Congress and the Education Convention, it is probable that the most valuable service of the Conference is the bringing together of people actuated by similar ideals, the friendships formed, the sense of unity strengthened, the inspiration given.

WORK OF OTHER DEPARTMENTS

The historical chapters have necessarily dealt in some detail with the work of the various Co-operative Union departments.

---

[1] *Modern Democracies*, Vol. 1. Bryce.

Hence it is only necessary here to give a general summary of the work of departments which have not been described in dealing with the organisation of the Union.

Finance Department

Besides the administration of the finances of the Co-operative Union and of various " special funds," this department provides various advisory services to retail societies on financial policy, on capital accumulation and employment, loans, interest rates, depreciation, liquidity, development projects.

Taxation Department

The British fiscal system has become so complicated that only experts can understand it. Moreover, each year there are fiscal changes which create new problems, not the least being the proper interpretation of the Finance Acts. As a consequence the Union, as earlier chapters showed, had to develop a specialist service to assist societies with their taxation problems.

A vast, and unique body of knowledge of retail societies' taxation problems, has been acquired by the Department as a result of its long and wide experience in computing returns and negotiating with the Inland Revenue. This is of great service to retail societies, and scores of thousands of pounds are saved to societies each year in tax repayments alone. General advice on fiscal problems is presented to all societies, and guidance on specific problems is sought by individual societies and given. Some societies place their taxation affairs in the hands of the Department.

Legal Department

With activities as wide and numerous as those of the Co-operative Movement, legislation affects it at numerous points. A retail society, for instance, is involved in legal relations with its members as members, embodied in the Industrial and Provident Societies Acts, but these by no means cover all its legal obligations. It is involved in all those of a trader, buying and selling, and so affected by the huge body of commercial law. It is also an employer of labour, and subject to all the law governing the employment of labour. It is often a landlord, and sometimes a tenant, affected by the laws related to Property, Landlord and Tenant. It is involved in road transport, it has innumerable relations and contacts with the public, and so is affected by all the laws relating thereto.

No co-operative official could possibly have the knowledge and grasp of all the laws related to his society's activities. He needs a general knowledge sufficient to make him aware when a legal problem is involved and an understanding to induce him to seek legal advice.

The Co-operative Union provides such advice. More so even than with other departments (for the Union's earliest work was with legal problems) long experience has accumulated a vast specialist knowledge of the legal problems of retail societies. It also retains the services of a firm of solicitors in Manchester, and of another in Glasgow because of the differences in Scottish and English law. The Department is responsible for the framing of the Model Rules and also is required to give advice on partial or complete amendments of rules, the interpretation of rules, the transfers of engagements and amalgamations.

Editorial Department

This department is responsible for the publication of the *Co-operative Review*, the official organ of the Union, and a wide range of other publications, reports, pamphlets and books, including the *Co-operative Gazette* and *Co-operative Directory*. The *Gazette* is published about once a week and is an invaluable source of information for societies' officials, mainly on trading matters; and most of the textbooks on co-operative subjects, including this book, have been produced by the Editorial Department.

The Department also publishes the Congress Report and the ancillary Congress literature.

Press relations are also maintained by the Editorial Department, answering inquiries from the national Press, circulating information to newspapers and news agencies, and keeping in touch with national and local references to the Movement. This entails the scrutiny of about 25,000 newspaper clippings each year.

Publications Department

The Publications Department sells books, pamphlets, stationery and other material. The books and pamphlets include not only co-operative publications but also many from outside publishers, and are sold to co-operative societies, educational establishments, students, libraries and the general public.

Most of the stationery produced by the department is for use by co-operative societies in their everyday work. Examples are hire purchase agreement forms and repayment books, log sheets for transport departments, and contracts of employment. Stationery is also produced for students in co-operative classes.

The Department organises the awards scheme for the best retail co-operative publicity of the year. The Union's Advertising Awards are aimed at improving the standard of co-operative publicity. Besides awarding diplomas for the best individual entries, the Union presents a challenge trophy to the society submitting the best batch of entries.

Statistical Department

The prime task of this Department is the compilation of the Annual Co-operative Statistics, which are invaluable, even indispensable, to any serious student of the Co-operative Movement. Published annually they give the figures of membership, analyses of capital liabilities and assets, number of employees, amount of sales, productions, interest, net surplus, average rate of dividend, grants for education of every retail society in the country, and of all other societies which are members of the Co-operative Union.

Moreover, these statistics are grouped in Regions and in Sections, totals for each of these being given and brought together in Sectional and National tables of totals and averages in the Summary of Co-operative Statistics. Necessary comparisons are thus made possible, societies can compare their contemporary position in regard to capital, reserves, trade, surplus, etc., with those of other societies in their Region or Section, or with those of a similar size, they can make comparisons with the past and so discover trends in their own and other societies and they can consider whether the position of their own society and its trends are satisfactory or not.

On a Sectional or National level any rational discussion of the Movement's business problems would be impossible without this data. The compilation, however, is a formidable task, involving the scrutiny and analysis of every balance sheet of every society. Apart from the figures of Regional and Sectional totals and education grants, this results in at least 29,000 items being given.

The Department provides essential information for every other Union department, and for the work of every Union committee. For these purposes other important statistics are compiled, many too confidential for publication, but which are necessary for the knowledge and understanding on which advice to individual societies and to the Movement as a whole is given. Figures for departmental trade, wages cost per £ of sales, average sales per employee and the relationship of stock to sales, for instance, are found, involving monthly schemes of departmental sales, stocks and credit trade. Special research schemes and surveys, costing schemes and the analysis of departmental accounts for individual societies are also undertaken. Statistics issued by other bodies, e.g., Census of Distribution, are also considered, interpreted and their bearing on co-operative matters decided.

CONCLUSION

From the above description the organisation and work of the Co-operative Union may appear complicated, as indeed they are. When however the scope and increasing variety of the functions it performs and the variety of organisations and interests which need to be represented or consulted are considered, complication will be seen to be inevitable. Efficiency is not necessarily improved by simplification, the higher organisms are much more complicated than the lower.

The efficiency of the Co-operative Union is shown in its effectiveness in fulfilling the will of its members. This requires democratic machinery to ascertain that will and to ensure it is carried out. As the quotation which heads this chapter states, complicated administrative machinery is the inevitable result. Moreover, as the Movement grows the demands upon the Co-operative Union will increase and its machinery become still more complicated. Administration only remains simple if an organisation is lifeless, whereas increasing complication is a consequence and is significant of growth.

AGRICULTURAL CO-OPERATION

" Feed and fertiliser business, cattle marketing and egg packing are in themselves rather uninspiring things . . . what Co-operation must do is to associate spiritual and mental values with the provision of material necessities."

Professor C. R. Fay.

" It is not enough to organise farmers in a district for one purpose only . . . in a credit society, a dairy society, a fruit society, a bacon factory or a co-operative store. All these may be and must be beginnings; but if they do not develop and absorb all rural business into their organisation they will have little effect on character. The specialised society only affects economic efficiency. The evolution of humanity beyond its present level depends absolutely on its power to unite and create true social organisms."

G. W. Russell.

INTRODUCTION

SO far co-operative organisations which compose the British Co-operative Movement, i.e., pursue a common ideal and are parts of an historical process beginning with Owenism have been considered. These do not, however, include all the agricultural societies, most of which, although undoubtedly co-operative and having relations with organisations of the Co-operative Movement, are not inspired by the same social ideals whose common pursuit made these co-operative organisations into a social movement, the British Co-operative Movement.

This has not been due to any lack of interest in or concern with agriculture by the British Co-operative Movement. Co-operation in agriculture was part of Owen's scheme. The most successful attempt to establish an Owenite Community was at Ralahine, an Irish peasant village, in 1831, the story of which was written by its secretary E. T. Craig and published in the 'eighties as throwing light upon the Irish land and labour question, and suggesting a solution—co-operative farming.

Other Owenites, Dr. King, the Rochdale Pioneers, the Redemptionists also looked to the acquiring of land for the practice of co-operative agriculture. Attempts continued to be made, including the Jumbo Farm, near Oldham, founded in 1851 and continuing for 10 years, during which it also served as a place for meetings and for co-operative festivals and gatherings of co-operators from the Oldham, Middleton and Rochdale districts, and which played some part in the origins of the C.W.S.

Co-operative agriculture was the subject of papers, discussions and resolutions at Co-operative Congresses, but all this produced very little. Even today almost the only substantial undertakings by co-operative enterprise in the actual running of farms in Great Britain are those of consumer Co-operation, i.e., of the wholesale and retail societies. The C.W.S. is one of the largest farmers and fruit growers in Great Britain; in 1958 farming 34,000 acres. Forty-nine retail societies farmed 24,708 acres. What is generally referred to as Agricultural Co-operation is not Co-operation in agriculture, but the co-operation of agriculturists in undertaking for themselves services, such as provision of credit, supply of requisites, marketing of produce, which had either been disintegrated or were in course of disintegration, from agriculture proper.

THE NEED FOR AGRICULTURAL CO-OPERATION

In most countries the typical peasant holding is very small. Generally, both in Great Britain and abroad, the typical farm is the family farm, that is a farm depending for its labour principally upon that of the farmer and his family. There are, of course, farms which employ many workers, but the number of wage earners employed has tended to decrease, in Great Britain, from 849,000 in June, 1948, to 672,000 in June, 1959. In other parts of the world, typical holdings are much smaller and so is the proportion of hired workers.

The family farm's continued existence is due to the farmer and his family being more careful and conscientious than is hired labour, ready to work harder and longer, or at any time required. There are, however, also disadvantages. The farmer's income may be derived from the sale of one or two crops in the year, and these may fail due to pests, disease, drought, flood, and frost. Prices may fall, and his income suffer due to nature being too bountiful and his markets glutted. Also he has often insufficient capital to farm efficiently, and without economic reserves a bad year may plunge him into hopeless indebtedness.

Also, although agricultural operations may be more economically performed on a small scale, this may not be true of many of the associated services. The production of some of the requisites of farming such as seed, fertilisers, petroleum, machinery, needs to be on a large scale, so does the marketing of the products and the processes preparatory to marketing, such as the grading of eggs, the canning of fruit, the making of butter or cheese or the curing of bacon.

These problems have been met by developments of the capitalist system. The prospects of profit have induced merchants to provide the farmers' requisites, buying on a large scale and selling on a small to the individual cultivators, purchasing the small individual harvests or products of small farmers, and bulking them for sale, often for export. Factories and packing stations may be established on a large scale to perform the preparatory processes, their raw material being the product of numerous small farmers. Credit is provided by merchants and moneylenders.

These developments have not provided a satisfactory solution. Sometimes they have resulted in swarms of middlemen, agents, dealers, speculators, all taking profits and adding to the price the final consumer must pay, often very much higher than the primary producer received. In time of war such systems cannot be tolerated, countries cannot afford the wastage of resources involved, nor dare risk the discontent arising from profit-making enterprise taking advantage of the opportunities provided to extort profit from consumers.

Whilst consumers are exploited at one end of the chain of distribution, however, the primary producer is exploited at the other. The more dependent he becomes on others to provide the requisites of production and to find a market for his product, the weaker his position and often the worse his condition becomes. He is in an inferior bargaining position to those from whom he buys and to whom he sells. In each case he is dealing in small quantities with those who are dealing in large. It matters little to the big merchant whether or not he buys the produce of any individual farmer, it may be a matter of survival to the farmer that he sells. In some instances, one merchant is not only the one buyer and seller, but the local moneylender as well.

Nominally, the farmer is independent, owns his own land and the other instruments of production and employs himself and his family. Actually he may be heavily in debt, paying extortionate rates of interest on loans, paying extortionate prices for goods, cheated in both purchase and sale by false weight and measure, beaten down to a miserable price for his produce.

Such evils are more prevalent and obvious in countries other than Great Britain. The typical British farmer is in a bigger way of business than is the typical peasant overseas, he is in the midst of the best market for agricultural produce in the world, he enjoys facilities of transport and communication which lessen his dependence on any one buyer or seller. His credit needs, except perhaps in the case of the very small man, are met readily and cheaply through an efficient banking system and a comparatively abundant supply of capital, and there is always the opportunity to escape to urban life and employment. Nevertheless, although in smaller measure and of less seriousness, the same evils exist.

AGRICULTURAL CO-OPERATION

Co-operation provides solutions to the problems facing the farmer and governments of many countries are seeking to promote agricultural co-operation. The United Nations Conference on Food and Agriculture in 1943, recognised its importance in improving the lot of people engaged in agriculture, in increasing production and in lowering the costs of distribution.

By co-operating, individual farmers can obtain capital and credit easier and cheaper, they can perform for themselves those functions which require to be performed on a large scale. " Self help by mutual aid," enables them to retain control over activities associated with agriculture, which otherwise are undertaken by others who are thereby in a position to exploit them.

Agricultural co-operation has been exceptionally prolific in the forms of society it has engendered. The principal purposes for which they have been established are, the provision of credit; the supply of requisites of farming, this involving their co-operative purchase or production; the marketing of the products of the members, sometimes involving processing; insurance; the holding of pools of machinery, transport and implements, for individual use; irrigation and electrification, education and research. Some societies perform more than one function, some perform most, so that classification of societies by function becomes difficult and can be misleading.

AGRICULTURAL CO-OPERATIVE CREDIT
SOCIETIES

The agricultural credit society is the most numerous form in the world. All are derived from the original Raiffeisen system, although there have been many variants, not always improvements. F. W. Raiffeisen, a German burgomaster, originated the first society at Flammersfeld in 1849. His ultimate aim was to raise the moral stature of the peasant. At the time the peasantry were demoralised. He believed this demoralisation was due to the hopeless indebtedness in which they were sunk, and his societies were established to free the peasant from such indebtedness.

Peasant indebtedness is world wide and reaches back to ancient times, the Old Testament gives evidence of its existence and recognises its evil. This indebtedness may be due to improvidence, or to misfortune. But apart from misfortune, the normal needs and circumstances of agriculturists also create a need for credit. Raiffeisen's remedy was to free the peasants from indebtedness. If a small number of them formed an association, this would be able to borrow as an association in order to lend to the individual members. The aggregate credit needs of the members would constitute a sum which would make such a loan attractive business to reputable banks, the security for the loan would be the entire property of the members. Credit however is only maintained if promises to pay are met, so that the success of a credit association depended on its punctual repayment of loans. This required that the loans of the association to individual members were also punctually repaid. If they were to be repaid they must be good loans, so the essential features of the Raiffeisen system were to ensure that only good loans were made.

Associations must be so small that each member had a good knowledge of the character and prospects of every other member, democratically elected and responsible committees would manage and supervise, there must be guarantors for each loan made, and the purpose of a loan must be stated and approved. Each member was also subject to unlimited liability for the society's debts; this stimulated care in electing the right committeemen and in granting loans and in supervising their use.

The Raiffeisen system would allow loans only for productive purposes, for these would provide the means to redeem the debt incurred, loans for other purposes would add to the peasant's burden of indebtedness without increasing his capacity to bear it. Good credit rather than cheap credit was desired. Originally there was no share capital, but a law of 1889 compelled them to have it. The associations were non-profit making. All surpluses were put to reserves, and reserves never shared out even if the association were dissolved.

Credit societies of the Raiffeisen type were established in Europe and Asia before 1914, and are found in most agricultural countries. In 1961 the International Co-operative Alliance estimated there were 280,000 credit societies with 40 million members in the world, the bulk being in India and Pakistan, but the movement was as well established in countries with smaller populations, such as France, Austria, Ceylon, and Finland. They

have played a minor part in the British Isles for, apart from
Ireland, the circumstances favouring their establishment were
absent.

Comparison with Rochdale Co-operation reveals some similar
features. There is the common feature of all co-operative societies,
that is the association of the users of a service to supply that
service for their own benefit. Rochdale societies are associations
of consumers, run for the benefit of consumers, not of suppliers.
The credit society is an association of borrowers run for the
benefit of borrowers, not of moneylenders. As it does not distribute any surplus it is non-profit making—so that credit societies
as well as societies on the Rochdale system are non-profit making
enterprises. Both are democratically controlled, both are non-
profit making and membership is voluntary. A co-operative
credit society thus embodies the fundamental Rochdale Principles.

Some people find the existence of a credit society a contradiction
of the Rochdale principle of No Credit, but if the purpose of the
Rochdale principle and of the credit society are examined, so
far from a contradiction a similarity of aim is apparent. The
Rochdale principle was intended to promote thrift and free its
members from indebtedness, the Raiffeisen society has the same
objectives, and is equally resolute in refusing credit for purposes
of consumption.

CO-OPERATIVE REQUISITE OR SUPPLY SOCIETIES

The co-operation of agriculturists to supply themselves with
the requisites of production offers similar advantages to those
offered to final consumers by retail co-operative societies.
Merchants, of course, have undertaken to provide these requisites,
but not always to the satisfaction of the user. By co-operation
not only are the users able to undertake these services for themselves and so keep the merchants' hands out of their pockets,
but they are able to control quality, and quality of seed or
fertiliser is much more important to the user than it is to the
merchant.

In some cases, these societies have proceeded to produce
requisites for themselves, extending to sources of supply as consumers' societies have done.

The societies are run on similar lines to consumers' societies,
although a low price policy is more attractive to the farmer than
is dividend on purchases, and since the trade is in productive
goods, credit facilities are more necessary. Moreover, their trade
is of a more specialised type and with a narrower range than that

of final consumers' societies so that the risks of loss through price fluctuations are greater and so therefore is the need to build up strong reserves.

CO-OPERATIVE MARKETING SOCIETIES

Marketing societies are established so that producers can undertake the marketing of their own produce. It is generally beyond the capacity of the individual producer to do this as there are generally preparatory processes, or transport and handling, for instance, when the markets are far distant, which require it to be done on a large scale. A number of small producers may associate and form a marketing society which by handling their combined produce can operate on an economical scale. Federations of such societies may be large enough to undertake the largest scale operations, such as export with depots and sales campaigns in other countries.

By so doing they by-pass the profit-seeking middlemen, eliminate much competitive muddle and waste, and often not only benefit the producer by obtaining better prices and creating more reliable markets, but also benefit the consumer by improved quality grading, improved packing, giving a more reliable supply and lowering prices. Advances on produce received but awaiting sale may also be made, thus meeting some of the producers' credit needs. The lower prices to consumers and the higher prices to producers are made possible by the elimination of the waste in capitalist distribution.

These societies also operate on the approved co-operative principles. They are run, of course, in the interests of those who use their services, i.e., the producers. In their cases, therefore, surpluses are not divided in proportion to purchases but in proportion to the value of the produce they have delivered to the society. This accords with the Rochdale principle of division of the surplus between the members in proportion to their transactions with the society.

Consumers, however, have some fear that the interests of consumers and producers may conflict, that producers through the development of marketing societies into international organisations could create monopolies and pursue monopolist policies to the detriment of the consumer. This fear of monopolies is shown by the Co-operative Union statements on Agricultural Marketing Policy 1952, and on Co-operative Policy on the Agricultural Marketing Acts, 1958.

The above are the main types of co-operative societies of agriculturists. As pointed out earlier, large numbers of societies are not satisfactorily placed in these classifications for they may perform more than one function, one society may provide credit, supply requisites, market produce, and engage in other activities also. Circumstances generally determine whether the multi-purpose or the specialised society is preferred, though it may be significant that Denmark, famous for the success and efficiency of co-operative marketing, has a preference for the specialised society.

DIFFICULTIES IN GREAT BRITAIN

There were few attempts at co-operation by agriculturists in England during the nineteenth century. One reason was that no idealist appeared capable of inspiring English farmers. This, however, would have been difficult as the English agricultural system was not conducive to co-operation. Landowners often supplied much of the capital and not a little of the brains and the enterprise, but their tenant farmers were generally not in a position to dare to promote or adopt developments disagreeable to their landlords, although there were landlords favourable to agricultural co-operation.

Nor did they constitute a social class, for they varied considerably in status and resources, from the gentleman farmer down to the small self-employed man scratching a bare living from a few acres. Rarely were there communities of small producers producing the same product, with consequent common interests in marketing and supply, strong and obvious enough to induce them to organise for mutual aid. Homogeneity of interest, indispensable to co-operation, was lacking. Also, as Professor Clapham suggested in his *Economic History of Modern Britain*, the differences in status and resources favoured the English individualist temper and snob tradition, and the man whose main aim was to climb a status higher was unlikely to make a good co-operator. There was, in short, no homogeneous group in which individuals indentified the good of their fellows with that of their own.

THE IRISH MOVEMENT

Circumstances were different in Ireland. This was a country of small peasants, bound together by common grievances agains absentee landlords and a strong desire for Irish national independence. The Great Agricultural Depression which afflicted British agriculture in general during the last quarter of the nineteenth century had created a strong opinion that the large-scale farm was a mistake and that small holdings should be encouraged. This was easier done in Ireland than in England, and legislation

o

in 1895 and 1903 converted Ireland from a country of peasant tenants to one of peasant proprietors.

Landlordism, however, was only one of the evils afflicting the Irish peasant; he was heavily in debt, exploited by merchant moneylenders, and suffered from the lack of an efficient marketing system and the inefficiency of his own farming methods. The only means of improving his condition was co-operation. Whilst he remained an individualist, freedom and competence were beyond his reach.

Circumstances, however, in themselves do not create movements. These require men not only capable of analysing the problems presented by circumstances and realising what is needed to solve them, but also capable of making others aware and inspiring them to make the necessary efforts. Horace Plunkett was such a man. He had been interested in Co-operation when young, establishing a village retail society, the Dunsany Co-operative Society in 1878. After a period of ranching in the U.S.A., he returned to Ireland in 1889. He had long been impressed by what working people had accomplished by Co-operation in Great Britain and believed that it could also be the answer to many of Ireland's troubles.

In 1888, arising from an Irish Exhibition in London, the Irish Co-operative Aid Association was formed, supported by some British co-operators, notably E. V. Neale. Plunkett joined this and became its leading figure. The support of the Co-operative Union was gained, and after visits to Ireland by J. C. Gray, an Irish Section of the Co-operative Union was formed, Plunkett was its chairman and R. A. Anderson its secretary.

Co-operative Creameries

The C.W.S. had been buying butter from Ireland for a generation. New methods of butter making had been introduced in Denmark, however, and Danish butter was driving Irish out of the market. All the C.W.S. buyers in Ireland were instructed to advise the Irish to adopt the Danish method. This meant creameries. In Denmark many of the creameries were co-operative, owned and controlled by the farmers. Some, among them Plunkett, saw the possibility of developing Co-operation in Ireland through the establishment of co-operative creameries, and the task of persuading Irish farmers to get together for the purpose was undertaken. The first was started in 1889 at Drumcollogher. Its rules were drawn up by J. C. Gray of the Co-operative Union, among its promotors was W. L. Stokes, the C.W.S. butter buyer at Limerick, and the C.W.S. took up some shares in this and similar undertakings. During the next five years 50 creameries, 10 requisite societies and a credit society were established.

Opposition from business interests and from various movements in the tangled web of Irish political and social life was encountered, but the most serious difficulties were the ignorance, timidity, hopelessness and mutual suspicions of the farmers themselves. The task began to outrun the resources of Plunkett and his supporters. An advisory and propagandist body was necessary, so the Irish Agricultural Organisation Society was founded as such in 1894. Plunkett was its chairman and R. A. Anderson, also secretary of the Irish Section of the Co-operative Union, was its secretary. The agricultural societies were too poor to finance it, it had to be supported by Plunkett's generosity, private subscriptions, and later by government grants.

Dispute with the C.W.S.

Trouble arose when the C.W.S. took over a co-operative creamery at Castlemahan, which was in serious financial difficulties. Its members were split by political quarrels which resulted in some refusing to send their milk to the creamery, and the creamery was on the point of being sold to a private firm. The matter was raised at the Co-operative Congress of 1894, and the action of the C.W.S. tacitly upheld. It was discussed again as part of a wider question raised in a resolution moved by Plunkett at the Congress of 1895. This resolution expressed the opinion that the acquisition or establishment of creameries in Ireland by the C.W.S. would " largely destroy the work of the Irish Section, which has succeeded in organising farm workers and farm labourers in co-operative societies to conduct the business on the lines advocated by the Co-operative Movement."

There was a heated debate, for the issues at stake were of principle, of the right of the consumer to organise and control the production of goods for his consumption, and in this case whether the C.W.S., the consumers' organisation, had the right to own creameries to serve its own members. On the other hand, Plunkett feared that C.W.S. creameries would prevent the development of the type of Co-operation which he believed was most needed in Ireland. It was not simply a question of prices and division of profits. Plunkett, in common with co-operators such as Owen, King, the Christian Socialists, Raiffeisen, believed that the practice of Co-operation developed desirable moral qualities. As C.W.S. creameries did not involve the farmers in a co-operative relationship they would not promote those desirable qualities. The Irish farmer looked solely to the price he would get for his milk, and nothing else; he had no idea of accepting any responsibility, or showing any mutual trust in the principles co-operators spend their lives in advocating. If the C.W.S. persisted, Co-operation in Ireland would be stamped out.

To the suggestion that farmers had abandoned the idea of forming a society and preferred to deal with a C.W.S. creamery he replied: " The people would always abandon an idea if they could get out of the trouble of doing the thing for themselves. If anyone else would do it, they would give up Co-operation."

The Irish Section thereafter met but once, to dissolve itself " in view of the apparent approval by Congress of the action of the Wholesale."

Numerous creameries were established in Ireland, many by private firms, but only those of the C.W.S. were attacked by the I.A.O.S. as organisations exploiting the Irish farmer. Friction continued, as did losses by the C.W.S., which failed to dispose of all the creameries in a complete transfer in negotiations with the I.A.O.S. in 1904 and 1907. So the C.W.S. proceeded to dispose of them one by one. Preference was given to I.A.O.S. societies, but by the end of 1912 when most had been sold, of the 34 main creameries and 51 auxiliaries which had passed out of C.W.S. hands, about one-third only went to various kinds of agricultural co-operative societies. The rest went to private firms.

The I.C.A.S.

Another co-operative organisation had been founded in 1892, The Irish Co-operative Agency Society, a federation of co-operative creameries to market their butter. It opened offices in Manchester to deal directly with British retail societies, and so overlapped with the C.W.S. Just as the full benefits of co-operative wholesale buying depend upon the loyalty of retail societies, so also do those of co-operative federal marketing depend upon the loyalty of the producing societies. In each case trouble arose in the early days through the unwillingness of societies' officials to use the federal services. The I.C.A.S. was handicapped by the disloyalty of the creamery societies; they only made use of the Agency if they could not sell their butter otherwise. The creamery managers also fancied their skill in salesmanship and feared centralised selling would make their skill redundant. The root difficulty, of course, was in trying to manage co-operative business with private business mentality. Other forms of Co-operation have met this same difficulty.

The conflict of interests, as seen, came to a head in the Congress of 1895, when Plunkett failed to persuade it to agree to his views, and the Irish Sectional Board resigned, resulting in the dissolution of the Irish Section. The I.A.O.S., however, continued, and widened its activities, engaging a staff of accountants to audit societies' accounts and providing technical advice. A weekly journal, *The Irish Homestead*, started publication in 1895. Its editor, writing as A.E., was George William Russell, a well known poet and artist. The journal exercised a good deal of influence not confined to Ireland, for it gave not only technical advice, often of temporary value and narrow interest, but also philosophical reflections on the meaning and purpose of Co-operation and idealistic visions which were limited neither by time, country nor form of organisation. In common with other great co-operators, Owen, King, the Christian Socialists, Raiffeisen, he regarded the ultimate purpose of Co-operation to be the improvement of character.

The development of supply societies soon brought realisation of the need for a federal wholesale. For a time the I.C.A.S. served, then in 1897 a separate agency was set up and this was transformed into the Irish Agricultural Society in 1898. It was handicapped by lack of capital and loyalty, but achieved good work in breaking manufacturers' rings in machinery and fertilisers and in improving the reliability of seed. Its testing and certification of seed compelled private merchants to do likewise.

By 1900 the main outlines of development were clear. Co-operative marketing was extended from creameries to eggs and poultry, cattle marketing, bacon factories and slaughter-houses. Supply societies extended their range of trade to include all manner of machines, plant and equipment, tools, fertilisers, insecticides, feeds, etc. Unsuccessful attempts to start cottage industries in embroidery, knitting, and lace making were made. All in all, Co-operation made a good contribution to Irish rural life. What could be done was demonstrated at Templecrone in Donegal, vividly described in *My Story* by "Paddy the Cope," although the core of the movement which revolutionised this village was a retail society, helped by the S.C.W.S., along with the propaganda of Russell.

The early history of agricultural Co-operation in Ireland is described because it was a starting point of an agricultural Co-operative Movement in the United Kingdom, and indeed its influence was even more widespread. Ireland was a demonstration centre of a co-operative way of dealing with a world-wide problem, that of maintaining a rural way of life and culture whilst agriculture was being transformed by industrial and commercial revolution. And the problem of agricultural producer and consumer relations also emerged.

EARLY GROWTH IN ENGLAND

In England, for reasons already given, little progress was made. E. O. Greening's Agricultural and Horticultural Association, founded in 1868, continued to be engaged in propaganda for agricultural Co-operation and in some business by supplying agricultural requisites to its members. But in 1900 there were only 19 societies with 4,814 members, and a trade of £121,416, plus some enterprises with co-operative rules although registered as companies. In that year, however, W. L. Charleton of Newark founded the British Agricultural Organisation Society. In 1901, it changed its name to the Agricultural Organisation Society, had headquarters in London and modelled itself on the I.A.O.S. The Co-operative Union subscribed to it, and had two representatives on its Board of Governors. The Congress of 1904 expressed approval of its aims and activities.

Requisite societies grew most rapidly and they soon outnumbered all other types. By 1914 there were 274 requisite societies with a membership of 30,000 and 129 marketing societies with 10,000 members. Attempts were made to promote intertrading between the consumer and the agricultural Movements. In 1906, a joint committee representative of the Co-operative Union, the C.W.S., the A.O.S., the I.A.O.S., and the Scottish A.O.S. (Scotland formed its own organisation in 1905) was set up for the purpose of arranging conferences and promoting intertrading, and efforts continued to be made until 1919.

The agricultural societies and the C.W.S. could not agree upon the conditions of inter-trading; on how free should the C.W.S. be to buy from others, whether the C.W.S. should provide them with a guaranteed market; what guarantees of qualities, prices and supplies it was reasonable for the C.W.S. to demand. The Co-operative Union General Survey Committee's principal recommendations regarding agriculture were that the Wholesale Societies should increase their farming and that there should be a development of inter-trading between the consumer and agricultural Movements on a world-wide scale.

INTER-WAR DIFFICULTIES

The post-war slump beginning in 1920 resulted in severe losses and depression in agriculture, and government economies. These put the A.O.S. into financial difficulties. The society was dependent partly upon subscriptions from its affiliated societies and partly upon government grants. Financial independence often proves best in the long run, dependence upon grants may lead to developments and commitments which may be ruinous if the grants are withdrawn. This was the experience of the A.O.S. As the amounts granted were cut down from time to time and eventually withdrawn the members did not welcome the increase in subscriptions thereby made necessary and the A.O.S. was dissolved in 1924. In the same year the Agricultural Wholesale Society was also brought to an end. This had originated from a trading advisory committee of the A.O.S., it undertook wholesale trading in 1905, became the Farmers' Central Trading Board in 1912 and transformed itself into the Agricultural Wholesale Society in 1918. It was never very successful; losses between £50,000 and £60,000 a year were suffered for five years. It was unfortunate in being caught by the 1922 slump so soon after its establishment.

The Consumer Movement then attempted to meet the difficulties in which the agricultural societies were placed. The C.W.S. developed its agricultural department for the supply of agricultural requisites and also assisted many agricultural societies by trading and other credits and by improving their accounts and business methods. Appreciation of the assistance given was expressed in the Year Book of Agricultural Co-operation 1943-1944, which stated that the far-reaching activities of the C.W.S. had made possible the abundant supply of agricultural requisites to the agricultural societies " which before the war provided an abundant alternative supply of artificial manures and feeding stuffs. This supply is an example of true Co-operation and has been of the greatest possible assistance to the farmers' societies." It was also a safeguard against monopolistic temptations of big business.

James McFadyen, the Managing Secretary of a marketing society (and later President of Ipswich Co-operative Society, a member of the Central Board of the Co-operative Union, and a Director of the C.W.S.) writing of the difficult years in the 'twenties, found the root cause in the farmers' disloyalty to their societies. They looked on the societies as mere trading organisations, were unwilling to provide capital or trade regularly and consistently with the societies, preferring to build up a direct trade for their best produce and to dump the remainder on their societies. Loyalty is more essential to the success of marketing societies than to any other, and it is not surprising that such farmers were incapable of successfully operating them. His society suffered heavy losses, and in 1926 its reserves went. It

recovered, but would have failed to do so but for " the valuable
trading relationships with the consumers' Movement in general and
the C.W.S. in particular." Many societies had similar experiences.

Relations with the Co-operative Union

The General Survey Committee in 1920 had recommended that
the Co-operative Union establish an agricultural section. In
1924, the Linlithgow Committee, rather lukewarmly recommended
agricultural Co-operation and the establishment of trading
relations between " the industrial Co-operative Movement and
producers' co-operative organisations." Shortly afterwards, the
Ministry of Agriculture approached the Joint Parliamentary
Committee to see if it could assist the Ministry in giving effect
to the recommendations of the Linlithgow Committee. After
consideration with members of the United Board and the C.W.S.
it was decided to establish a special Agricultural Propaganda
Department of the Co-operative Union " able to spread co-
operative ideas among agriculturists, to promote the formation
of co-operative agricultural societies of different types, and
generally to do work formerly undertaken by the English Agricultural Organisation Society."

In 1925 Congress approved a resolution to establish such a
department with an Agricultural Adviser at its head. This was a
joint department with the C.W.S., until 1927, when the latter
withdrew. As previously shown this Co-operative Union department actually developed into one mainly concerned with advising
retail societies on the running of their farms and dairies and with
proposed schemes and operations of Marketing Boards. But the
first intentions were to fill partly the void created by the disappearance of the A.O.S.

The National Farmers' Union

The Ministry of Agriculture helped by instituting a Co-operation
and Markets Branch, which undertook research into Co-operation
and agricultural business, advised on projected undertakings and
occasionally made loans for marketing purposes. Many societies
sought advice from the National Farmers' Union, which had
taken over the maintenance of a register of agricultural co-
operative societies, and had " somewhat reluctantly agreed to
set up a Co-operative Committee, ready to advise, but abstaining
from propaganda." This Committee did, however, make some
useful enquiries, drew up new sets of model rules, and secured
some legislative improvements. The N.F.U. also obtained in 1928
a grant from the Government of £35,000 to assist in the settlement

of affairs of societies consequent upon the collapse of the Agricultural Wholesale Society in 1924.

When the events subsequent to the collapse of the A.O.S. are reviewed it might appear that it would have been cheaper and less troublesome for the Government to have continued its grants and kept the A.O.S. in being. On the other hand, it was questionable whether public money should be continued to be expended on services which the farmers did not value sufficiently to pay for. It even appeared that agricultural Co-operation had a stronger appeal to the consumer Co-operative Movement's idealistic sentiments than it had to farmers' or to farmers' organisations' business interests.

One body specifically concerned with agricultural Co-operation, however, remained, and this was the Horace Plunkett Foundation.[1] It was set up in 1919 " to promote the systematic study of the principles and methods of agricultural and industrial Co-operation," and became the research and information centre of the agricultural Movement. In 1928 it commenced to issue its annual *The Year Book of Agricultural Co-operation*, which is one of the best sources of information regarding agricultural Co-operation in all parts of the world.

Conference of 1930

This body in 1930 convened a conference of societies, principally concerned with the leaderless position of their Movement. Most of them were members of the N.F.U., but this gave them neither representation nor responsibility in the government of the Movement, nor any voice in formulating or even commenting upon policies affecting their own Movement. There was no promotional activity, no propaganda, no assistance to weak or new societies. A few were members of the Co-operative Union, but these felt themselves to be " submerged minorities " in their Sections. If they decided to set up an independent body, they desired to know what their relations would be with the N.F.U., and the Co-operative Union. If they did not set up an independent body they desired to improve their position in either or both of these organisations, to approach which a committee was appointed.

The Co-operative Union was willing, subject to the approval of Congress, to set up a separate Agricultural Section of the Co-operative Union, and the succeeding Bournemouth Congress agreed that this should be done when the number of affiliated societies justified the step. The N.F.U., was non-committal in response to approaches but called a conference of societies.

---

[1] Now the Plunkett Foundation for Agricultural Studies.

Terms were submitted by the N.F.U. which, although improving the position, fell a long way short of what the committee desired. So the Co-operative Union terms were recommended for acceptance.

The agricultural societies, however, were in a dilemma. On the one hand were the actual and potential services of the C.W.S. and the Co-operative Union, and the advantages of becoming part of the British Co-operative Movement. On the other there was loyalty to the N.F.U., " not unmixed with fear of its active hostility to the Co-operative Movement in the event of a breach." The second conference of societies convened to consider the Committee's report defeated its recommendation " that the terms of affiliation proposed by the Co-operative Union should be accepted as fully meeting the desires of the societies," by three votes, but more than a quarter of those present abstained from voting.

Inability of the delegates to make up their minds or lack of courage to act thereon was then shown by the passing of the companion resolution " that the terms offered by the N.F.U., although not fully meeting the requirements of the Societies should nevertheless be accepted." This was approved by less than a quarter of the delegates, the rest abstained from voting. Thus this resolution carried with less support than the one which was defeated.

Nevertheless the conferences were not without value. The N.F.U. had to attempt to justify its action or inaction regarding agricultural Co-operation and was stimulated to cultivate closer relations. The N.F.U. also was in a dilemma, for many of its members were indifferent or hostile to the Co-operative Movement.

AGRICULTURAL CO-OPERATIVE MANAGERS' ASSOCIATION

The need for an independent co-operative organisation however continued, and steps towards this were taken in 1936 by the formation of the Agricultural Co-operative Managers' Association. Its being and activities strengthened the unity of societies and also helped to make people aware that there was an agricultural Co-operative Movement. Yet it could not claim to speak for that Movement as it did not directly represent the committees or the members of the societies.

AGRICULTURAL CO-OPERATIVE ASSOCIATION

During the war, efforts were made to establish a representative central organisation and in 1944 a conference was held to discuss its formation. The old problem of relations with the N.F.U. emerged—the desire for the agricultural Co-operative Movement to have control over its own affairs balanced against the unwillingness or fear to sever the link with the N.F.U. A scheme was eventually drawn up and adopted in 1945 which established The Agricultural Co-operative Association.

All agricultural societies registered under the Industrial and Provident Societies Acts were eligible for membership, and other special organisations, concerned with the promotion of Co-operation could be admitted. The Association had five geographical regions, each of which elected four members to a Central Committee. This could add to its number by co-opting seven special members, two of whom must be members of the Co-operation Committee of the N.F.U. This Committee of the N.F.U. was also reconstituted and consisted of the members of the Central Committee of the A.C.A., three members of the Agricultural Managers' Association, eight members of the Council of the N.F.U. and two members of the Welsh Agricultural Organisation Society.

The Association was financed by subscriptions of member societies graduated on trade turnover, sufficient to make it financially independent. Nevertheless there was considerable integration with the N.F.U., shown by the composition of the Central Committee of the A.C.A., and the Co-operation Committee of the N.F.U. There was also a demarcation of functions, the A.C.A. to deal with matters of a domestic or technical character, while the N.F.U. Co-operation Committee dealt with matters of policy and questions affecting the Movement as a whole. The N.F.U. also exercised control over expenditure of funds and had some control over policy and the appointment of staff of the A.C.A.

This scheme, however, did not run smoothly. The N.F.U. made proposals which the A.C.A. was unable to accept; they indicated " a fundamental difference between the two organisations in essence." In 1954 negotiations between the two bodies came to an end.

The chairman of the A.C.A. explained the situation as follows, " The N.F.U. wish all the effective functions which A.C.A. was formed to carry out, to be assigned to an organisation whose controlling body consists half of people effectively appointed by the N.F.U., and half appointed by the societies, this body being itself at least in some measure in subordination to another body which is appointed solely by N.F.U. . . . The A.C.A. view of the N.F.U. scheme is that it necessarily involves the views of the societies on what are essentially their own affairs being swamped by the much greater weight of the N.F.U. and puts the control of agricultural Co-operation into the hands of people who, however well intentioned, have other interests to serve. The N.F.U view of the A.C.A. proposal is that it does not give the N.F.U. control of agricultural Co-operation and that they must control everything to do with agriculture."

The whole position was then aggravated by the unilateral action of the N.F.U. in setting up a Farmers' Central Organisation. Only fifty societies became members of this organisation, and the N.F.U. failed to gain and exercise the control of agricultural Co-operation which it desired.

REORGANISATION

In 1956 a new body, the Agricultural Central Co-operative Association, was registered. The Farmers' Central Organisation was wound up and the A.C.A. transferred its engagements to the A.C.C.A. This new body was essentially a compromise between the A.C.A. and the N.F.U. Although the A.C.C.A. was set up as a separate body, the N.F.U. achieved a considerable degree of control by an arrangement under which the Union, acting through the N.F.U. Development Company, appointed a third of the members of the A.C.C.A. Council and secured a third of the votes at general meetings of the Association. Over the next few years, however, the A.C.C.A. and the N.F.U. worked in fairly close harmony.

But in 1964, the A.C.C.A. Council decided that the time was ripe for an expert survey of farmers' Co-operation in England and Dr. Joseph Knapp, Administrator of the Farmer Co-operative Service of the United States Department of Agriculture, was invited to prepare a report. Among the major recommendations in that report, published in 1965, was one to reorganise the A.C.C.A. as a fully independent co-operative organisation with increased financial support from members and government financial assistance for research and education. Subsequently, in 1966, the A.C.C.A. once more became the Agricultural Co-operative Association with Council members elected exclusively by co-operatives and no nominated members. Liaison with the N.F.U. is now carried on through a Joint Committee.

New possibilities for agricultural co-operatives through government action were opened up by part of the 1967 Agricultural Act which provided for the setting up of a Central Council for Agricultural and Horticultural Co-operation, to be partly appointed by the Minister and partly selected by agricultural co-operatives and the farmers' unions throughout the U.K. This Council began work in 1967 and in time it is envisaged that it will have general oversight of agricultural co-operative development in the U.K. and that it will have the power to make grants for the development of Co-operation in marketing and production as well as for educational purposes.

WALES AND SCOTLAND

Meanwhile the agricultural organisations in Wales and Scotland had been free from many of the troubles afflicting the English Movement. The structure of agriculture was more favourable in both these countries and there was not the apathy or hostility of farmers to Co-operation. The Scottish A.O.S. was set up in 1905. It took over the Scottish National Poultry Organisation in 1907 and flourished. In 1913, however, it suffered a split, a new body, The Scottish Small Holders' Association, being formed. This set up a subsidiary " Scottish Central Marts " with its own retail shops for the sale of small-holders' produce, also a Scottish Central Land Bank and a Scottish Insurance Society for livestock.

The slump following the war of 1914–1918 put an end to Scottish Central Marts and the independent existence of the bank and insurance society. The Scottish A.O.S. survived the slump, and so did the Welsh Agricultural Organisation Society which had separated from the A.O.S. in 1922. There had been considerable independence previously so the separation was neither difficult nor unexpected. It was, however, seriously affected by the collapse of the A.O.S. and A.W.S. in 1924, not least by an increase in the distrust of central organisations.

But for the faith and tenacity of a few societies and some individual idealists, including Professor Ashby and the Department of Agricultural Economics of the Aberystwyth University College of Wales, the W.A.O.S. would have sunk. A Joint Scheme of the W.A.O.S. and the Department enabled advisory and educational services to be continued.

In the 'thirties it still struggled, assisted by some State grants, but prevented by lack of money from undertaking necessary activities. The societies continued to be in difficulties. Egg and poultry societies disappeared one by one, and rock bottom was reached in 1933. There was then a gradual improvement and during the war a rapid one. Membership, capital and trade increased, and with them the position and status of the W.A.O.S. improved.

FEDERATION OF AGRICULTURAL CO-OPERATIVES

Before the war " Round Table Meetings " were held and attended by representatives of the Agricultural Organisations of England, Wales, Scotland, Ireland, and Ulster, the N.F.U., the Agricultural Co-operative Managers' Association and the Horace Plunkett Foundation.

These were revived in 1947 and it was decided to form and register a British Isles Federation of Agricultural Co-operative Societies, which was accomplished in 1949, later assuming the title of Federation of Agricultural Co-operatives of Great Britain and Ireland. It was for mutual consultation, education and propaganda, joint action on questions affecting the Co-operative Movement and the channel for direct representation on the International Federation of Agricultural Producers.

POST-WAR PROSPERITY AND GROWTH

A common impression before the war was that agricultural Co-operation in Great Britain had failed. This was never true, although the inter-war years justified a pessimistic view of its prospects. Yet it grew and flourished after the war as never before.

Membership in England increased from 108,000 in 1946 to 301,240 in 1967 which, allowing for duplication of membership, probably means that two out of every three farmers are members of agricultural co-operatives compared with one in five in 1930 and one in two in 1946. Trade increased from £25 million in 1946 to £246 million in 1967.

Requisites (or supply) societies have always been the strongest and are still so accounting for £143 million of turnover. These societies have not confined themselves to the supply of requisites, however, but have undertaken many other services including marketing. Of their £143 million turnover in 1967 £111 million was accounted for by requisite sales, the rest was largely marketing. Nearly all the requisites societies traded in grain and potatoes, for instance, and almost a quarter of the trade in eggs was handled by these societies. Many of these societies, of which there were 70 in 1967, might be better described as multi-purpose or general purpose societies.

Conversely many marketing societies, of which there were 134, were also engaged in the selling of requisites. Out of a total turnover for marketing societies of £61 million, £4½ million was accounted for by requisite sales. By far the most important of the commodities which they marketed was eggs and poultry which accounted for £32 million of their sales. In order of importance then came deadstock (£12 million), livestock (£3 million) and wool (£2 million).

Some Problems of Growth

The size of societies increased—24 of the 70 requisite societies had 92 per cent turnover out of the £143 million total turnover of the group, and 16 societies accounted for 84 per cent of the total turnover. It is common in other parts of the world for the primary societies to be small and local in character, and for them to form federal societies to undertake activities which require a larger scale than is possible for a small society. In England this has not taken place. Some societies have grown, been enter-prising, installed plant or undertaken activities which require a larger market and have proceeded to acquire that market by extending their area of operations and increasing their member-ship.

This type of development obviously results in overlapping and competition between societies. Also it makes democratic control increasingly difficult. A large society may sprawl over several counties, members having little contact with or knowledge of each other. General meetings which even a reasonable proportion could attend without involving a fair amount of individual expense and time spent are impossible (in some instances it would involve journeys of scores or even more than 100 miles). Unless members have a strong sense of membership, of belonging to the society, they will not make the necessary efforts, and it is very unlikely that in such societies the members will have a sense of membership sufficiently strong.

The farmer member generally looks upon a society as he does upon any other business organisation, he is not loyal on principle, and thus many of the economies of Co-operation are lost, e.g., a sure market enables future operations to be safely planned to reduce waste, speculative risks are cut out, and the need for and expenses of " salesmanship " reduced. If members' loyalty can-not be relied on the society has to adopt similar methods to other business organisations to get trade, and is subject to the same speculative risks. If run with efficiency equal to that of com-petitive businesses the society will benefit the farmer member by the return to him of the profit which would otherwise have gone into a private merchant's pocket, and by providing him with a very valuable safeguard against monopolistic exploitation. But the real economic gains of Co-operation are not realised. More important, the social gains, the spiritual and mental values emphasised by Professor Fay, the prospect of which inspired the pioneers of the Movement, men like Plunkett and Russell, are completely lost.

RELATIONS WITH THE CONSUMER MOVEMENT

There have been several close contacts between the agricultural and the consumer Movement, and some important ones with the C.W.S. The C.W.S. sold various goods to the requisites societies, e.g., feeding stuffs, fertilisers, seed, amounting to about half of their requirements turnover. The C.W.S. has also bought from them such goods as home-grown grain, eggs, fruit and vegetables. Some societies have accounts with the Co-operative Bank, which not only helped many in the past financially but also with valuable advice. Some have also insured with the Co-operative Insurance Society. The C.W.S. has also joint control over and investments in a number of agricultural co-operative organisations. There was a joint committee for liaison between the C.W.S. and the Agricultural Co-operative Managers' Association, and in 1958 the Agricultural Finance Federation was set up to provide hire purchase facilities to members of agricultural co-operatives. Half the initial capital was subscribed by the C.W.S., the rest by affiliated societies.

The record of relations between the C.W.S. and the agricultural societies shows the practicability of harmonious co-existence and indeed the co-operation of producers' and consumers' organisations. Professor C. R. Fay stated, " the C.W.S. has played its part magnificently . . . the membership of the agricultural societies in the C.W.S. is not only profitable to them by way of service and dividend, but symptomatic of a better understanding in the future between the industrial and the rural population." The Co-operative Union also in several policy statements has firmly expressed itself in favour of the development of agricultural co-operative societies.

WALES AND SCOTLAND POST-WAR

In Wales also, post-war, the multi-purpose societies continued to account for the bulk (67 per cent in 1967) of the turnover, the marketing societies accounting for 30 per cent. As in England the marketing societies also generally engage to some extent in supply of requisites. Wales, however, has a less varied agriculture than England, its greater reliance on livestock makes for a greater proportionate demand for feeding stuffs, which improves the position of the requisite societies, but makes the development of co-operative marketing more difficult, since a large proportion of the produce, which is milk, is in the hands of the Milk Marketing Board. Although there are milk marketing societies in some parts of Wales, producers in other parts of Wales have not been free to emulate them.

Although trade increased as compared with pre-war, when allowance is made for price changes the trade per member had fallen by 1955–1956. It appears that there was neither the strong loyalty nor the antipathy to co-operative societies which was found in pre-war days. All farmers shared their trade with several competitors, including the societies. This was rightly regarded as showing the need for the education of members.

The agricultural movement in Scotland is primarily a marketing one in contrast to England. Over three-quarters of the nearly £65 million turnover is done in marketing. Nearly half of all the eggs packed in Scotland are co-operatively handled and there is a substantial co-operative trade in livestock and wool. The bulk of the supply business in Scotland is done by three very large societies. The crofters' societies, most similar to the peasant societies in other countries, continued to meet difficulties arising from the nature of their products, difficulties of communication and, strange in Scots, weakness in business sense and administration.

LAND SETTLEMENT ASSOCIATION

One of the most interesting experiments and developments of agricultural Co-operation in this country is that of the estates of the Land Settlement Association. Originally the scheme was introduced to enable unemployed people to become self-supporting by cultivating small holdings, a Land Settlement Association being formed for the purpose in 1934, registered under the I. & P. Acts. The Government, deciding to float the scheme more quickly and in a larger way than was likely if it depended for finance upon shareholding and charitable contributions, invited the Association to undertake 1,000 holdings for which it would provide the whole of the capital.

By 1939 a 1,000 holdings had been acquired on 14 estates in 14 counties. On these, 440 tenants had been established and another 409 were on the estates undergoing preparatory training. The outbreak of war ended the problem of unemployment, and up to the present this has not returned, so that the original purpose of the scheme is no longer relevant.

Following the Agriculture Act of 1947, the scheme was reconstructed. The estates were transferred to the Government, and the debt of the Association to the Government cancelled. At the same time the Association became the Minister's agent for the administration of the small holdings estates and for the continued provision of their centralised services. The rules of the Association were amended to give effect to new objects—to provide holdings for men with agricultural experience (recognising a change which had in fact been made during the war), to relieve the producer of the problems of management so that he is free to devote his whole time to production, to provide services that it would be uneconomical for each individual to provide for himself.

Each estate is divided into small holdings, each of which has its house and buildings, such as glass house and piggery. For these the tenant pays rent. He cultivates his holding as an individual but is subject to certain specified obligations. Most of his requisites of production must be bought from the Association and his produce must be sold through it. Thus he is under an obligation, which is enforced as a condition of tenancy, to co-operate in buying and selling. Each estate is under a manager, employed by the Association. He is responsible for the organisation of the supply of requisites and of marketing, and also gives valuable advice to the tenants.

The supply of requisites involves a good deal more than purchase and sale, for the Association produces many of these on the estates, e.g., chicks, piglets, plants. By so doing it can improve and maintain strains, prevent the introduction of disease, and provide them better and more cheaply than could the individual tenant for himself, because, producing on a larger scale, it can use equipment out of the reach of the individual small producer and employ experts. The Association also has a central pool of equipment and labour, as tractors, ploughs, etc., on which the individual producer can draw.

It will be seen that individual interest and attention is maintained in those activities where it is best, but in those activities where a larger scale is necessary he is obliged to co-operate. Although it could be argued that this is a contravention of the voluntary principle it must be remembered that each tenant voluntarily enters the scheme with its obligations and can, if he so wishes, leave it. The manager of an estate is responsible, not to the tenants, but to the Association, which of course employs him. However, on nearly every estate there is a consultative committee consisting of the Estate Manager as chairman, a tenant as vice-chairman, the senior estate staff and elected tenants.

At national level satisfactory consultative machinery is more difficult to create. The difficult elements are the necessity of management remaining with the Executive Committee of the Association appointed by the Minister, the desire of the tenants to be associated with the management of the scheme (they have a national association), and the difficulty of finding experienced tenants, to whom time is very precious, willing to give time to attending management meetings in London.

Though the co-operative purist may criticise, there are good co-operative elements within the scheme, and in purpose and work it could be argued that it is co-operative. Moreover, these estates could evolve into something approaching co-operative communities, into organisations absorbing all rural business, the ideal of G. W. Russell.

The schemes have proved successful in a business sense. Although the co-operation is enforced, the economic gains are nevertheless made. And they are substantial. Over the five years ending in 1956 the average return to tenants of the 821 holdings, after paying all outgoings was about £600 per year, whereas the average earnings of a representative group of farms of 50 acres or less was £360 to £470. Thus the Association tenants of holdings of ten acres or less were much better off than the average small farmer of up to 50 acres of land. Some tenants fare better than others, in 1957 the tenants of one estate averaged £997, and of all the tenants of the Association, over 50 per cent made more than £600 per year, and 25 per cent exceeded £1,000.

NEED FOR EDUCATION

In all the agricultural societies, as in the consumers' societies also, the principal defects and weaknesses arise from the ignorance and consequent apathy and disloyalty of many members, and even of some directors and staffs. Professor C. R. Fay has written that " co-operative business, and every business in the final resort depends on the enthusiasm of its personnel. It is indeed desirable that directors should know why they co-operate, but it is even more important that the staffs of societies should know that Co-operation stands for something and promises something which will not be forthcoming if the personnel are not imbued with the right tradition. . . . The manager can be so keen on the expansion of his society that his attitude to his neighbours is distinctly unco-operative. No doubt in competitive industry the manager who goes after business at any price is doing what he is paid to do. This is not true of co-operation. A Co-operative manager can hurt Co-operation by developing it in the wrong way."

The central organisations of the agricultural societies are apparently well aware of the need for educating societies' staffs.

A grant of £25,000 in 1953 from the United States Mutual Security Administration Counterpart Funds was offered for the purpose of increasing productivity of agricultural co-operatives. On the advice of the Federation of Agricultural Co-operatives part of this was used to initiate a scheme, consisting of short correspondence courses integrated with short residential courses, which included not only " managerial " subjects, but of more moment, the principles and development of agricultural co-operatives.

This training scheme became self-supporting after three years. It was believed, probably rightly, that although the primary problem was to make its members conscious of co-operative principles, this could only be achieved if the staffs of co-operatives themselves believed in Co-operation and were technically efficient. Sales representatives and lorry drivers, for instance, are often the only direct contacts of the societies with their farmer members. With truly co-operative staffs, the way for the education of the member is prepared.

The Plunkett Foundation for Co-operative Studies has, of course, been actively engaged in publishing material on agricultural Co-operation, but this is more for the use of students and those already interested in the Movement. British agricultural Co-operation still needs idealists to inspire it to pursue not only better farming and better business, but also, in the fullest sense, better living.

17 INTERNATIONAL CO-OPERATION

> " Since the time of Robert Owen ... men have striven
> to establish International Co-operation ... it was
> worth while endeavouring to unite all men and all
> nations in peaceful labour for the good of humanity;
> all these men striving to give tangible form to an
> international co-operative alliance of all countries
> gathered patience and enthusiasm to work for this
> end from the absolute certainty that behind the
> hurly burly of class warfare, behind all the horrors
> of racial war, there lies a realm of justice, peace
> and brotherly love, the attainment of which is the
> highest destiny of our race."
>
> Dr. Hans Müller.

FROM the beginning the Co-operative Movement has had an
international outlook. Robert Owen, for instance, not only
appealed to all classes of all nations, but his most serious effort
to establish a co-operative community was not in the United
Kingdom, but in the United States of America. Again, the
success of the Rochdale Pioneers aroused a great deal of interest
in other countries, increased by the publication of Holyoake's
history of the society. This circulated all over the world and was
translated into many languages. Some Continental scholars and
reformers corresponded with the Rochdale co-operators and some
visited their Society. The Christian Socialists had many contacts
and friends overseas, their original co-operative ideas indeed
came from France, and later they looked to Germany for ideas
and information on co-operative banking. Other leading co-
operators such as G. J. Holyoake, Hodgson Pratt and Owen
Greening were active in various international movements, and
William Pare, actively engaged in pioneering co-operative enterprises from the first Birmingham Society in 1828 to the Co-
operative Congress in 1869, had worked as a commercial traveller
in the Scandinavian countries and had co-operative friends there.

It is not surprising therefore that advantage was taken of the
opportunity presented by the convening of the Congress of 1869

to include prominent co-operators in other countries and to emphasise to British co-operators that their Movement was not limited by national boundaries. Eighteen foreign co-operators were made members of the Arrangement Committee. Among them were Professor V. A. Huber, one of the earliest and most eminent of German co-operative theorists, Dr. E. Pfeiffer, pioneer of German consumer Co-operation, Louis Blanc, pioneer of French producer societies and social democracy, H. Valleroux, French co-operative writer, Professor Vignano, pioneer of Co-operation in Italy, Pastor Sonne of Denmark, Axel Krook of Sweden, Dr. Vogt of Switzerland, and Ion Perdicaris of Greece (he gave a paper to Congress on " Educational Establishments "). William Pare, secretary to the Congress, attended as the delegate of a Norwegian Society, the Eidsfoss Iron Works Co-operative Society.

INTEREST OF THE BRITISH MOVEMENT

That the conveners of the Congress intended to keep the international nature of the Co-operative Movement to the forefront is further shown by the arrangement of Congress procedure, the chairman's opening address being followed by the reading of papers on Co-operation in Denmark, France, Germany, Sweden and Switzerland, written by eminent co-operators in those countries. It was also the expressed intention of the Arrangement Committee that the Congress should discuss " forming an Organisation of all Co-operative Societies and Co-operators at Home and Abroad." This was not, however, carried out.

Interest in Co-operation abroad continued to be maintained and shown by the inclusion of " Foreign Reports " in Congress Reports. In 1870 a paper for discussion on " International Co-operation " should have been given to Congress, but it was not forthcoming. The chairman (the Rev. W. N. Molesworth, the " Co-operative Parson " of Rochdale), however, led a discussion on the subject, describing co-operative establishments he had visited on the Continent and giving evidence of the spread of Co-operation in various parts of the world, and a resolution was carried which expressed the hope " that a friendly correspondence may be established between the Co-operators in Great Britain and those engaged in the work of Co-operation elsewhere, so that they may be encouraged by each others' experience and advice."

The continued sending of reports and papers by foreign co-operators to the British Movement, of course, indicates a mutual interest in Co-operation in all countries, and it was natural that some should begin to consider the possibilities of co-operation between the national Movements for mutual advantage. Correspondence took place between G. W. A. Wright, Commissioner of the National Grange (a farmers' co-operative movement in the U.S.A.) and E. V. Neale in 1876, in which Wright proposed the establishment of an Anglo-American Co-operative Company to facilitate inter-trading between British co-operative societies and the Grange co-operative societies in the United States of America. This proposal came to nothing, but it is indicative that international Co-operation was already in the air.

APPROACH OF E. de BOYVE

The first step on the way to the establishment of the International Co-operative Alliance, however, is usually taken to be the message from French co-operators expressing the desire to enter into relations with British co-operators, given by Harold Cox to the Derby Co-operative Congress in 1884. The moving spirit, the indispensable idealist without whom progress is never made, in France at this time was Edouard de Boyve who was responsible for starting the famous retail society, " Emancipation " at Nimes in 1883. He was also active with tongue and pen in propagating the co-operative ideal, and in making a movement out of French retail societies, which up to then had been advocated and supported only on account of the economic advantages they offered to members.

Lacking the unifying and driving force of a social ideal, they had little interest in or concern with each other, each was untroubled by anything but its own immediate interests. De Boyve interested others, and inspired them to break through this " philistine " conception of the Co-operative Movement and realise its ideals, duties, social importance and evolutionary possibilities. He realised the need to form a national federation of French societies and sought the assistance of E. V. Neale and the British Co-operative Union to accomplish this.

Assistance was given, including the attendance by Neale and Johnston as delegates to the first French Congress at Paris in 1885. This was the first time the British Movement had been represented at a foreign congress in an official capacity. The hope had been expressed that the time would come when French and British co-operators would form a great union in which they would work together, not only to satisfy their material, but above all, their ideal needs. Differences upon ideals, however, were to be the biggest obstacles to the founding of an international co-operative organisation.

In 1886 de Boyve attended and addressed the Plymouth Congress, and at the Lyons Congress in the same year, presided over by Professor Charles Gide, one of the great formative figures of Co-operation, the intention was expressed of establishing an International Co-operative Alliance. A Congress at Milan projected a scheme for national committees with a general central office. Committees were formed in Great Britain, France and Italy, but they never met and nothing practical was done.

In the opinion of Dr. Hans Müller the reasons for this failure were the over ambitious objects; it was to decide matters of dispute in economic theories and methods, bring about social and international peace, counterbalance revolutionary socialism and guide socialist movements in all countries into the channels of Christian social reform. The movements, apart from the British, were in their infancy and far too weak and inexperienced to embark on a programme with these professed objectives.

INFLUENCE OF E. V. NEALE

E. V. Neale, however, sought to put international Co-operation to the service of what he regarded as the living interests of Co-operation and so in Müller's opinion was the true founder of international co-operative organisation. Unfortunately, Neale's opinion of what were the living interests of Co-operation did not agree with those of some other co-operators. Neale's idea of the purpose of the Co-operative Movement was still that which induced him to enter it—the reconciling of the interests of capital and labour by associations of workmen employing themselves. It will be remembered, however, that at this time a great struggle was taking place in the British Movement between the advocates of producer and consumer Co-operation, and Neale sought to use international Co-operation in this struggle.

But the " Foreign Inquiry Committee " of the Co-operative Union set up by Congress in accordance with de Boyve's scheme included J. T. W. Mitchell, the powerful opponent of producer Co-operation. Neale met this difficulty by never convening the committee, explaining that " the time had hardly arrived when it was practicable to formulate a statement of principles and methods pursued by co-operators in their efforts to produce social reform which might be accepted in the different countries where branches of the International Union exist."

The continued failure of the Foreign Inquiry Committee to meet led to its non-reappointment in 1890, but the international personal contacts were still there. In 1891 Neale retired from his position as General Secretary of the Co-operative Union and turned his attention to the founding of an International Co-operative Alliance. In 1892, he met de Boyve at the Rochdale Congress and expressed the opinion that no progress could be made owing to the English Wholesale. Holding that the Co-operative International must be completely independent, it was decided to call an international alliance into being without the active participation of the Co-operative Union. A preliminary committee was to meet of " an international alliance of the friends of co-operative production."

It was consequently a group of private persons, not representatives of co-operative organisations, who now attempted to establish a co-operative international body. Their appeal for support criticised consumer Co-operation and stated the case for producer Co-operation. It was sent to, and met a favourable response from individual co-operators, factory managers, social politicians and productive societies. For the Alliance was not to be confined to co-operative societies " but shall include all firms and companies which accept the principle of the participation of the worker in profit as part of their constitution or systematic practice, and all persons, whether heads of industrial bodies or not, who signify their approval of this principle by becoming members of the Alliance." According to this statement, capitalist concerns with profit-sharing schemes would have been eligible for membership of the Alliance, whilst most British co-operative societies and the C.W.S. would not.

A meeting was held at the Crystal Palace Festival in 1892, at which a programme presented by Greening was almost devoid of co-operative content. However, it was decided that an international alliance should be formed and a provisional council appointed consisting of Neale, Holyoake, Greening, Albert Grey (later Earl Grey), Mrs. Lawrenson and Miss Tournier. It was also decided to hold the first international Congress in conjunction with the Crystal Palace Festival in 1893.

HENRY WOLFF'S EFFORTS

Neale died on September 16th, 1892, a great loss to the " friends of co-operative production." His place was taken by Henry Wolff, who, although of English birth, had lived a long time in Germany, and was actively concerned in agricultural Co-operation, especially credit societies and co-operative banks. (His books on co-operative banking are the classic works on the subject.) He had consequently a good knowledge of continental Co-operation, but knew little of the British Movement. He realised, however, that the aim of profit-sharing was too narrow for an organisation claiming to be an international co-operative alliance. He urged that the programme should be extended to " embrace everything that is co-operative, in any shape or form," and Greening agreed.

Wolff was active and energetic and invited the leaders of co-operative credit associations to the International Congress. Six of them attended, from France, Italy, Belgium and Germany. There were also individual British co-operators present and representatives of British producer societies, but not of consumer societies. Although it was decided that the meeting should not constitute a congress, important steps were taken. The name of the projected organisation was changed to The International Co-operative Alliance, it was not to be open to all who favoured profit-sharing, but was to be an international federation of co-operative societies. An executive committee was appointed, consisting of Holyoake, Greening, Earl Grey, Hodgson Pratt, Mrs. Lawrenson and Miss Tournier. This committee was to be regarded as the representative of the British Co-operative Movement, and was to contact the Co-operative Union and the English Women's Guild.

Wolff proceeded to contact societies all over the Continent, but was rebuffed by the British Co-operative Union, and found its aloofness an obstacle to his continental efforts, for the Co-operative Union was regarded as the British Movement. The Co-operative Union declined to accept the invitation to join the London Committee on the grounds that all such action should emanate from the Union as the recognised centre of Co-operation in this country. The Union felt that it would not be consulting the dignity of the Union by consenting to its being ranked, in such an important matter, as being of no more weight than any individual sympathiser with the Movement. The Union, therefore, informed its continental correspondents, in answer to their inquiries, that the Union was not in any way connected with the proposed International Co-operative Alliance, and that in that sense the British section was not representative of co-operators in this country.

However, an International and Foreign Inquiry Committee was appointed to make full inquiries into the question of an International Alliance. It met the London Committee, which had now realised it could not organise an international congress without Co-operative Union support and agreed to support it in organising such a congress on condition that the Co-operative Union was recognised as the only legitimate representative of British societies.

EARLY HISTORY OF THE I.C.A.

In August, 1895, the first International Co-operative Congress was held. Greening and Wolff had worked hard and secured the attendance or moral support of any and everybody likely to be interested, including lords, bishops, professors, social reformers and members of Parliament, delegates from the Peace Society, the Independent Labour Party, the Social Democratic Federation, the Labour Church and the Christian Social Union. Earl Grey gave the opening address and declared the principal question to be discussed was the profit-sharing principle, but Greening, with a better understanding, made a clever speech which avoided such controversial issues, and declared " let us tolerate every variety of organisation which can fairly be recognised as co-operative."

Important steps were taken towards the framing of a constitution, although a fierce debate took place, on what the I.C.A. should be, which almost wrecked the project. Eventually the Congress accepted as Article I, that " An International Co-operative Alliance is created between the associations now or hereafter adhering to the work commenced by the late Vansittart Neale and his friends to promote Co-operation and profit-sharing in all their forms. The resolutions of the first International Congress (London, August 19th to 23rd, 1895) shall serve as guides for the preparation of statutes for the Alliance and its operations."

EARLY CONGRESSES

The British Congress at Woolwich in 1896 agreed that the Union should join the Alliance and support its efforts with all the means in its power. Without such support the Alliance would have sunk owing to lack of financial support, for in the first years almost the entire expenses of the Alliance were met by British contributions. At the I.C.A. Congress of 1896, the total subscriptions received amounted to £158 17s. 0d., and of this Great Britain had subscribed £153, Denmark and the United States £2 each, Barbados £1, and France 17/–.

The second International Congress (1896) held in Paris, was much more of a co-operative affair, although there were delegates from profit-sharing firms. France, of course, supplied most of the delegates, next came Great Britain (27), Italy (8), Holland (7), Belgium (4), Germany (2), Spain (2), Russia (1), Switzerland (1), Barbados (1). The most important work of this Congress was the making of a constitution. Disaster was once more narrowly averted, for the profit-sharing enthusiasts nearly succeeded in

carrying rules which would have made many forms of Co-
operation ineligible for membership, including the British
societies which provided the cash.

The third Congress, 1897, was held at Delft, and was not as
well attended as the second. British delegates feared the Congress
was becoming simply an international debating club, and believed
this was due to individuals being eligible for membership. Thus
" all sorts of people given to speechifying or suffering from ideas
of self reform, whose main object was to direct the attention of
the Assembly to their own special whim rather than to forward
Co-operation, found their way into the Congresses " (Müller).

At the next Congress (Paris 1900) the British Co-operative
Union was successful in carrying a resolution abolishing individual
membership in all those countries where Co-operative Unions
existed. This took the wind out of the sails of the profit-sharing
section, which consisted largely of individual enthusiasts in
Britain and France.

The following Congress held in 1902 was in Manchester. Both
the C.W.S. and the S.C.W.S. had joined the Alliance, and continental co-operators were impressed by the tangible evidence of
the success of British consumer Co-operation. An attempt to
create a special profit-sharing section of the Alliance failed, for
it met not only the opposition of consumer co-operatives, but
also of the new generation of socialists, a French delegate holding
that profit-sharing was a trick of the capitalists to lull the workers
in order to weaken their trade union organisation. This was the
end of the profit-sharing element in the I.C.A., and the end of the
first phase of its life.

CHANGING PURPOSES

Professor Charles Gide, in his historical account of the I.C.A.
speaks of this as its " Bourgeois Period," its sponsors in Britain
and France were bourgeois and so was its programme. " These
men . . . by no means shared with the distributive societies the
desire to create what I have later on called the ' Co-operative
Republic,' i.e., to abolish profits and institute a new economic
order. They sought simply the reconciliation of capital and
labour and social peace, and they saw no better means of realising
that ideal than the principle of profit-sharing. . . . They were
equally sympathetic with the credit societies which enabled
artisans and small masters, not to become independent, since they
were that already, but to maintain their independence and not
fall to the level of mere wage earners, sympathetic to the masters'
institutions, even when they had nothing co-operative in their

constitution except the participation of their workers in the profits."

The next period Gide terms " The Socialist Period." As the profit-sharing advocates disappeared, consumers' Co-operation became increasingly influential in the Alliance. Socialism was also growing rapidly in Great Britain and the Continent; and socialists sought to absorb working class movements, such as Trade Unionism and Co-operation, in the Socialist Movement. This, however, was also resisted, some co-operators insisting on the right of the Co-operative Movement to autonomy, to its own self expression as a Movement different from what had come to be regarded as the Socialist Movement (often better termed " étatism ").

Gide pointed out some of these differences, the share capital, interest, open and voluntary membership, the absence of collectivist expropriation, the absence of the class conflict " for the obvious reason that the consumer does not represent any class." The International Socialist Congress at Copenhagen, 1910, recognised the right of the Co-operative Movement to act independently and autonomously side by side with Trade Unionist, Socialist and political Movements.

DISSENSION

Socialistic objectives, however, aroused dissension in the Alliance. At the Budapest Congress in 1904, Dr. Hans Müller (Secretary of the Union of Swiss Distributive Societies, and later General Secretary of the I.C.A.), expressed views on the desirability of covering the country with a network of societies, arousing the consciousness of solidarity amongst consumers, fostering popular education, forming unions and central agencies for co-operative purchase, and emphasising the general objective of organising a nation's consumption so as to eliminate the profits of capitalist trading, and to build up a new economic and social order which would enlarge the liberty of the individual and the people as a whole.

Although these views were applauded they aroused the opposition of Dr. Cruger, director of the German Union of Schulze-Delitsch societies. He declared that the German distributive societies did not desire to organise consumers in opposition to capitalist trading or seek to replace the existing order of things. His opposition was supported by Klingenbiel, representative of the German Raiffeisen Union, who stated that his Union did not encourage distributive societies, and believed in the importance of maintaining a commercial and industrial middle class and not encouraging co-operative developments which would injure that class. The director of the Austrian Union of Schulze-Delitsch societies also expressed similar views. But the debate showed that the majority regarded the Co-operative Movement as anti-capitalist.

Another debate on whether State aid to the Co-operative Movement was permissible, showed the general inclination that it should only be " within moderate limits," and " only as a temporary support " and a majority favoured the total rejection of State aid.

The effect of these debates was the breakaway of the agricultural organisations for they either enjoyed State aid or desired it, and of the Schulze-Delitsch Unions of Germany and Austria. The withdrawal of the agricultural and credit societies was believed by some to strengthen the Alliance for it made a common basis of principle easier to find. Consumers' organisations now predominated.

PUBLICATIONS AND NEW RULES

In 1907, at Cremona, William Maxwell, chairman of the S.C.W.S., was elected President of the I.C.A., in succession to H. W. Wolff. Dr. Hans Müller became secretary and the I.C.A. commenced the issue of its valuable publications, a monthly bulletin in English, French and German, the *International Co-operative Bibliography*, the *International Directory of the Co-operative Press* and in 1910, the first *Year Book of International Co-operation*.

The eighth Congress, at Hamburg, 1910, effected a comprehensive revision of rules. The desire of many continental co-operators to make the I.C.A. a federation only of national co-operative organisations was resisted by Great Britain. There were several hundred individual societies affiliated to the I.C.A., most of them British, and their support, moral and financial, was vital to the Alliance.

1913 PEACE RESOLUTION

The Congress of 1913 was notable for the hopes and plans for international Co-operation and for a famous peace resolution. It was a long resolution, which expressed the view that not only was peace an essential condition for the development of Co-operation but that the progress of Co-operation formed one of the most valuable guarantees of the world's peace.

That such a resolution was followed shortly by a war in which most of the nations represented were engaged on opposite sides invites cynicism. But co-operators at the time did not take this attitude, they believed, " It was effective in maintaining the spirit of association and friendship among the co-operators of the various countries, belligerent, as well as allied and neutral."

There was certainly evidence of a friendship between and a confidence in each other and in the sentiments expressed in 1913 by leading co-operators such as G. D. C. Goedhart (Holland), Maxwell (Scotland), Von Elm (Germany), Albert Thomas (France), O. Dehli (Norway), which facilitated the revival of the I.C.A. after the war.

GREAT WAR, 1914–1918

The 1914–1918 war interrupted the activities and growth of the I.C.A.; many doubted if it could survive such a struggle, in which the nations of the principal members of the Alliance waged merciless war on each other. Dr. Müller had resigned as General Secretary in 1913, and his successor, H. J. May, did a great work in holding the Alliance together during the war and rebuilding it during the peace. Co-operators in neutral countries communicated with each other and with those in belligerent countries, the bulletin continued to be issued in identical English, French and German text (from Hamburg), so that there was a fair knowledge and understanding of what was happening to Co-operation in the various countries.

A Conference of the central co-operative organisations of the allied countries was held in Paris in 1916 to prepare for the resumption of Alliance activities after the war. The I.C.A. itself did not take part, fearing that to do so might be misunderstood by the Co-operative Movements in neutral and belligerent countries.

Three important questions were discussed: Economic policy, during and after the war; Responsibility toward co-operative societies which had suffered during the War; and the organisation of an International Co-operative Wholesale Society. On the last question the establishing of an international statistical bureau as the first step towards establishing an International Co-operative Wholesale Society was approved in principle.

AFTER-WAR CONFERENCES

A second inter-allied conference was held in 1919, again at Paris, the I.C.A. being represented in a consultative capacity. In June, 1919, a third conference, attended by representatives from twenty countries, included neutrals and some from newly created states (Armenia, Czechoslovakia, Finland, Georgia,

Latvia, Lithuania, Poland, Ukraine). The main questions were international economic policy after the war; the organisation of commercial relations between the Wholesale Societies; when, how and under what conditions could the activities of the I.C.A be resumed.

Some good work was done on these questions, but the I.C.A. regarded the maintenance of the Alliance as neutral ground as most important and so would not call a meeting of the Central Committee, and still less Congress, until all members could attend. Thus these conferences, although serving very valuable purposes, had not the status or authority of the I.C.A.

REVIVAL OF THE I.C.A. AFTER WORLD WAR I

Steps to revive the I.C.A., however, were taken; first the meeting of the Executive in August, 1919, then of the Central Committee in April, 1920. Important decisions had to be made on the position of newly created national co-operative organisations, revisions of rules, date and place of the next International Congress, participation in the Council of the International Labour Office, attitude to the economic blockade of Russia, attitude to the treatment of co-operative organisations in Russia. This last question was to cause a good deal of concern and discussion at the succeeding Congress, and for a long time afterwards.

When the tides of war had receded it was gradually realised that much of the world of 1914 had disappeared. Old empires which had dominated and intimidated Europe had broken up into new independent sovereign states. The ideal of self-determination was in part served thereby, but many new problems arose.

Extreme nationalism, which divides people into fearful, suspicious and jealous groups, was given its head. Each new state meant additional political boundaries, and economic nationalism made these into ever-rising barriers of tariffs, currency, and other restrictions upon trade. There were far more restrictions on and obstacles to the movement of goods, men and ideas after the 1914–1918 war than before it. Also there was great instability, no new state could feel itself firmly grounded, and there were also revolutions, counter revolutions, and the fear of them.

Under these disturbed conditions it was not surprising that the world economy of pre-1914 did not revive, that unemployment, crises, bankruptcies and what appeared to be permanent depression, ravaged Europe, intensifying the economic nationalism which was in great measure responsible for the trouble.

Yet immediately after the war there was a great optimism and hope of international organisation, a general realisation that many political, economic and social problems could only be solved by international action. The foundation of the League of Nations and the International Labour Office seemed as though governments also realised it, and that internationalism was going to replace the old nationalism and imperialism.

Leading co-operators desired the national Co-operative Movements to organise and take advantage of the opportunities presented by the new international world. Professor Gide who had presided over the war-time and post-war conferences, had advocated, and got the conferences to agree upon, the desirability of a new system of international trade in place of either capitalistic free trade or protectionism, both of which were dangerous to peace. He desired organised exchange based on co-operative principles.

But sovereign states, even when organised in a League of Nations, were incapable of considering problems other than from the aspect of power politics. International trade to them was not exchange for mutual benefit, but a kind of cold war in which markets were attacked or defended, captured or lost. Their attitude in fact was pre-Adam Smith.

BASLE CONGRESS, 1921

However, when the first post-war Congress met at Basle in 1921, hopes and prospects of a better international era were still bright. Co-operation had grown much in many countries during the war and co-operators had greater confidence in themselves and in their organisation and methods. Under the severe stress of war they had seen private enterprise and competition unable to meet the strain and discarded as wasteful, inefficient and unadaptable. Many also found that they were by no means inferior to big businessmen in organising and administering affairs for the general welfare. Consequently there was the desire to establish and develop co-operative international organisations to further co-operative progress. Progressive co-operators increasingly regarded co-operative problems from an international aspect.

The Congress at Basle 1921, was attended by over 400 delegates from 23 different states. Its most important work was the revision of rules, constitution and statement of aims. These are dealt with later in this chapter, but they included detailed items for international action such as the convening of international congresses, the publication of journals, books and pamphlets, a regular press exchange, a library of co-operative literature, the promotion of International Co-operative Trading and of International Co-operative Banking, the establishment of a central

P

bureau of statistics and information, the promotion of relations with other international organisations. Efforts were made to fulfil these purposes.

In large measure the Basle Congress laid down the pattern to which the Alliance has since conformed, in spite of the havoc wrought upon the Co-operative Movement by totalitarianism, a second world war and the cold war which followed it. The subsequent history of the Alliance is dealt with in describing that pattern and its development. Changes there have been, of course, but these have generally been developments along the lines laid down at Basle and in furtherance of the aim of the Alliance decided on there.

TOTALITARIAN STATES AND THE I.C.A.

A major problem faced at Basle and subsequent Congresses arose from the Russian Revolutions of March and October 1917. These and subsequent events, such as the Brest-Litovsk treaty, liberated formerly subject peoples and created new states, Esthonia, Latvia, Lithuania, Finland, the Ukraine, Georgia, Poland. As these developed their own co-operative organisations they desired independent membership of the Alliance. This was not difficult to provide, the major difficulty was with the co-operative organisation in the U.S.S.R. itself.

Some co-operators objected to the treatment of the Co-operative Movement in Russia by the Communist Party Government, and the Central Committee of the Alliance at the conferences held preceding the Basle Congress, refused to recognise the *de facto* condition of Co-operation in Russia as being in conformity with the constitution of the Alliance, and protested against " all the measures which have deprived all the Russian co-operative organisations of their independence and full autonomy."

The issue had to be faced by the need for a decision on who should represent the Russian organisations—the representatives elected in accordance with the rules before the Revolution, but who had fled from Russia and were cut off from the co-operative organisations there, or new representatives appointed by the new regime. The Executive Committee decided to recognise the Centrosoyus (the central co-operative organisation in Russia) as the only authority entitled to nominate members representing Russia to the Central Committee and to appoint delegates to Congress.

The Central Committee, however, did not agree with the Executive (which at that time consisted entirely of British members) on this matter and moved an amendment to enable it to be debated.

The debate was mainly concerned with whether Centrosoyus was a genuine co-operative organisation or not. But the view of the Executive prevailed, although against powerful opposition, that if there were to be a Russian membership of the Alliance, it was bound to be of the Russian organisations which then existed, and that "the form and constitution of the Board and of the All Russian Central Union is primarily a matter for the decision and approval of the Russian co-operators in Russia."

There was also the desire to prevent the Co-operative International being split as the Socialist and the Trade Union Internationals had been split by a Communist splintering. There was a hope that in time the objectionable features would disappear and the co-operative organisations in Russia would once more become an indisputable Co-operative Movement.

U.S.S.R. AND THE I.C.A.

Russian interest in the Alliance, which seemed considerable at first, apparently declined after 1927, the number of its delegates to I.C.A. Congresses dropping from 78 at Stockholm (1927) to 23 at Vienna (1930) to 10 at London (1934) and six at Paris (1937), and after the London Congress, Centrosoyus was seldom represented at Executive or Central Committee meetings.

In 1935 a Soviet decree ordered the liquidation of all the consumers' co-operative societies in the towns and the transference of all their property to the State Trading Department. Centrosoyus also had its powers as the Central Organisation for the import of all consumption goods for retail distribution withdrawn and transferred to the State Trading Department. This extinction of urban co-operative societies by State decree increased doubts of the genuine co-operative character of the Co-operative Movement in the U.S.S.R., and the I.C.A. General Secretary sought, unsuccessfully, to obtain information and a statement on the question from Centrosoyus. A U.S.S.R. delegate at the Congress of 1937 defended the decree on the ground that it made no difference to Soviet trade whether co-operative shops were handed over to the state trading organisation or vice versa, and denied that the decree was an instrument of policy tending to the elimination of the Co-operative Movement.

ITALIAN FASCISM

The Co-operative Movement, was being attacked, its character forcibly changed, and sometimes its property seized and the Movement liquidated by other totalitarian states. Mussolini seized power in Italy in 1922 and quickly attacked the Movement.

By 1925 only 1,000 societies remained of the 8,000 societies existing and contributing to Lega Nazionale (the Italian co-operative union) in 1922. Of the thousands of societies which had disappeared some had been forcibly joined to the Fascist organisation, many co-operators had fled the country, hundreds had been killed or injured.

In 1925, a decree dissolved the Lega Nazionale and a Fascist " co-operative chief " took over. Fascist officials replaced the elected committees of societies, and a body " the Superior Council " could dissolve any co-operative society which did not conform to the discipline imposed by the Fascists or it could replace its Board of Management by a Commissioner. Nevertheless, the Fascist leaders of Italy put forth " every effort to clothe their spoil with the semblance of a genuine movement, with the intention of holding it up to the world as a respectable member of the International Co-operative Family." (I.C.A. Report 1927.) Not surprisingly Italian membership of the Alliance ceased.

NAZISM

Even more serious were the consequences of Hitler's rise to power and the Nazification of Germany. There were about 1,100 consumers' societies with $4\frac{1}{2}$ million members in Germany in 1930; they experienced difficulties from the great economic crisis and depression of 1930–1933, unemployment forcing members to withdraw their savings from the societies. But voluntary Co-operation could have no place in a totalitarian state, the agricultural societies were absorbed into a food and agricultural organisation (Reichanahrstand); the People's Banks and Handworkers' Societies as well as the Housing Societies were restricted and discouraged; the consumers' societies were dissolved (1935–1941).

In 1934 an authoritarian regime (Dollfuss-Schnuschnigg) was established in Austria and the I.C.A. successfully sought to secure some freedom of action for the Co-operative Movement there on condition that it kept out of politics; the later appropriation of Austria by Germany caused the severance of the Austrian movement from the I.C.A.

In Spain the defeat of the Spanish Republican Government by the Franco insurgents and the establishment of the Franco dictatorship, led to the dissolution of the Co-operative Movement in its old form.

EFFECTS OF THE SECOND WORLD WAR

The second world war brought further disasters. Germany's subjection of Czechoslovakia caused the dissolution of the federation of the consumers' Movement there. The invasion and carving up of Poland, the conquest of Latvia, Lithuania and Esthonia by the U.S.S.R. resulted in the disappearance of independent co-operative organisations in those countries.

As other European countries, Belgium, Holland, France, Denmark, Norway, and the Balkan countries were subdued by Germany, and Japan became a belligerent, the number of countries in effective membership with the I.C.A. was seriously reduced. The I.C.A. was affected to a greater extent by the second world war than by the first, only two neutral European countries, Sweden and Switzerland, could serve as channels of communication, and Europe was occupied by powers hostile to the Co-operative Movement.

On the other hand Co-operative Movements in the free world flourished and grew. The prospects for International Co-operation also brightened as steps to post-war international action began to be made, and the valuable part which could be played by Co-operative Movements in post-war reconstruction was obviously realised by allied governments and inter allied organisations.

HOT SPRINGS RESOLUTION, 1943

The United Nations Conference on Food and Agriculture at Hot Springs in 1943 in its " Final Act " passed a resolution which declared:

" Whereas

1. The Co-operative Movement has been of very great importance in many countries, both to urban and rural populations, especially in agricultural districts, where farming is based on small units and in urban areas of low income families.

2. The proper functioning of co-operative societies may facilitate adjustments of agricultural production and distribution, as members have confidence in the recommendations and guidance of their own co-operative organisations, which they know operate in the interests of their members and of society in general.

3. The democratic control and educational programme which are features of the Co-operative Movement can play a vital part in the training of good citizens, and assist in inducing a sound conception of economic matters.

The United Nations Conference on Food and Agriculture recommends

1. That, in order to make it possible for people to help themselves in lowering costs of production and costs of distribution and marketing

(a) All countries study the possibilities of the further establishment of producer and consumer co-operative societies in order to render necessary production, marketing, purchasing, finance and other services.

(b) Each nation examine its laws, regulations and institutions to determine if legal or institutional obstacles to co-operative development exist, in order to make desirable adjustments.

(c) Full information as to the present development of co-operatives in different countries be made available through the permanent organisation recommended in Resolution II."

The " Final Act," was signed by the delegations of the 44 nations represented at the Conference, including that of Great Britain. Although the above was only one resolution out of 33, such a resolution by such a body was of great value, for it not only showed an appreciation of the worth of Co-operation but also showed an intention that Co-operation should assist in the work of post-war reconstruction.

The permanent organisation recommended was set up and termed the United Nations Food and Agricultural Organisation, (F.A.O.) which eventually set up a Committee on Co-operation. The I.C.A. was admitted to consultative status with this body and is represented at conferences convened by it.

CO-OPERATION IN THE COMMONWEALTH

Many governments took the pledge to assist the promotion and development of co-operative societies seriously. The British Government did a great deal in its overseas territories. An Adviser on Co-operation was appointed in the Colonial Office, the territories were circularised instructing them to further co-operative societies, and a model Co-operative Law and Model Rules were drawn up.

The various territories were encouraged to create Co-operative Departments to promote, advise, inspect and guide co-operative societies. These departments gradually developed staffs experienced in such work; many were sent to the British Co-operative College to gain a wider knowledge and understanding of the Co-operative Movement. These Co-operative Departments have played an invaluable part in the development of Co-operation in these territories. In many there would have been no co-operative societies but for them, and in all they have probably been responsible for keeping the societies on the right lines so that they developed into sound as well as flourishing movements.

THE I.C.A. AND POST-WAR TOTALITARIANISM

As after the first world war, hopes and prospects of international action were disappointed and dimmed by the inability of national governments to co-operate. Peace depends on a harmony of interests and it was soon evident that the defeat of the Fascist powers had not removed all the causes of discord. Two great hostile political camps developed in the world and although the exhaustion consequent upon the second world war and the fear of mutual destruction from nuclear warfare has probably prevented another, a " cold war," in which the sapping and mining of social and political structure was a principal weapon, has continued to be waged.

International organisations are obvious fields for such warfare; it split the international trade union movement newly enrolled after the war in the World Federation of Trade Unions. The International Co-operative Alliance has had to face the pre-war question of whether Movements in totalitarian countries could be genuinely co-operative or not.

The problem is more serious than it was before the war. In some countries, previously independent, Co-operative Movements have been reorganised on the Communist model and there is the possibility of their number increasing by conquest or subversion. These Co-operative Movements are no longer independent, but have become instruments of the State and the Communist Party. Consequently the views expressed and the influence sought by these organisations in the Alliance, are not those of independent co-operative organisations, but of political forces of which they are the instruments. There is the danger, therefore, of the Alliance being used for the purposes of party politics, with a consequent splitting, for many of its affiliated organisations would refuse to remain in membership with a body used as an instrument for political ends.

STATEMENT OF PRINCIPLES, 1949

In 1949 the Alliance Executive clarified the situation to some extent by a statement of principles essential to genuine co-operative activity. This stated:

(i) " Co-operative organisations must be open to everybody who desires and is able to employ their services, without any discrimination on political, religious or racial grounds

(ii) The organisation of co-operatives must be democratic at all levels: that is to say, they must have the right to elect their committees or other governing bodies without any intervention or pressure from outside, and all members of co-operatives must have the same rights and be able to form and express their opinions freely

(iii) Co-operative organisations must be completely free and independent and must be able to take up a position with regard to all the problems which affect their own interests, or the general interests, independent of the State and public authorities generally, as well as of private organisations (political parties).

In countries where the right of free association is denied and where any divergent opinions are suppressed, free and independent organisations cannot exist. It is only in this way that the Co-operative Movement can be in a position to fight against oppression in all its forms and for the liberation of all the social groups, and thus contribute to ensuring peace, and in this way only will a real co-operative system based on mutual self help materialise."

REFUSAL OF MEMBERSHIP

On these grounds the applications for membership by some organisations within authoritarian states have been rejected. The policy was attacked by the Soviet representatives at the Helsinki meeting of the Central Committee in 1950, and at the I.C.A. Congresses since. In each case the Executive policy has been approved by Congress. At Paris indeed the Congress also approved the decision of the Executive that if any affiliated organisation at any time voluntarily or involuntarily effected a change which meant it no longer complied with the statutory conditions of membership it made itself liable to be excluded from membership by the Central Committee.

Thus the I.C.A. decided to admit to membership only societies which were genuinely independent. Yet it has also allowed those organisations which were already members and already instruments of government to remain in membership, although it was not prepared to accept changes which would add to their number. This policy of the I.C.A. has been attacked by some as infringing the principle of political neutrality. The defence against this charge is that it is necessary in order to preserve political neutrality.

Nevertheless, since 1963 the Movements of two eastern European countries have managed to persuade the Alliance that they are sufficiently free of government control to be admitted to membership so that now only one major European Communist power, East Germany, is excluded from membership.

INFANT MOVEMENTS

Complications arose with the rise of Co-operative Movements in the emergent countries, for these were often created and assisted by their governments, and although moving towards independence could not be regarded as having arrived there whilst dependent on government assistance and control. Yet the Alliance rightly felt that these infant Movements should be assisted and encouraged to join the world co-operative family. This problem was met by the introduction of Associate Membership as a temporary stage on the way to full membership. Associate members can take part in and enjoy many of the I.C.A. activities and services, but have no power in making I.C.A. decisions.

It will have been gathered that the I.C.A. has been forced by pressure of circumstances to define its aims, purpose, principles, more clearly than have other co-operative organisations. These definitions, however, are important to all. After this brief sketch of its history it is now possible to understand the constitution of the Alliance.

AIM OF THE I.C.A.

From the earliest days the I.C.A. was compelled to consider what it should mean by " co-operative," and what should be the purpose of the Alliance. It will be remembered that the question was fiercely debated by the profit-sharing advocates, later by the consumer co-operatives and the credit and agricultural societies, and later still by the co-operative organisations of totalitarian countries.

The Basle Congress defined the aim of the Alliance as follows: " The International Co-operative Alliance, in continuance of the work of the Rochdale Pioneers, seeks in complete independence and by its own methods, to substitute for the present competitive regime of private interest a co-operative system in the interests of the whole community and based upon mutual self help." Slight changes were later made to state the meaning more explicitly and clearly. The aim now reads: " . . . in continuance of the work of the Rochdale Pioneers and in accordance with Co-operative Principles, seeks, in complete independence and by its own methods, to substitute for the profit-making regime a co-operative system organised in the interests of the whole community and based upon mutual self help." (Article 1 of the Rules of the I.C.A.)

This definition of aim expresses the realisation of the historical continuity of the Co-operative Movement's pursuit of its ideals and adherence to its principles which make it a Movement, and emphasises its " complete independence." Without such independence the I.C.A. could not continue, for the national organisations of any country would not remain in membership of an international organisation which was not independent of political and religious movements they could not support.

Hence this independence is stressed again in Article 7. "The I.C.A. regards Co-operation as neutral ground on which people holding the most varied opinions and professing the most diverse creeds may meet and act in common. The I.C.A. shall not associate itself with any political or religious organisation. Such independence, on which the unity of the International Co-operative Movement depends, shall be maintained in all the meetings and in all publications of the I.C.A."

OBJECTS

The objects of the Alliance are enumerated in greater detail in Article 3.

(1) To be the universal representative of co-operative organisations of all types which in practice observe the Co-operative principles.

(2) To propagate co-operative principles and methods throughout the world.

(3) To promote Co-operation in all countries.

(4) To safeguard the interests of the Co-operative Movement in all its forms.

(5) To maintain good relations between its affiliated organisations.

(6) To promote friendly and economic relations between the co-operative organisations of all types, nationally and internationally.

(7) To work for the establishment of lasting peace and security through co-operative efforts.

The above objects leave the meaning of "co-operative" undefined. The Basle Congress sought to identify it with "the work of the Rochdale Pioneers," but this was far too vague and indefinite. To remedy this the I.C.A. has undertaken two enquiries into the Rochdale Principles. The reports of the first were debated and accepted by the Congresses of 1934 and 1937. Subsequent doubts and disagreements led to another enquiry being undertaken in the 1960's and the report of that enquiry was accepted by the 1966 Congress. As these have been described in earlier chapters, it is unnecessary to deal with them again here.

But the definition of principles had its effect on the Alliance, for they were taken as a guide in amending the rules regarding eligibility of organisations for admission to its membership.

" By doing so it safeguarded the future unity of the I.C.A. Henceforth only those which observed the essential principles in spirit and in practice could join it and take part in shaping its policy." (W. P. Watkins.)

MEMBERSHIP OF THE I.C.A.

Article 8 stated the conditions of eligibility—associations of persons or co-operative organisations which observe the aims of the I.C.A. and the policy laid down by its Congress. " Any association of persons, irrespective of its legal constitution, shall be recognised as a co-operative society provided that it has for its object the economic and social betterment of its members by means of the exploitation of an enterprise based upon mutual aid, and that it conforms to the Co-operative Principles as established by the Rochdale Pioneers and as reformulated by the 23rd Congress of the I.C.A." (See Chapter 12.)

Subject to compliance with these conditions the types of association eligible for membership include National Unions of Co-operative Societies, National Federations of Co-operative Unions, Regional Unions of Co-operative Societies, Recognised Auxiliary Organisations of affiliated National Unions or Federations, Consumers' Co-operative Societies, Retail or Wholesale, Co-operative Societies of Industrial Producers or Artisanal Co-operatives, Agricultural or Fishery Co-operative Societies, Co-operative Credit Societies, Co-operative Banks, Co-operative Assurance Societies, Housing and Building Societies, other Associations of persons or Associations which have as their aim the promotion of Co-operation."

From this it will be gathered that the I.C.A. is open to every form of genuine co-operative organisation.

Applications for membership are made to the Executive of the I.C.A. which may possibly consult the National Union, if such Union is already a member of the I.C.A., or another member in the same country, before giving its decision. The General Secretary must make all appropriate inquiries as to suitability before the application is submitted to the Executive. If the application is rejected the organisation concerned has the right of appeal to the Central Committee.

MEMBERS' RIGHTS

Members, subject to the fulfilment of their financial obligations have the right to take part in Congress, to nominate representatives to the Central Committee, to submit proposals for consideration by the Executive, Central Committee, or Congress, to receive from the Secretariat of the I.C.A. all appropriate services, advice, etc.

Members, of course, have obligations which may be summarised as:— observing and forwarding the aims and policy of the I.C.A., as defined in its rules and laid down by Congress; to supply the I.C.A. with their Annual Report; to provide the I.C.A. library with a *gratis* copy of all literary works published by them and information of any published works of interest to the I.C.A.; to appoint a correspondent who will keep the I.C.A. informed of national co-operative developments, legislation or actions of public authorities which affect the Co-operative Movement; and to pay the annual membership subscription.

ASSOCIATE MEMBERSHIP

Associate membership is permitted to organisations whose aims and activities are satisfactory, but which, owing to their early stage of development are receiving outside support and have not yet complete control of their affairs. This form of membership, however, is a transitional stage to full membership. Associate members have the right to receive *gratis* the publications of the I.C.A.; to nominate an observer to Central Committee meetings without the right to speak or vote; to nominate an observer to Congress without the right to vote, but with the right to speak subject to the consent of Congress; and to receive from the Secretariat all appropriate services, advice, etc.

Subscriptions for National, Regional and National Auxiliary Organisations are on a uniform rate; for other organisations there is a scale based on membership. Collective membership can be acquired by a National Federation paying a flat rate for itself and a further sum in respect of each national organisation in its membership and a contribution graduated according to membership. There is a maximum limit to the amount a national organisation is obliged to pay. The subscription of each Associate member is fixed by the Executive.

CHANGES IN MEMBERSHIP

The composition of the membership of the Alliance changed before 1914 by the gradual elimination of individual membership (finally abolished at Basle, 1921), the growing representative membership, the increasing predominance of consumer organisations and the withdrawal of the German and Austrian Agricultural and Artisanal Unions. In 1913, there were 3,926 societies in membership which had about 20 million members, and 3,698 of these societies were consumer organisations, so that the consumer type was predominant; nevertheless there were strong agricultural organisations in membership in Austria, Denmark, Finland, Hungary, Italy, Norway, Russia, and Servia.

The Great War of 1914–1918 and its immediate aftermath of new states with their respective national co-operative organisations, resulted in an increase in the number of I.C.A. member organisations, while there was a general growth of Co-operation resulting in an increase of the individual members of affiliated organisations. In the 'twenties, however, the I.C.A. remained almost overwhelmingly European, 40 per cent of its affiliated membership was in thirteen countries of Northern, Central and Western Europe; outside Europe there were affiliated co-operative organisations in only Canada, U.S.A. and Japan.

In the 'thirties, membership suffered from the rise and conquests of totalitarianism, Italy and Portugal had been lost in the 'twenties, they were followed by the German consumer organisations, Austria, the German speaking societies of Czechoslovakia, Spain, and the halving of Russian membership by the decree of 1935 which ended the urban consumer societies.

The Second World War resulted in further losses, either by the conquest of countries and the destruction of their national organisations or by the establishment of systems which made them ineligible for membership of the I.C.A. On the other hand Co-operation was extending and growing elsewhere, and an increasing number of organisations from continents other than Europe were becoming members of the Alliance, mainly from Asia. Many of these organisations were of various forms connected with agriculture, and the Alliance became increasingly what some had originally hoped it would be, an alliance of all forms of co-operative activity.

After the war the destruction of some of the Fascist dictatorships enabled the Co-operative Movements in those countries to revive and enter once more the fold of the I.C.A. But in other countries subjected to totalitarian forms the co-operative organisations were for some time unable to satisfy the I.C.A.'s conditions of eligibility although all but one has now been able to do so. In any case, the rapid growth of co-operative organisations in all parts of the world has made the I.C.A. into a world-wide organisation with a world outlook.

Figures published by the I.C.A. in 1969 showed that it included 143 directly affiliated organisations in 60 countries, and some 230 million members grouped in 578,000 societies.

Its geographical distribution was as follows:

	Members
Europe	120,900,000
Asia	73,100,000
America	33,700,000
Africa	1,800,000
Oceania	1,000,000

The different types of society had the following membership in 1967:

Type of Society	Members
Consumers	113,410,500
Agricultural	38,497,800
Credit	69,358,600
Building and Housing	5,531,800
Productive and Artisanal	3,950,600
Fishery	1,481,200
Miscellaneous	6,286,200

The U.S.S.R., with 55 million members, had more members than any other single country; India came next with 47 million, then the U.S.A. with 24 million, Japan with 16 million and Great Britain with 13 million. Organisations of 60 different countries were in membership, although co-operative organisations exist in over a hundred countries. In numbers and scope the I.C.A. is the biggest voluntary international organisation in the world.

CONSTITUTION

The constitution of the I.C.A. is similar to that of co-operative unions of societies, framed to give fair representation of the constituent members and adequate democratic control.

Its supreme governing body is a Congress of delegates of its affiliated organisations, held every three years. At each Congress a Central Committee is appointed, each national organisation being entitled to one representative on this committee and additional members for each £400 of annual subscriptions up to a maximum of eight members. Among the most important functions of the Central Committee is the election of a President, two Vice-Presidents and eleven others, who together form the Executive Committee. No country may have more than two representatives on the Executive, excluding the President.

The International Congress brings together delegates of various forms of co-operative organisations from all over the world. With such diversity of membership each delegate meets new and strange opinions, approaches and problems, which stimulate and widen the mind. But as matters are discussed, formally and informally, an underlying, common philosophy becomes evident and the realisation of this, together with the contacts and friendships made, promotes the sense of international co-operative fellowship which is one of the prime purposes of the Alliance.

CONGRESS WORK AND PROCEDURE

The work of Congress includes a discussion of a Report to Congress, submitted by the Central Committee, which reviews the activities of the I.C.A. since the previous Congress. It also discusses motions submitted by the Central Committee or affiliated organisations. Congress is the supreme authority of the I.C.A., alone has power to amend the rules of the I.C.A., and its policy declarations are binding, unless and until some succeeding Congress declares otherwise.

Organisations are entitled to one vote for each delegate. They may, however, entrust all their votes to fewer delegates provided that no delegate holds more then ten votes. Delegates are restricted to two for each national organisation, and in the cases of " collective membership " to an extra delegate for each 25,000 members enrolled in their affiliated societies. To prevent any single country exercising a predominance of voting power, however, a rule (Article 23) restricts the voting power of the organisations of one country, or a union of countries, to one-fifth of the total voting power of Congress.

Proceedings are carried on in the four official languages of the Alliance; English, French, German and Russian, and they are now simultaneously translated.

CENTRAL COMMITTEE

Immediately after Congress the Central Committee meets to elect the President, Vice-Presidents and members of the Executive. According to rule, the Central Committee must meet at least once each year, and also hold a meeting immediately before and after each Congress. Its chief duties are the carrying out of the programme of the I.C.A., determined by Congress; the election of the Executive, President and Vice-Presidents; the appointment of Director, General Secretary and other principal officials; the appointment of auditor; confirmation of the budget submitted by the Executive; decision of the agenda and date of Congress; the appointment of a Congress Committee for each Congress, and dealing with appeals and exclusion of members.

I.C.A. EXECUTIVE

The I.C.A. Executive's duties are to admit or reject applications for membership; to draw up a budget for confirmation by the Central Committee and control expenditure; to prepare the agenda for meetings of the Central Committee; to prepare and organise Congress; to present an annual report to the Central Committee; to direct the collaboration of the I.C.A. with United Nations organisations and other bodies with which the I.C.A. has established relations; to control the affairs of the I.C.A. between the meetings of the Central Committee; and to deal with questions submitted to it by the Central Committee.

At one time the rules of the Alliance required that the Executive should meet at least every three months, but at present it is only required to " meet as often as circumstances demand," although it seldom meets more than four times in any year.

SECRETARIAT

The secretariat operates from the headquarters of the Alliance in London. It is headed by a Director who is responsible " for the necessary action to give effect to the decisions of the Congress, the Central Committee and the Executive, and for the control of the affairs of the I.C.A. between meetings of the Executive." This involves controlling the use of finances according to the budget, and the work of the personnel, the establishments and the activities of the Alliance; advising and taking part in the meetings of the committees; arranging and preparing documentation for the Congresses and committees of the Alliance; representing the I.C.A. when required at meetings of United Nations organisations and other bodies; and maintaining relations between the I.C.A. and its members and visiting national Movements.

Between 1948 and 1963 there was, in addition to the Director, a General Secretary responsible for general secretarial functions, but since 1963 the work of the Secretariat has been the sole responsibility of the Director and it has been divided into three main departments—Administration; Research, Statistics and Documentation; and Education, Press, Publicity and Films. Then, in addition to the heads of these departments, there are Secretaries for Housing, for Agriculture and for Women Co-operators.

Owing to the scattered nature of the Alliance membership, meetings of its authorities cannot be frequent, and a good deal of initiative and consequent responsibility inevitably rests with the various officials.

WORK OF THE ALLIANCE

At the headquarters of the Alliance a research section is concerned with collecting and compiling statistics relating to all the organisations belonging to the Alliance, with co-ordinating the research activities of national movements by compiling joint research returns, and with particular pieces of research of particular co-operative interest, such as on methods of dividend accounting, on co-operative advertising, on Co-operatives and Development Strategy and so on.

A valuable library on Co-operation and related social subjects had been built up and is, of course, ever growing. The library consists not only of books, but of files of journals, reports and other publications of its affiliated organisations, of collections of photographs, newspaper cuttings and documents. Some hundreds of co-operative journals and other periodicals are regularly received and are available for study. Select bibliographies have been made in response to special requests by co-operative organisations and others.

An International Summer School is held annually, each year in a different country. This also helps to promote international understanding and fellowship among co-operators from many countries.

Since the Congress resolutions at Paris and Stockholm, in 1954 and 1957, the Alliance has assisted the young Co-operative Movements in the emergent territories, not only by written advice but also by provision of education material and equipment, personal visits and inquiry into conditions and problems, and the provision of expert assistance, sometimes for lengthy periods. There is a great need for work of this kind, but as yet the financial resources of the I.C.A. are woefully inadequate for it to attempt any but a minute fraction of what requires to be done.

PUBLICATIONS

A great deal of the research and collection of information by the I.C.A. is, of course, for its own use and that of its affiliated organisations, but it also publishes much which is of value to all who are interested in Co-operation. The best known of its publications is the " Review of International Co-operation," an illustrated bi-monthly published in English, French, German, and, since 1968, Spanish. It is the official organ of the I.C.A., describes its current activities, co-operative developments in various parts of the world, international developments, and discusses problems arising from ideas and trends.

The Reports of the International Congresses are mines of information, giving not only reports of the activities of the I.C.A. and its auxiliary organisations, but the discussions on resolutions and papers which reveal co-operative thought on various topics and give indications of a co-operative social philosophy.

One of the most highly regarded of the I.C.A.'s regular publications was " Cartel," a quarterly review in English and French. It was mainly concerned with monopoly in all its aspects, garnering and providing information thereon which was valuable not only to co-operators, but to economists, government departments, trade unions, and banks. When it closed, due to financial circumstances, in 1964, there was a steady demand for back numbers from universities all over the world.

From its inception in 1962, the " Consumer Affairs Bulletin " (which covers some of the same ground that " Cartel " and the " Economic News Service " used to) has steadily advanced in its object of arousing interest in consumer questions and has provided an ever-increasing volume of material on consumer information and protection. Although the Bulletin is naturally aimed at consumers as members of co-operative societies, it is often read and consulted by people outside the Movement interested in consumer affairs.

The " Co-operative News Service " gives current information on co-operative developments in various parts of the world and the "Agricultural Co-operative Bulletin " provides useful news and information on the rather more specialised area of agricultural co-operation.

Less frequent publications include the " Statistics of Affiliated Organisations " published triennially, " International Co-operation " which describes the activities of the national organisations for stated periods, " Directory of the Co-operative Press " containing details of virtually all the journals in the Movement, and the " Film Bulletin " giving details of silent and sound films used in co-operative propaganda and education.

WHOLESALING

Some of the earliest approaches of co-operators in one country to those of another visualised inter-trading. As Co-operative Movements developed in size, scope and variety, the possibilities of international co-operative action in many fields were presented. To explore possibilities and promote action where desirable, auxiliary committees were set up. The first of these was to promote inter-trading between wholesale societies. Some saw a similarity between the development of retail societies necessitating the establishment of national wholesales and the development of national wholesale societies trading in world markets necessitating the establishment of an International Co-operative Wholesale Society.

An organisation with this name was constituted in 1924, but it was not even an embryo, its functions consisting merely of the collection of information and preparation of statistics on matters affecting trade and their circulation to national wholesales.

Succeeding steps were intended, similar to some of the schemes suggested for wholesale trading in England in the 1850's, of grouping of orders and one wholesale acting as agent and buying for the rest, then, as confidence and loyalty grew, the establishment of an International Co-operative Trading Agency, and later a fully developed International Organisation, producing and holding stocks ready for sale to the various national wholesales, owned and controlled by them.

The International Co-operative Trading Agency established in 1937 was one of the casualties of the second world war. In the post-war period, restrictions on international trade were so many and severe, and further developments of national economic planning so probable and likely to increase them, that revival was difficult. An attempt was made but it ceased operations in 1952.

The need for organised co-operative international trading has not, however, disappeared and in fact the prospect is more encouraging now than it has been for some time. Two international organisations have now been operating in Europe for some years. One, " Nordisk Andelsforbund " (N.A.F.), is a federation of the wholesale societies of Finland, Denmark, Sweden, Norway and Iceland which exports and imports. And in the countries of the European Economic Community there is the " Community of National Organisations of Consumers' Co-operatives in the Common Market "—Euroco-op—which has done something to co-ordinate the demand of wholesale societies in these countries and has recently entered the production of biscuits on behalf of its member organisations.

On a wider front, the I.C.A. in 1956 formed a new auxiliary committee on wholesaling—the Co-operative Wholesale Committee. Generally speaking, the activities of the Committee can be said to be the collection and distribution of information; the exchange of experience; and the promotion of co-operative trade. Since 1965 these three functions have neatly come together in the attempts of the Committee to collaborate on and co-ordinate the demand for certain commodities from their eighteen member organisations. Consequently coffee buying, for example, is being increasingly channelled through the N.A.F. office in Brazil, tea through the British Co-operative Tea Society, canned fruit through the N.A.F. in San Francisco and the C.W.S. in Sydney. At the same time, expert groups in non-foods have been working to map out common interests, fix the assortment for joint buying and undertake the common purchases in the most effective way.

A further development has been the decision to merge the Wholesale Committee with another auxiliary committee of the Alliance, the Committee on Retail Distribution, established in 1958. This amalgamation is being effected because of the general trend towards an integration of wholesaling and retailing and also because the members of the two committees were much the same. The merger will create the International Organisation for Consumer Co-operative Distributive Trades—Interco-op—whose main object will be to promote and improve the economic efficiency of affiliated organisations, firstly by developing and intensifying economic collaboration on the wholesale and production levels and circulating information and advice on topics of common interest, and secondly by keeping informed on all distributive problems on the co-operative retail level, arranging the exchange of experiences gained in this field, and intensifying and cultivating mutual contacts between the co-operative retail societies.

PETROLEUM

The International Co-operative Petroleum Association may indicate a line of advance. It arose from the development of the production and refining of petroleum with its by-products by the Consumers' Co-operative Association in the U.S.A., largely to meet the needs of farmers. The output of by-products, such as lubricating oils, however, far exceeded the requirements of the Movement in the U.S.A. Co-operators there saw a solution of the problem in the establishment of an international co-operative society producing and distributing petroleum and its products. Proposed at a meeting of the I.C.W.S. in Paris in 1937, it was not regarded as immediately practicable. In 1945, however, the Americans raised the matter again, and a special sub-committee was appointed to go into details and prepare a plan. This was put before the I.C.A. Congress at Zurich in 1946 and approved.

Co-operative organisations in twenty countries soon joined and subscribed an initial capital of $1 million. The S.C.W.S. was in this from the start and the C.W.S. joined in 1947, and was allocated one seat on a board of eight directors. In 1969, I.C.P.A. consisted of 41 co-operative organisations in 24 countries. Its headquarters are in New York, and its president is a Swede, its vice-president an American, the secretary an American, and other directors are from Ceylon, Holland, France and Switzerland. Both consumer and agricultural societies are members, and the biggest customers for its products are Holland, Sweden, Egypt and Ceylon. Significant developments have been the opening in 1963 of an I.C.P.A. lubricating oil blending plant in Holland, the first international co-operative manufacturing facility and since then it has supervised the building of a similar plant in Ceylon for the Ceylon Petroleum Corporation, an I.C.P.A. member. Since 1968, the I.C.P.A. has been an individual member of the I.C.A. and is therefore no longer listed as an auxiliary committee. It is in fact one of five international organisations that are members of the I.C.A.

BANKING

A Committee on International Banking was set up in 1922 to bring together the directors and managers of the co-operative central banks and credit institutions to exchange information, discuss policy and work out methods of inter-co-operative banking. Activities were suspended after 1932 due to the world depression and failure of the " Banque des Co-operatives de France." Banking statistics of all banks adhering to the committee are circulated from Manchester. It was intended to lead to the establishment of an International Co-operative Bank, and a decision to establish such a bank was made in 1956. Little was done on the decision, however, until 1965 when the existing International Co-operative Bank in Basle was reorganised as a limited company (but with co-operative shareholders retaining majority control) with an increase in capital from something over one million Swiss francs to ten millions. In 1967, the International Co-operative Banking Company Ltd.—INGEBA—was awarded the status of a " Bank " by the Swiss Banking Commission. It is hoped that INGEBA will create the conditions for the collaboration of all co-operative organisations and Banks at the international level and generally increase the proportion of foreign financial business that co-operatives do through co-operative sources.

INSURANCE

A Committee for International Co-operative Insurance was also set up in 1922. At first it confined itself to a study of problems and the possibilities of co-operation between the national co-operative insurance organisations. The studies and interchange of information have proved valuable and they continue, but two problems have dominated its discussion throughout its life—nationalisation and international re-insurance.

In 1948, 1951 and 1957, protests against the nationalisation of co-operative insurance were made, to the effect " that while nationalisation is understandable for social insurance, such as state pensions, co-operative methods offer better terms and conditions for the insured in other branches of business than a state monopoly system. Co-operative insurance operates without seeking private profit, guarantees control by the insured, and avoids all the undesirable features of private as well as state capitalism."

Insurers often find it necessary on grounds of prudence to lessen their risks by re-insuring with other insurance organisations. This necessity obliges co-operative insurance societies to turn to the capitalist market. To avoid this the originators of the committee hoped to establish an International Society of Co-operative Re-insurance. This proved to be too big and difficult a step to take before the war; after the war its possibility was re-examined. It was found to be premature, but a less ambitious step in that direction was made by the creation of a Re-insurance Bureau, operating since 1949, and this facilitated the making of contracts by which many of the societies insure each others' risks.

In addition to the Re-insurance Bureau, there are now two additional bodies. One is Allnations, a corporation registered in the U.S.A. whose directors are the Executive of the Insurance Committee and whose shareholders are the members of the Committee. The function of this organisation is to give temporary financial assistance to new insurance co-operatives in developing countries. The other is the Insurance Development Bureau which is intended to provide technical assistance and advice to the same kinds of organisation where the financial assistance from All-nations needs to be supplemented.

ARTISANAL CO-OPERATIVES

The Committee of Representatives of Workers' Productive and Artisanal Co-operatives was proposed before the second world war, but not created until after it. These societies have perhaps more in common with the originators of the Alliance than have any others, but they are less numerous. The activities of the

Committee have been very practical—the holding of technical courses, the detailed study of occupations in which these societies are engaged, the publication of monographs thereon in English, French and German, and a study of the possibilities of social rehabilitation by co-operatives of the disabled or maimed. Contacts and the exchange of experiences, sometimes of technicians, have increased the knowledge of techniques and of successfully running a co-operative society, of great value to societies in the less developed countries.

HOUSING

Although Co-operative Housing has only been of slight interest to the British Co-operative Movement since 1914, this has not been so to Movements in other parts of the world. Before the second world war, co-operative housing societies were playing an important part in the housing of various continental countries. After the war they played an even greater one.

So important had they become and such were the prospects that the I.C.A. Congress of 1951 created an International Committee on Housing. It concerned itself with inquiries into, studies of and discussion upon general and co-operative housing problems, and the development of contacts with infant housing co-operatives in countries outside Europe and also with co-operative and non-co-operative organisations interested in housing problems.

A study on *Housing Finance in Western Europe* which was published in English, French and German, was well received not only by Co-operative Movements in various parts of the world but also by the International Labour Office and the Economic Commission for Europe Housing Committee. Other studies were on building materials, speculation in real estate, and the role of housing societies.

Model rules for co-operative housing societies were compiled by Dr. E. Bodien of the German Federal Republic. The collection and dissemination of statistics of Housing Co-operatives is undertaken by the I.C.A. Secretariat.

An observer of the committee regularly attended meetings of the Housing Committee of the Economic Commission for Europe, and there are close contacts and relations between the I.C.A. Committee on Housing, the I.L.O., and the E.C.E. Housing Committee.

AGRICULTURE

Although consumer Co-operation was at one time overwhelmingly dominant in the Alliance, this is no longer so, and the

increasing membership and influence of agricultural co-operatives on the Alliance has been welcomed by the British Movement.
It desires indeed the development of genuine agricultural co-
operatives in the British Isles, the Wholesale Societies have
assisted them in the past and continue to do so, and membership
of the Co-operative Union is open to them.

There is a recognition of the need for a co-operative organisation to cover all forms of co-operatives, for not only have they
many common interests and problems but also their respective
developments involve increasing inter-relations which raise their
own problems. It is desirable that these problems be anticipated,
discussed and resolved by co-operators approaching them from
the standpoint of a common interest and mutual advantage, and
not from the standpoint of individual or sectional gain irrespective
of the effects on others. The first co-operative efforts in many of
the less developed territories are in agriculture so that the I.C.A.'s
interest and concern is not solely that involved in seeking to
represent the world co-operative movement, but also in furthering
and assisting pioneering co-operative projects of every kind.

In 1951 agricultural Co-operation so interested the Alliance
that an International Committee on Agricultural Co-operation
was established. Various organisations were represented on this
committee, e.g., agricultural, credit and consumer organisations.
Attempts were made to interest other agricultural co-operative
organisations in the idea of the I.C.A., but this was not easy.
Agricultural co-operative organisations have often become little
other than business organisations, concerned with purely sectional
interests, devoid of any social ideals, oblivious of the common
good. This position, of course, presents a problem to be solved,
not a sorry state of affairs to be accepted. The problem is how
to bring such organisations into the Co-operative Movement.

Thus among the prime activities of the Committee were attempts
to establish contacts and relations with other co-operative agricultural organisations. Among the means designed to this end were
the increased study of and concern with agricultural questions
by the I.C.A. It was thought that the provision of a special
section of the Secretariat to be concerned with agricultural Co-
operation, capable of providing expert technical advice, would
assist. Agriculture, however, covers such a vast ground of
different crops, conditions of climate, soil, pests, disease, etc., that
it would be impossible for the I.C.A. to provide technical advice.
Moreover governments' agricultural departments, university
departments and agricultural institutions the world over are
already engaged in this work. But there is a great need for

specialist assistance and advice in promoting, establishing and developing agricultural *co-operative* societies. Recognising this, the I.C.A. engaged a specialist in this field in 1957.

Consequently the membership of the Committee has grown substantially. In 1957 there were 14 co-operative organisations from 12 countries represented on the committee. By 1968, this had risen to 37 organisations from 27 countries. Attention is being given to a number of problems including those of the co-operative processing of agricultural goods and its contribution to co-operative development, the finance of co-operatives at the international level, and other problems connected with agricultural and fishermen's co-operatives.

REGIONAL ACTIVITIES

A new venture for the Alliance since 1960 has been its work on a regional basis, most developed in South East Asia where a Regional Office and an Education Centre were opened in New Delhi. At the end of 1963 the two were amalgamated into the one institution whose functions are to serve the general purposes of the I.C.A.; to contribute to the execution of I.C.A. policy in all its aspects; to supplement the existing means by which organisations are able to keep in touch with one another; to give information and guidance on requests for technical assistance and to maintain contact with projects in the course of execution; to co-ordinate the work initiated by the Alliance and its members in the organisation of conferences, seminars, and working groups; and to represent the Alliance in its relations with national government departments and international organisations in South East Asia.

In pursuit of these ends, a number of activities have been built up, such as international, regional, and national conferences and seminars, research has been sponsored into matters of regional interest, a number of publications have been issued, technical assistance and consultative services have been made increasingly available to I.C.A. members in the region and a comprehensive library is being built up.

Subsequently, in 1968, an I.C.A. Office for East and Central Africa was opened in Tanzania and the Alliance maintains very close contact with the Organisation of the Co-operatives of America, itself a member of the Alliance, an organisation to co-ordinate and develop the work of co-operatives in Latin America.

The work being done in South East Asia and East Africa is to a large extent being made possible by the generosity of the Swedish

Co-operative Movement. About four-fifths of the funds of the South East Asian Regional Office, for example, come from Sweden. While the Co-operative Movement recognises the responsibility of more developed countries and movements towards those which are less developed, they also recognise the benefits of self-help and there is a growing awareness among the countries in South East Asia of the need to contribute increasingly towards financing the activities of the Regional Office and Education Centre.

INTERNATIONAL DAY AND THE RAINBOW FLAG

Although the I.C.A. is an association of representative co-operative organisations, it realises that all rest upon a base of co-operating individuals and so it is desirable that these should know of the I.C.A., and realise they are part of it. To recall the ideals and principles of the Movement to the millions of co-operators the world over, to inspire them and renew their loyalty to express the sense of international solidarity, to publicise the achievements, obligations to and promise of the Alliance, International Co-operative Day was instituted in 1923. With a brief interval, this has always been celebrated on the first Saturday or Sunday in July, usually by festivals consisting of demonstrations, processions, speeches, field days and so forth.

On that day Canadians, Africans, Indians, Pakistanis, Japanese, Germans, French, Swedes, Danes, British and co-operators in the rest of the 47 countries in membership with the Alliance, assemble in towns and villages to express their sense of international fellowship, hope for international peace, faith in a common ideal and adherence to a common body of principles. For a period, brief though it may be, these co-operators, differing in race, nationality, religion, have a sense of unity and human brotherhood.

A common feature in all these festivals on International Co-operative Day is the display of the Rainbow Flag, bunting and badges. The rainbow, or seven colours of the spectrum, was adopted in 1923 as the flag or colours of the I.C.A. There was a desire for a flag " at once dignified, artistic, and above all, expressive of the idea of International Co-operation." Opinions of what is dignified and artistic change from generation to generation and differ between individuals, so that general agreement thereon is difficult to obtain.

In the case of an International Co-operative Flag it was still more difficult because of national sentiments and the desire to avoid infringing political neutrality. The colours must not resemble any national flag or colours, for instance, nor must they be indentified with any political movement, as would red or white.

Professor Gide provided the solution, a flag embracing all the colours and thus expressing International Co-operation, and he hoped in the form of a rainbow, thus expressing faith in the future of mankind. The idea is said to have been originally conceived by Fourier, the French socialist thinker, corresponding to and contemporary with Robert Owen.

RELATIONS WITH THE I.L.O.

Various international organisations have been established whose scope makes them of concern to Co-operative Movements. It is desirable that they should be able to have contact and relations with these organisations on an international level. The International Co-operative Alliance enables this to be done.

Among the earliest and most important of these is the International Labour Office, created by the Treaty of Versailles, the only enduring constructive effort of that treaty. Its purpose was to consider and make international agreements regulating and improving industrial and social conditions. In this work representatives of capital and labour were to be associated with representatives of governments. The surprising success of the I.L.O. is often regarded as due to the zeal and ability of its first Director-General, Albert Thomas. Thomas was an old and fervent co-operator, well aware of how standards of living had been and could be improved by the development of consumers' and agricultural Co-operation. Consequently, in order to spread and hasten the development of Co-operation he instituted in the I.L.O. a special Co-operative Section.

With the resources at its disposal this Section did great work; it collected and distributed information about co-operative institutions the world over; it supplied information and advice to governments on Co-operation, and it brought together co-operative organisations on the international level. The I.L.O. was a considerable factor in promoting the development of various forms of Co-operation in many parts of the world and in promoting international co-operative relations. Among the most promising of these was the convening of a joint committee of Consumers' and Agricultural Co-operatives to discuss methods of practical collaboration.

Meanwhile the I.C.A. strove to obtain co-operative representation on the governing body of the I.L.O., but this proved impossible without a revision of the Peace Treaty. There was a need for co-operative points of view to be expressed, for these frequently differed from those of both employers' and workers' representatives. This was recognised by inviting international co-operative organisations to appoint representatives in an advisory capacity when discussions either affected co-operative interests or were on matters in which co-operators had special experience and knowledge.

During the second world war the I.C.A. made a successful request to be allowed an observer at the International Labour Conference (1944). The constitution of the I.L.O. was altered so that I.C.A. representatives would be regularly admitted to the Conference as observers, and a committee of the I.L.O. was created to consist of representatives of the main kinds of co-operative organisations.

RELATIONS WITH THE UNITED NATIONS

Besides the I.L.O., the I.C.A. was in contact with the Economic Section of the League of Nations, and the general secretary addressed the International Economic Conference at Geneva in 1927, and later served as a consultative member of the League Economic Committee. The permanent organisation set up as a result of the decisions of the Hot Springs Conference to which reference has already been made was the Food and Agriculture Organisation of the United Nations (F.A.O.). This also has a Co-operative Section and undertakes work very similar to that of the I.L.O. Both have been responsible for valuable publications on Co-operation in recent years.

The setting up of the United Nations Economic and Social Council (a body of the United Nations Organisation) presented an opportunity for the I.C.A. to request to be allowed to collaborate with the Council. The General Assembly of the United Nations decided to grant the request and recommended " that the Economic and Social Council should as soon as possible adopt suitable arrangements enabling the World Federation of Trade Unions and the International Co-operative Alliance . . . to collaborate for purposes of consultation with the Economic and Social Council."

The I.C.A. enjoys the highest consultative status, category A, with the Council. This gives it the right to appoint an observer to attend all public meetings of the Council, to circulate statements and suggestions within their competence of members of the Council, to submit proposals for inclusion in the provisional Agenda, and if accepted to present them orally before the Council and to participate in the meetings of the various Commissions.

It is also invited regularly to the Special Conferences convened by the Council and to meetings of the inter-governmental organisations such as the I.L.O. and U.N.E.S.C.O. The I.C.A. has been able, due to this status, to express its views to the Council on such matters as full employment, international trade, access to raw materials, use of the world's oil resources, control of restrictive business practices. Thus the Co-operative Movement is able to make its voice heard at the highest level.

INTERNATIONAL PEACE

The I.C.A. claims to have two principal aims, it seeks to link together the Co-operative Movements of different countries so that they form one expanding economic system, and it also seeks to create a world environment favourable to Co-operation by removing causes of economic strife and obstacles to mutual understanding and permanent peace. These aims are inter-dependent. The main obstacles to the international development of Co-operation are the artificial barriers erected by governments. These barriers are both cause and effect of economic nationalism and national economic planning. They are also expressive of mutual jealousies, suspicions, fears and hatreds.

It is not surprising that attempts to create some world order and peace by and through power organisations have been unsuccessful. A different approach seems necessary. Peace is not the mere absence of fighting, it is a harmony of interests wherein none is exploiting or seeking to exploit or injure others, it is justice and recognised as justice. Peace and justice are indivisible, for injustice is only possible if those suffering injustice feel themselves too weak for the time being to do otherwise than submit. This is what Hobbes described as a state of "passive war;" there is no actual fighting as in active war, but it is not peace.

The creation of world peace requires an approach to world problems from a world point of view. It would not be sufficient for a few leaders to take such a viewpoint, it would require large numbers of people in each nation to do so. Hence the need for the development of all manner of organisations world wide in scope, and for the increasingly intensive development of world wide community.

A world wide sense of community interest would probably be most easily developed by the furtherance of trading relations between people in the world. These relations are the easiest and generally the first to be entered into. The Free Trade Movement inspired by Cobden in the nineteenth century had ends higher than mere economic ones. A good deal of the driving force behind it came from the idealism of world peace. People who became accustomed to trading with each other would not stop at trading relations. They would know and understand each other, friendships would be made and a sense of community would gradually develop. As a consequence war would become unthinkable. It would also become impossible, for nations would become so dependent on each other that none would be able to make war without the assistance of the rest.

This seems a sound approach. Nations seek self-sufficiency either because they fear war or intend it, and the very search for self-sufficiency has been in itself a potent cause of war. The Free Trade Movement eventually failed to carry conviction because international trade was capitalistic, and so, rightly or wrongly, was suspected as a means by which some nations could exploit others.

The development of co-operative international trade, however, would be free of such suspicions. Conducted by international co-operative organisations on co-operative principles, it would be subject to democratic control by all those concerned. It would be non-profit making as profits would be returned in proportion to transactions. Open membership would enable any people to enter on the same terms as those already in. Voluntary membership would mean that the system was not forced on any people.

A brief example illustrates how the application of co-operative principles to international problems would assist their solution. A great danger to peace is conflict over possession or control of essential raw materials, especially oil. During the war a Swedish co-operator, Anders Hedberg, advocated that all the oil supplies of the world should be brought under the ownership and control of what would be a co-operative society, the members of which would be all nations. Every nation would have its voice in the government of the society and profits would be distributed among the nations according to the proportion of oil which each had purchased. The proposal was later brought before the United Nations and rejected, probably because nations possessing oil feared the loss of power to themselves which would result. Thus the jealousies and fears of nation states prevented a practical solution of a problem which will continue to endanger world peace.

The Co-operative Movements, however, the world over are accustomed to working together for common ends, to creating schemes for mutual advantage. Ideas of domination and exploitation are alien to their outlook. In these Co-operative Movements

are people with the necessary outlook and experience. Their
system enables international trade to be developed free from the
evils associated with capitalist trade. Hence the belief of many
co-operators that the development of international co-operative
organisations helps to create the world environment necessary
to world peace. This was one of the ideals for which the International Co-operative Alliance was founded. It is an ideal still
held.

18 TOWARDS THE CO-OPERATIVE COMMONWEALTH

" But where does all this co-operative activity lead? What is the goal for which co-operators are aiming? Is it merely a more efficient economic system? It is that; but it is something more. Is it a more satisfying economic system because it is more moral and because it solves most of the present day problems of industry and commerce? It is that; but it is something more, for Co-operation has other aims than economic ones. The earnest co-operator seeks to apply co-operative methods to all purposes of social life, and does so because he believes that in working with others for the common good, man's highest qualities are enlisted and developed; and in the employment and development of these qualities the man himself becomes a better man, and the quality of the human race is improved."

("*Co-operation*," Hall and Watkins.)

IT is sometimes argued that the Co-operative Movement was born of the squalor and misery of the Industrial Revolution and so has lost the reason for its existence as squalor and misery have disappeared. This argument is based upon a misunderstanding of both the origin and purpose of the Co-operative Movement. Squalor and misery certainly played a part in stimulating opposition to capitalism, but there were more positive and permanent elements involved in the generation of the Co-operative Movement. Its opposition to capitalism, for instance, was an opposition to the very spirit of capitalism, to the profit-making motive as well as to its consequences. This motive and its consequences remain, and so does the co-operative opposition.

Among these consequences are the inequitable distribution of wealth and income, inequitable because it corresponds neither with need nor merit. Much income is unearned by the recipients, and wealth and incomes may appreciate or depreciate as a result of changes in demand, social developments, inventions and discoveries, wars or political changes, for which the recipients are not responsible. Differences in wealth are important factors in every phase of life; they result in differences in power and influence in economic, social and political life. These differences are seldom socially beneficial in their effects, for the ability or good fortune to accumulate wealth is not by any means necessarily accompanied by the will or ability to use it well.

It has been argued, however, that although capitalism may not result in an equitable distribution of wealth, it is still justified because it so increases wealth that everybody is better off; even the poorest may be better off with a small slice of a big cake than an equal slice of a little one. The profit motive, it is held, acts as a spur to enterprise, favours the survival of the fittest and promotes economic progress. It is also held that the profit index is an index of social needs and preferences and induces productive resources to flow in the right proportion into the various channels of production to correspond with those needs and preferences.

Against this it may be argued that capitalism generates many restrictive practices which keep the cake smaller than it might be. There is a great deal of unearned income which permits idleness, and owing to the unequal distribution of income neither the price nor the profit index are a true measure of social needs. Neither is there the mobility of resources necessary to enable them to flow easily and quickly to correspond with social needs. The desire for individual gains (including wages, salaries, professional fees as well as profits and rents) results in practices and restrictions which hinder mobility.

Exploitation of Labour.

Moreover, profits may be increased by reducing wages, increasing the length of the working week, speeding up, and in general exploiting labour more severely. Trade union strength and industrial legislation now prevent the worst abuses, but the profit incentive to practise them is still there. Morever, capitalist society is divided into employers and employed, the interests of whom, as Adam Smith observed even in the 18th century, are by no means the same. There are consequent conflicts between capital and labour, which do not diminish even with improvements in wages and working conditions, for the fundamental causes of labour discontent are in the employer-employed relationship itself.

A. D. Lindsay [1] expressed this as follows: " The real quarrel which people have with profit-making is their quarrel with a system which specialises responsibility and those who have responsibility taken for them . . . our industrial system tends to make

---

[1] Christianity and Economics

Q

it easy for men to treat other men merely as means or instruments.
. . . What really concerns the wage earner is loss of status or
personal dignity in the sense that he feels he is a tool or instrument
and nothing more. The fundamental distinction in an industrial
society is not between rich and poor: it is between the employing
and the employed class, between those who take responsibility
and manage and organise and discipline, and those who have no
share in responsibility, who are managed, organised and
disciplined."

This relation and the discontent to which it gives rise is not
peculiar to industrial society, it is found in the armed services, in
nationalised industries, municipal enterprises, and in some co-
operative enterprises. The self-governing workshops of the
Christian Socialists and co-operative producer and co-operative
co-partnership societies were attempts to solve this problem, but
raised others. It is a problem which is likely to increase in gravity
as the working classes become better educated, unless as a result
of technical progress the length of the working week is so reduced
that the part of their lives spent in employment becomes of minor
importance.

Exploitation of the Consumer.

The profit motive is not only an incentive to exploit labour, it
is also an incentive to exploit the consumer. Legislation and
government inspection are even necessary to restrain or prevent
adulteration of foodstuffs dangerous to health, and the using of
false weights and measures. Nevertheless, adulteration of goods
intended to deceive the consumer as to quality and the use of
packs and containers to deceive as regards quantity are still
common commercial practice.

As production becomes mechanised it becomes more profitable,
in order to keep plant regularly employed, to produce goods
which will wear out quickly instead of those of lasting quality.
In cases where goods do not wear out quickly enough changes of
fashion may be stimulated or designs altered to induce consumers
to scrap the old and buy new. Sometimes the changes are for the
worse, and the competition in deception generally tends to
deterioration in the quality of products, at least as regards final
consumer goods for the final consumer generally lacks the
technical knowledge to choose wisely.

Many goods differ so little in quality that competition between
different brands becomes largely a competition in advertisement.
Advertising is so effective in stimulating demand that producers
tend to rely more upon it to create a demand for their products

than upon producing goods in response to consumer needs. Thus productive resources do not invariably flow into the channels corresponding to needs, demands are stimulated to conform to pre-determined supplies. As industrial progress enables existing wants to be satisfied by the expenditure of less resources if all resources are to continue to be employed then the surplus resources must be used to produce the means to satisfy new wants. This involves the discovery of new wants and the stimulation of the public to feel them. In deciding which new wants to stimulate, however, profit-seeking concerns do not consider which are likely to be good and which harmful but which can be most easily stimulated into profitable demands. All these consequences result in a wastage of resources.

Debasement of Moral Values

Co-operators have always held that the most serious evils resulting from the profit motive, however, are those upon character. This was, as was shown in the first chapter, the opinion of Robert Owen. Ruskin, when condemning the complex division of labour, remarked it to be a sad thing for a man's whole working life to be spent in making the thirtieth part of pins. It may be sadder still for it to be spent in making the worse appear the better by devising deceptive advertisements or in discovering additives to foodstuffs which will give deceptive flavourings and colourings.

Some of the evil effects on character may be lessened by the loss of the sense of personal responsibility. The artist or scientist engaged in lucrative yet anti-social activities may consider he has no responsibility for them, that such responsibility rests with his employers. The typical shareholder in a joint stock company may also feel that he has no responsibility for the way in which the company conducts the business and makes the profits in which he shares. As the company's board of directors may also consider that their prime duty is to make profits for the shareholders, and cannot allow any twinges of individual conscience to interfere with it, nobody feels morally responsible for the way in which the business is conducted. Moreover, they are subject to the dictates of competition. If competitors gain an advantage by a malpractice then they must adopt it to remain in business.

There is a common opinion that a malpractice is justified if everybody does it, a belief that anything is justified if it gives the public what it is supposed to want and an indifference to the consequences of economic decisions excepting those which affect profit. This lack of a sense of responsibility, of indifference to consequences, of assessing the worth of anything by its profitability is partly due to and partly cause of a loss of sense of values. A. D. Lindsay drew attention to the serious consequences of this, that the poisoning of the sense of what is valuable in life matters more than anything else, " for if our values go, no tinkering or mending of instruments will do any good."

It will be gathered that all these various ills arise from economic activities being directed to the wrong ends, to the making of profits instead of to the satisfaction of wants. Profit-seeking spoils everything it touches, the worst effects are on human character and relations, but art, culture, sport, craftsmanship, scenic beauty, also suffer. They lose their essence as they become in the popular term " commercialised," i.e. exploited for profit.

Different motives for economic behaviour are required for true and lasting social improvement. Consumers' Co-operation provides a different motive. The elimination of profit by its principles of fixed interest on capital and the division of surplus in proportion to transactions eliminates the profit motive and replaces it by the satisfaction of consumer needs. Democratic control, in which all members have equal voting power, keeps control in the hands of consumers, and co-operative enterprises are directed to the prime purpose of satisfying consumer needs.

This should affect designs and qualities of goods, advertising and salesmanship, and indeed to some extent has done so. That the full beneficial effects have not been realised is due to the fact that Co-operation still operates within a capitalist world, and its members, officials and staffs cannot remain unaffected by the general environment. There is, consequently, a constant struggle to prevent co-operative business from being perverted to capitalist aims and methods.

DESIRE FOR A CO-OPERATIVE COMMONWEALTH

Opposition to capitalism, however, is not the sole reason for the existence of the Co-operative Movement. It pursues ideals of its own. From its origin it has sought to create an economic and social order which, being favourable to the improvement of human character would be conducive to greater human happiness. In the first chapter the Owenite aims were summarised as equality, social ownership, just prices and the elimination of profit, the abolition of the profit motive and education in co-operative living. Robert Owen and his followers looked to the creation of co-operative village communities as the means to create a New Moral World " by placing all within arrangements of surroundings as will form the character, create the wealth and cordially unite all in one interest and feeling all over the world." Dr. King also held that the ultimate purpose of Co-operation was the improvement of the moral character and believed this would be accomplished by the practice of Co-operation, education and the development of co-operative communities.

The Rochdale Pioneers were, of course, Owenite idealists to whom the co-operative store was but the first step to their objective, the establishing of " a self-supporting home colony of united interests." During the 1850's the co-operative village community lost a good deal of its attractiveness as a means to the end sought. Economic and social developments made it obvious that the village community was on too small a scale and the development of co-operative societies showed it possible to evolve, not little village communities, but co-operative organisations on a national, and perhaps even on a supra-national, scale; of bit by bit transforming the existing system into a co-operative one.

E. V. Neale and T. Hughes had similar views and visions. They condemned the existing system of competition, as not merely wasteful, but injurious to character, held that work ought to be carried on, not upon a system of struggle but upon one of fellowship where the results of common labour would be distributed with equity. They desired the existing system to be replaced by a co-operative system. Co-operative distribution was the first step towards this better system, it would be followed by developments into wholesaling, production, importing, shipping and " thus we see the way opening to the quiet, gradual introduction of that world of co-operative union." (*Manual for Co-operation*, 1881, approved by the Co-operative Congress of that year.)

The desired co-operative economic and social order has come to be known as " The Co-operative Commonwealth." Sidney and Beatrice Webb frequently used the term. The Co-operative Congress of 1925 approved the inclusion in the objects of the Co-operative Union as stated in its rules, " the ultimate establishment of a Co-operative Commonwealth " and a condition of membership of the Co-operative Party is an affirmation of belief in it.

The ideal of a Co-operative Commonwealth has thus always been held by the Co-operative Movement in Great Britain, but it is not confined to the British Movement. Professor Gide, the great French co-operator, stated that " Co-operation, therefore, means nothing less than an economic system destined to supersede capitalism by mutual aid " and saw that each co-operative society " constitutes a little world organised in conformity with justice and social benefit, and that it is sufficient to let it develop spontaneously, either by growth or imitation, to realise in the more or less distant future the best of all possible worlds."

E. Poisson, also of France, explained the theory of the evolution of the Co-operative Movement into a Commonwealth. Anders Örne of Sweden believed the Co-operative Movement was the means to the evolution of a new economic and social order. So did Dr. Warbasse of the United States of America, who spoke of such an order as a Co-operative Democracy—" a democracy that would supersede both capitalist anarchy and collectivist state."

Lastly, the International Co-operative Alliance itself states in Article 1 of its rules that it, " in continuance of the work of the Rochdale Pioneers and in accordance with their principles, seeks, in complete independence and by its own methods, to substitute for the profit-making regime a co-operative system organised in the interests of the whole community and based upon mutual self-help."

Thus leading co-operators at various times and in various countries have expressed their faith in the creation of a Co-operative Commonwealth and the view that this is the end to which Co-operation moves, and to which its activities should be directed.

EVOLUTION OF THE CO-OPERATIVE COMMONWEALTH

The Owenites drew up plans for their communities in great detail, almost as the plans for machines or the organisation of a factory would be prepared. Karl Marx described this as "Utopian Socialism," for human society cannot be constructed to a plan or established at will. Human society evolves, and Marx held that a new order could only be generated by forces contained in the old. His " scientific socialism " was based on what he believed were the laws governing social evolution.

Some early co-operators, however, also had doubts about the Owenite method of drawing up a blueprint of an ideal order and then persuading people to adopt it. Dr. King, for instance, held that a Co-operative Community must be evolved from and by the development of co-operative societies, the process of development providing the knowledge and experience and forming the characters of people to fit them for a successful co-operative community.

The Rochdale Pioneers desired a co-operative community, it was " the concrete realities of the situation " which caused them to start with a store and adopt a scheme of development similar to that advocated by Dr. King. Later, as Ben Jones pointed out, a " Rochdale Plan " emerged, in which co-operative development was not of the store into a village community, but into national and international organisations. [1]

Hughes and Neale rejected the idea of ideal systems, they believed that such schemes were impracticable and in any case too rigid for human well-being and progress. They concerned themselves with ideals of conduct, of principles which should govern human relations. Circumstances differed and changed, the application of the same principles to different circumstances would produce different systems, it was therefore fatuous to make blueprints of systems; it was the principles which were important.

Utopian schemes became discredited in the late 19th century as theories of evolution came to be accepted and attention was directed to social evolution. Ideals of a better social order were not discarded but there was no longer the willingness to prepare blueprints of it. Attention was given to principles, to the embodiment of socialist principles in reforms and institutions dealing with economic and social problems, in the belief that a socialist order would gradually emerge thereby.

Co-operators had long discarded their ideas of Utopian communities, but they did not discard their idea of a Co-operative Commonwealth. They were no more willing, however, to prepare a detailed plan of such a Commonwealth than were State Socialists or Marxists to present detailed plans of their ideal orders. All such plans would have been Utopian.

The form of the Co-operative Commonwealth and the process of its evolution have received more attention in this century. In Chapter VIII some of the views of Sidney and Beatrice Webb, Leonard Woolf, Professor C. Gide, E. Poisson and A. Örne are described. The Webbs described their ideas for the constitution of a Socialist Commonwealth and the place of the Co-operative Movement within it. Their suggestions would be approved by most co-operators and are in accord with most co-operative thinking on the subject. Leonard Woolf outlined a Co-operative Commonwealth but his plan for attaining it was not acceptable to co-operators. He held that it should be created by political methods, and that the consumer co-operative system could be effected at any time by legislation. Gide, Poisson and Örne on the other hand believed that a Co-operative Commonwealth could, and would be evolved by co-operative evolution. Poisson devoted a whole book, the *Co-operative Republic*, to the subject and it is dealt with here more fully because it gives a theory of co-operative evolution with which most co-operators would probably agree.

---

[1] Co-operative Production. *B. Jones, 1894.*

Poisson's Laws

Poisson outlined a theory of social evolution showing the interrelation between economic progress and social change, how a new system gradually grows out of an old one. He claimed that " the institutions which form part of the essential conditions of a transformation of society are definitely to be found in the consumers' Co-operative Movement."

He stated what he termed " The Organic Laws of Co-operation" which he considered gave a definite character to a consumers' society. They were division of surplus in proportion to purchases, equality of members in control, sale at ordinary market prices, collectively-owned capital. Then he explained the " Laws of Co-operative Evolution."

First is the " Law of Indefinite Extensibility " according to which every consumers' society has within it the possibility of limitless extension, to which it is driven by natural impulse. It relates to the increase in membership and to its business operations. Societies usually begin by trading in a few goods, gradually the range of goods traded in is increased, department is added to department. Operations too big for the scale of the individual society are undertaken by a co-ordination of efforts through the establishing of federations. Wholesale societies based on the same principles as the primary societies are set up and the same tendencies to extension are manifested. Being on a larger scale there is a greater scope; they extend into industrial production, agriculture, finance. " Nothing, therefore, stays the extension of Co-operation; no sphere is closed to it; nothing indicates that it will not ultimately succeed. It obeys a law that impels it at all times and in all latitudes. Drawn into all kinds of enterprise, its law, its destiny, is to extend without limit in all economic spheres. Its driving power is its principle of progress and this principle itself springs from its organic laws."

The second law is, " The Adaptation of Co-operation to Economic Progress " and states, " The progress of consumers' societies conforms to the economic evolution of the existing society within the framework of which they operate and develop." They are most developed and most prosperous where capitalism is most highly developed and so are apparently involved in general economic progress, " following the evolution of that very capitalistic system to which in principle it is absolutely opposed." If true, this would, of course, support his theory of evolution. But he also held that Co-operation had a " Universal Adaptability." It developed a creative power of its own which operates in all social circumstances, so that consumers' societies were successfully operating in old civilisations and in transplanted civilisations; all races, all climates were suitable for Co-operation. The co-operative society was adapted to all natural states of society, not merely to the kind of society in which it first appeared.

Poisson's Hypothesis

The growth of co-operative enterprises led him to "The Hypothesis of the Co-operative Republic." This stated—" If retail societies succeeded in establishing themselves . . . in every place, omitting no town or district; if these retail societies were without exception affiliated to wholesale organisations and these wholesale organisations organised their own production and reached the stage of controlling industry from the sources of raw material to the last stages of manufacture; if the wholesales had gained control over transport by organising their own road transport, and acquiring railways and ships, if they had established co-operative banks and controlled all credit on behalf of co-operators; if they had acquired the land. . . . If in short, wholesale commerce, manufacture, finance and agriculture had been taken over by consumers' co-operative societies owning, controlling and organising them all. If all these hypotheses were realised, what would result? A completely new economic society would be established, and this we shall call the Co-operative Republic."

In this Republic the means of production and exchange would be the common property of consumers; profits, interest, rents, would consequently go to the consumer and there would be no parasitic classes living by owning. " Inequality of wealth, therefore, comes to an end, and the class struggle has no longer any object." There would be an end of economic disorder, crises, waste, unco-ordinated effort, neglect of general interests. Production would be for the known needs of consumers; " henceforward consumption will govern production and direct it."

But although a co-operative republic or commonwealth could be created by evolution, this creation was not automatic or inevitable: " It can be established only by men and women, by their will to unite, by the endeavour of consumers who have become co-operators. The rapidity of its attainment depends upon this moral factor. Knowledge of the purpose in view, and of those means which alone can accomplish it, constitute a second factor of the same kind."

Although the Co-operative Republic would be socialistic, the methods of attaining it would differ from those of political socialism, " for it claims to be establishing itself from now

onwards and day by day, and lends no credence to the notion of
a great upheaval which would mean no more than the seizure of
political power. The Co-operative Republic starts from society as
it now is. . . . It revolutionises other social relations. It begins as
private property and ends as public property. It substitutes the
administration of affairs for the government of men because it
tends to deprive the state of its compulsory attributes and
abolishes class divisions. It practises the ethics of solidarity and
brings to the front once more the national ethics of antiquity, the
pursuit of happiness and the love of life, because its basis is the
satisfaction of wants.

" In a sentence, the Co-operative Republic is shown to be self-
sufficient in its own field of action, and to contain in rudimentary
form the solution of the social problem, which it will accomplish
by its own natural and complete development."

Co-operative Considerations.

There is little in the above summary with which co-operators
of previous generations would disagree. Support for the views
expressed could easily be culled from the works of co-operative
leaders and thinkers in past times and in various countries. This
could not, however, be said of all the opinions expressed in
Poisson's book. For instance, he visualised the development of
one comprehensive national society, all the retail societies amalgamating into one and this taking over the wholesale societies
with all their activities. Some might consider such an organisation
to be undesirable as well as impracticable. It might be doubted
if one organisation could manage the hundreds of industries and
trades, the thousands of plants and workshops to meet the varying
needs of millions of people.

Poisson himself appears to have had doubts. He wrote:
" Unity must not be confused with centralisation. If the Co-
operative Republic were no more than a Co-operative Empire,
we should expect it to have an empire's defects, all its bureaucracy, machinery of coercion, and other weaknesses. . . . In
establishing organic unity we must allow for local differences and
regional interests as well as the needs of the central organisation.
Management and administration must be largely decentralised.
Room must be made for the widest autonomy, and control must
be as flexible as possible."

It may be observed that organic unity could be obtained by
other means than Poisson's monolithic society. Federal organisations, such as wholesale societies, co-operative unions, co-operative banks, etc., could develop an organic unity of various types

of societies, and important values associated with independence, such as self-reliance and effective democracy, could be retained.

Poisson's *Co-operative Republic* must not be regarded as covering the entire sector of social life, but only of that suitable for consumer control. This, in his opinion, did not extend to the administration of justice, the preservation of public order, national defence, the running of certain public services, and provision of various social services such as pensions, health services, family allowances. In short, the Co-operative Republic did not embrace the political state or such areas of social and individual life as aesthetics and religion.

His concept of a Co-operative Republic differed little from that of the Webb's Socialist Commonwealth. In each case the organisations to supply the means to satisfy consumers' wants are voluntary consumers' co-operative societies with unlimited rights to expand; in both there is what the Webbs termed an " unsocialised " sector, a political sector, and a public sector of economic administration.

The increasing development of state collectivism and of movements hoping to achieve socialism or other " isms " by increasing the powers and functions of the State have faced co-operators with the problem of the State presenting itself as a formidable obstacle to the Movement's progress. Chapters VII and XI related instances of these in the recent history of the British Movement, occasioning statements of policy by the Co-operative Union in 1950, 1953 and 1958, dealing with " The Place of the Co-operative Movement in a Collectivist Economy," " Social Ownership and Consumer Problems," and " Co-operation and Socialism." These, as the summaries given in Chapter XI show, insisted on the right of the Co-operative Movement to exist and grow.

CO-OPERATION AND THE STATE

Co-operators recognise the need for the State but they by no means worship it, nor do they believe that their ideals can be attained by the coercive powers of the State. Their ideals are to be attained by voluntary Co-operation, by encouraging and assisting people to help themselves by mutual aid, by people co-operating of their own free will. Individual freedom is necessary for the development of the mental and moral faculties, so that the co-operative ideal of improving and raising the mental and moral stature of man cannot be attained by other than free men and women.

Dr. William King, for instance, held that Co-operation was

essentially voluntary, that it should depend on no power but itself, that the interference of governments would be harmful.

Hughes and Neale wrote: " Our co-operators . . . do not ask the State to do anything for them, beyond giving them a fair field and standing aside while they do their own work in their own way. They want no State aid—they would be jealous of it if proffered " and " of one thing they must assert their undoubting conviction, that if the co-operative spirit, with the facilities of action now open to it, cannot succeed in forming a reformed social state, the existing state will be absolutely powerless to create a co-operative spirit."

Hall and Watkins expressed similar doubts of the State performing co-operators' tasks: " Purely political solutions of the social problems are seen to be impossible when it is remembered that people bred and trained in profit-seeking business, cannot be transformed by a stroke into public-spirited officers of State, and that educating the general public in its rights and duties is an even slower task."

Anders Örne gave a fairly comprehensive view—" Co-operation cannot, without betraying its very mission, place itself under the the economic guardianship of the State or allow itself to be transformed into an instrument of the State's general policy. It aims higher and further than national states. On the other hand Co-operation is in no way hostile to the State. It subordinates itself loyally and readily to national jurisdiction and considers that some such compulsory organisation as the State is, and will always be, indispensable for the protection of right and justice in the broadest sense, for ordinary education, for care of the sick and feeble, and for a number of other duties. But at the same time it considers free co-operation of the people preferable to compulsory satisfaction of material needs."

Dr. Warbasse was less convinced of the need for a State than were the European co-operators. To him the State was necessary because " as yet people do not think they can do without it. The lame man cannot suddenly be deprived of his crutch, nor the slave of his master. The lives of the people have been adjusted to the State." As, however, people learned to serve themselves instead of being served by the State or profit-making business, there was less need for the State. Thus, although States would be necessary for a long time to come, they would fade away as co-operative organisations of the people took their place, the functions of the State would grow less " and the vanishing point of the State will be the peaceful end toward which society should tend."

The "Co-operative Sector"

The *Co-operative Sector* by Dr. G. Fauquet reappraised the views of Gide and Poisson. He drew attention to the changed circumstances; capitalism was becoming less competitive and more monopolistic, the liberal State had disappeared, States were increasing their functions and powers, attempting to plan their respective economies and directly undertaking economic enterprises. " The Co-operative Movement can consequently no longer count as in the past upon an indefinite growth in the environment of economic liberty. It has now to adapt itself, by struggle in one place, by agreement in another, to the elements of a complex environment, partly free and partly organised."

Nations had come to have " mixed economies," consisting of four sectors. The Public Sector comprised state and municipal enterprises and the organs by which the State seeks to exercise a general control over the economy. In the Capitalist Sector all the enterprises were dominated by private capital which incurs the risks and takes the profits. The Private Sector proper (or pre-capitalist sector) comprised the innumerable non-capitalist units and activities of family economy and handicraft economy. The Co-operative Sector comprised all the forms of Co-operation already linked or tending to link themselves together socially and economically.

The Co-operative Sector has relations with the other four. It competes with the capitalist sector and yet has business relations with it, and many of its members are employed therein. The Private Sector is of minor importance in Great Britain, but is of very great importance in some countries. In these it is closely connected with the Co-operative Sector and the two may largely coincide, as marketing, supply, credit and other forms of co-operative society are formed within it. Relations with the Public Sector vary according to the type of State, in some they are completely subject to control by the State, and although the form of a co-operative society remains, the co-operative spirit has been completely expelled.

Assuming that the Public Sector is likely to increase, Fauquet considered what the attitude of co-operatives to such development should be. He believed that much of such development is desirable, public action being an effective means of controlling parts of the economic process strongly held by the capitalist economy and which could be captured by the co-operative economy only with great difficulty if at all.

The Public and Co-operative Sectors could be complementary

to each other. The State starts from the top and organises and commands downwards. Consequently, " it is far from the concrete realities of life, which present themselves to it as approximations and averages; it counts heads but knows nothing of persons." On the other hand Co-operation is organised from the bottom upwards, its little basic units are close to the individual person, the sovereignty of these little units locates the origin and exercise of power at the very origin of needs, man remains his own master and the organisation his servant. Co-operation is also voluntary whereas the State by its nature is coercive. There are spheres of action where coercion and centralisation would be ineffective or unsuitable. If the State invaded the whole of economic life it would be a monstrous system of tyranny. Co-operation with its highest levels of organisation working in conjunction with the State's organs of a centralised economy could remedy some of the State's defects and weaknesses.

As time went on Co-operation would continue to develop from the bottom upwards, and it is probable that there would be demands from consumers and workers for more effective democratic control of some of the State economic organisations and of more equitable means of dealing with their surpluses, i.e., demands to convert them into organisations similar to co-operative ones. Thus even in State-planned economies there is a possibility of co-operative growth and progress. Providing Co-operation retains its right to expand and grow, Co-operative Commonwealths similar to those visualised by Poisson and the Webbs are well within the bounds of possibility.

BUILDERS OF THE COMMONWEALTH

It may seem a far cry to these speculations upon a Co-operative Commonwealth from the contemporary work of the co-operative employee or the co-operative activities of the member. Yet the historical chapters have described great progress towards this Commonwealth, and although much of this was due to co-operative theorists, leaders and congresses, none of it would have been made but for the humbler activities of the millions of unknown co-operative members and employees.

The records of increases in membership, capital, trade and production, may appear dull and lifeless unless one appreciates what they represent. Each unit in the membership figure, for instance, represents a person and a person who made a decision to join a co-operative society. In 1844 there were 28 such persons, in 1960 there were 13 million.

Others of these statistics also refer to the results of individual decisions freely made by the millions of common people, alive and dead, who constitute the Co-operative Movement. The aggregate figures of membership, capital and trade and their growth are impressive, but they are the aggregates of very small individual contributions. Every individual contribution, whether in membership, capital, or trade, is a voluntary contribution, i.e., a result of a free and willing decision made by an individual person. Every such contribution is an advance towards the Commonwealth.

The Co-operative Commonwealth cannot be forced upon people, it can only grow as, how, when and where people desire it. But it is growth which each individual can directly assist day by day, without having to wait for general elections or revolutionary situations. Every time the housewife decides to buy from the co-operative society she is advancing the Commonwealth, every time she decides to buy elsewhere she is maintaining capitalism. Vital decisions of whether there shall be an advance to the Commonwealth or not are thus made daily by the millions of individuals who constitute the purchasing public.

Other vital decisions are made by people with money to save and invest. Co-operative enterprise cannot exist and develop without capital. Its capital does not come, and is unlikely to come, from big investors but from millions of small investors. The average member's investment, indeed every individual's investment in a co-operative society, is far too small to finance even a small business, but the association of the many small capitals forms a huge aggregate capital. In these days the savings of the millions of common people would be sufficient to finance co-operative enterprise on the widest fields and the largest scale. Yet there are many ardent socialists, willing to lay down their lives on the barricades, who will more readily stake their money in the football pools in the hope of winning some of that of their fellows than invest in their own co-operative businesses and so benefit all.

Likewise there are many people strongly opposed to the power wielded by " big business " and to the dictatorial position of the employer, who desire democratic control of economic life yet never take an interest nor part in the control of their co-operative societies, never look at the accounts or attend a general meeting. These shortcomings of many quite sincere people are generally due to ignorance; ignorance of co-operative purpose and possibilities, of the power which people can exercise when they co-operate, although as individuals they are impotent. It is one of the tasks of co-operative education to remove this ignorance.

Some people, although living in an environment which promotes and encourages individual selfishness and the disposition to determine their decisions by the comparative possibilities of individual gain, will become members of, invest in and buy from, co-operative societies because they believe that by so doing they are replacing an evil and unjust system by a better moral one. But this is not the case with most people. They join a co-operative society and buy from it because they are better off by so doing, they believe that they spend to better advantage, they invest in co-operative societies because the investments are safe and liquid.

These material benefits are largely due to Co-operation itself, for the more loyal co-operators are, the greater are the benefits in the long run. As co-operative societies, however, have increased in size, they have become increasingly dependent on the efficiency of their staffs. If co-operative business is to grow, even if it is to maintain itself, it must be more efficient than its capitalist competitors. Greater efficiency has to be proved to the sceptical or critical shopper considering the limited contents of her purse and comparing the prices, values and services of one shop with others. It is harder thus to prove the superiority of co-operative enterprise in the competitive market, than it is to prove the superiority of public enterprise on a public platform or in a parliamentary debate. But in the interests of the common good this is desirable; it ensures that co-operative enterprise only replaces capitalist enterprise where and when it is superior in economic efficiency.

Co-operative business efficiency depends very largely upon co-operative employees, from the executive officers downwards. This efficiency depends not only upon skill and knowledge but also upon zeal, and zeal depends upon the understanding and love of the purpose for which the Movement exists, as with Cromwell's Ironsides who were formidable because they knew what they fought for and loved what they knew. Co-operative employees should work for something besides a wage or salary, for their employment engages them in a Movement for a social ideal, not to make profits for a capitalist employer. Not only do they serve the current needs of common people without exploiting them, but their work is evolving a better economic and social order, one based upon social justice—a Co-operative Commonwealth.

CONCLUSION

This survey of the organisation of the British Co-operative Movement has shown amid all its complexities that the outstanding features are democratic. From the basic retail societies to the national federations they are governed from the bottom upwards. A retail society's board is elected by and from its members and is responsible to them, a responsibility frequently emphasised at its general meetings. The various federal bodies have boards elected by and from their constituent societies and responsible to them. Other features such as dividend on purchases and voluntary membership make the democratic control more effective and real. It is these features which have made federation successful. For they prevent some members dominating or making gains at the expense of the rest through federation.

A danger to all federations is the tendency to disintegrate as a result of a majority seeking to impose its will on, or to exploit a minority. These dangers are avoided in co-operative federations by their adherence to co-operative principles. Societies retain their autonomy and federal decisions are binding upon the federations but not upon the societies which compose them. There is no government from the top downwards in the Co-operative Movement.

These features make it difficult for those accustomed to power being concentrated at the top, whether in political governments or in business, to understand the Co-operative Movement. Similarly those accustomed to regard the purpose of business as profit-making find it difficult to understand co-operative business. The Co-operative Movement is no field for those who seek either power or wealth.

Democracy, however, is both difficult and dangerous. It requires the willingness and ability of each to see the common interest and to serve it. This is often lacking, not only in the rank and file members of retail societies, but also in the boards and officials of societies. This lack is generally due to a lack of understanding and this, in turn, to a lack of education in Co-operation.

On the other hand, the problems encountered would be still there even if the Movement lost its democracy, and it is doubtful if they would be any better dealt with. The observations of Edmund Burke on the bigger problems of government have a bearing on the smaller one of co-operative organisations :

" A work for social ends is to be only wrought by social means. There, mind must conspire with mind. Time is required to produce that union of minds which alone can produce all the good we aim at. Our patience will achieve more than our force . . . in my course I have known and, according to my measure, have co-operated with great men; and I have never yet seen any plan which has not been mended by the observations of those who were much inferior in understanding to the person who took the lead in the business. By a slow but well-sustained progress, the effect of each step is watched; the good or ill success of the first gives light to us in the second. . . . We see that the parts of the system do not clash. The evils latent in the most promising contrivances are provided for as they arise. One advantage is as little as possible sacrificed to another. We compensate, we reconcile, we balance. We are enabled to unite into a consistent whole the various anomalies and contending principles that are found in the minds and the affairs of men. From hence arises, not an excellence in simplicity, but one far superior, an excellence in composition." (*Reflections on the Revolution in France.*)

It is still somewhat Utopian to speculate on the organisation of a Co-operative Commonwealth for this will depend on circumstances and future circumstances are unknown. But one feature common to all the views of co-operative evolution and an ultimate commonwealth which have been considered is the acceptance of the soundness of Rochdale co-operative principles, so that it is reasonable to assume that the organisations of a Co-operative Commonwealth would embody and be based upon these. A discussion upon a Co-operative Commonwealth would be largely concerned with these principles, and their application, and with the development, that is the history, of the Co-operative Movement at home and abroad.

From a consideration of these matters it can be assumed that a system of Co-operation sufficiently comprehensive to justify the term of Co-operative Commonwealth would only evolve if it were freely and willingly desired. This depends, as Poisson stressed, upon the co-operative education of the people. Adherence to co-operative ideals and principles is only possible or likely if people understand them. With this adherence based upon understanding, co-operative societies of all kinds and sizes would be truly co-operative and people would become increasingly aware of the values of association and individual freedom.

It is probable that there would be a continually increasing variety of societies, for as the habit and practice of Co-operation grew, new types of society could be expected to be formed to meet new social needs. There would be housing societies, communities and settlements, productive societies, all manner of agricultural societies, societies for cultural, recreational and sporting activities, etc.

Most of these societies would also form federations, some of them international in scope. Consumers' societies from their nature would be the most common and have the largest and most widespread organisations, probably there would be world co-operative organisations for commerce, banking, insurance and transport. Each individual would probably be a member of several societies, taking an active part in those which interested him most. There would thus be many opportunities available for those wishing to take an active part in the democratic administration of affairs, and the sense of social responsibility would be widened and quickened.

Such a Commonwealth would not be a neat, orderly, comprehensively planned system, some Utopian dream come true. A community of true co-operators would not be content to have their lives or society moulded by or dependent upon some superior authority or centralised bureaucracy. They would be fertile of new ideas, with the initiative to thrust up spontaneously new societies and forms of social organisation. The Co-operative Commonwealth would be a viable society with the vigour and increasing diversity of a growing organism.

This would result from the increase in individual freedom and the realisation of what can be accomplished by association. For as the Webbs pointed out in their closing chapter of the *Consumers' Co-operative Movement*, " we multiply, vary and correlate democracies of producers and democracies of consumers . . . not for the sake of elaborating social machinery, but in order to lessen the toil and friction, the danger and disorder by which we are at present fettered; and thus to secure to each citizen the largest measure of liberty to live his own life according to his conscience, his talents, and his aspirations."

Appendix I.

BIOGRAPHICAL DICTIONARY

A compressed account of so large and complex a movement as the Co-operative Movement forces out of consideration the individuals, even the leading personalities, who constituted and made it. Yet the Movement's ideals, principles, systems of organisation and administration originated in the minds of individuals. It was individuals also who thought, decided, formed, established, developed, discussed and debated.

These brief biographical sketches are intended to give some idea of the manner of men and women who played important parts in the Co-operative Movement. It is impossible to deal with all, those selected are those whom students most frequently desire to know something about. In some cases, e.g., Robert Owen or the Webbs, it is easy to get a good deal of information, but in most of those dealt with here it is difficult, which also accounts for the inclusion of some.

Alexander, Earl, of Hillsborough, 1885-1965.—*Co-operative Politician.*

Born and bred in the west country. Left school at 13 and a year later was a clerk to the Bristol School Board. Studied part-time and by 1920 was in charge of higher education for Somerset County Education Department. Began his political life as a Liberal but was so radical that it was natural he should gravitate towards the still young Labour Party. Became Secretary of the Joint Parliamentary Committee 1920. Entered Parliament 1922 as Co-operative Member for Hillsborough thus being among the first Co-operative M.P.s. Served as a Cabinet Minister in the governments of Ramsey MacDonald, the Winston Churchill coalition and Clement Attlee. First Lord of the Admiralty 1929-31, 1940-47, Minister of Defence from 1947. Went to House of Lords in 1950 as Viscount Alexander, made an Earl 1963. Leader of the Opposition in the Lords 1955-65. As Secretary of the Parliamentary Committee, M.P., and peer "A.V." was tireless in his work for the Movement. In Parliament his name became synonymous with Co-operation.

Bamford, Samuel, 1848–1898.—*Editor of the " Co-operative News."*

Born near Rochdale. Education mainly in the Science and Art classes of the Rochdale Equitable Pioneers' Society. Appointed editor of the *Co-operative News* in 1875, then heavily in debt with a circulation of 11,000. At his death had its own buildings and plant and a circulation of 50,000. Exercised considerable influence on the development of the Movement during these years. Served also for nine years, three as president, on the committee of Manchester and Salford Society. Father of William Bamford, editor of *Co-operative News* and Annie Bamford Tomlinson, editor and founder of *Women's Outlook.*

Blandford, Thomas, 1861–1899.—*General Secretary of the C.P.F.*

Born at Curragh, Ireland. Employed as a warehouseman in London 1881, attended lectures at Men's and Women's College and commended by James Bonar, the economist. Joined the Labour Association in 1885 and thenceforward devoted himself to the cause of co-operative production. President of the Labour Association for two years. In 1894 was made Secretary of the Co-operative Productive Federation and then worked himself to death. In five years 1894–1899, fourteen new societies started in membership with the C.P.F.

Byron, Lady Noel, 1792–1860.—*Wife of the poet and friend to the early Co-operative Movement.*

Lady Noel Byron, nee Annabelle Milbanke, born Elemore Hall, Durham, of wealthy and well-connected parents. Married Lord Byron, the poet, 1815, one daughter, Ada, 1815, left him 1815, legal separation 1816. Spent remainder of her life in charitable works and assisting reform movements. A friend of Dr. Wm. King, who was tutor to her daughter at a salary of £300 a year and often served as her adviser. King found a house for her in Brighton, 1826, and she became interested in and an enthusiast for Co-operation. From 1828 onwards her name frequently appears in connection with co-operative efforts, she gave financial assistance to co-operative societies and co-operators and persuaded friends to do likewise. Probably helped with the publication of King's *Co-operator*. Assisted to establish societies in various parts of the country at Gatacre (Liverpool), Leicester, Huddersfield, Spitalfields, and in Sussex where she also tried to establish a wholesale organisation. She had a strong belief in the importance of education and founded an Industrial and Agricultural School at Ealing Grove, with the Owenite, E. T. Craig, in charge. Had previously thought of starting a school " on a Co-operative plan of education." Purchased a building at Bristol to enable Mary Carpenter to continue her reformatory.

Although enthusiastic for Co-operation, it was that of Dr. King, not of Robert Owen, which appealed to her. W. H. Brown described her as " the godmother of Co-operation." Her name is on the Reformers' Memorial, Kensal Green.

de Boyve, Edouard, 1840–1923.—*One of the originators of the I.C.A.*

French co-operator. English mother, read English co-operative journals. Settled at Nimes 1872, met Auguste Fabre. In 1879 joined in founding a co-operative bakery and in 1883 a consumers' society. Then proposed to establish a Co-operative Union. With the help of Neale and Holyoake was successful. Played an active and important part in establishing the International Co-operative Alliance and in its early history.

Campbell, Alexander, 1796–1873.—*Scottish Owenite, Co-operative and Trade Union Pioneer.*

Born Kintyre, Argyllshire. Apprenticed to joiner. Early disciple of Robert Owen. Member of Orbiston Community, jailed in Hamilton, 1828, for Orbiston debt. 1830, formed Glasgow Co-operative Society. 1831, pamphlet of lecture at Cambuslang " Address on Progress of the Co-operative System." Claim that this contained dividend on purchase idea has never been proved. 1832, delegate at London Co-operative Congress. Also active in Radical and Trade Union movements. Advocated Women's Suffrage during struggle for Reform Bill. 1834, secretary of Glasgow Carpenters' Union and Secretary of Glasgow United Committee of Trades. 1830–1831, editor of *Herald to the Trades Advocate*, 1833–1834 editor of *The Tradesman*. 1834, jailed for contravening Stamp Act. 1836, assisted formation of National Radical Association of Scotland. 1838, appointed Social Missionary. 1840, mobbed at Burslem. 1847, parliamentary candidate for Stockport, withdrew. 1848, editor of *Spirit of the Age*. 1856–1858, editor of *Weekly Chronicle*. 1863, editor of *Glasgow Sentinel*. 1858, Co-operative Association formed, Campbell chairman. Did much co-operative propaganda and founded societies at Cumbernauld and Lanark. Convened conference at Trongate to consider establishing a wholesale depot, took part in establishing the S.C.W.S., and was one of the supporters of the Co-operative Congress 1869. Helped to refound the Glasgow Trades Council, 1858. With MacDonald, the miners' leader, took a leading part in agitation for repeal of Master and Servants Act. Chairman of the Repeal Committee, 1864. On his initiative, a national trade union conference called in 1864, a precursor of the first Trades Union Congress.

Cooper, William, 1822–1868.—*One of the original Rochdale Pioneers.*

Handloom weaver, later stationer and account books maker. Owenite, Chartist, Secularist, Radical. Self-educated. Served as cashier of the Rochdale Society from its beginning to his death, as well as performing many other duties including that of superintendent of the stores from 1851. One of the first members of the Rochdale

District Co-operative Corn Mill Society, whose history he wrote. Took an active part in developing the Co-operative Movement corresponding with people at home and abroad, giving information and advice on the forming and management of co-operative societies. His correspondents ranged from Gladstone and university professors to working men requiring advice on how to start a society. Regarded as the best informed man in Britain regarding co-operative principles and methods of administration.

Much of the preparatory work in establishing the Co-operative Wholesale Society fell upon him, convening conferences, acting as secretary, and assisting Neale to draft the necessary changes in the Industrial and Provident Societies' Act. This was no light task, in two years it involved 1,600 postal communications, including letters, petition forms, circulars, receipts. He was one of the original 12 members of the C.W.S. Later he was equally active in establishing the Co-operative Insurance Company (the C.I.S.), and also serving as its first secretary.

" He conducted the Pioneers' office business, spoke at other societies' gatherings, filled the part of a co-operative union in answering innumerable letters of inquiry, and literally worked night and day." (Redfern).

" His life was active and unselfish and the remuneration he received was far less than he deserved. All his conduct seemed marked with an exact and unvarying conscientiousness." (Robertson).

" He spared himself no trouble; he gave the leisure of his mornings, of his mid-day, of his evenings and of his sabbaths, freely and ungrudgingly to sending replies to most distant or unknown persons in any part of the country or in any part of the world—he thought much higher of the benefits co-operative principles could render morally than of the pecuniary benefits they could confer." (Holyoake).

" Billy Cooper was a roystering sort of lad—a Lancashire lad with red hair, rather wiry, which used to stick up and look like a mop. . . . He was the finest example of a Pioneer that Co-operation ever had." (Ben Jones).

Craig, E. T., 1804–1894.—*Owenite, Manager of Ralahine.*

Born in Manchester 1804. Present at Peterloo. Fustian cutter. Member of the " Utility Society " 1825–1827, formed in Manchester for " intellectual and social improvement," an offshoot was a fustian cutters' co-operative society. Attended early Congresses. Started and edited *The Lancashire and Yorkshire Co-operator* 1831–1832. Organiser of the Ralahine Co-operative Community 1831–1833, his *History of Ralahine* translated into French, German and Italian. An originator of agricultural and industrial training schools, organised the first of the kind in this country under the auspices of Lady Noel Byron at Ealing in 1834. Numerous inventions. Various tracts on health. Editor of *Leamington Advertiser, Brighton Times, Oxford University Herald.* Agitated for renewal of Co-operative Congresses in the 'sixties. Present at the first of the modern series in 1869, and succeeding ones until 1889.

Davies, Margaret Llewellyn, 1862–1944.—*Secretary of the Co-operative Women's Guild.*

Father was John Llewellyn Davies, Rector of Marylebone, London, scholar and reformer, honorary chaplain to the Queen, a Christian Socialist who played an active part in the Working Men's College. Mother was daughter of Mr. Justice Compton, aunt was Miss Emily Davies, one of the founders of Girton College, Cambridge. M. L. Davies thus brought up in a Christian Socialist circle interested in education and feminist emancipation. Educated at Queen's College, London, and two years at Girton. With Miss Vaughan Nash tried to establish self-governing workshops for women, later studied and converted to the Rochdale system.

Joined Marylebone branch of the Co-operative Women's Guild 1887, became its secretary, elected to Central Committee 1889 and appointed General Secretary the same year. Father appointed Vicar of Kirby Lonsdale, West Riding, and M. L. Davies removed there, a room at the vicarage serving as the Guild Office. She had a commanding presence, was an inspiring orator and a fine leader. She led and urged the Guild and its members to take an active part in co-operative and civic life, to have wider interests and vision than women were then supposed to have, e.g., free trade, reform of the Poor Law, establishing of Trade Boards, and the minimum wage for co-operative employees' campaign.

She had ideas on co-operative education, many of which came to be adopted and was largely responsible for the Woolwich Congress 1896 setting up the famous inquiry into the educational work of the Movement. Had views of the place of the Co-operative Movement in the Labour Movement similar to those of the Webbs.

Largely through her efforts that the International Women's Guild was formed in 1921. When appointed General Secretary the Guild had 51 branches and about 1,800 members, when she retired in 1921 it had 1,023 branches and 52,000 members. Wrote many pamphlets and the History of the Co-operative Womens' Guild 1904. Was President of the Co-operative Congress 1922, the only woman to fill this office. Her Presidential speech showed a grasp and understanding of co-operative ideals and principles much above the average for these occasions.

Dent, John James, –1936.

Originally a bricklayer, gravitated to the Civil Service, attached to the Board of Trade as Labour Correspondent, later to the Ministry of Labour. 1919, appointed adviser on co-operative and social questions to the Development Commission and awarded a C.M.G. Throughout his life he was associated with the Movement. Among his friends were G. J. Holyoake, T. Hughes, E. V. Neale, Hodgson Pratt, and E. O. Greening. Member of the Central Board 1883–1893, attended fifty Congresses. One of the founders of the Co-operative Permanent Building Society, of which he was a director. Responsible for the establishment of several distributive and productive societies. For 47 years on the committee of the Tenant Co-operators Ltd. Also active with the Club and Institutes' Union, the Workers' Educational Association, and the London University Joint Committee of Tutorial Classes. A collector of books and periodicals on the early co-operative and socialist movements in Great Britain, much of which passed into possession of the Co-operative College.

Gide, Charles, 1847–1932.—*French economist and co-operator.*

Came of a Huguenot family, born at Uzés (Gard), where his father was a judge. 1872, obtained his Doctor's degree with a thesis on the collective law of associations. 1879, appointed to the chair of Political Economy at Bordeaux, left this for Montpellier in 1880. Devoted himself to socio-economic problems. Completed his *Principles of Political Economy* in 1883, which was to go through 27 editions in 49 languages. 1887, founded the *Review of Political Economy*. 1900, appointed to Chair of Comparative Social Economy at Paris. Entrusted with general report of the Social Economy Section of the Universal Exhibition of 1900. 1921, retired, but appointed to a Chair of Co-operation at the College de France 1922–1930. In 1913 awarded the Laveleye prize by the Royal Academy of Belgium, bestowed every six years by an international body of judges on the economist or lawyer " whose work as a whole shall have contributed most to the advancement of science."

In his youth interested in ideas of Fourier by a fellow student, Auguste Fabre, later discovered Co-operation in an article on the Rochdale Pioneers by Elie Reclus during 1867. Attracted by the Pioneers' solution to the socio-economic problem as being " not a revolutionary solution, but neither was it a lazy solution, and which carried a conviction as a formula of morality, truth and justice."

Edouard de Boyve's efforts to establish a Co-operative Union decided him to join in co-operative activities, and in 1886 presided over the second Co-operative Congress. He speedily gained a reputation as a theorist and expositor of co-operative doctrine. His views were mockingly referred to as the " School of Nimes," an epithet which became his glory. In 1902 made President of the Co-operative Union, and in 1903 elected to the Central Committee of the I.C.A. Played a great part in the I.C.A. both before 1914 and in reviving it after the Great War 1914–1918. His co-operative doctrines were firmly based on Rochdale principles, and his admiration for the Rochdale Pioneers inspired him to make a famous speech upon them which included what has been described as one of the finest passages in co-operative literature.

Works: *Principles of Political Economy, Institutions of Social Progress, Consumers'*

Co-operative Societies, Selected Works of Fourier, History of Economic Doctrines (in collaboration with M. Rist), *Lectures on Political Economy*.

Gray, J. C., 1854–1912.—*General Secretary of the Co-operative Union.*

Born at Ripley, Derbyshire, son of a Baptist minister. Began work as a railway clerk, became secretary of the Hebden Bridge Fustian Society, 1874 (a co-operative society taken over by the C.W.S. in 1918). Assistant secretary of the Co-operative Union in 1883 and General Secretary in 1891. Was concerned with the I.C.A. in its early days and was its joint honorary secretary with E. O. Greening. Is remembered as a first rate administrator and for his proposal, made in his presidential address to the Co-operative Congress of 1906, that all existing co-operative societies should be combined into one national society. He wrote many pamphlets and articles and a handbook on the Industrial and Provident Societies Act, 1893.

Greening, E. O., 1836–1923.

Born in Warrington. Educated at the Quakers' School, Manchester. Apprenticed to wireworking at 13 years of age, worked 12 hours a day. Soon engaged in reform movements. First public speech when 16 years of age at a meeting of the Anti-Slavery Society, Manchester, of which he became secretary. During the American Civil War he was an active propagandist for the northern states. One of the founders and honorary secretary of the Union and Emancipation Society, which had several leading co-operators among its members. Active in the agitations for manhood suffrage in the 'sixties, helping to found the Manchester and Salford Manhood Suffrage League (the northern section of the Reform League). Contested Halifax in the parliamentary election of 1868 as a working class candidate, opposing both Liberal and Conservative.

His reform activities brought him into contact with co-operators and he was actively engaged in the Co-operative Movement from the mid-'fifties onwards. Several of his co-operative acquaintances were old Owenites, among them Dr. J. Watts, James Hole, Wm. Pare, Galpin (Pare's son-in-law and member of the firm of Cassell, Petter and Galpin, then the biggest publishers in the world), Lloyd Jones, E. T. Craig, G. J. Holyoake, A. Pears (founder of the famous soap firm, reputed possessor of the finest collection of personal relics of Owen: Greening held that the recipe for Pears soap was given to Pears by Robert Owen). Was active in the events leading to the convening of the Co-operative Congress of 1869 and in the formation of the Co-operative Union, in whose affairs he was prominent. A member of its Central Board. Rarely missed a Congress until his death. Opened Holyoake House in 1911, the headquarters of the Union.

He had a hand in starting and running several industrial co-partnership enterprises. Also helped to form the Labour Association, was a member of its first Executive and its first treasurer 1884, became its President 1893. Also helped to form the Co-operative Productive Federation, 1882, as one of its seven original individual members. Started the Agricultural and Horticultural Association, 1868, and was its managing director until 1915. Edited its publications *The Agricultural Economist* and the *One and All Gardening Annual*.

Played a prominent part in the formation of the I.C.A., and as described in the text, was a member of its first council.

Believed co-operative societies should engage in matters other than trade, such as encouraging and supporting sport, art, and hobbies and undertaking varied educational activities. Persuaded Southern Sectional Board to run a Co-operative Institute, initiated the Crystal Palace Festival, 1887–1910 (entries reached 6,000, attendance was between 25,000 and 50,000). Always a keen educationist he advocated a Co-operative College in his inaugural address as President of Congress in 1904. Lectured at innumerable week-end schools and at summer schools, author of numerous pamphlets and articles and histories of several societies.

Greenwood, Abraham, 1824–1911.

Born at Rochdale, son of a small blanket manufacturer. Educated at his uncle's school near Leeds and at a Rochdale seminary. Trained in business of woolsorting. Was secretary of the Rochdale Chartist Association at the age of 18. Also acted as spare-time librarian of the People's Institute, which at that time had the biggest library in the town. Joined the Rochdale Pioneers in 1846 and was soon elected to its Management Committee. Keenly interested in its educational work in which he took an active part, an originator of its education department. His paper *The Education Department of the Rochdale Equitable Pioneers' Society*, 1877, was printed by the Co-operative Union, had a wide circulation, and some influence on other societies' educational activities.

Associated with the founding of the Rochdale Corn Mill Society and its first chairman. For a time acted as manager and put the society on its feet. During the 'fifties was concerned with the attempts at co-operative wholesale trading. His experience as chairman of the Pioneers' wholesale department gave him an insight into the problems and needs involved. Actively concerned with the steps to establish a wholesale society from 1860 onwards, his scheme for a wholesale society was largely adopted, as described in the text, and " Mr. Abraham Greenwood of Rochdale must be regarded as the original promoter of the Co-operative Wholesale Society " (C.W.S. advertisements in *The Co-operator*). He was one of the 12 original individual members and the first President, an office he held for seven years. Cashier and bank manager of the C.W.S., 1874–1898.

Also founder, director and for a time manager of the Co-operative Insurance Company (later the C.I.S.). Was one of the promoters of the Co-operative Newspaper Society (now the Co-operative Press Ltd.) and was its chairman for 25 years.

A member of the Central Board he was a well-known figure at Congresses and co-operative meetings of all kinds, at which he was often accompanied by his daughter, who in 1883 became one of the founders of the Women's Co-operative Guild.

Hall, Fred, 1878–1938.—*Adviser of Studies and first Principal of the Co-operative College.*

Born at Rochdale. At 13 years of age an office boy at John Bright and Bros., Rochdale, later assistant manager to a Wardle textile firm, then secretary, traveller and manager of an eyelet manufacturing firm. Meanwhile was teaching classes in Co-operation for the Rochdale Pioneers' Society, and in book-keeping and business methods in technical schools, and studying in University Extension Classes. Later studied at Manchester University where he graduated B.Com. in 1908 and M.A. in 1910. In 1910 appointed chief lecturer in commercial and industrial organisation at Belfast College of Technology (Queen's University) and in 1913 Professor in Commerce.

In 1906 he had been agitating for a Co-operative College. An article by him in Belfast Society's *Wheatsheaf*, 1911, resulted in his being asked to submit a paper on the subject to the Easter week-end conference at Leicester, 1912. This commenced an enthusiastic and organised movement to establish the college. In 1915 appointed Adviser of Studies to the Co-operative Union.

The great co-operative survey had commenced in 1915 and he speedily became associated with it, he enlarged its scope, sought to give it scientific precision, undertook responsibility for the statistical research and for many of the constructive proposals submitted to Congress. The Report of the Survey Committee was largely his work, and presented a policy which the Movement however only partly pursued. Much of the Independent Commission Report of 1958 repeated in essence what had been said in 1920.

Then and in the years which followed he re-organised and expanded the work of the Education Department, started and developed the Co-operative College, started and conducted a Co-operative International Summer School (later taken over by the I.C.A.), taught and lectured by day and night, at week-ends and summer schools, wrote many pamphlets and text-books, dealing mainly with education and business subjects, including *Handbook for Members of Co-operative Committees*, probably still found on many executive officers' desks, *Standard Co-operative Book-keeping*, three volumes, and with W. P. Watkins *Co-operation*.

He also linked the educational work of the Co-operative Movement with that of other educational bodies such as the Workers' Educational Association (being one of its earliest members and associated with it up to his death), Ruskin College, the

World Association for Adult Education and numerous others. Served on many committees, including Government ones, the most important of which was the Committee on National Debt and Taxation (the Colwyn Committee) and prepared memoranda and presented evidence before such committees and Royal Commissions.

" It can be said with truth that Fred Hall's influence on co-operative development and expansion throughout the post-war years was greater than the Co-operative Movement knew. As the Movement grew he did not alter. Always he was the same rugged, democratic, unpresumptuous son of Rochdale, one comparable with Charles Howarth, Samuel Ashworth, and J. T. W. Mitchell."—T. W. Mercer.

Hirst, T.,   –1833.

One of the originators of Huddersfield Society, 1829. Corresponded with Lady Noel Byron. Delegate to the first Congress, 1831, and to subsequent ones. A prominent and influential member of those Congresses, at times occupying the chair. Lectured on Co-operation in Lancashire and Yorkshire. His widow was assisted by Lady Noel Byron who also provided for the education of his two sons, each spending three years at E. T. Craig's school at Ealing Grove.

Holyoake, George Jacob, 1817–1906.—*Co-operator and Secularist.*

Born at Birmingham, son of an engineer, second of 13 children. Apprenticed as a tinsmith, also worked as a whitesmith. In 1834 attended a Mechanics' Institute, showing an aptitude for mathematics and making of instruments. Was teaching mathematics in 1837. In 1831 joined the Birmingham Reform League, beginning an active participation in political and social movements which continued throughout a long life. Attended meetings addressed by Robert Owen, 1837. In 1838 delivered his first lecture on Socialism and Co-operation and became a member of Owen's Association of All Classes of All Nations. Lectured at the Worcester Hall of Science, 1840 (Halls of Science were Owenite educational institutions). Went to Sheffield in 1841 to lecture and conduct a school for the Universal Community Society of Rational Religionists (then the title of the major organisation of Owenites). Tried and convicted on a charge of blasphemy in 1842 consequent upon a lecture at Cheltenham.

Went to London, 1843, and kept a shop for the sale of advanced literature. Secretary of Anti-persecution Union. Editor of *The Movement*. Continued lecturing on Owenism in various parts of the country, including one in Rochdale in 1843. In 1846 started *The Reasoner* which, in addition to its secularist opinions, also contained co-operative news and views. The term Secularist, invented by himself, was first used in it (Dec., 1846).

Started business of bookselling and publishing in 1853 and took a prominent part in the movement for the removal of the tax on newspapers and engaged in the movement for electoral reform. Secretary for the British Legion which went to Italy to assist Garibaldi. Corresponded with and a friend of Mazzini. Attempted to enter Parliament in 1857 for Tower Hamlets, 1868 for Birmingham, 1884 for Leicester. Spent last years of his life in Brighton, where he was President of the Liberal Association.

He had a life-long and generally active association with the Co-operative Movement and was friendly or well-acquainted with all the leading figures in it. One of the promoters of the 1869 Congress, he attended subsequent ones and spoke frequently, edited the reports of the proceedings of the third, fourth and fifth Congresses, presided at the seventh, and being a moving, eloquent orator addressed most co-operative occasions worthy of note. He contributed numerous articles to the press on co-operative topics and also wrote many pamphlets on co-operative subjects.

His books on Co-operation, *Self-Help by the People: History of Co-operation in Rochdale* 1858 (first appeared as a series of articles in the *Daily News*, 1855), *History of Co-operation in England*, two volumes, 1875–1879; *Self-Help a Hundred Years Ago*, 1888; *The Co-operative Movement To-day*, 1891, are little read today. None of them is good. He was far too unreliable for any historical work. Only the first, which dealt with the history of the Rochdale Pioneers is of any value, and this because it was such an effective and widespread piece of propaganda that it could not be ignored in a history of Co-operation. His other notable work is his *Sixty Years of An Agitator's Life*, two volumes, 1892, which gives interesting light on some 19th century movements, but whose value is also lessened by the unreliability of the author.

He had a prolific pen, and wrote on a variety of subjects, besides co-operative, such as manuals on grammar and mathematics, children's reading books, books on religion or irreligion, politics, trade unionism, biographies, overseas settlement. J. McCabe's biography lists 175 books and pamphlets by Holyoake.

In addition he edited several periodicals, 27 in all, some of which he started. Those of co-operative interest are *The Reasoner*, 1846–1872, especially a supplement, *The Reasoner Gazette; Co-operative and Secular News*, 1860, *The Counsellor*, 1861, *The Secular World and Social Economist*, 1862–1864, *The Industrial Partnerships Record*, 1867–1868 (in partnership with E. O. Greening) and its successor, *Social Economist*, 1868–1869.

His great age and his contacts with the earlier figures of the Co-operative Movement made him a revered figure in his last years. On his death the Movement levied itself threepence per member to provide a worthy memorial to him, this taking the form of a site and building to serve as the headquarters of the Co-operative Union and known as Holyoake House. There was an opinion that the name of E. V. Neale who did more than any other man to establish the Co-operative Union should have been associated with its headquarters, but this was not to be, and Neale's name in any case is inseparably connected with the Co-operative Union even if Holyoake's name is attached to the building it inhabits.

Howarth, Charles, 1814–1868.—*Rochdale Pioneer*.

Born at Rochdale, one of the original Pioneers and an active member of the No. 24 Branch which preceded the foundation of the Rochdale Society in 1844. Was one of the leading figures, and sometimes described as " the Constitution Maker of the Modern Co-operative Movement." With James Daly drew up the original rules of the Rochdale Society, and has been generally credited with inventing the device of dividend on purchases, though it is now known that others had preceded him with similar devices in other parts of the country. Was elected President of the society at its first quarterly meeting.

Also concerned with the Rochdale Co-operative Corn Mill whose rules he helped to compile. Took an active part in establishing the Co-operative Wholesale Society and was elected to its first Board of Directors, and in establishing the Co-operative Insurance Company, of which he was also a director. A cotton warper by trade, he was active in reform movements. Played a prominent part in the agitation for the Ten Hours Act, and was sent to London as a delegate to lobby the House of Commons.

Hughes, Thomas, 1822–1896.—*Christian Socialist*.

Born at Uffington, Berkshire. Went to Rugby School, 1833, his experiences at which provided the ground for the book by which he became best known—*Tom Brown's Schooldays*. From Rugby went to Oriel College, Oxford, graduated B.A., 1845. Called to the Bar 1848, Queen's Counsel, 1869, Judge of No. 9 County Court Circuit, Cheshire, 1882. One of the early group known as Christian Socialists, he remained associated with and active in the Co-operative Movement. Presided at the Co-operative Congress of 1869 and delivered the inaugural address, also at the fourth congress, and at the fifth and sixth occupied the chair for three and two days respectively.

His honesty and forthrightness earned him the respect of opponents. Took a prominent part in the great debates in the 'seventies and 'eighties on producer versus consumer Co-operation, championing the producer case. He and E. V. Neale were life-long friends.

Member of Parliament for Lambeth, 1865–1868, and for Frome, 1868–1874. Joint author with Neale of *A Manual for Co-operators*. In recognition of his services the Co-operative Movement founded the Hughes Scholarship, tenable at Oriel College, Oxford (later incorporated with a similar scholarship founded to commemorate E. V. Neale).

Jones, Ben, 1848–1947.

Born in Salford, son of a dyer's labourer. Began work at nine years of age as an errand boy but rose to position of book-keeper to the firm. In 1866 appointed assistant to Wm. Nuttall of the C.W.S., and in 1868 succeeded him as accountant. Was meanwhile studying at mechanics institutes and at Owen's College under Professor Stanley Jevons and served on Education Committee of Blackley Society. Became assistant salesman in 1870 and in 1871 was managing a department. When the C.W.S. opened its branch in London he was put in charge, and became one of the leaders of Co-operation in the South.

Did a great deal of propaganda and organising work in his leisure hours. Was a member of the Central Board from 1875 and acted as honorary secretary to the Southern Sectional Board, 1875–1894. Chairman of the Co-operative Aid Association. Founder of " The Tenant Co-operators' Society " the first co-operative housing society. Honorary secretary to the Joint Parliamentary Committee. First chairman of the London Committee of the C.P.S. Twice President of Congress.

Contested three parliamentary elections as a Labour candidate. For some years was one of the managers of two London Board Schools, correspondent and manager for evening classes, chairman of a working men's club. With A. D. Acland wrote *Working Men Co-operators*, 1883, which has gone through so many revised editions and served so many generations of co-operators that it is probably the most extensively read of any book on Co-operation. More important, however, was his *Co-operative Production*, 839 pp., 1894. The fruit of original research, it gives detailed accounts of almost every form of co-operative productive activity in the 19th century. A classic and mine of information.

Jones, Lloyd, 1811–1886.—*Owenite and Social Missionary*.

Born at Brandon, Northern Ireland. Fustian cutter. Went to Manchester, 1827. Engaged in the Co-operative Movement by 1832, largely due to influence of E. T. Craig. Lectured in Manchester and neighbouring towns. Soon one of the Owenite leaders. Elected to the Central Board of the Association of All Classes of All Nations, 1837, and appointed to the staff of the regular home missionaries, undertook propaganda and education in Lancashire, Yorkshire, London, and Scotland. The *New Moral World* contains numerous records of his activities.

Was brought into contact with E. V. Neale and assisted him in his ventures during the 'fifties. The text refers to his co-operative activities during this decade and during the 'sixties and 'seventies, which it will be seen were numerous, widespread and various. Linked pre-Rochdale Co-operation with the later Movement, and his many contacts with northern co-operators enabled him to link the Rochdale Movement of the north with that being promoted by Neale, Hughes and Ludlow in the metropolis. His long, wide and varied experience gave him a strong influence. One of those who brought the Congress of 1869 into being, and a frequent and influential speaker at succeeding ones.

Also active in trade unionism. Was secretary to a fustian cutters' trade union in 1827, but became more engaged in the later period of his life, serving as arbitrator to a number of trade unions in the 'seventies.

As with many social reformers in the 19th century he engaged in journalism. Contributed to the *New Moral World*, to the *Spirit of the Times* as " Cromwell," 1849, the *Spirit of the Age*, 1849–1850, the *Glasgow Sentinel*, 1850–1863, again as " Cromwell." Established the *Leeds Express*, 1857. Was connected with the *Beehive* (a Labour Paper of the 'seventies) until 1876, writing most of the leading articles, the *Newcastle Weekly*, the *Newcastle Daily Chronicle*, 1878, *Miners' Watchman and Labour Sentinel* as editor, the *Co-operative News*. Wrote a Life of Robert Owen. Stood for Parliament as a Radical. Advocated a People's Party.

King, Dr. William, 1786–1865.—*An originator of the Co-operative Movement*.

Born at Ipswich, son of the Rev. John King, of an old Richmond, Yorkshire, family. Educated at Ipswich Grammar School, Westminster, Oxford, Cambridge. 1809, graduated B.A., 1812, M.A. Fellow of Peterhouse. Intended for the Church, but could not agree with all the 39 articles. Studied medicine at St. Bartholomew's Hospital and in Paris. 1819, M.D. of Cambridge. 1820, Fellow of Royal College of Physicians. Married in 1821 and settled in Brighton. Active in social work in Brighton. 1823, instrumental in establishing an infant school. Acquainted with Elizabeth Fry and assisted her to form the Brighton Provident and District Society (the first visiting society in England). Chief promoter of the Brighton Mechanics' Institute, opened 1825 by Dr. King and Dr. Birkbeck (1776–1841, the founder of Mechanics' Institutes, a native of Settle, Yorkshire).

King conducted classes in mathematics and natural philosophy. These brought him in contact with men interested in Owenism. 1827, Brighton Co-operative Benevolent Fund Association and Brighton Co-operative Trading Association formed. A visit by the editor of the *Co-operative Magazine* in 1827 reported favourably upon these Brighton ventures. King's *Co-operator*, published 1828–1830 (first issue May, 1828) to assist these and other societies. This was his great contribution to co-operative thought and is dealt with in the text. Its worth and influence was such that some have credited King with being the father of Co-operation.

King withdrew from active participation in 1830, in spite of subsequent appeals from individual co-operators and from Congresses. Was friend and adviser to Lady Noel Byron and tutor to her daughter, she remained a great friend to the Co-operative Movement. Continued to be active in the life of Brighton and pursuing his medical career. 1826, was one of the Town Commissioners. 1842, appointed consulting physician to the Royal Sussex County Hospital. 1847, instrumental in forming the Brighton Medical Society. Was its first president, some lectures of his under its auspices published as Medical Essays.

Although King's association with the Co-operative Movement was so brief, his influence was such that it was never forgotten. Correspondence with him was published by the *Christian Socialist* and later by Pitman's *Co-operator*. Several references to him were made in speeches and correspondence by old co-operators reported in the *Co-operative News* in the 19th century. J. J. Dent stressed his importance in a lecture given to the Working Men's College, 1889, and later wrote a pamphlet outlining King's principles (published by the Co-operative Union in 1922).

Although he was never forgotten, however, he was considerably underrated. The first step to giving him his true place in co-operative history was a classic account of his *Co-operator* by Dr. Hans Müller in the I.C.A. Year Book in 1913. The second was the publication of *Dr. William King and the Co-operator*, 1828–1830 by T. W. Mercer (1922). This contains a brief biography of Dr. King, some of his correspondence, and most valuable, a reprint of all the 28 numbers of the *Co-operator*. It was issued again with some slight revisions edited by A. R. Downie under the title of *Co-operation's Prophet*.

Kingsley, The Rev. Charles, 1819–1875.—*Christian Socialist*.

Born at Holne vicarage, Devon. Educated at King's College, London; Magdalene College, Cambridge. Ordained 1842. Rector of Eversley 1844. Sympathised with the Chartists. A Christian Socialist, serving mainly with his pen. Contributed to *Politics for the People* and the *Christian Socialist*. His novels *Yeast* and *Alton Locke* were written to arouse people to the sufferings and injustices suffered by working people and his *Cheap Clothes and Nasty* to expose the sweating system.

With strong feelings, an independent mind but impulsive, he aroused much antagonism. Nevertheless he was successful as an author. His *Westward Ho*, *Hypatia*, *Hereward* and *The Water Babies* are still known and read. He became the most popular Cambridge lecturer as Regius Professor of Modern History at that university, and was appointed one of Her Majesty's Chaplains and Canon of Chester Cathedral. Keenly interested in science, he was a member of the Linnean and Geological societies and welcomed the Darwinian theory of evolution when it was still suspect or opposed by many churchmen and scientists.

Lawrenson, Mary E., 1851–1943.—*General Secretary Women's Co-operative Guild*.

Daughter of a Liverpool printer, eldest child of seven. Married J. Lawrenson, auditor of Woolwich Society. Served on education committee, organised and taught children's classes. One of the originators of the Women's Co-operative Guild. Drew up its first constitution, was a member of its first Central Committee, general secretary 1885–1889. Served on the Southern Sectional Board 1893–1894, 1896–1898, the first woman member of the Central Board.

Ludlow, John Malcolm Forbes, 1821–1911.—*Christian Socialist.*

Born in India, son of a British officer, educated in France, graduated B.Litt. at University of France, enrolled a member of Lincolns Inn 1843. A member of the Christian Socialist group, he attracted the rest of the group to Co-operation. Started and edited the *Christian Socialist*, and engaged in all the activities of the group, promoting productive societies and working men's associations, preparing the ground for the introduction and passing of the Industrial and Provident Societies' Act, 1852, establishing the Working Men's College and teaching there.

Was also interested in and sympathetic to trade unionism, wrote and spoke on its behalf, defended the trade unions during some big strikes, helped to collect and present evidence without which the passing of the Trade Union Act of 1871 would have been unlikely.

Assisted to convene the Co-operative Congress of 1869, wrote the preface to its Report, presented a paper and spoke on many subjects to it, played a prominent part in succeeding Congresses until 1875. Secretary to the Royal Commission on Friendly and Building Societies, 1874. Appointed Registrar of Friendly Societies, 1875.

Maxwell, Sir William, 1841–1922.—*Chairman of the S.C.W.S.*

Born in Glasgow. Began work as a messenger at 10 years of age. Attended evening classes. Apprenticed as a coach painter at 13. Had co-operative connections, his great uncle a keen Owenite. Maxwell corresponded with and was influenced by G. J. Holyoake and Lloyd Jones. Joined St. Cuthberts Co-operative Association, Edinburgh, 1872. In 1876 made secretary of the District Conference Association. A fine speaker and propagandist and did much to inspire the starting of new societies. Joined the Board of Directors of the S.C.W.S. in 1880 and was made its chairman in 1881. In 1893 elected to the Board of the Co-operative Newspaper Society.

Had imagination, enterprise and a social philosophy, and was one of the great formative influences of the Movement. A great opponent of sweating and a strong supporter of trade unionism. Shocked Congress in 1893 by exposure of wages and conditions of some co-operative employees. Helped to stimulate formation of the A.U.C.E. Supported profit sharing and participation of employees in management.

Believed in political action and sought to persuade the Co-operative Movement to further co-operative representation in Parliament and to fuse forces with the trade unions and the Labour Party. Parliamentary candidate for the Tradeston Division in General Election, 1901. His programme was anti-war, and included taxation of land values, nationalisation of liquor traffic, abolition of House of Lords, liberal old age pensions.

As a co-operative idealist he desired the Movement to extend co-operative production. He was largely responsible for the scheme of the S.C.W.S. industrial estate at Shieldhall, although his intention that a co-operative model village should be associated with it was not realised. He also played a great part in effecting the joint ventures of the S.C.W.S. and the C.W.S., in tea, coffee and cocoa.

In 1902, he was elected to the Central Committee of the I.C.A. and in 1907 was made its President, an office he held until 1921, when failing health necessitated his resignation.

Mercer, T. W., 1885–1947.—*Co-operative Journalist.*

Son of a Surrey agricultural labourer. Started work at 12 years of age in a grocer's shop. Entered co-operative service in his early twenties, became a branch manager and later took charge of Epsom Society when it was under the control of the C.W.S. Appointed Education Secretary to Plymouth Society. Contested the Moss Side Division in a parliamentary election. Appointed to teaching staff of the Co-operative College in its first days, but in 1922 was made editor of publications of the Co-operative Union, and was the first editor of the *Co-operative Review*. Rest of his life engaged as a journalist.

1927, appointed London representative of the *Co-operative News*, and at various times edited the *Millgate*, the *Co-operative Official* and the *Guildman*, Served on the National committees of the National Co-operative Men's Guild and the Co-operative Party. He had a very lively, though not always disciplined, mind and prolific pen. At his best was a very fine writer indeed. Wrote *Dr. William King and The Co-operator*, 1922, and *Towards The Co-operative Commonwealth*, 1936.

Mitchell, John Thomas Whitehead, 1828–1895.—*Chairman of the C.W.S.*

Born in Rochdale, mother a domestic servant who later kept a small beerhouse. Grandfather associated with the Rochdale Society of 1835 and a subscriber to Queenwood. Educated at a National School, started work at a cotton mill at 10 years of age, continued his secular education in Sunday classes. When 17 began to attend Sunday School, which had a marked effect on his life. Read little except the Bible which he knew well. Joined the Rochdale Pioneers' Society in 1853 and was elected to its management committee in 1856. Served also as part-time secretary to and on the Library Committee (which concerned itself with education). Helped to promote the Rochdale Co-operative Manufacturing Society and served on its committee 1860 and 1862 and then became its chairman until 1870. Acted as secretary to the Pioneers' Science and Art Classes, 1872–1873, 1881–1895. Elected to the Board of the C.W.S. in 1869 and became its chairman in 1874, an office he held until his death in 1895.

A strong, enterprising character, with personal qualities which commanded the respect of all, he largely shaped the policy and course of the C.W.S., and indeed of the Movement. All the major developments of the C.W.S. to his death bore his mark. He is generally credited with being the father of the idea of consumers' Co-operation, and although this may be disputed, it was certainly he who made the British Movement largely a consumers' one.

He attended the Co-operative Congress of 1869 and all succeeding ones to 1894. Elected to the Central Board in 1872, he was closely associated with the work of the Co-operative Union, He was a protagonist of the great debates on the control of co-operative production and profit-sharing during the 'seventies and 'eighties, opposing such redoubtable debaters as Hughes and Neale, and standing up to a keen examination of his consumer theory by Professor Alfred Marshall when giving evidence before the Royal Commission on Labour (1892). He presided at the Rochdale Co-operative Congress, 1892, and his presidential address expressed his ideals and outlined his ideas of a consumer theory.

An active temperance worker and superintendent of a Sunday School until his death. Politically he saw good and evil in both Conservatives and Liberals, but was a member of the Radical Reform Association and stood as a Liberal candidate in the Rochdale municipal elections in 1893 and 1894. His defeat on both occasions was largely due to the opposition of private traders. His programme would have been agreeable to the future Labour Party, advocating direct employment by the corporation on work for the corporation, a living wage for all, the abolition of the aldermanic bench.

Mitchell was a co-operator and could not have accommodated himself to either of the big parties of the day. In 1891 he had declared to Congress that it was absolutely necessary for co-operators as such to be represented in Parliament, the representatives to be sent apart from politics or religion. Nicknamed " Baron Wholesale," and reputed to have well feathered his nest during his 21 years as chairman of the C.W.S., (despite living simply in a Rochdale working man's house—15 John St.), he left—£350 17s. 8d.

His views were well summarised in a passage in his presidential address—" The three great forces for the improvement of mankind are religion, temperance and Co-operation, and as a commercial force, supported and sustained by the other two, Co-operation is the grandest, noblest, and most likely to be successful in the redemption of the industrial classes."

Molesworth, The Rev. W. Nassau, 1816–1890.—*Co-operative Clergyman.*

Born at Millbrook, Hants. Son of the Rev. J. E. N. Molesworth, Vicar of Rochdale, who was a Tory opponent of Rochdale radicals. Traced descent from the

Plantagenets. Educated Canterbury and Cambridge. Appointed Vicar of Spotland, a Rochdale district, in 1844. A high churchman, radical, historian, friend of Cobden and Bright and a great co-operator. Almost from the beginning took an interest in the Rochdale Pioneers' Society, gave advice and taught classes and was made arbitrator in 1862.

Attended and gave an address to the Co-operative Congress of 1869, and helped to promote international Co-operation as related in the text. Sometimes referred to as " the Co-operative Parson." In his memory the Society presented a sculptured bust of him to his church and J. T. W. Mitchell presented his portrait in oils to the Society. Author of *History of the Reform Bill*, 1864, and *History of England Since 1830*, three volumes, 1873.

Morgan, John Minter, 1782–1854.—*Christian Owenite*.

Born in London, father a wholesale stationer, who bequeathed him an ample fortune. One of the earliest adherents of Owen, a fervent Christian, was not deterred by Owen's denunciation of religions 1817. Published *On the Practicability of Owen's Plan*,1819, and defended against clerical attacks the right of Owen to give Sunday lectures, 1830. Did much to popularise Owen by expressing his social theories in a digestible form and perhaps by showing that they were not at variance with Christian doctrine. His most important work was *Hampden in the Nineteenth Century*, 1834, held by Holyoake to be his most extensively read book, but Beer (*History of British Socialism*) gives this palm to *The Revolt of the Bees*, 1826, stating that it was read much by working men and popular writers. The *Co-operative Magazine* gave lengthy extracts from it, and Harriet Martineau referred to it in the *Poor Man's Guardian*, 1832. It is probable that this book and its frontispiece suggested the beehive as a symbol of Co-operation, serving as such until recent times. Many co-operative halls and buildings still display it.

He made a fortune as a paper manufacturer. Prepared a scheme for a Church of England Self Supporting Village on Owenite lines, which he unfolded in a prospectus and explained to a meeting in Exeter Hall, 1842, approached Parliament and the clergy upon it 1843, tried to raise £60,000 to establish one, 1850, but little response. Constructed a model of his community which he exhibited at his home in Sackville Street, London. His community scheme is the chief topic of his *The Christian Commonwealth*, 1845, published in English and French. Founded the National Orphans' Home, 1849, admitted children left destitute by cholera epidemic. Wrote or edited other works in addition to those referred to above. In 1850 reprinted his own and some other selected works under the title of The Phoenix Library.

Mudie, George.—*Early Co-operator*.

Little known of his life. Did not complete his studies at Edinburgh and went into journalism. 1818–1819, on a Glasgow paper, went to London about 1820. Reporter to the *Morning Chronicle*, a Liberal paper, position said to be due to influence of James Mill. Mudie probably already an Owenite. 1821–1822, editor of the *Economist*, a weekly devoted to Owenite propaganda. It succeeded in gaining the attention of the London artisans and inspired the founding of the Co-operative and Economical Society in London, 1820.

Neale, Edward Vansittart, 1810—1892.—*Christian Socialist, co-operative idealist, and General Secretary of the Co-operative Union*.

Born at Bath, son of the Rev. E. Neale, family home Bisham Abbey. Educated Oriel College, 1827, graduated B.A., 1831, M.A., 1836, called to the Bar, 1837. Drawn into the Christian Socialist circle, member of the Council of Promoters of Societies for Promoting Working Men's Associations, 1850. His co-operative activities are referred to in the text. He served the Co-operative Movement longer and more continuously than any others of the circle, had a more comprehensive view and a better understanding of its potentialities. His legal ability served the Movement well, from the drafting of the I. & P. Act of 1852 until 1876 all the amendments to the Act were prepared wholly or in part by him. Drafted the rules for registration of such national co-operative organisations as the C.W.S., compiled the model rules for co-operative societies published by the Co-operative Union, and his advice was continually sought on legal questions by co-operative organisations.

One of the promoters of the Congress of 1869 and became secretary of the Central Board in 1872 (officially known as the Co-operative Union, 1875) at a nominal salary. Did great work in propaganda, in promoting societies and organisations and in guiding and advising new societies. One of the protagonists in the great debates of the 'seventies and 'eighties on consumer versus producer control of production. Was on the side of producer control. As he was one of the first to realise the need for national organisation in the 'fifties and 'sixties and was active in promoting it, so he was also one of the first to appreciate the possibilities of international Co-operation and sought to promote that also, being one of the principal founders of the I.C.A.

Long record as a promoter of co-operative organisations and of service on their managing boards, from the ventures of the early 'fifties such as the Co-operative League and the Central Co-operative Agency to the Co-operative Insurance Company, 1867, the Co-operative Newspaper Society, 1871, the Co-operative Productive Federation, 1882, the Agricultural and Horticultural Association, 1867.

Besides his contributions in legal, advisory, promotional and administrative activities, he was one of the principal co-operative thinkers. Congress reports from 1870 onwards, and 19 pamphlets on co-operative subjects, show his ability to discover and frame principles, to reveal the fundamental problems of co-operative development and to formulate schemes to solve them by the application of principles. With Hughes he wrote *A Manual for Co-operators* which is a classic on co-operative ethics and economics.

Throughout his association with the Co-operative Movement he proved himself not only a sincere idealist, but one who took practical action in attempts to achieve them, who not only framed principles but applied them. He paid a big price in so doing, losing £40,000 in the efforts to establish working men's associations for production in the 'fifties, and spending the last 20 years of his life as General Secretary of the Co-operative Union engaged in the hard uphill work of firmly establishing the organisation, in guiding and influencing the hundreds of societies which were still in their infancy, in struggling for social ideals, often against grubby and short-sighted materialism. For what must often have seemed a hopeless and thankless task, he lived the greater part of each week in Manchester lodgings, away from his family, when he might have spent those years in easy, gracious living at Bisham Abbey.

" His devotion to the Co-operative Movement and the priceless services which he rendered are known only to those who were honoured by his personal friendship; but his generosity and patience, his simplicity of heart, of faith amid failure, his bravery and selflessness have inspired others with enthusiasm and self sacrifice." (Extract from a resolution of the Central Board of the Co-operative Union.) A memorial to him was erected in the crypt of St. Paul's Cathedral, and a scholarship for the sons of co-operators tenable at Oriel College was endowed in his memory. He was one of the finest characters ever associated with the Co-operative Movement.

Örne, Anders, 1881–1956.—*Foremost theoretician of the Swedish Co-operative Movement.*

Born of a peasant family in Western Sweden and reared in a peasant economy. Graduated in philosophy at Uppsala University. 1907, editor of a Stockholm Labour journal and active in the Labour movement. 1910, appointed chief editor of publications of Ko-operativa Förbundet (Swedish Co-operative Union and Wholesale). 1916, appointed General Secretary of K.F. 1919, a member of the first chamber of the Riksdag (Swedish Parliament), and Under State-Secretary to the Ministry of Finance in Sweden's first Labour Government, and Minister of Communications and Transport in the second.

In 1926 left his co-operative employment to become Director of the Post Office, was Director of the National Debt Office Board, but retained an interest in and continued active in the Co-operative Movement. Member of the Administrative Council of K.F., President of Stockholm Society, and member of the Central Committee of the I.C.A., 1920–1956. His experience in both the co-operative and labour movements and as an elected leader and salaried official in both government and co-operative service give his opinions exceptional weight. These were firmly based on Rochdale principles. He expounded them in *Co-operative View on Society*, 1918; *The Seven Basic Principles*, 1919; *Co-operatism*, 1921; *The Co-operative Programme*, 1921; *Co-operative Ideals and Problems*, 1924 (long used by the Education Department of the British Co-operative Union) and over 30 pamphlets. Wrote and lectured on co-operative subjects, economics, political and social problems, and also produced several popular books on mathematics.

Owen, Robert, 1771-1858.—" *The Father of Co-operation,*" *of British Socialism, and much else.*

Born at Newtown, Montgomeryshire, sixth of seven children. Father a saddler, ironmonger and postmaster. Attended day school but at 10 years of age entered retail trade, first for a few weeks with his brother, a saddler in London, then with McGuffog, a linen draper at Stamford, for some time in a big drapery shop, Flint and Palmer, in London, and at the age of 18 at a haberdashers, Sattersfield, in St. Ann's Square, Manchester. Entered into partnership with a mechanic, Jones, in making spinning mules, then worked on his own. Gave this up to become manager of Drinkwater's cotton mill, later manager and partner of the Chorlton Twist Company. His life in Manchester had a great influence on his career, it not only gave him experience and knowledge of the factory system but he made friends with members of Manchester College and as a member of the Manchester Literary and Philosophical Society he had contacts with thinkers such as John Dalton, Coleridge, and Dr. Percival, whose work and report on factory life was the beginning of the movement for factory legislation. In this circle Owen heard economic and social theories discussed and from these discussions formulated theories of his own.

In 1799 he married Miss Dale, daughter of David Dale, the owner of the New Lanark cotton mills, and became manager of those mills for the New Lanark Twist Company (consisting of himself and two of his Manchester partners). He ran the business successfully and gained the reputation of a good practical businessman, but he also conducted his social experiments, in the education of children and improving working conditions, which he believed proved the soundness of his theory of character formation.

Then he attempted to have his theories applied on a larger scale, seeking to obtain legislation to improve factory conditions, which resulted in the disappointing Factory Act of 1819, and to have communities established. These were suggested by him to government and local authorities as a remedy for unemployment and poverty, though he had much higher and further objectives and sought to advance his opinions by pen and speech as described in the text.

His denunciation of all organised religions 1817 aroused a great deal of unnecessary antagonism, and handicapped co-operation for more than a generation. In 1819 and 1820 unsuccessfully contested the parliamentary election of Lanark Burghs. At the zenith of his manufacturing career he withdrew from business and devoted himself to the furtherance of his plans for communities. Undertook, and sank money in his communist experiments at New Harmony, U.S.A., 1825-1828, which failed. On his return to England, 1829, found the working classes were forming co-operative societies with the object of developing into communities, attended the first Co-operative Congress and was little impressed with the Movement or attracted by its methods. Became more enthusiastic as he saw possibilities of using the Movement for his scheme of National Equitable Labour Exchanges (opened the one at Grays Inn Road, 1832).

A brief and catastrophic incursion into trade unionism with the same end in view resulted in the formation and collapse of the Grand National Consolidated Trade Union, 1834. This period was designated by Owen as The Crisis, his journal under that name being followed by the *New Moral World*, 1834-1845. Owen then toured this country and many others, expounding his New Moral World, and forming associations to propagate it—The Association of All Classes of All Nations, the Universal Community Society of Rational Religionists, the Home Colonization Society. His views on marriage and religion aroused intense feeling and resulted in what Podmore refers to as The Holy War, 1839-1841. The last great community venture at Queenwood ended in failure. He became its governor with full powers in 1841, but conducted it extravagantly, expenditure anticipating income which failed to materialise. He resigned in 1842, but was invited to take over again in 1843. Matters went from bad to worse and the Congress of Rational Religionists of 1844 decided not to invite Owen to continue as President. This was practically the end although he continued to write and address petitions, to tour and to speak. About 1853 became a convert to Spiritualism.

Accepted an invitation to stand as parliamentary candidate for Marylebone in 1848, issued an election address which contains interesting items, not all of which would appeal to modern socialists. Contributed five papers for discussion at the National Association for the Promotion of Social Science meeting 1857, and travelled to and addressed its meeting at Liverpool, 1858. The effort was too much for him, although he rallied and a fortnight later was able to get to Newtown; he died there on Nov. 17th, 1858.

He was a voluminous writer, much of it boring and repetitive, although his earlier work and his autobiography are very readable. The *New View of Society* published in the Everyman's edition includes four essays on the Formation of Character, 1813–1814, and *Address to the Inhabitants of New Lanark*, 1816; *Observations on the Effect of the Manufacturing System, 1815; On the Employment of Children in Manufactories*, 1818; *To the British Manufacturers*, 1818; *An Address to the Working Classes*, 1819; *Report to the Committee of the Association for Relief of the Manufacturing and Labouring Poor*, 1817; *Letters Upon the Relief of the Poor*, 1817; *A Catechism of the New View of Society and Three Addresses*, 1817; *A Further Development of the Plan for the Relief of the Poor and the Emancipation of Mankind*, 1817; *Report to the County of Lanark*, 1820. With the exception of his autobiography this is the best of Owen.

There is a good introduction by G. D. H. Cole and a bibliography of Owen's works. *Robert Owen*, 1906, by Podmore is the most comprehensive biography of Owen; G. D. H. Cole's *Life of Robert Owen*, 1930, is shorter but very good; *Robert Owen* by Margaret Cole, 1953, is much shorter but contains all the essentials and is very readable. *Life, Times and Labours of Robert Owen*, Lloyd Jones (1889–1890) is found in many libraries and is, of course, by an admirer who knew him personally.

Pare, William, 1805–1873.—*Leading Owenite.*

Born in Birmingham, son of a cabinet maker, apprenticed to his father but became a reporter. Later a retailer of tobacco and cigars. Helped to start a Mechanics' Institute (later attended by G. J. Holyoake as a student). Took an active and leading part in Birmingham social and political life by attending meetings to promote Parliamentary Reform in 1819, in the agitation for repeal of the Test and Corporation Acts and for Roman Catholic Emancipation. Member of the Council of the Birmingham Political Union, 1830 (of its considerable secretarial work it was reported " All of it was managed by William Pare "). Led an agitation for the repeal of church rates, 1832. Secretary of the Reformers' Registration Society, 1835. Appointed the first Registrar of Birmingham in 1837. Member of the committee promoting the incorporation of the town and a member of its first council.

He was interested in Co-operation in 1827, being converted to Owenism by William Thompson of Cork. Following correspondence with Dr. William King of Brighton in 1828 and moved by the example of Brighton Society, a co-operative society was established in Birmingham in November, 1828. Pare maintained the correspondence and circulated copies of King's *Co-operator* in the Midlands and the North. In 1830 he lectured in Liverpool, Manchester, Bolton, Chester, and elsewhere.

Attended the first Co-operative Congress (Manchester) 1831, and convened the second (Birmingham) and acted as secretary. At the first Congress seconded the resolution to establish a wholesale organisation, was elected to a council for the ensuing year and drafted the address from the Congress to all the co-operative societies in the United Kingdom. He reported and edited most of these Congresses, among them the important third congress (London). From these reports Pare appears as the most frequent speaker, mover of the most resolutions, and undoubtedly among the most active and influential members, an acknowledged leader.

His many speeches reveal him to have a thorough grasp of Owenism and also a shrewdness and commonsense which perhaps appealed to those who disliked Owen's " metaphysics."

1829, started and edited the *Birmingham Co-operative Herald* and in 1833, the *Birmingham Labour Exchange Gazette*. A keen advocate of National Equitable Labour Exchanges he did much to get a Birmingham branch established. Was on the Management Council and chosen to represent the Exchange in Ireland, to arrange exchanges with Irish produce. Lectured upon Exchanges in Ireland, visited Ralahine, and took possession of estate of William Thompson (deceased). He was one of the trustees of the property of Thompson which had been bequeathed for co-operative purposes.

Pare was elected Vice-President of the Association of All Classes of All Nations and its subsidiary The National Community Friendly Society, 1835. Moved a resolution in the 1838 Congress to appoint missionaries, and was one of a committee of four to formulate a plan and make the appointments. Prepared and delivered an address from Congress to the Chartist Convention, 1838. His socialist opinions, however, aroused such feeling among some quarters in Birmingham that he was compelled to resign his position as Registrar and left Birmingham, 1842. Served as Governor of the Queenwood Community, 1842–1844. Between 1844–1846 worked as a railway statistician and prepared reports for presentation to Parliament on projected lines. Engaged in the management of ironworks, 1846–1865.

Appears to have travelled on business in Scandinavia during this period and to have spread co-operative ideas at the same time. Significant that he attended the modern series of Congresses as a delegate from a Norwegian society—The Eidesfoss Co-operative Society. The text describes his part in promoting the Congress of 1869. He acted as honorary secretary to this and to the Congresses of 1870, 1871, 1872, undertook the foreign correspondence, among the most interesting features of these Congress reports, and spoke frequently and gave addresses. Holyoake credits him with introducing into England the term Congress for deliberative meetings.

Author of *Claims of Capital and Labour*, *Plan for the Suppression of the Predatory Classes*, *Co-operative Agriculture*, and a history of Ralahine. Edited William Thompson's *Inquiry into the Principles of the Distribution of Wealth Most Conducive to Human Happiness*.

Pitman, Henry, 1826–1909.—*Editor of the " Co-operator."*

Born at Trowbridge, Wilts., youngest but one of eleven children. Sir Isaac Pitman was an elder brother, and whilst inventing, perfecting, and promulgating his system of phonography (shorthand) taught Henry, and his other brothers the system, and they engaged in writing, teaching, and lecturing upon it everywhere. Henry, after some years, became a newspaper reporter. Served as such on some Manchester papers including the *Manchester Guardian*, and his Manchester connections resulted in him assisting to start the *Co-operator* in 1860, he suggesting the name of the paper. After nine months' existence, in order to prevent the paper ceasing publication, he took its charge upon himself, liabilities included, and continued it until the publication of the *Co-operative News*.

The paper exercised a great influence during the important formative decade of the 'sixties, which saw the establishing of the C.W.S., the holding of Co-operative Congresses, the formation of the Co-operative Insurance Company, and the general bringing together of co-operative societies into national organisations. Pitman's *Co-operator* played a great part in starting and accomplishing these achievements as reference to the text will show. For 40 years he was the official reporter of the Co-operative Congresses, attending the Newcastle one in the year he died. He was active in many other reform movements—temperance, vegetarian, anti-tobacco and anti-vaccination—serving a prison sentence as an anti-vaccinator.

Plunkett, Sir Horace Curzon, 1854–1932.—*Pioneer of Agricultural Co-operation.*

Born at Sherborne House, Glos., third son of Lord Dunsany. Educated at Eton and University College, Oxford, graduated 1877. 1879, started ranching at Wyoming, U.S.A. Visited Ireland each year. 1888, article on Co-operative Stores in Ireland in the 19th century. 1889, returned to settle in Ireland. Visited U.S.A. each year. Opened campaign for agricultural Co-operation. 1891–1918, member of Congested District Board for Ireland. 1892, elected M.P. for South County Dublin, Unionist. 1894, promoted Irish Agricultural Organisation. President until 1899. In 1895, got Recess Committee convened which led to establishment of Department of Agriculture and Technical Instruction for Ireland, 1899. Plunkett its Vice-President until 1907. From 1907 till his death engaged in spreading the gospel of agricultural Co-operation. Re-elected President of I.H.O.S. Given Plunkett House, Merrion Square, Dublin, as a mark of esteem.

Keen on keeping Ireland within the United Kingdom. 1917–1918, Chairman of Irish Convention, 1919 founded Irish Dominion League. Accepted membership of Senate of Irish Free State, 1922, but his house burned down by political extremists, 1923. Settled in England. 1924, presided over conference on Agricultural Co-operation in the British Empire. 1925, visited South Africa. Died at Weybridge.

Wrote *Ireland in the New Century*, 1904; *Rural Life Problem of the U.S.A.*, 1910, also many pamphlets. These and his diary in care of Horace Plunkett Foundation, Doughty Street, London.

Poisson, E., 1882–1942.—*French Co-operator.*

Qualified as a lawyer but spent most of his life in service of the Socialist and Co-operative Movements. Was closely associated with the great French socialist leader Jean Jaures, and was with him when Jaures was assassinated in 1914. Became secretary of the French Co-operative Union in 1912, member of the Central Committee of the I.C.A. in 1913, elected to the executive of the I.C.A. in 1921, and became Vice-President, an office he held until his death in 1942.

Did great work towards unifying the French Movement and exercised much influence in the I.C.A., here also seeking to make the Alliance as comprehensive as possible without sacrificing principle. Was driven out of office by the fascists of France during the occupation. Wrote several books, much inspired by Professor C. Gide, such as *La Co operation et la Democratie, Une Programme d'Action, La Republique Co-operative* (translated into English by W. P. Watkins).

Pratt, Hodgson, 1824–1907.—*Co-operator and Internationalist.*

Born at Bath, educated at Haileybury College. Served in Indian Civil Service, 1846–1863. A friend of India, strove to break down racial barriers. A strong supporter of vernacular education as a step to self-government. Retired as result of a serious illness and contributed articles on Indian questions to the *Economist*. Assisted to form the National Indian Association and was its first honorary secretary, 1872.

Became interested in the work of the Working Men's Club and Institute Union (formed in 1862) and joined the Council of the Union, 1864. Active and interested in the Club movement for remainder of his life. His association with this movement brought him into contact with the Co-operative Movement. Friendly with Hughes, Neale, Ludlow, and Holyoake. On the committee which called the Congress of 1869 into being. A good linguist, with many friends on the Continent and was one of the earliest and most active advocates for international Co-operation. Worked incessantly in the 'seventies and 'eighties to establish societies in London. Honorary secretary of Southern Sectional Board, 1873. One of the three guarantors of the London Co-operative Agency, 1873. Prime mover in the establishment of the Guild of Co-operators, 1878. A warm supporter of Co-operative Co-partnership. One of the founders of the Co-operative Permanent Building Society, 1884.

In the opinion of J. J. Dent, did more than any other single man to promote Peace and Arbitration Societies in Great Britain and on the Continent. One of the founders and president for many years of the International Arbitration and Peace Association in London. Took an active part in establishing the International Federation for Arbitration and Peace, and the International League of Workers for Peace, 1883. In the 'eighties worked hard in promoting Peace Societies in Germany. Advocated the establishment in all countries of Councils of International Concord, non-official and non-governmental, to ascertain and publish the truth when false or dangerous accusations were made against a nation within the territory of another nation. Strongly opposed militarism.

A strong advocate of craft and technical training, recognising the need for this when few others did, also for the higher education of adult workmen and women, as early as 1870 addressing a Memorial to the Universities urging its provision. Also urged the Co-operative Movement to educate its members in private and public morality, social and political duty, history and literature, and its employees in technical, artistic and scientific subjects to make them first-class managers, overseers, foremen and clerks.

A Hodgson Pratt Memorial was founded in 1911 to keep alive his memory. It consisted of a fund from which essay prizes, scholarships and grants were made " to assist organisations carrying on work which Mr. Pratt would have supported had he been alive." The Co-operative Union and the Wholesale Societies were represented on the committee which administered the fund, which was augmented each year by contributions from co-operative societies, clubs and individuals. J. J. Dent acted as secretary until his retirement in 1930, when the Memorial Society was dissolved and its assets handed over to the Co-operative Union on condition that the capital fund should be kept intact, only the annual income to be spent, that an annual lecture be given in each Section in rotation, that annual scholarships to the Co-operative College and Summer and Week-end schools be awarded, that all such lectures and scholarships bear the title of Hodgson Pratt Memorial.

Rae, William Robert, 1858–1936.—*Educationist.*

Born in the Orkneys, educated Edinburgh University. Headmaster of Hendon School, Sunderland. Member of Central Board, 1898–1936; President of Congress, 1909; for 34 years chairman of the Education Department of the Co-operative Union, and for some years chairman of the Central Board and a Director of the Co-operative Press. These were critical years for co-operative education and much of the success achieved and related in the text was due to his vigour and zeal. He was also a magistrate, associated with the Temperance Movement, one of those associated with the founding of the Workers' Educational Association, chairman of the Sunderland Juvenile Advisory Committee, and organised a mission for boys in Sunderland. Of fine physique and commanding presence, a splendid and powerful orator blessed with the gift of humour, his personality was a great asset to co-operative education in general and to the Co-operative College in particular.

Raiffeisen, Friedrich Wilhelm, 1818–1888.—*Originator of Co-operative Credit Societies.*

Founder of the co-operative credit society movement. Son of the Burgomaster of Hamm, Westphalia. Educated at home, his short military career terminated by bad eyesight, he undertook a career of public service. 1845, Burgomaster of Weyerbusch; 1848, Burgomaster of Flammersfeld; 1854, Burgomaster of Heddersdorf. Desired to improve the character and lot of the peasants who were exploited by moneylenders and merchants. Established a co-operative bakery, then a cattle purchasing association and then the first village co-operative credit society at Flammersfeld. He engaged in propaganda and organisation to extend these credit institutions but at first they spread slowly, the second being founded at Heddersdorf, 1854, the third in 1862, and the fourth in 1868. By 1874 they were becoming well known and after 1880 they spread rapidly and not only in Germany. They spread and exist with some variations, all over the world wherever a free peasant economy is found.

Rochdale Pioneers.

An appendix to Cole's *Century of Co-operation* records the most comprehensive investigation yet made into the identities of the original Pioneers. Many who were associated with the venture at some time or other during 1844 cannot be so regarded, merely putting their names and doing nothing more. Those who were certainly members when the store opened and had contributed capital were:—

	Occupation		Age in 1844
Ashworth, George	Flannel Weaver		
Ashworth, Miles	Flannel Weaver	Chartist	54
Ashworth, Samuel	Flannel Weaver	Chartist	19
Bamford, James	Shoemaker		19
Bent, John	Tailor	Socialist	27
Brooks, David	Block Printer	Chartist	41
Chadwick, Thomas	Hatter		
Collier, John	Mill Engineer	Socialist	36
Cooper, William	Flannel Weaver	Socialist	24
Daly, James	Joiner	Socialist	
Hill, John	Hatter		30
Holt, James	Weaver		
Holt, John	Slubber	Chartist	
Howarth, Charles	Warper	Socialist	32
Maden, James	Flannel Weaver		41
Mallalieu, William	Cotton Band Manf'r	Socialist	48
Manock, James	Flannel Weaver	Chartist	46
Riley, James	Deviler		
Rudman, Benjamin	Flannel Weaver	Chartist	31
Scowcroft, John	Hawker	Chartist	59
Smith, Jos.	Woolsorter	Socialist	
Smithies, James	Woolsorter	Socialist	25
Standring, James	Flannel Weaver		40
Taylor, Robert	Flannel Weaver	Socialist	
Taylor, William	Power Loom Overlooker	Socialist	30
Tweedale, James	Clogger	Socialist	25
Whitehead, John	Weaver	Socialist	
Williams, William	Overlooker		

Names given in other lists include John Kershaw, Ann Tweedale, Samuel Tweedale, Charles Barnish, Benjamin Jordan. A list compiled by the Pioneers' Society in 1880 including those who had joined by the first quarterly meeting, January 6th, 1845, on the evidence of the minute book and " surviving originators " added many more —W. Walker, J. Dawson, J. Butterworth, W. Oldham, J. Crabtree, S. Allat, I. Clegg, W. Hellawell, J. Casson, J. Wilson, R. Lupton, G. Morton, J. Whatmough, R. Lees, A. Butterworth, C. Shaw. Many of these are found in the list of names in the Purchase Book referred to in *A Century of Co-operation*. If one accepts them, and their claim might be disputed, there would be 49 original Pioneers, not 28. Lists other than that of G. D. H. Cole include the arbitrators, C. Barnish, J. Garside, G. Healey, J. Lord, J. Wilkinson, none of whom however appear to have been members at the time, and it is probable that the intended nature of the office induced the selection of men sympathetic to, but outside, the Society.

William Robertson, a Rochdalian, on the staff of the *Manchester Guardian*, a local historian and author of a biography of John Bright, described some of them in the Handbook to the Rochdale Congress of 1892. " Smithies was a native of Huddersfield and had received a good education. On coming to Rochdale he was apprenticed to Mr. Phelps, wool stapler, and having served his time he set up in that business in the top storey of his house in Henland. Amongst those who met at his residence was Charles Howarth, a man of practical knowledge, who it will be remembered took a prominent part in the Co-operative Shop, No. 15 Toad Lane, and which had failed. James Daly, of Crook Street, off John Street, a joiner, was a native of the North of Ireland where his father was a sergeant of the militia. He worked for William Robinson, Drake Street, and acted afterwards in the capacity of foreman for Thomas Robinson. This native of the Emerald Isle was a good grammarian, arithmetician, mathematician and musician, and was a prominent member of the Oddfellows Society. William Cooper, handloom weaver and socialist, was an energetic young man, employed by Mr. Ashworth of Church Style. John Bent, a native of Davyhulme, near Flixton, was educated at Manchester Bluecoat School (Chetham's Hospital). He was apprenticed to the business of a tailor at Knutsford, became a socialist and lost £15 in the land scheme of Robert Owen, yet nevertheless he joined the aforementioned enthusiasts in forming a plan for the salvation of their fellow workmen. James Standring of Cloth Hall, a man of an enquiring turn of mind, had been a member of the former store, and very poor, for he had a large family, David Brooks, a block printer at Belfield and an enthusiastic Chartist, was also amongst the number, together with others."

Among these others were Miles Ashworth, the first president, a former Marine, one of the guard which escorted Napoleon in the *Bellerophon* to St. Helena; his son, Samuel Ashworth, the first shopman of the Society, later its manager, who resigned this position to become buyer for the C.W.S., 1867–1871; John Holt, first treasurer of the society and with David Brooks, entrusted with the first purchases, was formerly treasurer of the local Chartists; John Scowcroft was a Swedenborgian preacher and a speaker at a great demonstration during the strike of 1842 (Plug Plot). John Collier was a descendent of Tim Bobbin, the Lancashire dialect writer, and a member of a very radical family. He had a beehive (until recent times a generally recognised symbol of Co-operation) carved on his tombstone. James Daly in 1849 sailed with his wife and eight children to investigate the possibilities of starting a co-operative community in Texas, but he and his wife died on the voyage.

Many of these men served in various ways during the early days, James Tweedale and William Williams, for instance, collected the subscriptions to share capital by visiting the subscribers on Sunday mornings. Daly knocked up rude shelves prior to the opening of the store, and with Tweedale and Miles Ashworth cleaned the place up and prepared it for opening. Later some served on committees, not only of the Pioneers, but on those of the Corn Mill and the manufacturing society. Some who were not members by January, 1845, could be credited as Pioneers by the work they did in the early days of the Society's existence.

It may be noted that, of the original Pioneers, there were more than 28 and only a minority of them were weavers.

Smithies, James, 1819–1869.—*Rochdale Pioneer.*

An original Rochdale and C.W.S. Pioneer. Born in Huddersfield. Wool stapler. Active in the Co-operative Movement before 1844. His home a meeting-place for co-operators. Active in the formation and development of the Rochdale Society, serving as director, president, secretary, superintendent. Taught in the Toad Lane store on Sunday mornings. One of the promoters of the Rochdale Co-operative Manufacturing Society. A strong advocate of profit-sharing. Chosen by the Pioneers to fight the Inland Revenue Commissioners on income tax liability. One of the original members of the C.W.S., on its first Board and its first treasurer. Elected to the Rochdale Borough Council.

Holyoake described him as the chief of the Pioneers and in some respects the greatest, " it was Mr. Smithies' merriment which kept Co-operation in good countenance during the evil days. He laughed the Society into existence, gave the timid courage and made the grim-faced members genial. His happy nature, his wise tolerance, his boundless patience with dullness, ignorance and discontent made him exercise the great influence which kept the Society together."

Thompson, William, ? 1785–1833.—*Owenite.*

Native of Cork of which he was a prosperous landed proprietor. Corresponded with Jeremy Bentham and resided with him for many years after 1819. Came also under the influence of Owen. He combined the ethics of Bentham, the labour economics of Ricardo and the social views of Owen into a system of socialism. His most important work was a tome, *Inquiry into the Principles of the Distribution of Wealth most conducive to Human Happiness*, 1824, which is said to have fallen stillborn from the press. William Pare published an abridged version of it in 1850. Also wrote *An Inquiry into the Principles Most Conducive to Human Happiness*, 1824, *Labour Rewarded, or How to Secure the Whole Product of His Exertions*, 1827,

Practical Directions for the Speedy and Economical Establishment of Communities, 1830. These books reveal the direction of his thought and expound his socialism, the need for socialism, a description of his ideal community and ways and means of establishing them. He is generally regarded as being the finest intellect associated with the Owenite movement, attended the early Co-operative Congresses and was highly revered by them. He conceived and worked out the theory of surplus value. Also wrote *An Appeal of One Half of the Human Race, Women, Against the Pretensions of the Other Half, Men.*

Died at Clounksen, County Cork. Bequeathed most of his property to trustees (William Pare was one) for the purpose of propagating his principles and aiding their practical application. His library was to go to the first co-operative community established in Great Britain or Ireland. The will was disputed by relatives, and William Pare was still engaged in litigation upon it in 1850. His body was to be examined by a lecturer on anatomy and the skeleton preserved in an anatomical museum. Despite the objections of the local peasantry this was claimed to have been accomplished.

Wade, Dr. Arthur S.—*Owenite Vicar.*

Vicar of Warwick. Active in various Owenite societies in London, member of the National Union of the Working Classes, " a jovial, eccentric doctor of divinity, weighing some 20 stones, a prop and pillar of militant Owenism." Headed, " in full canonicals and the scarlet hood of a Doctor of Divinity " the monster procession of trade unionists (estimated by the *Times* at 30,000) to present a petition to Lord Melbourne against the sentencing of the Tolpuddle labourers. He was prominent in the Co-operative Congresses, especially the important Third Congress, 1832, where he smoothed over contentions arising from Owen's views on religion. He expressed himself in bold language in attacking the injustices suffered by the poor and is said at one time to have been inhibited from preaching by his bishop. A stone was erected to his memory in St. Nicholas churchyard, Warwick, by the Labour movement on the centenary of his death, 1835.

Warbasse, Dr. J. P., 1866-1957.—*American Co-operator.*

Born in Newton, New Jersey, of Danish descent. Graduated 1889, Colombia University's College of Physicians and Surgeons. Served as army surgeon in Spanish American War and consequently developed " a strong pacifist leaning." Distinguished in medicine and surgery, author of *Surgical Treatment*, three volumes, editor of *New York State Journal of Medicine* and *American Journal of Surgery.* In 1902 married Agnes Dyer (descendant of Samuel Adams). She was active in various social causes and served as unpaid secretary of the Co-operative League until 1928. The Warbasse's homes in Brooklyn and Cape Cod were rallying points for co-operators from all over the U.S.A. Engaged in several labour and social movements, participating in strikes, socialism, anarchism, the single tax movement. Meetings with Sir William Maxwell and A. Sonnichsen (leader in a New York Co-operative) converted him to Co-operation. Enthusiastic and energetic leader of the group which established the Co-operative League, 1916. Was its first President and remained in that office until 1941. Retired from medicine in 1919 to devote all his time to co-operative work. For the first 15 years of the League he was its financial mainstay. A strong adherent and advocate of Rochdale principles, opposing those who favoured modification and short cuts, emphasised importance of co-operative education. Edited and contributed to the League's periodical *Co-operation,* author of *Co-operative Democracy, Co-operative Education, The Doctor and the Public, What is Co-operation? Co-operation, a Way of Peace. Problems of Co-operation. Three Voyages* (his autobiography).

Webb, Sidney (1859-1947) and Beatrice (1858-1943).—(*Lord and Lady Passfield.*)

Sidney Webb, born in London, younger son of C. Webb, accountant, mother kept a hairdressing business. Left school at 16. 1875-1878, in city office of some colonial brokers. Studied in evening classes and entered Civil Service by open competition. 1878, second division clerk in War Office. 1879, in Surveyor of Taxes

Office. 1881, first division clerkship in Colonial Office. 1885, called to the Bar. 1886, graduated LL.B., London, with third class honours. 1879, became friendly with George Bernard Shaw, and joined the Fabian Society, 1885. Both were members of the Executive, and with Graham Wallas and Sidney Olivier, largely dominated the society for many years.

1887, wrote *Facts for Socialists* and contributed to the Fabian Essays, 1889. These were some of the most influential contributions to British Socialism. Met Beatrice Potter at the Co-operative Congress of 1890, where they came to "a working compact," and married 1892. Thenceforward they also constituted a working partnership of such a nature that it is necessary to consider their work, thought and activities jointly.

Beatrice Webb, née Potter, born at Standish House, near Gloucester, eighth of the nine daughters of Richard Potter, industrial and railway magnate, niece of T. B. Potter, Liberal M.P. for Rochdale. Educated at home. 1882, on death of mother, managed home and assisted father. Friendly with and interest in social and philosophical problems stimulated by Herbert Spencer. Active in London's "Society." Nearly married Joseph Chamberlain. Slummed, visited for Charity Organisation Society, assisted in research for *Inquiry Into the Life and Labour of the People of London* by Charles Booth (her cousin's husband). To get first hand knowledge of working class life lived with a working class family in Bacup, Lancashire, 1883. To get first hand knowledge of sweated industry worked as a "trouser hand" in the East End of London. Returned north to make an inquiry into the Co-operative Movement, the fruit of which was *The Co-operative Movement in Great Britain*, 1891. This was her first book, and although small, exercised a big and historic influence as related in the text. Sidney gave a paper to the Congress of 1891 on the best methods of bringing Co-operation within the reach of the people. Beatrice gave one on the Sweating System to the Rochdale Congress of 1892.

After their marriage they devoted themselves to political and research work, Beatrice having a comfortable "unearned income" which permitted this. Her study of the Co-operative Movement led them to undertake an inquiry into trade unionism, the result of which was their classic *History of Trade Unionism*, 1894, and *Industrial Democracy*, 1897. Their intention to make a scientific study of facts before coming to conclusions inevitably engaged them in formidable historical research, which may have been salutary to the many authorities who had expressed weighty opinions without such study. Their series on local government, indispensable to any serious student of local government or of social history, began with the publication of *The Manor and the Borough*, 1906, and proceeded through ten massive volumes to *English Poor Law History, The Last Hundred Years* in 1929.

Pursuing the Fabian policy of permeation, they sought to influence the leaders of all political parties to adopt socialist solutions to particular social problems, with some success. "For years the famous house at 41 Grosvenor Road was not so much a private house as an efficient manufactory of informed political opinion " (M. Cole). Beatrice's connections provided opportunities for the necessary contacts. Sidney was a member of the London County Council, 1892–1910, sat on 16 committees. His most important work was on education, particularly further education. A Technical Instruction Act, 1889, permitted County Councils to levy a rate for education of this kind. Webb persuaded the L.C.C. to set up a technical education committee with himself as chairman, and by further successful persuasion gradually enlarged the interpretation of "technical" until it included "the teaching of every conceivable subject other than ancient Greek and theology." This was the devious way employed to establish what he really aimed at, a system of adequate secondary education. He was made chairman of the L.C.C. Higher Education Committee. A Fabian, Henry Hutchinson, left £10,000 in trust to his daughter and Sidney Webb and three other members of the Fabian Society for the propaganda and advancement of the Society and its Socialism. As a result of Webb's broad vision a substantial part of this bequest was used to found The London School of Economics and Political Science in the belief that objective, hard thinking on scientific lines was what socialism most needed. Webb also did much in the reorganisation of London University and became a member of its Senate.

Beatrice was made a member of the Royal Commission on the Poor Law, 1905–1909, and largely dominated its proceedings. Although she was not able to persuade the majority to make the recommendations she desired, the majority report was different from what it would otherwise have been, and her Minority Report became one of the great state papers of British social history, one of the formative influences in shaping social policy during this century.

Beatrice founded the Fabian Research Department and Sidney founded the *New Statesman*, 1913, intending it to be an independent journal whose independent approach would lead intelligent readers to adopt socialist views. It published supplements on current problems, dealt with in a weighty and detailed way, among them a valuable one written by the Webbs on the Co-operative Movement.

The Great War, 1914–1918, brought both more directly into party politics. In 1915 he became a member of the Labour Party Executive and played the major part in drafting its new constitution and its programme, *Labour and the New Social Order*. Webb played a prominent part in the proceedings of the Sankey Commission on the Coal Industry. He, with Sir L. C. Money, R. H. Tawney and Robert Smillie, represented the Miners' Federation. The miners put him at the head of the poll for the Labour Executive in 1919, and in the parliamentary seat for Seaham Harbour, 1922. But the Webbs were still mainly concerned with research and the creation of informed opinion. They issued some important works to this end—a revised edition of the *History of Trade Unionism*, 1920, and on the request of the International Socialist Bureau, *A Constitution For the Socialist Commonwealth of Great Britain*, 1920; *The Consumers' Co-operative Movement*, 1921; *The Decay of Capitalist Civilisation*, 1923. Sidney was a member of the first Labour Government, 1924, as President of the Board of Trade.

In the second Labour Government, 1929–1931, he was made Colonial Secretary and initiated many good reforms although getting into difficulties over Palestine. Parliament did not appeal to him, he had been made a peer, 1929, to meet the requirements of the Labour government, assuming the title of Lord Passfield, his wife resolutely refusing to be addressed otherwise than as Mrs. Sidney Webb. After the fall of the Labour Government the pair turned to an intensive study of the U.S.S.R. In May, 1932, they arrived in Leningrad and returned in August of the same year. Both were well over 70 years of age, were treated as very important persons, and, as with most persons who visited the Soviet Union found what they went to find. The result was *Soviet Communism, A New Civilisation*, two volumes, 1935. Beatrice's last public position was President of the Fabian Society, 1939–1941. The Order of Merit was conferred on Sidney after the death of Beatrice in 1943, and in 1947 the ashes of both were laid in Westminster Abbey.

Beatrice wrote an autobiography of her early life in *My Apprenticeship*, 1929, which contains some very interesting material to the co-operative student, it was continued in *Our Partnership*, 1948, a posthumous publication, and carried down to 1932 in *Beatrice Webb's Diaries*, two volumes, edited by Margaret Cole. These works are of absorbing interest; they reveal the Labour Movement from the inside by a shrewd, knowledgeable and sympathetic but critical observer. Sidney and Beatrice Webb are important because of their work and influence upon all branches of the Labour movement from 1890 onwards. They were largely responsible for the conception of a Welfare State and " Another great service which the Webbs rendered to the Socialist Movement was by their exhaustive examination of Local Government and the Trade Union and Co-operative Movement. They gave a wider concept to democracy which had formerly been considered largely from the angle of parliamentary institutions." C. R. Attlee, Preface to *Beatrice and Sidney Webb*, by Margaret Cole.

Appendix II.

A letter published in the London newspapers, August 9th, 1817, reprinted in *The Life of Robert Owen* by Himself, contrasting conditions in the manufacturing towns with those in Owen's proposed villages.

" In the Manufacturing Towns—the poor and working classes now usually live in garrets or cellars, within narrow lanes or confined courts.

" In the Proposed Villages—the poor and working classes will live in dwellings formed into a large square, rendered in every way convenient, and usefully ornamented.

" In the Manufacturing Towns—they are surrounded with dirt, enveloped in smoke, and have seldom a pleasant object on which to fix their eye.

" In the Proposed Villages—they will be surrounded by gardens, have abundance of space in all directions to keep the air healthy and pleasant; they will have walks and plantations before them, within the square, and well cultivated grounds, kept in good order around, as far as the eye can reach.

" In the Manufacturing Towns—parents are oppressed with anxiety to secure the means of subsistence for themselves and children.

" In the Proposed Villages—in consequence of the principle of mutual co-operation being understood and practised to its full extent, the necessaries and comforts of life are enjoyed by all in abundance.

" In the Manufacturing Towns—each family has the care and trouble of going to market to supply their individual wants, and under every disadvantage.

" In the Proposed Villages—the same trouble will provide for 1,000 as is now required of one family; and all articles will be procured on the best terms.

" In the Manufacturing Towns—each family must have domestic arrangements for cooking, etc., and one person must be wholly occupied in preparing provisions, etc., for a family of ordinary numbers.

" In the Proposed Villages—the best provisions will be cooked in the best manner, under arrangements that will enable five or six individuals to prepare provisions for 1,000.

" In the Manufacturing Towns—the parents must toil from ten to sixteen hours a day to procure the wretched subsistence which they obtain for themselves and children and very often under circumstances the most unfavourable to health and natural enjoyments.

" In the Proposed Villages—the parents will be pleasantly and healthfully occupied not more than eight hours in the day.

" In the Manufacturing Towns—in bad times, which frequently occur, the parties experience a distress not easily to be described.

" In the Proposed Villages—in the event of sickness, the utmost care and attention will be experienced; every one, both from principle and interest, will be active and have pleasure in rendering the situation of the invalid as comfortable as possible.

" In the Manufacturing Towns—the early death of parents leaves the children orphans and subject to every evil.

" In the Proposed Villages—the early death of parents leaves the children in all respects well provided for and protected.

" In the Manufacturing Towns—the children are usually sickly and, as well as their parents, ill-clothed.

" In the Proposed Villages—the children will be ruddy and healthy, and, as well as their parents, neat, clean and properly clothed.

" In the Manufacturing Towns—the young children are much neglected and hourly acquire bad habits.

" In the Proposed Villages—the children will be well looked after, prevented from acquiring bad, and taught good habits.

" In the Manufacturing Towns—the education of the children is neglected.

" In the Proposed Villages—the children are well trained and informed.

" In the Manufacturing Towns—the children are sent early in life to some one trade or manufacture, usually of a very unhealthy nature, and at which they must attend from ten to sixteen hours a day.

"In the Proposed Villages—the children will be gradually instructed in gardening, agriculture, and some trade or manufacture, and only employed according to age and strength.

"In the Manufacturing Towns—the children are trained under ignorant persons, possessing many bad habits.

"In the Proposed Villages—the children will be trained by intelligent persons, possessing only good habits.

"In the Manufacturing Towns—scolding, coercion and punishments, are the usual instruments of training.

"In the Proposed Villages—kindness and good sense will be the only instruments of training.

"To proceed with the contrast would be endless; the mind of the reader will easily supply the remainder; suffice it therefore to say

"That the Manufacturing Towns are the abode of poverty, vice, crime and misery

"While the Proposed Villages will ever be the abode of abundance, active intelligence, correct conduct and happiness."

Appendix III.

Model Rules for Co-operative Societies in 1832, from the Report of the Third Co-operative Congress, held in London, April 23rd to 30th, 1832.

" The Rev. Mr. Dunn brought up the report of the committee appointed to draw up the rules and regulations for co-operative societies. It was as follows:—

1. Let it be universally understood that the grand ultimate object of all co-operative societies whether engaged in trading, manufacturing or agricultural pursuits, is community on land.

2. To effect this important purpose, a weekly subscription, either in money, goods, or labour, from a penny to any other amount agreed upon, is indispensably necessary to be continued from year to year, until a capital sufficient to accomplish the object of the society be accumulated.

3. The next preliminary step to be pursued as auxiliary to the former, will be for the society to purchase at wholesale price, articles of ordinary consumption, of the most genuine description, in order to be retailed at the market prices for the purpose of further accumulation. The adoption of these instructions will, of course, be regulated by the circumstances and inclinations of particular societies.

4. We would observe that the immediate benefit derivable from these societies, in their successful approximation to community, are, the mutual employment of members, the establishment of schools for the education of children, and of libraries and reading rooms for adults.

5. In order to ensure without any possibility of failure the successful consummation of these desirable objects, it is the unanimous decision of the delegates here assembled, that the capital accumulated by such associations should be rendered indivisible, and any trading societies formed for the accumulation of profits, with the view to making a dividend thereof at some future period, cannot be recognised by this congress as identified with the co-operative world, nor admitted into that great social family which is now rapidly advancing to a state of independent and equalized community.

6. It is deemed more especially essential in all the trading transactions of co-operative societies that credit shall be neither taken nor given; as deviation from this important principle has been the sole cause of the destruction of so many previous societies, and thus banefully operated to retard the general progress of co-operation. In order to carry this important measure into successful operation, the congress recommend that in case of want of employment among the members, means should be taken by the society, if possible, to provide them some employment, as local circumstances may admit. In cases of sickness, should there be no other sources of relief, pecuniary assistance may be given from the funds belonging to the society, or from individual subscription amongst the members.

7. The congress is of opinion that it is extremely inimical to the principles of co-operation, and productive of the most serious consequences, to permit an individual who is already a member of one society to become a member of another.

This report was unanimously adopted."

Appendix IV.

Letter from William Cooper to Professor Fawcett, November, 1866.

Rochdale Equitable Pioneers Society Limited,
Toad Lane, Rochdale.
November, 1866.

Worthy Professor Fawcett,

I will attempt to give some account of the above Society and its results to the Working or wage-receiving Classes.

At the latter end of the year 1843 and the beginning of 1844 the Flannel Weavers and Spinners in Rochdale and the neighbourhood appealed to their employers for an advance of wages; to which some of them complied and paid the increased rate for several weeks with the understanding that if the other employers did not advance also, at the end of the time agreed upon they would reduce again to the prices previously paid. The Weavers and Spinners turned out against some of the Firms who would not raise the rate of wages and they that struck work were supported by those who remained at work paying 2s. each weekly to maintain the Turn-outs. The Weavers and Spinners failed to obtain a general advance of wages partly because of the refusal and resistance offered to the rise by some of the employers, and partly because the Weavers and Spinners turned out in greater numbers than those who remained at work were able to support.

A few (say 30 or 40) of the weavers kept in the Union and continued to pay the 2s. per week even after the object for which they had been on strike had not been obtained.

Their idea was to collect a sum of money wherewith to commence the Manufacture of Flannels and thereby become their own employers, and independent of the Masters. After a time they began to see that 2s. per week from a few persons would not in a reasonable time raise a sufficient amount to begin manufacturing even on a small scale. Hence some began to fall off in their payments and others proposed to divide the amount collected. It happened in Rochdale—as in most other Towns—that there were then Societies of Chartists, Teetotalers and Socialists and each of these pleaded that theirs was the best plan for bettering the position of the Working Classes.

Some Owenites, O'Connorites, and Teetotalers met in a room to discuss and talk over their several remedies for the evils of Society. The Weavers (late turn-outs) also went to these meetings. The Teetotalers went in for everybody becoming abstainers from all intoxicating drinks and said that if the working classes saved the money spent on drink they would become well off, almost independent. The Chartists would have the people to agitate until they got the six points of the Charter, when, they said, having universal suffrage and the Government in their own hands they could remove and remedy wasteful and class misgovernment.

The Socialists advocated Co-operation and union amongst the working classes. Their ideas were to establish communities of each for all and all for each where the property should be held in common for the equal benefit of all.

As the weavers were not likely to commence Manufacturing very soon; that all men could not be persuaded in a day to become Teetotalers; that the ruling classes would be a long while before they granted the Charter; that competitive Society could not be converted into communities of united interests in a reasonable time; this question arose, what can and shall be done, and somebody or several persons said let us become our own shopkeepers. The Socialists had amongst themselves, a Society named the " Rational Sick and Burial Society " whose rules the would-be society of Co-operators borrowed. From these and the Friendly Societies Acts, rules were drawn up for the Society which was then and is now named the Rochdale Equitable Pioneers Society.

The Owenites or Socialists had the greatest share in framing the Rules and regulations for the Society; the Weavers, Chartists, and Teetotalers meeting along with the framers to approve and adopt or reject the same.

Mr. Charles Howarth sketched most of the rules in one of which it was provided to divide profits after paying interest on Capital and allowing for depreciation of

Fixed Stock, amongst the members in proportion to their purchases of goods from the Store.

To begin business with the Society had about 30 members and say £30 in money, one half of which sum had to be expended in repairing an old warehouse which was taken for a Shop, and fitting the same up with counter, shelves, Scales, Weights etc. With the (say £15) floating capital the Store was supplied (I must not say stocked) with Flour, Meal, Butter, Sugar, Soap, Candles at wholesale prices, which were sold to members at retail rates. The goods bought in were paid for in ready money, and when sold cash had to be paid down before being removed from the counter.

It was well that the Society was limited in its funds as with the little or scarcely any experience in trade a mistake might have been made in purchasing goods. Indeed it was talked over amongst the members—even before the Store was opened for business—about purchasing a winter's stock of potatoes; which I am persuaded would have been a speculation resulting in a loss to the Society—a serious matter to a new Society in its first attempt at trading.

When the Society had been in business six or seven years it did buy a winter's stock of potatoes which began to sprout or grow again, and some of them had to be sold at a reduced—considerably below cost—price. However, the Society had got pretty well established at this time and was dealing in other articles upon which a profit was being realised, so that the Potato loss had little effect on the Dividend or the Society.

The following table cut from the Rochdale Equitable Pioneers' Society Almanac for 1866 shows the position of the Society from year to year:

Operations of the R.E.P. Society

Year	Members	Funds £	Business £	Profits £
1844	28	28		
1845	74	181	710	22
1846	80	252	1,146	80
1847	110	286	1,924	72
1848	140	397	2,276	117
1849	390	1,193	6,611	561
1850	600	2,299	13,179	880
1851	630	2,785	17,638	990
1852	680	3,471	16,352	1,206
1853	720	5,848	22,760	1,674
1854	900	7,172	33,364	1,763
1855	1,400	11,032	44,902	3,106
1856	1,600	12,920	63,197	3,921
1857	1,850	15,142	79,788	5,470
1858	1,850	18,160	71,680	6,284
1859	2,703	27,060	104,012	10,739
1860	3,450	37,710	152,063	15,906
1861	3,900	42,925	176,206	18,020
1862	3,501	38,465	141,074	17,564
1863	4,013	49,361	158,632	19,671
1864	4,747	62,105	174,937	22,717
1865	5,326	78,779	196,234	25,156
		Total	1,478,685	155,919

Thus it will be seen that from December 1844 when the Society opened for business to Decr. 1865 the sum of £1,478,685 had been received for goods sold; and if we add £118,222 cash from sales up to June 19th 1866 we have £1,596,906 as the aggregate of the Society's business from its establishment.

The Table shows amount of profits to be £155,919 for the 21 years; add to which £14,651 realised up to June 19th 1866 and we get an aggregate of £170,570 as gain from trade since the Society commenced operations. £170,570 saved or made by one Society must have been highly beneficial to its members.

I am persuaded that the wage receiving classes of Rochdale are much more temperate, provident, self-dependent or independent and yet more considerate and reasonable in their relations to their employers, or those above them in social position, than they would have been had no Co-operative Society existed in Rochdale.

Every purchaser at the Society pays ready money for the goods he or she buys, which makes the members more thoughtful as to how they are expending their money so as not to exceed—but live within or below—their incomes, than is the habit amongst working men and women who go on credit with the Shopkeepers.

Some of these latter live within their earnings and even save money but the bulk of those who are in debt with the Shopkeeper must feel themselves tied and to some extent at his mercy, as the Shopkeeper in self protection has to put on a wholesome check or stop or limit the supplies to his more unfortunate or improvident customers. If Industrial and Provident Societies did nothing more than raise the people from general indebtedness to that of frugal, thoughtful, ready money trading they would have achieved no little amount of good to the working classes in particular; and such improved habits amongst the masses cannot be otherwise than beneficial to other classes of the community. But these Societies also foster a spirit of saving as they are the Savings Banks for the members thereof.

Take the late cotton famine as an illustration of provident Co-operation. The members of the Rochdale Equitable Pioneers Society had all of them deposits of a greater or less amount in the Society when the famine set in. The poor people in Rochdale who were not members of the Society were thrown on the parishes or voluntary relief funds almost immediately the Cotton Mills stopped working. Some of the members of the Society who had but small investments in the Society (mostly newly admitted to membership) had to withdraw their small sums to live upon; and when this was done, were necessitated to ask relief. Not so with the great number of the members, as they passed through the famine, I will not say unhurt, but without seeking or needing the aid of anybody. The following slip cut from our Society's Almanack 1866 bears on this point:

" We do not need to go back to the time when it commenced, to shew the firm position it has attained; but the fact that we have not only maintained our existence but actually progressed in a remarkable degree in one of the most severe and longest panics on record, is one convincing proof of its soundness, and of its strength.

In December, 1861, when the panic had commenced, the Cash received for Goods was £176,206; in 1865 it was £196,234; shewing an increase of £20,028. Our capital in 1861 was £42,295; in 1865 it was £78,778. Number of Members, in 1861 was, 3,900; in 1865, 5,326 shewing an increase during the panic of 1,426 Members. In 1862 we built a New Shop at Bluepits, at a cost of about £700; in 1863 we built a Slaughterhouse and Stables, at a cost of £1,000; in the same year a New Shop was erected at Pinfold, which cost £1,050; in 1864 another was built at Spotland Bridge, which cost £1,150; in 1864- 65 another was erected in Oldham-road for School-lane Branch, at the cost of £1,700; and lastly, in 1865, Buersill Branch was finished at the cost of £1,000; and to crown all, we have just commenced the excavation for a New Central Store in Toad Lane, which we have every reason to believe will be an ornament to the town. Since December, 1865, the total Withdrawals have been £83,638 5. 0d.; in the same time £1,841 3. 10d. has been appropriated for Educational purposes; and, notwithstanding the great distress in the past four years, £749 10. 4d. has been given away for charitable purposes.

From these figures some idea may be drawn as to what the society has been doing during the cotton famine. It will be seen that the society has not absolutely and entirely aimed at getting dividend and profit, but likewise the education and improvement of its Members, for if there is one feature more than another to which we can look with satisfaction and pleasure, it is the ample provision that is made for the diffusion of every class of knowledge and useful information on all the Sciences, Art and Literature of our time. We also entertain the hope that the day is not far distant when Schools will be established in connection with the society, to educate the rising generation of Co-operators.

Appendix V.

Extracts from the Laws and Objects of the Rochdale Society of Equitable Pioneers. 1844.

1. The objects and plans of this society are to form arrangements for the pecuniary benefit, and the improvement of the social and domestic condition of its members, by raising a sufficient amount of capital in shares of one pound each, to bring into operation the following plans and arrangements.

The establishment of a store for the sale of provisions and clothing, etc.

The building, purchasing or erecting a number of houses, in which those members desiring to assist each other in their domestic and social condition may reside.

To commence the manufacture of such articles as the society may determine upon, for the employment of such members as may be without employment, or who may be suffering in consequence of repeated reductions in their wages.

As a further benefit and security to the members of this society, the society shall purchase or rent an estate or estates of land, which shall be cultivated by the members who may be out of employment, or whose labour may be badly remunerated.

That as soon as practicable, this society shall proceed to arrange the powers of production, distribution, education and government, or in other words to establish a self supporting home colony of united interests, or assist other societies in establishing such colonies.

That for the promotion of sobriety, a Temperance Hotel be opened in one of the society's houses as soon as convenient.

2. That the government of the society shall be vested in a President, Treasurer and Secretary, three trustees and five directors, the President, Secretary, Treasurer and Trustees to be elected at the general meeting held in January, the directors to be elected at the July general meeting, any of them being eligible for re-election . . .

3. That two auditors be appointed . . . They shall audit the accounts of the society, see that they are correctly kept and balanced quarterly, and report the same to each quarterly meeting or be fined.

4. That the officers and board of directors shall meet every Thursday evening, at eight o'clock, in the Committee Room, Weavers' Arms, Yorkshire Street, Rochdale, for the transaction of the society's business, . . .

5. That general meetings of the members shall be holden on the first Monday in the months of January, April, July and October, at eight o'clock p.m., at which meetings the officers of this society shall make their quarterly financial report, in which report shall be specified the amount of funds, and value of stock possessed by the society.

6. That an annual general meeting be holden on the " First Market Tuesday " on which occasion a dinner shall be provided at a charge of one shilling each person, and one week's notice.

(*Rules 7, 8, 9, deal with the duties of President, Secretary and Treasurer, 10, 11 with those of Trustees*).

13. Any person desirous of becoming a member of this society shall be proposed and seconded by two members at a meeting of the officers and directors, and if approved by a majority of those present shall be eligible for election at the next weekly meeting. Each candidate shall pay the sum of one shilling as entrance money on being admitted to membership; shares may be paid by instalments of threepence per week on each share.

Any member neglecting to pay such instalments for three months shall, except in cases of sickness or want of employment, be fined in the sum of sixpence.

Any member neglecting to pay such instalment for six months shall be expelled, his or her share or shares be sold, and the remainder after paying all necessary expenses, returned to such expelled member. No member to have more than fifty shares.

14. That should the officers and members of this society find the conduct of any of its members to be injurious to the interests of the society, the president is hereby called upon to remonstrate with such member, and should any member after such remonstrance still pursue the same offensive line of conduct, such member shall

receive one month's notice of exclusion from this society, at the expiration of which time the offending member shall be expelled without further notice.

15. That should any member wish to withdraw from this society such member shall give one month's notice of such intention to the officers at the expiration of which time the member shall be at liberty to withdraw from the society, such liberty to continue in force until the next meeting of the board, but no longer.

16. That in all cases of exclusion or withdrawal from this society, previous to receiving the balance remaining (after paying all necessary expenses) for shares sold, the excluded or withdrawing party shall sign his or her name in a book kept by the society for that purpose, after which he or she shall have no further claim upon this society, nor shall this society have any further claim upon him or her.

17. (provided that a member withdrawing could retain possession of his shares " until they can be disposed of advantageously " for a period of twelve months, during which time no interest would be paid on them. It may be noted that shares were not withdrawable from the society).

18. That this society shall not be responsible for the debts of any of its members except to the amount of the share or shares held by a member. . . .

19. That in the case of a dispute between this society and any of its members, or members or persons claiming on account of a member finding himself aggrieved, or having any complaint against any member or officer, may apply to the officers or directors for redress, but should the party not receive satisfaction, appeal may be made to a general meeting of the members of the society, whose decision shall be final and binding, except reference be made to arbitration.

20. (dealt with appointment and duties of arbitrators).

21. That no person shall be allowed to purchase anything on behalf of this society, except those who are regularly appointed by the officers or members, and the officers of this society shall not in any case, nor on any pretence, purchase any articles except for ready money, neither shall they be allowed to sell any article or articles except for ready money. Any officer acting contrary to this law shall be fined in the sum of ten shillings, and be disqualified from performing the duties of such office.

22. That at each quarterly general meeting the officers in their financial statement shall publish the amount of profits realised by the society during the preceding quarter, which shall be divided thus: Interest at the rate of $3\frac{1}{2}$ per cent per annum shall be paid upon all shares paid up previous to the quarter's commencement; the remaining profits shall be paid to each member in proportion to the amount of money expended at the store.

23. (dealt with disposal of shares on death of a member).

24. That this society shall not be dissolved so long as the intents and purposes thereof, or any of them, remain to be carried into effect, without obtaining the votes of five-sixths of the then existing members of this society.

Management of the Store

25. That the store be opened to the public on the evenings of Mondays and Saturdays; on Monday from seven till nine; on Saturdays from six till eleven.

26. That all purchases be paid on delivery.

27. That a cashier and salesman be appointed to conduct the business of the store, each to serve six months alternately and be eligible for re-election.

28. The salesman shall weigh, measure and sell such articles and commodities as are to be disposed of at the store, but shall not receive payment for any goods sold.

29. The cashier shall receive payment for all goods purchased at the store: he shall give a receipt to each purchaser for the amount received, and keep a check of such receipt in a book provided for that purpose, he shall pay over to the secretary at the weekly meetings of the board, as a check on the cashier.

30. That purchasers be furnished with printed forms containing the names of such articles as are on sale at the store, these forms to be filled up by the purchaser and handed to the salesman when goods are required; the salesman shall hand in all such orders to the secretary at the weekly meetings of the board as a check on the cashier.

31. That the amount of money expended by each member during each quarter to be determined by the check receipts produced by each member.

32. That the cashier or salesman be fined one shilling for non-attendance at the proper time, unless 48 hours' notice be given to the president and secretary of inability to perform the duties of his or her office.

33. That the president and secretary be empowered to appoint a member to perform the duty of any officer not attending to his duty but that the board have power to alter such appointment should it be thought expedient to do so.

34. That the store be opened at the proper time by the president.

Miles Ashworth, President.
John Holt, Treasurer.
Charles Howarth.
James Standring.
James Daly, Secretary.

Supplement of Amended Laws of the First Department of the Rochdale Society of Equitable Pioneers, Held in Toad Lane, in the Parish of Rochdale, in the County of Lancaster.

Addition for the first law

That for the establishment of the store department a capital of one thousand pounds be raised in shares of one pound each, by not more than two hundred and fifty members. Each person on his or her admission to membership shall take out four shares in the capital, but should one thousand pounds be found not sufficient to carry out the business . . . it shall be lawful to augment the shares from four to five . . . (*remainder of a long rule is intended to bring about equality of share holdings*).

A new law to be placed or read between the 4th and 5th laws

That general meetings of the members be holden on the first and third Monday evenings in each month, the business to commence at eight o'clock, the four general quarterly meetings to be included. The business of these meetings to consist in the explanation of the principles, objects and laws of the society, to discuss the affairs and suggest any improvement for the consideration of the officers and board of directors. . . Members present at all general, quarterly and annual meetings to have each, one vote, and no more, in the decision of all questions. . .

Amendment of the 6th law

That on the general meeting held on the first Monday in October, it shall be decided whether a dinner or tea or either be provided, on the following " First Market Tuesday," to celebrate the anniversary and that if it be decided by a majority then present that one be provided, the whole of the members shall pay for the same whether they attend or not. . . No part of the expenses to come out of the funds.

Eleventh law

The eleventh law was repealed, and one substituted to deal with liabilities of officers.

Amendment of the 13th law

Any person desirous of becoming a member of this society, shall be proposed and seconded by two members at a general meeting of the members, and if approved of at the next general meeting by a majority then present shall be admitted to membership. . . Each person on the night of his admission, shall appear personally in the meeting room and state his willingness to take out four shares of one pound each, and to pay a deposit of not less than one shilling or threepence per share, and to pay not less than threepence per week after, and to allow all interests and profits that may be due to him to remain in the funds until he have four shares in the capital. . .

Amendment of the 22nd law

That the rate of interest be five pounds per cent per annum, instead of three and a half.

Amendment of the 24th law

This society shall not be dissolved so long as the intents and purposes or any of them remain to be carried into effect, without obtaining the votes of five-sixths *in value* of the then existing members of this society, and the consent of all members who may be under any responsibility on account of the society.

Laws repealed

That the 26th, 27th, 28th, 29th, 30th, 31st, 32nd, 33rd and 34th laws be repealed, and the management of the store left in the hands of the officers and board of directors.

That the sale of all shares of persons leaving the society be by ticket.

> Benjamin Rudman.
> Charles Howarth.
> James Tweedale.
> James Daly, Secretary.
> Certified August 7th, 1845.

Appendix VI.

Some extracts from minutes of the Rochdale Equitable Society of Pioneers in its early years.

First General Meeting, Sunday, August 11th, 1844

Resolved—1st   That the following persons be appointed to conduct the business of the Society now established

> Mr. Miles Ashworth, President
> Mr. John Holt, Treasurer
> Mr. James Daly, Secretary.

Resolved   That James Tweedale
> James Smithies
> James Holt
> James Bamford
> William Taylor

be appointed Directors.

Resolved   That Charles Howarth
> George Ashworth
> William Mallalieu

be appointed Trustees.

Resolved   That John Bent and Joseph Smith be appointed auditors.

Resolved   That James Wilkinson, Shoe Maker, High Street,
> Charles Barnish, Weaver, Spotland,
> George Healey, Hatter, Sudden Brow,
> John Garside, Cabinet Maker, High Street,
> John Lord, Weaver, Cronkey Shaw,

be arbitrators.

Meeting Held in the Social Institute on Thursday, August 15th, 1844

Resolved—1st   That the following Books be purchased, viz., a Minute Book, Register Book for the use of the Society.

> 2nd   That the Society date its establishment August 15th 1844.

> 3rd   That the law book relating to the Friendly Societies be purchased for the use of the society.

Meeting, August 29th, 1844

Resolved   That all fines go to the General Fund of the Society.

> That for the purpose of raising capital more rapidly, no interest upon any Share or Shares or profit arising from trade with the Store of the Society shall be drawn for the first twelve months after the Society commence active operations but shall be added to each man's Stock to form additional shares.

Board Meeting, November 21st, 1844

Resolved   That James Tweedale and George Ashworth wait on Mr. Dunlop and take the Warehouse if it can be taken for £12. 0. 0. and repaired by the Landlord.

Board Meeting, November 25th, 1844

Resolved   That Mr. Dunlop's Warehouse be taken on the following terms, viz., that the Society do the necessary repairs and pay £10. 0. 0. per year rent for a term of 3 years.

Board Meeting, November 28th, 1844

Resolved—1st   That James Tweedale, Miles Ashworth, James Daly be appointed to super ... the cause to repair the premises in Toad Lane.

> 2nd   That George Ashworth, Thomas Holt be appointed to purchase the necessary furniture for commencing business.

> 3rd   That George Ashworth purchase three forms for five shillings.

Board Meeting, December 12th, 1844

Resolved—3rd   That David Brooks and John Holt be the purchasers of stock for the society.
4th   That purchases consist in the following articles, Flour, Butter, Sugar and Oat Meal.

Board Meeting, Monday, December 16th, 1844

Resolved   That William Cooper be appointed cashier and Samuel Ashworth salesman and that each receive 3d. per hour for their labour.

Board Meeting, January 23rd, 1845

Resolved   That the Store Superintendent provide aprons and sleeves for the Salesmen.

Board Meeting, February 27th, 1845

Resolved—1st   That the Store be opened at the following times for the sale of goods
On Monday 4 to 9 o'clock
Wednesday 7 to 9, one servant
Thursday 8 to 10 one servant
Friday 7 to 9 one servant
Saturday 1 to 11 one servant until six

when another shall assist till 11 o'clock.

Quarterly Meeting, October 6th, 1845

Resolved   That to celebrate the Anniversary of the Society a tea party be held on First Market Tuesday at 5 o'clock in the afternoon, the price of admission to be for Gents 9d. each, Ladies 7d. each, all members will be compelled to pay for their tea whether they attend or not according to the amendment to 6th rule.

Quarterly Meeting, October 5th, 1846

Resolved   That we make Jas. Daly an offer of ten shillings per quarter as Secretary for keeping the Account of the Society.

Board Meeting, May 20th, 1847

Resolved   That Charles Shaw receive ten shillings per week until his capital be reduced to one pound, except he gets work before it is reduced so low.
That Benjamin Rudman made application for £10. 0. 0. and he having purchased many shares the board agreed to offer him £9. 14. 0. for the £10. 0. 0., he having purchased many at 18/6 per share.

General Meeting, February 4th, 1850

Resolved   2nd   That every Member shall have full liberty to speak his sentiments on all subjects when brought before the meetings at a proper time and in a proper manner and all subjects shall be legitimate when properly proposed.

Quarterly Meeting, July 1st, 1850

Resolved   That we invest some portion of our funds in the establishment of Corn Mill.
That we invest five shillings per member for every member as fixed stock in this Society in the Corn Mill Society.

Board Meeting, September 26th, 1850

Resolved   That letters be written to all Co-operative Stores informing them that a meeting will take place. Delegates to consider the best means of purchasing our goods together.

Board Meeting, November 28th, 1850

That the shop be opened for Wholesale on Mondays at 1 o'clock and Wm. Cooper and John Healey attend on the Wholesale customers.

Quarterly Meeting, April 2nd, 1855

Resolved—1st   That there be a permanent secretary on the premises.

2nd   That the Secretary's wage be 21/– per week and raised 1/– per quarter till it reach 25/– if he should be thought worth it.

3rd   That it be decided to-night who shall be secretary.   That William Cooper be the Secretary.

6th   That John K. Clegg be the nominal secretary.

Board Meeting, April 22nd, 1858

1st   That the servants of the Society have a Tea given them next Tuesday evening at 6 o'clock.

2nd   That the Board pay sixpence each for their tickets.

December 26th, 1862

That Dr. Molesworth, the Vicar of Rochdale, be appointed to act as arbitrator in place of the late John Garside.

Declined, and accepted by his son, Wm. N. Molesworth, Incumbent of Spotland.

Appendix VII.

The paper prepared by Abraham Greenwood on the establishment of a Wholesale Society. From *Co-operation*, Hall and Watkins.

Before proceeding to develop a scheme of a wholesale agency, permit me in the first place to glance at past efforts to accomplish the object we are this day met to discuss, viz., the desirability of aggregating the purchasing power of the co-operative stores, especially in Lancashire, Yorkshire, and adjoining counties.

The first attempt in this direction was made by the Christian Socialists, conspicuous amongst whom were Edward Vansittart Neale, Esq., Rev. F. D. Maurice, Rev. Charles Kingsley, J. M. Ludlow, Thomas Hughes, F. J. Furnivall, Joseph Woodin, and Lloyd Jones, Esquires. I am thus circumstantial in mentioning the names of these gentlemen, that their services in the early stages of the Co-operative Movement may be acknowledged; they not only wished well to, but, aided nobly by their well-known talents, and no less by their pecuniary assistance to, the cause of true co-operation. They instituted the " Central Co-operative Agency " for the purpose of counteracting the system of adulteration and fraud prevailing in trade, and for supplying to co-operative stores a quality of goods that could be relied upon and in the highest state of purity. The agency did not prove a success, but had to be given up, entailing a great loss to its promoters. There is still a remnant of the agency left, known by the firm of " Woodin and Co., Sherborne Lane, London."

The second effort was made by the " Equitable Pioneers' Society " in 1852, by initiating a " Wholesale Department." This department was originated for supplying goods to its members in large quantities, and also with a view to supplying the co-operative stores of Lancashire and Yorkshire, whose small capital did not enable them to purchase in the best market, nor command the services of what is indispensable to any store, a good buyer, who knew the markets, what, how, and where to buy. The Pioneers' Society invited other stores to co-operate in carrying out practically the idea of a wholesale establishment, offering at the same time to find the necessary amount of capital for carrying on the wholesale business, for which the Pioneers' Society would charge this department at the rate of 5 per cent per annum. A few stores did join, but they never gave that hearty support necessary to make the scheme thoroughly successful. Notwithstanding this counteracting influence, the " Wholesale Department " from the beginning paid interest not only on capital, but dividends to the members trading in this department. Had all concerned in this affair displayed shrewdness and persistence, the practicability of acting in concert in a matter of this kind would ere this have been demonstrated, and placed in the category of co-operative " facts."

However, after a time, the demon of all working-class movements hitherto—jealousy—crept in here. The stores dealing in the wholesale department of the Pioneers' Society thought that it had some advantage over them; while, on the other side, a large number of the members of the Pioneers' Society imagined they were giving privileges to the other stores, which a due regard to their immediate interests did not warrant them in bestowing. My opinion is that, had there been no other causes of failure than those mentioned, the " Central Co-operative Agency" and the " Equitable Pioneers' Wholesale Department " must inevitably have failed, from their efforts being too soon in the order of co-operative development.

Failures have their lessons, and, if read aright, lead on to success. The world seldom or never calculates how much it is indebted to failure for ultimate success. " Failures are with heroic minds the stepping-stones to success." At school our children are taught the lesson, and it is one we should learn in the co-operative school, that:—

> Once or twice, though we should fail,
>   Try again!
> If we would at last prevail,
>   Try again!
> If we strive 'tis no disgrace
> Though we do not win the race,
> What should we do in that case?
>   Try again!

An eminent philosophical writer has very appositely said with regard to failures: " It is far from being true, in the progress of knowledge, that after every failure we must recommence from the beginning. Every failure is a step to success, every detection of what is false directs us to what is true, every trial exhausts some tempting form of error. Not only so, but scarcely any attempt is entirely a failure; scarcely any theory, the result of steady thought, is altogether false; no tempting form of error is without some latent charm derived from truth." How often we hear men who never attempted anything for the good of their fellow-men taunt those who have with the failure of their efforts for the elevation of humanity. If failure does not command our admiration, it is very often entitled to our respect.

I have said that the " Central Co-operative Agency " and the " Pioneers' Whole-sale Department " failed from being too soon in the order of co-operative develop-ment. Let us see if the progress of Co-operation now offers ample room for success.

There were in England, when the " Central Co-operative Agency " was established, not more than 10 stores, and not more than 17 when the Rochdale Store established its " Wholesale Department." What a contrast—indicative of co-operative progress —these times present with those of 10 or 12 years ago! Now there are some hundreds of co-operative stores in the United Kingdom. In the June number of the *Co-operator* of last year there are enumerated upwards of 250 stores. There are in Lancashire, Yorkshire, and Cheshire alone 120 stores, numbering in the aggregate 40,000 members. 26 stores in the counties named did business to the amount of £800,000 in 1861. If we take the average weekly expenditure of the 40,000 members at 10s. each (this will be under the average) it will give an expenditure of £20,000 weekly, or an annual expenditure of £1,040,000.

No doubt from the statistics here given that the field for aggregative efforts has considerably expanded since the failures mentioned in the former part of this paper.

We have succeeded, too, in carrying through Parliament a measure affording facilities for, and sweeping away many legal impediments to, co-operative progress, enabling that to be done by direct sanction of law which had to be done previously by roundabout methods.

I will here place before the conference a calculation of the quantities of com-modities of the kind named in the tables required to supply the 40,000 members of the co-operative stores in these Northern districts. The calculations are made on the data of goods actually sold in one quarter at the Rochdale Pioneers' Society. There are 3,500 members belonging to the Rochdale Store, and, as the average consumption of groceries, &c., is higher per member than at most stores, I may reasonably take it for granted that the demand at the Pioneers' Store will equal one-tenth of the demand of the 40,000 members.

One Quarter's Consumption of Groceries, &c., at the Rochdale Equitable Pioneers' Store*		One Quarter's Consumption of 40,000 Members *pro rata*
Coffee	9,000 lb.	90,000 lb.
Tea	7,736 lb.	77,360 lb.
Tobacco	5,363 lb.	53,630 lb.
Snuff	141 lb.	1,410 lb.
Pepper	316 lb.	3,160 lb.
Sugar	1,819 cwt.	18,190 cwt.
Syrup and Treacle	520 cwt.	5,200 cwt.
Currants	140 cwt.	1,400 cwt.
Butter	932 cwt.	9,320 cwt.
Soap	440 cwt.	4,400 cwt.

* This and the following table pretend not to be strictly correct to fractions but sufficiently so for the purposes of this paper.

Now let us calculate, on the basis of the table given, what would be the weekly consumption of those articles named by the 40,000 members; also the weekly and yearly money value of the same.

Kind of Articles	One Week's Consumption	Weekly Money Value	Yearly Money Value
		£	£
Coffee	6,923 lb.	266	13,832
Tea	5,951 lb.	991	51,532
Tobacco	4,125 lb.	825	42,900
Snuff..............................	108 lb.	22	1,144
Pepper	243 cwt.	15	780
Sugar..............................	1,400 cwt.	3,500	182,000
Syrup, &c.	400 cwt.	350	18,200
Currants	107 cwt.	160	8,320
Butter	717 cwt.	3,440	178,880
Soap	338 cwt.	524	27,248
*Totals.....................	......	10,093	524,836

* I have taken the prices paid by the Rochdale store, and adjusted them to something like an average.

There are mentioned in the tables several articles, any one of which would in itself be sufficient to make an agency profitable. The agency might at the beginning supply those articles only which there was a sure profit upon. It will be seen from the statistics given that the present state of our Movement will permit, and in fact warrants, a further step being taken in co-operative progress. The problem for solution is to hit upon a plan which shall suit the present spirit and intelligence of the great body of co-operators.

Gentlemen, I submit to your criticism a plan which, I think will meet the requirements of our purpose.

PLAN.

The plan I propose is this: That an office be taken either at Liverpool or Manchester, as may be thought best suitable for the purpose. All stores joining the agency will be requested to act promptly in giving orders, and making remittances for goods to be bought on their account. Orders sent to the agency will be aggregated; the purchaser will then go to the markets, and there buy the quantity and quality of those articles required to supply the demand upon the agency. The purchaser, having bought, will give either printed or written directions to the houses from which the purchases are made to draft such number of tierces of sugar, puncheons of treacle, boxes of soap, boxes of candles, barrels of currants, and firkins of butter, &c., to the different stores on whose account they have been bought. On the plan of an agency there will be very little, if any, warehouse room required, and that little will be necessitated by very small stores not being able to purchase in bulk. Otherwise an office would amply suffice for the purposes of the agency. By far the greater portion of the goods bought will at once be sent on to the stores ordering them, and, where there is plenty of room for warehousing, any quantity of goods they need should be kept in stock.

Each store will be left to determine for itself when and to what amount of commodities it is proper to purchase at any time. Many stores have already acquired the knowledge of " when to buy," and those stores that have not so learned, it will be one of the duties of the agency to keep them well advised upon that matter. If a store thought proper to speculate in any article supplied through the agency, it will do so at its own risk. Whereas if the wholesale affair be made a trading concern it will necessitate ultimately the centralisation of some £50,000 sterling, with all the liabilities and contingencies of a trading establishment. On the other hand, an agency will secure all the advantages expected to accrue from the "Wholesale Depot" without any of its risks.

I wish to advert to an instance where, to some extent, the plan here propounded is carried out. There is the Rochdale Pioneers' Society, with its nine grocery branches, all supplied and managed from the central store in Toad Lane. The transactions of the Rochdale Store with its branches are done in this way: The head shopman at each branch store makes out a list of requirements for his branch on a form provided for the purpose, and sends it to the central place of business; then the manager gives directions to the railway or canal companies where the goods are lying to send such and such quantities of articles specified to such and such branch store named on the delivery order.

Now the central store stands in the same relation to its branches as an agency would to the store joining it. It will be almost as easy to manage an agency as it is to carry on the concern named. The mode will be very similar, but the time in getting goods through the agency will be a trifle longer, and the transactions very much larger (but only requiring the same amount of labour to work the agency as it does to work the Rochdale Store with its branches).

We have another case in point, in the Rochdale Corn Mill Society, of the beneficial working of a wholesale establishment. There are 60 co-operative stores who belong to the corn mill, from which they take wholly or in part the flour required for supplying their members. This co-operative arrangement permits the business of corn grinding to be much more economically and profitably done than any single store could of itself accomplish. The absurdity would be no greater did each of the 60 stores on its individual account purchase grain to manufacture into flour, as it is for each store to buy groceries singly. In the case of the corn mill we have exemplified the strength and benefit of concerted operations; in the case of the stores acting singly we have weakness. Isolation is the opposite of real co-operation, which is the combining, consulting, and so acting together of good and true men as to bring about those ameliorative conditions which shall lead to self-elevation by promoting the welfare of humanity, and a state "in which the good of the whole is tantamount to the highest kind of good for each."

It is indispensable to the well-working of any scheme, especially a co-operative one, that those who wish to be concerned should thoroughly understand the conditions upon which it is based, and their obligations relative thereto. A proper comprehension of the conditions and obligations at the commencement of this wholesale affair will obviate, in great degree, bickerings, ill-will, and regrets which often arise from want of a clear perception of the stipulations on which an undertaking is founded. People who conceive of an object different from what it really is, imagine themselves deceived, when the deception is not in the thing itself, but in their having conceived of the thing erroneously.

I respectfully submit to the conference a few stipulations on which an agency should be based.

COLLIGATING CONDITIONS.

1. That the good policy of dealing with and for ready money be strictly adhered to in all transactions of the agency.

I need not dwell on the necessity of this. It is one of the fundamental conditions of our success hitherto. One of the leading objects of Co-operation is to redeem the working classes from that state of indebtedness which has too long held them in a condition of slavishness.

2. That none but co-operative stores should be allowed to join the agency.

I do not like for my part that Co-operation be made a means of supporting the old system of shopkeeping. The sooner we can get the labouring classes out of their ancient mode of credit trading, the better for themselves in many ways. I have known shopkeepers take, and, in fact, are now taking, advantage of our co-operative arrangements for enabling them to maintain their position longer than they would otherwise be able to do against a better system. All co-operative efforts should tend exclusively for the promotion of genuine Co-operation. In saying this much allow me to disclaim any bad feeling towards the shopkeeping class. They have done the State some service, and my wish is that they may see the wisdom and propriety of transferring their small capitals to other investments, such as manufacturing companies, where they will command good interest, before their occupation is gone.

3. That each store joining the agency should pledge itself to deal exclusively with the agency in those articles which it supplies.

An agency cannot be carried on with thorough success if stores are allowed to go to and from the agency when they think proper. That would be a liberty incompatible with and jeopardise the existence of the agency. Kant has laid down a rule with regard to personal conduct which applies no less to societies of men: "So act that the rule on which thou actest would admit of being adopted by all rational beings." All who join the agency must be prepared, if need be, to make some sacrifice; and not, because the thing does not succeed at once, to back out of it. The Rochdale Pioneers' Society and the Brickfield Store, near Rochdale, at the commencement of the Corn Mill Society, passed resolutions to purchase flour from no other place, or otherwise the corn mill would have gone down. In those two instances the obligation of dealing with a concern (their own) that it might be a success, I am glad to say, was perfectly understood.

4. That a small percentage be charged to each store as commission on the amount of business done through the agency.

Stores should be supplied through the agency at the cost price of an article, plus the small commission to cover the expenses of the agency. The purpose in this is to keep the transactions of the agency as simple as it will permit. It strikes me very forcibly that making profits in connection with a wholesale affair is a superfluous piece of work. It would be absurd to put profits on goods bought merely to divide them by way of dividend.

It will be wholesome to leave as much local action to the stores as possible, and to have as little as possible of centralisation. Hence I would not presume in this respect to put stores in a state of pupilage by doing that for them which they are capable of doing for themselves, viz., to make members of co-operative societies, almost in spite of themselves, accumulate capital. This is a function which properly belongs to each individual store, and not to a wholesale concern.

5. The necessary amount of capital for carrying on the agency shall be raised *pro rata* on the number of members belonging to the stores joining the agency.

The amount of capital per member will be determined, in a measure, by the number of co-operative stores that may join the agency. Say that in good times there will be fully 40,000 members of co-operative stores in the counties previously named, at 2s. 6d. each member, these will give a total capital of £5,000. This sum will be ample for carrying on an agency.

6. That the stores pay their own carriage.

Each store now pays the carriage of goods from the places where they are purchased, and the stores should bear a like relation to the agency as they do to the markets where they now purchase, thus keeping the business of the agency free from transit charges.

What are the benefits we may legitimately expect from a wholesale agency?

1. Stores will be enabled through the agency to purchase more economically than heretofore by reaching the best markets.
2. Small stores and new stores are at once put in a good position by being placed directly (through the agency) in the best markets, thus enabling them to sell as cheap as any first-class shopkeeper.
3. As all stores will have the benefit of the best markets by means of the agency, it follows that dividends paid by the stores must be more equal than heretofore, and by the same means dividends will be considerably augmented.
4. Stores, especially large ones, will be able to carry on their business with less capital. Large stores will not, as now, be necessitated, in order to reach the minimum prices of the markets, to purchase goods they do not require for the immediate supply of their members.
5. Stores will be able to command the services of a good buyer, and will thus save a large amount of labour and expense by one purchaser buying for perhaps some 150 stores, while the great amount of blundering in purchasing at the commencement of a co-operative store will be obviated.

Appendix VIII.

Periodical Publications Bearing on Co-operation. Editors in brackets.

1821–1822	The Economist (George Mudie)
1823	The Political Economist and Universal Philanthropist
1825–1828	New Harmony Gazette (circulated U.S.A., R. D. Owen, Frances Wright, Wm. Owen, R. L. Jennings)
1825–1827	Register for the First Society of Adherents to Divine Revelation at Orbiston (Abram Combe)
1826–1827	Advocate of the Working Classes
1826–1830	Co-operative Magazine
1828–1830	The Co-operator (Dr. Wm. King)
1829–1830	The Associate and Co-operative Mirror
1829	The Union Exchange Gazette
1829–1830	The Birmingham Co-operative Herald (Wm. Pare)
1830	The Belfast Co-operative Advocate
1830	The Chester Co-operator
1830	Co-operative Miscellany
1830	The British Co-operator
1830	United Co-operative Trades Journal
1830–1835	The Poor Man's Guardian (Bronterre O'Brien)
1831–1832	The Lancashire Co-operator, later the Lancashire and Yorkshire Co-operator (T. Hurst)
1831–1832	Voice of the People (John Doherty)
1831–1832	The Pioneer (James Morrison)
1832–1834	The Crisis (R. Owen, E. Smith)
1832	Union Pilot and Co-operative Intelligencer
1832	Poor Man's Advocate (John Doherty)
1832	The Rational Reformer
1832–1834	The Tradesman, Trades Advocate, Liberator (Alex Campbell, circulating around Glasgow)
1833	Birmingham Labour Exchange Gazette (Wm. Pare)
1833	Gazette of Labour Exchanges
1834	Gazette of Exchange Bazaars
1834	Herald of the Rights of Industry
1834–1845	The New Moral World (R. Owen, G. A. Fleming)
1834–1838	The Shepherd (J. E. Smith)
1837–1838	Star in the East (James Hill)
1837–1852	The Northern Star (Feargus O'Connor)
1839	The Social Pioneer
1839	The Herald of the Future
1839–1840	The Working Bee
1840	Morning Star (Hugh Doherty)
1841–1842	Educational Circular and Communist Apostle (Henry Fry)
1841–1843	The London Phalanx (Hugh Doherty)
1841–1843	The Oracle of Reason
1842	The Union, a Monthly Record (G. A. Fleming)
1843–1844	New Age and Concordium Gazette
1843–1845	The Movement (G. J. Holyoake, M. Q. Ryall)
1844	Social Pioneer
1844–1845	The Communitist (in the U.S.A.)
1844–1849	Owen's Book of the New Moral World
1845	The Sunbeam
1845	The Moral World
1845	The Commonwealth, succeeded The Moral World (James Hill)
1845–1846	The Herald of Progress (John Cramp)
1846–1872	The Reasoner (G. J. Holyoake)
1847–1848	Herald of Redemption, later Herald of Co-operation (James Hole)
1848–1849	The Spirit of the Age (G. J. Holyoake)

1848	Apostle and Chronicle of the Communist Church (Goodwin Barnaby)
1848	Politics for the People (F. D. Maurice, J. M. Ludlow, etc.)
1850	Trades Advocate and Herald of Progress (Dr. John Watts)
1850–1853	The Leader
1850–1852	The Christian Socialist, later The Journal of Association (F. D. Maurice, J. M. Ludlow, etc.)
1850	People's Review
1850	Weekly Letters to the Human Race (R. Owen)
1850–1853	Robert Owen's Journal
1851–1852	The Operative (Wm. Newton)
1853	National Quarterly Review and Journal (R. Owen)
1855	English Republic (W. J. Linton)
1856–1858	Millenial Gazette (R. Owen)
1860–1871	The Co-operator (Henry Pitman)
1861–1877	The Beehive (G. Potter)
1862–1864	Secular World and Social Economist (G. J. Holyoake)
1863–1871	The Scottish Co-operator (merged into the Co-operative News. G. T. M'Innes)
1866	The Working Man (G. J. Holyoake)
1867–1868	Industrial Partnerships Record (G. J. Holyoake and E. O. Greening)
1868-1869	The Social Economist (G. J. Holyoake, E. O. Greening)
1871–	The Co-operative News (Bailey Walker, S. Bamford, W. M. Bamford, J. A. Flanagan, W. R. Richardson, F. Tootill, D. Boydell, F. Bruckshaw)
1875	Agricultural Economist (E. O. Greening)
1876–1884	Secular Review (G. J. Holyoake)
1883–1886	The Present Day (G. J. Holyoake)
1887	Brotherhood (G. B. Wallace)
1893	The Scottish Co-operator (Dr. H. Dyer, W. Reid, P. J. Haughney, R. Murray, A. W. Oakes)
1894	Labour Co-partnership
1895–1923	The Irish Homestead (G. W. Russell)
1896–1964	The Wheatsheaf, later the Home Magazine
1905–1953	Millgate Monthly (W. M. Bamford, C. E. Tomlinson)
1907–1960	Our Circle
1907–1915	Co-operation in Agriculture
1908–1920	The Co-operative Employee, continuing after 1920 as The New Dawn
1913–1914	The College Herald (F. Hall), later incorporated in The Co-operative Educator, 1917–1939
1916–1966	The Producer. (Discontinued for a period during the Second World War)
1919–1967	Woman's Outlook
1919–	The Co-operative Official (F. Hall, T. W. Mercer, N. H. Gregory, A. L. Sugar, I. Bennett)
1914–1920	The Co-operative Union Quarterly Review
1921–1923	The Co-operative Monthly (T. W. Mercer)
1926–	The Co-operative Review (T. W. Mercer, Edward Topham, K. Hulse)
1925–1960	Co-operative Productive Review
1968–	Co-operative Management and Marketing (F. Bruckshaw)

At the present time there are the following publications:—

Title	Publisher	Remarks
Co-operative News	Co-operative Press	General co-operative news and opinion (W).
Scottish Co-operator	Co-operative Press	Scottish co-operative news and opinion (W).
Co-operative Management and Marketing	Co-operative Press	Topics of special interest for committee members and officials (M).

Title	Publisher	Remarks
Co-operative Gazette	Co-operative Union	Information on legislation, regulations, etc.
Co-operative Review	Co-operative Union	The official organ of the Co-operative Union (M).

(Published as monthly supplement to Co-operative News and Scottish Co-operator.)

Title	Publisher	Remarks
Co-operative Congress Report	Co-operative Union	Annual Report of Work of the Co-operative Union, and Congress debates.
Co-operative Statistics	Co-operative Union	Statistics of every individual society (A).
Review of Co-operative Statistics	Co-operative Union	National statistics (A).
Co-operative Party "Platform"	Co-operative Union	Statement of the Party's views on current issues.

(Published as supplement to Co-operative News.)

Title	Publisher	Remarks
Co-operative Official	Nat. Assoc. of Co-op. Officials	Articles of professional interest to officials (M).

(Published as supplement to Co-operative Management and Marketing.)

Title	Publisher	Remarks
Review of International Co-operation	I.C.A.	Official organ of I.C.A. Information on co-operation anywhere in the world (M).
Co-operative News Service	I.C.A.	Current news of co-operation in various countries (F).

Appendix IX.

Principal Provisions of the Industrial and Provident Societies Acts.

N.B.—The rules of a society may limit some of the possibilities conferred by legislation, *e.g.*, some societies do not admit as members persons below 18 years of age.

1. Seven individuals (who must be at least 16 years of age), or two Industrial and Provident Societies, are required as the minimum number of members of an Industrial and Provident Society.

2. Societies and their rules (and any amendments thereto) are registered with the Registrar of Friendly Societies. The rules must contain provisions in respect of several matters mentioned in a schedule to the 1965 Act. The word " Limited " must be the last word of the name of a registered society. Registration gives a society the status of a corporate body that may sue or be sued in its own name and have perpetual succession. A society that may be registered under the Industrial and Provident Societies Acts is one for carrying on any industries or trades specified in or authorised by its rules, whether wholesale or retail, and including dealings of any description with land.

3. Every society must have a registered office to which all communications and notices are to be addressed.

4. Individuals and joint-stock companies may not hold more than £1,000 of share capital; but there is no limit to the shareholding of one registered society in another. (N.B.—The rules of a society usually fix the minimum number of shares and their value which a member must hold; and they sometimes fix a maximum below the £1,000 permitted by law.)

5. Loan capital may be accepted if authority is given in the rules, the amount that may be accepted and the security given being also determined by the authority given in the rules. (There is no legal limit beyond this to the amount of loan capital which any person may hold in a society.)

6. Share capital may be either transferable or withdrawable. A society with withdrawable share capital may not undertake the business of banking; but the receipt of not more than £2 in one deposit or £50 in all from any one depositor, payable on not less than two clear days' notice, does not constitute the business of banking in this connection.

7. The liability of every member, as member (*e.g.*, not as a purchaser) is limited to the number of shares he has taken up (the minimum being the number for membership) and this liability continues for one year after cessation of membership for such debts as were contracted before he ceased to be a member and if the contributions of existing members are insufficient to meet them.

8. Members have certain rights. They include:—
   (1) A right to purchase for a sum not exceeding two shillings a copy of the rules of his society (non-members also have this right);
   (2) A right to a copy of the last Annual Return forwarded to the Registrar of Friendly Societies (other persons interested in the funds of the society, *e.g.*, loanholders also have this right);
   (3) A right to inspect his own account in the books of his society; and also to inspect the books containing the names of the members of the society (it has been ruled that he can take copies of these names). (These rights are also shared by other persons having an interest in the funds of the society);
   (4) The right to nominate, in writing, any person(s) to whom the whole, or a specified part, of his property shall be paid at his decease. A nomination may be revoked or varied by a subsequent nomination but not by a will. Subsequent marriage revokes a nomination. (Provision is made to protect the State in regard to the payment of death duties.)

9. A registered society has certain obligations. They include:—

    (1) Having its accounts audited by a qualified Auditor once a year.

    (2) The forwarding to the Registrar of Friendly Societies, not later than 31st March in each year, of an Annual Return showing the receipts and expenditure, funds, and effects of the society, the Return being signed by the auditor(s) and accompanied by any report(s) issued by him (them) during the year.

    (3) The keeping of a copy of the last balance sheet for the time being, together with a report of the auditors, always hung up in a conspicuous place at the registered office of the society.

    (4) The preparation by a society undertaking the business of banking of a statement in specified form made up on the first Mondays in February and August each year, and hanging up a copy of this statement in a conspicuous position in its registered office and every other office or place of business belonging to it where the business of banking is carried on.

10. A member under 18 years of age may be secretary, but not a member of the committee, trustee, manager, or treasurer of the society.

11. By special resolution, a society may amalgamate with another society, transfer its engagements to another registered society willing to undertake them, convert itself into a company under the Companies Acts, or amalgamate with or transfer its engagements to such a company.

12. By ordinary resolution, a society may change its name.

13. Upon application from one-tenth of the whole number of members or of one hundred members if the membership exceeds one thousand the Registrar, with the consent of the Treasury, may (a) appoint an inspector or inspectors to examine into and report on the affairs of such society; or (b) call a special meeting of the society.

14. The term " officer " is explained as covering any treasurer, secretary, member of the committee, manager or servant, other than a servant appointed by the committee, of a society.

INDEX

Abbots, W., 180
Acland, A., 120
Acland, Mrs. A. C., 125
Address to Governments, 29
Adulteration, 52, 53, 68, 107, 327, 474, 475
Advertising, 158, 248, 307, 324, 328
Adviser of Studies (see F. Hall)
A. E. (see Russell, G. W.)
Agriculture, 88, 151–152, 218, 233–234, 274–275, 403–428, 463–465
Agricultural Act 1967, 420
Agricultural Co-operation, 380, 402–428, 433, 438, 463–465, 467
Agricultural Finance Federation, 424
Agricultural Societies, 159, 177, 204, 275, 286, 405, 422–425
Agricultural Credit Societies, 327, 405–407, 433
Agricultural and Horticultural Association, 414
Agricultural Marketing Acts, 151, 152, 274–276
Agricultural Marketing Boards, 151, 152, 274–276, 425
Agricultural Marketing Societies, 408–409, 422–423
Agricultural Organisation Society, 176, 414, 415, 416, 417
Agricultural Irish Organisation Society, 411, 412, 413, 414
Agricultural Scottish Organisation Society, 414, 421
Agricultural Welsh Organisation Society, 419, 421
Agricultural Supply Societies, 407–408, 422
Agricultural Wholesale Society, 415, 417
Agricultural Co-operative Managers' Association, 418, 419, 422, 424
Agricultural Co-operative Association, 418–420
Agricultural Central Co-operative Association, 420
Allan, William, 80, 81
Allnations, 462
Alexander, A.V., 192, 194, 217, 218, 231, 296, 492
Amalgamated Society of Engineers, 79, 80
Amalgamated Union of Co-operative Employees, 128–130, 197, 200
Amalgamation Survey, 290, 291, 352
Anderson, R. A., 410, 411
Applegarth, R., 81
Ashby, Prof., 421

Ashworth, G., 45, 49
Ashworth, M., 49, 511, 512
Ashworth, S., 57, 511, 512
Aspden, J., 42
Association of All Classes of All Nations, 37
Associate Membership of I.C.A., 452
Atlas Engineering Works, 64
Agricultural Co-operation, Year Books, 415, 417
Agricultural Co-operative Bulletin, 415
Agricultural Marketing Policy, Statement On (Co-operative Union, 1952), 268, 408
Alton Locke, C. Kingsley, 61

Bailey, J., 350
Balance of Trade and Payments, 231, 232, 239, 240
Balfour Committee, 149
Bamford, J., 49, 511
Bamford, S., 57, 84, 125, 492
Bamford, W. H., 492
Banking, 80, 104–106, 159
Banking Department (see C.W.S., and S.C.W.S.)
Bank of England, 233
Barlow Report, 235
Barnes, A., 231, 296
Barnish, C., 49, 511
Bastiat, 58
Bates, J., 68
Beaton, N., 171
Beer, M., 1, 8, 9
Bent, J., 45, 49, 511, 512
Bentham and Benthamism, 7, 10, 60, 95
Beveridge and Report, 234
Blanc, L., 69, 430
Blandford, Thomas, 115, 492
Blatchford, R., 95
Board of Trade, 192, 196, 210
Bodien, Dr. F., 463
Bonar, Prof., 113
Bonner, Arnold, 309
Bowley, Prof., 89
Boyve, E. de, 431–432, 493
Brickfield E. P. Society, 52
Brighton Co-operative Benevolent Fund Association, 23, 501
Brighton Co-operative Trading Association, 23, 501
Bright, John, 42, 54
British and Foreign Consolidation Association of Industry, 36
British Broadcasting Association, 229
British Isles Federation of Agricultural Co-operative Societies, 422

Brooks, David, 511
Brougham, Lord, 10
Brown, W. H., 493
Buchan, Mrs., 127
Buckley, Justice, 111
Burke, E., 59, 489
Bycroft, 131
Byron, Lady Noel, 32, 493
British Trade and Industry, (G. D. H.
    Cole), 89
British War Economy (Hancock and
    Gowing), 231

Campbell, A., 38, 75, 76, 85, 493
Campbells, G. and W., 91
Capital (see Co-operative), 24, 48, 50
Capitalism, 10, 205, 306, 307
Capital Gains, 312,
Carnegie, A., 93
Carpenter, E., 4
Carson, 29
Cash and Carry, 215, 230
Cash Trading, 326–327
Castlemahon, 411
Castle Street Tailors, 62, 63
Cattle Boycott, 112–113
Census of Distribution, 244, 255, 256
Central Board (see also Co-operative
    Union), 37, 62, 82
Central Co-operative Agency, 65, 68, 70
Centrosoyus, 442, 443
Chadwick, E., 8
Chain Stores, 290–291, 370
Charlton, W. L., 414
Chartist and Chartism, 38, 39, 43, 45, 51,
    60, 61, 195
Cheetham, T., 57, 72, 73, 75
Cheltenham Agreement, 192
Christianity, 24, 25, 26, 29, 92
Christian Socialism 26, 53, 60–62, 64, 66,
    68, 78, 81, 85, 86, 105,
    113, 127, 133, 204, 305,
    364, 411, 413, 429, 474
Churchill, W. S., 192, 218
City Region, 242–243
Clapham, Prof., 56, 409
Clynes, J. R., 139
Coalition Government, 145, 194
Coal, 145, 150, 178, 233
Cobden, R., 42
Cole, G. D. H., 41, 45, 228, 510
Collier, J., 41, 43, 45, 511, 512
Collectivism, 130, 268
Colonial Office, 301, 302, 446
Communities, 13 ff, 22, 25, 516
Communism, 442–443, 447
Comrades' Circles, 186
Company Law, 66, 90
Conciliation, 197, 200
Conservative, 67, 94, 132, 149, 279, 286

Consumer Advisory Councils, 249
Consumer Association, 249
Consumer Council, 249
Consumer Producer Controversy,
    133–136
Consumer Co-operation, 133, 134, 136,
    137, 202 ff, 207, 307, 404,
    408, 437, 463, 476
Conscription, 138, 141, 209, 231
Controls, 138 ff, 209–212, 232, 269
Co-ordination, 180
Cooper, Walter, 62, 63
Cooper, William, 44, 45, 53, 54, 57, 66,
    71, 72, 73, 75, 77, 493–
    494, 511–512, 519–521
Co-operative Aid Association, 114
Co-operative College,
    58, 118, 121, 123–124,
    180–182, 184, 187, 195,
    220, 221–222, 228, 297,
    300–302, 303, 348, 392,
    394, 446
Co-operative Commonwealth, 107, 183,
    205, 350, 380, 395, 472–
    491
Co-operative Conferences, 68, 70, 71, 72,
    73, 74, 76, 77, 81
Co-operative Congresses, Pre-Rochdale,
    23, 28–31, 35, 37, 39, 40,
    42, 45, 78, 80, 316, 518
Co-operative Congresses, Present Series,
    78–81, 82, 83, 84, 104–105,
    117, 118, 119, 121, 125,
    128, 129, 130, 131, 132,
    133, 142, 143, 156, 157,
    167, 171, 179, 180, 183,
    189, 192, 196, 198, 202,
    205, 206, 269, 270, 273,
    275, 279, 281, 282, 287,
    288, 290, 292, 293, 294,
    295, 297, 301, 370, 382–
    385, 388, 390, 393, 395,
    396, 397, 411, 413, 429,
    431, 433, 434, 477
Co-operative Corn Mills, 51–53
Co-operative Co-partnership,
    53, 113–115, 159, 172–173,
    227–228, 266–267, 474
Co-operative Dairies, 104
Co-operative Development Agency, 281
Co-operative Education Committees'
    Association, 176, 186
Co-operative Educational Fellowship,
    123, 351
Co-operative Elections, 317–319, 358–
    359, 372, 383
Co-operative Housing, 114
Co-operative Insurance Company, 54, 77
Co-operative Insurance Society, 109,
    172, 265, 374, 385, 424

541

Co-operative Managers' Association,
124, 129, 176
Co-operative Party,
143, 150, 174, 189–195,
218, 270, 272, 277, 278,
279, 295–297, 349–351,
385, 395–397, 477
— Conferences, 150, 190–191, 396–397
— Constitution, 189–190, 349–351
— Growth, 194, 218, 295, 395–397
— Policy, 191–192
— and Elections, 143, 194, 231, 295–296
— Relations with Labour Party, 192–
193, 218, 272, 296–297,
349–357
Co-operative Press (and Newspaper
Society), 28, 83, 128, 194–195, 270,
376–378
Co-operative Printing Society, 84
Co-operative Permanent Building
Society, 265–266
Co-operative Productive Federation,
113, 114, 121, 124, 172–
173, 227–228, 266–267,
270, 287–288, 293, 374–
376, 388
Co-operative Publications (Past and
Present), 534–536
Co-operative Secretaries' Association,
124, 129
Co-operative Retail Development
Society, 289, 290
Co-operative Tea Society, 374, 460
Co-operative Travel Service, 369
Co-operative Union, The, 68, 81–83, 86,
113, 117, 118, 133, 142,
157, 159, 160, 171, 174,
175–179, 185, 201, 215–
218, 228, 231, 260, 262,
268–302, 354, 366, 369,
370, 379–401, 414, 416,
417, 418, 424, 432, 434,
435, 436, 464, 477
— Constitution, 82–83, 175 ff, 269 ff,
380–388
— Central Board, 82, 105, 116, 119, 126,
133, 142, 157, 175, 181,
187, 270
— Central Executive, 270, 271, 280, 287,
289, 290, 293, 295, 375,
382, 383, 384, 385, 386,
387, 389, 395, 396
— Committee on Congress Procedure,
269
— Departments—
Agriculture, 159, 176–177, 217,
218, 417
Development and Advisory
Services, 271, 291, 294, 370
Dry Goods, 272, 294, 370

Editorial, 399
Education, 158, 175, 176, 180–187,
219, 270, 297–298, 303,
344, 349, 390–395
Finance, 178, 279, 289, 294, 398
Food Trades, 272, 294, 370
Legal, 178, 398
Labour, 176, 197, 216, 289, 388–390
Publications, 178, 216, 399–400
Research, 168, 176, 180, 224, 289
Statistical, 400
Taxation, 216, 279, 398
— District Associations, 176, 387
— Education Executive (Committee),
119, 120, 121, 122, 123,
124, 126, 222, 297, 298,
303, 391, 392, 393
— Economic and Taxation
Committee, 385
— Foreign Inquiry, 432
— General Purposes, 270, 272, 381, 434
— National Authority, 175, 193, 209,
269, 270, 272, 273
— National Executive, 175, 186, 270
— National Policy, 269, 277
— National Wages Board, 295, 388–390
— National Co-operative Education
Association, 297, 298, 299, 390,
391, 392, 393
— United Board, 83, 175, 177, 416
— Parliamentary Committee, 270
— Provincial Board, 82, 105
— Regional Councils, 387
— Sectional Boards, 82, 83, 116, 117,
119, 175, 199, 270, 271,
291, 297, 385, 386–387,
388
— Trade Advisory Committee, 272
— Joint Committees:—
Parliamentary, 217, 269, 270, 272,
276, 295, 386, 387, 416
Propaganda, 171
— Sections, 116, 161, 162, 163, 165, 166,
167, 250, 254
— Sectional Education Committees and
Councils, 121, 297, 298, 349, 391,
393
— Trade Associations, 177–178, 217,
270, 271, 388
Bakery, 388
Dry Goods, 388
Fuel, 178, 294, 388
Laundry, 388
Meat, 178, 388
Milk, 164, 177, 294, 388
Technical Panels, 178, 388
Co-operative Wholesaling, 68–77, 109–
111, 113, 134, 157, 159,
226, 328–329, 362–364,
529–534

Co-operative Wholesale Society,
72, 74, 76, 77, 81, 84, 96,
97, 103, 109, 119, 124,
132, 134, 135, 140, 169 ff,
181, 185, 196, 199, 206,
217, 224, 226–227, 228,
257, 262–265, 270, 275,
287–288, 290, 292, 293–
295, 302, 356–371, 385,
403, 410–412, 413, 415,
416, 418, 424, 433, 436,
460, 461

C.W.S. Bank, 104–106, 159, 170–171,
196, 264, 361–362, 369,
424
— Branches and Depots, 103
— Constitution, 75, 357–360
— Capital, 360–362
— Market Research, 257
— Production, 106–108, 109, 126, 134,
159, 170, 226, 263, 364–
365
— Retail Services, 171, 251–252, 365–371
— Trade, 169, 170, 262–264
— Inquiry Committee, 1953, 265
— Joint Re-organisation Committee,
264, 359
Co-operative Vigilance Committee, 112
Co-operative Youth Movement (and
Junior Classes), 120, 175, 186, 220–221,
298, 299, 347, 351
Co-ordination, 179–180, 287
Corporation Tax, 258, 277, 296
Cottrell, Mrs., 189
Council of Promoters, 62
Cox, H., 431
Craig, E. T., 77, 85, 402, 494
Crosland, C. A. R., 288
Crawford, Sharman, 44
Credit Societies, 405–407
Credit Trading, 26, 30, 47, 117, 165,
247–248, 326–327, 521
Creameries, 410–411
Cartel, 458
Census of Shops and Services (Co-opera-
tive Union, 1955), 343
Century of Co-operation (G. D. H. Cole),
45, 228, 511
Christian Socialist, The, 61, 63, 65, 68
Christian Socialism, Tracts on, 61
Christianity and Economics (A. D.
Lindsay), 85, 473
Clarion, The, 95
Conflicts of Capital and Labour (G.
Howell), 127
Consumer Affairs Bulletin, 458
Consumers' Co-operation (S. and B.
Webb), 137, 141, 202, 315, 323, 356,
359, 491

Consumers' Co-operation in Great Britain
(Carr-Saunders, Florence, and Peers),
206–208
Consumers' Co-operative Societies
(C. Gide), 203
*Constitution for a Socialist Common-
wealth* (S. and B. Webb), 202 ff, 233,
379
Co-operation (Hall and Watkins), 114,
118, 306, 379, 472, 529
Co-operation and the Future of Industry
(L. Woolf), 205–206
Co-operation and Socialism (L. Woolf),
205–206
Co-operation and Socialism (C.U. State-
ment, 1958), 284, 483
Co-operative Auxiliaries (Groombridge),
303
Co-operative Century (L. du Garde
Peach), 228
Co-operative Commercial Circular, 70
Co-operative Communities (Wm.
Thompson), 22
Co-operative Democracy (Warbasse), 478
Co-operative Gazette, 218, 399
Co-operative Ideals and Problems
(A. Orne), 203, 204–205, 306–307, 345
Co-operative Magazine, 22, 32
Co-operative Management and Marketing,
377
Co-operative Movement in Great Britain
(B. Potter), 135–136, 352
*Co-operative Movement in a Collectivist
Economy* (C.U., 1950), 483
Co-operative News, 57, 83–84, 110, 119,
125, 314, 377, 378
Co-operative News Service, 458
Co-operative Party Conference Report,
1935, 191
Co-operative Production (Ben Jones), 26,
86, 479
Co-operative Republic (E. Poisson), 203,
204, 308, 480–483
Co-operative Review, 31, 319, 399
Co-operative Sector (G. Fauquet),
485–486
Co-operative Stores, Report on,
1878–1879, 96–98
Co-operator, The, 1828–1830 (King's),
22–28, 30, 44, 47, 330
Co-operator, The, 1860–1871 (Pitman's),
72, 73, 75, 76, 77, 78, 83
Co-operators' Year Book, 115
Crisis, The, 33, 34, 36

Dalton, H., 235
Daly, James, 43, 45, 49, 511–512
Darling, George, 296
Davies, Miss M. L., 120, 126, 131, 494–
495

Deflation, 147
Deans, J., 112
Dehli, O., 439
Democracy, 29, 30, 136, 203, 205, 478
Democratic Control, 313–320, 324, 445, 447, 454, 478, 487–491
Dent, J. J., 495
Departmental Stores, 91, 135, 158, 161, 343
Devaluation, 233, 240
Devonport, Lord, 139
Dicey, A. V., 8
Dickens, Charles, 60
Dickson-Mabon, J., 296
Digby, Miss M., 288
Disraeli, B., 60
Distribution of Wealth and Income, 18–19, 237–238, 307, 472–473
Distributive Trades, 244
Dividend on Purchase (see also Retail Societies), 47, 49, 50, 75, 101–102, 203, 225, 273, 277, 321–324, 362, 364, 369–371, 408
Dividend Stamps, 261, 341
Doherty, J., 41
Domestic System, 3 ff, 307
Drumcollogher, 410
Dunsany Co-operative Society, 410

Early English Socialists, 9, 13
Easter Education Convention, 123, 136, 186, 220, 299, 392
Eastmans, 91
Economic Background, 2–6, 40, 44, 88–90, 137–140, 144–156, 209–215, 230–250
Economic Planning, 138, 144, 148, 149–152, 193, 201, 239
Economic Planning Board, 281–282
Edinburgh Central Co-operative Association, 76
Education, 92–93, 221, 234–235
Education (Co-operative), 25, 38, 43, 118–124, 158–161, 174, 180–187, 191, 219–222, 297–302, 314, 324–325, 329, 344–349, 390–395, 427–428
Education, Owen on, 16–17
Education, King on, 25
Education, Joint Council for Advance, 221
Edwards, J. C., 72, 73, 74, 75, 76, 77
Eldsfoss Co-operative Society, 508
Elliott, S. R., 195
Employees (Co-operative), 126, 128, 159, 197 ff, 201, 318–319, 324
Employee Representation, 159, 200–201, 203
Employment Exchanges, 211

Elections (Co-operative), (see Co-operative)
Elections (Parliamentary), 143, 295–296
English and Scottish Joint C.W.S., 169, 172, 374
Equality and Equity, 329
European Common Market, 279
Expenditure, Consumer, 153–154, 163, 212, 241–242
Excess Profits Duty, 142
Excess Profits Tax, 213, 216, 258, 277
Economic History of Modern Britain (Clapham), 56, 409
Economic News Service, 458
Economic Survey Report, 1938, 167–169
Edinburgh Review, 14

Fabian Socialism and Society, 94, 95, 131, 136, 157
Factory System, 4–6
Family Allowances, 134
Farmers' Central Trading Board, 415
Farmers' Central Organisation, 420
Farn, J. C., 84
Fascism, 443–444
Fauquet, Dr. G., 485–486
Fawcett, Prof., 44
Fay, Prof., 402, 424, 427
Finance Acts, 178, 194, 277
Federations, District, 259
Federations, Local, 261–262
Federation of Agricultural Co-operatives, 422, 428
Federation of British Industries, 281
Finch, John, 29, 31, 40, 61
Flammersfeld, 405
Fleming, 42
Flint and Palmers, 91
Florence, Prof. Sargant, 243
Food and Agriculture Organisation, 446
Food Control, 139, 209–210, 234
Food, Ministry of, 139, 140, 210
Foreign Trade, 88–89, 146, 148, 215, 230, 231, 232
Fourier, C., 62, 467
Fraternity, 330
Free Trade, 126, 146, 469
Freedom, 329, 448
Friendly Societies' Act, 66
Frugal Investment Clause, 66
Fabian Tracts, 95
Facing the Future Together (J. Bailey), 350
Food, Health, and Income (J. B. Orr), 154
Fresh Analysis of Rochdale Principles (Lambert), 308, 316, 320

Gaitskell, H. T. N., 288
Garnlwyd, 59
Gaskell, Mrs., 60

Garside, J., 43, 49
General Co-operative Survey and
  Report, 100, 102, 103, 109, 156–160,
          161, 194, 200, 201, 291,
          335, 346, 414, 416
General Meetings, 315–317, 320
General Strike, 196, 200
George, David Lloyd, 140
Gide, Prof. C., 58, 203–204, 306, 307–
          308, 311, 328–329, 432,
          436, 437, 441, 467, 477,
          479, 495–496
Gift Schemes, 111
Goedhart, G. D. C., 439
Gosling, R. G., 288
Gold Standard, 146, 147, 148
Government Control, 138
Grand National Consolidated Trades
  Union, 32, 35–37
Gray, J. C., 117, 410, 496
Great Depression, 89, 106, 113, 409
Green, T. H., 94
Greening, E. O., 81, 113, 123, 131, 134,
          414, 429, 433, 434, 435,
          496
Greenwood, A., 51, 52, 53, 54, 57, 71,
          72, 73, 74, 75, 76, 77, 81,
          83, 106, 125, 131, 496–
          497, 529
Grey, A. (Earl), 433, 434
Groombridge, B., 303
Guilds (Co-operative), 120, 123, 124–
          127, 128, 175, 176, 186,
          187–189, 218–219, 298,
          299, 302–303, 346, 351–
          352, 434, 494–495, 501–
          502

Hall, Fred, 57, 121, 123, 124, 157, 174,
          187, 205, 206, 305, 306,
          319, 336, 346, 497–498
Hall, Lady Margaret, 288
Hallsworth, J., 198
Halstead, R., 121
Hardie, Keir, 96
Hardie, Col. S. J. L., 288
Hammond, J. L. and B., 5
Harmony Hall (see Queenwood)
Harmsworth, A., 93
Healey, G., 44, 49, 511
Hedberg, A., 470
Health, 126
Herbert, Auberon, 118, 123, 328
Hilton, J., 72, 73, 75
Hire Purchase, 247–248, 296, 424
Hirst, T., 23, 28, 29, 498
Hitler, Adolf, 192, 444
Hole, J., 59, 79

Holyoake, G. J., 28, 34, 38, 41, 42, 48,
          56, 79, 80, 81, 97, 131,
          132, 303, 305, 335, 368,
          429, 433, 434, 498–499
Holyoake House, 117, 124, 181, 220, 227
Holt, James, 49, 511
Holt, John, 49, 511
Home and Colonial, 91
Home Colonisation Society, 38
Honest Trading, 42, 52, 53, 68, 96, 97,
          107, 108, 111, 203, 326,
          327–328, 365, 377, 381–
          382, 474–476
Hood, T., 60
Hooson, E., 72, 73
Hough, J. A., 165, 168, 224, 225
Hours and Wages Board, 197
Housing, 114, 235, 463
Hot Springs Conference, 445–446, 468
Howarth, Charles, 42, 45, 49, 52, 57, 72,
          73, 75, 499, 511
Howell, G., 113, 127
Huber, Prof. V. A., 430
Hughes, T., 60, 61, 66, 67, 85, 105, 106,
          113, 117, 134, 311, 477,
          479, 484, 499
Hume, J., 14, 18
Hungry Forties, 44
Handbook to I. and P. Acts (Chappenden),
          342
Handbook for Members of Management
  Committees (F. Hall), 206, 319, 336
Handbook to Rochdale Congress, 1892,
          511
Herald of Redemption and Herald of
  Co-operation, 59
History of British Trade Unionism (S.
  and B. Webb), 35, 36, 145
History of British Socialism (M. Beer),
          1, 8, 9
History of Economic Doctrines (Gide
  and Rist), 203
History of Rochdale Pioneers (G. J.
  Holyoake), 335
History of the Workers' Educational
  Association (T. W. Price), 121

Ideals, 305
Income Tax, 178, 194, 213, 277
Independent Commission of Inquiry,
          157, 253, 254, 255, 256,
          259, 287–288, 291, 320,
          328, 335, 352, 361, 365,
          370
Independent Labour Party, 95, 131, 435
Independent Retailers, 245, 255, 256
Industrial Bank, 106
Industrial Revolution, 3 ff, 87, 303, 472
Industrial Unionism, 89

Industrial and Provident Societies' Acts, 55, 66–68, 72, 73, 76, 77, 83, 106, 117, 286, 336, 341–342, 398, 419, 537–538
Inflation, 209, 231, 235, 239–240, 272, 298
INGEBA, 461
Insurance Development Bureau, 461
Interco-op, 460
International Co-operative Alliance, 49, 51, 58, 204, 308–309, 325, 406, 429–471
— Constitution, 435, 438, 454–457
— Congresses, 58, 309, 434–435, 441–442, 448–452, 454, 455, 457, 460, 463
— Membership, 448, 451–454
— Committees, 455–456, 460
— Objects, 436–438, 449–457
— Regional Office, 465
International Co-operative Banking, 441, 461
International Co-operative Insurance, 462
International Co-operative Petroleum Association, 460–461
International Co-operative Trade, 160, 441, 459
International Co-operative Trading Agency, 160, 459–460
International Co-operative Day, 466–467
International Co-operative Wholesale Society, 160, 439, 458–460
International Labour Office, 440, 441, 463, 467–468
International Federation of Agricultural Producers, 422
Irish Agricultural Organisation Society, 411, 412, 413, 414
Irish Co-operative Aid Association, 410
Irish Co-operative Agency Society, 412
Irish Agricultural Society, 413
Iron and Steel Boards Federation, 150
Irving, Sydney, 296
International Co-operative Alliance
— Congress Reports, 325, 458
— Review, 457
— Year Books, 438
Irish Homestead, 413
Irish Land and Labour Question (E. T. Craig), 402

Jack, D. T., 288
Jaures, J., 204
Jefferys, J. B., 91, 135, 288
Joint Committee of Trade Unions and Co-operators, 196, 198
Joint Committee on Technical Education, 185

Joint Industrial Council, 217
Joint Stock Companies, 90, 312, 319, 475
Joint Policy National Committee, 280, 295
Jones, Ben, 66, 86, 119, 125, 131, 478, 500
Jones, Lloyd, 34, 38, 43, 47, 59, 62, 65, 66, 69, 70, 79, 81, 83, 85, 105, 107, 110, 130, 131, 328, 329, 500
Jumbo Farm, 72, 403

Kerr, C. H. Bellenden, 66
Keynes, J. M. (Lord), 231
King, Dr. Wm., 22–28, 31, 32, 39, 40, 44, 46, 47, 59, 61, 85, 127, 204, 207, 306, 311, 330, 341, 364, 368, 403, 411, 413, 477, 478, 483, 500–501
Kingsley, C., 61, 68, 85, 501
Knapp, Dr. J., 420
Krook, Axel, 430
Kooperativa Förbundet, 214

Labour, 211, 473–474
Labour Association, 113
Labour Exchange Bank, 30
Labour Exchanges (Owenite), 32–35
Labour, Royal Commission On, 1892, 503
Labour Governments, 148, 192, 194, 205, 231–238, 269, 272–274, 277, 286, 296
Labour Movement, 128, 129, 130, 136, 195, 201, 205, 234
Labour Party, 89, 94, 95, 131, 132, 133, 145, 149, 192, 231–238, 272–274, 279, 296
Labour Representation Committee, 95
Laissez Faire, 138, 144, 207, 209, 303
Lambert, Prof. P., 308, 313, 316–317, 320
Lancs. and Yorks. Conference Association, 57, 78, 79, 81
Landlordism, 410
Land Settlement Association, 425–427
Lawrenson, Mrs. M., 125, 126, 433, 434, 501–502
Laws of Co-operative Evolution, 480
League of Nations, 192, 441
Lend Lease, 215, 230, 232
Lever, Sir Wm., 112
Liberal Party, 67, 83, 93, 94, 131, 149
Liberty (see Freedom)
Libraries, 38, 51, 93
Licensing, 273
Lega Nazionale, 444
Lindsay, A. D., 85, 305, 473
Linlithgow Committee, 416
Livsey, T., 43

Local Food Committees, 139
London Co-operative Board, 80, 81, 82
London Co-operative Congress, 1869,
78–81
Longfield, E., 72, 77
Lord, J., 49
Loyalty, 97, 109–111, 126, 158, 263, 321,
328–329, 353, 363–364,
415, 423–424, 488
Lovett, Wm., 27, 29
Ludlow, J. M. F., 61, 62, 66, 67, 68, 72,
81, 105, 113, 134, 502
Lowbands Farm, 72
Labour Believes in Britain, 283
Labour and the New Social Order, 145
Labour Rewarded (W. Thompson), 22
Life and Labour of the London Poor
(Mayhew), 60
Life of Robert Owen (Autobiography),
16, 17, 18, 19, 516
Life of Robert Owen (Podmore), 20
Life and Struggles (Wm. Lovett), 27
London Life in the Eighteenth Century
(George), 4

Macadam, E., 188
Mail Order, 158, 246–247
Mallalieu, Wm., 44, 45, 49
Malthus, 10, 18
Management, 110, 313, 316, 319–320,
334–339
Management Development Scheme, 301
Manock, J., 511
Mansbridge, A., 121, 122
Marcroft, Wm., 72, 73, 75, 77
Marketing Acts (see Agriculture)
Marketing Boards (see Agriculture)
Marshall, Alfred, 113, 204
Marshall, R. L. M., 297, 298
Marshall Plan, 232
Marriott, Rev. Jos., 42
Marx, Karl, 13, 131, 478
Maurice, F. D., 61, 68
Maxwell, Wm., 132, 438, 439, 502
May, H. J., 143, 439
McFadyen, J., 415
McInnes, J. T., 76, 77, 82
Mercer, T. W., 179, 502
Milk Marketing, 151
Military Service Tribunals, 141–142
Mill, James, 7, 10, 18, 60
Mill, J. S., 8, 58, 60, 66, 335
Ministry of Agriculture, 274–275, 416
Ministry of Food, 210, 217, 275, 276
Ministry of Health, 140
Ministry of Labour, 138, 211, 237
Ministry of Reconstruction, 140
Ministry of Transport, 296
Mitchell, J. T. W., 53, 54, 57, 71, 72, 80,
92, 131, 132, 135, 364,
432, 503

Model Rules, 30, 114, 399, 518
Molesworth, Rev. J. E. N., 57, 80, 105,
430, 503–504
Molony Committee on Consumer
Protection, 1959, 249, 274–275, 284,
296
Monopoly, 149, 150, 274–275, 284, 296
Morgan, J. M., 13, 51, 504
Morier, R. B. D., 105
Morrison, J., 36
Morrison, R. C., 231
Morrison, W., 80, 106
Mudie, G., 504
Multiples, 155–156, 161, 255–256
Müller, Hans, 429, 432, 436, 437, 439
Municipalisation, 205–208, 284
Murray, J. T., 288
Mussolini, 443
Manual for Co-operators (Hughes and
Neale), 117, 311, 477
Manual on University Extension (Sadler),
56
Manchester Guardian, 84, 511
Marketing Acts, Co-operative Policy On
(Co-operative Union, 1958), 275
Member Education Bulletin, 393
Merrie England (R. Blatchford), 95
Millgate, The, 195, 378
Modern Democracies (Bryce), 397
Modern Democratic State (Lindsay), 85
My Story, By Paddy the Cope (P.
Gallagher), 413

National Assistance, 234
National Community Friendly Society,
37
National Conciliation Board, 198–199,
389
National Co-operative Chemists,
370–371
National Co-operative Education
Association, 297, 298, 299, 390
National Co-operative Publishing
Society, 194
National Council of Hours and Wages
Boards, 216
National Council of Labour, 193, 279
National Debt, 214, 235
National Defence Contributions, 213
National Economic Development
Council, 239
National Educational Council, 175, 297
National Emergency Congress, 1917, 143
National Equitable Labour Exchanges,
32–37
National Farmers' Union, 275, 276, 416–
417, 418, 419, 420, 422
National Federal Organisation, 293
National Federation Negotiating
Committee, 264, 293–294

National Government, 148, 194
National Health Service, 234
National Income, 89, 237
Nationalisation, 145, 202, 205, 206, 272, 283, 284
National Insurance Scheme, 234, 273, 277, 297
National Union of Distributive and Allied Workers, 197, 198, 200
National Union of Co-operative Officials, 158
National Membership Scheme, 285–286
National Grange, 431
National Plan in 1965, 239
National Society, 203, 482
Nazism, 444
Neale, E. V., 53, 61, 64, 65, 66, 68, 69, 70, 72, 73, 75, 79, 82, 83, 86, 87, 104, 113, 117, 119, 125, 131, 134, 311, 410, 430, 432–433, 435, 477, 479, 484, 504–505
Neville, W. B., 177
New Harmony, 15, 22
New Lanark, 6, 9, 17, 75
New Moral World, 10, 37, 476
Newman, J. H., 61
Newnes, G., 93
Nîmes, 431
Nordisk Andelsforbund, 460
North-Eastern Co-operative Society, 292
North of England Newspaper Co., 84
North-West of England Co-operative Company, 28, 31, 32
Nuttall, Wm., 72, 83, 84, 119
New Moral World, The, 17, 36, 38, 42
New Philanthropy, The (Macadam), 188
New Statesman and Nation, 207
New View of Society (R. Owen), 10
Notes of a Tour in the Manufacturing Districts (W. Cooke Taylor), 5

Old Immoral World, 10, 20, 87
Olivier, S., 95
Open Membership, 312–313, 329, 470
Operation Facelift, 257, 264
Orbiston, 15, 75
Organic Laws of Co-operation, 480
Örne, Anders, 203, 204, 306–307, 308, 311, 312, 325, 345, 478, 479, 484, 505–506
Osborne Judgment, 94
Ouseburn Engineering Works, 106
Overlapping, 158, 290, 354, 423
Owen, Robert Dale, 19
Owen, Robert, 1–40, 85, 91, 352, 411, 413, 429, 467, 475, 476, 506–507
— on Communities, 13 ff, 516–517

— on Education, 16–17
— on Economists, 18–19
— on Factories, 3–11
— on Marriage, 20
— on Religion, 10, 19–20, 29
— on Unemployment, 11 ff
— on Profits and Prices, 12–13
Owenism, 1–40, 43, 45, 47, 75, 79, 80, 85, 105, 127, 133, 204, 270, 305, 306, 364, 402, 403, 477–478
Oxford Movement, 61
Observations on the Factory System (Owen), 3, 11

Padiham Commercial Mill Co., 64
Pahlmann, A., 31, 32
Palmer, R. A. (Lord Rusholme), 231
Pare, Wm., 23, 28, 70, 78, 79, 80, 81, 85, 87, 105, 117, 118, 123, 270, 429, 430, 507–508
Parliamentary Representation, 130, 131, 132, 133, 142, 194, 231, 296
Parliamentary Elections, 191, 231, 233
P.A.Y.E., 213
Peace, 192, 230, 438, 450, 469–471
Peach, L. du Garde, 228
Pearson, A., 93
Peasant Farming, 403–405
Pette, Ald. F., 288
Perdicaris, I., 430
Pfeiffer, Dr. E., 430
Pickup, A., 177
Pilling, A., 44
Pitman, H., 72, 77, 508
Place, F., 8, 10, 18
Planned Economy, 138
Planet Friendly Society, 172
Plebs League, 93
Plunkett, H. C., 410, 411, 412, 424, 508–509
Plunkett Foundation, 417, 422, 428
Points, 210, 225
Poisson, E., 203, 204, 308, 312, 478, 479–483, 490, 509
Political Neutrality, 30, 83–84, 130, 142, 326, 447, 448, 449–450
Population, 152–153, 242
Potter B. (see also Webb, S. and B.), 127, 135–136, 202, 331, 352
Post Office Savings Banks, 88, 214
Pratt, Hodgson, 123, 429, 434, 509–510
Press, The, 92, 195, 277
Prices, 33 ff, 139, 154, 241
Price Control, 139, 140, 210, 234, 239
Price Policy, 48, 272, 274, 322, 339–341
Price, W. T., 121
Principles (see also Rochdale), 305–330
Private Enterprise, 138
Private Sector, 485

Producer v. Consumer Controversy, 133–136
Producer Co-operation, 54, 106, 107, 113, 127, 128, 134, 136, 202 ff, 227, 228, 432, 433, 434
Production, Co-operative, 159, 180, 287
Profit, 24, 47
Profit Motive, 32 ff, 136, 140, 142, 206, 306, 307, 323–324, 449, 473, 476
Profit Sharing, 53, 54, 62, 113, 433, 434, 435, 436
Profits Tax, 273, 277, 296
Proprietary Articles Traders' Association, 90
Protection, 146, 148
Proudhon, 58
Provincial Board, 82, 105
Public Sector, 483, 485–486
Purchase Tax, 214, 236, 276, 278, 284, 296

Pioneer, The, 36
Place of the Co-operative Movement in a Collectivist Economy (Co-operative Union), 282, 312, 483
Plan or No Plan (B. Wootton), 152
Politics for the People, 61
Portrait of an Age (Young), 8
Principles of Political Economy (Gide), 203

Queenwood, 15, 37, 38, 43, 44, 47, 85
Quarterly Review, 22

Rae, W. R., 121, 123, 187, 510
Raiffeisen, F. W., 405, 406, 411, 413, 510
Rainbow Flag, 466–467
Ralahine, 15, 402, 494, 508
Rational Association Sick and Burial Society, 45
Rational Society, 32, 38
Rationalisation, 149 ff
Rationing, 140, 209–210, 234
Reconstruction, 144
Reclus, E., 495
Reddaway, Prof., 278
Redemption Societies, 59, 63
Redfern, P., 72
Reform Acts, 130
Regional Plan, 251, 291–292, 303, 352, 386, 387
Registrar of Friendly Societies, 74, 341, 342
Registrations, 225
Rent Restrictions, 154
Religious Neutrality, 30, 49, 326
Resale Price Maintenance, 249, 296

Retailing, 22, 90, 154–156, 244–250
Retail Societies, 96–103, 109, 158–169, 222–226, 250–251, 287, 289, 291, 331–355
— Accounts, 341–342
— Amalgamation of, 98, 158, 160, 169, 251, 290, 352
— Capital, 99–100, 126, 143, 159, 165–166, 215, 225–226, 258–260, 321, 332–334
— Credit, 97, 165, 225, 226, 253, 261, 326–327
— Committees, 101, 297, 298, 319–320, 334–336, 346–348, 349–351
— Constitution, 313–320, 334–339, 341–342
— Dividend, 96, 101–102, 159, 166, 216, 226, 260, 321–324, 339–341
— Interest, 320–321
— Membership, 97–99, 143, 158, 160, 250, 314, 332, 344
— Number of, 50, 59, 97, 251
— Officials, 101, 298, 319, 334, 337–339, 348–349
— Production, 102, 344
— Reserves, 99, 159, 166, 225–226, 258–259, 322, 324, 333
— Size, 97, 98, 160, 161, 168, 251, 352–354
— Trade, 96, 100–101, 144, 162–165, 167–169, 224–225, 342–344
— War Damage, 223–224
Rhonnda, Lord, 139
Rigby, J., 42
Ricardo, D., 10, 14, 18
Road and Rail Traffic Act, 150
Rudman, B., 511
Ruskin, 475
Ruskin College, 93
Rusholme, Lord (see R. A. Palmer), 231
Russell, G. W. (A. E.), 402, 413, 424, 427
Rochdale, 41
Rochdale Branch of Rational Society, 24, 39, 42, 43
Rochdale Friendly Co-operative Society, 42
Rochdale Co-operative Card Manufacturing Society, 54
Rochdale Co-operative Conference, 1856, 71
Rochdale Co-operative Congress, 1892, 303
Rochdale Co-operative Corn Mill, 51 ff, 71, 104, 532, 533
Rochdale Co-operative Manufacturing Society, 53, 54, 73

Rochdale System of Co-operation, 78, 81, 85, 86, 87, 96, 133, 135, 136, 304, 407, 478, 479
Rochdale Education Guild, 121
Rochdale Equitable Sick and Provident Society, 54
Rochdale Equitable Society of Pioneers, 41–58, 59, 70, 77, 99, 104, 106, 118, 125, 228, 316, 519–521, 526–528
— Date of Establishment, 50, 526
— Education, 55 ff
— First Officers, 49, 526
— Members, Original, 45, 511–512
— Objects, 46, 522
— Rules (see Rochdale Principles), 46 ff, 522–525
— Wholesaling, 54, 69–72, 527–528, 529–533
Rochdale People's Institute, 51
Rochdale Pioneers, 30, 41–58, 72, 203, 303, 305, 307, 310, 313, 317, 321, 326, 327, 364, 403, 429, 449, 450, 451, 477, 478, 510–512
Rochdale Pioneers' Centenary, 220, 222, 228–229
Rochdale Principles, 48, 49, 68, 203, 205, 305–330, 381, 407, 408, 449, 450, 451
Rochdale Plan (see Rochdale System)
Rochdale Savings Bank, 51, 60
Rochdale Social Institute, 50
Rochdale Weavers' Association, 50
Raw Materials Controls (Worswick), 211
Reasoner, The, 100
Reflections on the Revolution in France (E. Burke), 489
Report on Co-operative Auxiliaries, 1960 (Groombridge), 303
Report of Reorganisation Committee for Milk, 1933, 164
Report to the County of Lanark (Owen), 10, 19
Report of Departmental Committee on Income Tax, 1905, 323
Retail Trading in Great Britain (Jefferys), 91, 155
Reynolds News, 195, 377, 378
Rochdale Principles, A Fresh Analysis of (Lambert), 308, 316, 320

Sadler, M., 56
Salford Hatters, 63
San Garde, Dr., 319
Sankey Commission, 145
Savings, 24, 25, 51, 212, 214 ff, 273
Schulze, Delitsch, 105, 438

Sectional Boards (see Co-operative Union)
Self Employment, 25, 45, 474
Select Committee on Co-operative Stores, 1878–1879, 97–98
Self Service, 248, 343
Scottish Agricultural Organisation Society, 414, 421
Scottish Central Land Bank, 421
Scottish Co-operative Iron Works, 108
Scottish Co-operative Retail Services, 251, 252–253, 374
Scottish Co-operative Wholesale Society, 75–77, 105, 108–109, 112–113, 124, 132, 169 ff, 181, 200, 226–227, 262–265, 270, 287–288, 291, 292, 293–294, 357, 370, 371–374, 385, 436, 438, 461
— Banking Department, 264, 373
— Branches and Depots, 108
— Capital, 262
— Constitution, 371–373
— Foundation, 75–77
— Production, 108, 109, 159, 169, 171–172, 263
— Retail Branches, 251, 373
— Retailing, 109, 171, 172
— Review of Organisation, 264
— Trade, 109, 169, 262–263
Scottish National Poultry Organisation, 421
Scottish Smallholders' Association, 421
Scowcroft, James, 511
Selective Employment Tax, 240, 274, 277, 278–279, 280, 296, 300
Shares of Retail Trade, 245
Shaw, G. B., 95
Shoefayre Ltd., 370
Simm, J. S., 226
Simpson, G., 31
Skevington, J., 29
Slaney, R., 67
Smith, Adam, 7, 13, 473
Smith, J. E., 36
Smith, Jos., 45, 49
Smithies, James, 23, 42, 44, 45, 49, 53, 57, 69, 70, 72, 73, 75, 77, 125, 512
Social Democratic Federation, 94, 95, 96, 130, 435
Social Institutes, 38
Social Missionaries, 37, 38
Socialism, Owenite, 9, 13, 26, 37, 39, 42, 43, 89, 130, 478
Socialism, State, 94–96, 130, 131, 134, 136, 202, 205–208, 282–285, 306, 437, 479
Society Footwear Ltd., 370

Society for Promoting Industrial and Provident Societies, 70
Sonne, Pastor, 430
Spooner, Miss, 126
Special Committee on Government of the Co-operative Union, 1930, 175 ff
Special Congress, 1958, 288–289, 290, 335
State, The, 483–486
State Control, 138
Stanford Hall, 222, 297
Stonehouse, John, 296
Strikes, 145, 196, 198, 238, 244
Standring, J., 42, 511
Stokes, W. L., 410
Stuart, Prof., 56, 119
Sugar Commission, 141
Swansea Congress, 1917, 142
Summer Schools, 124, 185, 220
Supermarkets, 248, 343
Syndicalism, 89
Scottish Co-operator, The, 76, 314, 378
Social Ownership and Consumer Problems, 1953 (Co-operative Union), 283, 483
Signposts for the Sixties (Labour Party Policy Statement), 280
Staff Training and Education Bulletin, 393
Sunday Citizen, 377

Taylor, Wm., 45, 49
Tawney, R. H., 122
Taxation, 212–214, 236, 276–279
Technical Panels, 294
Temperance, 31–32, 45, 46
Templecrone, 413
Ten Year Plan, 167, 179–180, 228
Thomas, Albert, 439, 467
Thompson, W., 13, 19, 22, 28, 512–513
Toad Lane, 42, 50, 52, 56, 58
Totalitarian States, 442–444, 447–449, 453
Tournier, Miss, 433, 434
Town and Country Planning, 235
Trade Associations (see Co-operative Union)
Trade Unionism, 25, 28, 32, 35–37, 42, 79, 80, 94, 95, 115, 116, 129, 130, 136, 138, 145, 243, 282, 437
Trades Union Congress, 79, 95, 127, 128, 131, 133, 195–196, 198, 200, 221, 280, 281
Trades Unionism and Relations with the Co-operative Movement, 79, 80, 127–130, 195–201, 389–390
Travis, Dr., 79, 80
Tweddell, T., 132, 133

Tweedale, James, 511
Tweedale, Samuel, 511
Threading My Way (R. D. Owen), 19
Town Labourer (Hammond), 5
Towards Democracy (Carpenter), 4
Trade Unionism Today (Cole), 198
University Extension Journal, 121

Unemployment, 11–12, 89, 146–149, 191, 243
United Board (see Co-operative Union)
United Nations, 446, 468–469, 470
United Nations Conference on Food and Agriculture, 405, 445–446
United Nations Economic and Social Council, 468–469
United States of America Mutual Security Administration Counterpart Funds, 428
Universal Community of Rational Religionists, 38, 42
University Extension, 56, 93
University Survey, 206, 208
Utility Scheme, 210–211
Utopia, 306, 307, 478, 479, 490
Uthwatt Report, 235
Utilitarians, 6–8

Variety Store, 246
Varley, A., 171
Valleroux, H., 430
Vignana, Prof., 430
Villages of Co-operation, 10, 17, 516 (see Owen)
Vivian, H., 113
Voluntary Association, 205, 207, 486–487
Voluntary Chains, 246
Voluntary Membership, 309, 310–311, 329, 470
Voght, Dr., 430

Wages and Earnings, 89, 201, 202, 212, 237 ff, 241
Wade, Dr. A., 29, 513
Walker, Bailey, 84
Wallas, G., 95
War, 1914–1918, 137–144, 156, 439, 440, 444–445
War, 1939–1945, 209–229, 444–445
War Emergency Circular, 216
Warbasse, Dr. J. P., 478, 484, 513
Watkins, W. H., 118, 174
Watkins, W. P., 204, 451
Watts, Dr. J., 80, 84, 96, 105, 134
Weavers' Arms, 42, 47, 52
Webb, Catherine, 126

Webb, Sidney and Beatrice, 8, 35, 36, 95, 128, 135, 136, 137, 141, 145, 157, 179, 201, 202, 203, 205, 206, 207, 208, 233, 282, 288, 310, 315, 321, 323, 356, 359, 379, 477, 479, 483, 491, 513–515

Welsh Agricultural Organisation Society, 419, 421

Wheat Commission, 141

Whitehead, J., 44

Wilkinson, Miss E., 198, 202

Wilkinson, J., 49

Wood, C. E., 121

Woodcraft Folk, 186 ff

Wooden, Jones and Co. (see Central Co-operative Agency), 65

Wolff, H., 433–434, 435, 438

Woolf, L., 205–206, 207, 479

Women's Guilds (see Guilds)

Workers' Educational Association, 93, 121–122, 221, 347, 348

Workers' Productive and Artisanal Co-operatives, 462–463

Working Men's Associations, 62–66

Worswick, G. D. N., 211

Wright, G. W. A., 430

War Time Finance (J. S. Simm), 226

Wealth of Nations (Smith), 7, 13

Workers' Educational Association, Story of (Price), 121

Young, G. M., 8

Yeast (Kingsley), 61